Third Edition

Practical Argument
A Text and Anthology

Laurie G. Kirszner
University of the Sciences, Emeritus

Stephen R. Mandell
Drexel University

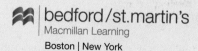

bedford/st.martin's
Macmillan Learning
Boston | New York

For Bedford/St. Martin's

Vice President, Editorial, Macmillan Learning Humanities: Edwin Hill
Editorial Director, English: Karen S. Henry
Senior Publisher for Composition, Business and Technical Writing, Developmental Writing: Leasa Burton
Executive Editor: John E. Sullivan III
Developmental Editor: Sherry Mooney
Production Editor: Matt Glazer
Media Producer: Sarah O'Connor
Production Supervisor: Lisa McDowell
Marketing Manager: Joy Fisher Williams
Assistant Editor: Jennifer Prince
Copy Editor: Diana Puglisi George
Indexer: Mary White
Photo Editor: Angela Boehler
Photo Researcher: Sheri Blaney
Permissions Editor: Christine Volboril
Senior Art Director: Anna Palchik
Text Design: Jerilyn Bockorick
Cover Design: John Callahan
Cover Photos: (bike) Science Photo Library/Getty Images; (backpack) SarapulSar38/Getty Images
Composition: Cenveo Publisher Services
Printing and Binding: RR Donnelley and Sons

Manufactured in the United States of America.

1 0 9 8 7 6
f e d c b a

For information, write: Bedford/St. Martin's, 75 Arlington Street, Boston, MA 02116   (617-399-4000)

ISBN 978-1-319-02856-5

In recent years, many college composition programs have integrated argumentation into their first-year writing sequence, and there are good reasons for this. Argumentation is central to academic and public discourse, so students who are skilled at argumentation are able to participate in the dynamic, ongoing discussions that take place both in their classrooms and in their communities. Clearly, argumentation teaches valuable critical-thinking skills that are necessary for academic success and for survival in today's media-driven society.

What has surprised and troubled us as teachers, however, is that many college argument texts are simply too difficult. Frequently, a divide exists between the pedagogy of these texts and students' ability to understand it. In many cases, technical terminology and excessively abstract discussions lead to confusion instead of clarity. The result is that students' worst fears are realized: instead of feeling that they are part of a discourse community, they see themselves as marginalized outsiders who will never be able to understand, let alone master, the principles of argumentation.

Recognizing that students struggle to master important principles of argumentative thinking and writing, we drew on our years of classroom experience to create an innovative book: *Practical Argument: A Text and Anthology*. In this third edition, *Practical Argument* remains a straightforward, accessible, and visually appealing introduction to argumentative writing that explains concepts in understandable, everyday language and illustrates them with examples that actually mean something to students. *Practical Argument* is an alternative for instructors who see currently available argument texts as too big, too complicated, and too intimidating for their students.

In short, our goal in this text is to demystify the study of argument. To this end, we focus on the things that students need to know, omitting the overly technical concepts they often struggle with. For example, *Practical Argument* emphasizes the basic principles of classical argument and downplays the more complex Toulmin logic, treating it as an alternative way of envisioning argument. *Practical Argument* works because its approach is "practical"; it helps students to make connections between what they learn in the classroom and what they experience outside of it. As they do so, they become comfortable with the rhetorical skills that are central to effective argumentation. We believe there's no other book like it.

Organization

Practical Argument, both a text and a reader, includes in one book every-thing students and instructors need for an argument course.

- **Part 1, Understanding Argument,** discusses the role of argument in everyday life and the value of studying argument, offers definitions of what argument is and is not, explains the means of persuasion (appeals to *logos*, *pathos*, and *ethos*), and defines and illustrates the basic elements of argument (thesis, evidence, refutation, and conclud-ing statement).

- **Part 2, Reading and Responding to Arguments,** explains and illus-trates critical thinking and reading; visual argument; writing a rhetori-cal analysis; logic and logical fallacies; and Rogerian argument, Toulmin logic, and oral arguments.

- **Part 3, Writing an Argumentative Essay,** traces and illustrates the process of planning, drafting, and revising an argumentative essay.

- **Part 4, Using Sources to Support Your Argument,** covers locating and evaluating print and online sources; summarizing, paraphrasing, quoting, and synthesizing sources; documenting sources in MLA style; and using sources reponsibly.

- **Part 5, Strategies for Argument,** explains and illustrates the most common kinds of arguments—definition arguments, cause-and-effect arguments, evaluation arguments, proposal arguments, and ethical arguments.

- **Part 6, Debates, Casebooks, and Classic Arguments,** includes both contemporary and classic arguments. The contemporary arguments are arranged in four pro-con debates and four in-depth casebooks on issues such as whether controversial sports mascots should be replaced and whether helicopter parents are ruining their children's lives. The eleven classic arguments include well-known pieces by writers such as Jonathan Swift, George Orwell, Betty Friedan, and Rachel Carson.

- **Appendixes.** Appendix A provides instruction on writing literary arguments, and Appendix B covers APA documentation style.

Key Features

Accessible in a Thoughtful Way

Practical Argument covers everything students need to know about argu-ment but doesn't overwhelm them. It limits technical vocabulary to what students and instructors actually need to understand and discuss key concepts in argument and argumentative writing. In short, *Practical Argument* is argument made accessible.

Argument Step by Step, Supported by Helpful Apparatus

Practical Argument takes students through a step-by-step process of reading and responding to others' arguments and writing, revising, and editing their own arguments. The book uses a classroom-tested, exercise-driven approach that encourages students to participate actively in their own learning process. Chapters progress in a clear, easy-to-understand sequence: students are asked to read arguments, identify their key elements, and develop a response to an issue in the form of a complete, documented argumentative essay based on in-book focused research.

Exercises and writing assignments for each selection provide guidance for students as they work toward creating a finished piece of writing. Throughout the text, checklists, grammar-in-context and summary boxes, and source and gloss notes provide support. In addition, more than a dozen unique templates for paragraph-length arguments—located with the end-of-chapter exercises—provide structures that students can use for guidance as they write definition arguments, cause-and-effect arguments, evaluation arguments, proposal arguments, and ethical arguments. Sentence templates also frequently appear in the questions that follow the readings, providing an opportunity for students to work up to arguments at the paragraph level.

A Thematically Focused Approach with Compelling Chapter Topics

Students learn best when they care about and are engaged in an issue. For this reason, *Practical Argument* uses readings and assignments to help students learn argumentation in the context of one high-interest contemporary issue per chapter. Chapter topics include media violence, free speech, online education, technology and privacy, student debt, and student safety—issues that have real meaning in students' lives.

Readings on Relevant and Interesting Issues

One hundred and twenty-one accessible professional readings—on issues that students will want to read about and debate—are presented in the text, including selections from journals and blogs. Topics include the advantages of two-year colleges, the concept of "humane" meat, and why undergraduate majors matter. Many visual selections enhance the readings throughout the book while seventeen sample student essays, more than in any other argument book, provide realistic models for student writers as well as additional student voices. Each student essay, including complete MLA and APA research papers, is annotated to further assist students through their own writing process. An additional twenty-four selections are organized as debates and casebooks on questions such as whether meat can be an ethical choice, whether controversial sports mascots should be replaced, and whether every American should go to college. A collection of eleven classic arguments offers more challenging approaches to enduring issues.

To help students better understand the context of the sources included in *Practical Argument*, each is marked with an icon that shows how it was originally presented.

Book   Magazine or journal   National newspaper   Speech

Poem   Student essay   Student newspaper   Website

An Open and Inviting Full-Color Design

The fresh, contemporary look of *Practical Argument* will engage students. This open, colorful design eliminates the sea of dense type that is typical of many other argument books. Over a hundred photographs and other visuals—such as graphic novel excerpts, cartoons, advertisements, templates, charts and graphs, Web pages, and fine art—provide appealing and instructive real-world examples. The use of open space and numerous images reinforces the currency of the book's themes and also creates an inviting and visually stimulating format.

Two Versions

Practical Argument is also available in a trimmed-down edition, *Practical Argument*, Short Third Edition. This version features a streamlined table of contents with fewer readings for the instructor who is looking to do more with less. *Practical Argument*, Short Third Edition, can also be packaged with the full LaunchPad. To order *Practical Argument*, Short Third Edition, use ISBN **978-1-319-03019-3**.

New to This Edition

Essays, Topics, and Images

The third edition includes sixty-eight engaging new professional essays on such timely topics as self-driving cars and free speech on college campuses. These essays have been carefully selected for their high-interest subject matter as well as for their effectiveness as sources and as teaching models for student writing.

Debates and Casebooks

New debate and casebook topics include whether bystanders have an obligation to intervene in an emergency, and whether it pays to study the humanities.

More Help with the Writing Process and Academic Writing

In response to instructor requests, we have expanded the templates, making them more useful to students and adding interactivity in the Launch-Pad; included additional annotations in the MLA paper to guide students in the integration of source material; simplified the coverage of Rogerian argument; and provided more background on the rhetorical situation. We have also provided more help with academic writing, including additional material on finding sources as well as expanded examples of MLA and APA documentation. We have substantially expanded our coverage of how to refute opposing arguments, providing students with a firm grasp of how to usefully incorporate conflicting viewpoints into their writing. Finally, a set of disciplinary contents has been included for instructors who want to browse the readings by disciplines outside of composition to help their students make connections to their other courses.

Get the Most Out of Your Course with *Practical Argument*

Bedford/St. Martin's offers resources and format choices that help you and your students get even more out of your book and course. To learn more about or to order any of the following products, contact your Macmillan sales representative, email sales support (**sales_support@bfwpub.com**), or look for *Practical Argument*, Third Edition, at **macmillanlearning.com**.

LaunchPad for Practical Argument: *Where Students Learn*

LaunchPad provides engaging content and new ways to get the most out of your book. Get an **interactive e-book** combined with **useful, highly relevant materials** in a fully customizable course space; then assign and mix our resources with yours.

- Auto-graded **reading quizzes, comprehension quizzes on argument topics**, and **interactive writing templates** help students to engage actively with the material you assign.

- **Pre-built units**—including readings, videos, quizzes, discussion groups, and more—are **easy to adapt and assign** by adding your own materials and mixing them with our high-quality multimedia content and ready-made assessment options, such as **LearningCurve** adaptive quizzing. The LearningCurve now includes argument modules focusing on topic, purpose, and audience; arguable claims; reasoning and logical fallacies; and persuasive appeals (*logos, pathos,* and *ethos*).

- LaunchPad also provides access to a **Gradebook** that provides a clear window on the performance of your whole class, individual students, and even results of individual assignments.

- A **streamlined interface** helps students focus on what's due, and social commenting tools let them **engage**, make connections, and learn from each other. Use LaunchPad on its own or integrate it with your school's learning management system so that your class is always on the same page.

To get the most out of your book, order LaunchPad for *Practical Argument* packaged with the print book. (LaunchPad for *Practical Argument* can also be purchased on its own.) An activation code is required. To order LaunchPad for *Practical Argument* with the print book, use ISBN **978-1-319-07353-4**.

Choose from Alternative Formats of Practical Argument

Bedford/St. Martin's offers a range of affordable formats, allowing students to choose the one that works best for them. For further details, look for *Practical Argument* at **macmillanlearning.com**.

- *Paperback brief edition* To order the paperback *Practical Argument*, Short Third Edition, use ISBN **978-1-319-03019-3**.

- *Other popular e-book formats* For details, visit **macmillanlearning .com/ebooks**.

Select Value Packages

Add value to your text by packaging one of the following resources with *Practical Argument*. To learn more about package options for any of the following products, contact your Bedford/St. Martin's sales representative or visit **macmillanlearning.com**.

Writer's Help 2.0 is a powerful online writing resource that helps students find answers whether they are searching for writing advice on their own or as part of an assignment.

- **Smart search**
  Built on research with more than 1,600 student writers, the smart search in Writer's Help 2.0 provides reliable results even when students use novice terms such as *flow* and *unstuck*.

- **Trusted content from our best-selling handbooks**
  Choose *Writer's Help 2.0, Hacker Version* or *Writer's Help 2.0, Lunsford Version* and ensure that students have clear advice and examples for all of their writing questions.

- **Adaptive exercises that engage students**
  Writer's Help 2.0 includes LearningCurve, game-like online quizzing that adapts to what students already know and helps them focus on what they need to learn.

Student access is packaged with *Practical Argument* at a significant discount. Order ISBN 978-1-319-07356-5 for *Writer's Help 2.0, Hacker Version* or ISBN 978-1-319-07355-8 for *Writer's Help 2.0, Lunsford Version* to ensure your students have easy access to online writing support. Students who rent a book or buy a used book can purchase access to Writer's Help 2.0 at **macmillanhighered.com/writershelp2**.

Instructors may request free access by registering as an instructor at **macmillanhighered.com/writershelp2**.

For technical support, visit **macmillanlearning.com/getsupport**.

Portfolio Keeping, **Third Edition, by Nedra Reynolds and Elizabeth Davis,** provides all the information students need to use the portfolio method successfully in a writing course. *Portfolio Teaching,* a companion guide for instructors, provides the practical information instructors and writing program administrators need to use the portfolio method successfully in a writing course. To order *Portfolio Keeping* packaged with this text, contact your sales representative for a package ISBN.

Instructor Resources

You have a lot to do in your course. Bedford/St. Martin's wants to make it easy for you to find the support you need—and to get it quickly.

Resources for Teaching Practical Argument is available as a PDF that can be downloaded from the Bedford/St. Martin's online catalog. In addition to chapter overviews and teaching tips, the instructor's manual includes sample syllabi, answers to questions that appear within the book, and suggested classroom activities.

Join Our Community! The Macmillan English Community is now Bedford/St. Martin's home for professional resources, featuring Bedford *Bits,* our popular blog site that offers new ideas for the composition classroom and composition teachers. Connect and converse with a growing team of Bedford authors and top scholars who blog on *Bits*: Andrea Lunsford, Nancy Sommers, Steve Bernhardt, Traci Gardner, Barclay Barrios, Jack Solomon, Susan Bernstein, Elizabeth Wardle, Doug Downs, Liz Losh, Jonathan Alexander, and Donna Winchell.

In addition, you'll find an expanding collection of additional resources that support your teaching.

- Sign up for webinars
- Download resources from our professional resources series that support your teaching
- Start a discussion
- Ask a question
- Follow your favorite members
- Review projects in the pipeline

Visit **community.macmillan.com** to join the conversation with your fellow teachers.

Acknowledgments

The following reviewers gave us valuable feedback: Joshua Beach, University of Texas at San Antonio; Jenny Billings Beaver, Rowan Cabarrus Community College; Jade Bittle, Rowan Cabarrus Community College; Shannon Blair, Central Piedmont Community College; Chris Blankenship, Emporia State University; Patricia Colella, Bunker Hill Community College; Jason DePolo, North Carolina A&T State University; Julie Dorris, Arkansas Northeastern College; Sarah Duerden, University of Sheffield; Alan Goldman, Massachusetts Bay Community College; Iris Harvey, Tarrant County Community College; Rebecca Hewett, California State University; Bruce Holmes, Stratford University; Anneliese Homan, State Fair Community College; Ann Hostestler, Goshen College; Elizabeth Hurston, Eastfield College; Ann Johnson, University of Nebraska at Omaha; Virginia Kearney, Baylor University; Audrey Lapointe, Cuyamaca College; Laurie Leach, Hawaii Pacific University; Vicki Martineau-Gilliam, National University; Gwendolyn Miller, University of Wisconsin–Parkside; Deborah Miller-Zournas, Stark State College; James Minor, South Piedmont Community College; Lani Montreal, Malcolm X College; Kathleen Moore, Community College of Vermont–Montpelier; Meltam Oztan, Kent State; Matt Pifer, Husson University; Cory Potter, Bethune-Cookman University; Mandy Reid, Indiana State University; Stuart Rosenberg, Cyprus College; Zahir Small, Santa Fe College; Kymberly Snelling, Metropolitan Community College–Ft. Omaha; Rosie Soy, Hudson County Community College; Andrea Spofford, Austin Peay State University; Wes Spratlin, Motlow State Community College; Cheli Turner, Greenville Technical College; Barbara Urban, Central Piedmont Community College–Levine Campus; and Sandra Zapp, Paradise Valley Community College.

We thank Jeff Ousborne, Deja Ruddick, Elizabeth Rice, and Michelle McSweeney for their valuable contributions to this text.

At Bedford/St. Martin's, Joan Feinberg, Denise Wydra, Karen Henry, Steve Scipione, Leasa Burton, and John Sullivan were involved and supportive from the start of the project. John, in particular, helped us shape this book and was with us every step of the way. In this third edition, we have had the pleasure of working with Sherry Mooney, our smart, talented, and creative editor. Her addition to our team has made *Practical Argument* a much better book. Matt Glazer patiently and efficiently shepherded the book through the production process. Others on our team included Jennifer Prince, who helped with many details; Joy Fisher Williams and Gillian Daniels, who were instrumental in marketing the book; Sheri Blaney, who found art and obtained permission for it; Christine Volboril, who handled text permissions; and our outstanding copy editor, Diana P. George. We are grateful for their help.

Finally, we would like to thank each other for lunches past—and for many, many lunches to come.

Laurie G. Kirszner
Stephen R. Mandell

BRIEF CONTENTS

CONTENTS

CONTENTS

PART

2 Reading and Responding to Arguments 57

3   Decoding Visual Arguments   83

4 Writing a Rhetorical Analysis   99

6 Rogerian Argument, Toulmin Logic, and Oral Arguments   191

PART

3 Writing an Argumentative Essay   251

7 Planning, Drafting, and Revising an Argumentative Essay   253

PART

4   Using Sources to Support Your Argument   285

8   Finding and Evaluating Sources   287

11 Using Sources Responsibly   369

13 Cause-and-Effect Arguments   467

14 Evaluation Arguments   517

15 Proposal Arguments   551

PART

6 Debates, Casebooks, and Classic Arguments   643

DEBATES

CLASSIC ARGUMENTS

25

DISCIPLINARY CONTENTS

Business/Economics

Education

Environmental Science

History

Law/Criminal Justice

Medicine/Nursing

Philosophy

Political Science

Psychology

Sociology

PART

1

Understanding
Argument

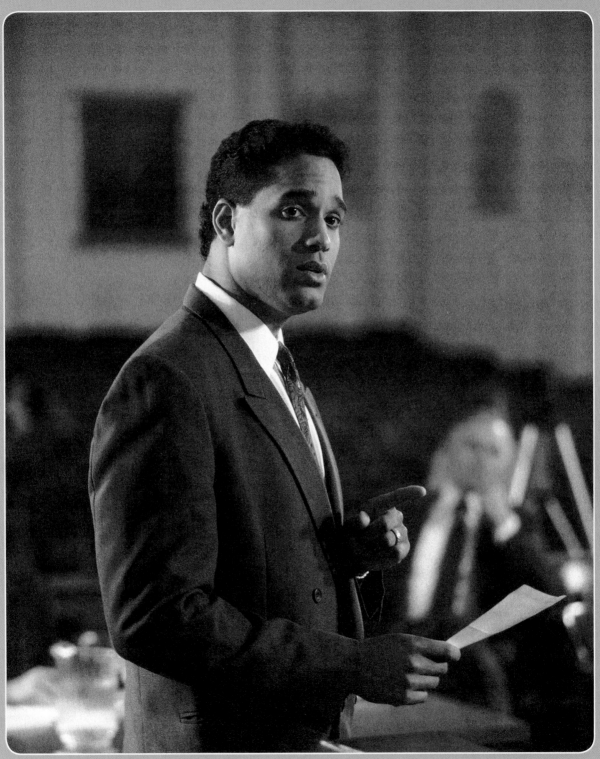

An Introduction to Argument

Recognizing Arguments

Arguments are everywhere. Whenever you turn on the television, read a newspaper or magazine, talk to friends and family, enter an online discussion, or engage in a debate in one of your classes, you encounter arguments. In fact, it is fair to say that much of the interaction that takes place in society involves argument. Consider, for example, a lawyer who tries to persuade a jury that a defendant is innocent, a doctor who wants to convince a patient to undergo a specific form of treatment, a lawmaker who wants to propose a piece of legislation, an executive who wants to institute a particular policy, an activist who wants to pursue a particular social agenda, a parent who wants to convince a child to study harder, a worker who wants to propose a more efficient way of performing a task, an employee who thinks that he or she deserves a raise, or a spokesperson in an infomercial whose goal is to sell something: all these people are engaging in argument.

In college, you encounter arguments on a daily basis; in fact, both class discussions and academic writing often take the form of argument. Consider, for example, the following questions that might be debated (and written about) in a first-year writing class:

- Do the benefits of fracking outweigh its risks?

- How free should free speech be?

- Are helicopter parents ruining their children's lives?

- How far should schools go to keep students safe?

- Do bystanders have an ethical responsibility to help in a crisis?

What these questions have in common is that they all call for argumentation. To answer these questions, students would be expected to state their opinions and support them.

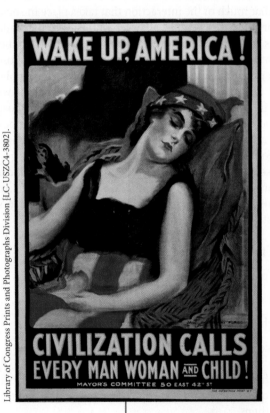

Wake Up, America! (1917) James Montgomery Flagg. Published by the Hegeman Print, New York/ Library of Congress Prints and Photographs Division [LC-USZC4-3802].

World War I propaganda poster (1917)

Defining Argument

Now for the obvious question: exactly what is an argument? Perhaps the best way to begin is by explaining what argument is *not*. An argument (at least an academic argument) is not a **quarrel** or an angry exchange. The object of argument is not to attack someone who disagrees with you or to beat an opponent into submission. For this reason, the shouting matches that you routinely see on television or hear on talk radio are not really arguments. Argument is also not **spin**—the positive or biased slant that politicians routinely put on facts—or **propaganda**—information (or misinformation) that is spread to support a particular viewpoint. Finally, argument is not just a contradiction or denial of someone else's position. Even if you establish that an opponent's position is wrong or misguided, you still have to establish that your own position has merit by presenting evidence to support it.

There is a basic difference between **formal arguments**—those that you develop in academic discussion and writing—and **informal arguments**—those that occur in daily life, where people often get into arguments about politics, sports, social issues, and personal relationships. These everyday disputes are often just verbal fights in which one person tries to outshout another. Although they sometimes include facts, they tend to rely primarily on emotion and unsupported opinions. Moreover, such everyday arguments do not have the formal structure of academic arguments: they do not establish a logical link between a particular viewpoint and reliable supporting evidence. There is also no real effort to address opposing arguments. In general, these arguments tend to be disorganized, emotional disputes that have more to do with criticizing an opponent than with advancing and supporting a position on an issue. Although such informal arguments can serve as starting points for helping you think about issues, they do not have the structure or the intellectual rigor of formal arguments.

So exactly what is an argument—or, more precisely, what is an academic argument? An **academic argument** is a type of formal argument that takes a stand, presents evidence, includes documentation, and uses logic to convince an audience to accept (or at least consider) the writer's position. Of course, academic arguments can get heated, but at their core they are civil exchanges. Writers of academic arguments strive to be fair and to show respect for others—especially for those who present opposing arguments.

Keep in mind that arguments take positions with which reasonable people may disagree. For this reason, an argument never actually proves anything. (If it did, there would be no argument.) The best that an argument can do is to convince other people to accept (or at least acknowledge) the validity of its position.

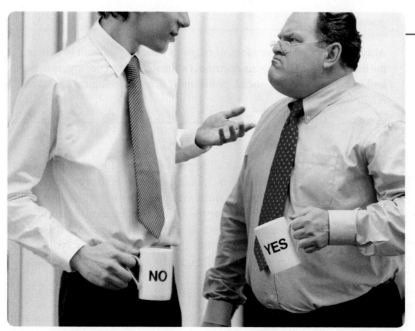

An angry exchange is not an academic argument.

Flying Colours Ltd./Getty Images

WHAT KINDS OF STATEMENTS ARE NOT DEBATABLE?

To be suitable for argument, a statement must be **debatable**: in other words, there must be conflicting opinions or conflicting facts that call the validity of the statement into question. For this reason, the following types of statements are generally *not* suitable for argument:

- **Statements of fact:** A statement of fact can be verified, so it is not debatable. For example, there is no point in arguing that your school makes instructors' lectures available as podcasts. This is a question of fact that can easily be checked. You can, however, argue that making instructors' lectures available as podcasts would (or would not) enhance education at your school. This is a debatable statement that can be supported by facts and examples.

- **Statements of personal preference or taste:** Expressions of personal preference or taste are not suitable for argument. For example, if you say that you don't like the taste of a particular soft drink, no one can legitimately argue that you are wrong. This statement is beyond dispute because it is a matter of personal taste. You could, however, argue that soft drinks should not be sold in school cafeterias because they contribute to obesity. To support this position, you would supply evidence—facts, statistics, and expert opinion.

> **NOTE**
>
> Although personal expressions of religious belief are difficult to debate, the interpretation of religious doctrine is a suitable subject for argument—and so are the political, social, philosophical, and theological effects of religion on society.

It is a mistake to think that all arguments have just two sides—one right side and one wrong side. In fact, many arguments that you encounter in college focus on issues that are quite complex. For example, if you were considering the question of whether the United States should ban torture, you could certainly answer this question with a yes or a no, but this would be an oversimplification. To examine the issue thoroughly, you would have to consider it from a number of angles:

- Should torture be banned in all situations?

- Should torture be used as a last resort to elicit information that could prevent an imminent attack?

- What actually constitutes torture? For example, is sleep deprivation torture? What about a slap on the face? Loud music? A cold cell? Are "enhanced interrogation techniques"—such as waterboarding—torture?

- Who should have the legal right to approve interrogation techniques?

If you were going to write an argument about this issue, you would have to take a position that adequately conveyed its complex nature—for example, "Although torture may be cruel and even inhuman, it is sometimes necessary." To do otherwise might be to commit the **either/or fallacy** (see p. 151)—to offer only two choices when there are actually many others.

Arguments in Real Life

In blogs, social media posts, work-related proposals, letters to the editor, emails to businesses, letters of complaint, and other types of communication, you formulate arguments that are calculated to influence readers. Many everyday situations call for argument:

- A proposal to the manager of the UPS store where you work to suggest a more efficient way of sorting packages

- A letter to your local newspaper in which you argue that creating a walking trail would be good use of your community's tax dollars

- An email to your child's principal asking her to extend after-school hours

- A letter to a credit card company in which you request an adjustment to your bill

- A blog post in which you argue that the federal government could do more to relieve the student loan burden

Because argument is so prevalent, the better your arguing skills, the better able you will be to function—not just in school but also in the wider world. When you have a clear thesis, convincing support, and effective refutation of opposing arguments, you establish your credibility and go a long way toward convincing readers that you are someone worth listening to.

Presenting a good argument does not guarantee that readers will accept your ideas. It does, however, help you to define an issue and to express your position clearly and logically. If you present yourself as a well-informed, reasonable person who is attuned to the needs of your readers—even those who disagree with you—you increase your chances of convincing your audience that your position is worth considering.

Arguments are also central to our democratic form of government. Whether the issue is taxation, health care, border control, the environment, abortion, gun ownership, energy prices, gay marriage, terrorism, or cyber-bullying, political candidates, media pundits, teachers, friends, and family members all try to influence the way we think. So in a real sense, argument is the way that all of us participate in the national (or even global) conversation about ideas that matter. The better you understand the methods of argumentation, the better able you will be to recognize, analyze, and respond to the arguments that you hear. By mastering the techniques of argument, you will become a clearer thinker, a more informed citizen, and a person who is better able to influence those around you.

Black Lives Matter
protest

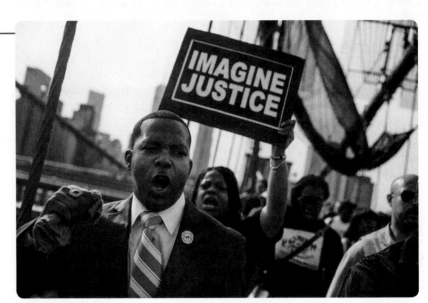

Andrew Burton/Getty Images

Winning and Losing Arguments

People often talk of "winning" and "losing" arguments, and of course, the aim of many arguments is to defeat an opponent. In televised political debates, candidates try to convince viewers that they should be elected. In a courtroom, a defense attorney tries to establish a client's innocence. In a job interview, a potential employee tries to convince an employer that he or she is the best-qualified applicant. However, the goal of an argument is not always to determine a winner and a loser. Sometimes the goal of an argument is to identify a problem and suggest solutions that could satisfy those who hold a number of different positions on an issue.

If, for example, you would like your college bookstore to lower the price of items (such as sweatshirts, coffee mugs, and backpacks) with a school logo, you could simply state your position and then support it with evidence. A more effective way of approaching this problem, however, might be to consider all points of view and find some middle ground. For example, how would lowering these prices affect the bookstore? A short conversation with the manager of the bookstore might reveal that the revenue generated by these products enables the bookstore to discount other items—such as art supplies and computers—as well as to hire student help. Therefore, decreasing the price of products with college logos would negatively affect some students. Even so, the high prices also make it difficult for some students to buy these items.

To address this problem, you could offer a compromise solution: the price of items with college logos could be lowered, but the price of other items—such as magazines and snacks—could be raised to make up the difference.

The Rhetorical Situation

In everyday use, the term *rhetoric* has distinctly negative connotations. When a speech is described as being nothing but *rhetoric*, the meaning is clear: the speech consists of empty words and phrases calculated to confuse and manipulate listeners. When writing instructors use the term *rhetoric*, however, it means something quite different: it refers to the choices someone makes to structure a message—written, oral, or visual.

The **rhetorical situation** refers to the factors that influence the creation of any type of communication—especially its words, images, and structure. Applied to argument, the rhetorical situation refers to five factors you should consider when planning an effective argument. Although every rhetorical situation is different, all rhetorical situations involve the following five elements:

- The writer
- The purpose
- The audience
- The question
- The context

Considering the Writer

Every argument begins with a writer, the person who creates the text. For this reason, it is important to understand how your biases or preconceptions could affect what you produce. For example, if you were home schooled, you might have very definite ideas about education. Likewise, a former Navy Seal might have preconceptions concerning the war in Afghanistan. Strongly held beliefs like these can, and often do, color your arguments. The following factors can affect the tone and content of an argument:

age

education

gender

ethnicity

cultural experiences

political affiliation

religion

sexuality

social standing

Before you plan an argument, ask yourself what preconceived ideas you may have about a particular topic. Do your beliefs prevent you from considering all sides of an issue, reaching a logical and fair conclusion, or acknowledging the validity of opposing arguments? It is important that you present yourself as a fair and open-minded person, one whom readers trust. For this reason, you should maintain a reasonable tone and avoid the use of words or phrases that indicate bias.

Considering the Purpose

A writer's **purpose** is his or her reason for writing. The purpose of an argument is to present a position and to change (or at least influence) people's ideas about an issue. In addition to this general purpose, a writer may have more specific goals. For example, you might want to criticize the actions of others or call into question a particular public policy. You may also want to take a stand on a controversial topic or convince readers that certain arguments are weak. Finally, you may want to propose a solution to a problem or convince readers to adopt a certain course of action.

When you write an argument, you may want to state your purpose directly—usually in your introduction. (Key words in your thesis statement can indicate the direction the argument will take as well as the points that you will discuss.) At other times, especially if you think readers will not readily accept your ideas, you may want to indicate your purpose later in your essay or simply imply it.

Considering the Audience

When you write argumentative essays, you don't write in a vacuum; you write for real people who may or may not agree with you. As you are writing, it is easy to forget this fact and address a general group of readers. However, doing this would be a mistake. Defining your audience and keeping this audience in mind as you write is important because it helps you decide what material to include and how to present it.

One way to define an audience is by its **traits**—the age, gender, interests, values, preconceptions, and level of education of audience members. Each of these traits influences how audience members will react to your ideas, and understanding them helps you determine how to construct your argument. For instance, suppose you were going to write an essay with the following thesis:

> Although college is expensive, its high cost is justified.

How you approach this subject would depend on the audience you were addressing. For example, college students, parents, and college administrators would have different ideas about the subject, different perspectives, different preconceptions, and different levels of knowledge. Therefore, the argument you write for each of these audiences would be different from the others in terms of content, organization, and type of appeal.

- **College students** have a local and personal perspective. They know the school and have definite ideas about the value of the education they are getting. Most likely, they come from different backgrounds and have varying financial needs. Depending on their majors, they have different expectations about employment (and salary) when they graduate. Even with these differences, however, these students share certain concerns. Many probably have jobs to help cover their expenses. Many also have student loans that they will need to start paying after graduation.

  An argumentative essay addressing this audience could focus on statistics and expert opinions that establish the worth of a college degree in terms of future employment, job satisfaction, and lifetime earnings.

- **Parents** probably have limited knowledge of the school and the specific classes their children are taking. They have expectations—both realistic and unrealistic—about the value of a college degree. Some parents may be able to help their children financially, and others may be unable to do so. Their own life experiences and backgrounds probably color their ideas about the value of a college education. For example, parents who have gone to college may have different ideas about the value of a degree from those who haven't.

  An argumentative essay addressing this audience could focus on the experience of other parents of college students. It could also include statistics that address students' future economic independence and economic security.

- **College administrators** have detailed knowledge about college and the economic value of a degree. They are responsible for attracting students, scheduling classes, maintaining educational standards, and providing support services. They are familiar with budget requirements, and they understand the financial pressures involved in running a school. They also know how tuition dollars are spent and how much state and federal aid the school needs to stay afloat. Although they are sympathetic to the plight of both students and parents, they have to work with limited resources.

An argumentative essay addressing this audience could focus on the need to make tuition more affordable by cutting costs and providing more student aid.

Another way to define an audience is to determine whether it is *friendly, hostile,* or *neutral.*

- A **friendly audience** is sympathetic to your argument. This audience might already agree with you or have an emotional or intellectual attachment to you or to your position. In this situation, you should emphasize points of agreement and reinforce the emotional bond that exists between you and the audience. Don't assume, however, that because this audience is receptive to your ideas, you do not have to address its concerns or provide support for your points. If readers suspect that you are avoiding important issues or that your evidence is weak, they will be less likely to take your argument seriously—even though they agree with you.

- A **hostile audience** disagrees with your position and does not accept the underlying assumptions of your argument. For this reason, you have to work hard to overcome their preconceived opinions, presenting your points clearly and logically and including a wide range of evidence. To show that you are a reasonable person, you should treat these readers with respect even though they happen to disagree with you. In addition, you should show that you have taken the time to consider their arguments and that you value their concerns. Even with all these efforts, however, the best you may be able to do is get them to admit that you have made some good points in support of your position.

- A **neutral audience** has no preconceived opinions about the issue you are going to discuss. (When you are writing an argument for a college class, you should assume that you are writing for a neutral audience.) For this reason, you need to provide background information about the issue and about the controversy surrounding it. You should also summarize opposing points of view, present them logically, and refute them effectively. This type of audience may not know much about an issue, but it is not necessarily composed of unsophisticated or unintelligent people. Moreover, even though such readers are neutral, you should assume that they are **skeptical**—that is, that they will question your assumptions and require supporting evidence before they accept your conclusions.

> **NOTE**
>
> Some audiences are so diverse that they are difficult to categorize. In this case, it is best to define the audience yourself—for example, *concerned parents*, *prudent consumers*, or *serious students*—and then address them accordingly.

Keep in mind that identifying a specific audience is not something that you do at the last minute. Because your audience determines the kind of argument you present, you should take the time to make this determination before you begin to write.

Considering the Question

All arguments begin with a question that you are going to answer. To be suitable for argument, this question must have more than one possible answer. If it does not, there is no basis for the argument. For example, there is no point trying to write an argumentative essay on the question of whether head injuries represent a danger for football players. The answer to this question is so obvious that no thoughtful person would argue that they are not. The question of whether the National Football League is doing enough to protect players from head injuries, however, is one on which reasonable people could disagree. Consider the following information:

- In recent years, the NFL has done much to reduce the number of serious head injuries.

- New protocols for the treatment of players who show signs of head trauma, stricter rules against helmet-to-helmet tackles, and the use of safer helmets have reduced the number of concussions.

- Even with these precautions, professional football players experience a high number of head injuries, with one in three players reporting negative effects—some quite serious—from repeated concussions.

Because there are solid arguments on both sides of this issue, you could write an effective argument in which you address this question.

Considering the Context

An argument takes place in a specific **context**—the set of circumstances that surrounds the issue. As you plan your argument, consider the social, historical, and cultural events that define the debate.

Assume that you were going to argue that the public school students in your hometown should be required to purchase iPads. Before you begin your argument, you should give readers the background—the context—they will need to understand the issue. For example, they should know that school officials have been debating the issue for over a year. School administrators say that given the advances in distance learning as well as the high quality of online resources, iPads will enhance the educational experience of students. They also say that it is time to bring the schools' instructional methods into the twenty-first century. Even so, some parents say that requiring the purchase of iPads will put an undue financial burden on them. In addition, teachers point out that a good deal of new material will have to be developed to take advantage of this method of instruction. Finally, not all students will have access at home to the high-speed Internet capacity necessary for this type of instruction.

If it is not too complicated, you can discuss the context of your argument in your introduction; if it requires more explanation, you can discuss it in your first body paragraph. If you do not establish this context early in your essay, however, readers will have a difficult time understanding the issue you are going to discuss and the points you are going to make.

Logos, Pathos, and Ethos

To be effective, your argument has to be persuasive. **Persuasion** is a general term that refers to how a speaker or writer influences an audience to adopt a particular belief or to follow a specific course of action.

In the fifth century BCE, the philosopher Aristotle considered the issue of persuasion. Ancient Greece was primarily an oral culture (as opposed to a written or print culture), so persuasive techniques were most often used in speeches. Public officials had to speak before a citizens' assembly, and people had to make their cases in front of various judicial bodies. The more persuasive the presentation, the better the speaker's chance of success. In *The Art of Rhetoric*, Aristotle examines the three different means of persuasion that a speaker can use to persuade listeners (or writers):

Aristotle

- The appeal to reason (*logos*)
- The appeal to the emotions (*pathos*)
- The appeal to authority (*ethos*)

The Appeal to Reason (Logos)

According to Aristotle, argument is the appeal to reason or logic (**logos**). He assumed that, at their core, human beings are logical and therefore would respond to a well-constructed argument. For Aristotle, appeals to reason focus primarily on the way that an argument is organized, and this organization is determined by formal logic, which uses deductive and inductive reasoning to reach valid conclusions. Aristotle believed that appeals to reason convince an audience that a conclusion is both valid and true (see Chapter 5 for a discussion of deductive and inductive reasoning and logic). Although Aristotle believed that ideally, all arguments should appeal to reason, he knew that given the realities of human nature, reason alone was not always enough. Therefore, when he discusses persuasion, he also discusses the appeals to *ethos* and *pathos*.

Logos *in Action*

Notice how the ad below for the Toyota Prius, a popular hybrid automobile, appeals primarily to reason. It uses facts as well as a logical explanation

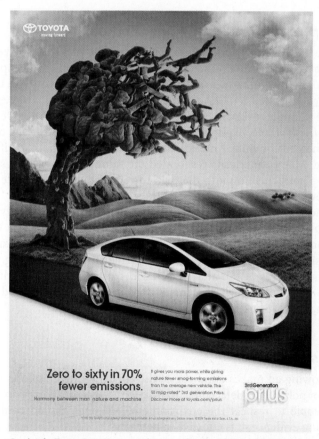

Car shot for Toyota Prius Harmony ad © Trevor Pearson. Background for Toyota Prius Harmony ad © Mark Holthusen Photography. Reproduced with permission of the photographers and Toyota Sales USA.

of how the car works to appeal to reason (as well as to the consumer's desire to help the environment).

You can assess the effectiveness of *logos* (the appeal to reason) in an argument by asking the following questions:

- Does the argument have a clear thesis? In other words, can you identify the main point the writer is trying to make?

- Does the argument include the facts, examples, and expert opinion needed to support the thesis?

- Is the argument well organized? Are the points the argument makes presented in logical order?

- Can you detect any errors in logic (**fallacies**) that undermine the argument's reasoning?

The Appeal to the Emotions (Pathos)

Aristotle knew that an appeal to the emotions (***pathos***) could be very persuasive because it adds a human dimension to an argument. By appealing to an audience's sympathies and by helping them to identify with the subject being discussed, emotional appeals can turn abstract concepts into concrete examples that can compel people to take action. After December 7, 1941, for example, explicit photographs of the Japanese attack on Pearl Harbor helped convince Americans that retaliation was both justified and desirable. Many Americans responded the same way when they saw pictures of planes crashing into the twin towers of the World Trade Center on September 11, 2001.

Although an appeal to the emotions can add to an already strong argument, it does not in itself constitute proof. Moreover, certain kinds of emotional appeals—appeals to fear, hatred, and prejudice, for example—are considered unfair and are not acceptable in college writing. In this sense, the pictures of the attacks on Pearl Harbor and the World Trade Center would be unfair arguments if they were not accompanied by evidence that established that retaliation was indeed necessary.

Pathos *in Action*

The following ad makes good use of the appeal to the emotions. Using a picture of polar bears defaced by graffiti, the ad includes a caption encouraging people to respect the environment. Although the ad contains no supporting evidence, it is effective nonetheless.

What will it take before we respect the planet?

Courtesy of WWF.org, reproduced with permission

You can assess the effectiveness of *pathos* (the appeal to the emotions) in an argument by asking the following questions:

- Does the argument include words or images designed to move readers?

- Does the argument use emotionally loaded language?

- Does the argument include vivid descriptions or striking examples calculated to appeal to readers' emotions?

- Are the values and beliefs of the writer apparent in the argument?

- Does the tone seem emotional?

The Appeal to Authority (Ethos)

Finally, Aristotle knew that the character and authority of a speaker or writer (***ethos***) could contribute to the persuasiveness of an argument. If the person making the argument is known to be honorable, truthful, knowledgeable, and trustworthy, audiences will likely accept what he or she is saying. If, on the other hand, the person is known to be deceitful, ignorant, dishonest, uninformed, or dishonorable, audiences will probably dismiss his or her argument—no matter how persuasive it might seem. Whenever you analyze an argument, you should try to determine whether the writer is worth listening to—in other words, whether the writer has **credibility**.

(For a discussion of how to establish credibility and demonstrate fairness in your own writing, see Chapter 7.)

Ethos *in Action*

The following ad uses an appeal to authority. It uses an endorsement by the popular tennis star Venus Williams to convince consumers to buy Reebok sneakers. (Recent studies suggest that consumers react positively to ads that feature products endorsed by famous athletes.)

You can assess the effectiveness of *ethos* (the appeal to authority) in an argument by asking the following questions:

- Does the person making the argument demonstrate knowledge of the subject?

- What steps does the person making the argument take to present its position as reasonable?

- Does the argument seem fair?

- If the argument includes sources, do they seem both reliable and credible? Does the argument include proper documentation?

- Does the person making the argument demonstrate respect for opposing viewpoints?

Venus Williams in an ad endorsing Reebok

AP Photo/Kathy Willens

The Rhetorical Triangle

The relationship among the three kinds of appeals in an argument is traditionally represented by a triangle.

LOGOS (reason)
Focuses on the text

ETHOS (authority)   *PATHOS* (emotions)
Focuses on the writer   *Focuses on the audience*

In the diagram above—called the **rhetorical triangle**—all sides of the triangle are equal, implying that the three appeals occur in an argument in equal measure. In reality, however, this is seldom true. Depending on the audience, purpose, and situation, an argument may include all three appeals or just one or two. Moreover, one argument might emphasize reason, another might stress the writer's authority (or credibility), and still another might appeal mainly to the emotions. (In each of these cases, one side of the rhetorical triangle would be longer than the others.) In academic writing, for example, the appeal to reason is used most often, and the appeal to the emotions is less common. As Aristotle recognized, however, the three appeals often work together (to varying degrees) to create an effective argument.

Each of the following paragraphs makes an argument against smoking, illustrating how the appeals are used in an argument. Although each paragraph includes all three of the appeals, one appeal outweighs the others. (Keep in mind that each paragraph is aimed at a different audience.)

APPEAL TO REASON (*LOGOS*)

Among young people, the dangers of smoking are clear. According to the World Health Organization, smoking can cause a variety of problems in young people—for example, lung problems and shortness of breath. Smoking also contributes to heart attacks, strokes, and coronary artery disease (72). In addition, teenage smokers have an increased risk of developing lung cancer as they get older (CDC). According to one study, teenage smokers see doctors or other health professionals at higher rates than those who do not smoke (Ardly 112). Finally, teenagers who smoke tend to abuse alcohol and marijuana as well as engage in other risky behaviors (CDC). Clearly, tobacco is a dangerous drug that has serious health risks for teenage smokers. In fact, some studies suggest that smoking takes thirteen to fourteen years off a person's life (American Cancer Society).

APPEAL TO THE EMOTIONS (*PATHOS*)

Every day, almost four thousand young people begin smoking cigarettes, and this number is growing (Family First Aid). Sadly, most of you have no idea what you are getting into. For one thing, smoking yellows your teeth, stains your fingers, and gives you bad breath. The smoke also gets into your hair and clothes and makes you smell. Also, smoking is addictive; once you start, it's hard to stop. After you've been smoking for a few years, you are hooked, and as television commercials for the nicotine patch show, you can have a hard time breaking the habit. Finally, smoking is dangerous. In the United States, one out of every five deaths can be attributed to smoking (Teen Health). If you have ever seen anyone dying of lung cancer, you understand how bad long-term smoking can be. Just look at the pictures on the Internet of diseased, blackened lungs, and it becomes clear that smoking does not make you look cool or sophisticated, no matter what cigarette advertising suggests.

APPEAL TO AUTHORITY (*ETHOS*)

My advice to those who are starting to smoke is to reconsider—before it's too late. I began using tobacco over ten years ago when I was in high school. At first, I started using snuff because I was on the baseball team and wanted to imitate the players in the major leagues. It wasn't long before I had graduated to cigarettes—first a few and then at least a pack a day. I heard the warnings from teachers and the counselors from the D.A.R.E. program, but they didn't do any good. I spent almost all my extra money on cigarettes. Occasionally, I would stop—sometimes for a few days, sometimes for a few weeks—but I always started again. Later, after I graduated, the health plan at my job covered smoking cessation treatment, so I tried everything—the patch, Chantix, therapy, and even hypnosis. Again, nothing worked. At last, after I had been married for four years, my wife sat me down and begged me to quit. Later that night, I threw away my cigarettes and haven't smoked since. Although I've gained some weight, I now breathe easier, and I am able to concentrate better than I could before. Had I known how difficult quitting was going to be, I never would have started in the first place.

When you write an argumentative essay, keep in mind that each type of appeal has its own particular strengths. Your purpose and audience as well as other elements of the rhetorical situation help you determine what strategy to use. Remember, however, that even though most effective arguments use a combination of appeals, one appeal predominates. For example, even though academic arguments may employ appeals to the emotions, they do so sparingly. Most often, they appeal primarily to reason by using facts and statistics—not emotions—to support their points.

 For more practice, see the LearningCurve on Persuasive Appeals (*pathos, ethos,* and *logos*) in the LaunchPad for *Practical Argument.*

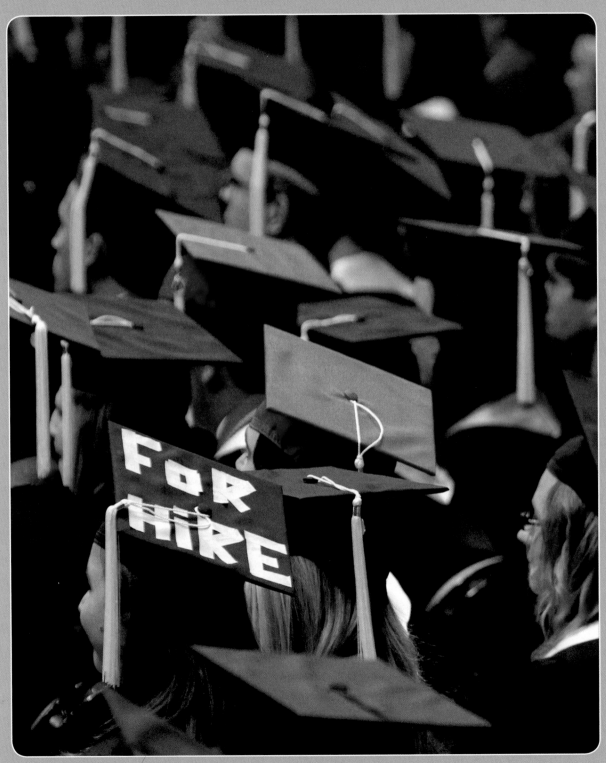

Butch Dill/AP Photos

1

The Four Pillars of Argument

Is a College Education Worth the Money?

In recent years, more and more high school graduates have been heading to college, convinced that higher education will enhance their future earning power. At the same time, the cost of a college education has been rising, and so has the amount of student-loan debt carried by college graduates. (During 2014, average tuition and fees at nonprofit private colleges rose 3.7 percent, to $31,231, while tuition for in-state students at four-year public schools went up 2.9 percent to $9,139. On average, 2015 graduates with student-loan debt owed over $35,000.) This situation has led some observers to wonder if the high cost of college actually pays off—not only in dollars but also in future job satisfaction. Will a college degree protect workers who are threatened by high unemployment, the rise of technology, the declining power of labor unions, and the trend toward outsourcing? Given the high financial cost of college, do the rewards of a college education—emotional and intellectual as well as financial—balance the sacrifices that students make in time and money? These and other questions have no easy answers.

Later in this chapter, you will be introduced to readings that highlight the pros and cons of investing in a college education, and you will be asked to write an argumentative essay in which you take a position on this controversial topic.

In a sense, you already know a lot more than you think you do about how to construct an argumentative essay. After all, an argumentative essay is a variation of the thesis-and-support essays that you have been writing in your college classes: you state a position on a topic, and then you support this position. However, argumentative essays also involve some special concerns in terms of structure, style, and purpose. Throughout this book, we introduce you to the unique features of argument. In this chapter, we focus on structure.

The Elements of Argument

An argumentative essay includes the same three sections—*introduction*, *body*, and *conclusion*—as any other essay. In an argumentative essay, however, the introduction includes an argumentative **thesis statement**, the body includes both the supporting **evidence** and the **refutation** of opposing arguments, and the conclusion includes a strong, convincing **concluding statement** that reinforces the position stated in the thesis.

The following diagram illustrates one way to organize an argumentative essay.

Introduction	Thesis statement
Body	Evidence
	Evidence
	Evidence
	Refutation of opposing arguments
Conclusion	Concluding statement

The elements of an argumentative essay are like the pillars of an ancient Greek temple. Together, the four elements—thesis statement, evidence, refutation of opposing arguments, and concluding statement—help you build a strong argument.

Ancient Greek temple

AP Photo/Alessandro Fucarini

Thesis Statement

A **thesis statement** is a single sentence that states your position on an issue. An argumentative essay must have an **argumentative thesis**—one that takes a firm stand. For example, on the issue of whether colleges should require all students to study a language other than English, your thesis statement could be any of the following (and other positions are also possible):

- Colleges should require all students to study a foreign language.
- Colleges should require all liberal arts majors to study a foreign language.
- Colleges should require all students to take Spanish, Chinese, or Farsi.
- Colleges should not require any students to study a foreign language.

An argumentative thesis must be **debatable**—that is, it must have at least two sides, stating a position with which some reasonable people might disagree. To confirm that your thesis is debatable, you should see if you can formulate an **antithesis**, or opposing argument. For example, the statement, "Our school has a foreign-language requirement" has no antithesis because it is simply a statement of fact; you could not take the opposite position because the facts would not support it. However, the following thesis statement takes a position that *is* debatable (and therefore suitable for an argumentative thesis):

THESIS	Our school should institute a foreign-language requirement.
ANTITHESIS	Our school should not institute a foreign-language requirement.

(For more on thesis statements, see Chapter 7.)

Evidence

Evidence is the material—facts, observations, expert opinion, examples, statistics, and so on—that supports your thesis statement. For example, you could support your position that foreign-language study should be required for all college students by arguing that this requirement will make them more employable, and you could cite employment statistics to support this point. Alternatively, you could use the opinion of an expert on the topic— for example, an experienced college language instructor—to support the opposite position, arguing that students without an interest in language study are wasting their time in such courses.

You will use both *facts* and *opinions* to support the points you make in your arguments. A **fact** is a statement that can be verified (proven to be true). An **opinion** is always open to debate because it is simply a personal judgment. Of course, the more knowledgeable the writer is, the more credible his or her opinion is. Thus, the opinion of a respected expert on language study will carry more weight than the opinion of a student with no particular expertise on the issue. However, if the student's opinion is supported by facts, it will be much more convincing than an unsupported opinion.

FACTS

- Some community colleges have no foreign-language requirements.

- Some selective liberal arts colleges require all students to take two years or more of foreign-language study.

- At some universities, undergraduates must take as many as fourteen foreign-language credits.

- Some schools grant credit for high school language classes, allowing these courses to fulfill the college foreign-language requirement.

UNSUPPORTED OPINIONS

- Foreign-language courses are not as important as math and science courses.

- Foreign-language study should be a top priority on university campuses.

- Engineering majors should not have to take a foreign-language course.

- It is not fair to force all students to study a foreign language.

SUPPORTED OPINIONS

- The university requires all students to take a full year of foreign-language study, but it is not doing enough to support those who need help. For example, it does not provide enough student tutors, and the language labs have no evening hours.

- According to Ruth Fuentes, chair of the Spanish department, nursing and criminal justice majors who take at least two years of Spanish have an easier time finding employment after graduation than students in those majors who do not study Spanish.

Refutation

Because every argument has more than one side, you should not assume that your readers will agree with you. On the contrary, readers usually need to be convinced that your position on an issue has merit.

This means that you need to do more than just provide sufficient evidence in support of your position; you also need to **refute** (disprove or call into question) arguments that challenge your position, possibly acknowledging the strengths of those opposing arguments and then pointing out their shortcomings. For example, if you take a position in favor of requiring foreign-language study for all college students, some readers might argue that college students already have to take too many required courses. After acknowledging the validity of this argument, you could refute it by pointing out that a required foreign-language course would not necessarily be a burden for students because it could replace another, less important required course. (For more on refutation, see Chapter 7.)

Concluding Statement

After you have provided convincing support for your position and refuted opposing arguments, you should end your essay with a strong **concluding statement** that reinforces your position. (The position that you want readers to remember is the one stated in your thesis, not the opposing arguments that you have refuted.) For example, you might conclude an essay in support of a foreign-language requirement by making a specific recommendation or by predicting the possible negative outcome of *not* implementing this requirement.

CHECKLIST

Does Your Argument Stand Up?

When you write an argumentative essay, check to make sure it includes all four of the elements you need to build a strong argument.

☐ Do you have an argumentative **thesis**?

☐ Do you include solid, convincing **evidence** to support your thesis?

☐ Do you include a **refutation** of the most compelling arguments against your position?

☐ Do you include a strong **concluding statement**?

⏺ The following student essay includes all four of the elements that are needed to build a convincing argument.

WHY FOREIGN-LANGUAGE STUDY SHOULD BE REQUIRED

NIA TUCKSON

Introduction

"What do you call someone who speaks three languages? Trilingual. 1 What do you call someone who speaks two languages? Bilingual. What do you call someone who speaks only one language? American." As this old joke illustrates, many Americans are unable to communicate in a language other than English. Given our global economy and American companies' need to conduct business with other countries, this problem needs to be addressed. A good first step is to require all college students to study a foreign language.

Thesis statement

First body paragraph: Evidence

After graduation, many students will work in fields in which speaking 2 (or reading) another language will be useful or even necessary. For example, health-care professionals will often be called on to communicate with patients who do not speak English; in fact, a patient's life may depend on their ability to do so. Those who work in business and finance may need to speak Mandarin or Japanese; those who have positions in the military or in the foreign service may need to speak Persian or Arabic. A working knowledge of one of these languages can help students succeed in their future careers, and it can also make them more employable.

Second body paragraph: Evidence

In addition to strengthening a résumé, foreign-language study can also 3 give students an understanding of another culture's history, art, and literature. Although such knowledge may never be "useful" in a student's career, it can certainly enrich the student's life. Too narrow a focus on career can turn college into a place that trains students rather than educates them. In contrast, expanding students' horizons to include subjects beyond those needed for their careers can better equip them to be lifelong learners.

Third body paragraph: Evidence

When they travel abroad, Americans who can speak a language 4 other than English will find that they are better able to understand people from other countries. As informal ambassadors for the United States, tourists have a responsibility to try to understand other languages and cultures. Too many Americans assume that their own country's language and culture are superior to all others. This shortsighted attitude is not likely to strengthen relationships between the United States and other nations. Understanding a country's language can help students to build bridges between themselves and others.

Some students say that learning a language is not easy and that it takes a great deal of time. College students are already overloaded with coursework, jobs, and family responsibilities, and a new academic requirement is certain to create problems. In fact, students may find that adding just six credits of language study will limit their opportunities to take advanced courses in their majors or to enroll in electives that interest them. However, this burden can be eased if other, less important course requirements—such as physical education—are eliminated to make room for the new requirement.

5 Fourth body paragraph: Refutation of opposing argument

Some students may also argue that they, not their school, should be able to decide what courses are most important to them. After all, a student who struggled in high school French and plans to major in computer science might understandably resist a foreign-language requirement. However, challenging college language courses might actually be more rewarding than high school courses were, and the student who struggled in high school French might actually enjoy a college-level French course (or study a different language). Finally, a student who initially plans to major in computer science may actually wind up majoring in something completely different—or taking a job in a country in which English is not spoken.

6 Fifth body paragraph: Refutation of opposing argument

Entering college students sometimes find it hard to envision their personal or professional futures or to imagine where their lives may take them. Still, a well-rounded education, including foreign-language study, can prepare them for many of the challenges that they will face. Colleges can help students keep their options open by requiring at least a year (and preferably two years) of foreign-language study. Instead of focusing narrowly on what interests them today, American college students should take the extra step to become bilingual—or even trilingual—in the future.

7 Conclusion

Concluding statement

⊘ EXERCISE 1.1

The following essay, "Raise the Drinking Age to Twenty-Five," by Andrew Herman, includes all four of the basic elements of argument discussed so far. Read the essay, and then answer the questions that follow it, consulting the diagram on page 24 if necessary.

This commentary appeared on August 22, 2007, on BG Views, a website for Bowling Green State University and the citizens of its community.

RAISE THE DRINKING AGE TO TWENTY-FIVE

ANDREW HERMAN

As a new school year begins, as dorms fill with new and returning students 1 alike, a single thought frequents the minds of every member of our population: newfound freedom from a summer of jobs and familial responsibilities.

But our return to school coexists with a possibly lethal counterpart: col- 2 lege drinking.

Nearly everyone is exposed to parties during college, and one would be hard 3 pressed to find a college party without alcohol. Most University students indicate in countless surveys they have used alcohol in a social setting before age 21.

It is startling just how ineffective current 4 laws have been at curbing underage drinking.

> "It is startling just how ineffective current laws have been."

A dramatic change is needed in the way 5 society addresses drinking and the way we enforce existing laws, and it can start with a simple change: making the drinking age 25.

Access and availability are the principal reasons underage drinking has 6 become easy to do. Not through direct availability, but through access to legal-aged "friends."

In a college setting, it is all but impossible not to know a person who is older 7 than 21 and willing to provide alcohol to younger students. Even if unintentional, there is no verification that each person who drinks is of the appropriate age.

However, it should be quite easy to ensure underage individuals don't have 8 access to alcohol. In reality, those who abstain from alcohol are in the minority. Countless people our age consider speeding tickets worse than an arrest for underage consumption.

Is it truly possible alcohol abuse has become so commonplace, so accept- 9 able, that people forget the facts?

Each year, 1,400 [college students] die from drinking too much. 600,000 10 are victims of alcohol-related physical assault and 17,000 are a result of drunken driving deaths, many being innocent bystanders.

Perhaps the most disturbing number: 70,000 people, overwhelmingly 11 female, are annually sexually assaulted in alcohol-related situations.

These numbers are difficult to grasp for the sheer prevalence of alcoholic 12 destruction. Yet, we, as college students, are responsible for an overwhelming portion of their incidence. It is difficult to imagine anyone would wish to assume the role of rapist, murderer, or victim. We all assume these things could never happen to us, but I am certain victims in these situations thought the same. The simple truth is that driving under the influence is the leading cause of death for teens. For 10- to 24-year-olds, alcohol is the fourth-leading cause of death, made so by factors ranging from alcohol poisoning to alcohol-related assault and murder.

For the sake of our friends, those we love, our futures, and ourselves, we must take a stand and we must do it now. 13

Advocates of lowering the drinking age assert only four countries worldwide maintain a "21 standard," and a gradual transition to alcohol is useful in reducing the systemic social problems of substance abuse. 14

If those under the age of 21 are misusing alcohol, it makes little sense to grant free rein to those individuals to use it legally. A parent who observes their children abusing the neighbor's dog would be irresponsible to get one of their own without altering such dangerous behavior. 15

Increasing the drinking age will help in the search for solutions to grievous alcoholic problems, making it far more difficult in college environments to find legal-aged providers. 16

By the time we are 25, with careers and possibly families of our own, there is no safety net to allow us to have a "Thirsty Thursday." But increasing the legal age is not all that needs to be done. Drinking to get drunk needs to exist as a social taboo rather than a doorway to popularity. 17

Peer pressure can become a tool to change this. What once was a factor greatly contributing to underage drinking can now become an instrument of good, seeking to end such a dangerous practice as excessive drinking. Laws on drinking ages, as any other law, need to be enforced with the energy and vigor each of us should expect. 18

Alcohol is not an inherently evil poison. It does have its place, as do all things in the great scheme of life. 19

But with alcohol comes the terrible risk of abuse with consequences many do not consider. All too often, these consequences include robbing someone of his life or loved one. All communities in the country, our own included, have been touched by such a tragedy. 20

Because of this, and the hundreds of thousands of victims each year in alcohol-related situations, I ask that you consider the very real possibility of taking the life of another due to irresponsible drinking. 21

If this is not enough, then take time to think, because that life could very well be your own. 22

Identifying the Elements of Argument

1. What is this essay's thesis? Restate it in your own words.

2. List the arguments Herman presents as evidence to support his thesis.

3. Summarize the opposing argument the essay identifies. Then, summarize Herman's refutation of this argument.

4. Restate the essay's concluding statement in your own words.

Is a College Education Worth the Money?

Reread the At Issue box on page 23, which summarizes questions raised on both sides of this issue. As the following sources illustrate, reasonable people may disagree about this controversial topic.

As you review the sources, you will be asked to answer some questions and to complete some simple activities. This work will help you understand both the content and the structure of the sources. When you have finished, you will be ready to write an essay in which you take a position on the topic "Is a College Education Worth the Money?"

Butch Dill/AP Photos

SOURCES

 David Leonhardt, "Is College Worth It? Clearly, New Data Say," p. 33

 Marty Nemko, "We Send Too Many Students to College," p. 37

 Jennie Le, "What Does It Mean to Be a College Grad?," p. 41

 Dale Stephens, "College Is a Waste of Time," p. 43

 Bridget Terry Long, "College Is Worth It—Some of the Time," p. 45

 Mary C. Daly and Leila Bengali, "Is It Still Worth Going to College?," p. 48

This essay appeared in the *New York Times* on May 27, 2014.

IS COLLEGE WORTH IT? CLEARLY, NEW DATA SAY

DAVID LEONHARDT

Rising Value of a College Degree

The pay of people with a four-year college degree has risen compared to that 1
of those with a high school degree but no college credit. The relative pay of
people who attended college without earning a four-year degree has stayed flat.

Ratio of average hourly pay, compared with pay of people with a high school degree

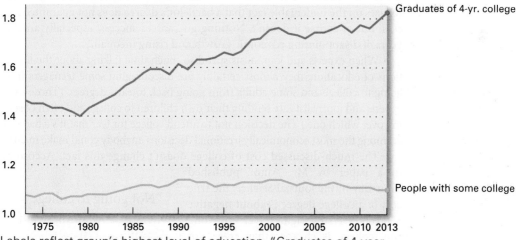

Labels reflect group's highest level of education. "Graduates of 4-year
college," for instance, excludes people with graduate degrees.

Data from: *New York Times* analysis of Economic Policy Institute data

Some newly minted college graduates struggle to find work. Others accept jobs 2
for which they feel overqualified. Student debt, meanwhile, has topped $1 trillion.

It's enough to create a wave of questions about whether a college educa- 3
tion is still worth it.

A new set of income statistics answers those questions quite clearly: Yes, col- 4
lege is worth it, and it's not even close. For all the struggles that many young college graduates face, a four-year degree has probably never been more valuable.

The pay gap between college graduates and everyone else reached a record 5
high last year, according to the new data, which is based on an analysis of Labor
Department statistics by the Economic Policy Institute in Washington. Americans with four-year college degrees made 98 percent more an hour on average in
2013 than people without a degree. That's up from 89 percent five years earlier,
85 percent a decade earlier, and 64 percent in the early 1980s.

The pay of people with a four-year college degree has risen compared to 6 that of those with a high school degree but no college credit. The relative pay of people who attended college without earning a four-year degree has stayed flat.

There is nothing inevitable about this trend. If there were more college 7 graduates than the economy needed, the pay gap would shrink. The gap's recent growth is especially notable because it has come after a rise in the number of college graduates, partly because many people went back to school during the Great Recession. That the pay gap has nonetheless continued growing means that we're still not producing enough of them.

"We have too few college graduates," says David Autor, an M.I.T. econo- 8 mist, who was not involved in the Economic Policy Institute's analysis. "We also have too few people who are prepared for college."

It's important to emphasize these shortfalls because public discussion 9 today—for which we in the news media deserve some responsibility—often focuses on the undeniable fact that a bachelor's degree does not guarantee success. But of course it doesn't. Nothing guarantees success, especially after 15 years of disappointing economic growth and rising inequality.

When experts and journalists spend so much time talking about the limita- 10 tions of education, they almost certainly are discouraging some teenagers from going to college and some adults from going back to earn degrees. (Those same experts and journalists are sending their own children to college and often obsessing over which one.) The decision not to attend college for fear that it's a bad deal is among the most economically irrational decisions anybody could make in 2014.

The much-discussed cost of college doesn't change this fact. According 11 to a paper by Mr. Autor published Thursday in the journal *Science*, the true cost of a college degree is about negative $500,000. That's right: Over the long run, college is cheaper than free. Not going to college will cost you about half a million dollars.

"Not going to college will cost you about half a million dollars."

Mr. Autor's paper—building on work by the economists Christopher Avery 12 and Sarah Turner—arrives at that figure first by calculating the very real cost of tuition and fees. This amount is then subtracted from the lifetime gap between the earnings of college graduates and high school graduates. After adjusting for inflation and the time value of money, the net cost of college is negative $500,000, roughly double what it was three decades ago.

This calculation is necessarily imprecise, because it can't control for 13 any pre-existing differences between college graduates and nongraduates— differences that would exist regardless of schooling. Yet other research, comparing otherwise similar people who did and did not graduate from college, has also found that education brings a huge return.

In a similar vein, the new Economic Policy Institute numbers show that 14 the benefits of college don't go just to graduates of elite colleges, who typically go on to earn graduate degrees. The wage gap between people with only a bachelor's degree and people without such a degree has also kept rising.

Tellingly, though, the wage premium for people who have attended college without earning a bachelor's degree—a group that includes community-college graduates—has not been rising. The big economic returns go to people with four-year degrees. Those returns underscore the importance of efforts to reduce the college dropout rate, such as those at the University of Texas, which Paul Tough described in a recent *Times Magazine* article. 15

But what about all those alarming stories you hear about indebted, jobless college graduates? 16

The anecdotes may be real, yet the conventional wisdom often exaggerates the problem. Among four-year college graduates who took out loans, average debt is about $25,000, a sum that is a tiny fraction of the economic benefits of college. (My own student debt, as it happens, was almost identical to this figure, in inflation-adjusted terms.) And the unemployment rate in April for people between 25 and 34 years old with a bachelor's degree was a mere 3 percent. 17

I find the data from the Economic Policy Institute especially telling because the institute—a left-leaning research group—makes a point of arguing that education is not the solution to all of the economy's problems. That is important, too. College graduates, like almost everyone else, are suffering from the economy's weak growth and from the disproportionate share of this growth flowing to the very richest households. 18

The average hourly wage for college graduates has risen only 1 percent over the last decade, to about $32.60. The pay gap has grown mostly because the average wage for everyone else has fallen—5 percent, to about $16.50. "To me, the picture is people in almost every kind of job not being able to see their wages grow," Lawrence Mishel, the institute's president, told me. "Wage growth essentially stopped in 2002." 19

From the country's perspective, education can be only part of the solution to our economic problems. We also need to find other means for lifting living standards—not to mention ways to provide good jobs for people without college degrees. 20

But from almost any individual's perspective, college is a no-brainer. It's the most reliable ticket to the middle class and beyond. Those who question the value of college tend to be those with the luxury of knowing their own children will be able to attend it. 21

Not so many decades ago, high school was considered the frontier of education. Some people even argued that it was a waste to encourage Americans from humble backgrounds to spend four years of life attending high school. Today, obviously, the notion that everyone should attend 13 years of school is indisputable. 22

But there is nothing magical about 13 years of education. As the economy becomes more technologically complex, the amount of education that people need will rise. At some point, 15 years or 17 years of education will make more sense as a universal goal. 23

That point, in fact, has already arrived. 24

⊃ AT ISSUE: SOURCES FOR STRUCTURING AN ARGUMENT

1. Paraphrase this essay's thesis statement by filling in the following template.

   Because _____ ,
   a four-year college degree is now more important than ever.

2. To support his position, Leonhardt relies largely on statistics. Where does he include other kinds of supporting evidence?

3. Look at the graph that follows paragraph 1, and read its caption. What does this image add to the essay? Would Leonhardt's argument have been as convincing without the graph? Why or why not?

4. In paragraph 8, Leonhardt quotes economist David Autor. How do you suppose Marty Nemko (p. 37) would respond to Autor's statements?

5. In paragraph 16, Leonhardt asks a question to introduce an argument opposed to his position. What is this argument? Does he refute it effectively in the discussion that follows?

6. In paragraph 22, Leonhardt begins his conclusion with an **analogy**. What two things is he comparing? What point is he making? Do you think this concluding strategy is effective? Why or why not? How else could he have ended his essay?

This undated essay is from MartyNemko.com.

WE SEND TOO MANY STUDENTS TO COLLEGE

MARTY NEMKO

Among my saddest moments as a career counselor is when I hear a story like 1
this: "I wasn't a good student in high school, but I wanted to prove to myself
that I can get a college diploma—I'd be the first one in my family to do it. But
it's been six years and I still have 45 units to go."

I have a hard time telling such people the killer statistic: According to the 2
U.S. Department of Education, if you graduated in the bottom 40 percent of
your high school class and went to college, 76 of 100 won't earn a diploma,
even if given 8½ years. Yet colleges admit and take the money from hundreds
of thousands of such students each year!

Even worse, most of those college dropouts leave college having learned 3
little of practical value (see below) and with devastated self-esteem and a
mountain of debt. Perhaps worst of all, those people rarely leave with a career
path likely to lead to more than McWages. So it's not surprising that when you
hop into a cab or walk into a restaurant, you're likely to meet workers who
spent years and their family's life savings on college, only to end up with a job
they could have done as a high school dropout.

Perhaps yet more surprising, even the high school students who are fully 4
qualified to attend college are increasingly unlikely to derive enough benefit to
justify the often six-figure cost and four to eight years it takes to graduate—and
only 40 percent of freshmen graduate in four years; 45 percent never graduate at
all. Colleges love to trumpet the statistic that, over their lifetimes, college graduates earn more than nongraduates. But that's terribly misleading because you
could lock the college-bound in a closet for four years and they'd earn more than
the pool of non-college-bound—they're brighter, more motivated, and have better family connections. Too, the past advantage of college graduates in the job
market is eroding: ever more students are going to college at the same time as
ever more employers are offshoring ever more professional jobs. So college graduates are forced to take some very nonprofessional jobs. For example, Jill Ple-
snarski holds a bachelor's degree in biology from the private ($160,000 published
total cost for four years) Moravian College. She had hoped to land a job as a
medical research lab tech, but those positions paid so little that she opted for a job
at a New Jersey sewage treatment plant. Today, although she's since been promoted, she must still occasionally wash down the tower that holds raw sewage.

Or take Brian Morris. After completing his bachelor's degree in liberal 5
arts from the University of California, Berkeley, he was unable to find a
decent-paying job, so he went yet deeper into debt to get a master's degree
from the private Mills College. Despite those degrees, the best job he could

land was teaching a three-month-long course for $3,000. At that point, Brian was married and had a baby, so to support them, he reluctantly took a job as a truck driver. Now Brian says, "I just *have* to get out of trucking."

Colleges are quick to argue that a college education is more about enlight- 6 enment than employment. That may be the biggest deception of all. There is a Grand Canyon of difference between what the colleges tout in their brochures and websites and the reality.

Colleges are businesses, and students are a cost item while research is a profit center. So colleges tend to educate students in the cheapest way possible: large lecture classes, with small classes staffed by rock-bottom-cost graduate students and, in some cases, even by undergraduate students. Professors who bring in big research dollars are almost always rewarded, while even a fine teacher who doesn't bring in the research bucks is often fired or relegated to the lowest rung: lecturer.

> "Colleges are businesses, and students are a cost item." 7

So, no surprise, in the definitive *Your First College Year* nationwide sur- 8 vey conducted by UCLA researchers (data collected in 2005, reported in 2007), only 16.4 percent of students were very satisfied with the overall quality of instruction they received and 28.2 percent were neutral, dissatisfied, or very dissatisfied. A follow-up survey of seniors found that 37 percent reported being "frequently bored in class," up from 27.5 percent as freshmen.

College students may be dissatisfied with instruction, but despite that, do 9 they learn? A 2006 study funded by the Pew Charitable Trusts found that 50 percent of college *seniors* failed a test that required them to do such basic tasks as interpret a table about exercise and blood pressure, understand the arguments of newspaper editorials, or compare credit card offers. Almost 20 percent of seniors had only basic quantitative skills. For example, the students could not estimate if their car had enough gas to get to the gas station.

What to do? Colleges, which receive billions of tax dollars with minimum 10 oversight, should be held at least as accountable as companies are. For example, when some Firestone tires were defective, the government nearly forced it out of business. Yet year after year, colleges turn out millions of defective products: students who drop out or graduate with far too little benefit for the time and money spent. Yet not only do the colleges escape punishment; they're rewarded with ever greater taxpayer-funded student grants and loans, which allow colleges to raise their tuitions yet higher.

What should parents and guardians do? 11

1. If your student's high school grades and SAT or ACT are in the bottom 12 half of his high school class, resist colleges' attempts to woo him. Their marketing to your child does *not* indicate that the colleges believe he will succeed there. Colleges make money whether or not a student learns, whether or not she graduates, and whether or not he finds good employment. If a physician recommended a treatment that cost a fortune and

required years of effort without disclosing the poor chances of it working, she'd be sued and lose in any court in the land. But colleges—one of America's most sacred cows—somehow seem immune.

So let the buyer beware. Consider nondegree options: 13

- Apprenticeship programs (a great portal to apprenticeship websites: www.khake.com/page58.html)

- Short career-preparation programs at community colleges

- The military

- On-the-job training, especially at the elbow of a successful small business owner

2. Let's say your student *is* in the top half of his high school class and is moti-   14
vated to attend college by more than the parties, being able to say she went to college, and the piece of paper. Then have her apply to perhaps a dozen colleges. Colleges vary less than you might think, yet financial aid awards can vary wildly. It's often wise to choose the college that requires you to pay the least cash and take on the smallest loan. College is among the few products where you don't get what you pay for—price does not indicate quality.

3. If your child is one of the rare breed who, on graduating high school, knows   15
what he wants to do and isn't unduly attracted to college academics or the *Animal House* environment that college dorms often are, then take solace in the fact that in deciding to forgo college, he is preceded by scores of others who have successfully taken that noncollege road less traveled. Examples: the three most successful entrepreneurs in the computer industry, Bill Gates, Michael Dell, and Apple cofounder Steve Wozniak, all do not have a college degree. Here are some others: Malcolm X, Rush Limbaugh, Barbra Streisand, PBS *NewsHour's* Nina Totenberg, Tom Hanks, Maya Angelou, Ted Turner, Ellen DeGeneres, former governor Jesse Ventura, IBM founder Thomas Watson, architect Frank Lloyd Wright, former Israeli president David Ben-Gurion, Woody Allen, Warren Beatty, Domino's pizza chain founder Tom Monaghan, folksinger Joan Baez, director Quentin Tarantino, ABC-TV's Peter Jennings, Wendy's founder Dave Thomas, Thomas Edison, Blockbuster Video founder and owner of the Miami Dolphins Wayne Huizenga, William Faulkner, Jane Austen, McDonald's founder Ray Kroc, Oracle founder Larry Ellison, Henry Ford, cosmetics magnate Helena Rubinstein, Benjamin Franklin, Alexander Graham Bell, Coco Chanel, Walter Cronkite, Walt Disney, Bob Dylan, Leonardo DiCaprio, cookie maker Debbi Fields, Sally Field, Jane Fonda, Buckminster Fuller, DreamWorks cofounder David Geffen, *Roots* author Alex Haley, Ernest Hemingway, Dustin Hoffman, famed anthropologist Richard Leakey, airplane inventors Wilbur and Orville Wright, Madonna, satirist H. L. Mencken, Martina Navratilova, Rosie O'Donnell, Nathan Pritikin (Pritikin diet), chef Wolfgang Puck, Robert

Redford, oil billionaire John D. Rockefeller, Eleanor Roosevelt, NBC mogul David Sarnoff, and seven U.S. presidents from Washington to Truman.

4. College is like a chain saw. Only in certain situations is it the right tool. 16 Encourage your child to choose the right tool for her post–high school experience.

⊙ AT ISSUE: SOURCES FOR STRUCTURING AN ARGUMENT

1. Which of the following statements best summarizes Nemko's position? Why?

   ■ "We Send Too Many Students to College" (title)

   ■ "There is a Grand Canyon of difference between what the colleges tout in their brochures and websites and the reality" (para. 6).

   ■ "Colleges, which receive billions of tax dollars with minimum oversight, should be held at least as accountable as companies are" (10).

   ■ "College is like a chain saw. Only in certain situations is it the right tool" (16).

2. Where does Nemko support his thesis with appeals to logic? Where does he appeal to the emotions? Where does he use an appeal to authority? Which of these three kinds of appeals do you find the most convincing? Why?

3. List the arguments Nemko uses to support his thesis in paragraphs 2–4.

4. In paragraph 4, Nemko says, "Colleges love to trumpet the statistic that, over their lifetimes, college graduates earn more than nongraduates." In paragraph 6, he says, "Colleges are quick to argue that a college education is more about enlightenment than employment." How does he refute these two opposing arguments? Are his refutations effective?

5. Nemko draws an analogy between colleges and businesses, identifying students as a "cost item" (7). Does this analogy—including his characterization of weak students as "defective products" (10)—work for you? Why or why not?

6. What specific solutions does Nemko propose for the problem he identifies? To whom does he address these suggestions—and, in fact, his entire argument?

7. Reread paragraph 15. Do you think the list of successful people who do not hold college degrees is effective support for Nemko's position? What kind of appeal does this paragraph make? How might you refute its argument?

This personal essay is from talk.onevietnam.org, where it appeared on May 9, 2011.

WHAT DOES IT MEAN TO BE A COLLEGE GRAD?

JENNIE LE

After May 14th, I will be a college graduate. By fall, there will be no more a cappella rehearsals, no more papers or exams, no more sleepless nights, no more weekday drinking, no more 1 AM milk tea runs, no more San Francisco Bay Area exploring. I won't be with the people I now see daily. I won't have the same job with the same awesome boss. I won't be singing under Sproul every Monday. I won't be booked with weekly gigs that take me all over California. I won't be lighting another VSA Culture Show.

I will also have new commitments: weekly dinner dates with my mom, brother/sister time with my other two brothers, job hunting and career building, car purchasing and maintenance. In essence, my life will be—or at least feel—completely different. From what college alumni have told me, I will soon miss my college days after they are gone.

But in the bigger picture, outside of the daily tasks, what does it mean to hold a college degree? My fellow graduating coworker and I discussed the importance (or lack thereof) of our college degrees: while I considered hanging up my two diplomas, she believed that having a bachelor's was so standard and insubstantial, only a professional degree is worth hanging up and showing off. Nowadays, holding a college degree (or two) seems like the norm; it's not a very outstanding feat.

> "Nowadays, holding a college degree (or two) seems like the norm."

However, I'd like to defend the power of earning a college degree. Although holding a degree isn't as powerful as it was in previous decades, stats still show that those who earn bachelor's degrees are likely to earn twice as much as those who don't. Also, only 27 percent of Americans can say they have a bachelor's degree or higher. Realistically, having a college degree will likely mean a comfortable living and the opportunity to move up at work and in life.

Personally, my degrees validate my mother's choice to leave Vietnam. She moved here for opportunity. She wasn't able to attend college here or in Vietnam or choose her occupation. But her hard work has allowed her children to become the first generation of Americans in the family to earn college degrees: she gave us the ability to make choices she wasn't privileged to make. Being the fourth and final kid to earn my degree in my family, my mom can now boast about having educated children who are making a name for themselves (a son who is a computer-superstar, a second son and future dentist studying at UCSF, another son who is earning his MBA and manages at Mattel, and a daughter who is thankful to have three brothers to mooch off of).

41

For me, this degree symbolizes my family being able to make and take the opportunities that we've been given in America, despite growing up with gang members down my street and a drug dealer across from my house. This degree will also mean that my children will have more opportunities because of my education, insight, knowledge, and support. 6

Even though a college degree isn't worth as much as it was in the past, it still shows that I—along with my fellow graduates and the 27 percent of Americans with a bachelor's or higher—will have opportunities unheard of a generation before us, showing everyone how important education is for our lives and our futures. 7

⊖ AT ISSUE: SOURCES FOR STRUCTURING AN ARGUMENT

1. What purpose do the first two paragraphs of this essay serve? Do you think they are necessary? Do you think they are interesting? How else could Le have opened her essay?

2. Where does Le state her thesis? Do you think she should have stated it more forcefully? Can you suggest a more effectively worded thesis statement for this essay?

3. In paragraph 3, Le summarizes an opposing argument. Paraphrase this argument. How does she refute it? Can you think of other arguments against her position that she should have addressed?

4. In paragraphs 5–6, Le includes an appeal to the emotions. Does she offer any other kind of supporting evidence? If so, where? What other kinds of evidence do you think she should include? Why?

5. Echoing a point she made in paragraph 4, Le begins her conclusion with "Even though a college degree isn't worth as much as it was in the past, . . ." Does this concluding statement undercut her argument, or is the information presented in paragraph 4 enough to address this potential problem?

This essay appeared on CNN.com on June 3, 2011.

COLLEGE IS A WASTE OF TIME

DALE STEPHENS

I have been awarded a golden ticket to the heart of Silicon Valley: the Thiel 1
Fellowship. The catch? For two years, I cannot be enrolled as a full-time student at an academic institution. For me, that's not an issue; I believe higher
education is broken.

I left college two months ago because it rewards conformity rather than 2
independence, competition rather than collaboration, regurgitation rather
than learning, and theory rather than application. Our creativity, innovation,
and curiosity are schooled out of us.

Failure is punished instead of seen as a learning opportunity. We think of 3
college as a stepping-stone to success rather than a means to gain knowledge.
College fails to empower us with the skills necessary to become productive
members of today's global entrepreneurial economy.

College is expensive. The College Board Policy Center found that the cost of 4
public university tuition is about 3.6 times higher today than it was 30 years ago,
adjusted for inflation. In the book *Academically Adrift*, sociology professors
Richard Arum and Josipa Roksa say that 36 percent of college graduates showed
no improvement in critical thinking, complex reasoning, or writing after four
years of college. Student loan debt in the United States, unforgivable in the case
of bankruptcy, outpaced credit card debt in 2010 and will top $1 trillion in 2011.

Fortunately, there are
productive alternatives to
college. Becoming the next
Mark Zuckerberg or mastering the phrase "Would you
like fries with that?" are not the only options.

> "Fortunately, there are productive alternatives to college."

The success of people who never completed or attended college makes us 6
question whether what we need to learn is taught in school. Learning by doing—in
life, not classrooms—is the best way to turn constant iteration into true innovation. We can be productive members of society without submitting to academic or
corporate institutions. We are the disruptive generation creating the "free agent
economy" built by entrepreneurs, creatives, consultants, and small businesses
envisioned by Daniel Pink in his book, *A Whole New Mind: Why Right Brainers
Will Rule the Future*.

We must encourage young people to consider paths outside college. 7
That's why I'm leading UnCollege: a social movement empowering individuals to take their education beyond the classroom. Imagine if millions of my
peers copying their professors' words verbatim started problem-solving in the
real world. Imagine if we started our own companies, our own projects, and

our own organizations. Imagine if we went back to learning as practiced in French salons, gathering to discuss, challenge, and support each other in improving the human condition.

A major function of college is to signal to potential employers that one is qualified to work. The Internet is replacing this signaling function. Employers are recruiting on LinkedIn, Facebook, StackOverflow, and Behance. People are hiring on Twitter, selling their skills on Google, and creating personal portfolios to showcase their talent. Because we can document our accomplishments and have them socially validated with tools such as LinkedIn Recommendations, we can turn experiences into opportunity. As more and more people graduate from college, employers are unable to discriminate among job seekers based on a college degree and can instead hire employees based on their talents. 8

Of course, some people want a formal education. I do not think everyone should leave college, but I challenge my peers to consider the opportunity cost of going to class. If you want to be a doctor, going to medical school is a wise choice. I do not recommend keeping cadavers in your garage. On the other hand, what else could you do during your next 50-minute class? How many e-mails could you answer? How many lines of code could you write? 9

Some might argue that college dropouts will sit in their parents' basements playing *Halo 2*, doing Jell-O shots, and smoking pot. These are valid but irrelevant concerns, for the people who indulge in drugs and alcohol do so before, during, and after college. It's not a question of authorities; it's a question of priorities. We who take our education outside and beyond the classroom understand how actions build a better world. We will change the world regardless of the letters after our names. 10

◉ AT ISSUE: SOURCES FOR STRUCTURING AN ARGUMENT

1. In paragraph 1, Stephens says, "I believe higher education is broken." Is this statement his essay's thesis? Explain.

2. List Stephens's criticisms of college education.

3. Why does Stephens begin by introducing himself as a winner of a Thiel Fellowship? Is this introductory strategy an appeal to *logos, ethos,* or *pathos*? Explain.

4. List the evidence that Stephens uses to support his position. Do you think this essay needs more supporting evidence? If so, what kind of support would you suggest Stephens add?

5. In paragraphs 9 and 10, Stephens considers possible arguments against his thesis. What are these opposing arguments? Does he refute them effectively?

6. Throughout this essay, Stephens uses the pronoun *we* (as well as the pronoun *I*). Do these first-person pronouns refer to college students in general? To certain kinds of students? To Thiel fellows? Explain.

This article first appeared in the online publication "Examining the Value of a College Degree," produced by PayScale.

COLLEGE IS WORTH IT—SOME OF THE TIME

BRIDGET TERRY LONG

Is it still worthwhile to attend college? This has been a constant question, and as an economist and higher education researcher, I can wholeheartedly say yes. The data are clear: individuals with at least some college education make more money than those with only a high school degree. And let us not forget about the non-monetary returns, such as better working conditions, lower rates of disability, and increased civic engagement.

However, the conversation has become more complicated as research has pointed to another important fact: yes, college is worth it, but not always. We no longer think that all educations are financially good investments—the specifics matter. The answer for any student depends upon three important factors: the college attended, the field of study, and the cost or debt taken.

> "We no longer think that all educations are financially good investments—the specifics matter."

First, the college a student attends makes a difference, as we can see from the Payscale data. But these recent data underscore a longer-term trend. In a 1999 study, a co-author and I documented increasing inequality among college-educated workers.[1] While those near the top of the income distribution (i.e., the 90th percentile) experienced larger returns to their educations over time, after accounting for inflation, those near the bottom of the distribution (i.e., the 10th percentile) earned less in 1995 than 1972. Our examination of the reasons behind these changes highlights the important role of increasing segregation in higher education, where the top students have become more and more concentrated at institutions with much greater resources. The colleges rated "most competitive" often spend more than three times per student than "less competitive" colleges.

However, selectivity rating alone does not necessarily predict which schools have the highest rates of student success. A 2009 study documents the fact that graduation rates differ not only by college selectivity but also within a selectivity group. For example, among colleges rated as "very competitive," six-year graduation rates averaged from 30 percent for the bottom 10 schools to 82 percent for the top 10 schools.[2] Selectivity does not necessarily guarantee high levels of degree completion.

---

[1]Hoxby, Caroline and Bridget Terry Long. (1999) "Explaining Rising Inequality among the College-Educated." National Bureau of Economic Research (NBER) Working Paper No. 6873.

[2]Hess, Frederick M., Mark Schneider, Kevin Carey, and Andrew P. Kelly. (2009) *Diplomas and Dropouts: Which Colleges Actually Graduate Their Students (and Which Don't).* American Enterprise Institute.

45

A large part of the problem to understanding which colleges are good 5
investments is the lack of good measures of college quality. Most existing
measures rely heavily on the academic achievements of students before they
even step foot on the college campus. Meanwhile, there are few measures of
the quality of the postsecondary learning experience or the value-added to
the student. Hence, we rely on indicators such as earnings and loan default
rates. While it is helpful to have this information to establish minimum
thresholds of what might be a financially worthwhile education, they are not
sufficient to help students compare possible colleges and make the decision
about where they, as individuals, might maximize their benefits.

The second thing that increasingly matters in college investments is the 6
field of study. While many students do not work in the field of their college
major, typically, students majoring in engineering and the sciences reap
the largest benefits. However, income is not the only thing that varies by
major: as emphasized by the Great Recession, unemployment rates also differ
by field of study. Interestingly, although education majors may not make the
most money, they have among the lowest unemployment rates.

The first two factors, the chosen college and major, focus on potential benefits, 7
but those benefits must be compared to costs to determine whether a college education is worthwhile. We focus most of our attention on price and debt load as a
measure of the burden of college costs. Debt is a reality of higher education today,
and some debt is fine if it makes possible a beneficial educational investment. However, the level of debt that is reasonable depends greatly on the school attended and
major. One might judge $10,000 of total debt for an engineering degree to be fine,
while the opposite would be true for a six-week certificate program.

Unfortunately, students typically have such poor counseling on how much 8
debt is appropriate given their plans, and with large levels of unmet financial
need, many turn to multiple sources of debt, such as credit cards and private
loans, without fully understanding how this will affect them over the longer term.
Moreover, recent graduates (or dropouts) fresh out of school have little apprecia-
tion for how their investments may pay off 10 years from now when their current
reality is living at home with their parents. In other words, it's difficult to inter-
nalize long-term benefits when the costs are so heavily weighed up front.

Ultimately, knowing whether college is a good investment depends on 9
which college, which major, at what price (or debt). Looking at the averages
is no longer as meaningful, given the importance of match for an individual
student with specific interests, talents, and resources. And while I would
underscore the fact that for the vast majority of students, most combinations
of college/major/debt they would choose are worthwhile investments, we
have reached a time when the benefits of college may not far exceed the costs
for increasing numbers of students.

Even if only a small percentage of investments are "bad"—ones in which 10
the college attended has low levels of success and gives credentials with little
value while making students take out large amounts of debt—we have reached
an enrollment level in which a small percentage translates into thousands and
thousands of students each year. And that is a problem that cannot be ignored.

⊙ AT ISSUE: SOURCES FOR STRUCTURING AN ARGUMENT

1. In paragraph 1, Long introduces herself as "an economist and higher education researcher." Why do you think she does this? Is she appealing here to *logos*, *ethos*, or *pathos*?

2. Long begins her essay with a question. What attitude toward college tuition does she assume her readers have? How can you tell? How else might she have opened her discussion?

3. According to Long, in what sense has "the conversation [about whether college is a worthwhile investment] become more complicated" (para. 2)? What "three important factors" does she consider?

4. Outline the structure of this essay, filling in the template below with Long's thesis statement and key points.

   Thesis statement:

   Support

   ■ *First important factor:* _____

   ■ *Second important factor:* _____

   ■ *Third important factor:* _____

5. In paragraphs 9 and 10, what does Long conclude about the value of a college education? What reservations does she have? How does the discussion in these paragraphs answer the question she asks in paragraph 1?

6. Could Long's entire essay be seen as a refutation of the position she takes in the essay's first paragraph? Explain.

7. If Long were making recommendations about how to solve the "problem that cannot be ignored" (10), what do you think she might recommend?

This economic letter was originally posted by the Federal Reserve Bank
of San Francisco at www.frbsf.org, where it appeared on May 5, 2014.

IS IT STILL WORTH GOING
TO COLLEGE?

MARY C. DALY AND LEILA BENGALI

Media accounts documenting the rising cost of a college education and rela-   1
tively bleak job prospects for new college graduates have raised questions
about whether a four-year college degree is still the right path for the average
American. In this *Economic Letter*, we examine whether going to college
remains a worthwhile investment. Using U.S. survey data, we compare annual
labor earnings of college graduates with those of individuals with only a high
school diploma. The data show college graduates outearn their high school
counterparts as much as in past decades. Comparing the earnings benefits of
college with the costs of attending a four-year program, we find that college is
still worth it. This means that, for the average student, tuition costs for the
majority of college education opportunities in the United States can be
recouped by age 40, after which college graduates continue to earn a return on
their investment in the form of higher lifetime wages.

Earnings Outcomes by Educational Attainment

A common way to track the value of going to college is to estimate a college   2
earnings premium, which is the amount college graduates earn relative to
high school graduates. We measure earnings for each year as the annual labor
income for the prior year, adjusted for inflation using the consumer price
index (CPI-U), reported in 2011 dollars. The earnings premium refers to the
difference between average annual labor income for high school and college
graduates. We use data on household heads and partners from the Panel
Study of Income Dynamics (PSID). The PSID is a longitudinal study that follows individuals living in the United States over a long time span. The survey
began in 1968 and now has more than 40 years of data including educational
attainment and labor market income. To focus on the value of a college
degree relative to less education, we exclude people with more than a four-
year degree.

Figure 1 shows the earnings premium relative to high school graduates   3
for individuals with a four-year college degree and for those with some college but no four-year degree. The payoff from a degree is apparent. Although
the premium has fluctuated over time, at its lowest in 1980 it was about
$15,750, meaning that individuals with a four-year college degree earned
about 43 percent more on average than those with only a high school degree.
In 2011, the latest data available in our sample, college graduates earned on
average about $20,050 (61 percent) more per year than high school graduates.

Over the entire sample period the college earnings premium has averaged about $20,300 (57 percent) per year. The premium is much smaller, although not zero, for workers with some college but no four-year degree.

Figure 1: Earnings Premium over High School Education

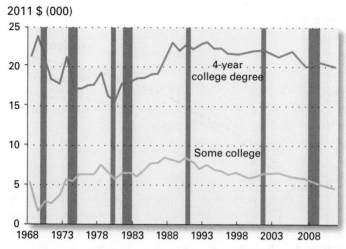

Data from: PSID and authors' calculations. Premium defined as difference in mean annual labor income. Blue bars denote NBER recession dates.

A potential shortcoming of the results in Figure 1 is that they combine the 4 earnings outcomes for all college graduates, regardless of when they earned a degree. This can be misleading if the value from a college education has varied across groups from different graduation decades, called "cohorts." To examine whether the college earnings premium has changed from one generation to the next, we take advantage of the fact that the PSID follows people over a long period of time, which allows us to track college graduation dates and subsequent earnings.

Using these data we compute the college earnings premium for three col- 5 lege graduate cohorts, namely those graduating in the 1950s–60s, the 1970s–80s, and the 1990s–2000s. The premium measures the difference between the average annual earnings of college graduates and high school graduates over their work lives. To account for the fact that high school graduates gain work experience during the four years they are not in college, we compare earnings of college graduates in each year since graduation to earnings of high school graduates in years since graduation plus four. We also adjust the estimates for any large annual fluctuations by using a three-year centered moving average, which plots a specific year as the average of earnings from that year, the year before, and the year after.

Figure 2 shows that the college earnings premium has risen consistently 6
across cohorts. Focusing on the most recent college graduates (1990s–2000s)
there is little evidence that the value of a college degree has declined over time,
and it has even risen somewhat for graduates five to ten years out of school.

Figure 2: College Earnings Premium by Graduation Decades

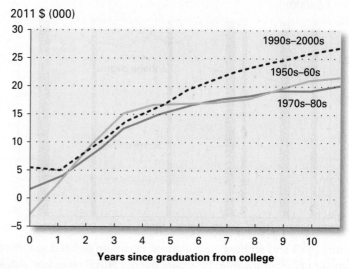

Data from: PSID and authors' calculations. Premium defined as
difference in mean annual labor income of college graduates in each
year since graduation and earnings of high school graduates in years
since graduation plus four. Values are three-year centered moving
averages of annual premiums.

The figure also shows that the gap in earnings between college and high 7
school graduates rises over the course of a worker's life. Comparing the earnings gap upon graduation with the earnings gap 10 years out of school illustrates this. For the 1990s–2000s cohort the initial gap was about $5,400, and in
10 years this gap had risen to about $26,800. Other analysis confirms that col-
lege graduates start with higher annual earnings, indicated by an initial earnings gap, and experience more rapid growth in earnings than members of
their age cohort with only a high school degree. This evidence tells us that the
value of a college education rises over a worker's life.

Of course, some of the variation in earnings between those with and with- 8
out a college degree could reflect other differences. Still, these simple estimates
are consistent with a large and rigorous literature documenting the substantial
premium earned by college graduates (Barrow and Rouse 2005, Card 2001,
Goldin and Katz 2008, and Cunha, Karahan, and Soares 2011). The main message from these and similar calculations is that on average the value of college
is high and not declining over time.

Finally, it is worth noting that the benefits of college over high school also 9
depend on employment, where college graduates also have an advantage. High
school graduates consistently face unemployment rates about twice as high as
those for college graduates, according to Bureau of Labor Statistics data. When
the labor market takes a turn for the worse, as during recessions, workers with
lower levels of education are especially hard-hit (Hoynes, Miller, and Schaller
2012). Thus, in good times and in bad, those with only a high school education
face a lower probability of employment, on top of lower average earnings once
employed.

The Cost of College

Although the value of college is apparent, 10
deciding whether it is worthwhile means
weighing the value against the costs of
attending. Indeed, much of the debate
about the value of college stems not from
the lack of demonstrated benefit but from
the overwhelming cost. A simple way to
measure the costs against the benefits is to
find the breakeven amount of annual
tuition that would make the average student indifferent between going to college
versus going directly to the workforce after high school.

> "Although the value of college is apparent, deciding whether it is worthwhile means weighing the value against the costs of attending."

To simplify the analysis, we assume that college lasts four years, students 11
enter college directly from high school, annual tuition is the same all four
years, and attendees have no earnings while in school. To focus on more
recent experiences yet still have enough data to measure earnings since graduation, we use the last two decades of graduates (1990s and 2000s) and again
smooth our estimates by using three-year centered moving averages.

We calculate the cost of college as four years of tuition plus the earnings 12
missed from choosing not to enter the workforce. To estimate what students
would have received had they worked, we use the average annual earnings of a
high school graduate zero, one, two, and three years since graduation.

To determine the benefit of going to college, we use the difference 13
between the average annual earnings of a college graduate with zero, one,
two, three, and so on, years of experience and the average annual earnings of
a high school graduate with four, five, six, seven, and so on years of experience. Because the costs of college are paid today but the benefits accrue over
many future years when a dollar earned will be worth less, we discount
future earnings by 6.67 percent, which is the average rate on an AAA bond
from 1990 to 2011.

With these pieces in place, we can calculate the breakeven amount of 14
tuition for the average college graduate for any number of years; allowing
more time to regain the costs will increase our calculated tuition ceiling.

If we assume that accumulated earnings between college graduates and non- 15
graduates will equalize 20 years after graduating from high school (at age 38), the

resulting estimate for breakeven annual tuition would be about $21,200. This amount may seem low compared to the astronomical costs for a year at some prestigious institutions; however, about 90 percent of students at public four-year colleges and about 20 percent of students at private nonprofit four-year colleges faced lower annual inflation-adjusted published tuition and fees in 2013–14 (College Board 2013). Although some colleges cost more, there is no definitive evidence that they produce far superior results for all students (Dale and Krueger 2011).

Table 1 shows more examples of maximum tuitions and the corresponding 16 percent of students who pay less for different combinations of breakeven years and discount rates. Note that the tuition estimates are those that make the costs and benefits of college equal. So, tuition amounts lower than our estimates make going to college strictly better in terms of earnings than not going to college.

Table 1: Maximum Tuitions by Breakeven Age and Discount Rates

	Breakeven age	
	33 (15 yrs after HS)	38 (20 yrs after HS)
Accumulated earnings with constant annual premium	$880,134	$830,816
Discount rate	Maximum tuition (% students paying less)	
5%	$14,385 (53–62%)	$29,111 (82–85%)
6.67%*	$9,869 (37–53%)	$21,217 (69–73%)
9%	$4,712 (0–6%)	$12,653 (53–62%)

*Average AAA bond rate 1990–2011 (rounded; Moody's).

Data from: PSID, College Board, and authors' calculations. Premia held constant 15 or 20 years after high school (HS) graduation. Percent range gives lower and upper bounds of the percent of full-time undergraduates at four-year institutions who faced lower annual inflation-adjusted published tuition and fees in 2013–14.

Although other individual factors might affect the net value of a college 17 education, earning a degree clearly remains a good investment for most young people. Moreover, once that investment is paid off, the extra income from the college earnings premium continues as a net gain to workers with a college degree. If we conservatively assume that the annual premium stays around $28,650, which is the premium 20 years after high school graduation for graduates in the 1990s–2000s, and accrues until the Social Security normal retirement age of 67, the college graduate would have made about $830,800 more than the high school graduate. These extra earnings can be spent, saved, or reinvested to pay for the college tuition of the graduate's children.

Conclusion

Although there are stories of people who skipped college and achieved finan- 18
cial success, for most Americans the path to higher future earnings involves a four-year college degree. We show that the value of a college degree remains high, and the average college graduate can recover the costs of attending in less than 20 years. Once the investment is paid for, it continues to pay dividends through the rest of the worker's life, leaving college graduates with substantially higher lifetime earnings than their peers with a high school degree. These findings suggest that redoubling the efforts to make college more accessible would be time and money well spent.

References

Barrow, L., and Rouse, C.E. (2005). "Does college still pay?" *The Economist's Voice* 2(4), pp. 1–8.

Card, D. (2001). "Estimating the return to schooling: progress on some persistent econometric problems." *Econometrica* 69(5), pp. 1127–1160.

College Board. (2013). "Trends in College Pricing 2013."

Cunha, F., Karahan, F., and Soares, I. (2011). "Returns to Skills and the College Premium." *Journal of Money, Credit, and Banking* 43(5), pp. 39–86.

Dale, S., and Krueger, A. (2011). "Estimating the Return to College Selectivity over the Career Using Administrative Earnings Data." *NBER Working Paper* 17159.

Goldin, C., and Katz, L. (2008). *The Race between Education and Technology.* Cambridge and London: The Belknap Press of Harvard University Press.

Hoynes, H., Miller, D., and Schaller, J. (2012). "Who Suffers During Recessions?" *Journal of Economic Perspectives* 26(3), pp. 27–48.

⊋ AT ISSUE: SOURCES FOR STRUCTURING AN ARGUMENT

1. Why does the title of this essay include the word "still"? What does *still* imply in this context?

2. This essay is an "economic letter" from the Federal Reserve Bank of San Francisco, and its language is more technical, and more math- and business-oriented, than that of the other readings in this chapter. In addition, this reading selection *looks* somewhat different from the others. What specific format features set this reading apart from others in the chapter?

3. What kind of supporting evidence do the writers use? Do you think they should have included any other kinds of support—for example, expert opinion? Why or why not?

4. In paragraph 10, the writers make a distinction between the "value of college" and the question of whether a college education is "worthwhile." Explain the distinction they make here.

5. For the most part, this report appeals to *logos* by presenting factual information. Does it also include appeals to *pathos* or *ethos*? If so, where? If not, should it have included these appeals?

TEMPLATE FOR STRUCTURING AN ARGUMENT

Write a one-paragraph argument in which you take a position on the topic of whether a college education is a good investment. Follow the template below, filling in the lines to create your argument.

Whether or not a college education is worth the money is a controversial topic. Some people believe that _____

_____

_____. Others challenge this position, claiming that _____

_____.

However, _____

_____. Although both sides of this issue have merit, it seems clear that a college education (is/is not) a worthwhile investment because _____

_____.

❍ EXERCISE 1.2

Interview two classmates on the topic of whether a college education is a worthwhile investment. Revise the one-paragraph argument that you drafted above so that it includes your classmates' views on the issue.

❍ EXERCISE 1.3

Write an essay on the topic "Is a College Education Worth the Money?" Cite the readings on pages 33–54, and be sure to document your sources and to include a works-cited page. (See Chapter 10 for information on documenting sources.)

❍ EXERCISE 1.4

Review the four-point checklist on page 27, and apply each question to your essay. Does your essay include all four elements of an argumentative essay? Add any missing elements. Then, label your essay's thesis statement, evidence, refutation of opposing arguments, and concluding statement.

❍ EXERCISE 1.5

Read the short essay that follows. What, if anything, do you think should be added to the writer's discussion to make it more convincing? Should anything be deleted or changed? Incorporating what you have learned about the structure and content of an effective argument, write a one-paragraph response to the essay.

This essay appeared on Businessweek.com in March 2011.

PRACTICAL EXPERIENCE TRUMPS FANCY DEGREES

TONY BRUMMEL

So you got great grades and earned your bachelor's degree? Congratulations. 1
You may have been better off failing college and then starting a venture and
figuring out why you didn't pass your classroom tests.

Being successful in business is absolutely not contingent on having a bach- 2
elor's degree—or any other type of degree, for that matter. A do-or-die work
ethic, passion, unwavering persistence, and vision mean more than anything
that can be taught in a classroom. How many college professors who teach
business have actually started a business?

I am the sole owner of the top independent rock
record label (according to Nielsen-published market
share). Historically, the music industry is thought of
as residing in New York City, Los Angeles, and
Nashville. But I have blazed my own trail, segregating my business in its own
petri dish here in Chicago. I started the business as a part-time venture in 1989
with $800 in seed capital. In 2009, Victory Records grossed $20 million. We've
released more than 500 albums, including platinum-selling records for the
groups Taking Back Sunday and Hawthorne Heights.

> "I have blazed my own trail." 3

Because I never went to college and didn't automatically have industry 4
contacts, I had to learn all of the business fundamentals through trial and error
when I started my own company. The skills I learned on my own have carried
me through 20 years of business. Making mistakes forces one to learn.

If you have a brand that people care about and loyal, hard-working 5
employees coupled with a robust network of smart financial advisers, fellow
entrepreneurs, and good legal backup, you will excel. There are plenty of people with degrees and MBAs who could read the books and earn their diplomas
but cannot apply what they learned to building a successful enterprise.

⟫ EXERCISE 1.6

Study the image that opens this chapter. What argument could it suggest
about the issue of whether a college education is worth the money?

PART

2

Reading and Responding to Arguments

Thinking and Reading Critically

Do Violent Media Images Trigger Violent Behavior?

In recent years, the popular media seem to have become increasingly violent. This is particularly true of visuals in video games and on some Internet sites, but graphically violent images also appear regularly in films, on TV, in comic books, and even in newspapers. Some research has suggested that these violent images can have a negative effect on those who view them, particularly on adolescents and young children. In fact, some media critics believe that these violent images have helped to create an increasingly violent culture, which in turn has inspired young people to commit violent crimes (including school shootings) such as the massacres at Virginia Tech in 2007 and Newtown, Connecticut, in 2012. The shooter who killed 12 people and injured 58 others at the premiere of *The Dark Knight Rises* in Aurora, Colorado, on July 20, 2012, was a devotee of violent role-playing video games, and some news reports emphasized that fact. Other observers, however, argue that violent media images are not to blame for such events—and that, in fact, these images may provide a safe outlet for aggression.

In this chapter and in the chapter that follows, you will be asked to read essays and study images that shed light on the relationship between media violence and violent behavior. In the process, you will learn critical-thinking and active reading strategies that will help you learn to examine and interpret texts and images.

Now that you understand the structure of an argumentative essay, you can turn your attention to reading arguments more closely. These arguments may be the subject of class discussion, or they may be source material for the essays you write. In any case, you will need to know how to get the most out of reading them.

Thinking Critically

When you **think critically**, you do not simply accept ideas at face value. Instead, you question these ideas, analyzing them in order to understand them better. You also challenge their underlying assumptions and form your own judgments about them. Throughout this book, discussions and readings encourage you to think critically. The box below shows you where in this text to find material that will help you develop your critical-thinking skills.

USING CRITICAL-THINKING SKILLS

Reading (see Chapter 2): When you read a text, you use critical-thinking skills to help you understand what the text says and what it suggests. You ask questions and look for answers, challenging the ideas you read and probing for information. *Previewing, highlighting,* and *annotating* are active reading strategies that require you to use critical-thinking skills.

Analyzing Visual Texts (see Chapter 3): When you examine an image, you use critical-thinking skills to help you understand what you are seeing, using previewing, highlighting, and annotating to help you analyze the image and interpret its persuasive message.

Writing a Rhetorical Analysis (see Chapter 4): When you write a rhetorical analysis of a text, you use critical-thinking skills to analyze its elements and to help you understand how the writer uses various appeals and rhetorical strategies to influence readers. Critical-thinking skills can also help you to understand the argument's context. Finally, you use critical-thinking skills to evaluate the overall effectiveness of the argument.

Analyzing an Argument's Logic (see Chapter 5): When you analyze an argument's logic, you use critical-thinking skills to help you understand the relationships among ideas and the form the argument takes as well as to determine whether its conclusions are both valid and true. You also use critical-thinking skills to identify any **logical fallacies** that may undermine the argument.

Writing an Essay (see Chapter 7): When you plan an essay, you use critical-thinking skills to probe a topic, to consider what you already know and what you need to find out, to identify your essay's main idea, and to decide how to support it—that is, which ideas to include and how to arrange them. As you draft and revise, you use critical-thinking skills to evaluate your supporting evidence, to make sure your arguments are reasonable and fair, and to decide whether ideas are arranged effectively within paragraphs and in the essay as a whole. *Freewriting, brainstorming, clustering*, and *outlining* are activities that require you to use critical-thinking skills.

Refuting Opposing Arguments (see Chapter 7): When you refute opposing arguments, you use critical-thinking skills to identify and evaluate arguments against your position—and to challenge or possibly argue against them.

Evaluating Sources (see Chapter 8): When you evaluate sources, you use critical-thinking skills to assess your sources in terms of their *accuracy, credibility, objectivity*, and *comprehensiveness* and to determine whether a source is trustworthy and appropriate for your purpose and audience.

Summarizing (see Chapter 9): When you summarize a passage, you use critical-thinking skills to identify the writer's main idea.

Paraphrasing (see Chapter 9): When you paraphrase a passage, you use critical-thinking skills to identify the writer's main idea, the most important supporting details and examples, and the ways in which key ideas are related.

Synthesizing (see Chapter 9): When you synthesize, you use critical-thinking skills to analyze sources and integrate them with your own ideas.

Reading Critically

When you read an argument, you should approach it with a critical eye. Contrary to what you may think, **reading critically** does not mean arguing with every idea you encounter. What it does mean is commenting on, questioning, and evaluating these ideas.

As a critical reader, you do not simply accept that what you are reading is true. Instead, you assess the accuracy of the facts in your sources, and you consider whether opinions are convincingly supported by evidence. You try to judge the appropriateness and reliability of a writer's sources, and you evaluate the scope and depth of the evidence and the relevance of that evidence to the topic. You also consider opposing arguments carefully, weighing them against the arguments developed in your sources. Finally, you watch out for possible **bias** in your sources—and you work hard to keep your own biases in check.

GUIDELINES FOR READING CRITICALLY

As a critical reader, you need to read carefully, keeping the following guidelines in mind:

- Assess the accuracy of a source's information.
- Be sure opinions are supported convincingly.
- Evaluate the supporting evidence.
- Consider opposing arguments.
- Be on the lookout for bias—in your sources and in yourself.

 LaunchPad
macmillan learning

For more practice, see the LearningCurve on Reading Critically in the LaunchPad for *Practical Argument*.

Becoming an Active Reader

Reading critically means being an active rather than a passive reader. Being an **active reader** means participating in the reading process by taking the time to preview a source and then to read it carefully, highlighting and annotating it. This process will prepare you to discuss the source with others and to respond in writing to what you have read.

Previewing

When you approach an argument for the first time, you **preview** it, skimming the argument to help you form a general impression of the writer's position on the issue, the argument's key supporting points, and the context for the writer's remarks.

Begin by looking at the title, the first paragraph (which often contains a thesis statement or overview), and the last paragraph (which often includes a concluding statement or a summary of the writer's key points). Also look at the topic sentences of the essay's body paragraphs. In addition, note any headings, words set in boldface or italic type, and bulleted or numbered lists in the body of the argument. If the argument includes visuals—charts, tables, graphs, photos, and so on—look at them as well. Finally, if an argument includes a headnote or background on the author or on the text, be sure to read this material. It can help you to understand the context in which the author is writing.

When you have finished previewing the argument, you should have a good general sense of what the writer wants to communicate.

Close Reading

Now, you are ready to read through the argument more carefully. As you read, look for words and phrases that help to shape the structure of the argument and signal the arrangement of the writer's ideas. These words and phrases will help you understand the flow of ideas as well as the content and emphasis of the argument.

COMPREHENSION CLUES

- Phrases that signal emphasis (the *primary* reason, the *most important* problem)

- Repeated words and phrases

- Words and phrases that signal addition (*also, in addition, furthermore*)

- Words and phrases that signal time sequence (*first, after that, next, then, finally*)

- Words and phrases that identify causes and effects (*because, as a result, for this reason*)

- Words and phrases that introduce examples (*for example, for instance*)

- Words and phrases that signal comparison (*likewise, similarly, in the same way*)

- Words and phrases that signal contrast (*although, in contrast, on the other hand*)

- Words and phrases that signal contradiction (*however, on the contrary*)

- Words and phrases that signal a move from general to specific (*in fact, specifically, in other words*)

- Words and phrases that introduce summaries or conclusions (*to sum up, in conclusion*)

⊝ EXERCISE 2.1

"Violent Media Is Good for Kids" is an essay by Gerard Jones, a comic book writer and author of several books about popular media. In this essay, which begins on the following page, Jones argues that violent comic books and video games serve a useful function for young people.

In preparation for class discussion and other activities that will be assigned later in this chapter, preview the essay. Then, read it carefully, and answer the questions that follow it.

This article appeared in *Mother Jones* on June 28, 2000.

VIOLENT MEDIA IS GOOD FOR KIDS

GERARD JONES

At 13 I was alone and afraid. Taught by my well-meaning, progressive, English-teacher parents that violence was wrong, that rage was something to be overcome and cooperation was always better than conflict, I suffocated my deepest fears and desires under a nice-boy persona. Placed in a small, experimental school that was wrong for me, afraid to join my peers in their bumptious rush into adolescent boy-hood, I withdrew into passivity and loneliness. My parents, not trusting the violent world of the late 1960s, built a wall between me and the crudest elements of American pop culture.

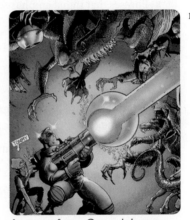

A scene from Gerard Jones and Will Jacobs's comic book *Monsters from Outer Space.*
© Gerard Jones, Gene Ha, Will Jacobs.

Then the Incredible Hulk smashed through it.

One of my mother's students convinced her that Marvel Comics, despite their apparent juvenility and violence, were in fact devoted to lofty messages of pacifism and tolerance. My mother borrowed some, thinking they'd be good for me. And so they were. But not because they preached lofty messages of benevolence. They were good for me because they were juvenile. And violent.

The character who caught me, and freed me, was the Hulk: overgendered and undersocialized, half-naked and half-witted, raging against a frightened world that misunderstood and persecuted him. Suddenly I had a fantasy self to carry my stifled rage and buried desire for power. I had a fantasy self who was a self: unafraid of his desires and the world's disapproval, unhesitating and effective in action. "Puny boy follow Hulk!" roared my fantasy self, and I followed.

I followed him to new friends—other sensitive geeks chasing their own inner brutes—and I followed him to the arrogant, self-exposing, self-assertive, superheroic decision to become a writer. Eventually, I left him behind, followed more sophisticated heroes, and finally my own lead along a twisting path to a career and an identity. In my 30s, I found myself writing action movies and comic books. I wrote some Hulk stories, and met the geek-geniuses who created him. I saw my own creations turned into action figures, cartoons, and computer games. I talked to the kids who read my stories. Across generations, genders, and ethnicities I kept seeing the same story: people pulling themselves out of emotional traps by immersing themselves in violent stories. People integrating the scariest, most fervently denied fragments of their psyches into fuller senses of selfhood through fantasies of superhuman combat and destruction.

I have watched my son living the same story—transforming himself into a 6 bloodthirsty dinosaur to embolden himself for the plunge into preschool, a Power Ranger to muscle through a social competition in kindergarten. In the first grade, his friends started climbing a tree at school. But he was afraid: of falling, of the centipedes crawling on the trunk, of sharp branches, of his friends' derision. I took my cue from his own fantasies and read him old Tarzan comics, rich in combat and bright with flashing knives. For two weeks he lived in them. Then he put them aside. And he climbed the tree.

A scene from Gerard Jones and Gene Ha's comic book *Oktane*. © Gerard Jones, Gene Ha, Will Jacobs.

But all the while, especially in the wake of 7 the recent burst of school shootings, I heard pop psychologists insisting that violent stories are harmful to kids, heard teachers begging parents to keep their kids away from "junk culture," heard a guilt-stricken friend with a son who loved Pokémon lament, "I've turned into the bad mom who lets her kid eat sugary cereal and watch cartoons!"

That's when I started the research.   8

"Fear, greed, power-hunger, rage: these 9 are aspects of our selves that we try not to experience in our lives but often want, even need, to experience vicariously through stories of others," writes Melanie Moore, Ph.D., a psychologist who works with urban teens. "Children need violent entertainment in order to explore the inescapable feelings that they've been taught to deny, and to reintegrate those feelings into a more whole, more complex, more resilient selfhood."

Moore consults to public schools and local 10 governments, and is also raising a daughter. For the past three years she and I have been studying the ways in which children use violent stories to meet their emotional and developmental needs—and the ways in which adults can help them use those stories healthily. With her help I developed *Power Play*, a program for helping young people improve their self-knowledge and sense of potency through heroic, combative storytelling.

We've found that every aspect of even the trashiest pop-culture story can 11 have its own developmental function. Pretending to have superhuman powers helps children conquer the feelings of powerlessness that inevitably come with being so young and small. The dual-identity concept at the heart of many superhero stories helps kids negotiate the conflicts between the inner self and the public self as they work through the early stages of socialization. Identification with a rebellious, even destructive, hero helps children learn to push back against a modern culture that cultivates fear and teaches dependency.

At its most fundamental level, what we call "creative violence"—head- 12
bonking cartoons, bloody video games, playground karate, toy guns—gives children a tool to master their rage. Children will feel rage. Even the sweetest and most civilized of them, even those whose parents read the better class of literary magazines, will feel rage. The world is uncontrollable and incomprehensible; mas-

> "Rage can be an energizing emotion."

tering it is a terrifying, enraging task. Rage can be an energizing emotion, a shot of courage to push us to resist greater threats, take more control, than we ever thought we could. But rage is also the emotion our culture distrusts the most. Most of us are taught early on to fear our own. Through immersion in imaginary combat and identification with a violent protagonist, children engage the rage they've stifled, come to fear it less, and become more capable of utilizing it against life's challenges.

I knew one little girl who went around exploding with fantasies so violent 13
that other moms would draw her mother aside to whisper, "I think you should know something about Emily. . . ." Her parents were separating, and she was small, an only child, a tomboy at an age when her classmates were dividing sharply along gender lines. On the playground she acted out *Sailor Moon*° fights, and in the classroom she wrote stories about people being stabbed with knives. The more adults tried to control her stories, the more she acted out the roles of her angry heroes: breaking rules, testing limits, roaring threats.

A Japanese cartoon series about magical girls

Then her mother and I started helping her tell her stories. She wrote them, 14
performed them, drew them like comics: sometimes bloody, sometimes tender, always blending the images of pop culture with her own most private fantasies. She came out of it just as fiery and strong, but more self-controlled and socially competent: a leader among her peers, the one student in her class who could truly pull boys and girls together.

The title character of *Oktane* gets nasty.
© Gerard Jones, Gene Ha, Will Jacobs.

I worked with an older girl, a 15
middle-class "nice girl," who held herself together through a chaotic family situation and a tumultuous adolescence with gangsta rap. In the mythologized street violence of Ice T, the rage and strutting of his music and lyrics, she found a theater of the mind in which she could

be powerful, ruthless, invulnerable. She avoided the heavy drug use that sank many of her peers, and flowered in college as a writer and political activist.

I'm not going to argue that violent entertainment is harmless. I think it has helped inspire some people to real-life violence. I am going to argue that it's helped hundreds of people for every one it's hurt, and that it can help far more if we learn to use it well. I am going to argue that our fear of "youth violence" isn't well-founded on reality, and that the fear can do more harm than the reality. We act as though our highest priority is to prevent our children from growing up into murderous thugs—but modern kids are far more likely to grow up too passive, too distrustful of themselves, too easily manipulated.

We send the message to our children in a hundred ways that their craving for imaginary gun battles and symbolic killings is wrong, or at least dangerous. Even when we don't call for censorship or forbid *Mortal Kombat*, we moan to other parents within our kids' earshot about the "awful violence" in the entertainment they love. We tell our kids that it isn't nice to play-fight, or we steer them from some monstrous action figure to a pro-social doll. Even in the most progressive households, where we make such a point of letting children feel what they feel, we rush to substitute an enlightened discussion for the raw material of rageful fantasy. In the process, we risk confusing them about their natural aggression in the same way the Victorians° confused their children about their sexuality. When we try to protect our children from their own feelings and fantasies, we shelter them not against violence but against power and selfhood.

The people who lived during the reign of Victoria (1819– 1901), queen of Great Britain and Ireland, who are often associated with prudish behavior.

Identifying the Elements of Argument

1. What is Jones's thesis? Restate it in your own words.

2. What arguments does Jones present as evidence in support of his thesis?

3. What arguments against his position does Jones identify? How does he refute them?

4. Paraphrase Jones's concluding statement.

Highlighting

After you read an argument, read through it again, this time highlighting as you read. When you **highlight**, you use underlining and symbols to identify the essay's most important points. (Note that the word *highlighting* does not necessarily refer to the underlining done with a yellow highlighter pen.) This active reading strategy will help you to understand the writer's ideas and to see connections among those ideas when you reread.

How do you know what to highlight? As a general rule, you look for the same signals that you looked for when you read the essay the first time—for example, the essay's thesis and topic sentences and the words and phrases that identify the writer's intent and emphasis. This time, however, you physically mark these elements and use various symbols to indicate your reactions to them.

SUGGESTIONS FOR HIGHLIGHTING

- Underline key ideas—for example, ideas stated in topic sentences.

- Box or circle words or phrases you want to remember.

- Place a check mark or a star next to an important idea.

- Place a double check mark or double star next to an especially significant idea.

- Draw lines or arrows to connect related ideas.

- Write a question mark near an unfamiliar reference or a word you need to look up.

- Number the writer's key supporting points or examples.

⊙ Here is how a student, Katherine Choi, highlighted the essay "When Life Imitates Video" by John Leo, which appears below. Choi was preparing to write an essay about the effects of media violence on children and adolescents. She began her highlighting by underlining and starring the thesis statement (para. 2). She then circled references to Leo's two key examples, "Colorado massacre" (1) and "Paducah, Ky." (7) and placed question marks beside them to remind herself to find out more about them. In addition, she underlined and starred some particularly important points (2, 8, 9) as well as what she identified as the essay's concluding statement (11).

This essay first appeared in *U.S. News & World Report* on May 3, 1999.

WHEN LIFE IMITATES VIDEO

JOHN LEO

Marching through a large building using various bombs and guns to pick off   1
victims is a conventional video-game scenario. In the Colorado massacre, Dylan Klebold and Eric Harris used pistol-grip shotguns, as in some video-arcade games. The pools of blood, screams of agony, and pleas for mercy must have been familiar—they are featured in some of the newer and more realistic kill-for-kicks games. "With each kill," the *Los Angeles Times* reported, "the

teens cackled and shouted as though playing one of the morbid video games they loved." And they ended their spree by shooting themselves in the head, the final act in the game *Postal*, and, in fact, the only way to end it.

Did the sensibilities created by the modern, video kill games play a role in the Littleton massacre? Apparently so. Note the cool and casual cruelty, the outlandish arsenal of weapons, the cheering and laughing while hunting down victims one by one. All of this seems to reflect the style and feel of the video killing games they played so often.

No, there isn't any direct connection between most murderous games and most murders. And yes, the primary responsibility for protecting children from dangerous games lies with their parents, many of whom like to blame the entertainment industry for their own failings.

But there is a cultural problem here: We are now a society in which the chief form of play for millions of youngsters is making large numbers of people die. Hurting and maiming others is the central fun activity in video games played so addictively by the young. A widely cited survey of 900 fourth-through eighth-grade students found that almost half of the children said their favorite electronic games involve violence. Can it be that all this constant training in make-believe killing has no social effects?

Dress rehearsal. The conventional argument is that this is a harmless activity among children who know the difference between fantasy and reality. But the games are often played by unstable youngsters unsure about the difference. Many of these have been maltreated or rejected and left alone most of the time (a precondition for playing the games obsessively). Adolescent feelings of resentment, powerlessness, and revenge pour into the killing games. In these children, the games can become a dress rehearsal for the real thing.

Psychologist David Grossman of Arkansas State University, a retired Army officer, thinks "point and shoot" video games have the same effect as military strategies used to break down a soldier's aversion to killing. During World War II, only 15 to 20 percent of all American soldiers fired their weapon in battle. Shooting games in which the target is a man-shaped outline, the Army found, made recruits more willing to "make killing a reflex action."

Video games are much more powerful versions of the military's primitive discovery about overcoming the reluctance to shoot. Grossman says Michael Carneal, the schoolboy shooter in Paducah, Ky, showed the effects of video- game lessons in killing. Carneal coolly shot nine times, hitting eight people, five of them in the head or neck. Head shots pay a bonus in many video games. Now the Marine Corps is adapting a version of *Doom*, the hyperviolent game played by one of the Littleton killers, for its own training purposes.

More realistic touches in video games help blur the boundary between fantasy and reality—guns carefully modeled on real ones, accurate-looking wounds, screams, and other sound effects, even the recoil of a heavy rifle. Some newer games seem intent on erasing children's empathy and concern for others. Once the intended victims of video slaughter were mostly gangsters or aliens. Now some games invite players to blow away ordinary people who have done nothing wrong—pedestrians, marching bands, an elderly woman with a walker. In these games, the shooter is not a hero, just a violent sociopath. One ad for a Sony game says: "Get in touch with your gun-toting, testosterone-pumping, cold-blooded murdering side."

These killings are supposed to be taken as harmless over-the-top jokes. 9
But the bottom line is that the young are being invited to enjoy the killing of vulnerable people picked at random. This looks like the final lesson in a course to eliminate any lingering resistance to killing.

SWAT teams and cops now turn up as the intended victims of some 10
video-game killings. This has the effect of exploiting resentments toward law enforcement and making real-life shooting of cops more likely. This sensibility turns up in the hit movie *Matrix*: world-saving hero Keanu Reeves, in a mandatory Goth-style, long black coat packed with countless heavy-duty guns, is forced to blow away huge numbers of uniformed law-enforcement people.

"We have to start worrying about what we are putting into the minds of 11
our young," says Grossman. "Pilots train on flight simulators, drivers on driving simulators, and now we have our children on murder simulators." If we want to avoid more Littleton-style massacres, we will begin taking the social effects of the killing games more seriously.

➲ EXERCISE 2.2

Look carefully at Katherine Choi's highlighting of John Leo's essay on pages 68–70. How would your own highlighting of this essay be similar to or different from hers?

➲ EXERCISE 2.3

Reread "Violent Media Is Good for Kids" (pp. 64–67). As you read, highlight the essay by underlining and starring important points, boxing or circling key words, writing question marks beside references that need further explanation, or drawing lines and arrows to connect related ideas.

Annotating

As you highlight, you should also annotate what you are reading. **Annotating** means making notes—of your questions, reactions, and ideas for discussion or writing—in the margins or between the lines. Keeping this kind of informal record of ideas as they occur to you will prepare you for class discussion and provide a useful source of material when you write.

As you read an argument and think critically about what you are reading, use the questions in the following checklist to help you make useful annotations.

CHECKLIST

Questions for Annotating

- ☐ What issue is the writer focusing on?
- ☐ Does the writer take a clear stand on this issue?
- ☐ What is the writer's thesis?
- ☐ What is the writer's purpose (his or her reason for writing)?
- ☐ What kind of audience is the writer addressing?
- ☐ Does the argument appear in a popular periodical or in a scholarly journal?
- ☐ Does the writer seem to assume readers will agree with the essay's position?

- ☐ What evidence does the writer use to support the essay's thesis? Does the writer include enough evidence?
- ☐ Does the writer consider (and refute) opposing arguments?
- ☐ Do you understand the writer's vocabulary?
- ☐ Do you understand the writer's references?
- ☐ Do you agree with the points the writer makes?
- ☐ Do the views the writer expresses agree or disagree with the views presented in other essays you have read?

The following pages, which reproduce Katherine Choi's highlighting of John Leo's essay on pages 68–70, also include her marginal annotations. In these annotations, Choi put Leo's thesis and some of his key points into her own words and recorded a few questions that she intended to explore further. She also added notes to clarify his references to two iconic school shootings. Finally, she identified arguments against Leo's position and his refutation of these arguments.

This essay first appeared in *U.S. News & World Report* on May 3, 1999.

WHEN LIFE IMITATES VIDEO
JOHN LEO

Marching through a large building using various bombs and guns to pick off victims is a conventional video-game scenario. In the (Colorado massacre) Dylan Klebold and Eric Harris used pistol-grip shotguns, as in some video-arcade games. The pools of blood, screams of agony, and pleas for mercy must have been familiar—they are featured in some of the newer and more realistic kill-for-kicks games. "With each kill," the *Los Angeles Times* reported, "the teens cackled and shouted as though playing one of the morbid video games they loved." And they ended their spree by shooting themselves in the head, the final act in the game *Postal*, and, in fact, the only way to end it.

Columbine H.S., 1999

Thesis
His position: "video kill games" can lead to violent behavior

✳

Did the sensibilities created by the modern, video kill games play a role 2 in the Littleton massacre? Apparently so. Note the cool and casual cruelty, the outlandish arsenal of weapons, the cheering and laughing while hunting down victims one by one. All of this seems to reflect the style and feel of the video killing games they played so often.

Opposing arguments

No, there isn't any direct connection between most murderous games and 3 most murders. And yes, the primary responsibility for protecting children from dangerous games lies with their parents, many of whom like to blame the entertainment industry for their own failings.

Refutation

True? ———————————

Date of survey?

(He means "training" does have negative effects, right?)

But there is a cultural problem here: We are now a society in which the 4 chief form of play for millions of youngsters is making large numbers of people die. Hurting and maiming others is the central fun activity in video games played so addictively by the young. A widely cited survey of 900 fourth-through eighth-grade students found that almost half of the children said their favorite electronic games involve violence. Can it be that all this constant training in make-believe killing has no social effects?

Opposing argument

Refutation

Dress rehearsal. The conventional argument is that this is a harmless 5 activity among children who know the difference between fantasy and reality. But the games are often played by unstable youngsters unsure about the difference. Many of these have been maltreated or rejected and left alone most of the time (a precondition for playing the games obsessively). Adolescent feelings of resentment, powerlessness, and revenge pour into the killing games. In these children, the games can become a dress rehearsal for the real thing.

Quotes psychologist (= authority)

Psychologist David Grossman of Arkansas State University, a retired 6 Army officer, thinks "point and shoot" video games have the same effect as military strategies used to break down a soldier's aversion to killing. During World War II, only 15 to 20 percent of all American soldiers fired their weapon in battle. Shooting games in which the target is a man-shaped outline, the Army found, made recruits more willing to "make killing a reflex action."

1997 ————————————

Video games are much more powerful versions of the military's primitive 7 discovery about overcoming the reluctance to shoot. Grossman says Michael Carneal, the schoolboy shooter in Paducah, Ky, showed the effects of video-game lessons in killing. Carneal coolly shot nine times, hitting eight people, five of them in the head or neck. Head shots pay a bonus in many video games. Now the Marine Corps is adapting a version of *Doom*, the hyperviolent game played by one of the Littleton killers, for its own training purposes.

✳

More realistic touches in video games help blur the boundary between 8 fantasy and reality—guns carefully modeled on real ones, accurate-looking wounds, screams, and other sound effects, even the recoil of a heavy rifle. Some newer games seem intent on erasing children's empathy and concern for others. Once the intended victims of video slaughter were mostly gangsters or aliens. Now some games invite players to blow away ordinary people who have done nothing wrong—pedestrians, marching bands, an elderly woman with a walker. In these games, the shooter is not a hero, just a violent sociopath.

One ad for a Sony game says: "Get in touch with your gun-toting, testosterone-pumping, cold-blooded murdering side."

These killings are supposed to be taken as harmless over-the-top jokes. But the bottom line is that the young are being invited to enjoy the killing of vulnerable people picked at random. This looks like the final lesson in a course to eliminate any lingering resistance to killing.   9

SWAT teams and cops now turn up as the intended victims of some video-game killings. This has the effect of exploiting resentments toward law enforcement and making real-life shooting of cops more likely. This sensibility turns up in the hit movie *Matrix*: world-saving hero Keanu Reeves, in a mandatory Goth-style, long black coat packed with countless heavy-duty guns, is forced to blow away huge numbers of uniformed law-enforcement people.   10

"We have to start worrying about what we are putting into the minds of our young," says Grossman. "Pilots train on flight simulators, drivers on driving simulators, and now we have our children on murder simulators." If we want to avoid more Littleton-style massacres, we will begin taking the social effects of the killing games more seriously.   11   *Recommendation for action*

⊘ EXERCISE 2.4

Reread Gerard Jones's "Violent Media Is Good for Kids" (pp. 64–67). As you read, refer to the "Questions for Annotating" checklist (p. 71), and use them as a guide as you write your own reactions and questions in the margins of Jones's essay. In your annotations, note where you agree or disagree with Jones, and briefly explain why. Quickly summarize any points that you think are particularly important. Look up any unfamiliar words or references you have identified, and write down brief definitions or explanations. Think about these annotations as you prepare to discuss the Jones essay in class (and, eventually, to write about it).

⊘ EXERCISE 2.5

Exchange books with another student, and read his or her highlighting and annotating. How are your written responses similar to the other student's? How are they different? Do your classmate's responses help you to see anything new about Jones's essay?

⊘ EXERCISE 2.6

The following letter to the editor of a college newspaper takes a position on the issue of how violent media—in this case, video games—influence young people. Read the letter, highlighting and annotating it.

Now, consider how this letter is similar to and different from Gerard Jones's essay (pp. 64–67). First, identify the writer's thesis, and restate it in your own words. Then, consider the benefits of the violent video games the writer identifies. Are these benefits the same as those Jones identifies?

In paragraph 4, the writer summarizes arguments against her position. Does Jones address any of these same arguments? If so, does he refute them in the same way this writer does? Finally, read the letter's last paragraph. How is this writer's purpose for writing different from Jones's?

This letter to the editor was published on October 22, 2003, in *Ka Leo o Hawai'i*, the student newspaper of the University of Hawaii at Manoa.

DON'T WITHHOLD VIOLENT GAMES

JESSICA ROBBINS

Entertainment and technology have changed. Video games today are more graphic and violent than they were a few years ago. There is a concern about children being influenced by the content of some of these video games. Some states have already passed laws which ban minors from the viewing or purchasing of these video games without an accompanying adult. I believe this law should not exist.

Today's technology has truly enriched our entertainment experience. Today's computer and game consoles are able to simulate shooting, killing, mutilation, and blood through video games. It was such a problem that in 1993 Congress passed a law prohibiting the sale or rental of adult video games to minors. A rating system on games, similar to that placed on movies, was put into place, which I support. This helps to identify the level of violence that a game might have. However, I do not believe that this rating should restrict people of any age from purchasing a game.

Currently there is no significant evidence that supports the argument that violent video games are a major contributing factor in criminal and violent behavior. Recognized universities such as MIT and UCLA described the law as misguided, citing that "most studies and experiments on video games containing violent content have not found adverse effects." In addition, there actually are benefits from playing video games. They provide a safe outlet for aggression and frustration, increased attention performance, along with spatial and coordination skills.

> "[T]here actually are benefits from playing video games."

Some argue that there is research that shows real-life video game play is 4
related to antisocial behavior and delinquency, and that there is need for a law
to prevent children from acting out these violent behaviors. This may be true,
but researchers have failed to indicate that this antisocial and aggressive
behavior is not mostly short-term. We should give children the benefit of the
doubt. Today's average child is competent and intelligent enough to recognize
the difference between the digital representation of a gun and a real 28-inch
military bazooka rocket launcher. They are also aware of the consequences of
using such weapons on real civilians.

Major software companies who create video games should write 5
Congress and protest this law on the basis of a nonexistent correlation
between violence and video games. If the law is modified to not restrict
these games to a particular age group, then these products will not be
unfairly singled out.

⊜ EXERCISE 2.7

The following document, a statement on media violence released by the
American Psychological Association (APA) in 2015, includes a list of
specific recommendations. What position does this document take? Draft
a thesis statement that summarizes this position. Then, consider how
Gerard Jones (pp. 64–67) would respond to this thesis—and to the APA's
specific recommendations.

This document was posted to APA.org to replace the outdated 1985 resolution on violence
on television.

VIOLENCE IN MASS MEDIA
AMERICAN PSYCHOLOGICAL ASSOCIATION

On the recommendation of the Board of Directors and the Board for the 1
Advancement of Psychology in the Public Interest, Council voted to adopt the
following resolution, as amended, as APA policy, replacing the 1985 resolution on television violence:

Whereas the consequences of aggressive and violent behavior have 2
brought human suffering, lost lives, and economic hardship to our society as
well as an atmosphere of anxiety, fear, and mistrust;

Whereas in recent years the level of violence in American society and 3
the level of violence portrayed in television, film, and video have escalated
markedly;

Whereas the great majority of research studies have found a relation 4 between viewing mass media violence and behaving aggressively;

Whereas the conclusion drawn on the basis of over 30 years of research 5 and a sizeable number of experimental and field investigations (Huston, et al., 1992; NIMH, 1982; Surgeon General, 1972) is that viewing mass media violence leads to increases in aggressive attitudes, values, and behavior, particularly in children, and has a long-lasting effect on behavior and personality, including criminal behavior;

Whereas viewing violence desensitizes the viewer to violence, resulting in 6 calloused attitudes regarding violence toward others and a decreased likelihood to take action on behalf of a victim when violence occurs;

Whereas viewing violence increases viewers' tendencies for becoming 7 involved with or exposing themselves to violence;

Whereas viewing violence increases fear of becoming a victim of violence, 8 with a resultant increase in self-protective behaviors and mistrust of others;

Whereas many children's television programs and films contain some 9 form of violence, and children's access to adult-oriented media violence is increasing as a result of new technological advances;

Therefore be it resolved that the American Psychological Association: 10

1. urges psychologists to inform the television and film industry personnel who are responsible for violent programming, their commercial advertisers, legislators, and the general public that viewing violence in the media produces aggressive and violent behavior in children who are susceptible to such effects;

2. encourages parents and other child care providers to monitor and supervise television, video, and film viewing by children;

3. supports the inclusion of clear and easy-to-use warning labels for violent material in television, video, and film programs to enable viewers to make informed choices;

4. supports the development of technologies that empower viewers to prevent the broadcast of violent material in their homes;

5. supports the development, implementation, and evaluation of school-based programs to educate children and youth regarding means for critically viewing, processing, and evaluating video and film portrayals of both aggressive and prosocial behaviors;

6. requests the television and film industry to reduce direct violence in "real life" fictional children's programming or violent incidents in cartoons and other television or film productions, and to provide more programming designed to mitigate possible effects of television and film violence, consistent with the guarantees of the First Amendment;

7. urges the television and film industry to foster programming that models prosocial behaviors and seeks to resolve the problem of violence in society;

8. offers to the television and film industry assistance in developing programs that illustrate psychological methods to control aggressive and violent behavior, and alternative strategies for dealing with conflict and anger;

9. supports revision of the Film Rating System to take into account violence content that is harmful to children and youth;

10. urges industry, government, and private foundations to develop and implement programs to enhance the critical viewing skills of teachers, parents, and children regarding media violence and how to prevent its negative effects;

11. recommends that the Federal Communications Commission (FCC) review, as a condition for license renewal, the programming and outreach efforts and accomplishments of television stations in helping to solve the problem of youth violence;

12. urges industry, government, and private foundations to support research activities aimed at the amelioration of the effects of high levels of mass media violence on children's attitudes and behavior (DeLeon, 1995).

Writing a Critical Response

Sometimes you will be asked to write a **critical response**—a paragraph or more in which you analyze ideas presented in an argument and express your reactions to them.

Before you can respond in writing to an argument, you need to be sure that you understand the writer's position and that you have a sense of how supporting ideas are arranged—and why. You also need to consider how convincingly the writer conveys his or her position.

If you have read the argument carefully, highlighting and annotating it according to the guidelines outlined in this chapter, you should have a good idea what the writer wants to communicate to readers as well as how successfully the argument makes its point.

Before you begin to write a critical response to an argument, you should consider the questions in the checklist on page 78.

Begin your critical response by identifying your source and its author; then, write a clear, concise summary of the writer's position. Next, analyze the argument's supporting points one by one, considering the strength of the evidence that is presented. Also consider whether the writer addresses all significant opposing arguments and whether those arguments are refuted convincingly. Quote, summarize, and paraphrase the writer's key points as you go along, being careful to quote accurately and not to misrepresent the writer's ideas or distort them by quoting out of context. (For information

CHECKLIST

Questions for Critical Reading

☐ What is the writer's general subject?

☐ What purpose does the writer have for presenting this argument?

☐ What is the writer's position?

☐ Does the writer support ideas mainly with facts or with opinion?

☐ What evidence does the writer present to support this position?

☐ Is the evidence convincing? Is there enough evidence?

☐ Does the writer present opposing ideas and refute them effectively?

☐ What kind of audience does the writer seem to be addressing?

☐ Does the writer see the audience as hostile, friendly, or neutral?

☐ Does the writer establish himself or herself as well informed? As a fair and reasonable person?

☐ Does the writer seem to exhibit bias? If so, how does this bias affect the argument?

on summarizing, paraphrasing, quoting, and synthesizing sources, see Chapter 9.) As you write, identify arguments you find unconvincing, poorly supported, or irrelevant. At the end of your critical response, sum up your assessment of the argument in a strong concluding statement.

🔽 Katherine Choi, the student who highlighted and annotated "When Life Imitates Video" by John Leo (pp. 71–73), used those notes to help her develop the following critical response to Leo's article.

RESPONSE TO "WHEN LIFE IMITATES VIDEO"

KATHERINE CHOI

Article's source and author identified

Summary of writer's position

Analysis of supporting evidence

In "When Life Imitates Video," John Leo takes the position that "video kill games" (para. 2) can actually lead to violent behavior. In fact, he suggests a cause-and-effect connection between such games and the notorious 1999 murder spree at Colorado's Columbine High School, which occurred shortly before Leo wrote his essay.   1

Although Leo acknowledges in paragraph 3 that there is no "direct connection" between video games and this crime and agrees that parents   2 bear the "primary responsibility" for keeping violent games out of the hands of their children, he insists that our culture is also responsible. He is very critical of our society's dependence on violent video games, which he considers "training in make-believe killing" (para 4). This argument is convincing, up to a point. The problem is that Leo's primary support for this argument is a reference to an unnamed "widely cited survey" (para. 4), for which he provides no date. In addition, his use of a weak rhetorical question at the end of paragraph 4 instead of a strong statement of his position does little to help to support his argument.

Leo cites an opposing argument at the beginning of paragraph 5— the "conventional argument" that video games are harmless because children can tell the difference between fantasy and reality. He refutes this argument with unsupported generalizations rather than with specifics, pointing out the possibility that the games will often be played by "unstable youngsters" who channel their "adolescent feelings of resentment, powerlessness, and revenge" into the games.

> 3 Analysis of Leo's discussion of an opposing argument

The key piece of supporting evidence for Leo's claim that video games are dangerous comes in paragraph 6 with the expert opinion of a psychology professor who is also a retired army officer. The professor, David Grossman, draws an analogy between adolescents' video games and military training games designed to encourage soldiers to shoot their enemies. Although this analogy is interesting, it is not necessarily valid. For one thing, the army training Grossman refers to took place during World War II; for another, the soldiers were aware that the games were preparing them for actual combat.

> 4 Analysis of supporting evidence

In paragraph 7, Leo goes on to cite Grossman's comments about the young shooter in a 1997 attack in Paducah, Kentucky, and the Marines' use of *Doom* to train soldiers. Again, both discussions are interesting, and both are relevant to the connection between video games and violence. The problem is that neither discussion establishes a cause-and-effect relationship between violent video games and violent acts.

> 5 Analysis of supporting evidence

It may be true, as Leo observes, that video games are becoming more and more violent and that the victims in these games are increasingly likely to be police officers. Still, Leo fails to make his point because he never establishes that real-life violence is also increasing; therefore, he is not able to demonstrate a causal connection. His concluding

> 6

statement—"If we want to avoid more Littleton-style massacres, we will begin taking the social effects of the killing games more seriously"—combines a frightening prediction and a strong recommendation for action. Unfortunately, although Leo's essay will frighten many readers, it does not convincingly establish the need for the action he recommends.

Concardidíng statement

Work Cited

Leo, John. "When Life Imitates Video." *Practical Argument*, 3rd ed., edited by Laurie G. Kirszner and Stephen R. Mandell. Bedford/St. Martin's, 2017, pp. 68–70.

TEMPLATE FOR WRITING A CRITICAL RESPONSE

Write a one-paragraph critical response to Gerard Jones's essay on pages 64–67. Use the following template to shape your paragraph.

According to Gerard Jones, violent media can actually have positive effects on young people because _____

_____

_____

_____. Jones also believes that violent media are a positive influence on children

because _____

_____.

Jones makes some good points. For example, he says that _____

_____

_____

_____. However, _____

_____

_____. All in

all, _____

_____.

⊖ EXERCISE 2.8

Expand the one-paragraph critical response that you wrote above into a more fully developed critical response to Gerard Jones's essay on pages 64–67. Refer to the highlighting and annotations that you did for Exercises 2.3 and 2.4. (If you like, you can expand your response with references to recent news events involving violent acts.)

Decoding Visual Arguments

AT ISSUE

Do Violent Media Images Trigger Violent Behavior? (continued)

In Chapter 2, you read essays focusing on whether violence on TV and in other popular media can be blamed (at least in part) for the violence in our society. Now, you will be introduced to a variety of visual texts that offer additional insights into this issue. At the same time, you will learn how to use the critical-reading strategies that you practiced in Chapter 2 to help you to **decode**, or interpret, visual texts and to use visuals as springboards for discussion and writing or as sources in your essays.

A **visual argument** can be an advertisement, a chart or graph or table, an infographic, a diagram, a Web page, a photograph, a drawing, or a painting. Like an argumentative essay, a visual argument can take a position. Unlike an argumentative essay, however, a visual argument communicates its position (and offers evidence to support that position) largely through images rather than words.

Thinking Critically about Visual Arguments

When you approach a visual argument—particularly one that will be the subject of class discussion or writing—you should do so with a critical eye. Your primary goal is to understand the point that the creator of the visual is trying to make, but you also need to understand how the message is conveyed. In addition, you need to evaluate whether the methods used to persuade the audience are both logical and convincing.

VISUALS VERSUS VISUAL ARGUMENTS

Not every visual is an argument; many simply present information. For example, a diagram of a hunting rifle, with its principal parts labeled, tells viewers what the weapon looks like and how it works. However, a photo of two toddlers playing with a hunting rifle could make a powerful argument about the need for gun safety. Conversely, a photo of a family hunting trip featuring a teenager proudly holding up a rifle while his parents look on approvingly might make a positive argument for access to guns.

Using Active Reading Strategies with Visual Arguments

As you learned in Chapter 2, being a critical reader involves responding actively to the text of an argument. The active reading strategies that you practiced in Chapter 2—*previewing, close reading, highlighting,* and *annotating*—can also be applied to visual arguments.

When you approach a visual argument, you should look for clues to its main idea, or message. Some visuals, particularly advertising images, include words (sometimes called *body copy*) as well, and this written text often conveys the main ideas of the argument. Apart from words, however, the images themselves can help you understand the visual's purpose, its intended audience, and the argument that it is making.

COMPREHENSION CLUES

- The individual images
- The relative distance between images (close together or far apart)
- The relative size of the images
- The relationship between images and background
- The use of empty space
- The use of color and shading (for example, contrast between light and dark)
- If people are pictured, their activities, gestures, facial expressions, positions, body language, dress, and so on

APPEALS: *LOGOS, PATHOS,* AND *ETHOS*

As you study a visual argument, you should consider the appeal (or appeals) that the visual uses to convince its audience.

- An ad produced by Mothers Against Drunk Drivers (MADD) that includes statistics about alcohol-related auto fatalities might appeal to logic (*logos*).

- Another MADD ad could appeal to the emotions (*pathos*) by showing photographs of an accident scene.

- Still another ad could appeal to authority (*ethos*) by featuring a well-known sports figure warning of the dangers of drunk driving.

(For more on these appeals, see pp. 14–21.)

The following illustration makes a strong visual argument, using the image of a young child holding a mutilated teddy bear to make an emotional appeal to those concerned about children's exposure to television violence.

This illustration by Todd Davidson first appeared in the *Age* newspaper, Melbourne, Australia, on March 22, 1998.

© Todd Davidson/Illustration Source

The visual on the previous page includes three dominant images: the child, the teddy bear, and a giant TV screen projecting an image of a hand holding a knife. The placement of the child in the center of the visual, with the teddy bear on one side and the knife on the other, suggests that the child (and, by extension, all children) is caught between the innocence of childhood and the violence depicted in the media. The hand holding the knife on the television screen is an extension of the child's actual arm, suggesting that the innocent world of the child is being taken over by the violent world of the media.

To emphasize this conflict between innocence and violence, the teddy bear is set against a dark background, while the TV, with its disturbing image, is paradoxically set against a light background. (The image of the child is split, with half against each background, suggesting the split between the two worlds the child is exposed to.) The child's gaze is directed at his mutilated teddy bear, apparently the victim of his own violent act. The expression on the child's face makes it clear that he does not understand the violence he is caught up in.

Because it treats subject matter that is familiar to most people—TV violence and children's vulnerability to it—this visual is easy to understand. Its powerful images are not difficult to interpret, and its message is straightforward: TV violence is, at least in part, responsible for real-world violence. The visual's accessibility suggests that it is aimed at a wide general audience (rather than, for example, child psychologists or media analysts).

The visual's purpose is somewhat more complex. It could be to criticize the media, to warn parents and others about the threat posed by media violence, or to encourage the audience to take action.

Now, turn your attention to the two graphs on the facing page. These graphs, which appeared in the 2012 *Washington Post* article "Ten-Country Comparison Suggests There's Little or No Link between Video Games and Gun Murders," by Max Fisher, appeal to logic by providing statistics as evidence to support the article's position. Thus, the graphs present a strong visual argument about the relationship between violent video games and crime—an argument that is more powerful than the argument the article alone would present.

The graphs use a simple, open design and a minimum of words to make their information accessible to most people who will look at them. The main idea, or message, they convey is summarized by the article's thesis statement, supporting the idea that contrary to expectations, the data suggest "a slight downward shift in violence as video game consumption increases."

This idea is likely to come as a surprise to most people, who might assume a causal relationship between violent video games and violent crime. However, as the graphs show, this is not the case. Thus, the graphs serve as a clear **refutation** of a commonly held assumption. Because the two graphs (and the article in which they appeared) present information that is intended to contradict the audience's probable assumptions, their purpose seems to be to convince people to change the way they look at video games.

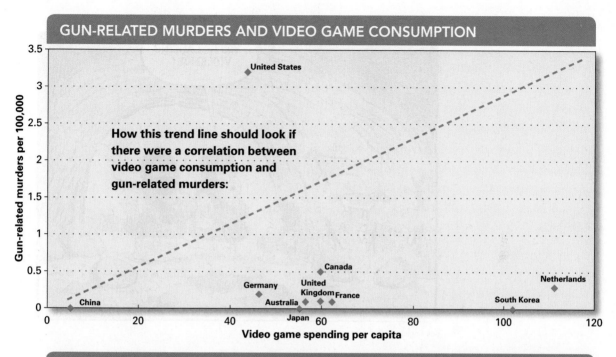

GUN-RELATED MURDERS AND VIDEO GAME CONSUMPTION

How this trend line should look if there were a correlation between video game consumption and gun-related murders:

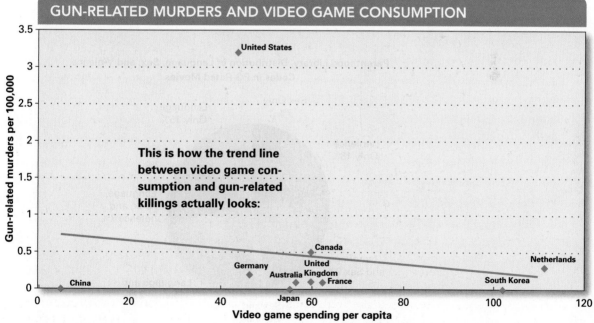

GUN-RELATED MURDERS AND VIDEO GAME CONSUMPTION

This is how the trend line between video game consumption and gun-related killings actually looks:

⊙ EXERCISE 3.1

Look at the visuals on the pages that follow, and then answer the questions on page 91.

Bob Engelhart, Violent Video Games

Bob Englehart. Courtesy of Cagle Cartoons.

Parenthood Library, Distribution of Language, Sex, and Violence Codes in PG-Rated Movies

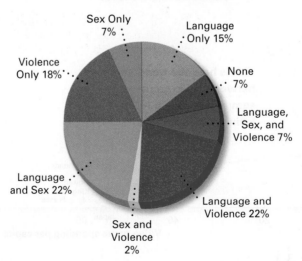

From Amy I. Nathanson & Joanne Cantor (1998), Protecting Children from Harmful Television: TV Ratings and the V-Chip. From Parenthood in America, University of Wisconsin–Madison General Library System.

Boy Playing Violent Video Game

Jochen Tack/imageBROKER/Agefotostock

Ways to Die in Children's Cartoons

A study in the *British Medical Journal* indicated that two thirds of cartoon movies included the deaths of characters, compared with half in adult films. Parents are five times as likely to die in cartoon films compared with adult dramas.

Type of Death, by Percentage of Films

Type of death	Children's animated films		Comparison films	
No on-screen deaths	33.3	▇▇	50.0	▇▇▇
Animal attacks	11.1	▇	0	
Falling	11.1	▇	33.3	▇▇
Other murder	8.9	▇	4.4	▮
Drowning	6.7	▇	1.1	▏
Gunshot	6.7	▇	14.4	▇
Magic	6.7	▇	0	
Illness/medical complications	4.4	▮	8.9	▇
Other injury	4.4	▮	2.2	▏
Stabbing/impaling	4.4	▮	2.2	▏
Motor vehicle crash	2.2	▏	8.9	▇
Killed in combat	0		3.3	▮
Suicide	0		1.1	▏

Lauren Dazzara, Why Gaming Is a Positive Element in Life

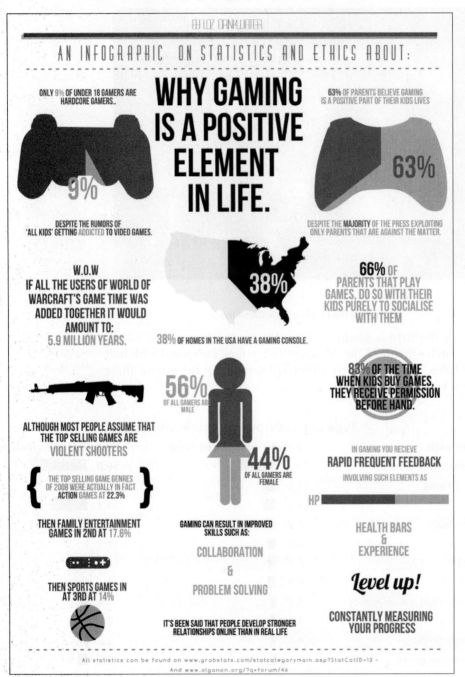

Identifying the Elements of a Visual Argument

1. Do you see all of the visuals on pages 87–90 as arguments, or do you think some were created solely to present information?

2. What main idea, or message, does each visual communicate? State the main idea of each visual in a single sentence.

3. What elements in each visual support this main idea?

4. If the visual includes words as well as images, are the words necessary?

5. What purpose does each visual seem designed to achieve?

6. What kind of audience do you think each visual is aimed at?

7. Does the visual appeal primarily to *logos, pathos*, or *ethos*?

8. Do you think the visual is effective? That is, is it likely to have the desired effect on its intended audience?

Highlighting and Annotating Visuals

Now, it is time to look more closely at visuals and to learn how to *highlight* and *annotate* them. Unlike highlighting and annotating a written text, marking a visual text involves focusing your primary attention not on any words that appear but on the images.

After previewing the visual by looking at its overall appearance, begin highlighting to identify key images—perhaps by starring, boxing, or circling them—and then consider drawing lines or arrows to connect related images. Next, go on to make annotations on the visual, commenting on the effectiveness of its individual images in communicating the message of the whole. As in the case of a written text, your annotations can be in the form of comments or questions.

The visual on the following page shows how a student, Jason Savona, highlighted and annotated an advertisement for *Grand Theft Auto IV*, a popular violent video game.

Rockstar North, Advertisement for *Grand Theft Auto IV*

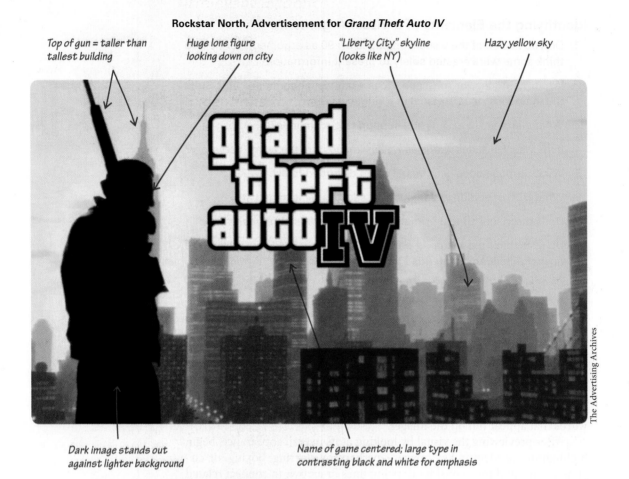

Top of gun = taller than tallest building

Huge lone figure looking down on city

"Liberty City" skyline (looks like NY)

Hazy yellow sky

Dark image stands out against lighter background

Name of game centered; large type in contrasting black and white for emphasis

The Advertising Archives

⊕ EXERCISE 3.2

Look at the visual on the following page, and then highlight and annotate it to identify its most important images and their relationship to one another. When you have finished, think about how the images work together to communicate a central message to the audience. What argument does this visual make?

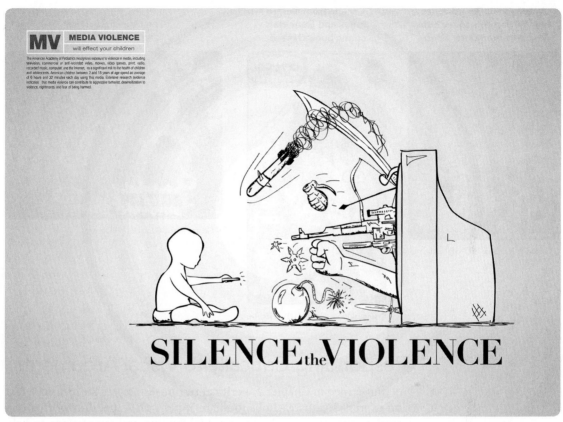

© Nate Londa

❯ EXERCISE 3.3

Interview a classmate about his or her experiences with video games—or with actual violence. Does your classmate see any links between the kinds of videos that are watched by friends and family members and the violence (or lack of violence) that occurs in his or her community? Write a paragraph summarizing your interview.

❯ EXERCISE 3.4

Study the following three visuals (and their captions), all of which appear in Gerard Jones's essay, "Violent Media Is Good for Kids" (pp. 64–67). Look at each visual with a critical eye, and then consider how effectively each one supports the central argument that Jones makes in his essay.

A scene from Gerard Jones and Will Jacobs's comic book *Monsters from Outer Space.*

© Gerard Jones, Gene Ha, Will Jacobs.

A scene from Gerard Jones and Gene Ha's comic book *Oktane.*

© Gerard Jones, Gene Ha, Will Jacobs.

The title character of *Oktane* gets nasty.

© Gerard Jones, Gene Ha, Will Jacobs.

Responding Critically to Visual Arguments

As you learned in Chapter 2, a **critical response** analyzes the ideas in a text and expresses your reactions to them. When you respond in writing to a visual argument, you rely on your highlighting and annotations to help you understand the writer's ideas and see how the words and images work together to make a particular point.

As you prepare to write a critical response to a visual argument, keep in mind the questions in the following checklist.

CHECKLIST

Questions for Responding to Visual Arguments

☐ In what source did the visual appear? What is the target audience for this source?

☐ For what kind of audience was the visual created? Hostile? Friendly? Neutral?

☐ For what purpose was the visual created?

☐ Who (or what organization) created the visual? What do you know about the background and goals of this person or group?

(*continued*)

- ☐ What issue is the visual addressing?
- ☐ What position does the visual take on this issue? How can you tell? Do you agree with this position?
- ☐ Does the visual include words? If so, are they necessary? What points do they make? Does the visual need more—or different— written text?
- ☐ Does the visual seem to be a *refutation*—that is, an argument against a particular position?
- ☐ Is the visual effective? Attractive? Interesting? Clear? Convincing?

When you write a critical response, begin by identifying the source and purpose of the visual. Then, state your reaction to the visual, and examine its elements one at a time, considering how effective each is and how well the various elements work together to create a convincing visual argument. End with a strong concluding statement that summarizes your reaction.

↻ The critical response that follows was written by the student who highlighted and annotated the advertisement for *Grand Theft Auto IV* on page 92.

RESPONSE TO *GRAND THEFT AUTO IV*
JASON SAVONA

The advertisement for *Grand Theft Auto IV* presents a disturbing preview of the game. Rather than highlighting the game's features and challenges, this ad promotes the game's violence. As a result, it appeals more to those who are looking for video games that depict murder and other crimes than to those who choose a video game on the basis of the skill it requires.

The "hero" of this game is Niko Bellic, a war veteran from Eastern Europe who has left his country to build a new life in the fictional Liberty City. Instead of finding peace, he has found a new kind of war. Now,

1   Identification of visual's source

Reaction to visual

2   Analysis of visual's elements

trapped in the corrupt world of organized crime, Bellic is willing to do whatever it takes to fight his way out. His idea of justice is vigilante justice: he makes his own rules. The ad conveys this sense of Bellic as a loner and an outsider by showing him as a larger-than-life figure standing tall and alone against a background of the Liberty City skyline.

In the ad, Niko Bellic holds a powerful weapon in his huge hands, 3 and the weapon extends higher than the tallest building behind it, dominating the picture. Clearly, Bellic means business. As viewers look at the picture, the dark image of the gun and the man who holds it comes to the foreground, and everything else—the light brown buildings, the city lights, the yellow sky—fades into the background. In the center, the name of the game is set in large black-and-white type that contrasts with the ad's hazy background, showing the importance of the product's name.

This image, clearly aimed at young players of violent video games, 4 would certainly be appealing to those who want to have a feeling of

Concluding statement   power. What it says is, "A weapon makes a person powerful." This is a very dangerous message.

TEMPLATE FOR RESPONDING TO VISUAL ARGUMENTS

Write a one-paragraph critical response to the visual you highlighted and annotated in Exercise 3.2 on pages 92–93. Use the following template to shape your paragraph.

The visual created by Nate Londa shows _____ _____.

This visual makes a powerful statement about _____. _____ The central image shows _____ _____

_____ The background enhances the central image because _____ _____.

_____ The visual includes words as well as images. These words suggest _____ _____.

The goal of the organization that posted the visual seems to be to _____ _____

_____ The visual (is/is not) effective because _____ _____.

➔ EXERCISE 3.5

Consulting the one-paragraph critical response that you wrote above, write a more fully developed critical response to the visual on page 93. Refer to the highlighting and annotating that you did for Exercise 3.2.

What Is a Rhetorical Analysis?

When you write a **rhetorical analysis,** you systematically examine the strategies a writer employs to achieve his or her purpose. In the process, you explain how these strategies work together to create an effective (or ineffective) argument. To carry out this task, you consider the argument's **rhetorical situation**, the writer's **means of persuasion**, and the **rhetorical strategies** that the writer uses.

OVERVIEW: "LETTER FROM BIRMINGHAM JAIL" BY MARTIN LUTHER KING JR.

Here and throughout the rest of this chapter, we will be analyzing "Letter from Birmingham Jail" by Martin Luther King Jr., which can be found online.

In 1963, civil rights leader Martin Luther King Jr. organized a series of nonviolent demonstrations to protest the climate of segregation that existed in Birmingham, Alabama. He and his followers met opposition not only from white moderates but also from some African-American clergymen who thought that King was a troublemaker. During the demonstrations, King was arrested and jailed for eight days. He wrote his "Letter from Birmingham Jail" on April 16, 1963, from the city jail in response to a public statement by eight white Alabama clergymen titled "A Call for Unity." This statement asked for an end to the demonstrations, which the clergymen called "untimely," "unwise," and "extreme." (Their letter was addressed to the "white and Negro" population of Birmingham, not to King, whom they considered an "outsider.")

King knew that the world was watching and that his response to the white clergymen would have both national and international significance. As a result, he used a variety of rhetorical strategies to convince readers that his demands were both valid and understandable and that contrary to the opinions of some, his actions were well within the mainstream of American social and political thought. Today, King's "Letter from Birmingham Jail" stands as a model of clear and highly effective argumentation.

Martin Luther King Jr.
in Birmingham Jail
(April 1963)

Considering the Rhetorical Situation

Arguments do not take place in isolation. They are written by real people
in response to a particular set of circumstances called the **rhetorical situation**
(see pp. 9–14). The rhetorical situation consists of the following five
elements:

- The writer
- The writer's purpose
- The writer's audience
- The question
- The context

By analyzing the rhetorical situation, you are able to determine why the writer made the choices he or she did and how these choices affect the argument.

ANALYZING THE RHETORICAL SITUATION

To help you analyze the rhetorical situation of an argument, look for information about the essay and its author.

1. **Look at the essay's headnote.** If the essay you are reading has a headnote, it can contain useful information about the writer, the issue being discussed, and the structure of the essay. For this reason, it is a good idea to read headnotes carefully.

2. **Look for clues within the essay.** The writer's use of particular words and phrases can sometimes provide information about his or her preconceptions as well as about the cultural context of the argument. Historical or cultural references can indicate what ideas or information the writer expects readers to have.

3. **Search the Web.** Often, just a few minutes online can give you a lot of useful information—such as the background of a particular debate or the biography of the writer. By looking at titles of the other books or essays the writer has written, you may also be able to get an idea of his or her biases or point of view.

The Writer

Begin by trying to determine whether anything in the writer's background (for example, the writer's education, experience, race, gender, political beliefs, religion, age, and experiences) has influenced the content of the argument. Also consider whether the writer seems to have any preconceptions about the subject.

ANALYZING THE WRITER

- What is the writer's background?

- How does the writer's background affect the content of the argument?

- What preconceptions about the subject does the writer seem to have?

If you were analyzing "Letter from Birmingham Jail," it would help to know that Martin Luther King Jr. was pastor of the Dexter Avenue Baptist Church in Montgomery, Alabama. In 1956, he organized a bus boycott that led to a United States Supreme Court decision that outlawed segregation on Alabama's buses. In addition, King was a leader of the Southern Christian Leadership Conference and strongly believed in nonviolent protest. His books include *Stride towards Freedom* (1958) and *Why We Can't Wait* (1964). His "I Have a Dream" speech, which he delivered on the steps of the Lincoln Memorial on August 28, 1963, is considered by scholars to be one of the most influential speeches of the twentieth century. In 1964, King won the Nobel Prize for peace.

In "Letter from Birmingham Jail," King addresses the injustices that he sees in America—especially in the South—and makes a strong case

"I Have a Dream" speech, Washington, D.C. (August 1963)

Hulton-Deutsch Collection/Corbis

for civil rights for all races. Throughout his argument, King includes numerous references to the Bible, to philosophers, and to political and religious thinkers. By doing so, he makes it clear to readers that he is aware of the social, cultural, religious, and political implications of his actions. Because he is a clergyman, King suggests that by battling injustice, he, like the apostle Paul, is doing God's work. This point is made clear in the following passage (para. 3):

> But more basically, I am in Birmingham because injustice is here. Just as the prophets of the eighth century B.C. left their villages and carried their "thus saith the Lord" far beyond the boundaries of their home towns, and just as the Apostle Paul left his village of Tarsus and carried the gospel of Jesus Christ to the far corners of the Greco-Roman world, so am I compelled to carry the gospel of freedom beyond my own home town. Like Paul, I must constantly respond to the Macedonian call for aid.

The Writer's Purpose

Next, consider what the writer hopes to achieve with his or her argument. In other words, ask yourself if the writer is trying to challenge people's ideas, persuade them to accept new points of view, or influence their behavior.

ANALYZING THE WRITER'S PURPOSE

- Does the writer state his or her purpose directly, or is the purpose implied?
- Is the writer's purpose simply to convince or to encourage action?
- Does the writer rely primarily on logic or on emotion?
- Does the writer have a hidden agenda?

It is clear that Martin Luther King Jr. wrote "Letter from Birmingham Jail" to convince readers that even though he had been arrested, his actions were both honorable and just. To get readers to understand that, like Henry David Thoreau, he is protesting laws that he considers wrong, he draws a distinction between just and unjust laws. For him, a law is just if it "squares with the moral law or the law of God" (16). A law is unjust if it "is out of harmony with the moral law" (16). As a clergyman and a civil rights leader, King believed that he had an obligation both to point out the immorality of unjust laws and to protest them—even if it meant going to jail.

The Writer's Audience

To analyze the writer's audience, begin by considering whether the writer seems to see readers as friendly, hostile, or neutral. (For a discussion of types of audiences, see pp. 10–13). Also, determine how much knowledge the writer assumes that readers have. Then, consider how the writer takes into account factors like the audience's race, religion, gender, education, age, and ethnicity. Next, decide what preconceptions the writer thinks readers have about the subject. Finally, see if the writer shares any common ground with readers.

ANALYZING THE WRITER'S AUDIENCE

- Who is the writer's intended audience?

- Does the writer see the audience as informed or uninformed?

- Does the writer see the audience as hostile, friendly, or neutral?

- What values does the writer think the audience holds?

- What does the writer seem to assume about the audience's background?

- On what points do the writer and the audience agree? On what points do they disagree?

In "Letter from Birmingham Jail," King aims his argument at more than one audience. First, he speaks directly to eight clergymen from Birmingham, who are at worst a hostile audience and at best a skeptical one. They consider King to be an outsider whose actions are "unwise and untimely" (1). Before addressing their concerns, King tries to establish common ground, referring to his readers as "fellow clergymen" and "my Christian and Jewish brothers." He then goes on to say that he wishes that the clergymen had supported his actions instead of criticizing them. King ends his letter on a conciliatory note by asking his readers to forgive him if he has overstated his case or been unduly harsh.

In addition to addressing clergymen, King also speaks to white moderates, who he assumes are sympathetic to his cause but concerned about his methods. He knows that he has to influence this segment of his audience if he is to gain wide support for his cause. For this reason, King uses a restrained tone and emphasizes the universality of his message, ending his letter with a plea that is calculated to console and inspire those people who need reassurance (50):

Let us all hope that the dark clouds of racial prejudice will soon pass away and the deep fog of misunderstanding will be lifted from our fear-drenched communities, and in some not too distant tomorrow the radiant stars of love and brotherhood will shine over our great nation with all their scintillating beauty.

The Question

Try to determine what question the writer is trying to answer. Is the question suitable for argument? Decide if there are good arguments on both sides of the issue. For example, what issue (or issues) is the writer confronting? Does he or she address them adequately?

ANALYZING THE QUESTION

- What is the central question of the argument?
- Are there solid arguments on both sides of the issue?
- Has the writer answered the question fully enough?

The question King attempts to answer in "Letter from Birmingham Jail" is why he has decided to come to Birmingham to lead protests. Because the answer to this question is complicated, King addresses a number of issues. Although his main concern is with racial segregation in Alabama, he also is troubled by the indifference of white moderates who have urged him to call off his protests. In addition, he feels that he needs to explain his actions (for example, engaging in nonviolent protests) and address those who doubt his motives. King answers his critics (as well as his central question) by saying that because the people of the United States are interconnected, the injustices in one state will eventually affect the entire country.

The Context

The **context** is the situation that creates the need for the argument. As you analyze an argument, try to determine the social, historical, economic, political, and cultural events that set the stage for the argument and the part that these events play in the argument itself.

ANALYZING THE CONTEXT

- What situation (or situations) set the stage for the argument?
- What social, economic, political, and cultural events triggered the argument?
- What historical references situate this argument in a particular place or time?

The immediate context of "Letter to Birmingham Jail" is well known: Martin Luther King Jr. wrote an open letter to eight white clergymen in which he defended his protests against racial segregation. However, the wider social and political context of the letter is less well known.

In 1896, the U.S. Supreme Court ruled in *Plessy v. Ferguson* that "separate but equal" accommodations on railroad cars gave African Americans the equal protection guaranteed by the Fourteenth Amendment of the U.S. Constitution. Well into the twentieth century, this decision was used to justify separate public facilities—including restrooms, water fountains, and even schools and hospitals—for blacks and whites.

In the mid-1950s, state support for segregation of the races and discrimination against African Americans had begun to be challenged. For example, Supreme Court decisions in 1954 and 1955 found that segregation in the public schools and other publicly financed locations was unconstitutional. At the same time, whites and blacks alike were calling for an end to racial discrimination. Their actions took the form of marches, boycotts, and sit-ins (organized nonviolent protests whose participants refused to move from a public area). Many whites, however, particularly in the South, strongly resisted any sudden changes in race relations.

King's demonstrations in Birmingham, Alabama, took place within this larger social and political context. His campaign was a continuation of the push for equal rights that had been gaining momentum in the United States for decades. King, along with the Southern Christian Leadership

Segregated water fountains in North Carolina (1950)

© Elliott Erwitt/Magnum

Conference, had dispatched hundreds of people to Birmingham to engage in nonviolent demonstrations against those who were determined to keep African Americans from gaining their full rights as citizens.

Considering the Means of Persuasion: *Logos, Pathos, Ethos*

In the introduction to this book, you learned how writers of argument use three means of persuasion—*logos*, *pathos*, and *ethos*—to appeal to readers. You also saw how the **rhetorical triangle** represents the way these three appeals come into play within an argument. (See p. 19 for more information about the rhetorical triangle.) Of course, the degree to which a writer uses each of these appeals depends on the rhetorical situation. Moreover, a single argument can use more than one appeal—for example, an important research source would involve both the logic of the argument (*logos*) and the credibility of the writer (*ethos*). In "Letter from Birmingham Jail," King uses all three appeals.

The Appeal to Reason (Logos)

In "Letter from Birmingham Jail," King attempts to demonstrate the logic of his position. In paragraph 15, for example, he says that there are two types of laws—just and unjust. He then points out that he has both a legal and a moral responsibility to "disobey unjust laws." In paragraph 16, King supports his position with references to various philosophers and theologians— for example, St. Thomas Aquinas, Martin Buber, and Paul Tillich. He also develops the logical argument that even though all Americans should obey the law, they are responsible to a higher moral authority—God.

The Appeal to the Emotions (Pathos)

Throughout "Letter from Birmingham Jail," King attempts to create sympathy for his cause. In paragraph 14, for example, he catalogues the injustices of life in the United States for African Americans. He makes a particularly emotional appeal by quoting a hypothetical five-year-old boy who might ask, "Daddy, why do white people treat colored people so mean?" In addition, he includes vivid images of racial injustice to provoke anger against those who deny African Americans equal rights. In this way, King creates sympathy (and possibly empathy) in readers.

The Appeal to Authority (Ethos)

To be persuasive, King has to establish his credibility. In paragraph 2, for example, he reminds readers that he is the president of the Southern Christian Leadership Conference, "an organization operating in every southern state." In paragraph 3, he compares himself to the apostle Paul, who carried the gospel "to the far corners of the Greco-Roman world." In addition, King attempts to show readers that what he is doing is well within the mainstream of American political and social thought. By alluding to Thomas Jefferson, Henry David Thoreau, and the 1954 U.S. Supreme Court decision that outlawed segregation in public schools, he tries to demonstrate that he is not the wild-eyed radical that some believe him to be. Thus, King establishes himself in both secular and religious terms as a leader who has the stature and the authority to present his case.

Considering the Writer's Rhetorical Strategies

Writers use various **rhetorical strategies** to present their ideas and opinions. Here are a few of the elements that you should examine when analyzing and evaluating an argument.

Thesis

The **thesis**—the main idea or claim that the argument supports—is of primary importance in every argument. When you analyze an argument, you should always ask, "What is the essay's thesis, and why does the writer state it as he or she does?" You should also consider at what point in the argument the thesis is stated and what the effect of this placement is.

In "Letter from Birmingham Jail," Martin Luther King Jr. begins by telling readers that he is "confined here in the Birmingham city jail" and that he is writing his letter to answer clergymen who have called his demonstrations "unwise and untimely." King clearly (and unapologetically) states his thesis ("But more basically, I am in Birmingham because injustice is here") at the beginning of the third paragraph, right after he explains his purpose, so that readers will have no doubt what his position is as they read the rest of his argument.

Organization

The **organization** of an argument—how a writer arranges ideas—is also important. For example, after stating his thesis, King tells readers why he is in Birmingham and what he hopes to accomplish: he wants unjust laws to be abolished and the 1954 Supreme Court ruling to be enforced. King then **refutes**—disproves or calls into question—the specific charges that were leveled at him by the white clergymen who want him to stop his protests.

The structure of "Letter from Birmingham Jail" enables King to make his points clearly, logically, and convincingly:

- King begins his argument by addressing the charge that his actions are untimely. If anything, says King, his actions are not timely enough: after all, African Americans have waited more than 340 years for their "constitutional and God-given rights" (14).

- He then addresses the issue of his willingness to break laws and makes the distinction between just and unjust laws.

- After chiding white moderates for not supporting his cause, he addresses their claim that he is extreme. According to King, this charge is false: if he had not embraced a philosophy of nonviolent protest, the streets of the South would "be flowing with blood" (29).

- King then makes the point that the contemporary church must recapture the "sacrificial spirit of the early church" (42). He does this by linking his struggle for freedom with the "sacred heritage of our nation and the eternal will of God" (44).

- King ends his argument by asserting both his humility and his unity with the white clergy.

Evidence

To convince an audience, a writer must support the thesis with **evidence**— facts, observations, expert opinion, and so on. King presents a great deal of evidence to support his arguments. For instance, he uses numerous examples (both historical and personal) as well as many references to philosophers, political thinkers, and theologians (such as Jesus, St. Paul, St. Augustine, Amos, Martin Luther, and Abraham Lincoln). According to King, these figures, who were once considered "extremists," were not afraid of "making waves" when the need arose. Now, however, they are well within the mainstream of social, political, and religious thought. King also presents reasons, facts, and quotations to support his points.

Stylistic Techniques

Writers also use stylistic techniques to make their arguments more memorable and more convincing. For example, in "Letter from Birmingham Jail," King uses figurative devices such as *similes*, *metaphors*, and *allusions* to enhance his argument.

Simile A **simile** is a figure of speech that compares two unlike things using the word *like* or *as*.

> Like a boil that can never be cured so long as it is covered up but must be opened with all its ugliness to the natural medicines of air and light, injustice must be exposed, . . . before it can be cured. (24)

> Isn't this like condemning a robbed man because his possession of money precipitated the evil act of robbery? (25)

Metaphor A **metaphor** is a comparison in which two dissimilar things are compared without the word *like* or *as*. A metaphor suggests that two things that are very different share a quality.

> Frankly, I have yet to engage in a direct-action campaign that was "well timed" in the view of those who have not suffered unduly from the disease of segregation. (13)

> [W]hen you see the vast majority of your twenty million Negro brothers smothering in an airtight cage of poverty . . . (14)

Allusion An **allusion** is a reference within a work to a person, literary or biblical text, or historical event in order to enlarge the context of the situation being written about. The writer expects readers to recognize the allusion and to make the connection to the text they are reading.

> I would agree with St. Augustine that "an unjust law is no law at all." (15)

> Of course, there is nothing new about this kind of civil disobedience. It was evidenced sublimely in the refusal of Shadrach, Meshach, and Abednego to obey the laws of Nebuchadnezzar, on the ground that a higher moral law was at stake. (21) [King expects his audience of clergymen to recognize this reference to the Book of Daniel in the Old Testament.]

In addition to those figurative devices, King uses stylistic techniques such as *parallelism*, *repetition*, and *rhetorical questions* to further his argument.

Parallelism **Parallelism**, the use of similar grammatical structures to emphasize related ideas, makes a passage easier to follow.

> In any nonviolent campaign there are four basic steps: collection of the facts to determine whether injustices exist; negotiation; self-purification; and direct action. (6)

> Shallow understanding from people of good will is more frustrating than absolute misunderstanding from people of ill will. Lukewarm acceptance is much more bewildering than outright rejection. (23)

> I wish you had commended the Negro sit-inners and demonstrators of Birmingham for their sublime courage, their willingness to suffer, and their amazing discipline in the midst of great provocation. (47)

Repetition Intentional **repetition** involves repeating a word or phrase for emphasis, clarity, or emotional impact.

> "Are you able to accept blows without retaliating?" "Are you able to endure the ordeal of jail?" (8)

> If I have said anything in this letter that overstates the truth and indicates an unreasonable impatience, I beg you to forgive me. If I have said anything that understates the truth and indicates my having patience that allows me to settle for anything less than brotherhood, I beg God to forgive me. (49)

Rhetorical questions A **rhetorical question** is a question that is asked to encourage readers to reflect on an issue, not to elicit a reply.

> One may well ask: "How can you advocate breaking some laws and obeying others?" (15)

> Will we be extremists for hate or for love? (31)

Assessing the Argument

No rhetorical analysis of an argument would be complete without an assessment of its effectiveness—whether the rhetorical strategies the writer uses create a clear and persuasive argument or whether they fall short. When you write a rhetorical analysis, you can begin with an assessment of the argument as a whole and go on to support it, or you can begin with a discussion of the various rhetorical strategies that the writer uses and then end with your assessment of the argument.

After analyzing "Letter from Birmingham Jail," you could reasonably conclude that King has written a highly effective argument that is likely to convince his readers that his presence in Birmingham is both justified and necessary. Using *logos, pathos,* and *ethos,* he constructs a multifaceted argument that is calculated to appeal to the various segments of his audience—Southern clergymen, white moderates, and African Americans. In addition, King uses similes, metaphors, and allusions to enrich his argument and to make it more memorable, and he uses parallelism, repetition, and rhetorical questions to emphasize ideas and to reinforce his points. Because it is so clear and powerful, King's argument—in particular, the distinction between just and unjust laws—addresses not only the injustices that were present in 1963 when it was written but also the injustices and inequalities that exist today. In this sense, King has written an argument that has broad significance beyond the audiences for which it was originally intended.

Preparing to Write a Rhetorical Analysis

As you read, ask the following questions:

☐ Who is the writer? Is there anything in the writer's background that might influence what is (or is not) included in the argument?

☐ What is the writer's purpose? What does the writer hope to achieve?

☐ What question has the writer decided to address? How broad is the question?

☐ What situation created the need for the argument?

☐ At what points in the argument does the writer appeal to logic? To the emotions? How does the writer try to establish his or her credibility?

☐ What is the argument's thesis? Where is it stated? Why?

☐ How does the writer organize the argument? How effective is this arrangement of ideas?

☐ What evidence does the writer use to support the argument? Does the writer use enough evidence?

☐ Does the writer use similes, metaphors, and allusions?

☐ Does the writer use parallelism, repetition, and rhetorical questions?

☐ Given your analysis, what is your overall assessment of the argument?

Sample Rhetorical Analysis

In preparation for a research paper, Deniz Bilgutay, a student in a writing class, read the following essay, "Terror's Purse Strings" by Dana Thomas, which makes an argument against buying counterfeit designer goods. Deniz then wrote the rhetorical analysis that appears on pages 115–117. (Deniz Bilgutay's research paper, "The High Cost of Cheap Counterfeit Goods," uses "Terror's Purse Strings" as a source. See Appendix B.)

This essay appeared in the *New York Times* on August 30, 2007.

TERROR'S PURSE STRINGS

DANA THOMAS

Luxury fashion designers are busily putting final touches on the handbags 1 they will present during the spring-summer 2008 women's wear shows, which begin next week in New York City's Bryant Park. To understand the importance of the handbag in fashion today consider this: According to consumer surveys conducted by Coach, the average American woman was buying two new handbags a year in 2000; by 2004, it was more than four. And the average luxury bag retails for 10 to 12 times its production cost.

"There is a kind of an obsession with bags," the designer Miuccia Prada 2
told me. "It's so easy to make money."

Counterfeiters agree. As soon as a handbag hits big, counterfeiters around the 3
globe churn out fake versions by the thousands. And they have no trouble selling
them. Shoppers descend on Canal Street in New York, Santee Alley in Los Angeles, and flea markets and purse parties around the country to pick up knockoffs
for one-tenth the legitimate bag's retail cost, then pass them off as real.

"Judges, prosecutors, defense attorneys shop here," a private investigator 4
told me as we toured the counterfeit section of Santee Alley. "Affluent people
from Newport Beach." According to a study by the British law firm Davenport
Lyons, two-thirds of British consumers are "proud to tell their family and
friends" that they bought fake luxury fashion items.

At least 11 percent of the world's clothing is fake, according to 2000 figures 5
from the Global Anti-Counterfeiting Group in Paris. Fashion is easy to copy:
counterfeiters buy the real items, take them apart, scan the pieces to make patterns, and produce almost-perfect fakes.

Most people think that buying an imitation handbag or wallet is harmless, a victimless
crime. But the counterfeiting rackets are run by
crime syndicates that also deal in narcotics,
weapons, child prostitution, human trafficking,

> "At least 11 percent 6
> of the world's
> clothing is fake ..."

An international criminal
police organization

and terrorism. Ronald K. Noble, the secretary general of Interpol,° told the
House of Representatives Committee on International Relations that profits
from the sale of counterfeit goods have gone to groups associated with Hezbollah, the Shiite terrorist group, paramilitary organizations in Northern Ireland,
and FARC, the Revolutionary Armed Forces of Colombia.

Sales of counterfeit T-shirts may have helped finance the 1993 World 7
Trade Center bombing, according to the International AntiCounterfeiting
Coalition. "Profits from counterfeiting are one of the three main sources of
income supporting international terrorism," said Magnus Ranstorp, a terrorism
expert at the University of St. Andrews, in Scotland.

Most fakes today are produced in China, a good many of them by children. 8
Children are sometimes sold or sent off by their families to work in clandestine factories that produce counterfeit luxury goods. Many in the West consider this an urban myth. But I have seen it myself.

On a warm winter afternoon in Guangzhou, I accompanied Chinese police 9
officers on a factory raid in a decrepit tenement. Inside, we found two dozen
children, ages 8 to 13, gluing and sewing together fake luxury-brand handbags.
The police confiscated everything, arrested the owner, and sent the children out.
Some punched their timecards, hoping to still get paid. (The average Chinese
factory worker earns about $120 a month; the counterfeit factory worker earns
half that or less.) As we made our way back to the police vans, the children threw
bottles and cans at us. They were now jobless and, because the factory owner
housed them, homeless. It was *Oliver Twist* in the 21st century.

What can we do to stop this? Much like the war on drugs, the effort to 10
protect luxury brands must go after the source: the counterfeit manufacturers.

The company that took me on the Chinese raid is one of the only luxury-goods makers that works directly with Chinese authorities to shut down factories, and it has one of the lowest rates of counterfeiting.

Luxury brands also need to teach consumers that the traffic in fake goods has many victims. But most companies refuse to speak publicly about counterfeiting—some won't even authenticate questionable items for concerned customers—believing, like Victorians,° that acknowledging despicable actions tarnishes their sterling reputations. 11

So it comes down to us. If we stop knowingly buying fakes, the supply chain will dry up and counterfeiters will go out of business. The crime syndicates will have far less money to finance their illicit activities and their terrorist plots. And the children? They can go home. 12

The people who lived during the reign of Victoria (1819–1901), queen of Great Britain and Ireland, who are often associated with prudish behavior

A POWERFUL CALL TO ACTION

DENIZ BILGUTAY

In her *New York Times* essay, "Terror's Purse Strings," writer Dana Thomas uses the opening of New York's fashion shows as an opportunity to expose a darker side of fashion—the impact of imitation designer goods. Thomas explains to her readers why buying counterfeit luxury items, like fake handbags, is a serious problem. Her first goal is to raise awareness of the dangerous ties between counterfeiters who sell fake luxury merchandise and international criminal organizations that support terrorism and child labor. Her second goal is to explain how people can be a part of the solution by refusing to buy the counterfeit goods that finance these criminal activities. By establishing her credibility, building her case slowly, and appealing to both logic and emotions, Thomas succeeds in writing an interesting and informative argument. 1

1 Context

Topic

Analysis of writer's purpose

Thesis statement: Assessment of essay

For Thomas's argument to work, she has to earn her readers' trust. She does so first by anticipating a sympathetic, well-intentioned, educated audience and then by establishing her own credibility. To avoid sounding accusatory, Thomas assumes that her readers are unaware of the problem posed by counterfeit goods. She demonstrates this by presenting basic factual information and by acknowledging what "most people think" or what "many in the West consider": that buying counterfeit goods is harmless. She also acknowledges her readers' high level of education by 2

2 Analysis of writer's audience

Writer's use of similes, metaphors, allusions

drawing comparisons with history and literature—specifically, the Victorians and *Oliver Twist*. To further earn the audience's trust, she uses her knowledge and position to gain credibility. As the Paris correspondent for *Newsweek* and as the author of a book on luxury goods, Thomas has credibility. Showing her familiarity with the world of fashion by referring to a conversation with renowned designer Miuccia Prada, she further establishes this credibility. Later in the article, she shares her experience of witnessing the abuse that accompanies the production of fake designer handbags. This anecdote allows her to say, "I've seen it myself," confirming her knowledge not just of the fashion world but also of the world of counterfeiting. Despite her authority, she does not distance herself from readers. In fact, she goes out of her way to identify with them, using informal style and first person, noting "it comes down to us" and asking what "we" can do.

In Thomas's argument, both the organization and the use of evidence 3 are effective. Thomas begins her article with statements that are easy to accept, and as she proceeds, she addresses more serious issues. In the first paragraph, she simply asks readers to "understand the importance of the handbag in fashion today." She demonstrates the wide-ranging influence and appeal of counterfeit designer goods, pointing out that "at least 11 percent of the world's clothing is fake." Thomas then makes the point that the act of purchasing these seemingly frivolous goods can actually have serious consequences. For example, crime syndicates and possibly even terrorist organizations actually run "the counterfeiting rackets" that produce these popular items. To support this point, she relies on two kinds of evidence—quotations from terrorism experts (specifically, the leader of a respected international police organization as well as a scholar in the field) and her own personal experience at a Chinese factory. Both kinds of evidence appeal to our emotions. Discussions of terrorism, especially those that recall the terrorist attacks on the United States, create fear. Descriptions of child labor in China encourage readers to feel sympathy.

Thomas waits until the end of her argument to present her thesis 4 because she assumes that her readers know little about the problem she is discussing. The one flaw in her argument is her failure to provide the evidence needed to establish connections between some causes and their effects. For example in paragraph 7, Thomas says that the sale of counterfeit T-shirts "may have helped finance the 1993 Word Trade Center bomb-

Writer's use of ethos

Analysis of the writer

Analysis of essay's organization

Writer's use of logos

Writer's use of evidence

Writer's use of pathos

Analysis of the essay's weakness

ing." By using the word *may*, she qualifies her claim and weakens her argument. The same is true when Thomas says that profits from the sale of counterfeit goods "have gone to groups associated with Hezbollah, the Shiite terrorist group." Readers are left to wonder what specific groups are "associated with Hezbollah" and whether these groups are in fact terrorist organizations. Without this information, her assertion remains unsupported. In spite of these shortcomings, Thomas's argument is clear and well organized. More definite links between causes and effects, however, would have made it more convincing than it is.

⊙ EXERCISE 4.1

Read the following essay, "Sweatshop Oppression," by Rajeev Ravisankar. Then, write a one-paragraph rhetorical analysis of the essay. Follow the template on page 119, filling in the blanks to create your analysis.

This opinion essay was published in the *Lantern*, the student newspaper of the Ohio State University, on April 19, 2006.

SWEATSHOP OPPRESSION

RAJEEV RAVISANKAR

Being the "poor" college students that we all are, many of us undoubtedly place an emphasis on finding the lowest prices. Some take this to the extreme and camp out in front of a massive retail store in the wee hours of the morning on Black Friday,° waiting for the opportunity to buy as much as we can for as little as possible.   1

The Friday after Thanksgiving, traditionally the biggest shopping day of the year

What often gets lost in this rampant, low-cost driven consumerism is the high human cost it takes to achieve lower and lower prices. Specifically, this means the extensive use of sweatshop labor.   2

Many of us are familiar with the term sweatshop,° but have difficulty really understanding how abhorrent the hours, wages, and conditions are. Many of these workers are forced to work 70–80 hours per week making pennies per hour. Workers are discouraged or intimidated from forming unions.   3

A work environment with long hours, low wages, and difficult or dangerous conditions

They must fulfill certain quotas for the day and stay extra hours (with no pay) if these are not fulfilled. Some are forced to sit in front of a machine for   4 hours as they are not permitted to take breaks unless the manager allows them to do so. Unsanitary bathrooms, poor ventilation, and extreme heat, upward of 90 degrees, are also prevalent. Child labor is utilized in some factories as well.

Facing mounting pressure from labor rights activists, trade unions, student protests, and human-rights groups, companies claimed that they would make improvements. Many of the aforementioned conditions, however, persist. In many cases, even a few pennies more could make a substantial difference in the lives of these workers. Of course, multinational corporations are not interested in giving charity; they are interested in doing anything to increase profits. Also, many consumers in the West refuse to pay a little bit more even if it would improve the lives of sweatshop workers. 5

> "[Corporations] are interested in doing anything to increase profits."

Free-market economic fundamentalists have argued that claims made by those who oppose sweatshops actually have a negative impact on the plight of the poor in the developing world. They suggest that by criticizing labor and human-rights conditions, anti-sweatshop activists have forced companies to pull out of some locations, resulting in workers losing their jobs. To shift the blame in this manner is to neglect a simple fact: Companies, not the anti-sweatshop protestors, make the decision to shift to locations where they can find cheaper labor and weaker labor restrictions. 6

Simply put, the onus should always be on companies such as Nike, Reebok, Adidas, Champion, Gap, Wal-Mart, etc. They are to blame for perpetuating a system of exploitation which seeks to get as much out of each worker for the least possible price. 7

By continuing to strive for lower wages and lower input costs, they are taking part in a phenomenon which has been described as "the race to the bottom." The continual decline of wages and working conditions will be accompanied by a lower standard of living. This hardly seems like the best way to bring the developing world out of the pits of poverty. 8

So what can we do about it? Currently, the total disregard for human well-being through sweatshop oppression is being addressed by a number of organizations, including University Students against Sweatshops. USAS seeks to make universities source their apparel in factories that respect workers' rights, especially the right to freely form unions. 9

According to an article in *The Nation*, universities purchase nearly "$3 billion in T-shirts, sweatshirts, caps, sneakers and sports uniforms adorned with their institutions' names and logos." Because brands do not want to risk losing this money, it puts pressure on them to provide living wages and reasonable conditions for workers. Campaigns such as this are necessary if we are to stop the long race to the bottom. 10

TEMPLATE FOR WRITING A RHETORICAL ANALYSIS

Ravisankar begins his essay by _____

_____

_____. The problem he identifies is _____

_____

_____. Ravisankar assumes his readers are _____

_____

_____. His purpose in this essay is to _____

_____

In order to accomplish this purpose, he appeals mainly to _____

_____

_____. He also appeals to _____

_____

In his essay, Ravisankar addresses the main argument against his thesis, the idea that _____

_____

_____

He refutes this argument by saying _____

_____

_____

Finally, he concludes by making the point that _____

_____

Overall, the argument Ravisankar makes is effective [or ineffective] because _____

_____

_____

◉ EXERCISE 4.2

Read the following essay, "Where Sweatshops Are a Dream," by Nicholas D. Kristof. Then, write a rhetorical analysis of Kristof's essay. Be sure to consider the rhetorical situation, the means of persuasion, and the writer's rhetorical strategies. End your rhetorical analysis with an assessment of the strengths and weaknesses of Kristof's argument.

This opinion column was published in the *New York Times* on January 15, 2009.

WHERE SWEATSHOPS
ARE A DREAM

NICHOLAS D. KRISTOF

Before Barack Obama and his team act on their talk about "labor standards," 1 I'd like to offer them a tour of the vast garbage dump here in Phnom Penh.

This is a Dante-like vision of hell. It's a mountain of festering refuse, a 2 half-hour hike across, emitting clouds of smoke from subterranean fires.

The miasma of toxic stink leaves you gasping, breezes batter you with 3 filth, and even the rats look forlorn. Then the smoke parts and you come across a child ambling barefoot, searching for old plastic cups that recyclers will buy for five cents a pound. Many families actually live in shacks on this smoking garbage.

Mr. Obama and the Democrats who favor labor standards in trade agree- 4 ments mean well, for they intend to fight back at oppressive sweatshops abroad. But while it shocks Americans to hear it, the central challenge in the poorest countries is not that sweatshops exploit too many people, but that they don't exploit enough.

Talk to these families in the dump, and a job in a sweatshop is a cherished 5 dream, an escalator out of poverty, the kind of gauzy if probably unrealistic ambition that parents everywhere often have for their children.

"I'd love to get a job in a factory," said Pim Srey Rath, a 19-year-old 6 woman scavenging for plastic. "At least that work is in the shade. Here is where it's hot."

Another woman, Vath Sam Oeun, hopes her 10-year-old boy, scavenging 7 beside her, grows up to get a factory job, partly because she has seen other children run over by garbage trucks. Her boy has never been to a doctor or a dentist and last bathed when he was 2, so a sweatshop job by comparison would be far more pleasant and less dangerous.

I'm glad that many Americans are repulsed by the idea of importing products made by barely paid, barely legal workers in dangerous factories. Yet sweatshops are only a symptom of poverty, not a cause, and banning them closes off one route out of poverty. At a time of tremendous economic distress and protectionist pressures, there's a special danger that tighter labor standards will be used as an excuse to curb trade. 8

> "[S]weatshops are only a symptom of poverty, not a cause."

When I defend sweatshops, people always ask me: But would you want to 9 work in a sweatshop? No, of course not. But I would want even less to pull a rickshaw. In the hierarchy of jobs in poor countries, sweltering at a sewing machine isn't the bottom.

My views on sweatshops are shaped by years living in East Asia, watching 10 as living standards soared—including those in my wife's ancestral village in southern China—because of sweatshop jobs.

Manufacturing is one sector that can provide millions of jobs. Yet sweat- 11 shops usually go not to the poorest nations but to better-off countries with more reliable electricity and ports.

I often hear the argument: Labor standards can improve wages and work- 12 ing conditions, without greatly affecting the eventual retail cost of goods. That's true. But labor standards and "living wages" have a larger impact on production costs that companies are always trying to pare. The result is to push companies to operate more capital-intensive factories in better-off nations like Malaysia, rather than labor-intensive factories in poorer countries like Ghana or Cambodia.

Cambodia has, in fact, pursued an interesting experiment by working 13 with factories to establish decent labor standards and wages. It's a worthwhile idea, but one result of paying above-market wages is that those in charge of hiring often demand bribes—sometimes a month's salary—in exchange for a job. In addition, these standards add to production costs, so some factories have closed because of the global economic crisis and the difficulty of compet- ing internationally.

The best way to help people in the poorest countries isn't to campaign 14 against sweatshops but to promote manufacturing there. One of the best things America could do for Africa would be to strengthen our program to encourage African imports, called AGOA, and nudge Europe to match it.

Among people who work in development, many strongly believe (but few 15 dare say very loudly) that one of the best hopes for the poorest countries would be to build their manufacturing industries. But global campaigns against sweatshops make that less likely.

Look, I know that Americans have a hard time accepting that sweatshops 16 can help people. But take it from 13-year-old Neuo Chanthou, who earns a bit less than $1 a day scavenging in the dump. She's wearing a "Playboy" shirt and hat that she found amid the filth, and she worries about her sister, who lost part of her hand when a garbage truck ran over her.

"It's dirty, hot, and smelly here," she said wistfully. "A factory is better." 17

5 Understanding Logic and Recognizing Logical Fallacies

How Free Should Free Speech Be?

Ask almost anyone what makes a society free and one of the answers will be free speech. The free expression of ideas is integral to freedom itself, and protecting that freedom is part of a democratic government's job: in a sense, this means that most people see free speech as one of the cornerstones of equality. Everyone's opinion can, and indeed must, be heard.

But what happens when those opinions are offensive, or even dangerous? If free speech has limits, is it still free? When we consider the question abstractly, it's very easy to say no. How can it be free if there are limits to how free it is, and who gets to decide those limits? It's dangerous to give anyone that kind of authority. After all, there is no shortage of historical evidence linking censorship with tyranny. When we think of limiting free speech, we think of totalitarian regimes, like Nazi Germany.

But what happens when the people arguing for the right to be heard are Nazis themselves? In places like Israel and France, where the legacy of Nazi Germany is still all too real, there are some

things you simply cannot say. Anti-Semitic language is considered "hate speech," and those who perpetuate it face stiff fines, if not imprisonment. It might seem outrageous to those of us who live in the United States. If you live in Israel, however, chances are that the legacy of the Holocaust is not that far away. And there are people in France who can still remember the day Nazi troops marched into Paris. Should they have to listen to what neo-Nazis have to say?

On American college campuses, free speech is often considered fundamental to a liberal education, and in many ways, encountering ideas that make you feel uncomfortable is a necessary part of a college education. But the question of free speech is easy to answer when it's theoretical: when the issue is made tangible by racist language or by a discussion of a traumatic experience, it becomes much more difficult to navigate. For example, should African-American students have to listen to "the n-word" in a discussion of *Huckleberry Finn*? Should a nineteen-year-old rape survivor have to sit through a

(continued)

(*continued*)

discussion of rape in American literature? Advocates of unlimited free speech respond to these objections by pointing out that censorship is a slippery slope: once you can penalize a person for saying something hateful, there will be no end to the subjects that will be off-limits.

Later in this chapter, you will be asked to think more about this issue. You will be given several sources to consider and asked to write a logical argument that takes a position on how free free speech should be.

The word *logic* comes from the Greek word *logos*, roughly translated as "word," "thought," "principle," or "reason." **Logic** is concerned with the principles of correct reasoning. By studying logic, you learn the rules that determine the validity of arguments. In other words, logic enables you to tell whether a conclusion correctly follows from a set of statements or assumptions.

Why should you study logic? One answer is that logic enables you to make valid points and draw sound conclusions. An understanding of logic also enables you to evaluate the arguments of others. When you understand the basic principles of logic, you know how to tell the difference between a strong argument and a weak argument—between one that is well reasoned and one that is not. This ability can help you cut through the tangle of jumbled thought that characterizes many of the arguments you encounter daily—on television, radio, and the Internet; in the press; and from friends. Finally, logic enables you to communicate clearly and forcefully. Understanding the characteristics of good arguments helps you to present your own ideas in a coherent and even compelling way.

Kobe Bryant, who played for the Los Angeles Lakers, arguing with a referee

Mark Ralston/Getty

Specific rules determine the criteria you use to develop (and to evaluate) arguments logically. For this reason, you should become familiar with the basic principles of *deductive* and *inductive reasoning*—two important ways information is organized in argumentative essays. (Keep in mind that a single argumentative essay might contain both deductive reasoning and inductive reasoning. For the sake of clarity, however, we will discuss them separately.)

Thomas Jefferson

What Is Deductive Reasoning?

Most of us use deductive reasoning every day—at home, in school, on the job, and in our communities— usually without even realizing it.

Deductive reasoning begins with **premises**— statements or assumptions on which an argument is based or from which conclusions are drawn. Deductive reasoning moves from general statements, or premises, to specific conclusions. The process of deduction has traditionally been illustrated with a **syllogism**, which consists of a *major premise*, a *minor premise*, and a *conclusion*:

MAJOR PREMISE	All Americans are guaranteed freedom of speech by the Constitution.
MINOR PREMISE	Sarah is an American.
CONCLUSION	Therefore, Sarah is guaranteed freedom of speech.

A syllogism begins with a **major premise**—a general statement that relates two terms. It then moves to a **minor premise**—an example of the statement that was made in the major premise. If these two premises are linked correctly, a **conclusion** that is supported by the two premises logically follows. (Notice that the conclusion in the syllogism above contains no terms that do not appear in the major and minor premises.) The strength of deductive reasoning is that if readers accept the major and minor premises, the conclusion must necessarily follow.

Thomas Jefferson used deductive reasoning in the Declaration of Independence. When, in 1776, the Continental Congress asked him to draft this document, Jefferson knew that he had to write a powerful argument that would convince the world that the American colonies were justified in breaking away from England. He knew how compelling a deductive argument could be, and so he organized the Declaration of Independence to reflect the traditional structure of deductive logic. It contains a major premise, a minor premise (supported by evidence), and a conclusion. Expressed as a syllogism, here is the argument that Jefferson used:

MAJOR PREMISE	When a government oppresses people, the people have a right to rebel against that government.
MINOR PREMISE	The government of England oppresses the American people.
CONCLUSION	Therefore, the American people have the right to rebel against the government of England.

In practice, deductive arguments are more complicated than the simple three-part syllogism suggests. Still, it is important to understand the basic structure of a syllogism because a syllogism enables you to map out your argument, to test it, and to see if it makes sense.

Constructing Sound Syllogisms

A syllogism is **valid** when its conclusion follows logically from its premises. A syllogism is **true** when the premises are consistent with the facts. To be **sound**, a syllogism must be *both* valid and true.

Consider the following valid syllogism:

MAJOR PREMISE	All state universities must accommodate disabled students.
MINOR PREMISE	UCLA is a state university.
CONCLUSION	Therefore, UCLA must accommodate disabled students.

In the valid syllogism above, both the major premise and the minor premise are factual statements. If both these premises are true, then the conclusion must also be true. Because the syllogism is both valid and true, it is also sound.

However, a syllogism can be valid without being true. For example, look at the following syllogism:

MAJOR PREMISE	All recipients of support services are wealthy.
MINOR PREMISE	Dillon is a recipient of support services.
CONCLUSION	Therefore, Dillon is wealthy.

As illogical as it may seem, this syllogism is valid: its conclusion follows logically from its premises. The major premise states that *recipients of support services*—all such *recipients*—are wealthy. However, this premise is clearly false: some recipients of support services may be wealthy, but more are probably not. For this reason, even though the syllogism is valid, it is not true.

Keep in mind that validity is a test of an argument's structure, not of its soundness. Even if a syllogism's major and minor premises are true, its conclusion may not necessarily be valid.

Consider the following examples of invalid syllogisms.

Syllogism with an Illogical Middle Term

A syllogism with an illogical middle term cannot be valid. The **middle term** of a syllogism is the term that occurs in both the major and minor premises but not in the conclusion. (It links the major term and the minor term together in the syllogism.) A middle term of a valid syllogism must refer to *all* members of the designated class or group—for example, *all* dogs, *all* people, *all* men, or *all* women.

Consider the following invalid syllogism:

MAJOR PREMISE	All dogs are mammals.
MINOR PREMISE	Some mammals are porpoises.
CONCLUSION	Therefore, some porpoises are dogs.

Even though the statements in the major and minor premises are true, the syllogism is not valid. *Mammals* is the middle term because it appears in both the major and minor premises. However, because the middle term *mammal* does not refer to *all mammals*, it cannot logically lead to a valid conclusion.

In the syllogism that follows, the middle term *does* refer to all members of the designated group, so the syllogism is valid:

MAJOR PREMISE	All dogs are mammals.
MINOR PREMISE	Ralph is a dog.
CONCLUSION	Therefore, Ralph is a mammal.

Syllogism with a Key Term Whose Meaning Shifts

A syllogism that contains a key term whose meaning shifts cannot be valid. For this reason, the meaning of a key term must remain consistent throughout the syllogism.

Consider the following invalid syllogism:

MAJOR PREMISE	Only man is capable of analytical reasoning.
MINOR PREMISE	Anna is not a man.
CONCLUSION	Therefore, Anna is not capable of analytical reasoning.

In the major premise, *man* refers to mankind—that is, to all human beings. In the minor premise, however, *man* refers to males. In the following valid syllogism, the key terms remain consistent:

MAJOR PREMISE	All educated human beings are capable of analytical reasoning.
MINOR PREMISE	Anna is an educated human being.
CONCLUSION	Therefore, Anna is capable of analytical reasoning.

Syllogism with Negative Premise

If *either* premise in a syllogism is negative, then the conclusion must also be negative.

The following syllogism is not valid:

MAJOR PREMISE	Only senators can vote on legislation.
MINOR PREMISE	No students are senators.
CONCLUSION	Therefore, students can vote on legislation.

Because one of the premises of the syllogism above is negative ("No students are senators"), the only possible valid conclusion must also be negative ("Therefore, no students can vote on legislation").

If *both* premises are negative, however, the syllogism cannot have a valid conclusion:

MAJOR PREMISE	Disabled students may not be denied special help.
MINOR PREMISE	Jen is not a disabled student.
CONCLUSION	Therefore, Jen may not be denied special help.

In the syllogism above, both premises are negative. For this reason, the syllogism cannot have a valid conclusion. (How can Jen deserve special help if she is not a disabled student?) To have a valid conclusion, this syllogism must have only one negative premise:

MAJOR PREMISE	Disabled students may not be denied special help.
MINOR PREMISE	Jen is a disabled student.
CONCLUSION	Therefore, Jen may not be denied special help.

Recognizing Enthymemes

An **enthymeme** is a syllogism with one or two parts of its argument—usually, the major premise—missing. In everyday life, we often leave out parts of arguments—most of the time because we think they are so obvious (or clearly implied) that they don't need to be stated. We assume that the people hearing or reading the arguments will easily be able to fill in the missing parts.

Many enthymemes are presented as a conclusion plus a reason. Consider the following enthymeme:

Robert has lied, so he cannot be trusted.

In the statement above, the minor premise and the conclusion are stated, but the major premise is only implied. Once the missing term has been supplied, the logical structure of the enthymeme becomes clear:

MAJOR PREMISE	People who lie cannot be trusted.
MINOR PREMISE	Robert has lied.
CONCLUSION	Therefore, Robert cannot be trusted.

It is important to identify enthymemes in arguments you read because some writers, knowing that readers often accept enthymemes uncritically, use them intentionally to unfairly influence readers.

Consider this enthymeme:

Because Liz receives a tuition grant, she should work.

Although some readers might challenge this statement, others will accept it uncritically. When you supply the missing premise, however, the underlying assumptions of the enthymeme become clear—and open to question:

MAJOR PREMISE   All students who receive tuition grants should work.

MINOR PREMISE   Liz receives a tuition grant.

CONCLUSION   Therefore, Liz should work.

Perhaps some people who receive tuition grants should work, but should everyone? What about those who are ill or who have disabilities? What about those who participate in varsity sports or have unpaid internships? The enthymeme oversimplifies the issue and should not be accepted at face value.

At first glance, the following enthymeme might seem to make sense:

North Korea is ruled by a dictator, so it should be invaded.

However, consider the same enthymeme with the missing term supplied:

MAJOR PREMISE   All countries governed by dictators should be invaded.

MINOR PREMISE   North Korea is a country governed by a dictator.

CONCLUSION   Therefore, North Korea should be invaded.

Once the missing major premise has been supplied, the flaws in the argument become clear. Should *all* nations governed by dictators be invaded? Who should do the invading? Who would make this decision? What would be the consequences of such a policy? As this enthymeme illustrates, if the major premise of a deductive argument is questionable, then the rest of the argument will also be flawed.

BUMPER-STICKER THINKING

Bumper stickers often take the form of enthymemes:

- Self-control beats birth control.
- Peace is patriotic.
- A woman's place is in the House . . . and in the Senate.
- Ban cruel traps.
- Evolution is a theory—kind of like gravity.

- I work and pay taxes so wealthy people don't have to.

- The Bible says it, I believe it, that settles it.

- No one needs a mink coat except a mink.

- Celebrate diversity.

Most often, bumper stickers state just the conclusion of an argument and omit both the major and minor premises. Careful readers, however, will supply the missing premises and thus determine whether the argument is sound.

Bumper stickers on a car. © Dave G. Houser/Corbis.

◑ EXERCISE 5.1

Read the following paragraph. Then, restate its main argument as a syllogism.

Drunk Driving Should Be Legalized

In ordering states to enforce tougher drunk driving standards by making it a crime to drive with a blood-alcohol concentration of .08 percent or higher, government has been permitted to criminalize the content of drivers' blood instead of their actions. The assumption that a driver who has been drinking automatically presents a danger to society even when no harm has been caused is a blatant violation of civil liberties. Government should not be concerned with the probability and propensity of a drinking driver to cause an accident; rather, laws should deal only with actions that damage person or property. Until they actually commit a crime, drunk drivers should be liberated from the force of the law. (From "Legalize Drunk Driving," by Llewellyn H. Rockwell Jr., WorldNetDaily.com)

⊙ EXERCISE 5.2

Read the following paragraphs. Then, answer the questions that follow.

Animals Are Equal to Humans

According to the United Nations, a person may not be killed, exploited, cruelly treated, intimidated, or imprisoned for no good reason. Put another way, people should be able to live in peace, according to their own needs and preferences.

Who should have these rights? Do they apply to people of all races? Children? People who are brain damaged or senile? The declaration makes it clear that basic rights apply to everyone. To make a slave of someone who is intellectually handicapped or of a different race is no more justifiable than to make a slave of anyone else.

The reason why these rights apply to everyone is simple: regardless of our differences, we all experience a life with its mosaic of thoughts and feelings. This applies equally to the princess and the hobo, the brain surgeon and the dunce. Our value as individuals arises from this capacity to experience life, not because of any intelligence or usefulness to others. Every person has an inherent value, and deserves to be treated with respect in order to make the most of their unique life experience. (Excerpted from "Human and Animal Rights," by Animal Liberation.org)

1. What unstated assumptions about the subject does the writer make? Does the writer expect readers to accept these assumptions? How can you tell?

2. What kind of supporting evidence does the writer provide?

3. What is the major premise of this argument?

4. Express the argument that is presented in these paragraphs as a syllogism.

5. Evaluate the syllogism you constructed. Is it true? Is it valid? Is it sound?

⊙ EXERCISE 5.3

Read the following five arguments, and determine whether each is sound. (To help you evaluate the arguments, you may want to try arranging them as syllogisms.)

1. All humans are mortal. Max is human. Therefore, Max is mortal.

2. Alison should order eggs or oatmeal for breakfast. She won't order eggs, so she should order oatmeal.

3. The cafeteria does not serve meat loaf on Friday. Today is not Friday. Therefore, the cafeteria will not serve meat loaf.

4. All reptiles are cold-blooded. Geckos are reptiles. Therefore, geckos are cold-blooded.

5. All triangles have three equal sides. The figure on the board is a triangle. Therefore, it must have three equal sides.

⊘ EXERCISE 5.4

Read the following ten enthymemes, which come from bumper stickers. Supply the missing premises, and then evaluate the logic of each argument.

1. If you love your pet, don't eat meat.

2. War is terrorism.

3. Real men don't ask for directions.

4. Immigration is the sincerest form of flattery.

5. I eat local because I can.

6. Don't blame me; I voted for the other guy.

7. I read banned books.

8. Love is the only solution.

9. It's a child, not a choice.

10. Think. It's patriotic.

Writing Deductive Arguments

Deductive arguments begin with a general principle and reach a specific conclusion. They develop that principle with logical arguments that are supported by evidence—facts, observations, the opinions of experts, and so on. Keep in mind that no single structure is suitable for all deductive (or inductive) arguments. Different issues and different audiences will determine how you arrange your ideas.

In general, deductive essays can be structured in the following way:

INTRODUCTION	Presents an overview of the issue
	States the thesis
BODY	Presents evidence: point 1 in support of the thesis
	Presents evidence: point 2 in support of the thesis
	Presents evidence: point 3 in support of the thesis
	Refutes the arguments against the thesis
CONCLUSION	Brings argument to a close
	Concluding statement reinforces the thesis

⊖ **EXERCISE 5.5**

The following student essay, "College Should Be for Everyone," includes all the elements of a deductive argument. The student who wrote this essay was responding to the question, "Should everyone be encouraged to go to college?" After you read the essay, answer the questions on pages 136–137, consulting the outline on page 133 if necessary.

COLLEGE SHOULD BE FOR EVERYONE

CRYSTAL SANCHEZ

Overview of issue

Until the middle of the twentieth century, college was largely for the   1
rich. The G.I. Bill, which paid for the education of veterans returning from World War II, helped to change this situation. By 1956, nearly half of those who had served in World War II, almost 7.8 million people, had taken advantage of this benefit (U.S. Department of Veterans Affairs). Even today, however, college graduates are still a minority of the population. According to the U.S. Census Bureau, only 27.5 percent of Americans age twenty-five or older have a bachelor's degree. In many ways, this situa-tion is not good for the country. Why should college be just for the privi-

Thesis statement

leged few? Because a college education provides important benefits, such as increased wages for our citizens and a stronger democracy for our nation, every U.S. citizen should have the opportunity to attend college.

Evidence: Point 1

One reason everyone should have the opportunity to go to college is   2
that a college education gives people a chance to discover what they are good at. It is hard for people to know if they are interested in statistics or public policy or marketing unless they have the chance to explore these sub-jects. College—and only college—can give them this opportunity. Where else can a person be exposed to a large number of courses taught by experts in a variety of disciplines? Such exposure can open new areas of interest and lead to a much wider set of career options—and thus to a better life (Stout). Without college, most people have limited options and never realize their true potential. Although life and work experiences can teach a person a lot of things, the best education is the broad kind that college offers.

Evidence: Point 2

Another reason everyone should have the opportunity to go to   3
college is that more and more jobs are being phased out or moved over-seas. Americans should go to college to develop the skills that they will

need to get the best jobs that will remain in the United States. Over the last few decades, midlevel jobs have been steadily disappearing. If this trend continues, the American workforce will be divided in two. One part will consist of low-wage, low-skill service jobs, such as those in food preparation and retail sales, and the other part will be high-skill, high-wage jobs, such as those in management and professional fields like business and engineering. According to a recent report, to compete in the future job market, Americans will need the skills that colleges teach. Future workers will need to be problem solvers who can think both critically and creatively and who can adapt to unpredictable situations. They will also need a global awareness, knowledge of many cultures and disciplines, and the ability to communicate in different forms of media. To master these skills, Americans have to be college educated ("Ten Skills for the Future Workforce").

Perhaps the best reason everyone should have the opportunity to go to college is that education is an essential component of a democratic society. Those without the ability to understand and analyze news reports are not capable of contributing to the social, political, and economic growth of the country. Democracy requires informed citizens who will be able to analyze complicated issues in areas such as finance, education, and public health; weigh competing claims of those running for public office; and assess the job performance of elected officials. By providing students with the opportunity to study subjects such as history, philosophy, English, and political science, colleges and universities help them to acquire the critical-thinking skills that they will need to participate fully in American democracy.

    4   Evidence: Point 3

Some people oppose the idea that everyone should have the opportunity to attend college. One objection is that educational resources are limited. Some say that if students enter colleges in great numbers they will overwhelm the higher-education system (Stout). This argument exaggerates the problem. As with any other product, if demand rises, supply will rise to meet that demand. In addition, with today's extensive distance-learning options and the availability of open educational resources—free, high-quality, digital materials—it will be possible to educate large numbers of students at a reasonable cost ("Open Educational Resources"). Another objection to encouraging everyone to attend college is that underprepared students will require so much help that they will take time and attention away from better students. This argument is actually a red herring.° Most schools already provide resources, such as tutoring and

    5   Refutation of opposing arguments

An irrelevant side issue used as a diversion

writing centers, for students who need them. With some additional funding, these schools could expand the services they already provide. This course of action will be expensive, but it is a lot less expensive than leaving millions of young people unprepared for jobs of the future.

A college education gave the returning veterans of World War II   6 many opportunities and increased their value to the nation. Today, a college education could do the same for many citizens. This country has an obligation to offer all students access to an affordable and useful education. Not only will the students benefit personally, but the nation will also. If we do not adequately prepare students for the future, then we will all suffer the consequences.

Concluding statement

Works Cited

"Open Educational Resources." *Center for American Progress*, 7 Feb. 2012, www.americanprogress.org/issues/labor/news/2012 /02/07/11114/open-educational-resources/.

Stout, Chris. "Top Five Reasons Why You Should Choose to Go to College." *Ezine Articles*, 2008, ezinearticles.com/?Top-Five-Reasons-Why-You-Should-Choose-To-Go-To-College&id=384395.

"Ten Skills for the Future Workforce." *The Atlantic,* 22 June 2011, www.theatlantic.com/education/archive/2011/06/ten-skills-for-future -work/473484/.

United States, Census Bureau. "Bachelor's Degree Attainment Tops 30 Percent for the First Time, Census Bureau Reports." *US Census Bureau Newsroom*, 23 Feb. 2012, www.census.gov/newsroom /releases/archives/education/cb12-33.html.

---, Department of Veterans Affairs. "Born of Controversy: The GI Bill of Rights." *GI Bill History*, 20 Oct. 2008, www.va.gov/opa/publications /celebrate/gi-bill.pdf.

Identifying the Elements of a Deductive Argument

1. Paraphrase this essay's thesis.

2. What arguments does the writer present as evidence to support her thesis? Which do you think is the strongest argument? Which is the weakest?

3. What opposing arguments does the writer address? What other opposing arguments could she have addressed?

4. What points does the conclusion emphasize? Do you think that any other points should be emphasized?

5. Construct a syllogism that expresses the essay's argument. Then, check your syllogism to make sure it is sound.

What Is Inductive Reasoning?

Inductive reasoning begins with specific observations (or evidence) and goes on to draw a general conclusion. You can see how induction works by looking at the following list of observations:

- Nearly 80 percent of ocean pollution comes from runoff.

- Runoff pollution can make ocean water unsafe for fish and people.

- In some areas, runoff pollution has forced beaches to be closed.

- Drinking water can be contaminated by runoff.

- More than one third of shellfish growing in waters in the United States are contaminated by runoff.

- Each year, millions of dollars are spent to restore polluted areas.

- There is a causal relationship between agricultural runoff and water-borne organisms that damage fish.

After studying these observations, you can use inductive reasoning to reach the conclusion that runoff pollution (rainwater that becomes polluted after

Sign warning of contaminated water

© Krista Kennella/ZUMA PRESS

it comes in contact with earth-bound pollutants such as fertilizer, pet waste, sewage, and pesticides) is a problem that must be addressed.

Children learn about the world by using inductive reasoning. For example, very young children see that if they push a light switch up, the lights in a room go on. If they repeat this action over and over, they reach the conclusion that every time they push a switch, the lights will go on. Of course, this conclusion does not always follow. For example, the light bulb may be burned out or the switch may be damaged. Even so, their conclusion usually holds true. Children also use induction to generalize about what is safe and what is dangerous. If every time they meet a dog, the encounter is pleasant, they begin to think that all dogs are friendly. If at some point, however, a dog snaps at them, they question the strength of their conclusion and modify their behavior accordingly.

Scientists also use induction. In 1620, Sir Francis Bacon first proposed the **scientific method**—a way of using induction to find answers to questions. When using the scientific method, a researcher proposes a hypothe-

REACHING INDUCTIVE CONCLUSIONS

Here are some of the ways you can use inductive reasoning to reach conclusions:

- **Particular to general:** This form of induction occurs when you reach a general conclusion based on particular pieces of evidence. For example, suppose you walk into a bathroom and see that the mirrors are fogged. You also notice that the bathtub has drops of water on its sides and that the bathroom floor is wet. In addition, you see a damp towel draped over the sink. Putting all these observations together, you conclude that someone has recently taken a bath. (Detectives use induction when gathering clues to solve a crime.)

- **General to general:** This form of induction occurs when you draw a conclusion based on the consistency of your observations. For example, if you determine that Apple Inc. has made good products for a long time, you conclude it will continue to make good products.

- **General to particular:** This form of induction occurs when you draw a conclusion based on what you generally know to be true. For example, if you believe that cars made by the Ford Motor Company are reliable, then you conclude that a Ford Focus will be a reliable car.

- **Particular to particular:** This form of induction occurs when you assume that because something works in one situation, it will also work in another similar situation. For example, if Krazy Glue fixed the broken handle of one cup, then you conclude it will probably fix the broken handle of another cup.

sis and then makes a series of observations to test this hypothesis. Based on these observations, the researcher arrives at a conclusion that confirms, modifies, or disproves the hypothesis.

Making Inferences

Unlike deduction, which reaches a conclusion based on information provided by the major and minor premises, induction uses what you know to make a statement about something that you don't know. While deductive arguments can be judged in absolute terms (they are either **valid** or **invalid**), inductive arguments are judged in relative terms (they are either **strong** or **weak**).

You reach an inductive conclusion by making an **inference**—a statement about what is unknown based on what is known. (In other words, you look at the evidence and try to figure out what is going on.) For this reason, there is always a gap between your observations and your conclusion. To bridge this gap, you have to make an **inductive leap**—a stretch of the imagination that enables you to draw an acceptable conclusion. Therefore, inductive conclusions are never certain (as deductive conclusions are) but only probable. The more evidence you provide, the stronger and more probable your conclusions (and your argument) are.

Public-opinion polls illustrate how inferences are used to reach inductive conclusions. Politicians and news organizations routinely use public-opinion polls to assess support (or lack of support) for a particular policy, proposal, or political candidate. After surveying a sample population—registered voters, for example—pollsters reach conclusions based on their responses. In other words, by asking questions and studying the responses of a sample group of people, pollsters make inferences about the larger group—for example, which political candidate is ahead and by how much. How solid these inferences are depends to a great extent on the sample populations the pollsters survey. In an election, for example, a poll of randomly chosen individuals will be less accurate than a poll of registered voters or likely voters. In addition, other factors (such as the size of the sample and the way questions are worded) can determine the relative strength of the inductive conclusion.

As with all inferences, a gap exists between a poll's data—the responses to the questions—and the conclusion. The larger and more representative the sample, the smaller the inductive leap necessary to reach a conclusion and the more accurate the poll. If the gap between the data and the conclusion is too big, however, the pollsters will be accused of making a **hasty generalization** (see p. 150). Remember, no matter how much support you present, an inductive conclusion is only probable, never certain. The best you can do is present a convincing case and hope that your audience will accept it.

Constructing Strong Inductive Arguments

When you use inductive reasoning, your conclusion is only as strong as the **evidence**—the facts, details, or examples—that you use to support it. For this reason, you should be on the lookout for the following problems that can occur when you try to reach an inductive conclusion.

Generalization Too Broad

The conclusion you state cannot go beyond the scope of your evidence. Your evidence must support your generalization. For instance, you cannot survey just three international students in your school and conclude that the school does not go far enough to accommodate international students. To reach such a conclusion, you would have to consider a large number of international students.

Insufficient Evidence

The evidence on which you base an inductive conclusion must be **representative**, not atypical or biased. For example, you cannot conclude that students are satisfied with the course offerings at your school by sampling just first-year students. To be valid, your conclusion should be based on responses from a cross section of students from all years.

Irrelevant Evidence

Your evidence has to support your conclusion. If it does not, it is **irrelevant**. For example, if you assert that many adjunct faculty members make substantial contributions to your school, your supporting examples must be adjunct faculty, not tenured or junior faculty.

Exceptions to the Rule

There is always a chance that you will overlook an exception that may affect the strength of your conclusion. For example, not everyone who has a disability needs special accommodations, and not everyone who requires special accommodations needs the same services. For this reason, you should avoid using words like *every*, *all*, and *always* and instead use words like *most*, *many*, and *usually*.

⤳ EXERCISE 5.6

Read the following arguments, and decide whether each is a deductive argument or an inductive argument and write "D" or "I" on the lines below.

1. Freedom of speech is a central principle of our form of government. For this reason, students should be allowed to wear T-shirts that call for the legalization of marijuana. _____

2. The Chevy Cruze Eco gets twenty-seven miles a gallon in the city and forty-six miles a gallon on the highway. The Honda Accord gets twenty-seven miles a gallon in the city and thirty-six miles a gallon on the highway. Therefore, it makes more sense for me to buy the Chevy Cruze Eco. _____

3. In Edgar Allan Poe's short story "The Cask of Amontillado," Montresor flatters Fortunato. He lures him to his vaults where he stores wine. Montresor then gets Fortunato drunk and chains him to the wall of a crypt. Finally, Montresor uncovers a pile of building material and walls up the entrance to the crypt. Clearly, Montresor has carefully planned to murder Fortunato for a very long time. _____

4. All people should have the right to die with dignity. Garrett is a terminally ill patient, so he should have access to doctor-assisted suicide. _____

5. Last week, we found unacceptably high levels of pollution in the ocean. On Monday, we also found high levels of pollution. Today, we found even higher levels of pollution. We should close the ocean beaches to swimmers until we can find the source of this problem. _____

⬏ EXERCISE 5.7

Read the following arguments. Then, decide whether they are deductive or inductive. If they are inductive arguments, evaluate their strength. If they are deductive arguments, evaluate their soundness.

1. *The Farmer's Almanac* says that this winter will be very cold. The National Weather Service also predicts that this winter will be very cold. So, this should be a cold winter.

2. Many walled towns in Europe do not let people drive cars into their centers. San Gimignano is a walled town in Europe. It is likely that we will not be able to drive our car into its center.

3. The window at the back of the house is broken. There is a baseball on the floor. A few minutes ago, I saw two boys playing catch in a neighbor's yard. They must have thrown the ball through the window.

4. Every time I go to the beach I get sunburned. I guess I should stop going to the beach.

5. All my instructors have advanced degrees. George Martin is one of my instructors. Therefore, George Martin has an advanced degree.

6. My last two boyfriends cheated on me. All men are terrible.

7. I read a study published by a pharmaceutical company that said that Accutane was safe. Maybe the government was too quick to pull this drug off the market.

8. Chase is not very good-looking, and he dresses badly. I don't know how he can be a good architect.

9. No fictional character has ever had a fan club. Harry Potter does, but he is the exception.

10. Two weeks ago, my instructor refused to accept a late paper. She did the same thing last week. Yesterday, she also told someone that because his paper was late, she wouldn't accept it. I'd better get my paper in on time.

⊙ EXERCISE 5.8

Read the inductive paragraph below, written by student Pooja Vaidya, and answer the questions that follow it.

Years ago, when my friend took me to a game between the Philadelphia Eagles and the Dallas Cowboys in Philadelphia, I learned a little bit about American football and a lot about the behavior of football fans. Many of the Philadelphia fans were dressed in green and white football jerseys, each with a player's name and number on the back. One fan had his face painted green and wore a green cape with a large white *E* on it. He ran up and down the aisles in his section and led cheers. When the team was ahead, everyone joined in. When the team fell behind, this fan literally fell on his knees, cried, and begged the people in the stands to support the Eagles. (After the game, several people asked him for his autograph.) A group of six fans sat without shirts. They wore green wigs, and each had one letter of the team's name painted on his bare chest. Even though the temperature was below freezing, none of these fans ever put on his shirt. Before the game, many fans had been drinking at tailgate parties in the parking lot, and as the game progressed, they continued to drink beer in the stadium. By the beginning of the second half, fights were breaking out all over the stadium. Guards grabbed the people who were fighting and escorted them to a holding area under the stadium where a judge held "Eagles Court." At one point, a fan wearing a Dallas jersey tried to sit down in the row behind me. Some of the Eagles fans were so threatening that the police had to escort the Dallas fan out of the stands for his own protection. When the game ended in an Eagles victory, the fans sang the team's fight song as they left the stadium. I concluded that for many

Eagles fans, a day at the stadium is an opportunity to engage in behavior that in any other context would be unacceptable and even abnormal.

1. Which of the following statements could you *not* conclude from this paragraph?

   a. All Eagles fans act in outrageous ways at games.

   b. At football games, the fans in the stands can be as violent as the players on the field.

   c. The atmosphere at the stadium causes otherwise normal people to act abnormally.

   d. Spectator sports encourage fans to act in abnormal ways.

   e. Some people get so caught up in the excitement of a game that they act in uncharacteristic ways.

2. Paraphrase the writer's conclusion. What evidence is provided to support this conclusion?

3. What additional evidence could the writer have provided? Is this additional evidence necessary, or does the conclusion stand without it?

4. The writer makes an inductive leap to reach the paragraph's conclusion. Do you think this leap is too great?

5. Does this paragraph make a strong inductive argument? Why or why not?

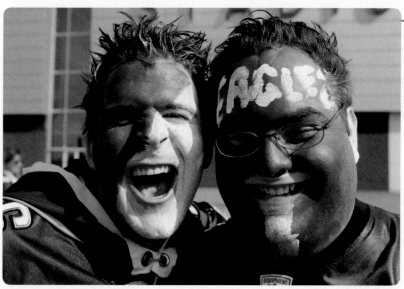

Philadelphia Eagles fans

© Chris Graythen/Getty Images Sports

Writing Inductive Arguments

Inductive arguments begin with evidence (specific facts, observations, expert opinion, and so on), draw inferences from the evidence, and reach a conclusion by making an inductive leap. Keep in mind that inductive arguments are only as strong as the link between the evidence and the conclusion, so the stronger this link is, the stronger the argument will be.

Inductive essays frequently have the following structure:

INTRODUCTION	Presents the issue
	States the thesis
BODY	Presents evidence: facts, observations, expert opinion, and so on
	Draws inferences from the evidence
	Refutes the arguments against the thesis
CONCLUSION	Brings argument to a close
	Concluding statement reinforces the thesis

⊘ EXERCISE 5.9

The following essay includes all the elements of an inductive argument. After you read the essay, answer the questions on page 146, consulting the outline above if necessary.

This essay appeared in *Slate* on September 2, 2006.

PLEASE DO NOT FEED THE HUMANS

WILLIAM SALETAN

Dug

In 1894, Congress established Labor Day to honor those who "from rude 1 nature have delved° and carved all the grandeur we behold." In the century since, the grandeur of human achievement has multiplied. Over the past four decades, global population has doubled, but food output, driven by increases in productivity, has outpaced it. Poverty, infant mortality, and hunger are receding. For the first time in our planet's history, a species no longer lives at the mercy of scarcity. We have learned to feed ourselves.

We've learned so well, in fact, that we're getting fat. Not just the United 2 States or Europe, but the whole world. Egyptian, Mexican, and South African women are now as fat as Americans. Far more Filipino adults are now overweight than underweight. In China, one in five adults is too heavy, and the rate of overweight children is 28 times higher than it was two decades ago. In Thailand, Kuwait, and Tunisia, obesity, diabetes, and heart disease are soaring.

Hunger is far from conquered. But since 1990, the global rate of malnutri- 3
tion has declined an average of 1.7 percent a year. Based on data from the
World Health Organization and the U.N. Food and Agriculture Organization,
for every two people who are malnourished, three are now overweight or
obese. Among women, even in most African countries, overweight has sur-
passed underweight. The balance of peril is shifting.

Fat is no longer a rich man's disease. For middle- and high-income Amer- 4
icans, the obesity rate is 29 percent. For low-income Americans, it's 35 percent.
Among middle- and high-income kids aged 15 to 17, the rate of overweight is
14 percent. Among low-income kids in the same age bracket, it's
23 percent. Globally, weight has tended to rise with income. But a study in
Vancouver, Canada, published three months ago, found that preschoolers in
"food-insecure" households were twice as likely as other kids to be overweight
or obese. In Brazilian cities, the poor have become fatter than the rich.

Technologically, this is a triumph. In the early days of our species, even the 5
rich starved. Barry Popkin, a nutritional epidemiologist at the University of
North Carolina, divides history into several epochs. In the hunter-gatherer era,
if we didn't find food, we died. In the agricultural era, if our crops perished, we
died. In the industrial era, famine receded, but infectious diseases killed us.
Now we've achieved such control over nature that we're dying not of starvation
or infection, but of abundance. Nature isn't killing us. We're killing ourselves.

You don't have to go hungry anymore; we can fill you with fats and carbs 6
more cheaply than ever. You don't have to chase your food; we can bring it to
you. You don't have to cook it; we can deliver it ready-to-eat. You don't have
to eat it before it spoils; we can pump it full of preservatives so it lasts forever.
You don't even have to stop when you're full. We've got so much food to sell,
we want you to keep eating.

What happened in America is happening everywhere, only faster. Fewer 7
farmers' markets, more processed food. Fewer whole grains, more refined
ones. More sweeteners, salt, and trans fats. Cheaper meat, more animal fat.
Less cooking, more eating out. Bigger portions, more snacks.

Kentucky Fried Chicken and Pizza Hut are spreading across the planet. 8
Coca-Cola is in more than 200 countries. Half of McDonald's business is
overseas. In China, animal-fat intake has tripled in 20 years. By 2020, meat
consumption in developing countries will grow by 106 million metric tons,
outstripping growth in developed countries by a factor of more than five.
Forty years ago, to afford a high-fat diet, your country needed a gross national
product per capita of nearly $1,500. Now the price is half that. You no longer
have to be rich to die a rich man's death.

Soon, it'll be a poor man's death. The rich have Whole Foods, gyms, and per- 9
sonal trainers. The poor have 7-Eleven, Popeye's, and streets unsafe for walking.
When money's tight, you feed your kids at Wendy's and stock up on macaroni and
cheese. At a lunch buffet, you do what your ancestors did: store all the fat you can.

That's the punch line: Technology has changed everything but us. We 10
evolved to survive scarcity. We crave fat. We're quick to gain weight and slow

to lose it. Double what you serve us, and we'll double what we eat. Thanks to technology, the deprivation that made these traits useful is gone. So is the link between flavors and nutrients. The modern food industry can sell you sweetness without fruit, salt without protein, creaminess without milk. We can fatten you and starve you at the same time.

> "We evolved to survive scarcity."

And that's just the diet side of the equation. Before technology, adult men had 11 to expend about 3,000 calories a day. Now they expend about 2,000. Look at the new Segway scooter. The original model relieved you of the need to walk, pedal, or balance. With the new one, you don't even have to turn the handlebars or start it manually. In theory, Segway is replacing the car. In practice, it's replacing the body.

In country after country, service jobs are replacing hard labor. The folks 12 who field your customer service calls in Bangalore are sitting at desks. Nearly everyone in China has a television set. Remember when Chinese rode bikes? In the past six years, the number of cars there has grown from six million to 20 million. More than one in seven Chinese has a motorized vehicle, and households with such vehicles have an obesity rate 80 percent higher than their peers.

The answer to these trends is simple. We have to exercise more and 13 change the food we eat, donate, and subsidize. Next year, for example, the U.S. Women, Infants, and Children program, which subsidizes groceries for impoverished youngsters, will begin to pay for fruits and vegetables. For 32 years, the program has fed toddlers eggs and cheese but not one vegetable. And we wonder why poor kids are fat.

The hard part is changing our mentality. We have a distorted body image. 14 We're so used to not having enough, as a species, that we can't believe the problem is too much. From China to Africa to Latin America, people are trying to fatten their kids. I just got back from a vacation with my Jewish mother and Jewish mother-in-law. They told me I need to eat more.

The other thing blinding us is liberal guilt. We're so caught up in the idea 15 of giving that we can't see the importance of changing behavior rather than filling bellies. We know better than to feed buttered popcorn to zoo animals, yet we send it to a food bank and call ourselves humanitarians. Maybe we should ask what our fellow humans actually need.

Identifying the Elements of an Inductive Argument

1. What is this essay's thesis? Restate it in your own words.

2. Why do you think Saletan places the thesis where he does?

3. What evidence does Saletan use to support his conclusion?

4. What inductive leap does Saletan make to reach his conclusion? Do you think he should have included more evidence?

5. Overall, do you think Saletan's inductive argument is relatively strong or weak? Explain.

Recognizing Logical Fallacies

When you write arguments in college, you follow certain rules that ensure fairness. Not everyone who writes arguments is fair or thorough, however. Sometimes you will encounter arguments in which writers attack the opposition's intelligence or patriotism and base their arguments on questionable (or even false) assumptions. As convincing as these arguments can sometimes seem, they are not valid because they contain **fallacies**—errors in reasoning that undermine the logic of an argument. Familiarizing yourself with the most common logical fallacies can help you to evaluate the arguments of others and to construct better, more effective arguments of your own.

The following pages define and illustrate some logical fallacies that you should learn to recognize and avoid.

Begging the Question

The fallacy of **begging the question** assumes that a statement is self-evident (or true) when it actually requires proof. A conclusion based on such assumptions cannot be valid. For example, someone who is very religious could structure an argument the following way:

MAJOR PREMISE	Everything in the Bible is true.
MINOR PREMISE	The Bible says that Noah built an ark.
CONCLUSION	Therefore, Noah's Ark really existed.

A person can accept the conclusion of this syllogism only if he or she also accepts the major premise, which has not been proven true. Some people might find this line of reasoning convincing, but others would not—even if they were religious.

Begging the question occurs any time someone presents a debatable statement as if it were true. For example, look at the following statement:

> You have unfairly limited my right of free speech by refusing to print my editorial in the college newspaper.

This statement begs the question because it assumes what it should be proving—that refusing to print an editorial violates a person's right to free speech.

Circular Reasoning

Closely related to begging the question, **circular reasoning** occurs when someone supports a statement by restating it in different terms. Consider the following statement:

> Stealing is wrong because it is illegal.

Waterfall, by M. C. Escher. The artwork creates the illusion of water flowing uphill and in a circle. Circular reasoning occurs when the conclusion of an argument is the same as one of the premises.

The conclusion of the statement on the previous page is essentially the same as its beginning: stealing (which is illegal) is against the law. In other words, the argument goes in a circle.

Here are some other examples of circular reasoning:

- Lincoln was a great president because he is the best president we ever had.

- I am for equal rights for women because I am a feminist.

- Illegal immigrants should be deported because they are breaking the law.

All of the statements above have one thing in common: they attempt to support a statement by simply repeating the statement in different words.

Weak Analogy

An **analogy** is a comparison between two items (or concepts)—one familiar and one unfamiliar. When you make an analogy, you explain the unfamiliar item by comparing it to the familiar item.

Although analogies can be effective in arguments, they have limitations. For example, a senator who opposed a government bailout of the financial industry in 2008 made the following argument:

This bailout is doomed from the start. It's like pouring milk into a leaking bucket. As long as you keep pouring milk, the bucket stays full. But when you stop, the milk runs out the hole in the bottom of the bucket. What we're doing is throwing money into a big bucket and not fixing the hole. We have to find the underlying problems that have caused this part of our economy to get in trouble and pass legislation to solve them.

The problem with using analogies such as this one is that analogies are never perfect. There is always a difference between the two things being compared. The larger this difference, the weaker the analogy—and the weaker the argument that it supports. For example, someone could point out to the senator that the financial industry—and by extension, the whole economy—is much more complex and multifaceted than a leaking bucket. To analyze the economy, the senator would have to expand his discussion beyond this single analogy (which cannot carry the weight of the entire argument) as well as supply the evidence to support his contention that the bailout was a mistake from the start.

Ad Hominem Fallacy (Personal Attack)

The **ad hominem fallacy** occurs when someone attacks the character or the motives of a person instead of focusing on the issues. This line of reasoning is illogical because it focuses attention on the person making the argument, sidestepping the argument itself.

Consider the following statement:

> Dr. Thomson, I'm not sure why we should believe anything you have to say about this community health center. Last year, you left your husband for another man.

The above attack on Dr. Thomson's character is irrelevant; it has nothing to do with her ideas about the community health center. Sometimes, however, a person's character may have a direct relation to the issue. For example, if Dr. Thomson had invested in a company that supplied medical equipment to the health center, this fact would have been relevant to the issue at hand.

The ad hominem fallacy also occurs when you attempt to undermine an argument by associating it with individuals who are easily attacked. For example, consider this statement:

> I think your plan to provide universal heath care is interesting. I'm sure Marx and Lenin would agree with you.

Instead of focusing on the specific provisions of the health-care plan, the opposition unfairly associates it with the ideas of Karl Marx and Vladimir Lenin, two well-known Communists.

Creating a Straw Man

This fallacy most likely got its name from the use of straw dummies in military and boxing training. When writers create a **straw man**, they present a weak argument that can easily be refuted. Instead of attacking the real issue, they focus on a weaker issue and give the impression that they have effectively refuted an opponent's argument. Frequently, the straw man is an extreme or oversimplified version of the opponent's actual position. For example, during a debate about raising the minimum wage, a senator made the following comment:

> Those who oppose raising the minimum wage are heartless. They obviously don't care if children starve.

The Granger Collection

Ad hominem attack against Charles Darwin, originator of the theory of evolution by natural selection

© SOTK2011/Alamy

Instead of focusing on the minimum wage, the senator misrepresents the opposing position so that it appears cruel. As this example shows, the straw man fallacy is dishonest because it intentionally distorts an opponent's position to mislead readers.

Hasty or Sweeping Generalization (Jumping to a Conclusion)

A **hasty or sweeping generalization** (also called **jumping to a conclusion**) occurs when someone reaches a conclusion that is based on too little evidence. Many people commit this fallacy without realizing it. For example, when Richard Nixon was elected president in 1972, film critic Pauline Kael is supposed to have remarked, "How can that be? No one I know voted for Nixon!" The general idea behind this statement is that if Kael's acquaintances didn't vote for Nixon, then neither did most other people. This assumption is flawed because it is based on a small sample.

Sometimes people make hasty generalizations because they strongly favor one point of view over another. At other times, a hasty generalization is simply the result of sloppy thinking. For example, it is easier for a student to simply say that an instructor is an unusually hard grader than to survey the instructor's classes to see if this conclusion is warranted (or to consider other reasons for his or her poor performance in a course).

Either/Or Fallacy (False Dilemma)

The **either/or fallacy** (also called a **false dilemma**) occurs when a person says that there are just two choices when there are actually more. In many cases, the person committing this fallacy tries to force a conclusion by presenting just two choices, one of which is clearly more desirable than the other. (Parents do this with young children all the time: "Eat your carrots, or go to bed.")

Politicians frequently engage in this fallacy. For example, according to some politicians, you are either pro-life or pro-choice, pro–gun control or anti–gun control, pro-stem-cell research or anti-stem-cell research. Many people, however, are actually somewhere in the middle, taking a much more nuanced approach to complicated issues.

Consider the following statement:

> I can't believe you voted against the bill to build a wall along the southern border of the United States. Either you're for protecting our border, or you're against it.

This statement is an example of the either/or fallacy. The person who voted against the bill might be against the wall but not against all immigration restrictions. The person might favor loose restrictions for some people (for example, migrant workers) and strong restrictions for others (for example, drug smugglers). By limiting the options to just two, the speaker oversimplifies the situation and attempts to force the listener to accept a fallacious argument.

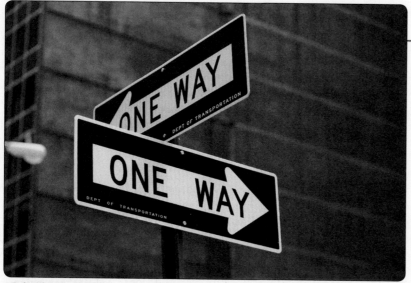

© Ferhat/Shutterstock.com

The either/or fallacy occurs when a writer presents just two choices when there are actually more.

Equivocation

The fallacy of **equivocation** occurs when a key term has one meaning in one part of an argument and another meaning in another part. (When a term is used **unequivocally**, it has the same meaning throughout the argument.) Consider the following old joke:

> The sign said, "Fine for parking here," so because it was fine, I parked there.

Obviously, the word *fine* has two different meanings in this sentence. The first time it is used, it means "money paid as a penalty." The second time, it means "good" or "satisfactory."

Most words have more than one meaning, so it is important not to confuse the various meanings. For an argument to work, a key term has to have the same meaning every time it appears in the argument. If the meaning shifts during the course of the argument, then the argument cannot be sound.

Consider the following statement:

> This is supposed to be a free country, but nothing worth having is ever free.

In this statement, the meaning of a key term shifts. The first time the word *free* is used, it means "not under the control of another." The second time, it means "without charge."

Red Herring

This fallacy gets its name from the practice of dragging a smoked fish across the trail of a fox to mask its scent during a fox hunt. As a result, the hounds lose the scent and are thrown off the track. The **red herring** fallacy occurs when a person raises an irrelevant side issue to divert attention from the real issue. Used skillfully, this fallacy can distract an audience and change the focus of an argument.

Political campaigns are good sources of examples of the red herring fallacy. Consider this example from the 2016 presidential race:

> I know that Donald Trump says that he is for the "little guy," but he lives in a three-story penthouse in the middle of Manhattan. How can we believe that his policies will help the average American?

The focus of his argument should have been on Trump's policies, not on the fact that he lives in a penthouse.

Here is another red herring fallacy from the 2016 political campaign:

Person trying to follow the argument.

The actual issue being argued.

Red herring, a distraction not related to the argument.

> Hillary Clinton wants us to vote for her, but she will be sixty-nine when she becomes president. I think that this is a problem.

Again, the focus of these remarks should have been on Clinton's qualifications, not on her age.

Slippery Slope

The **slippery-slope** fallacy occurs when a person argues that one thing will inevitably result from another. (Other names for the slippery-slope fallacy are the **foot-in-the-door fallacy** and the **floodgates fallacy**.) Both these names suggest that once you permit certain acts, you inevitably permit additional acts that eventually lead to disastrous consequences. Typically, the slippery-slope fallacy presents a series of increasingly unacceptable events that lead to an inevitable, unpleasant conclusion. (Usually, there is no evidence that such a sequence will actually occur.)

We encounter examples of the slippery-slope fallacy almost daily. During a debate on same-sex marriage, for example, an opponent advanced this line of reasoning:

> If we allow gay marriage, then there is nothing to stop polygamy. And once we allow this, where will it stop? Will we have to legalize incest—or even bestiality?

Whether or not you support same-sex marriage, you should recognize the fallacy of this slippery-slope reasoning. By the last sentence of the passage above, the assertions have become so outrageous that they approach parody. People can certainly debate this issue, but not in such a dishonest and highly emotional way.

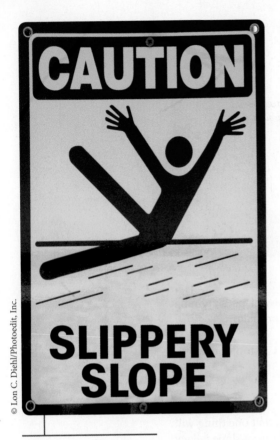

© Lon C. Diehl/Photoedit, Inc.

Beware the slippery-slope fallacy

You Also (Tu Quoque)

The **you also** fallacy asserts that a statement is false because it is inconsistent with what the speaker has said or done. In other words, a person is attacked for doing what he or she is arguing against. Parents often encounter this fallacy when they argue with their teenage children. By introducing an irrelevant point— "You did it too"—the children attempt to distract parents and put them on the defensive:

- How can you tell me not to smoke when you used to smoke?

- Don't yell at me for drinking. I bet you had a few beers before you were twenty-one.

- Why do I have to be home by midnight? Didn't you stay out late when you were my age?

Arguments such as these are irrelevant. People fail to follow their own advice, but that does not mean that their points have no merit. (Of course, not following their own advice does undermine their credibility.)

Appeal to Doubtful Authority

Writers of research papers frequently use the ideas of recognized authorities to strengthen their arguments. However, the sources offered as evidence need to be both respected and credible. The **appeal to doubtful authority** occurs when people use the ideas of nonexperts to support their arguments.

Not everyone who speaks as an expert is actually an authority on a particular issue. For example, when movie stars or recording artists give their opinions about politics, climate change, or foreign affairs— things they may know little about—they are not speaking as experts; therefore, they have no authority. (They *are* experts, however, when they discuss the film or music industries.) A similar situation occurs with the pundits who appear on television news shows. Some of these individuals have solid credentials in the fields they discuss, but others offer opinions even though they know little about the subjects. Unfortunately, many viewers accept the pronouncements of these "experts" uncritically and think it is acceptable to cite them to support their own arguments.

How do you determine whether a person you read about or hear is really an authority? First, make sure that the person actually has expertise in the field he or she is discussing. You can do this by checking his

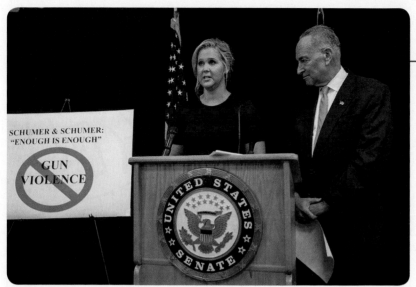

© Andrew Burton/Getty Images

Comedian/actor Amy Schumer boosts her credibility on the issue of gun control by appearing with her cousin, Senator Charles Schumer.

or her credentials on the Internet. Second, make sure that the person is not biased. No one is entirely free from bias, but the bias should not be so extreme that it undermines the person's authority. Finally, make sure that you can confirm what the so-called expert says or writes. Check one or two pieces of information in other sources, such as a basic reference text or encyclopedia. Determine if others—especially recognized experts in the field—confirm this information. If there are major points of discrepancy, dig further to make sure you are dealing with a legitimate authority.

Misuse of Statistics

The **misuse of statistics** occurs when data are misrepresented. Statistics can be used persuasively in an argument, but sometimes they are distorted—intentionally or unintentionally—to make a point. For example, a classic ad for toothpaste claims that four out of five dentists recommend Crest toothpaste. What the ad neglects to mention is the number of dentists who were questioned. If the company surveyed several thousand dentists, then this statistic would be meaningful. If the company surveyed only ten, however, it would not be.

Misleading statistics can be much subtler (and much more complicated) than the example above. For example, one year, there were 16,653 alcohol-related deaths in the United States. According to the National Highway Traffic Safety Administration (NHTSA), 12,892 of these 16,653 alcohol-related deaths involved at least one driver or passenger

"That's what I want to say. See if you can find some statistics to prove it."

Cartoonstock.com

who was legally drunk. Of the 12,892 deaths, 7,326 were the drivers themselves, and 1,594 were legally drunk pedestrians. The remaining 3,972 fatalities were nonintoxicated drivers, passengers, or nonoccupants. These 3,972 fatalities call the total number into question because the NHTSA does not indicate which drivers were at fault. In other words, if a sober driver ran a red light and killed a legally drunk driver, the NHTSA classified this death as alcohol-related. For this reason, the original number of alcohol-related deaths—16,653—is somewhat misleading. (The statistic becomes even more questionable when you consider that a person is automatically classified as intoxicated if he or she refuses to take a sobriety test.)

Post Hoc, Ergo Propter Hoc (After This, Therefore Because of This)

The **post hoc** fallacy asserts that because two events occur closely in time, one event must cause the other. Professional athletes commit the post hoc fallacy all the time. For example, one major league pitcher wears the same shirt every time he has an important game. Because he has won several big games while wearing this shirt, he believes it brings him luck.

Many events seem to follow a sequential pattern even though they actually do not. For example, some people refuse to get a flu shot because they say that the last time they got one, they came down with the flu. Even though there is no scientific basis for this link, many people insist that it is true. (The more probable explanation for this situation is that the flu vaccination takes at least two weeks to take effect, so it is possible for someone to be infected by the flu virus before the vaccine starts working.)

Another health-related issue also illustrates the post hoc fallacy. Recently, the U.S. Food and Drug Administration (FDA) studied several natural supplements that claim to cure the common cold. Because the study showed that these products were not effective, the FDA ordered the manufacturers to stop making false claims. Despite this fact, however, many people still buy these products. When questioned, they say the medications actually work. Again, the explanation for this phenomenon is simple. Most colds last just a few days. As the FDA pointed out in its report, people who took the medications would have begun feeling better with or without them.

Non Sequitur (It Does Not Follow)

The **non sequitur** fallacy occurs when a conclusion does not follow from the premises. Frequently, the conclusion is supported by weak or irrelevant evidence—or by no evidence at all. Consider the following statement:

> Megan drives an expensive car, so she must be earning a lot of money.

Megan might drive an expensive car, but this is not evidence that she has a high salary. She could, for example, be leasing the car or paying it off over a five-year period, or it could have been a gift.

Non sequiturs are common in political arguments. Consider this statement:

> Gangs, drugs, and extreme violence plague today's prisons. The only way to address this issue is to release all nonviolent offenders as soon as possible.

This assessment of the prison system may be accurate, but it doesn't follow that because of this situation, all nonviolent offenders should be released immediately.

Scientific arguments also contain non sequiturs. Consider the following statement that was made during a debate on climate change:

> Recently, the polar ice caps have thickened, and the temperature of the oceans has stabilized. Obviously, we don't need to do more to address climate change.

A non sequitur
fallacy

NON SEQUITUR © 2006 Wiley Ink, Inc. Dist. By UNIVERSAL UCLICK. Reprinted with permission.
All rights reserved.

Even if you accept the facts of this argument, you need to see more evidence before you can conclude that no action against climate change is necessary. For example, the cooling trend could be temporary, or other areas of the earth could still be growing warmer.

Bandwagon Fallacy

The **bandwagon fallacy** occurs when you try to convince people that something is true because it is widely held to be true. It is easy to see the problem with this line of reasoning. Hundreds of years ago, most people believed that the sun revolved around the earth and that the earth was flat. As we know, the fact that many people held these beliefs did not make them true.

The underlying assumption of the bandwagon fallacy is that the more people who believe something, the more likely it is to be true. Without supporting evidence, however, this form of argument cannot be valid. For example, consider the following statement made by a driver who was stopped by the police for speeding:

> Officer, I didn't do anything wrong. Everyone around me was going the same speed.

As the police officer was quick to point out, the driver's argument missed the point: he was doing fifty-five miles an hour in a thirty-five-mile-an-hour zone, and the fact that other drivers were also speeding was irrelevant. If the driver had been able to demonstrate that the police officer was mistaken—that he was driving more slowly or that the speed limit was actually sixty miles an hour—then his argument would have had merit. In this case, the fact that other drivers were going the same speed would be relevant because it would support his contention.

The bandwagon fallacy

Cartoonstock.com

Since most people want to go along with the crowd, the bandwagon fallacy can be very effective. For this reason, advertisers use it all the time. For example, a book publisher will say that a book has been on the *New York Times* bestseller list for ten weeks, and a pharmaceutical company will say that its brand of aspirin outsells other brands four to one. These appeals are irrelevant, however, because they don't address the central questions: Is the book actually worth reading? Is one brand of aspirin really better than other brands?

⟩ EXERCISE 5.10

Determine which of the following statements are logical arguments and which are fallacies. If the statement is not logical, identify the fallacy that best applies.

1. Almost all the students I talked to said that they didn't like the senator. I'm sure he'll lose the election on Tuesday.

2. This car has a noisy engine; therefore, it must create a lot of pollution.

3. I don't know how Professor Resnick can be such a hard grader. He's always late for class.

4. A vote for the bill to limit gun sales in the city is a vote against the Second Amendment.

5. It's only fair to pay your fair share of taxes.

6. I had an internship at a government agency last summer, and no one there worked very hard. Government workers are lazy.

7. It's a clear principle of law that people are not allowed to yell "Fire!" in a crowded theater. By permitting protestors to hold a rally downtown, Judge Cohen is allowing them to do just that.

8. Of course this person is guilty. He wouldn't be in jail if he weren't a criminal.

9. Schools are like families; therefore, teachers (like parents) should be allowed to discipline their kids.

10. Everybody knows that staying out in the rain can make you sick.

11. When we had a draft in the 1960s, the crime rate was low. We should bring back the draft.

12. I'm not a doctor, but I play one on TV. I recommend Vicks Formula 44 cough syrup.

13. Some people are complaining about public schools, so there must be a problem.

14. If you aren't part of the solution, you're part of the problem.

15. All people are mortal. James is a person. Therefore, James is mortal.

16. I don't know why you gave me an F for handing in someone else's essay. Didn't you ever copy something from someone else?

17. First, the government stops us from buying assault rifles. Then, it limits the number of handguns we can buy. What will come next? Soon, they'll try to take away all our guns.

18. Shakespeare was the world's greatest playwright; therefore, *Macbeth* must be a great play.

19. Last month, I bought a new computer. Yesterday, I installed some new software. This morning, my computer wouldn't start up. The new software must be causing the problem.

20. Ellen DeGeneres is against testing pharmaceutical and cosmetics products on animals, and that's good enough for me.

❯ EXERCISE 5.11

Read the following essay, and identify as many logical fallacies in it as you can. Make sure you identify each fallacy by name and are able to explain the flaws in the writer's arguments.

This essay is from Buchanan.org, where it appeared on October 31, 1994.

IMMIGRATION TIME-OUT

PATRICK J. BUCHANAN

Proposition 187 "is an outrage. It is unconstitutional. It is nativist. It is racist."

—Al Hunt, *Capital Gang*, CNN

That outburst by my columnist colleague, about California's Prop. 187— 1 which would cut off social welfare benefits to illegal aliens—suggests that this savage quarrel is about more than just money. Indeed, the roots of this dispute over Prop. 187 are grounded in the warring ideas that we Americans hold about the deepest, most divisive issues of our time: ethnicity, nation, culture.

What do we want the America of the years 2000, 2020, and 2050 to 2 be like? Do we have the right to shape the character of the country our grandchildren will live in? Or is that to be decided by whoever, outside America, decides to come here?

By 2050, we are instructed by the chancellor of the University of California at Berkeley, Chang Lin-Tin, "the majority of Americans will trace their roots to Latin America, Africa, Asia, the Middle East, and Pacific Islands." 3

Now, any man or woman, of any nation or ancestry can come here—and become a good American. 4

We know that from our history. But by my arithmetic, the chancellor is saying Hispanics, Asians, and Africans will increase their present number of 65 million by at least 100 million in 60 years, a population growth larger than all of Mexico today. 5

What will that mean for America? Well, South Texas and Southern California will be almost exclusively Hispanic. Each will have tens of millions of people whose linguistic, historic, and cultural roots are in Mexico. Like Eastern Ukraine, where 10 million Russian-speaking "Ukrainians" now look impatiently to Moscow, not Kiev, as their cultural capital, America could see, in a decade, demands for Quebec-like status for Southern California. Already there is a rumbling among militants for outright secession. A sea of Mexican flags was prominent in that L.A. rally against Prop. 187, and Mexican officials are openly urging their kinsmen in California to vote it down. 6

If no cutoff is imposed on social benefits for those who breach our borders, and break our laws, the message will go out to a desperate world: America is wide open. All you need do is get there, and get in. 7

Consequences will ensue. Crowding together immigrant and minority populations in our major cities must bring greater conflict. We saw that in the 1992 L.A. riot. Blacks and Hispanics have lately collided in D.C.'s Adams-Morgan neighborhood, supposedly the most tolerant and progressive section of Washington. The issue: bilingual education. Unlike 20 years ago, ethnic conflict is today on almost every front page. 8

Before Mr. Chang's vision is realized, the United States will have at least two official languages. Today's steady outmigration of "Anglos" or "Euro-Americans," as whites are now called, from Southern Florida and Southern California, will continue. The 50 states will need constant redrawing of political lines to ensure proportional representation. Already we have created the first "apartheid districts" in America's South. 9

Ethnic militancy and solidarity are on the rise in the United States; the old institutions of assimilation are not doing their work as they once did; the Melting Pot is in need of repair. On campuses we hear demands for separate dorms, eating rooms, clubs, etc., by black, white, Hispanic, and Asian students. If this is where the campus is headed, where are our cities going? 10

> "Ethnic militancy and solidarity are on the rise."

If America is to survive as "one nation, one people," we need to call a 11 "time-out" on immigration, to assimilate the tens of millions who have lately arrived. We need to get to know one another, to live together, to learn together America's language, history, culture, and traditions of tolerance, to become a new national family, before we add a hundred million more. And we need soon to bring down the curtain on this idea of hyphenated-Americanism.

If we lack the courage to make the decisions—as to what our country will 12 look like in 2050—others will make those decisions for us, not all of whom share our love of the America that seems to be fading away.

⊙ EXERCISE 5.12

Choose three of the fallacies that you identified in "Immigration Time-Out" for Exercise 5.11. Rewrite each statement in the form of a logical argument.

LaunchPad
macmillan learning

For more practice, see the LearningCurve on Reasoning and Logical Fallacies in the Launch-pad for *Practical Argument*.

How Free Should Free Speech Be?

SAVE FREEDOM OF SPEECH

BUY WAR BONDS

Printed by permission of the
Norman Rockwell Family Agency.
Copyright 1943 the Norman
Rockwell Family Entities.

Go back to page 123, and reread the At Issue box that gives background on how free free speech should be. As the following sources illustrate, this question has a number of possible answers.

As you read this source material, you will be asked to answer questions and to complete some simple activities. This work will help you understand both the content and the structure of the sources. When you are finished, you will be ready to write an argument—either inductive or deductive—that takes a new position on how free free speech should actually be.

SOURCES

This article originally appeared on TheDailyBeast.com on January 1, 2014.

SHOULD NEO-NAZIS BE ALLOWED FREE SPEECH?

THANE ROSENBAUM

Over the past several weeks, free speech has gotten costlier—at least in France 1 and Israel.

In France, Dieudonne M'Bala M'Bala, an anti-Semitic stand-up comic 2 infamous for popularizing the quenelle, an inverted Nazi salute, was banned from performing in two cities. M'Bala M'Bala has been repeatedly fined for hate speech, and this was not the first time his act was perceived as a threat to public order.

Meanwhile, Israel's parliament is soon to pass a bill outlawing the word 3 Nazi for non-educational purposes. Indeed, any slur against another that invokes the Third Reich could land the speaker in jail for six months with a fine of $29,000. The Israelis are concerned about both the rise of anti-Semitism globally, and the trivialization of the Holocaust—even locally.

To Americans, these actions in France and Israel seem positively un- 4 democratic. The First Amendment would never prohibit the quenelle, regardless of its symbolic meaning. And any lover of *Seinfeld* would regard banning the "Soup Nazi" episode as scandalously un-American. After all, in 1977 a federal court upheld the right of neo-Nazis to goose-step right through the town of Skokie, Illinois, which had a disproportionately large number of Holocaust survivors as residents. And more recently, the Supreme Court upheld the right of a church group opposed to gays serving in the military to picket the funeral of a dead marine with signs that read, "God Hates Fags."

While what is happening in France and Israel is wholly foreign to Ameri- 5 cans, perhaps it's time to consider whether these and other countries may be right. Perhaps America's fixation on free speech has gone too far.

Actually, the United States is an outlier among democracies in granting 6 such generous free speech guarantees. Six European countries, along with Brazil, prohibit the use of Nazi symbols and flags. Many more countries have outlawed Holocaust denial. Indeed, even encouraging racial discrimination in France is a crime. In pluralistic nations like these with clashing cultures and historical tragedies not shared by all, mutual respect and civility helps keep the peace and avoids unnecessary mental trauma.

Yet, even in the United States, free speech is not unlimited. Certain pro- 7 scribed categories have always existed—libel, slander and defamation, obscenity, "fighting words," and the "incitement of imminent lawlessness"—where the First Amendment does not protect the speaker, where the right to speak is curtailed for reasons of general welfare and public safety. There is no freedom to shout "fire" in a crowded theater. Hate crime statutes exist in many jurisdictions where bias-motivated crimes are given more severe penalties. In 2003, the Supreme Court held that speech intended to intimidate, such as cross burning, might not receive First Amendment protection.

Yet, the confusion is that in placing limits on speech we privilege physical 8 over emotional harm. Indeed, we have an entire legal system, and an attitude toward speech, that takes its cue from a nursery rhyme: "Sticks and stones can break my bones but names can never hurt me."

All of us know, however, and despite what we tell our children, names do, 9 indeed, hurt. And recent studies in universities such as Purdue, UCLA, Michigan, Toronto, Arizona, Maryland, and Macquarie University in New South Wales show, among other things, through brain scans and controlled studies with participants who were subjected to both physical and emotional pain, that emotional harm is equal in intensity to that experienced by the body, and is even more long-lasting and traumatic. Physical pain subsides; emotional pain, when recalled, is relived.

Pain has a shared circuitry in the human brain, and it makes no distinc- 10 tion between being hit in the face and losing face (or having a broken heart) as a result of bereavement, betrayal, social exclusion, and grave insult. Emotional distress can, in fact, make the body sick. Indeed, research has shown that pain relief medication can work equally well for both physical and emotional injury.

We impose speed limits on driving and regulate food and drugs because we know that the costs of not doing so can lead to accidents and harm. Why should speech be exempt from public welfare concerns when its social costs can be even more injurious? 11

> "We impose speed limits on driving and regulate food and drugs because we know that the costs of not doing so can lead to accidents and harm."

In the marketplace of ideas, there is a difference between trying to persuade and trying to injure. One can object to gays in the military without ruining the one moment a father has to bury his son; 12 neo-Nazis can long for the Third Reich without re-traumatizing Hitler's victims; one can oppose Affirmative Action without burning a cross on an African-American's lawn.

Of course, everything is a matter of degree. Juries are faced with similar 13 ambiguities when it comes to physical injury. No one knows for certain whether the plaintiff wearing a neck brace can't actually run the New York Marathon. We tolerate the fake slip and fall, but we feel absolutely helpless in evaluating whether words and gestures intended to harm actually do cause harm. Jurors are as capable of working through these uncertainties in the area of emotional harms as they are in the realm of physical injury.

Free speech should not stand in the way of common decency. No right 14 should be so freely and recklessly exercised that it becomes an impediment to civil society, making it so that others are made to feel less free, their private space and peace invaded, their sensitivities cruelly trampled upon.

AT ISSUE: HOW FREE SHOULD FREE SPEECH BE?

1. Rosenbaum waits until the end of paragraph 6 to state his thesis. Why? What information does he include in paragraphs 1–5? How does this material set the stage for the rest of the essay?

2. Rosenbaum develops his argument with both inductive and deductive reasoning. Where does he use each strategy?

3. What evidence does Rosenbaum use to support his thesis? Should he have included more evidence? If so, what kind?

4. In paragraph 11, Rosenbaum makes a comparison between regulating free speech and regulating driving and food and drugs. How strong is this **analogy**? At what points (if any) does this comparison break down?

5. Where does Rosenbaum address arguments against his position? Does he refute these arguments? What other opposing arguments could he have addressed?

6. What point does Rosenbaum reinforce in his conclusion? What other points could he have emphasized?

This op-ed originally ran in the *Wall Street Journal* on September 24, 2014.

THE UNFREE SPEECH MOVEMENT

SOL STERN

This fall the University of California at Berkeley is celebrating the 50th anni- 1
versary of the Free Speech Movement, a student-led protest against campus
restrictions on political activities that made headlines and inspired imitators
around the country. I played a small part in the Free Speech Movement, and
some of those returning for the reunion were once my friends, but I won't be
joining them.

Though the movement promised greater intellectual and political free- 2
dom on campus, the result has been the opposite. The great irony is that while
Berkeley now honors the memory of the Free Speech Movement, it exercises
more thought control over students than the hated institution that we rose up
against half a century ago.

We early-1960s radicals believed ourselves anointed as a new "tell it like it 3
is" generation. We promised to transcend the "smelly old orthodoxies" (in
George Orwell's phrase) of Cold War liberalism and class-based, authoritarian
leftism. Leading students into the university administration building for the
first mass protest, Mario Savio, the Free Speech Movement's brilliant leader
from Queens, New York, famously said: "There's a time when the operation of
the machine becomes so odious—makes you so sick at heart—that you can't
take part. . . . And you've got to indicate to the people who run it, to the people who own it that unless you're free, the machine will be prevented from
working at all."

The Berkeley "machine" now promotes Free Speech Movement kitsch. 4
The steps in front of Sproul Hall, the central administration building where
more than 700 students were arrested on Dec. 2, 1964, have been renamed the
Mario Savio Steps. One of the campus dining halls is called the Free Speech
Movement Cafe, its walls covered with photographs and mementos of the glo-
rious semester of struggle. The university requires freshmen to read an admiring biography of Savio, who died in 1996, written by New York University
professor and Berkeley graduate Robert Cohen.

Yet intellectual diversity is hardly embraced. Every undergraduate under- 5
goes a form of indoctrination with a required course on the "theoretical or
analytical issues relevant to understanding race, culture, and ethnicity in
American society," administered by the university's Division of Equity and
Inclusion.

How did this Orwellian inversion occur? It happened in part because the 6
Free Speech Movement's fight for free speech was always a charade. The struggle was really about using the campus as a base for radical politics. I was a

27-year-old New Left graduate student at the time. Savio was a 22-year-old sophomore. He liked to compare the Free Speech Movement to the civil-rights struggle—conflating the essentially liberal Berkeley administration with the Bull Connors of the racist South.

During one demonstration Savio suggested that the campus cops who 7 had arrested a protesting student were "poor policemen" who only "have a job to do." Another student then shouted out: "Just like Eichmann." "Yeah. Very good. It's very, you know, like Adolf Eichmann," Savio replied. "He had a job to do. He fit into the machinery."

I realized years later that this moment may have been the beginning of the 8 1960s radicals' perversion of ordinary political language, like the spelling "Amerika" or seeing hope and progress in Third World dictatorships.

Before that 1964–65 academic year, most of us radical students could not 9 have imagined a campus rebellion. Why revolt against an institution that until then offered such a pleasant sanctuary? But then Berkeley administrators made an incredibly stupid decision to establish new rules regarding political activities on campus. Student clubs were no longer allowed to set up tables in front of the Bancroft Avenue campus entrance to solicit funds and recruit new members.

The clubs had used this 40-foot strip of sidewalk for years on the 10 assumption that it was the property of the City of Berkeley and thus constitutionally protected against speech restrictions. But the university claimed ownership to justify the new rules. When some students refused to comply, the administration compounded its blunder by resorting to the campus police. Not surprisingly, the students pushed back, using civil-disobedience tactics learned fighting for civil rights in the South.

The Free Speech Movement was born on Oct. 1, 1964, when police tried 11 to arrest a recent Berkeley graduate, Jack Weinberg, who was back on campus after a summer as a civil-rights worker in Mississippi. He had set up a table on the Bancroft strip for the Berkeley chapter of the Congress of Racial Equality (CORE). Dozens of students spontaneously sat down around the police car, preventing it from leaving the campus. A 32-hour standoff ensued, with hundreds of students camped around the car.

Mario Savio, also back from Mississippi, took off his shoes, climbed onto 12 the roof of the police car, and launched into an impromptu speech explaining why the students had to resist the immoral new rules. Thus began months of sporadic protests, the occupation of Sproul Hall on Dec. 2 (ended by mass arrests), national media attention, and Berkeley's eventual capitulation.

That should have ended the matter. Savio soon left the political arena, saying that he had no interest in becoming a permanent student leader. But others had mastered the new world of political theater, understood the weakness of American liberalism, and soon turned their ire on the Vietnam War.

> "But others had mastered the new world of political theater, understood the weakness of American liberalism, and soon turned their ire on the Vietnam War." 13

169

Mario Savio at a victory rally on the University of California campus in Berkeley (December 9, 1964)

AP Photo.

The radical movement that the Free Speech Movement spawned eventu- 14 ally descended into violence and mindless anti-Americanism. The movement waned in the 1970s as the war wound down—but by then protesters had begun their infiltration of university faculties and administrations they had once decried. "Tenured radicals," in *New Criterion* editor Roger Kimball's phrase, now dominate most professional organizations in the humanities and social studies. Unlike our old liberal professors, who dealt respectfully with the ideas advanced by my generation of New Left students, today's radical professors insist on ideological conformity and don't take kindly to dissent by conservative students. Visits by speakers who might not toe the liberal line—recently including former Secretary of State Condoleezza Rice and Islamism critic Ayaan Hirsi Ali—spark protests and letter-writing campaigns by students in tandem with their professors until the speaker withdraws or the invitation is canceled.

On Oct. 1 at Berkeley, by contrast, one of the honored speakers at the Free 15 Speech Movement anniversary rally on Sproul Plaza will be Bettina Aptheker, who is now a feminist-studies professor at the University of California at Santa Cruz.

Writing in the Berkeley alumni magazine about the anniversary, Ms. 16 Aptheker noted that the First Amendment was "written by white, propertied men in the 18th century, who never likely imagined that it might apply to women, and/or people of color, and/or all those who were not propertied, and even, perhaps, not citizens, and/or undocumented immigrants. . . . In other words, freedom of speech is a Constitutional guarantee, but who gets to exercise it without the chilling restraints of censure depends very much on one's location in the political and social cartography. We [Free Speech Movement] veterans were too young and inexperienced in 1964 to know this, but we do now, and we speak with a new awareness, a new consciousness, and a new urgency that the wisdom of a true freedom is inexorably tied to who exercises power and for what ends." Read it and weep—for the Free Speech Movement anniversary, for the ideal of an intellectually open university, and for America.

⊘AT ISSUE: HOW FREE SHOULD FREE SPEECH BE?

1. In your own words, summarize Stern's thesis. Where does he state it?

2. At what point (or points) in the essay does Stern appeal to *ethos*? How effective is this appeal?

3. In paragraph 4, Stern says, "The Berkeley 'machine' now promotes Free Speech Movement kitsch." First, look up the meaning of *kitsch*. Then, explain what Stern means by this statement.

4. Stern supports his points with examples drawn from his own experience. Is this enough? What other kinds of evidence could he have used?

5. In paragraph 5, Stern says that every undergraduate at Berkeley "undergoes a form of indoctrination." What does he mean? Does Stern make a valid point, or is he **begging the question**?

6. Why does Stern discuss Bettina Aptheker in paragraphs 15–16? Could he be accused of making an **ad hominem** attack? Why or why not?

This code came out of a June 1992 meeting of the American Association of University Professors.

ON FREEDOM OF EXPRESSION AND CAMPUS SPEECH CODES

AMERICAN ASSOCIATION OF UNIVERSITY PROFESSORS

Freedom of thought and expression is essential to any institution of higher learning. Universities and colleges exist not only to transmit existing knowledge. Equally, they interpret, explore, and expand that knowledge by testing the old and proposing the new.

This mission guides learning outside the classroom quite as much as in class, and often inspires vigorous debate on those social, economic, and political issues that arouse the strongest passions. In the process, views will be expressed that may seem to many wrong, distasteful, or offensive. Such is the nature of freedom to sift and winnow ideas.

On a campus that is free and open, no idea can be banned or forbidden. No viewpoint or message may be deemed so hateful or disturbing that it may not be expressed.

> "On a campus that is free and open, no idea can be banned or forbidden."

Universities and colleges are also communities, often of a residential character. Most campuses have recently sought to become more diverse, and more reflective of the larger community, by attracting students, faculty, and staff from groups that were historically excluded or underrepresented. Such gains as they have made are recent, modest, and tenuous. The campus climate can profoundly affect an institution's continued diversity. Hostility or intolerance to persons who differ from the majority (especially if seemingly condoned by the institution) may undermine the confidence of new members of the community. Civility is always fragile and can easily be destroyed.

In response to verbal assaults and use of hateful language some campuses have felt it necessary to forbid the expression of racist, sexist, homophobic, or ethnically demeaning speech, along with conduct or behavior that harasses. Several reasons are offered in support of banning such expression. Individuals and groups that have been victims of such expression feel an understandable outrage. They claim that the academic progress of minority and majority alike may suffer if fears, tensions, and conflicts spawned by slurs and insults create an environment inimical to learning. These arguments, grounded in the need to foster an atmosphere respectful of and welcome to all persons, strike a deeply responsive chord in the academy. But, while we can acknowledge both the weight of these concerns and the thoughtfulness of those persuaded of the need for regulation, rules that ban or punish speech based upon its content cannot be justified. An institution of higher learning fails to fulfill its mission if it asserts the power to proscribe ideas—and racial or ethnic slurs, sexist epithets, or homophobic insults almost always express ideas, however repugnant. Indeed, by proscribing any ideas, a university sets an example that profoundly disserves its academic mission. Some may seek to defend a distinction between the regulation of the content of speech and the regulation of the manner (or style) of speech. We find this distinction untenable in practice because offensive style or opprobrious phrases may in fact have been chosen precisely for their expressive power. As the United States Supreme Court has said in the course of rejecting criminal sanctions for offensive words: Words are often chosen as much for their emotive as their cognitive force. We cannot sanction the view that the Constitution, while solicitous of the cognitive content of individual speech, has little or no regard for that emotive function which, practically speaking, may often be the more important element of the overall message sought to be communicated. The line between substance and style is thus too uncertain to sustain the pressure that will inevitably be brought to bear upon disciplinary rules that attempt to regulate speech. Proponents of speech codes sometimes reply that the value of emotive language of this type is of such a low order that, on balance, suppression is justified by the harm suffered by those who are directly affected, and by the general damage done to the learning environment. Yet a college or university sets a perilous course if it seeks to differentiate between high-value and low-value speech, or to choose which groups are to be protected by curbing the speech of others. A speech code unavoidably implies an institutional competence to distinguish permissible expression of hateful thought from what is proscribed as thoughtless hate. Institutions would also have to justify shielding some, but not other, targets of offensive language—not to political preference, to religious but not to philosophical creed, or perhaps even to some but not to other religious affiliations. Starting down this path creates an even greater risk that groups not originally protected may later demand similar solicitude—demands the institution that began the process of banning some speech is ill equipped to resist.

Distinctions of this type are neither practicable nor principled; their very 6 fragility underscores why institutions devoted to freedom of thought and expression ought not adopt an institutionalized coercion of silence.

Moreover, banning speech often avoids consideration of means more 7 compatible with the mission of an academic institution by which to deal with incivility, intolerance, offensive speech, and harassing behavior:

1. Institutions should adopt and invoke a range of measures that penalize conduct and behavior, rather than speech, such as rules against defacing property, physical intimidation or harassment, or disruption of campus activities. All members of the campus community should be made aware of such rules, and administrators should be ready to use them in preference to speech-directed sanctions.

2. Colleges and universities should stress the means they use best—to educate—including the development of courses and other curricular and co-curricular experiences designed to increase student understanding

and to deter offensive or intolerant speech or conduct. Such institutions should, of course, be free (indeed encouraged) to condemn manifestations of intolerance and discrimination, whether physical or verbal.

3. The governing board and the administration have a special duty not only to set an outstanding example of tolerance, but also to challenge boldly and condemn immediately serious breaches of civility.

4. Members of the faculty, too, have a major role; their voices may be critical in condemning intolerance, and their actions may set examples for understanding, making clear to their students that civility and tolerance are hallmarks of educated men and women.

5. Student personnel administrators have in some ways the most demanding role of all, for hate speech occurs most often in dormitories, locker-rooms, cafeterias, and student centers. Persons who guide this part of campus life should set high standards of their own for tolerance and should make unmistakably clear the harm that uncivil or intolerant speech inflicts.

To some persons who support speech codes, measures like these—relying as 8 they do on suasion rather than sanctions—may seem inadequate. But freedom of expression requires toleration of "ideas we hate," as Justice Holmes put it. The underlying principle does not change because the demand is to silence a hateful speaker, or because it comes from within the academy. Free speech is not simply an aspect of the educational enterprise to be weighed against other desirable ends. It is the very precondition of the academic enterprise itself.

⊘ AT ISSUE: HOW FREE SHOULD FREE SPEECH BE?

1. The writers of this statement rely primarily on deductive reasoning. Construct a syllogism that includes the selection's major premise, minor premise, and conclusion.

2. At what audience is this statement aimed—students, instructors, administrators, or the general public? How do you know?

3. What problem do the writers address? Where do they present their solution?

4. In paragraph 5, the writers discuss the major arguments against their position. Why do they address opposing arguments so early in the selection? How effectively do the writers refute these arguments?

5. Paragraph 7 is followed by a numbered list. What information is in this list? Why did the writers decide to set it off in this way?

6. What do the writers mean when they say that free speech "is the very precondition of the academic exercise itself" (para. 8)?

This essay first appeared in the *Washington Post* on February 20, 2015.

PROGRESSIVE IDEAS HAVE KILLED FREE SPEECH ON CAMPUS

WENDY KAMINER

Is an academic discussion of free speech potentially traumatic? A recent panel 1 for Smith College alumnae aimed at "challenging the ideological echo chamber" elicited this ominous "trigger/content warning" when a transcript appeared in the campus newspaper: "Racism/racial slurs, ableist slurs, anti-semitic language, anti-Muslim/Islamophobic language, anti-immigrant language, sexist/misogynistic slurs, references to race-based violence, references to antisemitic violence."

No one on this panel, in which I participated, trafficked in slurs. So what 2 prompted the warning?

Smith President Kathleen McCartney had joked, "We're just wild and 3 crazy, aren't we?" In the transcript, "crazy" was replaced by the notation: "[ableist slur]."

One of my fellow panelists mentioned that the State Department had for a 4 time banned the words "jihad," "Islamist," and "caliphate"—which the transcript flagged as "anti-Muslim/Islamophobic language."

I described the case of a Brandeis professor disciplined for saying "wet- 5 back" while explaining its use as a pejorative. The word was replaced in the transcript by "[anti-Latin@/anti-immigrant slur]." Discussing the teaching of *Huckleberry Finn*, I questioned the use of euphemisms such as "the n-word" and, in doing so, uttered that forbidden word. I described what I thought was the obvious difference between quoting a word in the context of discussing language, literature, or prejudice and hurling it as an epithet.

Two of the panelists challenged me. The audience of 300 to 400 people 6 listened to our spirited, friendly debate—and didn't appear angry or shocked. But back on campus, I was quickly branded a racist, and I was charged in the Huffington Post with committing "an explicit act of racial violence." McCartney subsequently apologized that "some students and faculty were hurt" and made to "feel unsafe" by my remarks.

Unsafe? These days, when students talk about threats to their safety and 7 demand access to "safe spaces," they're often talking about the threat of unwelcome speech and demanding protection from the emotional disturbances sparked by unsettling ideas. It's not just rape that some women on campus fear: It's discussions of rape. At Brown University, a scheduled debate between two feminists about rape culture was criticized for, as the *Brown Daily Herald* put it, undermining "the University's mission to create a safe and supportive environment for survivors." In a school-wide e-mail, Brown President Christina Paxon emphasized her belief in the existence of rape culture and invited students to an alternative lecture, to be given at the same time as the debate. And the *Daily Herald* reported that students who feared being "attacked by the viewpoints" offered at the debate could instead "find a safe space" among "sexual assault peer educators, women peer counselors and staff" during the same time slot. Presumably they all shared the same viewpoints and could be trusted not to "attack" anyone with their ideas.

How did we get here? How did a verbal defense of free speech become 8 tantamount to a hate crime and offensive words become the equivalent of physical assaults?

> "How did a verbal defense of free speech become tantamount to a hate crime and offensive words become the equivalent of physical assaults?"

You can credit—or blame—progres- 9 sives for this enthusiastic embrace of censorship. It reflects, in part, the influence of three popular movements dating back decades: the feminist anti-porn crusades, the pop-psychology recovery movement, and the emergence of multiculturalism on college campuses.

In the 1980s, law professor Catharine 10 MacKinnon and writer Andrea Dworkin showed the way, popularizing a view of free speech as a barrier to equality. These two impassioned feminists framed pornography—its production, distribution, and consumption—as an assault on women. They devised a novel definition of pornography as a violation of women's civil rights, and championed a model anti-porn ordinance that would authorize civil actions by any woman "aggrieved" by pornography. In 1984, the city of Indianapolis adopted the measure, defining pornography as a "discriminatory practice," but it was quickly struck down in federal court as unconstitutional. "Indianapolis justifies the ordinance on the ground that pornography affects thoughts," the court noted. "This is thought control."

So MacKinnnon and Dworkin lost that battle, but their successors are 11 winning the war. Their view of allegedly offensive or demeaning speech as a civil rights violation, and their conflation of words and actions, have helped shape campus speech and harassment codes and nurtured progressive hostility toward free speech.

The recovery movement, which flourished in the late '80s and early '90s, 12 adopted a similarly dire view of unwelcome speech. Words wound, anti-porn feminists and recovering co-dependents agreed. Self-appointed recovery experts, such as the best-selling author John Bradshaw, promoted the belief that most of us are victims of abuse, in one form or another. They broadened the definition of abuse to include a range of common, normal childhood experiences, including being chastised or ignored by your parents on occasion. From this perspective, we are all fragile and easily damaged by presumptively hurtful speech, and censorship looks like a moral necessity.

These ideas were readily absorbed on college campuses embarking on a 13 commendable drive for diversity. Multiculturalists sought to protect historically disadvantaged students from speech considered racist, sexist, homophobic or otherwise discriminatory. Like abuse, oppression was defined broadly. I remember the first time, in the early '90s, that I heard a Harvard student describe herself as oppressed, as a woman of color. She hadn't been systematically deprived of fundamental rights and liberties. After all, she'd been admitted to Harvard. But she had been offended and unsettled by certain attitudes and remarks. Did she have good reason to take offense? That was an irrelevant question. Popular therapeutic culture defined verbal "assaults" and other forms of discrimination by the subjective, emotional responses of self-proclaimed victims.

This reliance on subjectivity, in the interest of equality, is a recipe for 14 arbitrary, discriminatory enforcement practices, with far-reaching effects on individual liberty. The tendency to take subjective allegations of victimization at face value—instrumental in contemporary censorship campaigns—also leads to the presumption of guilt and disregard for due process in the progressive approach to alleged sexual assaults on campus.

This is a dangerously misguided approach to justice. "Feeling realities" 15 belong in a therapist's office. Incorporated into laws and regulations, they lead to the soft authoritarianism that now governs many American campuses. Instead of advancing equality, it's teaching future generations of leaders the "virtues" of autocracy.

⊘ AT ISSUE: HOW FREE SHOULD FREE SPEECH BE?

1. Should Kaminer have given more background information about the problem she discusses? What additional information could she have provided?

2. Kaminer devotes the first six paragraphs of her essay to describing a panel discussion. Why do you think she begins her essay in this way? How does this discussion prepare readers for the rest of the essay?

3. In paragraph 8, Kaminer asks two questions. What is the function of these questions?

4. According to Kaminer, what are "feeling realities" (para. 15)? In what sense are "feeling realities" harmful?

5. Does Kaminer ever establish that the situation she discusses is widespread enough to be a problem? Could she be accused of setting up a **straw man**?

6. What does Kaminer want to accomplish? Is her purpose to convince readers of something? To move them to action? What is your reaction to her essay?

This opinion piece was originally published on March 21, 2015, in the *New York Times*.

IN COLLEGE AND HIDING FROM SCARY IDEAS

JUDITH SHULEVITZ

Katherine Byron, a senior at Brown University and a member of its Sexual 1 Assault Task Force, considers it her duty to make Brown a safe place for rape victims, free from anything that might prompt memories of trauma.

So when she heard last fall that a student group had organized a debate about 2 campus sexual assault between Jessica Valenti, the founder of feministing.com, and Wendy McElroy, a libertarian, and that Ms. McElroy was likely to criticize the term "rape culture," Ms. Byron was alarmed. "Bringing in a speaker like that could serve to invalidate people's experiences," she told me. It could be "damaging."

Ms. Byron and some fellow task force members secured a meeting with 3 administrators. Not long after, Brown's president, Christina H. Paxson, announced that the university would hold a simultaneous, competing talk to provide "research and facts" about "the role of culture in sexual assault." Meanwhile, student volunteers put up posters advertising that a "safe space" would be available for anyone who found the debate too upsetting.

The safe space, Ms. Byron explained, was intended to give people who 4 might find comments "troubling" or "triggering," a place to recuperate. The room was equipped with cookies, coloring books, bubbles, Play-Doh, calming music, pillows, blankets, and a video of frolicking puppies, as well as students and staff members trained to deal with trauma. Emma Hall, a junior, rape survivor, and "sexual assault peer educator" who helped set up the room and worked in it during the debate, estimates that a couple of dozen people used it. At one point she went to the lecture hall—it was packed—but after a while, she had to return to the safe space. "I was feeling bombarded by a lot of viewpoints that really go against my dearly and closely held beliefs," Ms. Hall said.

Safe spaces are an expression of the conviction, increasingly prevalent 5 among college students, that their schools should keep them from being "bombarded" by discomfiting or distressing viewpoints. Think of the safe space as the live-action version of the better-known trigger warning, a notice put on top of a syllabus or an assigned reading to alert students to the presence of potentially disturbing material.

Some people trace safe spaces back to the feminist consciousness-raising 6 groups of the 1960s and 1970s, others to the gay and lesbian movement of the early 1990s. In most cases, safe spaces are innocuous gatherings of like-minded people who agree to refrain from ridicule, criticism, or what they term microaggressions—subtle displays of racial or sexual bias—so that everyone can relax enough to explore the nuances of, say, a fluid gender identity. As long as all parties consent to such restrictions, these little islands of self-restraint seem like a perfectly fine idea.

But the notion that ticklish conversations must be scrubbed clean of controversy has a way of leaking out

> "As long as all parties consent to such restrictions, these little islands of self-restraint seem like a perfectly fine idea."   7

and spreading. Once you designate some spaces as safe, you imply that the rest are unsafe. It follows that they should be made safer.

This logic clearly informed a campaign undertaken this fall by a Colum- 8 bia University student group called Everyone Allied Against Homophobia that consisted of slipping a flier under the door of every dorm room on campus. The headline of the flier stated, "I want this space to be a safer space." The text below instructed students to tape the fliers to their windows. The group's vice president then had the flier published in the *Columbia Daily Spectator*, the student newspaper, along with an editorial asserting that "making spaces safer is about learning how to be kind to each other."

A junior named Adam Shapiro decided he didn't want his room to be a 9 safer space. He printed up his own flier calling it a dangerous space and had that, too, published in the *Columbia Daily Spectator*. "Kindness alone won't allow us to gain more insight into truth," he wrote. In an interview, Mr. Shapiro said, "If the point of a safe space is therapy for people who feel victimized by traumatization, that sounds like a great mission." But a safe-space mentality has begun infiltrating classrooms, he said, making both professors and students loath to say anything that might hurt someone's feelings. "I don't see how you can have a therapeutic space that's also an intellectual space," he said.

I'm old enough to remember a time when college students objected to 10 providing a platform to certain speakers because they were deemed politically unacceptable. Now students worry whether acts of speech or pieces of writing may put them in emotional peril. Two weeks ago, students at Northwestern University marched to protest an article by Laura Kipnis, a professor in the university's School of Communication. Professor Kipnis had criticized— O.K., ridiculed—what she called the sexual paranoia pervading campus life.

The protesters carried mattresses and demanded that the administration 11 condemn the essay. One student complained that Professor Kipnis was "erasing the very traumatic experience" of victims who spoke out. An organizer of the demonstration said, "we need to be setting aside spaces to talk" about "victim-blaming." Last Wednesday, Northwestern's president, Morton O. Schapiro, wrote an op-ed article in the *Wall Street Journal* affirming his commitment to academic freedom. But plenty of others at universities are willing to dignify students' fears, citing threats to their stability as reasons to cancel debates, disinvite commencement speakers, and apologize for so-called mistakes.

At Oxford University's Christ Church college in November, the college cen- 12 sors (a "censor" being more or less the Oxford equivalent of an undergraduate dean) canceled a debate on abortion after campus feminists threatened to disrupt it because both would-be debaters were men. "I'm relieved the censors have made this decision," said the treasurer of Christ Church's student union, who had pressed for the cancellation. "It clearly makes the most sense for the safety—both physical and mental—of the students who live and work in Christ Church."

A year and a half ago, a Hampshire College student group disinvited an 13 Afrofunk band that had been attacked on social media for having too many white musicians; the vitriolic discussion had made students feel "unsafe."

Last fall, the president of Smith College, Kathleen McCartney, apologized 14 for causing students and faculty to be "hurt" when she failed to object to a racial epithet uttered by a fellow panel member at an alumnae event in New York. The offender was the free-speech advocate Wendy Kaminer, who had been arguing against the use of the euphemism "the n-word" when teaching American history or *The Adventures of Huckleberry Finn*. In the uproar that followed, the Student Government Association wrote a letter declaring that "if Smith is unsafe for one student, it is unsafe for all students."

"It's amazing to me that they can't distinguish between racist speech and 15 speech about racist speech, between racism and discussions of racism," Ms. Kaminer said in an email.

The confusion is telling, though. It shows that while keeping college-level 16 discussions "safe" may feel good to the hypersensitive, it's bad for them and for everyone else. People ought to go to college to sharpen their wits and broaden their field of vision. Shield them from unfamiliar ideas, and they'll never learn the discipline of seeing the world as other people see it. They'll be unprepared for the social and intellectual headwinds that will hit them as soon as they step off the campuses whose climates they have so carefully controlled. What will they do when they hear opinions they've learned to shrink from? If they want to change the world, how will they learn to persuade people to join them?

Only a few of the students want stronger anti-hate-speech codes. Mostly 17 they ask for things like mandatory training sessions and stricter enforcement of existing rules. Still, it's disconcerting to see students clamor for a kind of intrusive supervision that would have outraged students a few generations ago. But those were hardier souls. Now students' needs are anticipated by a small army of service professionals—mental health counselors, student-life deans, and the like. This new bureaucracy may be exacerbating students' "self-infantilization," as Judith Shapiro, the former president of Barnard College, suggested in an essay for *Inside Higher Ed*.

But why are students so eager to self-infantilize? Their parents should 18 probably share the blame. Eric Posner, a professor at the University of Chicago Law School, wrote on *Slate* last month that although universities cosset students more than they used to, that's what they have to do, because today's under-graduates are more puerile than their predecessors. "Perhaps overprogrammed children engineered to the specifications of college admissions offices no longer experience the risks and challenges that

> "Their parents should probably share the blame."

breed maturity," he wrote. But "if college students are children, then they should be protected like children."

Another reason students resort to the quasi-medicalized terminology of trauma is that it forces administrators to respond. Universities are in a double bind. They're required by two civil-rights statutes, Title VII and Title IX, to ensure that their campuses don't create a "hostile environment" for women and other groups subject to harassment. However, universities are not supposed to go too far in suppressing free speech, either. If a university cancels a talk or punishes a professor and a lawsuit ensues, history suggests that the university will lose. But if officials don't censure or don't prevent speech that may inflict psychological damage on a member of a protected class, they risk fostering a hostile environment and prompting an investigation. As a result, students who say they feel unsafe are more likely to be heard than students who demand censorship on other grounds. 19

The theory that vulnerable students should be guaranteed psychological security has roots in a body of legal thought elaborated in the 1980s and 1990s and still read today. Feminist and anti-racist legal scholars argued that the First Amendment should not safeguard language that inflicted emotional injury through racist or sexist stigmatization. One scholar, Mari J. Matsuda, was particularly insistent that college students not be subjected to "the violence of the word" because many of them "are away from home for the first time and at a vulnerable stage of psychological development." If they're targeted and the university does nothing to help them, they will be "left to their own resources in coping with the damage wrought." That might have, she wrote, "lifelong repercussions." 20

Perhaps. But Ms. Matsuda doesn't seem to have considered the possibility that insulating students could also make them, well, insular. A few weeks ago, Zineb El Rhazoui, a journalist at *Charlie Hebdo*, spoke at the University of Chicago, protected by the security guards she has traveled with since supporters of the Islamic State issued death threats against her. During the question-and-answer period, a Muslim student stood up to object to the newspaper's apparent disrespect for Muslims and to express her dislike of the phrase "I am Charlie." 21

Ms. El Rhazoui replied, somewhat irritably, "Being Charlie Hebdo means to die because of a drawing," and not everyone has the guts to do that (although she didn't use the word guts). She lives under constant threat, Ms. El Rhazoui said. The student answered that she felt threatened, too. 22

A few days later, a guest editorialist in the student newspaper took Ms. El Rhazoui to task. She had failed to ensure "that others felt safe enough to express dissenting opinions." Ms. El Rhazoui's "relative position of power," the writer continued, had granted her a "free pass to make condescending attacks on a member of the university." In a letter to the editor, the president and the vice president of the University of Chicago French Club, which had sponsored the talk, shot back, saying, "El Rhazoui is an immigrant, a woman, Arab, a human-rights activist who has known exile, and a journalist living in very real fear of death. She was invited to speak precisely because her right to do so is, quite literally, under threat." 23

181

You'd be hard-pressed to avoid the conclusion that the student and her 24 defender had burrowed so deep inside their cocoons, were so overcome by their own fragility, that they couldn't see that it was Ms. El Rhazoui who was in need of a safer space.

⊙ AT ISSUE: HOW FREE SHOULD FREE SPEECH BE?

1. What are "safe spaces"? According to Shulevitz, what is the problem of designating "some spaces as safe" (para. 7)?

2. In paragraph 9, Shulevitz quotes Adam Shapiro, a student, who says, "I don't see how you can have a therapeutic space that's also an intellectual space." What does Shapiro mean? Do you agree with him?

3. Does Shulevitz use inductive or deductive reasoning to make her case? Why do you think that she chose this strategy?

4. Where does Shulevitz discuss arguments against her position? Does she present these arguments fairly? Explain.

5. Does Shulevitz appeal mainly to *ethos, pathos,* or *logos*?

6. In paragraph 17, Shulevitz says, "Only a few of the students want stronger anti-hate-speech codes." Does this admission undercut her argument? Why or why not?

This essay was posted on Slate.com on February 12, 2015.

UNIVERSITIES ARE RIGHT TO CRACK DOWN ON SPEECH AND BEHAVIOR

ERIC POSNER

Lately, a moral panic about speech and sexual activity in universities has 1 reached a crescendo. Universities have strengthened rules prohibiting offensive speech typically targeted at racial, ethnic, and sexual minorities; taken it upon themselves to issue "trigger warnings" to students when courses offer content that might upset them; banned sexual acts that fall short of rape under criminal law but are on the borderline of coercion; and limited due process protections of students accused of violating these rules.

Most liberals celebrate these developments, yet with a certain uneasiness. 2 Few of them want to apply these protections to society at large. Conservatives and libertarians are up in arms. They see these rules as an assault on free speech and individual liberty. They think universities are treating students like children. And they are right. But they have also not considered that the justification for these policies may lie hidden in plain sight: that students *are* children. Not in terms of age, but in terms of maturity. Even in college, they must be protected like children while being prepared to be adults.

There is a popular, romantic notion that students receive their university 3 education through free and open debate about the issues of the day. Nothing could be farther from the truth. Students who enter college know hardly anything at all—that's why they need an education. Classroom teachers know students won't learn anything if they blab on about their opinions. Teachers are dictators who carefully control what students say to one another. It's not just that sincere expressions of opinion about same-sex marriage or campaign finance reform are out of place in chemistry and math class. They are out of place even in philosophy and politics classes, where the goal is to educate students (usually about academic texts and theories), not to listen to them spout off. And while professors sometimes believe there is pedagogical value in allowing students to express their political opinions in the context of some text, professors (or at least, good professors) carefully manipulate their students so that the discussion serves pedagogical ends.

That's why the contretemps about a recent incident at Marquette Univer- 4 sity is far less alarming than libertarians think. An inexperienced instructor was teaching a class on the philosophy of John Rawls, and a student in the class argued that same-sex marriage was consistent with Rawls' philosophy. When another student told the teacher outside of class that he disagreed, the teacher responded that she would not permit a student to oppose same-sex marriage in class because that might offend gay students.

While I believe that the teacher mishandled the student's complaint, 5 she was justified in dismissing it. The purpose of the class was to teach Rawls' theory of justice, not to debate the merits of same-sex marriage. The fact that a student injected same-sex marriage into the discussion does not mean that the class was required to discuss it. The professor might reasonably have believed that the students would gain a better understanding of Rawls' theory if they thought about how it applied to issues less divisive and hence less likely to distract students from the academic merits of the theory.

Teaching is tricky. Everyone understands that a class is a failure if stu- 6 dents refuse to learn because they feel bullied or intimidated, or if ideological arguments break out that have nothing to do with understanding an idea. It is the responsibility of the professor to conduct the class in such a way that maximal learning occurs, not maximal speech. That's why no teacher would permit students to launch into anti-Semitic diatribes in a class about the Holocaust, however sincerely the speaker might think that Jews were responsible for the Holocaust or the Holocaust did not take place. And even a teacher less scrupulous about avoiding offense to gay people would draw a line if a student in the Rawls class wanted to argue that Jim Crow or legalization of pedophilia is entailed by the principles of justice. While advocates of freedom of speech like to claim that falsehoods get squeezed out in the "marketplace of ideas," in classrooms they just receive an F.

> "It is the responsibility of the professor to conduct the class in such a way that maximal learning occurs, not maximal speech."

Most of the debate about speech codes, which frequently prohibit stu- 7 dents from making offensive comments to one another, concerns speech outside of class. Two points should be made. First, students who are unhappy with the codes and values on campus can take their views to forums outside of campus—to the town square, for example. The campus is an extension of the classroom, and so while the restrictions in the classroom are enforced less vigorously, the underlying pedagogical objective of avoiding intimidation remains intact.

Second, and more important—at least for libertarian partisans of the free 8 market—the universities are simply catering to demand in the marketplace for education. While critics sometimes give the impression that lefty professors and clueless administrators originated the speech and sex codes, the truth is that universities adopted them because that's what most students want. If students want to learn biology and art history in an environment where they needn't worry about being offended or raped, why shouldn't they? As long as universities are free to choose whatever rules they want, students with different views can sort themselves into universities with different rules. Indeed, students who want the greatest speech protections can attend public universities, which (unlike private universities) are governed by the First Amendment.

Libertarians might reflect on the irony that the private market, in which they normally put faith, reflects a preference among students for speech restrictions.

And this brings me to the most important overlooked fact about speech 9 and sex code debates. Society seems to be moving the age of majority from 18 to 21 or 22. We are increasingly treating college-age students as quasi-children who need protection from some of life's harsh realities while they complete the larval stage of their lives. Many critics of these codes discern this transformation but misinterpret it. They complain that universities are treating adults like children. The problem is that universities have been treating children like adults.

A lot of the controversies about campus life become clearer from this 10 perspective. Youngsters do dumb things. They suffer from lack of impulse control. They fail to say no to a sexual encounter they do not want, or they misinterpret a *no* as *yes*, or in public debate they undermine their own arguments by being needlessly offensive. Scientific research confirms that brain development continues well into a person's 20s. High schools are accustomed to dealing with the cognitive limitations of their charges. They see their mission as advancing the autonomy of students rather than assuming that it is already in place. They socialize as well as educate children to act civilly by punishing them if they don't. Universities have gradually realized that they must take the same approach to college students.

One naturally wonders why this has become necessary. Perhaps over- 11 programmed children engineered to the specifications of college admissions offices no longer experience the risks and challenges that breed maturity. Or maybe in our ever-more technologically advanced society, the responsibilities of adulthood must be delayed until the completion of a more extended period of education.

Yet college students have not always enjoyed so much autonomy. The 12 modern freedoms of college students date back only to the 1960s, when a wave of anti-authoritarianism, inspired by the Vietnam War and the civil rights movement, swept away strict campus codes in an era of single-sex dorms. The modern speech and sex codes have surfaced as those waters recede back to sea. What is most interesting is that this reaction comes not from parents and administrators, but from students themselves, who, apparently recognizing that their parents and schools have not fully prepared them for independence, want universities to resume their traditional role *in loco parentis*.

If all this is true, then maybe we can declare a truce in the culture wars 13 over education. If college students are children, then they should be protected like children. Libertarians should take heart that the market in private education offers students a diverse assortment of ideological cultures in which they can be indoctrinated. Conservatives should rejoice that moral instruction and social control have been reintroduced to the universities after a 40-year drought. Both groups should be pleased that students are kept from harm's way, and kept from doing harm, until they are ready to accept the responsibilities of adults.

⊃ AT ISSUE: HOW FREE SHOULD FREE SPEECH BE?

1. This article begins with a series of examples. Are these examples self-evident, or does Posner need to supply more material—for example, source information or evidence that the policies he mentions are widespread?

2. In paragraph 2, Posner says, "Most liberals celebrate these developments." He then goes on to talk about conservatives and libertarians. What logical fallacy does he seem to be committing?

3. In paragraph 3, Posner says, "Teachers are dictators who carefully control what students say to one another." Do you agree? How could you refute this statement?

4. What is Posner's purpose in writing this essay? Does he want to present information, change people's ideas, or move readers to action? Do you think that he achieves his purpose? Explain.

5. Posner makes a number of unsupported general statements in this essay. For example, in paragraph 8, he says that universities adopted speech and sex codes "because that's what most students want." Identify two or three of these general statements, and determine what kinds of evidence Posner would need to support them.

6. In his conclusion, Posner speculates on why universities should assume the responsibility of socializing students. Do you agree? Why or why not?

TEMPLATE FOR WRITING A DEDUCTIVE ARGUMENT

Write a one-paragraph **deductive** argument in which you argue *against* your school imposing speech codes. Follow the template below, filling in the blanks to create your argument.

> One of the basic principles of the United States government is the constitutional guarantee of freedom of speech. With few exceptions, all Americans _____
> _____
> _____. In college _____
> _____.
> For example, _____
> _____. By having the right to express themselves freely,
> _____
> _____
> _____. Therefore, _____
> _____.
> Not everyone agrees with this view, however. Some people argue that _____
> _____
> _____
> _____. This argument misses the point. When a university limits the
> speech of some students because others may be upset by their comments, _____
> _____
> _____.
> For this reason, colleges should _____
> _____
> _____.

TEMPLATE FOR WRITING AN INDUCTIVE ARGUMENT

Write a one-paragraph **inductive** argument in which you argue *in favor of* your school imposing speech codes. Follow the template below, filling in the blanks to create your argument.

The number of students demanding protection from distasteful ideas is growing yearly. Some students complain that _____ _____ _____. These students want _____ _____. A number of studies have shown that so-called safe spaces and trigger warnings go a long way toward calming students' fears and creating a hospitable learning environment. For example, some students _____ _____. As a result, _____ _____ _____. The best way for colleges to deal with this problem is to _____ _____.

Free speech advocates, however, argue that _____ _____ _____ _____. Although this may be true, _____ _____ _____.

For this reason, it would make sense to _____ _____ _____.

⟳ EXERCISE 5.13

Interview several of your classmates as well as one or two of your instructors about how free free speech should be. Then, edit the deductive and inductive arguments you wrote using the templates above so that they include some of these comments.

● EXERCISE 5.14

Write an essay in which you take a position on the question, "Should Universities Be Able to Place Limits on Free Speech?" Make sure that your essay is organized primarily as either a deductive argument or an inductive argument. Use the readings on pages 165–186 as source material, and be sure to document all information that you get from these sources. (See Chapter 10 for information on documenting sources.)

● EXERCISE 5.15

Review the logical fallacies discussed on pages 147–160. Then, reread the essay you wrote for Exercise 5.14, and check to see if it contains any fallacies. Underline any fallacies you find, and identify them by name. Then, rewrite each statement so it expresses a logical argument. Finally, revise your draft to eliminate any fallacies you found.

● EXERCISE 5.16

Review the four pillars of argument discussed in Chapter 1. Does your essay include all four elements of an effective argument? Add anything that is missing. Then, label the key elements of your essay.

6

Rogerian Argument, Toulmin Logic, and Oral Arguments

Is Online Education Better Than Classroom Education?

Chances are good that you have either taken an online course, or that you know someone who has. The National Center for Education Statistics found that as of 2014, one in four undergraduate students took at least one online course, and that number is expected to more than double in the coming years. In fact, from 2012 to 2013, online courses accounted for nearly three-quarters of the increase in enrollment for colleges in the United States. Given these facts, some educators wonder if students in online courses are getting what they pay for. Is online instruction as effective as meeting regularly on campus?

The appeal of online education is clear. For students, online education offers flexible scheduling, more time for work or family, and extra money, because online courses eliminate the need to commute to and from school. For colleges and universities, online education programs are cost-effective and profitable because they enable schools to reach new student populations, both nationally and internationally, without the expense of classrooms, offices, libraries, and bookstores.

But despite the advantages of online education, questions remain about its efficacy. For example, some educators ask if virtual classrooms are able to duplicate the dynamic educational atmosphere of face-to-face instruction. Others question whether students learn as well from education delivered by technology as they do from classroom instruction. Still others point out that because online instruction requires more self-discipline than on-campus classes, students find it easy to procrastinate and fall behind on their work.

Later in this chapter, you will be asked to think more about this issue. You will be given several sources to consider and asked to write an argument—using one of the three approaches discussed in this chapter—that takes a position on whether online education is better than classroom instruction.

A confrontational
argument

BloomImage/Getty Images

Understanding Rogerian Argument

The traditional model of argument is **confrontational**—characterized by conflict and opposition. This has been the tradition since Aristotle wrote about argument in ancient Greece. The end result of this model of argument is that someone is a winner and someone is a loser or someone is right and someone is wrong.

Arguments do not always have to be confrontational, however. In fact, the twentieth-century psychologist Carl Rogers contended that in many situations, this method of arguing can actually be counterproductive, making it impossible for two people to reach agreement. According to Rogers, attacking opponents and telling them that they are wrong or misguided puts them on the defensive. The result of this tactic is frequently ill will, anger, hostility—and conflict. If you are trying to negotiate an agreement or convince someone to do something, these are exactly the responses that you do not want. To solve this problem, Rogers developed a new approach to argument—one that emphasizes cooperation over confrontation.

Rogerian argument begins with the assumption that people of good will can find solutions to problems that they have in common. Rogers recommends that you consider those with whom you disagree as colleagues, not opponents. Instead of entering into the adversarial relationship that is assumed in classical argument, Rogerian argument encourages you to enter into a cooperative relationship in which both you and your readers search for **common ground**—points of agreement about a problem. By taking this approach, you are more likely to find a solution that will satisfy everyone.

Structuring Rogerian Arguments

Consider the following situation. Assume that you bought a video game console that stopped working one week after the warranty expired. Also assume that the manager of the store where you purchased the game console has refused to exchange it for another console. His point is that because the warranty has expired, the store has no obligation to take the product back. As a last resort, you write a letter to the game console's manufacturer. If you were writing a traditional argument, you would state your thesis—"It is clear that I should receive a new game console"—and then present arguments to support your position. You would also refute opposing arguments, and you would end your letter with a strong concluding statement.

Because Rogerian arguments begin with different assumptions, however, they are structured differently from classical arguments. In a Rogerian argument, you would begin by establishing common ground—by pointing out the concerns you and the video game console's manufacturer share. For example, you could say that as a consumer, you want to buy merchandise that will work as advertised. If the company satisfies your needs, you will continue to buy its products. This goal is shared by the manufacturer. Therefore, instead of beginning with a thesis statement that demands a yes or no response, you would point out that you and the manufacturer share an interest in solving your problem.

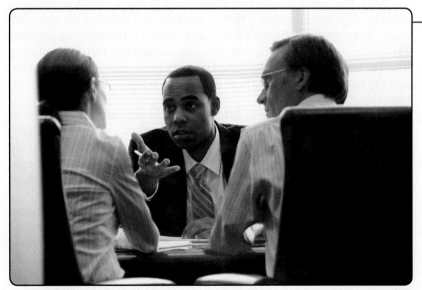

Establishing common ground

© Jose Luis Pelaez/Getty Images

Rogerian argument could resolve your problem.

© shvili/iStock/Getty Images

Next, you would describe *in neutral terms*—using impartial, unbiased language—the manufacturer's view of the problem, defining the manufacturer's concerns and attempting to move toward a compromise position. For example, you would explain that you understand that the company wants to make a high-quality product that will satisfy customers. You would also say that you understand that despite the company's best efforts, mistakes sometimes happen.

In the next section of your letter, you would present your own view of the problem fairly and objectively. This section plays a major role in convincing the manufacturer that your position has merit. Here, you should also try to concede the strengths of the manufacturer's viewpoint. For example, you can say that although you understand that warranties have time limits, your case has some unique circumstances that justify your claim.

Then you would explain how the manufacturer would benefit from granting your request. Perhaps you could point out that you have been satisfied with other products made by this manufacturer and expect to purchase more in the future. You could also say that instead of requesting a new game console, you would be glad to send the console back to the factory to be repaired. This suggestion shows that you are fair and willing to compromise.

Finally, your Rogerian argument would reinforce your position and end with a concluding statement that emphasizes the idea that you are certain that the manufacturer wants to settle this matter fairly.

⊃ EXERCISE 6.1

Read through the At Issue topics listed in this book's table of contents. Choose one topic, and then do the following:

1. Summarize your own position on the issue.

2. In a few sentences, summarize the main concerns of someone who holds the opposite position.

3. Identify some common ground that you and someone who holds the opposite position might have.

4. Write a sentence that explains how your position on the issue might benefit individuals (including those who hold opposing views) or society in general.

Writing Rogerian Arguments

Rogerian arguments are typically used to address issues that are open to compromise. By making it clear that you understand and respect the opinions of others, you avoid an "I win / you lose" situation and demonstrate empathy and respect for all points of view. In this sense, Rogerian arguments are more like negotiations than classical arguments. Thus, in a Rogerian argument, you spend a good deal of time defining the common ground that exists between you and those with whom you disagree. Ideally, you demonstrate that it is possible to reach a consensus, one that represents the common ground that exists between opposing sides. The more successful you are in accomplishing this goal, the more persuasive your argument will be. Of course with some issues—usually the most polarizing—a consensus is difficult or even impossible to achieve. In these cases, the best you can hope for is to convince people to agree on just one or two points. With other issues, however, you will be able to demonstrate to readers how they would benefit by moving toward your position.

> **NOTE**
>
> Although the Rogerian approach to argument can be used to develop a whole essay, it can also be part of a more traditional argument. In this case, it frequently appears in the refutation section, where opposing arguments are addressed.

In general, a Rogerian argument can be structured in the following way:

INTRODUCTION   Introduces the problem, pointing out how both the writer and reader are affected (establishes common ground)

BODY   Presents the reader's view of the problem

     Presents the writer's view of the problem (includes evidence to support the writer's viewpoint)

     Shows how the reader would benefit from moving toward the writer's position (includes evidence to support the writer's viewpoint)

     Lays out possible compromises that would benefit both reader and writer (includes evidence to support the writer's viewpoint)

CONCLUSION   Strong concluding statement reinforces the thesis and emphasizes compromise

⊙ EXERCISE 6.2

The following student essay includes all the elements of a Rogerian argument. This essay was written in response to the question, "Is it fair for instructors to require students to turn off their cell phones in class?" After you read the essay, answer the questions on page 199, consulting the outline above if necessary.

WHY CELL PHONES DO NOT BELONG IN THE CLASSROOM

ZOYA KAHN

Some college students think it is unfair for instructors to require   1
them to turn off their cell phones during class. Because they are accustomed to constant cell phone access, they don't understand how such a rule is justified. Granted, a strict, no-exceptions policy requiring that cell phones be turned off all over campus is not fair, but neither is a policy that prevents instructors from imposing restrictions ("Official Notices").

Common ground   Both students and instructors know that cell phone use—including texting—during class can be disruptive. In addition, most would agree that the primary goal of a university is to create a respectful learning environment and that cell phone use during class undercuts this goal. For this reason, it is in everyone's interest for instructors to institute policies that require students to turn off cell phones during class.

Thesis statement

Many students believe that requiring them to turn off their cell phones is unfair because it makes them feel less safe. Students are understandably concerned that, with their phones turned off, they will be unreachable during an emergency. For example, text message alerts are part of the emergency response system for most universities. Similarly, cell phones are a way for friends and family to contact students if there is an emergency. For these reasons, many students think that they should be free to make their own decisions concerning cell use. They believe that by turning their phones to vibrate or silent mode, they are showing respect for their classmates. As one student points out, "Only a small percentage of students will misuse their phones. Then, why should every student have to sacrifice for someone's mistakes?" (SchoolBook). After all, most students are honest and courteous. However, those few students who are determined to misuse their phones will do so, regardless of the school's phone policy.

2

Reader's view of the problem

To protect the integrity of the school's learning environment, instructors are justified in requiring students to turn off their phones. Recent studies have shown how distracting cell phones can be during a class. For example, a ringing cell phone significantly impairs students' performance, and a vibrating phone can be just as distracting (End et al. 56–57). In addition, texting in class decreases students' ability to focus, lowers test performance, and lessens students' retention of class material (Tindell and Bohlander 2). According to a recent study, most students believe that texting causes problems, "including a negative impact on classroom learning for the person who is texting, and distraction for those sitting nearby" (Tindell and Bohlander 4). Even more disturbing, cell phones enable some students to cheat. Students can use cell phones to text test questions and answers, to search the Web, and to photograph exams. Although asking students to turn off their phones will not prevent all these problems, it will reduce the abuses, and this will benefit the majority of students.

3 Writer's view of the situation

Benefits for reader of
writer's position

Students have good reasons for wanting to keep their phones on,   4
but there are even better reasons for accepting some reasonable restrictions. First, when students use cell phones during class, they distract
themselves (as well as their classmates) and undermine everyone's ability to learn. Second, having their cell phones on gives students a false
sense of security. A leading cell phone company has found that cell
phones can actually "detract from school safety and crisis preparedness" in numerous ways. For example, the use of cell phones during a
crisis can overload the cell phone system and make it useless. In addition, cell phones make it easy for students to spread rumors and, in
some cases, cell phone use has created more panic than the incidents
that actually caused the rumors ("Cell Phones").

Possible compromise

One possible compromise is for instructors to join with students to   5
create cell phone policies that take into consideration various situations
and settings. For example, instructors could require students to turn off
their phones only during exams. Instructors could also try to find ways
to engage students by using cell phone technology in the classroom.
For example, in some schools teachers take advantage of the various
functions available on most cell phones—calculators, cameras, diction-
aries, and Internet browsers ("Cell Phones"). In addition, schools should
consider implementing alternative emergency alert systems. Such com-
promises would ensure safety, limit possible disruptions, reduce the
potential for academic dishonesty, and enhance learning.

It is understandable that students want instructors to permit the   6
use of cell phones during class, but it is also fair for instructors to ask
students to turn them off. Although instructors should be able to
restrict cell phone use, they should also make sure that students understand the need for this policy. It is in everyone's best interest to protect
the integrity of the classroom and to make sure that learning is not

Concluding statement

compromised by cell phone use. To ensure the success of their education, students should be willing to turn off their phones.

Works Cited

"Cell Phones and Text Messaging in Schools." *National School Safety
and Security Services*, 2012, www.schoolsecurity.org/trends/cell
-phones-and-text-messaging-in-schools/.

End, Christian M., Shaye Worthman, Mary Bridget Mathews, and Katharina
    Wetterau. "Costly Cell Phones: The Impact of Cell Phone Rings on Aca-
    demic Performance." *Teaching of Psychology*, vol. 37, no. 1, 2010, pp.
    55–57. *Academic Search Complete*, doi: 10.1080/00986280903425912.
"Official Notices." UCLA Registrar's Office, Department of Student
    Affairs, 24 Oct. 2011, www.registrar.ucla.edu/soc/notices.htm.
SchoolBook. "Time to Repeal the Cell Phone Ban, Students Say." New
    York Public Radio, 2 Nov. 2011, www.wnyc.org/story/303205-time
    -to-repeal-the-cellphone-ban-students-say/.
Tindell, Deborah R., and Robert W. Bohlander. "The Use and Abuse of
    Cell Phones and Text Messaging in the Classroom: A Survey of Col-
    lege Students." *College Teaching*, vol. 60, no. 1, 2012, pp. 1–9. *ERIC
    Institute of Education Services*, eric.ed.gov/?id=EJ951966.

Identifying the Elements of a Rogerian Argument

1. How does the writer attempt to establish common ground? Do you think she is successful?

2. What evidence does the writer supply to support her position?

3. Other than reinforcing the writer's position, what else is the conclusion trying to accomplish?

4. How does the concluding statement reinforce agreement and compromise?

5. How would this essay be different if it were written as a traditional (as opposed to a Rogerian) argument?

Understanding Toulmin Logic

Another way of describing the structure of argument was introduced by the philosopher Stephen Toulmin in his book *The Uses of Argument* (1958). Toulmin observed that although formal logic is effective for analyzing classical arguments, it is inadequate for describing the arguments you encounter in everyday life. Although Toulmin was primarily concerned with the structures of arguments at the level of sentences or paragraphs, his model is also useful when dealing with longer arguments.

In its simplest terms, a **Toulmin argument** has three parts—the *claim*, the *grounds*, and the *warrant*. The **claim** is the main point of the essay—usually stated as the thesis. The **grounds** are the evidence that a writer uses to support the claim. The **warrant** is the **inference**—either stated or implied—that connects the claim to the grounds.

A basic argument using Toulmin logic would have the following structure.

CLAIM	Online education should be a part of all students' education.
GROUNDS	Students who take advantage of online education get better grades and report less stress than students who do not.
WARRANT	Online education is a valuable educational option.

Notice that the three-part structure above resembles the **syllogism** that is the backbone of classical argument. (See pp. 125–129 for a discussion of syllogisms.)

> **NOTE**
>
> When you use Toulmin logic to construct an argument, you still use deductive and inductive reasoning. You arrive at your claim inductively from facts, observations, and examples, and you connect the grounds and the warrant to your claim deductively.

Constructing Toulmin Arguments

Real arguments—those you encounter in print or online every day—are not as simple as the three-part model above implies. To be convincing, arguments often contain additional parts. To account for the demands of everyday debates, Toulmin expanded his model to include the following six interconnected elements.

CLAIM	The **claim** is the main point of your essay. It is a debatable statement that the rest of the essay will support.
	Online education should be a part of all students' education.
GROUNDS	The **grounds** are the concrete evidence that a writer uses to support the claim. These are the facts and observations that support the thesis. They can also be the opinions of experts that you locate when you do research.
	Studies show that students who take advantage of online education often get better grades than students who do not.

Research indicates that students who take advantage of online education are under less stress than those who are not.

WARRANT

The **warrant** is the inference that links the claim with the grounds. The warrant is often an unstated assumption. Ideally, the warrant should be an idea with which your readers will agree. (If they do not agree with it, you will need to supply **backing**.)

Online education is a valuable educational option.

BACKING

The **backing** consists of statements that support the warrant.

My own experience with online education was positive. Not only did it enable me to schedule classes around my job, but it also enabled me to work at my own pace in my courses.

QUALIFIERS

The **qualifiers** are statements that limit the claim. For example, they can be the real-world conditions under which the claim is true. These qualifiers can include words such as *most, few, some, sometimes, occasionally, often,* and *usually*.

Online education should be a required part of most students' education.

REBUTTALS

The **rebuttals** are exceptions to the claim. They are counterarguments that identify the situations where the claim does not hold true.

Some people argue that online education deprives students of an interactive classroom experience, but a course chat room can give students a similar opportunity to interact with their classmates.

⊙ EXERCISE 6.3

Look through this book's table of contents, and select an At Issue topic that interests you (ideally, one that you know something about). Write a sentence that states your position on this issue. (In terms of Toulmin argument, this statement is the *claim*.)

Then, supply as many of the expanded Toulmin model elements as you can, consulting the description of these elements above.

Claim: _____

_____

Grounds: _____

_____

_____

Warrant: _____

_____

_____

Backing: _____

_____

Qualifiers: _____

_____

_____

Rebuttals: _____

_____

Writing Toulmin Arguments

One of the strengths of the Toulmin model is that it emphasizes that presenting effective arguments involves more than stating ideas in absolute terms. Unlike the classical model of argument, the Toulmin model encourages writers to make realistic and convincing points by including claims and qualifiers and by addressing opposing arguments in down-to-earth and constructive ways. In a sense, this method of constructing an argument reminds writers that arguments do not exist in a vacuum. They are often quite subtle and are aimed at real readers who may or may not agree with them.

In general, a Toulmin argument can be organized in the following way:

INTRODUCTION	Introduces the problem
	States the claim (and possibly the qualifier)
BODY	Possibly states the warrant
	Presents the backing that supports the warrant
	Presents the grounds that support the claim
	Presents the conditions of rebuttal
	States the qualifiers
CONCLUSION	Brings the argument to a close
	Strong concluding statement reinforces the claim

⊙ EXERCISE 6.4

The following student essay, which includes all the elements of a Toulmin argument, was written in response to the question, "Are cheerleaders athletes?" After you read the essay, answer the questions on page 205, consulting the outline on the previous page if necessary.

COMPETITIVE CHEERLEADERS ARE ATHLETES

JEN DAVIS

Recently, the call to make competitive cheerleading an official   1
college sport and to recognize cheerleaders as athletes has gotten
stronger. Critics of this proposal maintain that cheerleading is simply
entertainment that occurs on the sidelines of real sporting events.
According to them, although cheerleading may show strength and skill,
it is not a competitive activity. This view of cheerleading, however,
misses the point. Because competitive cheerleading pits teams against
each other in physically and technically demanding athletic contests,
it should be recognized as a sport. For this reason, those who participate   Claim and qualifier
in the sport of competitive cheerleading should be considered athletes.

Acknowledging cheerleaders as athletes gives them the respect   2 Warrant
and support they deserve. Many people associate cheerleading with   Backing
pom-poms and short skirts and ignore the strength and skill competitive
cheerleading requires. Like athletes in other female-dominated sports,
cheerleaders unfortunately have had to fight to be taken seriously. For   Grounds
example, Title IX, the law that mandates gender equity in college
sports, does not recognize competitive cheerleading as a sport. This
situation demonstrates a very narrow definition of sports, one that
needs to be updated. As one women's sports advocate explains,
"What we consider sports are things that men have traditionally
played" (qtd. in Thomas). For this reason, women's versions of long-
accepted men's sports—such as basketball, soccer, and track—are easy
for people to respect and to support. Competitive cheerleading, however, departs from this model and is not seen as a sport even though

those who compete in it are skilled, accomplished athletes. As one coach points out, the athleticism of cheerleading is undeniable: "We don't throw balls, we throw people. And we catch them" (qtd. in Thomas).

Backing

Grounds

Recent proposals to rename competitive cheerleading "stunt" or "team acrobatics and tumbling" are an effort to reshape people's ideas about what cheerleaders actually do. Although some cheerleading squads have kept to their original purpose—to lead fans in cheering on their teams—competitive teams practice rigorously, maintain impressive levels of physical fitness, and risk serious injuries. Like other sports, competitive cheerleading involves extraordinary feats of strength and skill. Cheerleaders perform elaborate floor routines and ambitious stunts, including flips from multilevel human pyramids. Competitive cheerleaders also do what all athletes must do: they compete. Even a critic concedes that cheerleading could be "considered a sport when cheerleading groups compete against one another" (Sandler). Competitive cheerleading teams do just that; they enter competitive contests, are judged, and emerge as winners or losers.

Rebuttal

Qualifiers

Those in authority, however, are slow to realize that cheerleading is a sport. In 2010, a federal judge declared that competitive cheerleading was "too underdeveloped and disorganized" to qualify as a legitimate varsity sport under Title IX (Tigay). This ruling was shortsighted. Before competitive cheerleading can develop as a sport, it needs to be *acknowledged* as a sport. Without their schools' financial support, cheerleading teams cannot recruit, offer scholarships, or host competitions. To address this situation, several national groups are asking the National Collegiate Athletic Association (NCAA) to designate competitive cheerleading as an "emerging sport." By doing this, the NCAA would show its support and help competitive cheerleading to develop and eventually to flourish. This does not mean, however, that all cheerleaders are athletes or that all cheerleading is a sport. In addition, the NCAA does have reason to be cautious when it comes to redefining competitive cheerleading. Some schools have taken sideline cheerleading teams and recategorized them just so they could comply with Title IX. These efforts to sidestep the purpose of the law are, as one expert puts it, "obviously transparent and unethical" (Tigay). Even so, fear of possible abuse should not keep the NCAA from doing what is right and giving legitimate athletes the respect and support they deserve.

Competitive cheerleaders are athletes in every sense of the word. They are aggressive, highly skilled, physically fit competitors. For this reason, they deserve to be acknowledged as athletes under Title IX and supported by their schools and by the NCAA. Biased and outdated ideas about what is (and what is not) a sport should not keep competitive cheerleading from being recognized as the sport it is. As one proponent puts it, "Adding flexibility to the definition of college athletes is a common sense move that everyone can cheer for" ("Bona Fide"). It is time to give competitive cheerleaders the support and recognition they deserve.

5

Concluding statement

Works Cited

"Bona Fide Athletes." *USA Today*, 16 Oct. 2009, www.usatoday.com /story/opinion/2019/10/16/bona-fide-athletes/81582044/. Editorial.

Sandler, Bernice R. "Certain Types of Competition Define Sports." *USA Today*, 22 Oct. 2009, usatoday30.usatoday.com/printedition /news/20091022/letters22_st2.art.htm.

Thomas, Katie. "Born on the Sideline, Cheering Clamors to Be a Sport." *New York Times*, 22 May 2011, www.nytimes.com/2011/05/23/sports /gender-games-born-on-sideline-cheering-clamors-to-be-sport.html.

Tigay, Chanan. "Is Cheerleading a Sport Protected by Title IX?" *CQ Researcher*, 25 Mar. 2011, p. 276. library.cqpress.com/cqresearcher /document.php?id=cqresrre2011032500.

Identifying the Elements of a Toulmin Argument

1. Summarize the position this essay takes as a three-part argument that includes the claim, the grounds, and the warrant.

2. Do you think the writer includes enough backing for her claim? What other supporting evidence could she have included?

3. Find the qualifier in the essay. How does it limit the argument? How else could the writer have qualified the argument?

4. Do you think the writer addresses enough objections to her claim? What other arguments could she have addressed?

5. Based on your reading of this essay, what advantages do you think Toulmin logic offers to writers? What disadvantages does it present?

Understanding Oral Arguments

Many everyday arguments—in school, on the job, or in your community—are presented orally. In many ways, an oral argument is similar to a written one: it has an introduction, a body, and a conclusion, and it addresses and refutes opposing points of view. In other, more subtle ways, however, an oral argument is different from a written one. Before you plan and deliver an oral argument, you should be aware of these differences.

The major difference between an oral argument and a written one is that an audience cannot reread an oral argument to clarify information. Listeners have to understand an oral argument the first time they hear it. To help your listeners, you need to design your presentation with this limitation in mind, considering the following guidelines:

- **An oral argument should contain verbal signals that help guide listeners.** Transitional phrases such as "My first point," "My second point," and "Let me sum up" are useful in oral arguments, where listeners do not have a written text in front of them. They alert listeners to information to come and signal shifts from one point to another.

- **An oral argument should use simple, direct language and avoid long sentences.** Complicated sentences that contain elevated language and numerous technical terms are difficult for listeners to follow. For this reason, your sentences should be straightforward and easy to understand.

- **An oral argument should repeat key information.** A traditional rule of thumb for oral arguments is, "Tell listeners what you're going to tell them; then tell it to them; finally, tell them what you've told them." In other words, in the introduction of an oral argument, tell your listeners what they are going to hear; in the body, discuss your points, one at a time; and finally, in your conclusion, restate your points. This intentional repetition ensures that your listeners follow (and remember) your points.

- **An oral argument should include visuals.** Visual aids can make your argument easier to follow. You can use visuals to identify your points as you discuss them. You can also use visuals—for example, charts, graphs, or tables—to clarify or reinforce key points as well as to add interest. Carefully selected visuals help increase the chances that what you are saying will be remembered.

Planning an Oral Argument

The work you do to plan your presentation is as important as the presentation itself. Here is some advice to consider as you plan your oral argument:

1. **Choose your topic wisely.** Select a topic that is somewhat controversial so listeners will want to hear your views. You can create interest in a topic, but it is easier to appeal to listeners if they are already interested in what you have to say. In addition, try to choose a topic that you know something about. Even though you will probably do some research, the process will be much easier if you are already familiar with the basic issues.

2. **Know your audience.** Consider your audience and its needs before you begin to plan your presentation. For example, how much do listeners already know about your topic? Are they well informed, or do they know little about it? If listeners are unfamiliar with your topic, you will have to supply background information and definitions of key terms. If they already know a lot, you can dispense with this material and discuss your subject in more depth. Also, assess your audience members' likely response to your presentation. Will they be receptive? Hostile? Neutral? The answers to these questions will help you decide which arguments will most likely be effective (and which will not).

3. **Know your time limit.** Most oral presentations have a time limit. If you run over your allotted time, you risk boring or annoying your listeners. If you finish too soon, it will seem as if you don't know much about your subject. As you prepare your argument, include all the information that you can cover within your time limit. Keep in mind

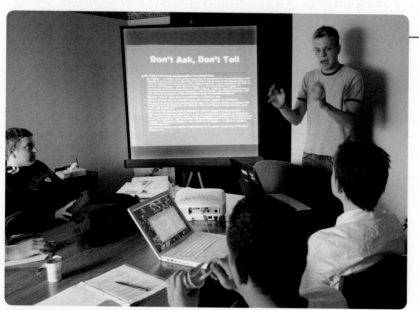

Visual aids can help listeners follow an oral presentation.

Ann Heisenfelt/AP Photo

that you will not be able to go into as much detail in a short speech as you will in a long speech, so plan accordingly.

4. **Identify your thesis statement.** Like a written argument, an oral argument should have a debatable thesis statement. Keep this statement simple, and make sure that it clearly conveys your position. Remember that in an oral argument, your listeners have to understand your thesis the first time they hear it. (See Chapter 7 for more on developing a thesis statement.)

5. **Gather support for your thesis.** Assume that your listeners are **skeptical**, that is, that they are not easily convinced. Even if you think that your audience is friendly, you still need to make a persuasive case. Don't make the mistake of thinking that listeners will automatically accept all your ideas just because they agree with your main point. For this reason, you need to support your thesis with compelling evidence if you expect listeners to conclude that your position is valid. Supporting evidence can be in the form of facts, observations, expert opinion, or statistics. Some of your support can come from your own experiences, but most will come from your research.

6. **Acknowledge your sources.** Remember that all of the information you get from your research needs to be acknowledged. As you deliver your presentation, let listeners know where the information you are using comes from—for example, "According to a 2015 editorial in the *New York Times* . . ." or "As Kenneth Davis says in his book *America's Hidden History*. . . ." This strategy enhances your credibility by showing that you are well informed about your topic. (Including source information also helps you protect yourself from unintentional **plagiarism**. See Chapter 11.)

7. **Prepare your speaking notes.** Effective speakers do not read their speeches. Instead, they prepare **speaking notes**—often on index cards—that list the points they want to make. (Microsoft's PowerPoint, as well as some other presentation software packages, has a section on each slide for speaking notes. Although the notes are displayed on the computer screen, they are not visible to the audience.) These notes guide you as you speak, so you should make sure that there are not too many of them and that they contain just key information. (If you use note cards, it is a good idea to number them so that you can be sure that they are in the correct order.)

8. **Prepare visual aids.** Visual aids help you to communicate your thesis and your supporting points more effectively. Visuals increase interest in your presentation, and they also strengthen your argument by reinforcing your points and making them easier for listeners to follow and to understand. In addition, visuals can help establish your credibility and thus improve the persuasiveness of your argument.

You can use the following types of visual aids in your presentations:

- Diagrams
- Photographs
- Slides
- Smartboards, flip charts
- Overhead transparencies
- Document cameras
- Handouts, objects

In order moving clockwise from top left:
© deomis/Shutterstock.com; © Peter Vaclavek/
Shutterstock.com; © Tarapong Siri/
Shutterstock.com; © deomis/Shutterstock.com

In addition to these kinds of visual aids, you can also use **presentation software**, such as Microsoft's PowerPoint or the Web-based application *Prezi* (Prezi.com). With presentation software, you can easily create visually appealing and persuasive slides. You can insert scanned photographs or drawings into slides, or you can cut and paste charts, graphs, and tables into them. You can even include YouTube videos and MP3 files. Keep in mind, however, that the images, videos, or sound files that you use must support your thesis; if they are irrelevant, they will distract or confuse your listeners. (See pp. 218–221 for examples of PowerPoint slides.)

9. **Practice your presentation.** As a general rule, you should spend as much time rehearsing your speech as you do preparing it. In other words, practice, practice, practice. Be sure you know the order in which you will present your points and when you will move from one visual to another. Rehearse your speech aloud with just your speaking notes and your visuals until you are confident that you can get through your presentation effectively. Try to anticipate any problems that may arise with your visuals, and solve them at this stage of the process. If possible, practice your speech in the room in which you will actually deliver it. Bring along a friend, and ask for feedback. Finally, cut or add material as needed until you are certain that you can stay within your time limit.

CHECKLIST

Designing and Displaying Visuals

☐ Use images that are large enough for your audience to see and that will reproduce clearly.

(continued)

☐ Make lettering large enough for your audience to see. Use 40- to 50-point type for titles, 25- to 30-point type for major points, and 20- to 25-point type for less important points.

☐ Use bulleted lists, not full sentences or paragraphs.

☐ Put no more than three or four points on a single visual.

☐ Make sure there is a clear contrast between your lettering and the background.

☐ Don't show your listeners the visual before you begin to speak about it. Display the visual only when you discuss it.

☐ Face your listeners when you discuss a visual. Even if you point to the screen, always look at your listeners. Never turn your back on your audience.

☐ Introduce and discuss each visual. Don't simply show or read the visual to your audience. Always tell listeners more than they can read or see for themselves.

☐ Don't use elaborate visuals or special effects that will distract your audience.

⊙ EXERCISE 6.5

Look through the table of contents of this book, and select three At Issue topics that interest you. Imagine that you are planning to deliver an oral argument to a group of college students on each of these topics. For each topic, list three visual aids you could use to enhance your presentation.

Delivering Oral Arguments

Delivery is the most important part of a speech. The way you speak, your interaction with the audience, your posture, and your eye contact all affect your overall presentation. In short, a confident, controlled speaker will have a positive impact on an audience, while a speaker who fumbles with note cards, speaks in a shaky voice, or seems disorganized will lose credibility. To make sure that your listeners see you as a credible, reliable source of information, follow these guidelines:

1. **Accept nervousness.** For most people, nervousness is part of the speech process. The trick is to convert this nervousness into energy that you can channel into your speech. The first step in dealing with nervousness is to make sure that you have rehearsed enough. If you have prepared adequately, you will probably be able to handle any problem you may encounter. If you make a mistake, you can correct it. If you forget something, you can fit it in later.

DEALING WITH NERVOUSNESS

If nervousness is a problem, the following strategies can help you to relax:

- **Breathe deeply.** Take a few deep breaths before you begin speaking. Research has shown that increased oxygen has a calming effect on the brain.

- **Use visualization.** Imagine yourself delivering a successful speech, and fix this image in your mind. It can help dispel anxiety.

- **Empty your mind.** Consciously try to eliminate all negative thoughts. Think of your mind as a room full of furniture. Imagine yourself removing each piece of furniture until the room is empty.

- **Drink water.** Before you begin to speak, take a few sips of water. Doing so will eliminate the dry mouth that is a result of nervousness. Don't, however, drink water during your speech.

- **Keep things in perspective.** Remember, your speech is a minor event in your life. Nothing that you do or say will affect you significantly.

2. **Look at your audience.** When you speak, look directly at the members of your audience. At the beginning of the speech, make eye contact with a few audience members who seem to be responding positively. As your speech progresses, look directly at as many audience members as you can. Try to sweep the entire room. Don't focus excessively on a single person or on a single section of your audience.

3. **Speak naturally.** Your presentation should sound like a conversation, not a performance. This is not to suggest that your presentation should include slang, ungrammatical constructions, or colloquialisms; it should conform to the rules of standard English. The trick is to maintain the appearance of a conversation while following the conventions of public speaking. Achieving this balance takes practice, but it is a goal worth pursuing.

4. **Speak slowly.** When you give a presentation, you should speak more slowly than you do in normal conversation. This strategy gives listeners time to process what they hear—and gives you time to think about what you are saying.

5. **Speak clearly and correctly.** As you deliver your presentation, speak clearly. Do not drop endings, and be careful to pronounce words correctly. Look up the pronunciation of unfamiliar words in a dictionary, or

ask your instructor for help. If you go though an entire speech pronouncing a key term or a name incorrectly, your listeners will question your competence.

6. **Move purposefully.** As you deliver your speech, don't pace, move your hands erratically, or play with your note cards. Try to stand in one spot, with both feet flat on the floor. Move only when necessary—for example, to point to a visual or to display an object. If you intend to distribute printed material to your listeners, do so only when you are going to discuss it. (Try to arrange in advance for someone else to give out your handouts.) If you are not going to refer to the material in your presentation, wait until you have finished your speech before you distribute it. Depending on the level of formality of your presentation and the size of your audience, you may want to stand directly in front of your audience or behind a podium.

7. **Be prepared for the unexpected.** Don't get flustered if things don't go exactly as you planned. If you forget material, work it in later. If you make a mistake, correct it without apologizing. Most of the time, listeners will not realize that something has gone wrong unless you call attention to it. If someone in the audience looks bored, don't worry. You might consider changing your pace or your volume, but keep in mind that the person's reaction might have nothing to do with your presentation. He or she might be tired, preoccupied, or just a poor listener.

Remember to project confidence and control as you speak.

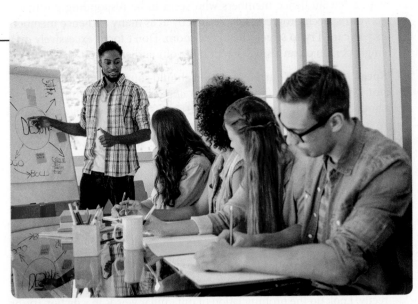

© Wavebreak Media/Agefotostock

8. **Leave time for questions.** End your presentation by asking if your listeners have any questions. As you answer questions, keep in mind the following advice:

   - *Be prepared.* Make sure you have anticipated the obvious counterarguments to your position, and be prepared to address them. In addition, prepare a list of websites or other resources that you can refer your audience to for more information.

   - *Repeat a question before you answer it.* This technique enables everyone in the audience to hear the question, and it also gives you time to think of an answer.

   - *Keep control of interchanges.* If a questioner repeatedly challenges your answer or monopolizes the conversation, say that you will be glad to discuss the matter with him or her after your presentation is finished.

   - *Be honest.* Answer questions honestly and forthrightly. If you don't know the answer to a question, say so. Tell the questioner you will locate the information that he or she wants and send it by email. Above all, do not volunteer information that you are not sure is correct.

   - *Use the last question to summarize.* When you get to the last question, end your answer by restating the main point of your argument.

Composing an Oral Argument

The written text of an oral argument is organized just as any other argument is: it has an introduction that gives the background of the issue and states the thesis, it has a body that presents evidence that supports the thesis, it identifies and refutes arguments against the thesis, and it ends with a concluding statement.

In general, an oral argument can be structured in the following way:

INTRODUCTION	Presents the background of the issue
	States the thesis
BODY	Presents evidence: Point 1 in support of the thesis
	Presents evidence: Point 2 in support of the thesis
	Presents evidence: Point 3 in support of the thesis
	Refutes opposing arguments
CONCLUSION	Brings the argument to a close
	Concluding statement restates thesis
	Speaker asks for questions

⊙ **EXERCISE 6.6**

The following oral argument was presented by a student in a speech course in response to the assignment, "Argue for or against the advantages of a 'gap year' between high school and college." (Her PowerPoint slides appear at the end of the speech.) After you read this argument, answer the questions on page 221, consulting the outline on the previous page if necessary.

AN ARGUMENT IN SUPPORT OF THE "GAP YEAR"

CHANTEE STEELE

College: even the word sounded wonderful when I was in high   1 school. Everyone told me it would be the best time of my life. They told me that I would take courses in exciting new subjects and that I'd make lifelong friends. [Show slide 1.] What they didn't tell me was that I would be anxious, confused, and uncertain about my major and about my future. Although this is only my second year in college, I've already changed my major once, and to be honest, I'm still not sure I've made the right decision. But during the process of changing majors, my adviser gave me some reading material that included information about a "gap year." A gap year is a year off between high school and college when students focus on work or community service and learn about themselves—something that would have benefited me. Although gaining popularity in the United States, the gap year still suggests images of spoiled rich kids who want to play for a year before going to college. According to educator Christina Wood, however, in the United Kingdom a gap year is common; it is seen as a time for personal growth that

Thesis statement   helps students mature (36). [Show slide 2.] In fact, 230,000 British students take a gap year before going to college. As the rest of my speech will show, a well-planned gap year gives students time to mature, to explore potential careers, and to volunteer or travel.

Evidence: Point 1 in support of thesis   [Show slide 3.] Apparently I'm not alone in my uncertainty about my   2 major or about my future. As Holly Bull, a professional gap-year counselor, explains, "The National Research Center for College and University Admissions estimates that over 50 percent of students switch majors at least once" (8). As they go from high school to college, most students have little time to think about what to do with their lives. A gap year before college would give them time to learn more about themselves. According to Wood, "Gap years provide valuable life experiences and maturity so students are more ready to focus on their studies when they return" (37). A year off would give some students the perspective they need to mature and to feel more confident about their decisions. Bull agrees, noting that the gap year helps students choose or confirm the area of study they want to pursue, that it makes them "instantly more mature," and that it "boosts their excitement about learning" (7–8).

The gap year gives students many options to explore before going to college. [Show slide 4.] This slide shows just some of the resources students can use as they prepare for their gap year. As you can see, they can explore opportunities for employment, education, and volunteer work. There are even resources for students who are undecided. As David Lesesne, the dean of admissions at Sewanee, says, "Some students do very interesting and enriching things: hike the Appalachian Trail, herd sheep in Crete, play in a rock band, [or even] attend school in Guatemala" (qtd. in Wood 37). Many other students, especially in these economic hard times, use the gap year to earn money to offset the high cost of their education (Wood 35).

3 Evidence: Point 2 in support of thesis

Taking a gap year can also help students to get into better colleges. According to an article by the dean of admissions at Harvard, "Occasionally students are admitted to Harvard or other colleges in part because they accomplished something unusual during a year off" (Fitzsimmons, McGrath, and Ducey). Depending on the scope of their service or work, a gap year could enable students to earn scholarships that they were not eligible for before. In fact, some colleges actually recommend that students take time off after high school. Harvard is one of several U.S. colleges that "encourages admitted students to defer enrollment for one year to travel, pursue a special project or activity, work, or spend time in another meaningful way" (Fitzsimmons, McGrath, and Ducey). Furthermore, evidence shows that a gap year can help students to be more successful after they begin in college. One Middlebury College admissions officer has calculated that "a single gap semester was the strongest predictor of academic success at his school"

4 Evidence: Point 3 in support of thesis

(Bull 7). Given this support for the gap year and given the resources that are now available to help students plan it, the negative attitudes about it in the United States are beginning to change.

Refutation of opposing arguments

In spite of these benefits, parental concerns about "slackerdom" and money are common. Supporters of the gap year acknowledge that students have to be motivated to make the most of their experiences. Clearly, the gap year is not for everyone. For example, students who are not self-motivated may not benefit from a gap year. In addition, parents worry about how much money the gap year will cost them. This is a real concern when you add the year off to the expense of four years of college (Wood 37). However, if finances are a serious concern, students can spend their gap year working in their own communities or taking advantage of a paid experience like AmeriCorps—which, as the AmeriCorps website shows, covers students' room and board *and* offers an educational stipend after students complete the program. [Show slide 5.] Additionally, parents and students should consider the time and money that is wasted when a student who is not ready for college starts school and then drops out.   5

After considering the benefits of a gap year, I have concluded that more students should postpone college for a year. Many students (like me) are uncertain about their goals. We welcome new opportunities and are eager to learn from new experiences and may find a year of service both emotionally and intellectually rewarding. Given another year to mature, many of us would return to school with a greater sense of purpose, focus, and clarity. In some cases, the gap year could actually help us get into better schools and possibly get more financial aid. If we intend to take the college experience seriously, spending a gap year learning about our interests and abilities would help us to become better, more confident, and ultimately more focused students. [Show slide 6.]   6

Concluding statement

Are there any questions?   7

Works Cited

Bull, Holly. "Navigating a Gap Year." *TeenLife*, Feb. 2011, pp. 6–9.

Fitzsimmons, William, et al. "Time Out or Burn Out for the Next Generation." *Harvard College Office of Admissions*, 2011, college.harvard .edu/admissions/preparing-college/should-i-take-time.

Wood, Christina. "Should You Take a 'Gap Year'?" *Careers and Colleges*, Fall 2007, pp. 36–37.

Slide 1

© Ana Blazic/istockphoto.com

Slide 2

230,000 students between 18 and 25 take a Gap Year in the U.K.

—Tom Griffiths, founder and director of GapYear.com

(qtd. in Christina Wood, "Should You Take a 'Gap Year'?," *Careers and Colleges*, Fall 2007)

Slide 3

50% of students change their major at least once.
—National Research Center for College
and University Admissions

Slide 4

A Few Links for the Potential "Gapster"

(links from Holly Bull, "The Possibilities of the Gap
Year," *Chronicle of Higher Education* 52.44 [2006])

Employment

Cool Works: CoolWorks.com (domestic jobs)

Working Abroad: WorkingAbroad.org (jobs overseas)

Education

Global Routes: GlobalRoutes.org (semester-long courses)

Sea-mester: Seamester.com (sea voyage programs)

Volunteer Work

AmeriCorps: AmeriCorps.gov

City Year: CityYear.org

Thoughtful Texts for Fence Sitters

Karl Haigler and Rae Nelson, *The Gap-Year
    Advantage* (Macmillan, 2005)

Colin Hall, *Taking Time Off* (Princeton Review, 2003)

Charlotte Hindle and Joe Bindloss, *The Gap Year
    Book* (Lonely Planet, 2005)

Slide 5

Courtesy of Corporation for National and Community Service. Reproduced by permission.

Slide 6

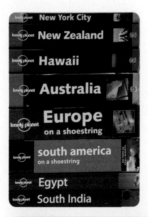

In order moving clockwise from top left: © Roger Cracknell 01/classic/Alamy; © Ben Blankenburg/iStock/Getty Images; © Steve Stock/Alamy; David Cordner/Getty Images

Identifying the Elements of an Oral Argument

1. Where does this oral argument include verbal signals to help guide readers?

2. Does this oral argument use simple, direct language? What sections of the speech, if any, could be made simpler?

3. Where does this oral argument repeat key information for emphasis? Is there any other information that you think should have been repeated?

4. What opposing arguments does the speaker identify? Does she refute them convincingly?

5. How effective are the visuals that accompany the text of this oral argument? Are there enough visuals? Are they placed correctly? What other information do you think could have been displayed in a visual?

6. What questions would you ask this speaker at the end of her speech?

Is Online Education Better Than Classroom Education?

© Karl Dolenc/iStock/Getty Images

Go back to page 191, and reread the At Issue box, which gives background about whether online education is better than classroom instruction. As the following sources illustrate, this question has a number of possible answers.

After you review the sources listed below, you will be asked to answer some questions and to complete some simple activities. This work will help you to understand both the content and the structure of the sources. When you are finished, you will be ready to develop an argument—using one of the three alternative approaches to argument discussed in this chapter—that takes a position on whether online education is better than classroom learning.

SOURCES

The Evolution of Online Schooling

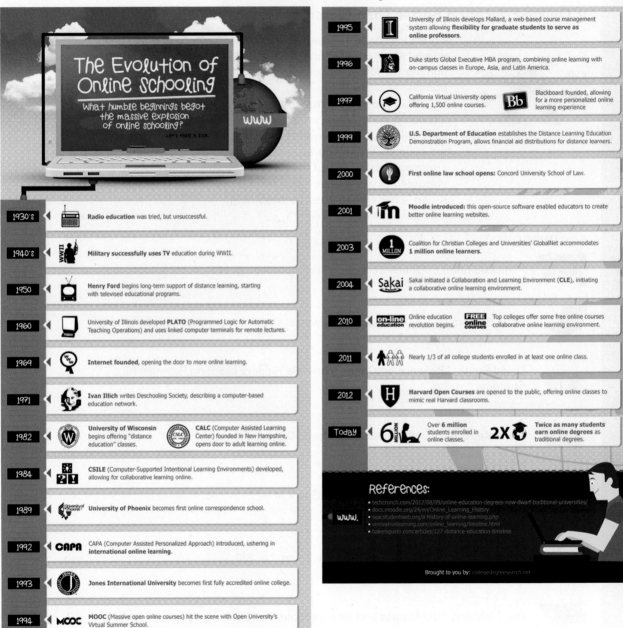

The Evolution of Online Schooling

What humble beginnings begot the massive explosion of online schooling?

Let's take a look.

www

1930's Radio education was tried, but unsuccessful.

1940's Military successfully uses TV education during WWII.

1950 Henry Ford begins long-term support of distance learning, starting with televised educational programs.

1960 University of Illinois developed PLATO (Programmed Logic for Automatic Teaching Operations) and uses linked computer terminals for remote lectures.

1969 Internet founded, opening the door to more online learning.

1971 Ivan Illich writes Deschooling Society, describing a computer-based education network.

1982 University of Wisconsin begins offering "distance education" classes. CALC (Computer Assisted Learning Center) founded in New Hampshire, opens door to adult learning online.

1984 CSILE (Computer-Supported Intentional Learning Environments) developed, allowing for collaborative learning online.

1989 University of Phoenix becomes first online correspondence school.

1992 CAPA (Computer Assisted Personalized Approach) introduced, ushering in international online learning.

1993 Jones International University becomes first fully accredited online college.

1994 MOOC (Massive open online courses) hit the scene with Open University's Virtual Summer School.

1995 University of Illinois develops Mallard, a web-based course management system allowing flexibility for graduate students to serve as online professors.

1996 Duke starts Global Executive MBA program, combining online learning with on-campus classes in Europe, Asia, and Latin America.

1997 California Virtual University opens offering 1,500 online courses. Blackboard founded, allowing for a more personalized online learning experience

1999 U.S. Department of Education establishes the Distance Learning Education Demonstration Program, allows financial aid distributions for distance learners.

2000 First online law school opens: Concord University School of Law.

2001 Moodle introduced: this open-source software enabled educators to create better online learning websites.

2003 Coalition for Christian Colleges and Universities' GlobalNet accommodates 1 million online learners.

2004 Sakai initiated a Collaboration and Learning Environment (CLE), initiating a collaborative online learning environment.

2010 Online education revolution begins. Top colleges offer some free online courses collaborative online learning environment.

2011 Nearly 1/3 of all college students enrolled in at least one online class.

2012 Harvard Open Courses are opened to the public, offering online classes to mimic real Harvard classrooms.

Today Over 6 million students enrolled in online classes. Twice as many students earn online degrees as traditional degrees.

References:
- techcrunch.com/2012/08/09/online-education-degrees-now-dwarf-traditional-universities/
- docs.moodle.org/24/en/Online_Learning_History
- seacstudentweb.org/a-history-of-online-learning.php
- innovativelearning.com/online_learning/timeline.html
- bakersguide.com/articles/127-distance-education-timeline

Brought to you by: collegedegreesearch.net

www.collegedegreesearch.net

⊙ AT ISSUE: SOURCES FOR USING ALTERNATIVE APPROACHES TO ARGUMENT

1. What is the purpose of this infographic? How successful is it in achieving this purpose?

2. What kind of audience does this infographic seem to be addressing? How can you tell?

3. What is this infographic's main idea or message? Write a one-sentence summary of this main idea.

4. Where does the infographic appeal to *ethos*? Is this appeal necessary? Why or why not?

5. How clear is this infographic? What other arrangement (or arrangements) of words, numbers, color, and spacing could have been used?

6. If you were going to write an argumentative essay in favor of online education, which information in this infographic would you find most useful? Which information would you find least useful? Explain.

This essay is from the online newspaper *Community College Times*. It appeared on November 16, 2011.

THE RISKS AND REWARDS OF ONLINE LEARNING

CHRIS BUSTAMANTE

In 2008, investors wanted to buy Rio Salado College, the nation's largest online public community college headquartered in Tempe, Ariz. The offer was more than $400 million with plans to convert it into a national, for-profit, online school. 1

Rio Salado wasn't for sale, but the offer proved how much demand exists for serving students who find traditional education systems inconvenient and need the flexibility of online formats. 2

Online learning may not be the first thing that comes to mind when community colleges consider providing support for student success. But that mindset is changing. It has to. The 2011 Sloan Survey of Online Learning reported that more than six million college students in the fall of 2010 took at least one online course, comprising nearly one-third of all college and university students. The growth rate in online course enrollment far exceeds the growth rate of the overall higher education student population. 3

Still, there is healthy skepticism about the proliferation of online learning and views still differ about its value. According to surveys by the Pew Research Center and the *Chronicle of Higher Education*, less than 30 percent of the public believes that online and classroom courses provide the same educational value. Half of college presidents share that belief. 4

Any way you look at it, online learning is an increasingly vital part of producing the number of qualified graduates needed to meet future workforce demands—when it is done correctly. 5

A Calculated Risk

In 1996, Rio Salado, one of 10 Maricopa Community Colleges, took a calculated risk and began offering courses online—16 to start—just when the Internet was taking off. Critics at the time challenged the quality of online education and claimed that students wouldn't adjust well to such a radical change in their learning environment. But Maricopa and Rio Salado pushed ahead, determined to create an innovative, nontraditional, and nimble approach that is responsive to and supportive of changing student needs. 6

The risks have proven to be worth it. While no one could have predicted the economic environment that students and higher education face today, making the decision to move online proved to be provident for the college and students. Rio Salado extended educational access to students who found traditional college to be out of reach in Arizona, nationwide, and around the world. 7

The college currently serves nearly 70,000 students each year, with more than 41,000 enrolled in 600-plus online courses.

Keeping Costs Down

To keep costs down, Rio Salado supports more than 60 certificate and degree 8 programs with just 22 residential faculty and more than 1,400 adjunct faculty. Our "one-course, many sections" model uses a master course approved by the resident faculty and taught by adjunct faculty in more than 6,000 course sections. The college's cost to educate students is as much as 48 percent less than peer institutions nationwide.

Without the expense of a traditional campus, Rio Salado has been able to 9 focus on building and improving its RioLearn platform, a customized learning management system that provides access to course-related resources, instructors, fellow students, and other support services.

Focused on Student Support

Meeting students' needs means providing access to robust, comprehensive 10 support services that are customized for their complex lifestyles, whether they are a working adult, an active military student accessing their coursework online, or someone taking in-person classes in adult basic education, incarcerated reentry, early college, or workforce training programs. Today's students need the resources of round-the-clock instructional and technology helpdesks, tutoring, and virtual library services. Additionally, we never cancel an online class and offer the flexibility of 48 start dates a year.

Students also need real-time support to keep them on track. Predictive 11 analytic technology allows the college to monitor online student engagement and predict by the eighth day of class the level of success students will have in a course. When needed, instructors facilitate interventions to minimize risks and support successful course completion.

Building a culture of unified support focused on completion won't hap- 12 pen overnight. It took 30 years for Rio Salado to get to this point. Our upside-down faculty model has made it possible for the college to adapt a corporate "systems approach," and all Rio Salado staff and faculty participate in a training program to instill a unified commitment to helping students complete their degree programs.

Technical Challenges

Staying ahead of the online curve comes with its share of challenges. Rio Salado 13 had to build its own learning management system because there wasn't one available that would support all of the features that our faculty and students wanted. In partnership with Microsoft and Dell, RioLearn was designed to be scalable to more than 100,000 students.

However, a few years ago, it didn't fully support Mac users. Although stu- 14 dents could access their coursework, they had to switch Internet browsers to do so. A new version of RioLearn was launched in 2010 to help students access their courses, regardless of the platform they are using.

225

We've also learned that many of our students are co-enrolled in traditional 15
colleges and universities. They come to Rio Salado for flexibility, affordability,
and convenience to accelerate their degree on their terms. They bank credits and
ultimately transfer those credits to complete their degrees at another institution.

A recent report examines Rio Salado's efforts and the experience and per- 16
spectives of more than 30 institutions throughout the U.S. addressing similar
challenges to ensure student success—especially for low-income, minority,
and adult students—and pursuing promising approaches to increase college
completion rates.

Reimagining the System

Our country can't continue to allow millions of people who are college mate- 17
rial to fall through the cracks. We must find new, convenient, and high-quality
educational options for students who might
otherwise have missed out on a college education. That means serving more students in
more places—especially where college enrollments have been capped—through efforts
such as online early college initiatives, by cre-
ating cohorts at the high-school level and developing open-source courses.

> "We must find new, convenient, and high-quality educational options for students."

With tuition rising faster than the rate of inflation, and the best-paying jobs 18
requiring some form of postsecondary degree, specialized certification, or licen-
sure, we have to find solutions that lower costs for students. We need to innovate. We need new models of education to leverage public resources through
private and public partnerships and increase the capacity to serve nontraditional
students through productive and cost-efficient means.

It's encouraging to see the rapid growth in affordable online learning. It 19
has broken down the barriers of time, distance, and affordability without sacrificing high-quality academics. But shoring up its credibility and value for
students means heeding some of the lessons learned over the past 15 years.
The stakes for getting it right are certainly high and getting higher.

⊘ AT ISSUE: SOURCES FOR USING ALTERNATIVE APPROACHES TO ARGUMENT

1. According to Bustamante, "[T]here is healthy skepticism about the proliferation of online learning" (para. 4). What does he mean? What reservations, if any, do you have about the rise of online education?

2. In this essay, where does the claim appear? How is this claim quali-fied? How does the qualifier set up the rest of the essay?

3. Bustamante's article focuses on the development of one school's online education program. Do you think the risks and rewards he dis-cusses also apply to other schools' online offerings? What factors might account for any differences in other schools' experiences with online learning?

4. What is Bustamante's purpose? What does he want readers to take away from his essay?

5. Does Bustamante ever address opposing arguments? If he does, where? If he does not, should he have addressed them? Explain.

6. What does Bustamante mean when he says that we must reimagine the system of higher education? What problems does he see with the current educational system? How will online education help solve these problems?

This essay was published in the *Daily Nebraskan*, the student newspaper of the University of Nebraska, on November 29, 2011.

RELIANCE ON ONLINE MATERIALS HINDERS LEARNING POTENTIAL FOR STUDENTS

DAVID SMITH

Students of today should be thankful for the . . . plethora of ways available for them to learn. Compared to our grandparents, parents, and even older siblings, we have access to modes of communication and education that would not have been possible even 10 years ago. 1

Students today, not just in college but in high school, middle school, and elementary school, take in and process astounding amounts of information on a daily basis. We have access to TV and the Internet, social media outlets such as Twitter and Facebook, and a nearly inexhaustible supply of ways to keep in contact with and learn about one another. 2

This variety has begun to work its way into academia, as well; more and more, it seems, organized instruction is moving beyond the classroom and into cyberspace. Pencils and paper, once the sole staples of the educational experience, are slowly being ousted by keyboards, webcams, and online dropboxes. 3

Here at the University of Nebraska–Lincoln, this growing prevalence is easy to see. Just look at Blackboard and how some courses are completely dependent upon it. Blackboard has everything from grade tracking and homework assignments to the administration of quizzes and exams. 4

Look at MyRED, which now handles everything from class enrollment and scheduling to residence hall contracts and meal plans. 5

Look at things such as the Love Library's EBSCO search engine, which gives students access to a greater wealth of information than even the most practiced scholar would know what to do with, and online courses such as the Keller Plan, which allow students to complete coursework and earn credit without having to leave their dorm rooms. 6

> "While the Internet has certainly made learning easier, has it made it better?"

It's clear to even the most casual observer that taking in and processing information is far easier for the students of today than it was for the students of 100, 50, or even 10 years ago. 7

But it begs the question: While the Internet has certainly made learning easier, has it made it better? Not necessarily. 8

Think for a moment about the fundamental differences between a traditional course, taught in a classroom, and one conducted entirely via Blackboard's online services. 9

In the former, students are bound by structure and organization. They 10 must attend class on a regular basis or suffer the consequences, typically (though not always) complete regular homework assignments for points, and are constantly reminded of the work that needs to be done by the ever-present figure (or specter) of the professor.

Such is not the case with classes taken outside the classroom. The 11 instructions for such courses are, at least in my experience, pared down to the following: "Read this by this date, this by this date, and this by this date. There are quizzes on Day X, Day Y, and Day Z, and the final exam can be taken at any time during finals week in the testing center. Have a nice semester."

Now, I know that college is supposed to be a place of greater expectations, 12 of increased responsibilities and better time management skills. I get that, I really do. But the sad truth is that all too often, giving a student that kind of freedom doesn't end well.

By removing the sense of structure from a course, you remove the stu- 13 dent's notion that he or she is under any sort of pressure, any sort of time constraint. By removing a constantly present instructor, you remove what is, in many cases, the sole source of motivation students have to do well in a class. You take away the sense of urgency, the sense of immediate requirement, and by extension the student's drive.

Readings are put off or forgotten, material review sessions (if there are 14 any) are blown off or missed, and quizzes and exams are ultimately bombed. More often than not, the student will get caught up with work from the other, more traditional courses on their schedule—the ones they remember they have homework in because it was assigned in class this afternoon or the ones they have to study for because the professor reminded them about the upcoming exam the other day. Unfortunately, another marked difference between traditional and online courses is that the latters are typically far less forgiving when it comes to things such as deadlines and extensions, making it next to impossible for students to get out of the holes they dig themselves into.

The Internet is a powerful tool. It allows us to share, distribute, and 15 absorb more information in a single year than our ancestors absorbed in a lifetime, and its capacity to do those things is constantly growing. What people, educators in particular, need to realize is that no matter how power-ful a tool it becomes, the Internet should never become anything more than that: a tool.

There will never be an adequate online substitute for the watchful eye 16 and the stern voice of a professor, or the pressure of an exam time limit that is about to expire, or the dismay and subsequent motivation to improve that can come from a handed-back assignment with a failing grade scrawled on it.

Now . . . off to class. 17

⊙ AT ISSUE: SOURCES FOR USING ALTERNATIVE APPROACHES TO ARGUMENT

1. Paragraph 8 expresses Smith's thesis in the form of a question and answer. Paraphrase this thesis statement in one sentence.

2. Why does Smith spend his first seven paragraphs discussing the amount of information currently available to students?

3. In paragraph 8, Smith says that his previous statement "begs the question." What does he mean? Is this statement actually an example of **begging the question**? Explain.

4. How, according to Smith, is online education different from classroom learning? What problems does Smith identify with online learning?

5. In paragraph 13, Smith says that online courses remove "the sense of structure from a course." What evidence does he present to support this statement?

6. What does Smith mean in paragraph 15 when he says that what we "need to realize is that no matter how powerful a tool it becomes, the Internet should never become anything more than that: a tool"? What is he warning against here?

7. Where does Smith use the techniques of Rogerian argument? Does he use these techniques often enough? Does he use them effectively? Explain.

8. In paragraph 16, Smith says, "There will never be an adequate online substitute for the watchful eye and the stern voice of a professor." Do you agree? Do you think this highlights a disadvantage of online education (as Smith intends) or an advantage?

This essay is from the October 9, 2011, edition of the *Daily Trojan*, the student newspaper of the University of Southern California.

ONLINE EDUCATION NEEDS CONNECTION

ELENA KADVANY

From the most trivial of issues (who went to what party this weekend?) to the most traditional of society's establishments (newspapers, music and book industries, Postal Service), the Internet has transformed our lives. But one area remains to be revolutionized digitally: education. 1

Online education is on the rise, pitting those who support the idea of a virtual university for its ability to increase access and revenue against those who believe there is no substitute for real-time, traditional educational experiences. 2

There's one thing wrong with the entire conversation, however: Viewing online education as a new higher-education business model that must supplant the current system is a close-minded view. Why not look at it as a means by which we can strengthen and innovate education by blending digital and traditional elements? 3

Online education began mostly as distance-learning programs for graduate degrees that lend themselves to the medium like engineering or business. 4

USC's Viterbi School of Engineering has a well-established Distance Education Network that offers more than 30 master's degree programs. 5

Now, in times of financial crisis, schools across the country, especially in California, are searching for ways to reinvent themselves. This has led to an expansion of digital courses into the undergraduate sphere. 6

But there is a distinct danger in allowing finance-driven ideas to dominate the dialogue about schools' futures and education in general, especially for undergraduates whose educational experiences and life tracks are so defined by their first four years on a campus. 7

> "[T]here is a distinct danger in allowing finance-driven ideas to dominate."

This is not to say that universities should completely reject online learning. It's great to be able to listen to lectures at home or gain access to classes you can't physically attend or afford. 8

Higher learning, however, is about a level of personal interaction and commitment that can't be re-created online. 9

Before transferring to USC, I spent a semester at the University of San Francisco, where I took a hybrid service-learning Spanish class. It combined conventional in-class instruction twice a week with a once-a-week class online with Blackboard, in addition to a requirement of outside community service hours. 10

231

This kind of blending shows the innovative potential universities should 11 recognize and seize. The idea of a virtual university should not replace the traditional, but instead should merge with it.

For undergraduates, hybrid classes could be incredibly valuable and much 12 more engaging for a generation that spends so much time online.

Some of the University of California schools have submitted courses in 13 response to an online education pilot project proposed by the University's Office of the President.

Sebastian Thrun, a professor at Stanford University renowned for leading 14 the team that built Google's self-driving car, now offers a free online course, "Introduction to Artificial Intelligence." Enrollment in this class has jumped from 58,000 to 130,000 across the world in the past month, according to the *New York Times*. USC is lucky enough to have generous alumni that keep it more than afloat financially. But as many universities choose to go digital, USC might want to follow suit.

The potential of all things online is vast. And there's no match for the 15 value of real-time, person-to-person educational experiences.

There's no reason universities can't take advantage of both. 16

⊘ AT ISSUE: SOURCES FOR USING ALTERNATIVE APPROACHES TO ARGUMENT

1. In paragraph 2, Kadvany says that online education pits those who support virtual education against those who support traditional classroom education. Do the essays in this At Issue section confirm or challenge Kadvany's point? Explain.

2. In paragraph 3, Kadvany says that it is wrong to view online education as a "higher-education business model" that will displace classroom education. Why does she use the term "business model"? Does she expect this term to have positive or negative connotations for her readers? How can you tell?

3. How has the financial crisis helped to promote the idea of online education? According to Kadvany, what is the danger of letting "finance-driven ideas" (para. 7) dominate the conversation about education?

4. In paragraph 9, Kadvany says that the personal interaction and commitment that characterize higher learning "can't be re-created online." What evidence does she present to support this statement? How convincing is this evidence? What additional evidence could she have used?

5. Does Kadvany ever use the techniques of Rogerian argument? If so, where? If not, should she have used them?

This essay is from the December 14, 2011, edition of the *MetroWest Daily News.*

SHORT DISTANCE LEARNING

JOHN CRISP

The end of the semester at my college always inclines me toward reflection, 1
relief, and mild melancholy. I suspect my students feel the same way, with
more inclination, perhaps, toward relief. Five classes have met with me about
30 times each over the course of 15 weeks, five communities of individuals
that materialize, coalesce, and disperse in a few months.

Whatever its merits, I've never developed 2
much enthusiasm for online learning. Its
proponents contend that a community of
learners can develop among students scattered
by geography but connected by the Internet,
and I'm not in a position to say they're wrong.

> "I've never developed much enthusiasm for online learning."

In fact, my purpose isn't to disparage online education. Along with the 3
trend toward a part-time professoriate, the proliferation of online education is
probably the most prominent tendency in higher education during the last
decade.

Still, I prefer the face-to-face classroom, which seems to me to preserve a 4
fine touch of humanity that warrants reflection during this week of final
exams.

Who was in my classes this semester? Many are traditional students, fresh 5
from high school and on their way to a four-year college or university, after a
sojourn at my community college. Many are bright, capable, and articulate.
Others are shy and reserved. A few are sullen or downright surly. But they're
not always my most interesting students.

Consider the young woman who, a decade after high school, finds herself 6
slogging through a developmental writing course before she can even attempt
freshman composition. Pardon the cliché, but sometimes you do see a light go
on in a student. She begins to listen to her instructor's and classmates' every
word, to take notes and to think, to become absorbed in her writing, which
over the course of the semester really does get better.

It doesn't always work like that, by any means. Other students are tak- 7
ing my developmental writing class for the second or third time. I like
them, but they miss too much class. Some of them have tattoos that betray
their gangbanger history; some have been thieves and some have been in
prison. And how well can you learn to write amid the violence and futility
in the barrio?

Many of them say that's all in the past now, and I believe them. Will they 8
pass this semester? I'm not sure. If they don't, what will become of them?

Momentous life passages occurred as the classes proceeded: At least two ⁹ women in my five classes this semester were pregnant and one gave birth. Two students died. One young man, a veteran who had survived tours in Iraq and Afghanistan, was killed in the second week of the semester, hit by a car while out for his morning jog.

In mid-semester, a young woman in the same class lost control of her car ¹⁰ on the way home from school and died in a one-vehicle rollover. When I told the class the next week that she wouldn't be coming back, there were some tears. So we learned about more than just writing this semester.

A middle-aged woman expressed conservative religious beliefs then ¹¹ admitted that she spent two years in prison for marijuana possession. Several veterans can't sleep at night and some of them drink too much. A young man came to class so depressed that I took him to one of the college's counselors, and he never came back.

Another young man and a young woman sat on opposite sides of the class ¹² and never spoke up or spoke to anyone else. Then they began to sit together and talk to each other. A lot. Now I occasionally see them around the campus together. Does that happen in online classes?

In short, it's all there, a rich mixture of human experiences in one ephem- ¹³ eral microcosm: birth, mating, sickness, death, frustration, laughter, story-telling, aspiration, failure, and learning.

Good luck, students; the pleasure was mine. ¹⁴

⊙ AT ISSUE: SOURCES FOR USING ALTERNATIVE APPROACHES TO ARGUMENT

1. Where does Crisp attempt to establish his credibility? How effective is this appeal to *ethos*?

2. To whom is Crisp addressing his argument? Teachers? Students? Parents? Administrators? Others? How do you know?

3. In paragraph 3, Crisp says that his purpose "isn't to disparage online education." What is his purpose?

4. In paragraph 4, Crisp says that he prefers traditional classroom instruction because it preserves "a fine touch of humanity." What does he mean? What evidence does he present in paragraphs 5–12 to support this point? How convincing is this evidence?

5. Draw a **rhetorical triangle** (p. 19) that represents the relative importance of the various appeals in this essay. Which appeal does the longest side of the triangle represent? Which does the shortest side represent? Do you think this is a good balance?

6. In paragraph 2, Crisp briefly addresses an opposing argument. Does he accurately characterize the case for online learning? Should he have spent more time addressing opposing arguments?

7. Crisp ends his essay with a single sentence. Is this sentence an effective concluding statement? Why or why not?

8. Suppose Crisp wanted to present his ideas in a speech. What parts of his essay would you suggest he expand? What parts would you advise him to condense or delete? What visuals would you suggest he include?

This article was originally published in *Liberal Education* in the Fall 2013 issue.

A PLEA FOR CLOSE LEARNING

SCOTT L. NEWSTOK

"At the School" (1910), French postcard envisioning learning in the year 2000. Private Collection © Look and Learn/Bridgeman Images.

What an exciting year for distance learning! Cutting-edge communication 1 systems allowed universities to escape the tired confines of face-to-face education. Bold new technologies made it possible for thousands of geographically dispersed students to enroll in world-class courses.

Innovative assessment mechanisms let professors supervise their pupils 2 remotely. All this progress was good for business, too. Private entrepreneurs leapt at the chance to compete in the new distance-learning marketplace, while Ivy League universities bustled to keep pace.

True, a few naysayers fretted about declining student attention spans and 3 low course-completion rates. But who could object to the expansively democratic goal of bringing first-rate education to more people than ever before? The new pedagogical tools promised to be not only more affordable than traditional classes, but also more effective at measuring student progress. In the words of one prominent expert, the average distance learner "knows more of the subject, and knows it better, than the student who has covered the same ground in the classroom." Indeed, "the day is coming when the work done [via distance learning] will be greater in amount than that done in the class-rooms of our colleges." The future of education was finally here.

2013, right? Think again: 1885. The commentator quoted above was Yale classicist (and future University of Chicago President) William Rainey Harper, evaluating *correspondence courses*. That's right: you've got (snail) mail. Journalist Nicholas Carr has chronicled the recurrent boosterism about mass mediated education over the last century: the phonograph, instructional radio, televised lectures. All were heralded as transformative educational tools in their day. This should give us pause as we recognize that massive open online courses, or MOOCs, are but the latest iteration of distance learning.

> "This should give us pause as we recognize that massive open online courses, or MOOCs, are but the latest iteration of distance learning."

In response to the current enthusiasm for MOOCs, skeptical faculty (Aaron Bady, Ian Bogost, and Jonathan Rees, among many others) have begun questioning venture capitalists eager for new markets and legislators eager to dismantle public funding for American higher education. Some people pushing for MOOCs, to their credit, speak from laudably egalitarian impulses to provide access for disadvantaged students. *But to what are they being given access?* Are broadcast lectures and online discussions the sum of a liberal education? Or is it something more than "content" delivery?

"Close Learning"

To state the obvious: there's a personal, human element to liberal education, what John Henry Newman once called "the living voice, the breathing form, the expressive countenance" (2001, 14). We who cherish personalized instruction would benefit from a pithy phrase to defend and promote this millennia-tested practice. I propose that we begin calling it *close learning*, a term that evokes the laborious, time-consuming, and costly but irreplaceable proximity between teacher and student. Close learning exposes the stark deficiencies of mass distance learning, such as MOOCs, and its haste to reduce dynamism, responsiveness, presence.

Techno-utopians seem surprised that "blended" or "flipped" classrooms—combining out-of-class media with in-person discussions—are more effective than their online-only counterparts, or that one-on-one tutoring strengthens the utility of MOOCs. In spite of all the hype about interactivity, "lecturing" à la MOOCs merely extends the cliché of the static, one-sided lecture hall, where distance learning begins after the first row. As the philosopher Scott Samuelson (2013) suggests, "The forces driving online education, particularly MOOCs, aren't moving us toward close learning. We should begin by recognizing that close learning is the goal and then measure all versions of our courses by that standard. Many giant lecture-hall courses are going to be found wanting, as will many online courses, and all (or almost all) MOOCs. In the end, we're still going to need a lot of face-to-face learning if we want to promote close learning."

237

The old-fashioned Socratic seminar is where we actually find interactive 8 learning and open-ended inquiry. In the close learning of the live seminar, spontaneity rules. Both students and teachers are always at a crossroads, collaboratively deciding where to go and where to stop; how to navigate and how to detour; and how to close the distance between a topic and the people discussing it. For the seminar to work, certain limits are required (most centrally, a limit in size). But these finite limits enable the infinity of questioning that is close learning. MOOCs claim to abolish those limits, while they paradoxically reinstate them. Their naïve model assumes that there is always total transparency, that passively seeing (watching a lecture or a virtual simulation) is learning.

A Columbia University neuroscientist, Stuart Firestein, recently published a 9 polemical book titled *Ignorance: How It Drives Science*. Discouraged by students regurgitating his lectures without internalizing the complexity of scientific inquiry, Firestein created a seminar to which he invited his colleagues to discuss what they don't know. As Firestein repeatedly emphasizes, it is informed ignorance, not information, that is the genuine "engine" of knowledge. His seminar reminds us that mere data transmission from teacher to student doesn't produce liberal learning. It's the ability to interact, to think hard thoughts alongside other people.

In a seminar, a student can ask for clarification, and challenge a teacher; a 10 teacher can shift course when spirits are flagging; a stray thought can spark a new insight. Isn't this the kind of nonconformist "thinking outside the box" that business leaders adore? So why is there such a rush to freeze knowledge and distribute it in a frozen form? Even Coursera cofounder Andrew Ng concedes that the real value of a college education "isn't just the content. . . . The real value is the interactions with professors and other, equally bright students" (quoted in Oremus 2012).

The business world recognizes the virtues of proximity in its own human 11 resource management. (The phrase "corporate campus" acknowledges as much.) Witness, for example, Yahoo's controversial decision to eliminate telecommuting and require employees to be present in the office. CEO Marissa Mayer's memo reads as a mini-manifesto for close learning: "To become the absolute best place to work, communication and collaboration will be important, so we need to be working side-by-side. That is why it is critical that we are all present in our offices. Some of the best decisions and insights come from hallway and cafeteria discussions, meeting new people, and impromptu team meetings. Speed and quality are often sacrificed when we work from home. We need to be one Yahoo!, and that starts with physically being together" (quoted in Swisher 2013).

Why do boards of directors still go through the effort of convening in 12 person? Why, in spite of all the fantasies about "working from anywhere" are "creative classes" still concentrating in proximity to one another: the entertainment industry in Los Angeles, information technology in the Bay Area, financial capital in New York City? The powerful and the wealthy are well aware that computers can accelerate the exchange of information and facilitate "training," but not the development of knowledge, much less wisdom.

Close learning transcends disciplines. In every field, students must incline 13 toward their subjects: leaning into a sentence, to craft it most persuasively; leaning into an archival document, to determine an uncertain provenance; leaning into a musical score, to poise the body for performance; leaning into a data set, to discern emerging patterns; leaning into a laboratory instrument, to interpret what is viewed. MOOCs, in contrast, encourage students and faculty to lean back, not to cultivate the disciplined attention necessary to engage fully in a complex task. Low completion rates for MOOCs (still hovering around 10 percent) speak for themselves.

Technology as Supplement

Devotion to close learning should not be mistaken for an anti-technology 14
stance. (Contrary to a common misperception, the original Luddites simply wanted machines that made high-quality goods, run by trained workers who were adequately compensated.) I teach Shakespeare, supposedly one of the mustiest of topics. Yet my students navigate the vast resources of the Internet, evaluate recorded performances, wrestle with facsimiles of original publications, listen to pertinent podcasts, survey decades of scholarship in digitized form, circulate their drafts electronically, explore the cultural topography of early modern London, and contemplate the historical richness of the English language. Close learning is entirely compatible with engaging in meaningful conversations outside the classroom: faculty can correspond regularly with students via e-mail and keep in close contact via all kinds of new media. But this is all in service of close learning, and the payoff comes in the classroom.

Teachers have always employed "technology"—including the book, one 15
of the most flexible and dynamic learning technologies ever created. But let's not fixate upon technology for technology's sake, or delude ourselves into thinking that better technology overcomes bad teaching. At no stage of education does technology, no matter how novel, ever replace human attention. Close learning can't be automated or scaled up.

As retrograde as it might sound, gathering humans in a room with real 16
time for dialogue still matters. As educators, we must remind ourselves—not to mention our legislators, our boards, our administrators, our alumni, our students, and our students' parents—of the inescapable fact that our "product" is close learning. This is why savvy parents have always invested in intensive human interaction for their children. (Tellingly, parents from Silicon Valley deliberately restrict their children's access to electronic distractions, so that they might experience the free play of mind essential to human development.)

What remains to be seen is whether we value this kind of close learning at 17
all levels of education enough to defend it, and fund it, for a wider circle of Americans—or whether we will continue to permit the circle to contract, excluding a genuinely transformative intellectual experience from those without means. Proponents of distance education have always boasted that they provide access, but are they providing access to *close learning*?

References
Firestein, S. 2012. *Ignorance: How It Drives Science.* New York: Oxford University Press.

Newman, J. H. 2001. "What Is a University?" In *Rise and Progress of Universities and Benedictine Essays,* edited by M. K. Tilman, 6–17. Notre Dame, IN: University of Notre Dame Press.

Oremus, W. 2014. "The New Public Ivies: Will Online Education Startups like Coursera End the Era of Expensive Higher Education?" *Slate,* July 17, http://www.slate.com/articles/technology/future_tense/2012/07 /coursera_udacity_edx_will_free_online_ ivy_league_courses_end _the_era_of_expensive_ higher_ed_.html.

Swisher, K. 2013. " 'Physically Together': Here's the Internal Yahoo No-Work-from-Home Memo for Remote Workers and Maybe More." *AllThingsD,* February 22. http://allthingsd.com/20130222/physically -together-heres-the-internal-yahoo-no-work-from-home-memo-which -extends-beyond-remote-workers.

⊘ AT ISSUE: SOURCES FOR USING ALTERNATIVE APPROACHES TO ARGUMENT

1. What effect does Newstok want his introduction to have on readers? How can you tell? In your opinion, is his strategy successful?

2. In paragraph 5, Newstok asks whether an education "is something more than 'content' delivery." What does he mean?

3. According to Newstok, what is "close learning" (para. 6)? What are its advantages over online education?

4. Where does Newstok address the major arguments against his position? How effectively does he refute them?

5. Use Toulmin logic to analyze Newstok's essay, identifying the argument's claim, its grounds, and its warrant. Does Newstok appeal only to *logos*, or does he also appeal to *pathos* and *ethos*? Explain.

6. Is Newstok's argument primarily deductive or inductive? Why do you think that he chose this structure?

This essay originally appeared in the January 2013 issue of *Techniques*.

OLD FLAMES AND NEW BEACONS

RAY MCNULTY

A few years ago, I saw a video of a pop concert. It looked just like concerts of 1 my youth: a well-lit stage amid a darkened crowd flecked with small wavering lights. I laughed when I realized, however, that the swaying glow was coming not from cigarette lighters but from LCD screens.

This juxtaposition of old flames and new beacons reminds me of distance 2 learning. Once the realm of correspondence schools, whose matchbook cover advertisements promised the chance to learn from home, distance learning has evolved into myriad interactive opportunities that cater to the spectrum of learners' needs. Striking a match on the correspondence school model, technology has ignited a virtual wildfire of prospects for education.

Educators have long pondered the technology question. Most of their stu- 3 dents know nothing firsthand about, or can scarcely remember, a time before laptops and cellphones. Yet, though they recognize the value of technology, many educators still do not take full advantage of it in their teaching. They are flummoxed by what they perceive as an all-or-nothing choice. If they integrate virtual learning strategies,

> "They are flummoxed by what they perceive as an all-or-nothing choice."

will they work themselves into obsolescence? If they maintain the status quo, will they be able to fully engage students? These are understandable questions, but I do not believe the answer is mutually exclusive.

Light Sources

Emerging teaching models combine the best of classroom methods with the 4 litheness of online learning to offer more pathways to learning for more students. Three particularly strong new models of this ilk are gaining popularity in American education: flipped classroom, blended classroom, and supported distance learning. Technology-infused, these learning models suit all types of curricula, including career and technical education (CTE), which leads the way in applied learning by keeping current with technological advances across disciplines. They also echo CTE's core goal of providing learners with relevant skills and knowledge to prepare them for successful careers.

The flipped classroom model reverses the traditional lecture/application 5 cycle. Educators post recorded lectures online and assign digital materials to further students' understanding. Pre-class work by students frees teachers to focus class meetings on discussions to reinforce understanding and hands-on activities for practice in application. Continuous access to lectures supports rigor in learning by enabling students to review lessons, in whole or in part, as many times as needed to grasp content. Relevancy is heightened through increased opportunities for hands-on activities. Further, when students have greater responsibility for content, they practice essential skills, such as self-motivation and time management, which become additional assets for employability and career success.

The blended classroom model involves mixing in-class lectures with online assignments, giving students opportunities for both group and independent learning. Classroom and online activities are balanced depending on content and learning goals. This model works particularly well for large or especially diverse groups of learners because it supports differentiated instruction to ensure that all students not only meet expectations but are also stretched in their learning. 6

Supported distance learning—technology-delivered coursework with low or no classroom residency requirements—is education's fastest growing sector. The National Center for Education Statistics reports that between 2005 and 2010, distance learning course enrollment among American public high school students increased by 77 percent to 1.3 million students, representing 53 percent of public high school districts. An estimated 18 percent of undergraduates will enroll in distance learning for 80 percent or more of their coursework by 2013, according to coursehero.com. 7

Snuffing Out the Myths

The rising popularity of online learning models invites a hard look at the myths and realities of what these approaches offer. 8

First, there is the erroneous perception that distance learning is only for adults. Distance and hybrid learning options are relevant across levels, from high school to graduate to career advancement programs, and capture more nontraditional students. The flexibility appeals to learners for many reasons. Some are encouraged—sometimes subsidized—by employers, others are self-motivated for career entry, advancement, or change. Others are pursuing new dreams. Learners who struggle in traditional programs find that asynchronous delivery and other elements of distance learning allow them to eliminate obstacles and forge pathways to learning success. 9

A recent Penn Foster blog asked students for feedback about why they had chosen distance learning. Some responses were expected: people with jam-packed lives sought portability and flexibility, employers were paying the fees, and lower costs. Others revealed simple but important personal reasons. One student shared that fluorescent classroom lighting gave her headaches; working at home eliminated the issue. Many respondents mentioned that music—from classical to classic rock—helped them concentrate. Several posters were happy to leave behind noisy classrooms, social pressures, and bullying. For many students, learning had become joyful and purposeful instead of forced. 10

Another myth: when it comes to employability, online learning cre- 11
dentials are not valid or valuable. Every consumer service sector has highs
and lows in quality. Some remote courses are designed well and led by great
teachers; some are not. Some programs are accredited; others are not. Wise
students research options to ensure that courses or programs support their
academic needs and professional goals. Industries often work on content
development with reputable programs—traditional and online—to ensure
courses align with industry standards in many fields. Some top-rated companies now look to online learning to enhance employees' credentials
while keeping them engaged in the workforce. Employers also recognize
the value in skills required to successfully complete online programs, such
as self-motivation, task focus, ability to work independently, and time
management.

Then there is the idea that hybrid and distance learning work only for 12
purely "academic" subjects, not for courses or programs that require hands-on
time in labs, practicums, or internships for credentialing. A good example of
success in distance learning for a hands-on profession is Penn Foster's veteri-
nary technician program. Our vet tech students complete accredited coursework online with support from peers and advisors. When they are ready for
internships, an advisor helps connect them with an onsite learning position
with one of the school's many partners. The approach works: 100 percent of
Penn Foster's vet tech students have passed the independent credentialing
exams required for employment in the field.

The vet tech program debunks the notion that distance learners must go 13
it alone, without the valuable and vibrant dialog with teachers and peers or
well-appointed libraries and other learning resources available on traditional
campuses. Flipped and blended classrooms feature classroom or campus time,
so these concerns are irrelevant to those models.

Students enrolled in well-supported distance learning need not worry 14
about isolation either. Quality distance learning programs provide many
options for students to engage with peers and teachers through online forums,
via email, by phone, and, sometimes, in person with local classmates. In the
vet tech program, students regularly connect with peers in online forums, and
they work closely, if remotely, with advisors throughout the program, especially when it comes time to arrange for internships.

Tending to the Future

The go-it-alone myth strikes a chord with many educators. If students have 15
the main responsibility for their learning, what is the teacher's role? Changes
in teaching theory and practice do not change the qualities of a good teacher.
The most effective teachers are still those who are most inspired by the possibility and responsibility of helping to shape the future and who aspire to
inspire their students. Certainly, distance and hybrid learning models change
the educator's role, but they do not negate it. High-quality programs and

courses rely on good teachers who continually seek ways to engage all types of learners so they can succeed not only in the world they live in now, but also in the one they are only beginning to dream up.

Teaching distance or hybrid model classes is different, but it offers some unique advantages. 16

In distance learning, the biggest practical differences for teachers tend to be asynchronistic teaching cycles and limited (or no) face-to-face time. Because distance learners set their own pace, teachers may find they are working with more students concurrently than is possible in a classroom. Staggered learning timelines make this possible, and many educators enjoy simultaneously teaching various stages of their lessons rather than following a sequential path for a set term. Although in-person contact is reduced, there are many opportunities for one-to-one contact by phone and online. 17

Flipped and blended classrooms shift the educator's role from a "sage on the stage" to one of an applied learning coach. With students taking on more pre-class prep, educators have more time to facilitate discussions and hands-on activities. 18

One of the most exciting advantages these dynamic models have for teachers is the flexibility to explore "next practices," innovative and sometimes as-yet untested ideas that may (or may not) evolve into best practices. Next practices speak to the ideals of what education can accomplish, and these teaching models support the creativity educators need to think ahead to those ideals. 19

In fact, it's a bit like switching from cigarette lighters to LCD screens at a concert. The old flame was good in its time, but technology offers a new beacon. As an educator, how will you choose to light up learning? 20

⊙ AT ISSUE: SOURCES FOR USING ALTERNATIVE APPROACHES TO ARGUMENT

1. Explain the essay's title.

2. Regarding technology, how does McNulty characterize students? How does he characterize instructors? Based on your experiences, are these characterizations fair? Accurate? Explain.

3. Define the following terms that McNulty introduces in paragraph 4.

   - Flipped classroom

   - Blended classroom

   - Supported distance learning

   Why does he discuss these new models of instruction? How does his discussion prepare readers for the rest of his essay?

244

4. Much of this essay involves "snuffing out the myths" (para. 8) associated with online learning. What are these myths? How successfully does McNulty refute them?

5. Throughout his essay, McNulty uses headings. What is the purpose of these headings? Do they help readers, or do they just get in the way? Explain.

6. Who is McNulty's intended audience? How can you tell?

This piece first appeared online at HybridPedagogy.com on January 5, 2012.

TRADING CLASSROOM AUTHORITY FOR ONLINE COMMUNITY

PETE RORABAUGH

Early web commenters referred to the Internet as a primitive, lawless place like 1
the "Wild West." Plenty still needs to change to make certain parts of the web more civil and useful, but some aspect of the "Wild West" spirit is applicable to a discussion of student-directed learning. Too much civilization and society makes us compartmentalized and complacent. The West was a challenging place for European immigrants because it required an expansive sense of responsibility. You could no longer be just an apothecary or a cobbler. You had to provide for your own food and shelter from the resources around you; you had to decide just "what to do" with all this freedom.

Digital culture is having a similar effect on the practice of education, and that's 2
a good thing. Students have to own their learning more. They can't just follow the dotted line on the ground that leads to their assignment, their grade, their degree.

Consider four core values for the classroom in general and the online 3
classroom: **show up**, **be curious**, **collaborate**, and **contribute**. The online classroom is more student-directed in the sense that students are more "on their own" than they are in a traditional classroom. With more authors, contexts, and platforms to consider, digital media literacy insists that students filter, evaluate, and prioritize information with more critical proficiency than traditional students. Traditional students could trust the stability of the worksheet and the textbook. Digital education by its mere existence insists on more progressive practices for teachers and students. Digital culture has already started affecting dominant cultural epistemology° by shifting some focus away from experts and giving it to participants.

A type of philosophy focused on the study of knowledge

Students in the digital environment, whether in a hybrid or fully online 4
classroom, carry more responsibility for their own progress. To succeed, they have to monitor their own progress more directly, engage with the insights of their peers, and ponder the external relevance of their work. A revolution is growing online that takes this trend to an extreme—digital citizens are building educational communities without institutions. "Learning" no longer means, or needs to mean, "going to school." It can just mean developing good observation and critical thinking skills.

> "A revolution is growing online that takes this trend to an extreme—digital citizens are building educational communities without institutions."

What this means for the online classroom is twofold: **1.** We recognize and 5
communicate the shift from a follow-the-leader framework to a framework in

which the authority is more equally distributed between teacher and students. **2.** We have to model this new approach to learning in our classrooms (whether analog or digital). Students might be happy to see the culture of experts and talking heads dissolve, but if they want to be part of the revolution then they have to be ready to share the work that the experts used to do. For example, we might have students blogging publicly instead of submitting their work to the instructor as a one-to-one transaction. In this move, students become content creators, instead of content consumers—creators of their own educations instead of consumers—textbook creators instead of consumers.

Traditional classrooms, the ones inspired by factories, create ideal students 6 who follow instructions well. ("Changing Education Paradigms," a video from RSA animate, offers a cogent argument for this shift in thinking about education.) The web and digital culture create ideal citizens who investigate things "just because." These students reach for *Wikipedia* or Google Maps on their iPhones to get immediate clarification when they need help. Our online classrooms should harness this educational holster mentality. Don't understand something? Ask the class, email a group of professionals, call the company, interview your grandmother. And this is the beauty of digital and critical pedagogy; when it's done right, it connects us to each other and to the world.

◯ AT ISSUE: SOURCES FOR USING ALTERNATIVE APPROACHES TO ARGUMENT

1. Rorabaugh begins his essay by comparing the Internet to the Wild West. In what respects is this **analogy** valid? In what respects is it not?

2. Where in this essay does the claim appear? How is the claim qualified? How does the qualifier set up the rest of the essay?

3. Rorabaugh makes a number of statements that he assumes are self-evident. For example, in paragraph 2 he says that in the online classroom "[s]tudents have to own their learning more," and in paragraph 3 he says, "The online classroom is more student-directed." Identify other statements like these. Are they really self-evident, or do they require support?

4. Rorabaugh is clearly a supporter of online learning. Does this prevent him from seeing problems associated with online learning? Explain.

5. What preconceptions about online learning does Rorabaugh assume his readers have? How do you know?

6. Suppose Rorabaugh wanted to rewrite his essay as a Rogerian argument. What changes in his essay's tone and emphasis would he have to make?

TEMPLATE FOR WRITING A ROGERIAN ARGUMENT

Write a one-paragraph **Rogerian** argument in which you argue that the drawbacks of online education have to be addressed before it can be successful. Follow the template below, filling in the blanks to create your argument.

> With more and more students taking online courses, both the students and the colleges benefit. For example, _____
> _____
> _____. In addition, _____
> _____.
> However, online education does have some drawbacks. For instance, _____
> _____
> _____.
> These problems could be easily solved. First, _____
> _____. Second, _____
> _____.
> If these problems are addressed, both students and colleges would benefit because _____
> _____.

TEMPLATE FOR WRITING A TOULMIN ARGUMENT

Write a one-paragraph **Toulmin** argument in which you argue in favor of online education. Follow the template below, filling in the blanks to create your argument.

> Many colleges and universities have instituted online education programs. These programs are the best way _____ _____.
>
> If colleges are going to meet the rising demand for education, they _____ _____ _____.
>
> The online course I took _____ _____ _____.
>
> Recent studies show that _____ _____. In addition, _____ _____. However, some people argue that _____ _____ _____. They also say that _____ _____.
>
> These arguments _____ _____.
>
> For this reason, online education is _____ _____ _____.

⬢ EXERCISE 6.7

Discuss your ideas about online learning with one or two of your classmates. Consider both the strengths and the limitations of this method of teaching. What types of classes do you think it is best suited for? Which classes do you think it would not work for? Then, edit the Rogerian and Toulmin arguments that you wrote on the previous templates so that they include some of these comments.

⊜ EXERCISE 6.8

Write an argumentative essay on the topic, "Is Online Education Better Than Classroom Education?" Use the principles of either Rogerian argument or Toulmin logic to structure your essay. Cite sources in the Reading and Writing about the Issue section on pages 222–247, and be sure to document the sources you use and to include a works-cited page. (See Chapter 10 for information on documenting sources.)

⊜ EXERCISE 6.9

Review the four pillars of argument that are discussed in Chapter 1. Does your essay include all four elements of an effective argument? Add anything that is missing. Then, label the elements of your argument.

⊜ EXERCISE 6.10

Assume that you have been asked to present the information in the essay you wrote for Exercise 6.8 as an oral argument. What information would you include? What information would you eliminate? Find two or three visuals that you would use when you deliver your speech. Then, make an outline of your speech and indicate at what points you would display these visuals.

Writing an Argumentative Essay

free!

2014/2015
UC SANTA CRUZ

Campus Food & Garden Guide

Where to find sustainable food at UC Santa Cruz and discover ways to engage in your campus and community food system!

FOOD SYSTEMS WORKING GROUP

DINING HALLS • CAMPUS EATERIES • CAMPUS GARDENS • FOOD SYSTEMS RELATED ACADEMIC COURSES • STUDENT AND COMMUNITY ORGANIZATIONS • VOLUNTEER OPPORTUNITIES • STUDENT INTERNSHIPS & PROJECTS • FARMERS' MARKETS

9TH EDITION

7 Planning, Drafting, and Revising an Argumentative Essay

AT ISSUE

Should College Campuses Go Green?

In recent years, more and more American colleges and universities have become "green campuses," emphasizing **sustainability**—the use of systems and materials that will not deplete the earth's natural resources. Various schools have taken steps such as the following:

- Placing an emphasis on recycling and reducing nonbiodegradable waste

- Creating green buildings and using eco-friendly materials in construction projects

- Instituting new curricula in environmental science

- Monitoring their greenhouse gas emissions and evaluating their carbon footprint

- Growing crops on campus to feed students

- Hiring full-time "sustainability directors"

- Encouraging students to use bikes instead of cars

- Purchasing wind-generated electricity to supply the campus's energy

- Eliminating trays in college cafeterias

Although many schools have launched ambitious programs and projects to reduce their energy dependence, some have been more cautious, citing the high cost of such programs and the need to allocate resources elsewhere. Moreover, some critics of the green movement object to the notion that colleges should help to make students "sustainability literate." Such critics consider the green movement to be an expression of political correctness that at best does no more than pay lip service to the problem and at worst threatens academic freedom by furthering a political agenda.

The question remains whether the green movement that is spreading rapidly across college campuses is here to stay or just a fad—or something between these two extremes. This chapter takes you through the process of writing an argumentative essay on the topic of whether college campuses should go green. (Exercises guide you through the process of writing your own argumentative essay on a topic of your choice.)

Before you can write a convincing argumentative essay, you need to understand the **writing process**. You are probably already familiar with the basic outline of this process, which includes *planning, drafting,* and *revising.* This chapter reviews this familiar process and explains how it applies to the specific demands of writing an argument.

Choosing a Topic

The first step in planning an argumentative essay is to choose a topic you can write about. Your goal is to select a topic that you have some emotional stake in—not simply one that interests you. If you are going to spend hours planning, writing, and revising an essay, then you should care about your topic. At the same time, you should be able to keep an open mind about your topic and be willing to consider various viewpoints. Your topic also should be narrow enough to fit the boundaries of your assignment—the time you have to work on the essay and its length and scope.

Typically, your instructor will give you a general assignment, such as the following.

> **Assignment**
> Write a three- to five-page argumentative essay on a topic related to college services, programs, facilities, or curricula.

The first thing you need to do is narrow this general assignment to a topic, focusing on one particular campus service, program, facility, or curriculum. You could choose to write about any number of topics—financial aid, the writing center, athletics, the general education curriculum—taking a position, for example, on who should receive financial aid, whether to expand the mission of the writing center, whether college athletes should receive a salary, or why general education requirements are important for business majors.

If you are interested in the environment, however, you might decide to write about the green movement that is spreading across college campuses, perhaps using your observations of your own campus's programs and policies to support your position.

> **Topic**
> The green movement on college campuses

TOPICS TO AVOID

Certain kinds of topics are not appropriate for argumentative essays. For one thing, some topics are just not arguable. For example, you could not write an argumentative essay on a statement of fact, such as the fact that many colleges saw their endowments decline after the financial crisis of 2008. (A fact is not debatable, so there can be no argument.)

Some familiar topics also present problems. These issues—the death penalty, abortion rights, and so on—are important (after all, that's why they are written about so often), but finding an original argument on either side of the debate can be a challenge. For example, you might have a hard time finding something new to say that would convince some readers that the death penalty is immoral or that abortion is a woman's right. In many people's minds, these issues are "settled." When you write on topics such as these, some readers' strong religious or cultural beliefs are likely to prevent them from considering your arguments, however well supported they might be.

Finally, topics that are very narrow or depend on subjective value judgments—or that take a stand on issues readers simply will not care much about, such as whether one particular video game or TV reality show is more entertaining than another—are unlikely to engage your audience (even if these topics are compelling to you and your friends).

⊖ EXERCISE 7.1

In response to the boxed assignment on the previous page, list ten topics that you could write about. Then, cross out any that do not meet the following criteria:

- The topic interests you.

- You know something about the topic.

- You care about the topic.

- You are able to keep an open mind about the topic.

- The topic fits the boundaries of your assignment.

Now, choose one topic to write an essay about.

For more practice, see the LearningCurve on Recognizing Topics and Main Ideas in the LaunchPad for *Practical Argument*.

Thinking about Your Topic

Before you can start to do research, develop a thesis statement, or plan the structure of your argument, you need to think a bit about the topic you have chosen. You can use *invention strategies,* such as **freewriting** (writing without stopping for a predetermined time), **brainstorming** (making quick notes on your topic), or **clustering** (creating a diagram to map out your thoughts) to help you discover ideas you might write about. You can also explore ideas in a writing journal or in conversations with friends, classmates, family members, or instructors.

Freewriting

> People say green is good, but I'm not sure why. Do we really need a separate, smelly container for composting? Won't the food decompose just as fast in a landfill? In middle school, we learned about the "three Rs" to save the environment—one was Recycle, but I forget the other two. Renew? Reuse? Remember? Whatever. OK, I know not to throw trash on the ground, and I know we're supposed to separate trash and recycling, etc. I get that. But does all this time and effort really do any good?

Brainstorming

Clustering

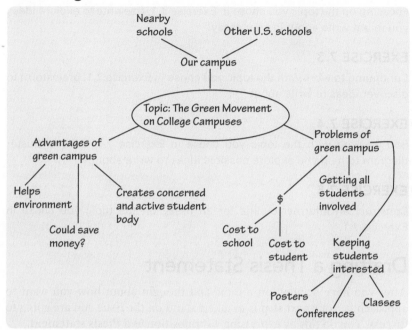

When you finish exploring ideas, you should be able to construct a quick **informal outline** that lists the ideas you plan to discuss.

Informal Outline

Topic: The Green Movement on College Campuses
    History/background
        National
        Our campus
    Positive aspects
        Helps environment
        Attracts new students
    Negative aspects
        Cost
        Enforcement
    Future

By grouping your ideas and arranging them in a logical order, an informal outline like the one above can help lead you to a thesis statement that expresses the position you will take on the issue.

⊙ EXERCISE 7.2

Focusing on the topic you chose in Exercise 7.1, freewrite to explore ideas you might write about in your essay.

⊙ EXERCISE 7.3

Continuing to work with the topic you chose in Exercise 7.1, brainstorm to discover ideas to write about.

⊙ EXERCISE 7.4

Still working with the topic you chose in Exercise 7.1, draw a cluster diagram to help you explore possible ideas to write about.

⊙ EXERCISE 7.5

Construct an informal outline for an essay on the topic you chose in Exercise 7.1.

Drafting a Thesis Statement

After you have decided on a topic and thought about how you want to approach it, your next step is to take a stand on the issue you are going to discuss. You do this by expressing your position as a **thesis statement**.

A thesis statement is the central element of any argumentative essay. It tells readers what your position is and perhaps also indicates why you are taking this position and how you plan to support it. As you draft your thesis statement, keep the following guidelines in mind:

- An argumentative thesis statement is not simply a statement of your topic; rather, it expresses the point you will make about your topic.

  TOPIC   The green movement on college campuses

  THESIS STATEMENT   College campuses should go green.

- An argumentative thesis statement should be specific, clearly indicating to readers exactly what position you will take in your essay.

  TOO GENERAL   Colleges need to do more to get students involved in environmental issues.

  REVISED   Colleges should institute programs and classes to show students the importance of using sustainable resources.

- An argumentative thesis statement should get right to the point, avoiding wordy, repetitive language.

WORDY	Because issues that revolve around the environment are so crucial and important, colleges should do more to increase student involvement in campus projects that are concerned with sustainability.
REVISED	Because environmental issues are so important, colleges should take steps to involve students in campus sustainability projects.

■ Many argumentative thesis statements include words such as *should* and *should not*.

- College campuses should _____.
- Because _____, colleges should _____.
- Even though _____, colleges should not _____.

> **NOTE**
>
> At this point, any thesis that you come up with is tentative. As you think about your topic and as you read about it, you will very likely modify your thesis statement, perhaps expanding or narrowing its scope, rewording it to make it more precise, or even changing your position. Still, the thesis statement that you decide on at this point can help you focus your exploration of your topic.

TENTATIVE THESIS STATEMENT

College campuses should go green.

⊘ EXERCISE 7.6

List five possible thesis statements for the topic you chose in Exercise 7.1. (To help you see your topic in several different ways, you might experiment by drafting at least one thesis statement that evaluates, one that considers causes and/or effects, and one that proposes a solution to a problem.) Which thesis statement seems most promising for your essay? Why?

Understanding Your Purpose and Audience

When you write an argument, your primary purpose is to convince your audience to accept your position. Sometimes you will have other goals as well. For example, you might want to change readers' ideas about an issue, perhaps by challenging a commonly held assumption, or even to move readers to take some action in support of your position.

To make the best possible case to your audience, you need to understand who your audience is—what knowledge, values, beliefs, and opinions your readers might have. You will also need to have some idea whether your audience is likely to be receptive, hostile, or neutral to the ideas you propose.

In most cases, it makes sense to assume that your readers are receptive but **skeptical**—that they have open minds but still need to be convinced. However, if you are writing about a topic that is very controversial, you will need to assume that at least some of your readers will not support your position and may, in fact, be hostile to it. If this is the case, they will be scrutinizing your arguments very carefully, looking for opportunities to argue against them. Your goal in this case is not necessarily to win readers over but to make them more receptive to your position—or at least to get them to admit that you have made a good case even though they may disagree with you. At the same time, you also have to work to convince those who probably agree with you or those who are neutral (perhaps because the issue you are discussing is something they haven't thought much about).

An audience of first-year college students who are used to the idea that sound environmental practices make sense might find the idea of a green campus appealing—and, in fact, natural and obvious. An audience of faculty or older students might be more skeptical, realizing that the benefits of green practices might be offset by the time and expense they could involve. College administrators might find the long-term goal of a green campus attractive (and see it as a strong recruitment tool), but they might also be somewhat hostile to your position, anticipating the considerable expense that would be involved. If you wrote an argument on the topic of green campuses, you would need to consider these positions—and, if possible, address them.

⊘ EXERCISE 7.7

Consider how different audiences might respond to the thesis statement you found the most promising in Exercise 7.6. Identify five possible groups of readers on your college campus—for example, athletes, history majors, or part-time faculty. Would you expect each group to be receptive, hostile, or neutral to your position? Why?

 LaunchPad   For more practice, see the LearningCurve on
macmillan learning   Topic, Purpose, and Audience in the Launch-
Pad for *Practical Argument*.

Gathering Evidence

After you have a sense of who your audience will be and how these readers might react to your thesis, you can begin to collect **evidence** to support your thesis. As you look for evidence, you need to evaluate the usefulness and relevance of each of your sources, and you need to be alert for possible bias.

Evaluating the Evidence in Your Sources

As you read each potential source, consider the quality of the supporting evidence that the writer marshals to support his or her position. The more compelling the evidence, the more willing you should be to accept the writer's ideas—and, perhaps, to integrate these ideas into your own essay.

> **NOTE**
>
> Don't forget that if you use any of your sources' ideas, you must document them. See Chapter 10 for information on MLA documentation format and Appendix B for information on APA documentation format.

To be convincing, the evidence that is presented in the sources you review should be *accurate, relevant, representative,* and *sufficient:*

- **Accurate** evidence comes from reliable sources that are quoted carefully—and not misrepresented by being quoted out of context.

- **Relevant** evidence applies specifically (not just tangentially) to the topic under discussion.

- **Representative** evidence is drawn from a fair range of sources, not just those that support the writer's position.

- **Sufficient** evidence is enough facts, statistics, expert opinion, and so on to support the essay's thesis.

(For more detailed information on evaluating sources, see Chapter 8.)

> **NOTE**
>
> Remember, the evidence you use to support your own arguments should also satisfy the four criteria listed above.

Detecting Bias in Your Sources

As you select sources, you should be alert for **bias**—a writer's use of preconceived ideas (rather than factual evidence) as support for his or her arguments. A writer who demonstrates bias may not be trustworthy, and you should approach such a writer's arguments with skepticism. To determine whether a writer is biased, follow these guidelines:

- *Consider what a writer explicitly tells you* about his or her beliefs or opinions. For example, if a writer mentions that he or she is a lifelong member of the Sierra Club, a vegan, and the owner of a house heated by solar energy, then you should consider the possibility that he or she might downplay (or even disregard) valid arguments against a green campus rather than presenting a balanced view.

- *Look for slanted language.* For example, a writer who mocks supporters of environmental issues as *politically correct* or uses pejorative terms such as *hippies* for environmentalists should not earn your trust.

- *Consider the supporting evidence* the writer chooses. Does the writer present only examples that support his or her position and ignore valid opposing arguments? Does the writer quote only those experts who agree with his or her position—for example, only pro- (or only anti-) environmental writers? A writer who does this is presenting an unbalanced (and therefore biased) case.

- *Consider the writer's tone.* A writer whose tone is angry, bitter, or sarcastic should be suspect.

- *Consider any overtly offensive statements or characterizations* that a writer makes. A writer who makes negative assumptions about college students (for example, characterizing them as selfish and self-involved and therefore dismissing their commitment to campus environmental projects) should be viewed with skepticism.

> **NOTE**
>
> Be aware of any biases you hold that might affect the strength or logic of your own arguments. See "Being Fair," page 268.

⊙ EXERCISE 7.8

What evidence might you use to support the thesis statement you decided on in Exercise 7.6?

⊙ EXERCISE 7.9

In writing an essay that supports the thesis statement you have been working with in this chapter, you might find it difficult to remain objective. What biases do you have that you might have to watch for as you research and write about your topic?

⊙ EXERCISE 7.10

Gather evidence to support your thesis statement, evaluating each source carefully (consulting Chapter 8 as necessary). Be on the lookout for bias in your sources.

> ## USING ANALOGIES AS EVIDENCE
>
> An **analogy** is an extended comparison between two items, situations, or concepts on the basis of a number of shared characteristics. This kind of comparison explains a difficult or unfamiliar concept in terms of something more familiar. **Argument by analogy** is a strategy that makes the case that a position about an issue is valid because it is analogous to a comparable position on another issue—a position you expect your readers to accept. For example, you could develop a comparison between the relatively recent green campus movement and the earlier movement to make campuses fully accessible for students with disabilities.
>
> However, this kind of argument has limitations. For more information, see the discussion of weak analogy in Chapter 5.

Refuting Opposing Arguments

As you plan your essay and read sources that will supply your supporting evidence, you will encounter evidence that contradicts your position. You may be tempted to ignore this evidence, but if you do, your argument will not be very convincing. Instead, as you review your sources, identify the most convincing arguments against your position and prepare yourself to **refute** them (that is, disprove them or call them into question), showing them to be illogical, unfair, or untrue. Indicating to readers that you are willing to address these arguments—and that you can respond effectively to them—will help convince them to accept your position.

Of course, simply saying that your opponent's position is "wrong" or "stupid" is not convincing. You need to summarize opposing arguments accurately and clearly identify their weaknesses. In the case of a strong opposing argument, be sure to acknowledge its strengths before you refute it; if you do not, readers may see you as uninformed or unfair. For example, you could refute the argument that a green campus is too expensive by acknowledging that although expenditures are high at first, in the long run, a green campus is not all that costly considering its benefits. Also be careful not to create a **straw man**—that is, do not distort an opposing argument by oversimplifying it so it can be easily refuted (for example, claiming that environmentalists believe that sustainability should always be a college's first priority in its decisions about allocating resources). This unfair tactic will discourage readers from trusting you and thus will undermine your credibility.

Strategies for Refuting Opposing Arguments

In order to do a convincing job of refuting an argument that challenges your position, you need to consider where such an argument might be weak and on what basis you could refute it.

WEAKNESS IN OPPOSING ARGUMENT	REFUTATION STRATEGY
Factual errors or contrary-to-fact statements	Identify and correct the errors, perhaps explaining how they call the writer's credibility into question
Insufficient support	Point out that more facts and examples are needed; note the kind of support (for example, statistics) that is missing.
Illogical reasoning	Identify fallacies in the writer's argument, and explain why the logic is flawed. For example, is the writer setting up a straw man or employing the either/or fallacy? (See Chapter 5 for more on logic.)
Exaggerated or overstated claims	Identify exaggerated statements, and explain why they overstate the case.
Biased statements	Identify biased statements, and show how they exhibit the writer's bias. (See page 261, "Detecting Bias in Your Sources.")
Irrelevant arguments	Identify irrelevant points and explain why they are not pertinent to the writer's argument.

⊘ EXERCISE 7.11

Read paragraphs 7 and 8 of the student essay on page 283. Summarize the opposing argument presented in each of these paragraphs. Then, consulting the list above, identify the specific weakness of each opposing argument. Finally, explain the strategy the student writer uses to refute the argument.

Revising Your Thesis Statement

Before you can begin to draft your argumentative essay and even before you can start to arrange your ideas, you need to revise your tentative thesis statement so it says exactly what you want it to say. After you have gathered and evaluated evidence to support your position and considered the merits of opposing ideas, you are ready to refocus your thesis and state it in more definite terms. Although a tentative thesis statement such as

"College campuses should go green" is a good start, the thesis that guides your essay's structure should be more specific. In fact, it will be most useful as a guide if its phrasing actually acknowledges opposing arguments.

> **REVISED THESIS STATEMENT**
>
> *Despite the expense, colleges should make every effort to create green campuses because doing so improves their own educational environment, ensures their own institution's survival, and helps solve the global climate crisis.*

⊘ EXERCISE 7.12

Consulting the sources you gathered in Exercise 7.10, list all the arguments against the position in your thesis statement. Then, list possible refutations of each of these arguments. When you have finished, revise your thesis statement so that it is more specific, acknowledging the most important argument against your position.

After you have revised your thesis statement, you will have a concise blueprint for the essay you are going to write. At this point, you will be ready to plan your essay's structure and write a first draft.

Structuring Your Essay

As you learned in Chapter 1, an argumentative essay, like other essays, includes an introduction, a body, and a conclusion. In the introduction of an argumentative essay, you state your thesis; in the body paragraphs, you present evidence to support your thesis and you address opposing arguments; and in your conclusion, you bring your argument to a close and reinforce your thesis with a strong concluding statement. As you have seen, these four elements—thesis, evidence, refutation, and concluding statement—are like the four pillars of the ancient Greek temple, supporting your argument so that it will stand up to scrutiny.

> ## SUPPLYING BACKGROUND INFORMATION
>
> Depending on what you think your readers know—and what you think they need to know—you might decide to include a background paragraph that supplies information about the issue you are discussing. For example, in an essay about green campuses, you might briefly sum up the history of the U.S. environmental movement and trace its rise on college campuses. If you decide to include a background paragraph, it should be placed right after your introduction, where it can prepare readers for the discussion to follow.

Understanding basic essay structure can help you as you shape your essay. You should also know how to use induction and deduction, how to identify a strategy for your argument, and how to construct a formal outline.

Using Induction and Deduction

Many argumentative essays are structured either **inductively** or **deductively**. (See Chapter 5 for explanations of induction and deduction.) For example, the body of an essay with the thesis statement that is shown on page 265 could have either of the following two general structures:

INDUCTIVE STRUCTURE

- Colleges are taking a number of steps to follow green practices.
- Through these efforts, campuses have become more environmentally responsible, and their programs and practices have made a positive difference.
- Because these efforts are helping to save the planet, they should be expanded.

DEDUCTIVE STRUCTURE

- Saving the planet is vital.
- Green campuses can help to save the planet.
- Therefore, colleges should create green campuses.

These structures offer two options for arranging material in your essay. Many argumentative essays, however, combine induction and deduction or use other strategies to shape their ideas.

Identifying a Strategy for Your Argument

There are a variety of different ways to structure an argument, and the strategy you use depends on what you want your argument to accomplish. In this text, we discuss five options for presenting material: *definition arguments*, *cause-and-effect arguments*, *evaluation arguments*, *proposal arguments*, and *ethical arguments*.

Any of the five options listed above could guide you as you develop an essay on green campuses:

- You could structure your essay as a **definition argument**, explaining the concept of a green campus and giving examples to show how it operates.

- You could structure your essay as a **cause-and-effect argument**, showing how establishing a green campus could have positive results for students and for the campus.

■ You could structure your essay as an **evaluation argument**, assessing the strengths and weaknesses of various programs and policies designed to create and sustain a green campus.

■ You could structure your essay as a **proposal argument**, recommending a particular program, service, or course of action and showing how it can support a green campus.

■ You could structure your essay as an **ethical argument**, explaining why creating a green campus is the right thing to do from a moral or ethical standpoint.

Constructing a Formal Outline

If you like, you can construct a **formal outline** before you begin your draft. (Later on, you can also construct an outline of your finished paper to check the logic of its structure.) A formal outline, which is more detailed and more logically organized than the informal outline shown on page 257, presents your main points and supporting details in the order in which you will discuss them.

A formal outline of the first body paragraph of the student essay on page 280 would look like this:

I. Background of the term *green*
  A. 1960s environmental movement
    1. Political agenda
    2. Environmental agenda
  B. Today's movements
    1. Eco-friendly practices
    2. Green values

Following a formal outline makes the drafting process flow smoothly, but many writers find it hard to predict exactly what details they will use for support or how they will develop their arguments. In fact, your first draft is likely to move away from your outline as you develop your ideas. Still, if you are the kind of writer who prefers to know where you are going before you start on your way, you will probably consider the time you devote to outlining to be time well spent.

◔ EXERCISE 7.13

Look back at the thesis you decided on earlier in this chapter, and review the evidence you collected to support it. Then, construct a formal outline for your argumentative essay.

Establishing Credibility

Before you begin drafting your essay, you need to think about how to approach your topic and your audience. The essay you write will use a combination of logical, emotional, and ethical appeals, and you will have to be careful to use these appeals reasonably. (See pp. 14–21 for information on these appeals.) As you write, you will concentrate on establishing yourself as well-informed, reasonable, and fair.

Being Well-Informed

If you expect your readers to accept your ideas, you will need to establish yourself as someone they should believe and trust. This involves showing your audience that you have a good command of your material—that is, that you know what you are talking about.

If you want readers to listen to what you are saying, you need to earn their respect by showing them that you have done your research, that you have collected evidence that supports your argument, and that you understand the most compelling arguments against your position. For example, discussing your own experiences as a member of a campus or community environmental group, your observations at a Greenpeace convention, and essays and editorials that you have read on both sides of the issue will encourage your audience to accept your ideas on the subject of green campuses.

Being Reasonable

Even if your evidence is strong, your argument will not be convincing if it does not seem reasonable. One way to present yourself as a reasonable person is to **establish common ground** with your readers, stressing possible points of agreement instead of attacking those who might disagree with your position. For example, saying, "We all want our planet to survive" is a more effective strategy than saying, "Those who do not support the concept of a green campus are out to destroy our planet." (For more on establishing common ground, see the discussion of Rogerian argument in Chapter 6.)

Another way to present yourself as a reasonable person is to **maintain a reasonable tone**. Try to avoid absolutes (words like *always* and *never*); instead, use more conciliatory language (*in many cases, much of the time,* and so on). Try not to use words and phrases like *obviously* or *as anyone can see* to introduce points whose strength may be obvious only to you. Do not brand opponents of your position as misguided, uninformed, or deluded; remember, some of your readers may hold opposing positions and will not appreciate your unfavorable portrayal of them.

Finally, be very careful to treat your readers with respect, addressing them as your intellectual equals. Avoid statements that might insult them or their beliefs ("Although some ignorant or misguided people may still think . . ."). And never assume that your readers know less about your topic than you do; they may actually know a good deal more.

Being Fair

If you want readers to respect your point of view, you need to demonstrate respect for them by being fair. It is not enough to support your ideas convincingly and maintain a reasonable tone. You also need to avoid unfair tactics in your argument and take care to avoid **bias**.

In particular, you should be careful not to *distort evidence, quote out of context, slant evidence, make unfair appeals,* or *use logical fallacies.* These unfair tactics may influence some readers in the short term, but in the long run such tactics will alienate your audience.

- **Do not distort evidence. Distorting** (or misrepresenting) **evidence** is an unfair tactic. It is not ethical or fair, for example, to present your opponent's views inaccurately or to exaggerate his or her position and then argue against it. If you want to argue that green programs on college campuses are a good idea, it is not fair to attack someone who expresses reservations about their cost by writing, "Mr. McNamara's concerns about cost reveal that he has basic doubts about saving the planet." (His concerns reveal no such thing.) It is, however, fair to acknowledge your opponent's reasonable concerns about cost and then go on to argue that the long-term benefits of such programs justify their expense.

- **Do not quote out of context.** It is perfectly fair to challenge someone's stated position. It is not fair, however, to misrepresent that position by **quoting out of context**—that is, by taking the words out of the original setting in which they appeared. For example, if a college dean says, "For schools with limited resources, it may be more important to allocate resources to academic programs than to environmental projects," you are quoting the dean's remarks out of context if you say, "According to Dean Levering, it is 'more important to allocate resources to academic programs than to environmental projects.'"

- **Do not slant evidence.** An argument based on slanted evidence is not fair. **Slanting** involves choosing only evidence that supports your position and ignoring evidence that challenges it. This tactic makes your position seem stronger than it actually is. Another kind of slanting involves using biased language to unfairly characterize your opponents or their positions—for example, using a dismissive term such as *tree hugger* to describe a concerned environmentalist.

- **Do not make unfair appeals.** If you want your readers to accept your ideas, you need to avoid **unfair appeals** to the emotions, such as appeals to your audience's fears or prejudices. For example, if you try to convince readers of the importance of using green building materials by saying, "Construction projects that do not use green materials doom future generations to a planet that cannot sustain itself," you are likely to push neutral (or even receptive) readers to skepticism or to outright hostility.

- **Do not use logical fallacies.** Using **logical fallacies** (flawed arguments) in your writing will alienate your readers. (See Chapter 5 for information about logical fallacies.)

MAINTAINING YOUR CREDIBILITY

Be careful to avoid phrases that undercut your credibility ("Although this is not a subject I know much about") and to avoid apologies ("This is just my opinion"). Be as clear, direct, and forceful as you can, showing readers you are confident as well as knowledgeable. And, of course, be sure to proofread carefully: grammatical and mechanical errors and typos will weaken your credibility.

Drafting Your Essay

Once you understand how to approach your topic and your audience, you will be ready to draft your essay. At this point, you will have selected the sources you will use to support your position as well as identified the strongest arguments against your position (and decided how to refute them). You may also have prepared a formal outline (or perhaps just a list of points to follow).

As you draft your argumentative essay, keep the following guidelines in mind:

- **Follow the general structure of an argumentative essay.** State your thesis in your first paragraph, and discuss each major point in a separate paragraph, moving from least to most important point to emphasize your strongest argument. Introduce each body paragraph with a clearly worded topic sentence. Discuss each opposing argument in a separate paragraph, and be sure your refutation appears directly after your mention of each opposing argument. Finally, don't forget to include a strong concluding statement in your essay's last paragraph.

- **Decide how to arrange your material.** As you draft your essay, you may notice that it is turning out to be an ethical argument, an evaluation argument, or another kind of argument that you recognize. If this is the case, you might want to ask your instructor how you can arrange your material so it is consistent with this type of argument.

- **Use evidence effectively.** As you make your points, select the evidence that supports your argument most convincingly. As you write, summarize or paraphrase relevant information from your sources, and respond to this information in your own voice, supplementing material that you find in your sources with your own original ideas and conclusions. (For information on finding and evaluating sources, see Chapter 8; for information on integrating source material, see Chapter 9.)

- **Use coordination and subordination to make your meaning clear.** Readers shouldn't have to guess how two points are connected; you should use coordination and subordination to show them the relationship between ideas.

Choose **coordinating conjunctions**—*and, but, or, nor, for, so,* and *yet*—carefully, making sure you are using the right word for your purpose. (Use *and* to show addition; *but, for,* or *yet* to show contradiction; *or* to present alternatives; and *so* to indicate a causal relationship.)

Choose **subordinating conjunctions**—*although, because,* and so on—carefully, and place them so that your emphasis will be clear. Consider the following two sentences.

> Achieving a green campus is vitally important. Creating a green campus is expensive.

If you want to stress the idea that green measures are called for, you would connect the two sentences like this:

> Although creating a green campus is expensive, achieving a green campus is vitally important.

If, however, you want to place emphasis on the high cost, you would connect the two sentences as follows:

> Although achieving a green campus is vitally important, creating a green campus is expensive.

- **Include transitional words and phrases.** Be sure you have enough transitions to guide your readers through your discussion. Supply signals that move readers smoothly from sentence to sentence and paragraph to paragraph, and choose signals that make sense in the context of your discussion.

SUGGESTED TRANSITIONS FOR ARGUMENT

- To show causal relationships: *because, as a result, for this reason*

- To indicate sequence: *first, second, third; then; next; finally*

- To introduce additional points: *also, another, in addition, furthermore, moreover*

- To move from general to specific: *for example, for instance, in short, in other words*

- To identify an opposing argument: *however, although, even though, despite*

- To grant the validity of an opposing argument: *certainly, admittedly, granted, of course*

- To introduce a refutation: *however, nevertheless, nonetheless, still*

GRAMMAR IN CONTEXT

Using Parallelism

As you draft your argumentative essay, you should express corresponding words, phrases, and clauses in **parallel** terms. The use of matching parts of speech to express corresponding ideas strengthens your argument's impact because it enables readers to follow your line of thought.

In particular, use parallelism in sentences that highlight *paired items* or *items in a series.*

- **Paired Items**

UNCLEAR	Creating a green campus is important because <u>it sets</u> an example for students and the <u>environment will be protected</u>.
PARALLEL	Creating a green campus is important because it <u>sets</u> an example for students and <u>protects</u> the environment.

- **Items in a Series**

UNCLEAR	Students can do their part to support a green campus in four ways—by <u>avoiding</u> bottled water, use of electricity <u>should be limited</u>, and they <u>can recycle</u> packaging and also <u>educating</u> themselves about environmental issues is a good strategy.
PARALLEL	Students can do their part to support a green campus in four ways—by <u>avoiding</u> bottled water, by <u>limiting</u> use of electricity, by <u>recycling</u> packaging, and by <u>educating</u> themselves about environmental issues.

- **Define your terms.** If the key terms of your argument have multiple meanings—as *green* does—be sure to indicate what the term means in the context of your argument. Terms like *environmentally friendly, climate change, environmentally responsible, sustainable,* and *sustainability literacy* may mean very different things to different readers.

- **Use clear language.** An argument is no place for vague language or wordy phrasing. If you want readers to understand your points, your writing should be clear and direct. Avoid vague words like *good, bad, right,* and *wrong,* which are really just unsupported judgments that do nothing to help you make your case. Also avoid wordy phrases such as *revolves around* and *is concerned with,* particularly in your thesis statement and topic sentences.

- **Finally, show your confidence and your mastery of your material.** Avoid qualifying your statements with phrases such as *I think, I* *believe, it seems to me,* and *in my opinion.* These qualifiers weaken your argument by suggesting that you are unsure of your material or that the statements that follow may not be true.

 LaunchPad For more practice, see the LearningCurve on Par-
macmillan learning   allelism in the LaunchPad for *Practical Argument.*

❍ EXERCISE 7.14

Keeping the above guidelines in mind, write a draft of an argumentative essay that develops the thesis statement you have been working with.

Revising Your Essay

After you have written a draft of your essay, you will need to revise it. **Revision** is "re-seeing"—looking carefully and critically at the draft you have written. Revision is different from editing and proofreading (discussed on p. 278), which focus on grammar, punctuation, mechanics, and the like. In fact, revision can involve substantial reworking of your essay's structure and content. The strategies discussed on the pages that follow can help you revise your arguments.

Asking Questions

Asking some basic questions, such as those in the three checklists that follow, can help you as you revise.

CHECKLIST

> **Questions about Your Essay's Purpose and Audience**
>
> ☐ What was your primary purpose in writing this essay? What other purposes did you have?
>
> ☐ What appeals, strategies, and evidence did you use to accomplish your goals?
>
> ☐ Who is the audience for your essay? Do you see your readers as receptive, hostile, or neutral to your position?
>
> ☐ What basic knowledge do you think your readers have about your topic? Did you provide enough background for them?
>
> ☐ What biases do you think your readers have? Have you addressed these biases in your essay?
>
> ☐ What do you think your readers believed about your topic before reading your essay?
>
> ☐ What do you want readers to believe now that they have read your essay?

> **CHECKLIST**
>
> ### Questions about Your Essay's Structure and Style
>
> ☐ Do you have a clearly stated thesis?
>
> ☐ Are your topic sentences clear and concise?
>
> ☐ Do you provide all necessary background and definitions?
>
> ☐ Do you refute opposing arguments effectively?
>
> ☐ Do you include enough transitional words and phrases to guide readers smoothly through your discussion?
>
> ☐ Have you avoided vague language and wordy phrasing?
>
> ☐ Do you have a strong concluding statement?

> **CHECKLIST**
>
> ### Questions about Your Essay's Supporting Evidence
>
> ☐ Do you support your opinions with *evidence*—facts, observations, examples, statistics, expert opinion, and so on?
>
> ☐ Do you have enough evidence to support your thesis?
>
> ☐ Do the sources you rely on present information accurately and without bias?
>
> ☐ Are your sources' discussions directly relevant to your topic?
>
> ☐ Have you consulted sources that represent a wide range of viewpoints, including sources that challenge your position?

The answers to the questions in the checklists may lead you to revise your essay's content, structure, and style. For example, you may want to look for additional sources that can provide the kind of supporting evidence you need. Or, you may notice you need to revise the structure of your essay, perhaps rearranging your points so that the most important point is placed last, for emphasis. You may also want to revise your essay's introduction and conclusion, sharpening your thesis statement or adding a stronger concluding statement. Finally, you may decide to add more background material to help your readers understand the issue you are writing about or to help them take a more favorable view of your position.

Using Outlines and Templates

To check the logic of your essay's structure, you can prepare a revision outline or consult a template.

- To make sure your essay's key points are arranged logically and supported convincingly, you can construct a **formal outline** of your draft. (See p. 267 for information on formal outlines.) This outline will indicate whether you need to discuss any additional points, add supporting evidence, or refute an opposing argument more fully. It will also show you if paragraphs are arranged in a logical order.

- To make sure your argument flows smoothly from thesis statement to evidence to refutation of opposing arguments to concluding statement, you can refer to one of the paragraph **templates** that appear throughout this book. These templates can help you to construct a one-paragraph summary of your essay.

Getting Feedback

After you have done as much as you can on your own, it is time to get feedback from your instructor and (with your instructor's permission) from your school's writing center or from other students in your class.

Instructor Feedback You can get feedback from your instructor in a variety of different ways. For example, your instructor may ask you to email a draft of your paper to him or her with some specific questions ("Do I need paragraph 3, or do I have enough evidence without it?" "Does my thesis statement need to be more specific?"). The instructor will then reply with corrections and recommendations. If your instructor prefers a traditional face-to-face conference, you may still want to email your draft ahead of time to give him or her a chance to read it before your meeting.

Writing Center Feedback You can also get feedback from a writing center tutor, who can be either a student or a professional. The tutor can give you another point of view about your paper's content and organization and also help you focus on specific questions of style, grammar, punctuation, and mechanics. (Keep in mind, however, that a tutor will not edit or proofread your paper for you; that is your job.)

Peer Review Finally, you can get feedback from your classmates. **Peer review** can be an informal process in which you ask a classmate for advice, or it can be a more structured process, involving small groups working with copies of students' work. Peer review can also be conducted electronically. For example, students can exchange drafts by email or respond to one another's drafts that are posted on the course website. They can also use Word's comment tool, as illustrated in the following example.

DRAFT

Comment [LB]: Your first two sentences are a little abrupt. Maybe you could ease into your argument more slowly?

Comment [KS]: I like these two questions. They really got me thinking.

Comment [PL]: Could you be more specific? I'm not sure what you mean.

Comment [PL]: You definitely talk about this in your paper, but you also talk about other reasons to go green. You might consider revising this thesis statement so it matches your argument.

Colleges and universities have no excuse for ignoring the threat of global climate change. Campus leaders need to push beyond efforts to recycle or compost and instead become models of sustainability. Already, many universities are hard at work demonstrating that reducing their institution's environmental impact is not only possible but worthwhile. They are overhauling their entire infrastructure, their buildings, systems, and even curriculum. While many students, faculty, staff, and administrators are excited by these new challenges, some still question this need to go green. Is it worth the money? Is it promoting "a moral and behavioral agenda rather than an educational one"? (Butcher). In fact, greening will ultimately save institutions money while providing their students with a good education. Colleges should make every effort to create green campuses because by doing so they will help solve the global climate crisis.

FINAL VERSION

Over the last few years, the pressure to go green has led colleges and universities to make big changes. The threats posed by global climate change are inspiring campus leaders to push beyond efforts to recycle to become models of sustainability. Today, in the interest of reducing their environmental impact, many campuses are seeking to overhaul their entire infrastructure—their buildings, their systems, and even their curriculum. While many students, faculty, staff, and administrators are excited by these new challenges, some question this need to go green. Is it worth the money? Is it promoting "a moral and behavioral agenda rather than an educational one"? (Butcher). In fact, greening will ultimately save institutions money while providing their students with the educational opportunities necessary to help them solve the crisis of their generation. Despite the expense, colleges should make every effort to create green campuses because by doing so they will improve their own educational environment, ensure their own institution's survival, and help solve the global climate crisis.

GUIDELINES FOR PEER REVIEW

Remember that the peer-review process involves *giving* feedback as well as receiving it. When you respond to a classmate's work, follow these guidelines:

- Be very specific when making suggestions, clearly identifying errors, inconsistencies, redundancy, or areas that need further development.

- Be tactful and supportive when pointing out problems.

- Give praise and encouragement whenever possible.

- Be generous with your suggestions for improvement.

⊘ EXERCISE 7.15

Following the guidelines for revision discussed earlier, get some feedback from others, and then revise your argumentative essay.

Adding Visuals

After you have gotten feedback about the ideas in your paper, you might want to consider adding a **visual**—such as a chart, graph, table, photo, or diagram—to help you make a point more forcefully. For example, in a paper on the green campus movement, you could include anything from photos of students recycling to a chart comparing energy use at different schools. Sometimes a visual can be so specific, so attractive, or so dramatic that its impact will be greater than words would be. At other times, a visual can expand and support a verbal argument.

You can create a visual yourself, or you can download one from the Internet, beginning your search with Google Images. If you download a visual and paste it into your paper, be sure to include a reference to the visual in your discussion to show readers how it supports your argument.

NOTE

Don't forget to label your visual with a figure number, to use proper documentation, and to include a caption explaining what the visual shows, as the student paper that begins on page 280 does. (For information on how to document visuals, see Chapter 10.)

Polishing Your Essay

The final step in the writing process is putting the finishing touches on your essay. At this point, your goal is to make sure that your essay is well organized, convincing, and clearly written, with no distracting grammatical or mechanical errors.

Editing

When you **edit** your revised draft, you review your essay's overall structure, style, and sentence construction, but you focus on grammar, punctuation, and mechanics. Editing is an important step in the writing process because an interesting, logically organized argument will not be convincing if readers are distracted by run-ons and fragments, confusingly placed modifiers, or incorrect verb forms. (Remember, your grammar checker will spot some grammatical errors, but it will miss many others.)

GRAMMAR IN CONTEXT

Pronoun-Antecedent Agreement

A pronoun must always agree in number with its **antecedent**, the word to which it refers. Every pronoun must clearly refer to a particular antecedent.

CONFUSING	College administrators, faculty members, and staff members must work hard to show every student that a green campus will benefit <u>them</u>.
REVISED	College administrators, faculty members, and staff members must work hard to show every student that a green campus will benefit <u>him or her</u>.

 LaunchPad macmillan learning   For more practice, see the LearningCurve on Nouns and Pronouns in the LaunchPad for *Practical Argument.*

Proofreading

When you **proofread** your revised and edited draft, you carefully read every word, trying to spot any remaining punctuation or mechanical errors, as well as any typographical errors (typos) or misspellings that your spell checker may have missed. (Remember, a spell checker will not flag a correctly spelled word that is used incorrectly.)

GRAMMAR IN CONTEXT

Contractions versus Possessive Pronouns

Be especially careful not to confuse the contractions *it's, who's, they're,* and *you're* with the possessive forms *its, whose, their,* and *your.*

INCORRECT	<u>Its</u> not always clear <u>who's</u> responsibility it is to promote green initiatives on campus.
CORRECT	<u>It's</u> not always clear <u>whose</u> responsibility it is to promote green initiatives on campus.

Choosing a Title

After you have edited and proofread your essay, you need to give it a title. Ideally, your title should create interest and give readers clear information about the subject of your essay. It should also be appropriate for your topic. A serious topic calls for a serious title, and a thoughtfully presented argument deserves a thoughtfully selected title.

A title does not need to surprise or shock readers. It also should not be long and wordy or something many readers will not understand. A simple statement of your topic ("Going Green") or of your position on the issue ("College Campuses Should Go Green") is usually all that is needed. If you like, you can use a quotation from one of your sources as a title ("Green Is Good").

⊙ EXERCISE 7.16

Evaluate the suitability and effectiveness of the following titles for an argumentative essay on green campuses. Be prepared to explain the strengths and weaknesses of each title.

- Green Campuses
- It's Not Easy Being Green
- The Lean, Clean, Green Machine
- What Students Can Do to Make Their Campuses More Environmentally Responsible
- Why All Campuses Should Be Green Campuses
- Planting the Seeds of the Green Campus Movement
- The Green Campus: An Idea Whose Time Has Come

Checking Format

Finally, make sure that your essay follows your instructor's guidelines for documentation style and manuscript format. (The student paper on p. 280 follows MLA style and manuscript format. For additional sample essays illustrating MLA and APA documentation style and manuscript format, see Chapter 10 and Appendix B, respectively.)

⟳ The following student essay, "Going Green," argues that colleges should make every effort to create green campuses.

GOING GREEN
SHAWN HOLTON

Introduction

Over the last few years, the pressure to go green has led colleges 1
and universities to make big changes. The threats posed by climate
change are encouraging campus leaders to push beyond early efforts,
such as recycling, to become models of sustainability. Today, in the
interest of reducing their environmental impact, many campuses are
seeking to overhaul their entire infrastructure. Although many students,
faculty, staff, and administrators are excited by these new challenges,
some question this need to go green. Is it worth the money? Is it
promoting "a moral and behavioral agenda rather than an educational
one"? (Butcher). In fact, greening will ultimately save institutions money
while providing their students with the educational opportunities
necessary to help them solve the crisis of their generation. Colleges

Thesis statement

should make every effort to create green campuses because by doing so
they will improve their own educational environment, ensure their own
institution's survival, and help solve the global climate crisis.

Body paragraph:
Background of green
movement

Although the green movement has been around for many years, 2
green has become a buzzword only relatively recently. Green political
parties and groups began forming in the 1960s to promote environmentalist goals ("Environmentalism"). These groups fought for "grassroots
democracy, social justice, and nonviolence" in addition to environmental protections and were "self-consciously activist and unconventional"
in their strategies ("Environmentalism"). Today, however, *green* denotes
much more than a political movement; it has become a catchall word
for anything eco-friendly. People use *green* to describe everything from
fuel-efficient cars to fume-free house paint. Green values have become
more mainstream in response to evidence that human activities, particularly those that result in greenhouse-gas emissions, may be causing
global warming at a dramatic rate ("Call for Climate Leadership" 4). To
fight this climate change, many individuals, businesses, and organizations are choosing to go green, making sustainability and preservation
of the environment a priority.

Greening a college campus means moving toward a sustainable campus that works to conserve the earth's natural resources. It means reducing the university's carbon footprint by focusing on energy efficiency in every aspect of campus life. This is no small task. Although replacing incandescent light bulbs with compact fluorescent ones and offering more locally grown food in dining halls are valuable steps, meaningful sustainability requires more comprehensive changes. For example, universities also need to invest in alternative energy sources, construct new buildings and remodel old ones, and work to reduce campus demand for nonrenewable products. Although these changes will eventually save universities money, in most cases, the institutions will need to spend money now to reduce costs in the long term. To achieve this transformation, many colleges are—individually or in cooperation with other schools—establishing formal "climate commitments," setting specific goals, and developing tools to track their investments and evaluate their progress.

3 Body paragraph: Definition of *green* as it applies to colleges

Despite these challenges, there are many compelling reasons to act now. Saving money on operating costs, thus making the school more competitive in the long term, is an appealing incentive. In fact, many schools have made solid and sometimes immediate gains by greening some aspect of their campus. For example, by changing its parking and transit systems to encourage more carpooling, biking, and walking, Cornell University has saved 417,000 gallons of fuel and cut costs by $36 million over the last twelve years ("Call for Climate Leadership" 10). By installing geothermal wells and replacing its old power plant with a geothermal pump system, the University of Central Missouri is saving 31 percent in energy costs, according to a case study in *Climate Neutral Campus Report* (Trane). These changes were not merely a social, or even a political, response, but a necessary part of updating the campus. Betty Roberts, the UCM vice president for administration, was faced with the problem of how to "make a change for the benefit of the institution . . . with no money." After saving several million dollars by choosing to go green, Roberts naturally reported that the school was "very happy!" with its decision (qtd. in Trane). There is more to be gained than just savings, however. Oberlin College not only saves money by generating its own solar energy (as shown in Fig. 1) but also makes money by selling its excess electricity back to the local power company (Petersen). Many other schools have taken similar steps, with similarly positive results.

4 Body paragraph: First argument in support of thesis

Body paragraph:
Second argument
in support of
thesis

AP Photo/The Morning Journal/Paul M. Walsh.

Fig. 1. Solar panels on the roof of the Adam Joseph Lewis Center for Environmental Studies, Oberlin College. 2008. Oberlin.edu.

Attracting the attention of the media, donors, and—most significantly—prospective students is another practical reason for schools to go green. As one researcher explains, "There is enough evidence nationwide to detect an arms-race of sorts among universities competing for green status" (Krizek et al. 27). The *Princeton Review* now includes a "green rating," and according to recent studies, more than two thirds of college applicants say that they consider green ratings when choosing a school (Krizek et al. 27). A school's commitment to the environment can also bring in large private donations. For example, Carnegie Mellon University attracted $1.7 million from the National Science Foundation for its new Center for Sustainable Engineering (Egan). The University of California, Davis, will be receiving up to $25 million from the Chevron Corporation to research biofuel technology ("Call for Climate Leadership" 10). While greening certainly costs money, a green commitment can also help a school remain financially viable.

Body paragraph: Third
argument in support of
thesis

In addition to these practical reasons for going green, universities also have another, perhaps more important, reason to promote and model sustainability: doing so may help solve the climate crisis. Although an individual school's reduction of emissions may not noticeably affect global warming, its graduates will be in a position to make a huge impact. College is a critical time in most students' personal and professional development. Students are making choices about what kind of adults they will be, and they are also receiving the training, education, and experience that they will need to succeed in the working world. If universities can offer time, space, and incentives—both in and out of the classroom—to help students develop creative ways to live sustainably, these schools have the potential to change the thinking and habits of a whole generation.

5

6

Many critics of greening claim that becoming environmentally friendly is too expensive and will result in higher tuition and fees. However, often a very small increase in fees, as little as a few dollars a semester, can be enough to help a school institute significant change. For example, at the University of Colorado–Boulder, a student-initiated $1 increase in fees allowed the school to purchase enough wind power to reduce its carbon emissions by 12 million pounds ("Call for Climate Leadership" 9). Significantly, the students were the ones who voted to increase their own fees to achieve a greener campus. Although university faculty and administrators' commitment to sustainability is critical for any program's success, few green initiatives will succeed without the enthusiastic support of the student body. Ultimately, students have the power. If they think their school is spending too much on green projects, then they can make a change or choose to go elsewhere.

7 Refutation of first opposing argument

Other critics of the trend toward greener campuses believe that schools with commitments to sustainability are dictating how students should live rather than encouraging free thought. As one critic says, "Once [sustainability literacy] is enshrined in a university's public pronouncements or private articles, then the institution has diminished its commitment to academic inquiry" (Butcher). This kind of criticism overlooks the fact that figuring out how to achieve sustainability requires and will continue to require rigorous critical thinking and creativity. Why not apply the academic skills of inquiry, analysis, and problem solving to the biggest problem of our day? Not doing so would be irresponsible and would confirm the perception that universities are ivory towers of irrelevant knowledge. In fact, the presence of sustainability as both a goal and a subject of study has the potential to reaffirm academia's place at the center of civil society.

8 Refutation of second opposing argument

Creating a green campus is a difficult task, but universities must rise to the challenge or face the consequences. If they do not commit to changing their ways, they will become less and less able to compete for students and for funding. If they refuse to make a comprehensive commitment to sustainability, they also risk irrelevance at best and institutional collapse at worst. Finally, by not rising to the challenge, they will be giving up the opportunity to establish themselves as leaders in addressing the climate crisis. As the coalition of American College and

9 Conclusion

Concluding statement

University Presidents states in its Climate Commitment, "No other institution has the influence, the critical mass and the diversity of skills needed to successfully reverse global warming" ("Call for Climate Leadership" 13). Now is the time for schools to make the choice and pledge to go green.

Works Cited

Butcher, Jim. "Keep the Green Moral Agenda off Campus." *Times Higher Education*, 19 Oct. 2007, www.timeshighereducation.com/news /keep-the-green-moral-agenda-off-campus/310853.article.

"A Call for Climate Leadership." *American College and University Presidents Climate Commitment*, Aug. 2009, www2 .presidentsclimatecommitment.org/html/documents/ACUPCC _InfoPacketv2.pdf

Egan, Timothy. "The Greening of America's Campuses." *New York Times*, 8 Jan. 2006, www.nytimes.com/2006/01/08/education /edlife/egan_environment.html?scp=1&amp%3Bsq=The&_r=0.

"Environmentalism." *Encyclopaedia Britannica Online*, 2015, www.britannica.com/topic/environmentalism.

Krizek, Kevin J., Dave Newport, James White, and Alan R. Townsend. "Higher Education's Sustainability Imperative: How to Practically Respond?" *International Journal of Sustainability in Higher Education*, vol. 13, no. 1, 2012, pp. 1 -33. DOI: 10.1108/14676371211190281.

Petersen, John. "A Green Curriculum Involves Everyone on Campus." *Chronicle of Higher Education*, vol. 54, no. 41, 2008, p. A25. *ERIC Institute of Education Services*, eric.ed.gov/?id=EJ801316.

Trane. "University of Central Missouri." *Climate Neutral Campus Report*, Kyoto Publishing, 14 Aug. 2009, secondnature.org/wp-content /uploads/09-8-14_ClimateNeutralCampusReportReleased.pdf.

⊙ EXERCISE 7.17

Find a visual that will strengthen your argument, and add it to your essay. Be sure to document it appropriately and to include a descriptive caption. Then, edit and proofread your paper, paying special attention to parenthetical documentation and your works-cited page. When you have finished, add a title, and print out a final copy of your essay.

4

Using Sources to Support Your Argument

Finding and Evaluating Sources

Is Technology a Serious Threat to Our Privacy?

It is increasingly common to share personal details on social media and online dating sites. The number of people who have profiles on online sites is staggering: Facebook currently has over 1.44 billion users worldwide, Twitter has over 236 million users, and Instagram has 300 million. Even newer apps like Yik Yak have millions of users, and one in five adults between the ages of twenty-five and thirty-four have used an online dating site. Studies have shown that the longer people use these sites, the more information they reveal without thinking about the possible consequences.

According to a 2015 Huffington Post report, 25 percent of Facebook users don't bother using their privacy settings. In addition, 63 percent of Facebook profiles are set on "visible to the public," meaning that anyone can access information. Even more disturbing is that every time a user visits a site with a "like" button, Facebook gets a notice, even if the user doesn't push the button. Not

surprisingly, the Internet has become the primary tool for those who want to access personal information: employers routinely use social-networking sites to find out about job candidates, advertisers buy their data to target consumers, and cybercriminals use information from these sites to steal users' identities.

In response to complaints, the federal government has begun to focus on the issue of cyberprivacy. As a result of pressure from the Federal Trade Commission, Facebook, Twitter, and Google have agreed to submit to privacy audits, and in response to complaints by users, Mark Zuckerberg, creator of Facebook, has repeatedly revised the site's privacy policies. Although privacy audits expose important weaknesses, critics claim that the only way to absolutely ensure privacy is for people to disengage from social media entirely and to avoid sharing personal information online. Others disagree, saying that social networks are a fact of

(continued)

(*continued*)

life and that people have to learn to use them responsibly. In other words, people should have no expectation of privacy when they post information about themselves online.

Later in this chapter, you will be asked to evaluate a number of research sources to determine if they are acceptable for an argumentative essay on the topic of technology and privacy. In Chapter 9, you will learn how to integrate sources into an essay on this general topic. In Chapter 10, you will see an MLA paper on one aspect of the topic: whether it is ethical for employers to access information posted on job applicants' social-networking sites. Finally, in Chapter 11, you will learn how to use sources responsibly while considering the question "Where should we draw the line with plagiarism?"

Finding Sources

In some argumentative essays, you can use your own ideas as evidence in support of your position. In many others, however, you have to do **research**—collect information (in both print and electronic form) from magazines, newspapers, books, journals, and other sources—to supplement your own ideas.

The obvious question is, "How does research help you to construct better arguments?" The answer is that research enables you to explore the ideas of others, consider multiple points of view, and expand your view of your subject. As you do so, you get a sense of the issues surrounding your topic, and as a result, you are able to develop a strong thesis and collect the facts, examples, statistics, quotations, and expert opinion that you will need to support your points. In addition, by taking the time to find reliable, up-to-date sources, you demonstrate to readers that your discussion is credible and that you are someone worth listening to. In short, doing research enables you to construct intelligent, authoritative, and convincing arguments.

Finding Information in the Library

When most students do research, they immediately go to the Internet—or, more specifically, to the Web. Unfortunately, by doing this, they ignore the most reliable source of high-quality information available to them: their college library.

Your college library contains both print and electronic resources that you cannot find anywhere else. Although the Internet gives you access to an almost unlimited amount of material, it does not offer the consistently high level of reliable information found in your college library. For this reason, you should always begin your research by surveying the resources of the library.

The best way to access your college library is to visit its website, which is the gateway to a great deal of information—for example, its online catalog, electronic databases, and reference works.

> **The Online Catalog:** The **online catalog** lists all the books, journals, newspapers, magazines, and other material housed in the library. Once you gain access to this catalog, you can type in keywords that will lead you to sources related to your topic.

NOTE

Many libraries have a **discovery service** that enables you to use a single search box to access a wide variety of content—for example, the physical items held by a library, content from e-books, journal articles, government documents, and electronic databases. Most discovery services return high-quality results quickly and (like Google) rank them according to relevancy.

> **Online Databases:** All college libraries subscribe to **databases**— collections of digital information that you access through a keyword search. The library's online databases enable you to retrieve bibliographic citations as well as the full text of articles from hundreds of publications. Some of these databases—for example, *Expanded Academic ASAP* and *Proquest Research Library*—provide information on a wide variety of topics. Others—for example, *Business Source Premier* and *Sociological Abstracts*—provide information on a particular subject area. Before selecting a database, check with the reference librarian to determine which will be most useful for your topic.
>
> **Reference Works:** All libraries contain **reference works**—sources of accurate and reliable information such as dictionaries, encyclopedias, and almanacs. These reference works are available both in print and in electronic form. **General encyclopedias**—such as the *New Encyclopaedia Britannica* and the *Columbia Encyclopedia*—provide general information on a wide variety of topics. **Specialized reference works**—such as *Facts on File* and the *World Almanac*—and **special encyclopedias**—such as the *Encyclopedia of Law and Economics*— offer detailed information on specific topics.

NOTE

Although a general encyclopedia can provide an overview of your topic, encyclopedia articles do not usually treat topics in enough depth for college-level research. Be sure to check your instructor's guidelines before you use a general encyclopedia in your research.

Finding Information on the Internet

Although the Internet gives you access to a vast amount of information, it has its limitations. For one thing, because anyone can publish on the Web, you cannot be sure if the information found there is trustworthy, timely, or authoritative. Of course, there are reliable sources of information on the Web. For example, the information on your college library's website is reliable. In addition, Google Scholar provides links to some scholarly sources that are as good as those found in a college library's databases. Even so, you have to approach this material with caution; some articles accessed through Google Scholar are pay-per-view, and others are not current or comprehensive.

A **search engine**—such as Google or Bing—helps you to locate and to view documents that you search for with keywords. Different types of search engines are suitable for different purposes:

- **General-Purpose Search Engines: General-purpose search engines** retrieve information on a great number of topics. They cast the widest possible net and bring in the widest variety of information. The disadvantage of general-purpose search engines is that you get a great deal of irrelevant material. Because each search engine has its own unique characteristics, you should try a few of them to see which you prefer. The most popular general-purpose search engines are Google, Bing, Yahoo!, Ask, and AOL Search.

- **Specialized Search Engines: Specialized search engines** focus on specific subject areas or on a specific type of content. The advantage of specialized search engines is that they eliminate the need for you to wade through pages of irrelevant material. By focusing your search on a specific subject area, you are more likely to locate information on your particular topic. (You are able to narrow your search to a specific subject area when you use a general-purpose search engine, but a specialized search engine narrows your search for you.) You can find a list of specialized search engines on the Search Engine List (thesearchenginelist.com).

- **Metasearch Engines:** Because each search engine works differently, results can (and do) vary. For this reason, if you limit yourself to a single search engine, you can miss a great deal of useful information. **Metasearch engines** solve this problem by taking the results of several search engines and presenting them in a simple, no-nonsense format. The most popular metasearch engines are Dogpile, Kartoo, Mamma, Surfwax, Yippy, and Zoo.

Evaluating Sources

Whenever you locate a source—print or electronic—you should always take the time to evaluate it. When you **evaluate** a source, you assess the

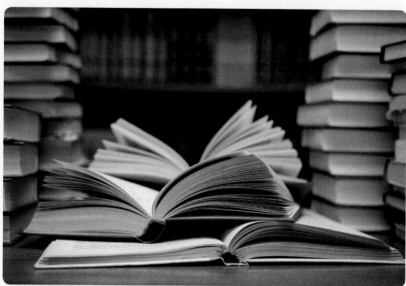

Sources must be evaluated carefully.

Viorika Prikhodko/iStock/Getty Images

objectivity of the author, the credibility of the source, and its relevance to your argument. (Although a librarian or an instructor has screened the print and electronic sources in your college library for general accuracy and trustworthiness, you cannot simply assume that these sources are suitable for your particular writing project.)

Material that you access online presents particular problems. Because anyone can publish on the Internet, the information you find there has to be evaluated carefully for accuracy. Although some material on the Internet (for example, journal articles that are published in both print and digital format) is reliable, other material (for example, personal websites and blogs) may be unreliable and unsuitable for your research. To be reasonably certain that the information you are accessing is appropriate, you have to approach it critically.

As you locate sources, make sure that they are suitable for your research. (Remember, if you use an untrustworthy source, you undercut your credibility.)

To evaluate sources, you use the same process that you use when you evaluate anything else. For example, if you are thinking about buying a laptop computer, you use several criteria to help you make your decision—for example, price, speed, memory, reliability, and availability of technical support. The same is true for evaluating research sources. You can use the following criteria to decide whether a source is appropriate for your research:

- Accuracy
- Credibility

- Objectivity

- Currency

- Comprehensiveness

- Authority

The illustrations on page 293 show where to find information that can help you evaluate a source.

Accuracy A source is **accurate** when it is factual and free of errors. One way to judge the accuracy of a source is to compare the information it contains to that same information in several other sources. If a source has factual errors, then it probably includes other types of errors as well. Needless to say, errors in spelling and grammar should also cause you to question a source's general accuracy.

You can also judge the accuracy of a source by checking to see if the author cites sources for the information that is discussed. Documentation can help readers determine both the quality of information in a source and the range of sources used. It can also show readers what sources a writer has failed to consult. (Failure to cite an important book or article should cause you to question the writer's familiarity with a subject.) If possible, verify the legitimacy of some of the books and articles that a writer cites by seeing what you can find out about them online. If a source has caused a great deal of debate or if it is disreputable, you will probably be able to find information about the source by researching it on Google.

Credibility A source is **credible** when it is believable. You can begin checking a source's credibility by determining where a book or article was published. If a university press published the book, you can be reasonably certain that it was **peer reviewed**—read by experts in the field to confirm the accuracy of the information. If a commercial press published the book, you will have to consider other criteria—the author's reputation and the date of publication, for example—to determine quality. If your source is an article, see if it appears in a **scholarly journal**—a periodical aimed at experts in a particular field—or in a **popular magazine**—a periodical aimed at general readers. Journal articles are almost always acceptable research sources because they are usually documented, peer reviewed, and written by experts. (They can, however, be difficult for general readers to understand.) Articles in high-level popular magazines, such as the *Atlantic* and the *Economist*, may also be suitable—provided experts wrote them. However, articles in lower-level popular magazines—such as *Sports Illustrated* and *Time*—may be easy to understand, but they are seldom acceptable sources for research.

You can determine how well respected a source is by reading reviews written by critics. You can find reviews of books by consulting *Book*

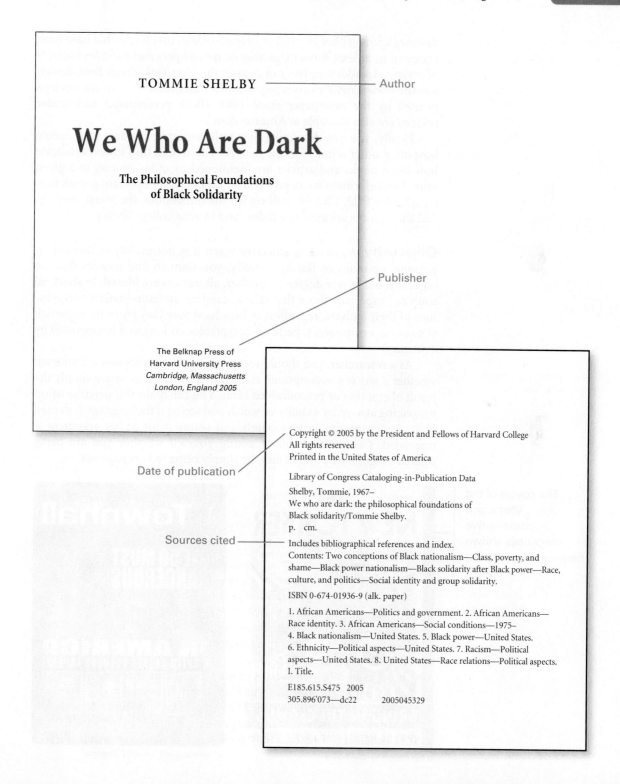

TOMMIE SHELBY ———————— Author

We Who Are Dark

**The Philosophical Foundations
of Black Solidarity**

———— Publisher

The Belknap Press of
Harvard University Press
Cambridge, Massachusetts
London, England 2005

Date of publication ————

Sources cited ————

Library of Congress Cataloging-in-Publication Data

Shelby, Tommie, 1967–
We who are dark: the philosophical foundations of
Black solidarity/Tommie Shelby.
p. cm.

Includes bibliographical references and index.
Contents: Two conceptions of Black nationalism—Class, poverty, and
shame—Black power nationalism—Black solidarity after Black power—Race,
culture, and politics—Social identity and group solidarity.

ISBN 0-674-01936-9 (alk. paper)

1. African Americans—Politics and government. 2. African Americans—
Race identity. 3. African Americans—Social conditions—1975–
4. Black nationalism—United States. 5. Black power—United States.
6. Ethnicity—Political aspects—United States. 7. Racism—Political
aspects—United States. 8. United States—Race relations—Political aspects.
I. Title.

E185.615.S475 2005
305.896'073—dc22   2005045329

Review Digest—either in print or online—which lists books that have been reviewed in at least three magazines or newspapers and includes excerpts of reviews. In addition, you can consult the *New York Times Book Review* website—www.nytimes.com/pages/books/index.html—to access reviews printed by the newspaper since 1981. (Both professional and reader reviews are also available at Amazon.com.)

Finally, you can determine how well respected a source is by seeing how often other scholars in the field refer to it. **Citation indexes** indicate how often books and articles are mentioned by other sources in a given year. This information can give you an idea of how important a work is in a particular field. Citation indexes for the humanities, the social sciences, and the sciences are available online and in your college library.

Objectivity A source is **objective** when it is not unduly influenced by personal opinions or feelings. Ideally, you want to find sources that are objective, but to one degree or another, all sources are **biased**. In short, all sources—especially those that take a stand on an issue—reflect the opinions of their authors, regardless of how hard they may try to be impartial. (Of course, an opinion is perfectly acceptable—as long as it is supported by evidence.)

As a researcher, you should recognize that bias exists and ask yourself whether a writer's assumptions are justified by the facts or are simply the result of emotion or preconceived ideas. You can make this determination by looking at a writer's choice of words and seeing if the language is slanted or by reviewing the writer's points and seeing if his or her argument is one-sided. Get in the habit of asking yourself whether you are being offered a legitimate point of view or simply being fed propaganda.

The covers of the liberal and conservative magazines shown here suggest different biases.

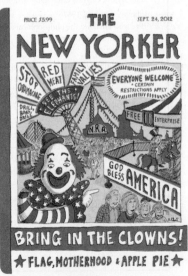

© Roz Chast/The New Yorker

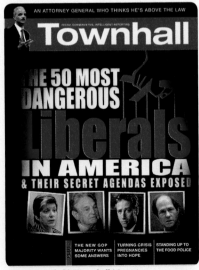

© Yasamin Khalili/Townhall Magazine

Currency A source is **current** when it is up-to-date. (For a book, you can find the date of publication on the copyright page, as above. For an article, you can find the date on the front cover of the magazine or journal.) If you are dealing with a scientific subject, the date of publication can be very important. Older sources might contain outdated information, so you want to use the most up-to-date source that you can find. For other subjects—literary criticism, for example—the currency of the information may not be as important as it is in the sciences.

Comprehensiveness A source is **comprehensive** when it covers a subject in sufficient depth. The first thing to consider is whether the source deals specifically with your subject. (If it treats your subject only briefly, it will probably not be useful.) Does it treat your subject in enough detail? Does the source include the background information that you need to understand the discussion? Does the source mention other important sources that discuss your subject? Are facts and interpretations supported by the other sources you have read, or are there major points of disagreement? Finally, does the author include documentation?

How comprehensive a source needs to be depends on your purpose and audience as well as on your writing assignment. For a short essay for an introductory course, editorials from the *New York Times* or the *Wall Street Journal* might give you enough information to support your argument. If you are writing a longer essay, however, you might need to consult journal articles (and possibly books) about your subject.

Authority A source has **authority** when a writer has the expertise to write about a subject. Always try to determine if the author is a recognized authority or simply a person who has decided to write about a particular topic. For example, what other books or articles has the author written? Has your instructor ever mentioned the author's name? Is the author mentioned in your textbook? Has the author published other works on the same subject or on related subjects? (You can find this information on Amazon.com.)

You should also determine if the author has an academic affiliation. Is he or she a faculty member at a respected college or university? Do other established scholars have a high opinion of the author? You can often find this information by using a search engine such as Google or by consulting one of the following directories:

Contemporary Authors

Directory of American Scholars

International Who's Who

National Faculty Directory

Who's Who in America

Wilson Biographies Plus Illustrated

⊙ EXERCISE 8.1

Assume that you are preparing to write an argumentative essay on the topic of whether information posted on social-networking sites threatens privacy. Read the sources that follow, and evaluate each source for accuracy, credibility, objectivity, currency, comprehensiveness, and authority.

- Nicholas Thompson, "Bigger Brother: The Exponential Law of Privacy Loss"

- *USA Today* editorial board, "Time to Enact 'Do Not Track'"

- Rebecca MacKinnon, "Privacy and Facebook"

This essay appeared in the December 5, 2011, edition of the *New Yorker*.

BIGGER BROTHER: THE EXPONENTIAL LAW OF PRIVACY LOSS

NICHOLAS THOMPSON

This past Tuesday, Facebook made a deal with the F.T.C.: from now on, the social-networking company can no longer humbug us about privacy. If we're told that something we post on the site will be private, it will stay that way, unless we give Facebook permission to make it public. Or at least sort of. For a while. Facebook has been relentless in its effort to make more of what it knows about us—the music we listen to, the photos we take, the friends we have—available to more people, and it will surely figure out creative ways, F.T.C. or no F.T.C., to further that campaign. The company's leadership sincerely believes that the more we share the better the world will be. Mark Zuckerberg, the C.E.O., has said that in ten years we'll share a thousand times as much as we do now. That seems to be both an observation and a goal.

Meanwhile, Zynga has announced that it's going to raise about a billion dollars in an impending I.P.O. Zynga makes social games like *FarmVille*, in which people harvest and sell virtual tomatoes. The games sound inane to non-players, and Zynga employees claim that their workplace is run like a labor camp; yet the company is worth perhaps ten billion dollars. Why? Partly because they collect and analyze fifteen terabytes of data a day from their users. They watch carefully in order to learn how to hook people and what enticements to offer someone frustrated about his slow-growing tomato crop. (There's a segment from *Bloomberg West* in which an analyst compares Zynga to a drug dealer.) According to Zynga's recent S.E.C. filings, its total number of players is stagnant, but the amount of money it can extract from each one is growing. Data is the currency of the Web right now. Whoever has the most detailed data about you will get rich. Zynga has great data, and Zynga is about to get very rich.

> "Whoever has the most detailed data about you will get rich."

Last week also brought the news that a company called Carrier IQ has 3 installed software on about a hundred and fifty million phones that lets it and its customers—such as Sprint, A.T. & T., and Apple—know an awful lot about you. It tracks location, stores the numbers you dial, and even records the Websites you browse when you're not connected to a cell network. The point of the software is to help the phone companies improve their networks and serve you better. But this is done in a mysterious (and perhaps nefarious) way. Most people don't know they have it, and it's not easy to remove. It's also not clear exactly what it's recording, though a bevy of new lawsuits and government investigations will now try to figure that out. At the very least, there's one more company that you've never heard of that knows a heck of a lot about you. "The excuse proffered thus far—improved service—is at best feeble when compared to the extent of the potential invasion of privacy," Stephen Wicker, a professor in electrical and computer engineering at Cornell, told me.

These are just three stories from the past seven days. There'll surely be 4 more soon. Together, they've made me think of something I'll call The Exponential Law of Privacy Loss (or TELPL, pronounced "tell people"). The more we do online, the better companies get at tracking us, and the more accurate and detailed the data they glean from us becomes. The amount of data that they have grows exponentially over time.

It's impossible to exactly measure what percent of our time is spent con- 5 nected to the Internet: texting, shopping, surfing, browsing, sleeping. But, my best estimation is that, a few years ago, we lived roughly ten percent of our lives online, and companies captured about ten percent of what we did. Now it's about thirty percent, and the companies capture thirty percent of that—which means roughly nine times as much as a few years ago. Eventually, when we live seventy percent of our lives online, digital companies will capture and store about seventy percent of that. I'm not sure what will happen to the formula when we spend our entire lives online. Ideally, we won't get there.

This tracking isn't all bad; it may not even be mostly bad. People keep 6 letting Facebook broadcast more of their preferences and habits, and they love it. The more that advertisers know about you, the more willing they are to do things like buy advertisements on Websites, supporting journalism such as this. Carrier IQ makes our phones more efficient, and I have yet to hear of any specific harm done to any specific person by their system. Still, the Law is real. The F.T.C. can slow things down, but only a little. All of us are still becoming corporate data at an ever faster rate, for better and for worse.

This editorial was published in *USA Today* on December 11, 2011.

TIME TO ENACT "DO NOT TRACK"

USA TODAY EDITORIAL BOARD

Facebook's 800 million users are probably feeling a little more secure since the social media giant agreed to privacy measures forced by the Federal Trade Commission (FTC) late last month. But they'd be wise to stay cautious. Plenty of incentive for mischief remains, and not only on Facebook.

The agreement requires Facebook to stop letting users mark their profile information as private and then making it public without their permission. Facebook also promised that it will warn users of privacy policy changes before enacting them.

But the agreement won't stop Facebook from monitoring and sharing users' Web-browsing habits, which is a way for the company and others like it to make money. It's an unsatisfying ending to a two-year investigation, but more important, it's a marker of how difficult it will be to maintain privacy in an increasingly wired world.

The weakness in the FTC's agreement is that it didn't establish any guidelines about Internet tracking, the method by which Facebook collects data about its users even when they're not on the network itself. As company representatives recently acknowledged to *USA Today*, Facebook automatically compiles a log of every Web page its users visit that has a Facebook plug-in, such as the ubiquitous "like" button.

Other online giants, such as Google and Yahoo, use similar methods to monitor users' Web-browsing. This lets them tailor their pages and advertisements to appeal to different visitors.

Online tracking companies, which help sites compile these browsing records, claim that your personal details are not connected to your name, meaning your privacy is not compromised when they share information with advertisers or others. But as the *Wall Street Journal* discovered last year, at least one tracking company collected Web surfers' names and other personally identifiable information and passed it on to clients.

The implication is that tracking companies and advertisers could know your name, e-mail address, hometown, medical history, political affiliation, and more. Such information could be used in troubling ways. A health insurance company, for example, could guess your medical conditions. Or a potential employer could find out whether you spend your time gambling online.

> "Such information could be used in troubling ways."

1

2

3

4

5

6

7

If you don't like that prospect, your only option is to use a Web browser that 8 offers a "Do Not Track" mechanism, such as Mozilla Firefox or Internet Explorer 9. Once you activate the feature, it signals websites you visit indicating that you do not want your data tracked by third parties. But existing Do Not Track mechanisms can't control what websites do; they can only communicate your preference.

That's why the FTC has called for a tougher and more universal version of 9 Do Not Track, a move that the online advertising industry argues would hamper Internet innovation. These fears are overblown. Behavioral advertising, which targets viewers based on their Web-browsing history, is large and growing, but it still accounts for less than 5% of all online advertising. So ads that rely on tracking are hardly the Internet's only revenue stream.

Measures that would create a legally enforceable Do Not Track mechanism 10 or otherwise address privacy concerns are languishing in Congress. Lawmakers should give Web users more tools to control their personal information. Until that happens, your online habits will reveal much more about you than just what you put on your Facebook profile.

This essay is from MacKinnon's book *Consent of the Networked* (2012).

PRIVACY AND FACEBOOK

REBECCA MACKINNON

As protests mounted in reaction to Iran's presidential elections on June 12, 1 2009, Facebook actively encouraged members of the pro-opposition Green Movement to use the social networking platform. By mid-June, more than four hundred members of Facebook's fast-growing Farsi-speaking community volunteered their time to create a Farsi version of Facebook. Thanks to efforts by Facebook enthusiasts all around the world, the platform has been made accessible in seventy languages—including many languages spoken in countries where regimes are known not to tolerate dissent.

Then in December 2009, Facebook made a sudden and unexpected alteration 2 of its privacy settings. On December 9, to be precise, people who logged in got an automatic pop-up message announcing major changes. Until that day, it was possible to keep one's list of Facebook "friends" hidden not only from the general Internet-surfing public but also from one another. That changed overnight without warning. An array of information that Facebook previously had treated as private, suddenly and without warning became publicly available information by default. This included a user's profile picture, name, gender, current city, what professional and regional "networks" one belonged to within Facebook, the "causes" one had signed on to support, and one's entire list of Facebook friends.

The changes were driven by Facebook's need to monetize the service 3 but were also consistent with founder Mark Zuckerberg's strong personal conviction that people everywhere should be open about their lives and actions. In Iran, where authorities were known to be using information and contacts obtained from people's Facebook accounts while interrogating Green Movement activists detained from the summer of 2009 onward, the implications of the new privacy settings were truly frightening. Soon after the changes were made, an anonymous commenter on the technology news site ZDNet confirmed that Iranian users were deleting their accounts in horror:

> A number of my friends in Iran are active student protesters of the government. They use Facebook extensively to organize protests and meetings, but they had no choice but to delete their Facebook accounts today. They are terrified that their once private lists of friends are now available to "everyone" that wants to know. When that "everyone" happens to include the Iranian Revolutionary Guard and members of the Basij militia, willing to kidnap, arrest, or murder to stifle dissent, the consequences seem just a bit more serious than those faced from silly pictures and status updates. I realize this may not be an issue for the vast majority of American Facebook users, but it's just plain irresponsible to do this without first asking consent. It's even more egregious because Facebook threw out the original preference (the one that requested Facebook keep the list of friends private) and replaced it with a mandate, publicizing what was once private information—with no explicit consent. If given the choice to remain a Facebook user with those settings, or quit, my friends would have quit rather than risk that information being seen by the wrong people. Instead, Facebook published it anyways. It's a betrayal of trust for the sake of better targeted advertising.

The global outcry over the exposure of people's friend lists in December 4 2009 was so strong that within roughly a day after the dramatic change, Facebook made an adjustment so that users could once again hide their friend lists from public view. People's friends could still see one another, however, and there was no way to hide them. Everybody's "causes" and "pages" were still publicly exposed by default, another serious vulnerability for activists. People kept complaining—many by creating protest groups within Facebook itself, where hundreds of thousands of people from all around the world posted angry messages. The groups had names like "Facebook! Fix the Privacy Settings!" and "Hide Friend List and Fan Pages! We Need Better Privacy Controls!" and "We Want Our Old Privacy Settings Back!" Scrolling through these pages, you see people posting from all over the world, with large numbers of Arab, Persian, Turkish, Eastern European, and Chinese names.

> "People's friends could still see one another, however, and there was no way to hide them."

Eventually Facebook fixed this problem as well, adjusting the privacy 5 options so that information about what pages users follow, or groups they have joined, can be made private. Meanwhile, however, lives of people around the world had been endangered unnecessarily—not because any government pressured Facebook to make changes, but because Facebook had its own reasons and did not fully consider the implications for the service's most vulnerable users, in democratic and authoritarian countries alike.

⊃ EXERCISE 8.2

Write a one- or two-paragraph evaluation of each of the three sources you read for Exercise 8.1. Be sure to support your evaluation with specific references to the sources.

Evaluating Websites

The Internet is like a freewheeling frontier town in the old West. Occasionally, a federal marshal may pass through, but for the most part, there is no law and order, so you are on your own. On the Internet, literally anything goes— exaggerations, misinformation, errors, and even complete fabrications. Some websites contain reliable content, but many do not. The main reason for this situation is that there is no authority—as there is in a college library—who evaluates sites for accuracy and trustworthiness. That job falls to you, the user.

Another problem is that websites often lack important information. For example, a site may lack a date, a sponsoring organization, or even the name of the author of the page. For this reason, it is not always easy to evaluate the material you find there.

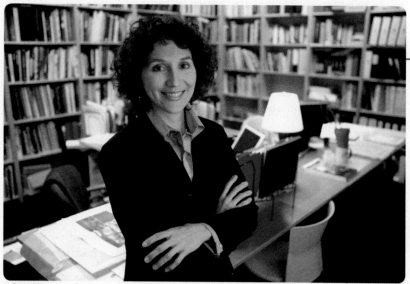

© Steve Hix/Somos Images/Corbis

Most sources found in a college library have been evaluated by a reference librarian for their suitability as research sources.

When you evaluate a website (especially when it is in the form of a blog or a series of posts), you need to begin by viewing it skeptically—unless you know for certain that it is reliable. In other words, assume that its information is questionable until you establish that it is not. Then apply the same criteria you use to evaluate any sources—*accuracy, credibility, objectivity, currency, comprehensiveness,* and *authority.*

The Web page pictured on page 303 shows where to find information that can help you evaluate a website.

Accuracy Information on a website is **accurate** when it is factual and free of errors. Information in the form of facts, opinions, statistics, and interpretations is everywhere on the Internet, and in the case of Wiki sites, this information is continually being rewritten and revised. Given the volume and variety of this material, it is a major challenge to determine its accuracy. You can assess the accuracy of information on a website by asking the following questions:

- **Does the site contain errors of fact?** Factual errors—inaccuracies that relate directly to the central point of the source—should immediately disqualify a site as a reliable source.

- **Does the site contain a list of references or any other type of documentation?** Reliable sources indicate where their information comes from. The authors know that people want to be sure that the information they are using is accurate and reliable. If a site provides no documentation, you should not trust the information it contains.

- **Does the site provide links to other sites?** Does the site have links to reliable websites that are created by respected authorities or sponsored by trustworthy institutions? If it does, then you can conclude that your source is at least trying to maintain a certain standard of quality.

- **Can you verify information?** A good test for accuracy is to try to verify key information on a site. You can do this by checking it in a reliable print source or on a good reference website such as *Encyclopedia.com.*

Credibility Information on a website is **credible** when it is believable. Just as you would not naively believe a stranger who approached you on the street, you should not automatically believe a site that you randomly encounter on the Web. You can assess the credibility of a website by asking the following questions:

- **Does the site list authors, directors, or editors?** Anonymity—whether on a website or on a blog—should be a red flag for a researcher who is considering using a source.

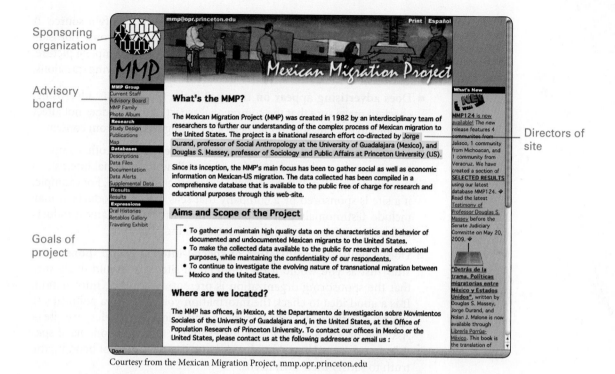

Courtesy from the Mexican Migration Project, mmp.opr.princeton.edu

- **Is the site refereed?** Does a panel of experts or an advisory board decide what material appears on the website? If not, what standards are used to determine the suitability of content?

- **Does the site contain errors in grammar, spelling, or punctuation?** If it does, you should be on the alert for other types of errors. If the people maintaining the site do not care enough to make sure that the site is free of small errors, you have to wonder if they will take the time to verify the accuracy of the information presented.

- **Does an organization sponsor the site?** If so, do you know (or can you find out) anything about the sponsoring organization? Use a search engine such as Google to determine the purpose and point of view of the organization.

Objectivity Information on a website is **objective** when it limits the amount of **bias** that it displays. Some sites—such as those that support a particular political position or social cause—make no secret of their biases. They present them clearly in their policy statements on their home pages. Others, however, try to hide their biases—for example, by referring only to sources that support a particular point of view and not mentioning those that do not.

Keep in mind that bias does not automatically disqualify a source. It should, however, alert you to the fact that you are seeing only one side of an issue and that you will have to look further to get a complete picture. You can assess the objectivity of a website by asking the following questions:

- **Does advertising appear on the site?** If the site contains advertising, check to make sure that the commercial aspect of the site does not affect its objectivity. The site should keep advertising separate from content.

- **Does a commercial entity sponsor the site?** A for-profit company may sponsor a website, but it should not allow commercial interests to determine content. If it does, there is a conflict of interest. For example, if a site is sponsored by a company that sells organic products, it may include testimonials that emphasize the virtues of organic products and ignore information that is skeptical of their benefits.

- **Does a political organization or special-interest group sponsor the site?** Just as you would for a commercial site, you should make sure that the sponsoring organization is presenting accurate information. It is a good idea to check the information you get from a political site against information you get from an educational or a reference site—*Ask.com* or *Encyclopedia.com*, for example. Organizations have specific agendas, and you should make sure that they are not bending the truth to satisfy their own needs.

- **Does the site link to strongly biased sites?** Even if a site seems trustworthy, it is a good idea to check some of its links. Just as you can judge people by the company they keep, you can also judge websites by the sites they link to. Links to overly biased sites should cause you to reevaluate the information on the original site.

USING A SITE'S URL TO ASSESS ITS OBJECTIVITY

A website's **URL** (uniform resource locator) can give you information that can help you assess the site's objectivity.

Look at the domain name to identify sponsorship. Knowing a site's purpose can help you determine whether a site is trying to sell you something or just trying to provide information. The last part of a site's URL can tell you whether a site is a commercial site (.com and .net), an educational site (.edu), a nonprofit site (.org), or a governmental site (.gov, .mil, and so on).

See if the URL has a tilde (~) in it. A tilde in a site's URL indicates that information was published by an individual and is unaffiliated with the sponsoring organization. Individuals can have their own agendas, which may be different from the agenda of the site on which their information appears or to which it is linked.

AVOIDING CONFIRMATION BIAS

Confirmation bias is a tendency that people have to accept information that supports their beliefs and to ignore information that does not. For example, people see false or inaccurate information on websites, and because it reinforces their political or social beliefs, they forward it to others. Eventually, this information becomes so widely distributed that people assume that it is true. Numerous studies have demonstrated how prevalent confirmation bias is. Consider the following examples:

- A student doing research for a paper chooses sources that support her thesis and ignores those that take the opposite position.

- A prosecutor interviews witnesses who establish the guilt of a suspect and overlooks those who do not.

- A researcher includes statistics that confirm his hypothesis and excludes statistics that do not.

When you write an argumentative essay, do not accept information just because it supports your thesis. Realize that you have an obligation to consider all sides of an issue, not just the side that reinforces your beliefs.

Currency Information on a website is **current** when it is up-to-date. Some sources—such as fiction and poetry—are timeless and therefore are useful whatever their age. Other sources, however—such as those in the hard sciences—must be current because advances in some disciplines can quickly make information outdated. For this reason, you should be aware of the shelf life of information in the discipline you are researching and choose information accordingly. You can assess the currency of a website by asking the following questions:

- **Does the website include the date when it was last updated?** As you look at Web pages, check the date on which they were created or updated. (Some websites automatically display the current date, so be careful not to confuse this date with the date the page was last updated.)

- **Are all links on the site live?** If a website is properly maintained, all the links it contains will be **live**—that is, a click on the link will take you to other websites. If a site contains a number of links that are not live, you should question its currency.

- **Is the information on the site up-to-date?** A site might have been updated, but this does not necessarily mean that it contains the most up-to-date information. In addition to checking when a website was last updated, look at the dates of the individual articles that appear on the site to make sure they are not outdated.

Comprehensiveness Information on a website is **comprehensive** when it covers a subject in depth. A site that presents itself as a comprehensive source should include (or link to) the most important sources of information that you need to understand a subject. (A site that leaves out a key source of information or that ignores opposing points of view cannot be called comprehensive.) You can assess the comprehensiveness of a website by asking the following questions:

- **Does the site provide in-depth coverage?** Articles in professional journals—which are available both in print and online—treat subjects in enough depth for college-level research. Other types of articles—especially those in popular magazines and in general encyclopedias, such as *Wikipedia*—are often too superficial (or untrustworthy) for college-level research.

- **Does the site provide information that is not available elsewhere?** The website should provide information that is not available from other sources. In other words, it should make a contribution to your knowledge and do more than simply repackage information from other sources.

- **Who is the intended audience for the site?** Knowing the target audience for a website can help you to assess a source's comprehensiveness. Is it aimed at general readers or at experts? Is it aimed at high school students or at college students? It stands to reason that a site that is aimed at experts or college students will include more detailed information than one that is aimed at general readers or high school students.

Authority Information on a website has **authority** when you can establish the legitimacy of both the author and the site. You can determine the authority of a source by asking the following questions:

- **Is the author an expert in the field that he or she is writing about?** What credentials does the author have? Does he or she have the expertise to write about the subject? Sometimes you can find this information on the website itself. For example, the site may contain an "About the Author" section or links to other publications by the author. If this information is not available, do a Web search with the author's name as a keyword. If you cannot confirm the author's expertise (or if the site has no listed author), you should not use material from the site.

- **What do the links show?** What information is revealed by the links on the site? Do they lead to reputable sites, or do they take you to sites that suggest that the author has a clear bias or a hidden agenda? Do other reliable sites link back to the site you are evaluating?

- **Is the site a serious publication?** Does it include information that enables you to judge its legitimacy? For example, does it include a statement of purpose? Does it provide information that enables you to determine the criteria for publication? Does the site have a board of advisers? Are these advisers experts? Does the site include a mailing address and a phone number? Can you determine if the site is the domain of a single individual or the effort of a group of individuals?

- **Does the site have a sponsor?** If so, is the site affiliated with a reputable institutional sponsor, such as a governmental, educational, or scholarly organization?

➲ EXERCISE 8.3

Consider the following two home pages—one from the website for the *Chronicle of Higher Education*, a publication aimed at college instructors and administrators, and the other from the website for *Glamour*, a publication aimed at general readers. Assume that on both websites, you have found articles about privacy and social-networking sites. Locate and label the information on each home page that would enable you to determine the suitability of using information from the site in your paper.

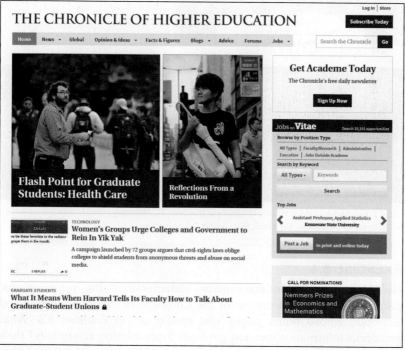

Courtesy of The Chronicle of Higher Education, www.chronicle.com; © Nabil K. Mark Photography; © Mark Leong/Redux

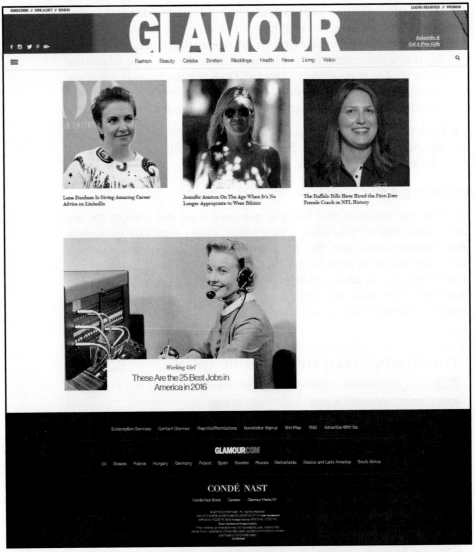

Courtesy of Glamour, © Conde Nast; Jason Merritt/Getty Images (Lena Dunham); TC: Wireimage/Getty Images (Jen Aniston); TR: AP/Wire Photo (Kathryn Smith); Bottom: Superstock/Getty Images (phone operator)

⊙ EXERCISE 8.4

Here are the **mission statements**—statements of the organizations' purposes—from the websites for the *Chronicle of Higher Education* and *Glamour,* whose home pages you considered in Exercise 8.3. What additional information can you get from these mission statements? How do they help you to evaluate the sites as well as the information that might appear on the sites?

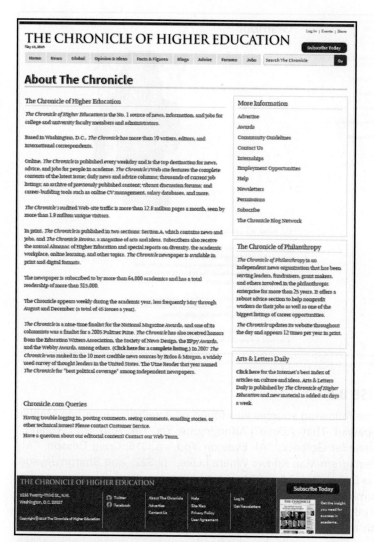

Courtesy of The Chronicle of Higher Education, www.chronicle.com

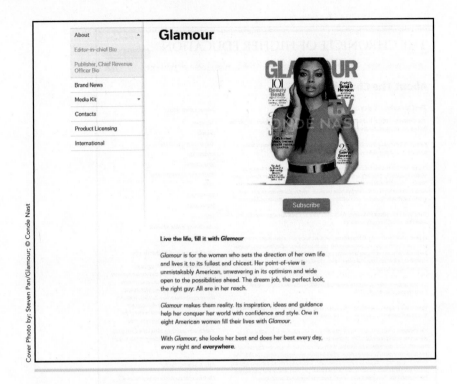

Cover Photo by: Steven Pan/Glamour; © Conde Nast

⊙ EXERCISE 8.5

Each of the following sources was found on a website: Jonathan Mahler, "Who Spewed That Abuse? Anonymous Yik Yak App Isn't Telling," p. 310; Jennifer Golbeck, "All Eyes on You," p. 316; Craig Desson, "My Creepy Instagram Map Knows Where I Live," p. 322; and Sharon Jayson, "Is Online Dating Safe?," p. 324.

Assume that you are preparing to write an essay on the topic of whether information posted on social-networking sites threatens privacy. First, visit the websites on which the articles appear, and evaluate each site for accuracy, credibility, objectivity, currency, comprehensiveness, and authority. Then, using the same criteria, evaluate each source.

This article originally ran in the *New York Times* on March 8, 2015.

WHO SPEWED THAT ABUSE? ANONYMOUS YIK YAK APP ISN'T TELLING

JONATHAN MAHLER

During a brief recess in an honors course at Eastern Michigan University last   1
fall, a teaching assistant approached the class's three female professors. "I think you need to see this," she said, tapping the icon of a furry yak on her iPhone.

The app opened, and the assistant began scrolling through the feed. 2
While the professors had been lecturing about post-apocalyptic culture,
some of the 230 or so freshmen in the auditorium had been having a separate conversation about them on a social media site called Yik Yak. There
were dozens of posts, most demeaning, many using crude, sexually explicit
language and imagery.

After class, one of the professors, Margaret Crouch, sent off a flurry of 3
emails—with screenshots of some of the worst messages attached—to various university officials, urging them to take some sort of action. "I have been defamed, my
reputation besmirched. I have been sexually harassed and verbally abused," she
wrote to her union representative. "I am about ready to hire a lawyer."

In the end, nothing much came of Ms. Crouch's efforts, for a simple rea- 4
son: Yik Yak is anonymous. There was no way for the school to know who was
responsible for the posts.

Eastern Michigan is one of a number of universities whose campuses have 5
been roiled by offensive "yaks." Since the app was introduced a little more
than a year ago, it has been used to issue threats of mass violence on more than
a dozen college campuses, including the University of North Carolina, Michigan State University, and Penn State. Racist, homophobic, and misogynist
"yaks" have generated controversy at many more, among them Clemson,
Emory, Colgate, and the University of Texas. At Kenyon College, a "yakker"
proposed a gang rape at the school's women's center.

In much the same way that Facebook swept through the dorm rooms of 6
America's college students a decade ago, Yik Yak is now taking their smartphones by storm. Its enormous popularity on campuses has made it the most
frequently downloaded anonymous social app in Apple's App Store, easily
surpassing competitors like Whisper and Secret. At times, it has been one of
the store's 10 most downloaded apps.

Like Facebook or Twitter, Yik Yak is a social media network, only without 7
user profiles. It does not sort messages according to friends or followers but by
geographic location or, in many cases, by university. Only posts within a 1.5-mile
radius appear, making Yik Yak well suited to college campuses. Think of it as a
virtual community bulletin board—or maybe a virtual bathroom wall at the
student union. It has become the go-to social feed for college students across
the country to commiserate about finals, to find a party, or to crack a joke
about a rival school.

Much of the chatter is harmless. Some of it is not. 8

"Yik Yak is the Wild West of anonymous 9
social apps," said Danielle Keats Citron, a law
professor at University of Maryland and the
author of *Hate Crimes in Cyberspace*. "It is
being increasingly used by young people in a
really intimidating and destructive way."

> "Much of the
> chatter is harmless.
> Some of it is not."

Colleges are largely powerless to deal with the havoc Yik Yak is wreak- 10
ing. The app's privacy policy prevents schools from identifying users

without a subpoena, court order, or search warrant, or an emergency request from a law-enforcement official with a compelling claim of imminent harm. Schools can block access to Yik Yak on their Wi-Fi networks, but banning a popular social media network is controversial in its own right, arguably tantamount to curtailing freedom of speech. And as a practical matter, it doesn't work anyway. Students can still use the app on their phones with their cell service.

Yik Yak was created in late 2013 by Tyler Droll and Brooks Buffington, fra- 11 ternity brothers who had recently graduated from Furman University in South Carolina. Mr. Droll majored in information technology and Mr. Buffington in accounting. Both 24, they came up with the idea after realizing that there were only a handful of popular Twitter accounts at Furman, almost all belonging to prominent students, like athletes. With Yik Yak, they say, they hoped to create a more democratic social media network, one where users didn't need a large number of followers or friends to have their posts read widely.

"We thought, 'Why can't we level the playing field and connect every- 12 one?'" said Mr. Droll, who withdrew from medical school a week before classes started to focus on the app.

"When we made this app, we really made it for the disenfranchised," 13 Mr. Buffington added.

Just as Mark Zuckerberg and his roommates introduced Facebook at 14 Harvard, Mr. Buffington and Mr. Droll rolled out their app at their alma mater, relying on fraternity brothers and other friends to get the word out.

Within a matter of months, Yik Yak was in use at 40 or so colleges in the 15 South. Then came spring break. Some early adopters shared the app with college students from all over the country at gathering places like Daytona Beach and Panama City. "And we just exploded," Mr. Buffington said.

Mr. Droll and Mr. Buffington started Yik Yak with a loan from Mr. Droll's 16 parents. (His parents also came up with the company's name, which was inspired by the 1958 song, "Yakety Yak.") In November, Yik Yak closed a $62 million round of financing led by one of Silicon Valley's biggest venture capital firms, Sequoia Capital, valuing the company at hundreds of millions of dollars.

The Yik Yak app is free. Like many tech start-ups, the company, based 17 in Atlanta, doesn't generate any revenue. Attracting advertisers could pose a challenge, given the nature of some of the app's content. For now, though, Mr. Droll and Mr. Buffington are focused on extending Yik Yak's reach by expanding overseas and moving beyond the college market, much as Facebook did.

Yik Yak's popularity among college students is part of a broader reaction 18 against more traditional social media sites like Facebook, which can encourage public posturing at the expense of honesty and authenticity.

"Share your thoughts with people around you while keeping your pri- 19 vacy," Yik Yak's home page says. It is an attractive concept to a generation of smartphone users who grew up in an era of social media—and are thus inclined to share—but who have also been warned repeatedly about the permanence of their digital footprint.

In a sense, Yik Yak is a descendant of JuicyCampus, an anonymous online 20 college message board that enjoyed a brief period of popularity several years ago. Matt Ivester, who founded JuicyCampus in 2007 and shut it in 2009 after it became a hotbed of gossip and cruelty, is skeptical of the claim that Yik Yak does much more than allow college students to say whatever they want, publicly and with impunity. "You can pretend that it is serving an important role on college campuses, but you can't pretend that it's not upsetting a lot of people and doing a lot of damage," he said. "When I started JuicyCampus, cyberbullying wasn't even a word in our vernacular. But these guys should know better."

Yik Yak's founders say the app's overnight success left them unprepared 21 for some of the problems that have arisen since its introduction. In response to complaints, they have made some changes to their product, for instance, adding filters to prevent full names from being posted. Certain keywords, like "Jewish," or "bomb," prompt this message: "Pump the brakes, this yak may contain threatening language. Now it's probably nothing and you're probably an awesome person but just know that Yik Yak and law enforcement take threats seriously. So you tell us, is this yak cool to post?"

In cases involving threats of mass violence, Yik Yak has cooperated with 22 authorities. Most recently, in November, local police traced the source of a yak—"I'm gonna [gun emoji] the school at 12:15 p.m. today"—to a dorm room at Michigan State University. The author, Matthew Mullen, a freshman, was arrested within two hours and pleaded guilty to making a false report or terrorist threat. He was spared jail time but sentenced to two years' probation and ordered to pay $800 to cover costs connected to the investigation.

In the absence of a specific, actionable threat, though, Yik Yak zealously 23 protects the identities of its users. The responsibility lies with the app's various communities to police themselves by "upvoting" or "downvoting" posts. If a yak receives a score of negative 5, it is removed. "Really, what it comes down to is that we try to empower the communities as much as we can," Mr. Droll said.

When Yik Yak appeared, it quickly spread across high schools and middle 24 schools, too, where the problems were even more rampant. After a rash of complaints last winter at a number of schools in Chicago, Mr. Droll and Mr. Buffington disabled the app throughout the city. They say they have since built virtual fences—or "geo-fences"—around about 90 percent of the nation's high schools and middle schools. Unlike barring Yik Yak from a Wi-Fi network, which has proved ineffective in limiting its use, these fences actually make it impossible to open the app on school grounds. Mr. Droll and Mr. Buffington also changed Yik Yak's age rating in the App Store from 12 and over to 17 and over.

Toward the end of last school year, almost every student at Phillips Exeter 25 Academy in New Hampshire had the app on his or her phone and checked it constantly to read the anonymous attacks on fellow students, faculty members, and deans.

"Please stop using Yik Yak immediately," Arthur Cosgrove, the dean of 26
residential life, wrote in an email to the student body. "Remove it from your
phones. It is doing us no good."

At Exeter's request, the company built a geo-fence around the school, but 27
it covered only a few buildings. Students continued using the app on different
parts of the sprawling campus.

"We made the app for college kids, but we quickly realized it was getting 28
into the hands of high schoolers, and high schoolers were not mature enough
to use it," Mr. Droll said.

The widespread abuse of Yik Yak on college campuses, though, suggests 29
that the distinction may be artificial. Last spring, Jordan Seman, then a sophomore at Middlebury College, was scrolling through Yik Yak in the dining hall
when she happened across a post comparing her to a "hippo" and making a
sexual reference about her. "It's so easy for anyone in any emotional state to
post something, whether that person is drunk or depressed or wants to get
revenge on someone," she said. "And then there are no consequences."

In this sense, the problem with Yik Yak is a familiar one. Anyone who has 30
browsed the comments of an Internet post is familiar with the sorts of intolerant, impulsive language that the cover of anonymity tends to invite. But Yik
Yak's particular design can produce especially harmful consequences.

"It's a problem with the Internet culture in general, but when you add this 31
hyper-local dimension to it, it takes on a more disturbing dimension," says
Elias Aboujaoude, a Stanford psychiatrist and the author of *Virtually You.*
"You don't know where the aggression is coming from, but you know it's very
close to you."

Jim Goetz, a partner at Sequoia Capital who recently joined Yik Yak's 32
board, said the app's history of misuse was a concern when his firm considered investing in the company. But he said he was confident that Mr. Droll
and Mr. Buffington were committed to ensuring more positive interactions on
Yik Yak, and that over time, the constructive voices would overwhelm the
destructive ones.

"It's certainly a challenge to the company," Mr. Goetz said. "It's not going 33
to go away in a couple of months."

Ms. Seman wrote about her experience being harassed on Yik Yak in the 34
school newspaper, the *Middlebury Campus,* prompting a schoolwide debate
over what to do about the app. Unable to reach a consensus, the paper's editorial board wrote two editorials, one urging a ban, the other arguing that the
problem wasn't Yik Yak but the larger issue of cyberbullying. (Middlebury has
not taken any action.)

Similar debates have played out at other schools. At Clemson, a group of 35
African-American students unsuccessfully lobbied the university to ban Yik
Yak when some racially offensive posts appeared after a campus march to protest the grand jury's decision not to indict a white police officer in the fatal
shooting of an unarmed black teenager in Ferguson, Mo. "We think that in the
educational community, First Amendment rights are very important," said

Leon Wiles, the school's chief diversity officer. "It's just problematic because you have young people who use it with no sense of responsibility."

During the fall, Maxwell Zoberman, the sophomore representative to the 36 student government at Emory, started noticing a growing number of yaks singling out various ethnic groups for abuse. "Fave game to play while driving around Emory: not hit an Asian with a truck," read one.

"Guys stop with all this hate. Let's just be thankful we arn't black," read 37 another.

After consulting the university's code, Mr. Zoberman discovered that state- 38 ments deemed derogatory to any particular group of people were not protected by the school's open expression policy, and were in fact in violation of its discriminatory harassment rules. Just because the statements were made on an anonymous social-media site should not, in his mind, prevent Emory from acting to enforce its own policies. "It didn't seem right that the school took one approach to hate speech in a physical medium and another one in a digital medium," he said.

Mr. Zoberman drafted a resolution to have Yik Yak disabled on the school's 39 Wi-Fi network. He recognized that this would not stop students from using the app, but he nevertheless felt it was important for the school to take a stand.

After Mr. Zoberman formally proposed his resolution to the student gov- 40 ernment, someone promptly posted about it on Yik Yak. "The reaction was swift and harsh," he said. "I seem to have redirected all of the fury of the anonymous forum. Yik Yak was just dominated with hateful and other aggressive posts specifically about me." One compared him to Hitler.

A few colleges have taken the almost purely symbolic step of barring Yik 41 Yak from their servers. John Brown University, a Christian college in Arkansas, did so after its Yik Yak feed was overrun with racist commentary during a march connected to the school's World Awareness Week. Administrators at Utica College in upstate New York blocked the app in December in response to a growing number of sexually graphic posts aimed at the school's transgender community.

In December, a group of 50 professors at Colgate University—which had 42 experienced a rash of racist comments on the app earlier in the fall—tried a different approach, flooding the app with positive posts.

Generally speaking, though, the options are limited. A student who felt that 43 he or she had been the target of an attack on Yik Yak could theoretically pursue defamation charges and subpoena the company to find out who had written the post. But it is a difficult situation to imagine, given the cost and murky legal issues involved. Schools will probably just stand back and hope that respect and civility prevail, that their communities really will learn to police themselves.

Yik Yak's founders say their start-up is just experiencing some growing pains. "It's definitely still a learning process for us," Mr. Buffington said, "and we're definitely still learning how to make the community more constructive."

> "Yik Yak's founders say their start-up is just experiencing some growing pains." 44

Golbeck's essay appeared in the September/October 2014 issue of *Psychology Today*.

ALL EYES ON YOU

JENNIFER GOLBECK

Every day, nearly everywhere I go, I'm being followed. That's not paranoia. It's 1
a fact. Consider:

On my local Washington, D.C., streets, I am constantly watched. The city 2
government alone has hundreds of traffic and surveillance cameras. And then
there are the cameras in parks, office buildings, ATM lobbies, and, of course,
around every federal building and landmark. On an average day, my image is
captured by well over 100 cameras.

When I'm online and using social media, a wealth of information about 3
my interests and routines is collected behind the scenes. I employ an add-on
on my browser that blocks companies from tracking my searches and visits. In
just one recent month, it reported blocking nearly 16,000 separate attempts to
access my data online.

I'm monitored offline, too. Anytime I use a reward card at a supermarket, 4
department store, or other retail outlet, my purchase is recorded, and the data
either sold to other marketers or used to predict my future purchases and guide
me to make them in that store. Department store tracking based on purchase
records can even conclude that a woman is pregnant and roughly when she is due.

My own devices report on me. I carry an iPhone, which tracks and records 5
my every movement. This will help me find my phone if I ever lose it (I haven't
yet), but it also provides Apple with a treasure trove of data about my daily habits.

Data on any call I place or email I send may be collected by the National 6
Security Agency. Recent news reports have revealed that the federal intelligence arm may be collecting metadata on phone and Internet traffic—when
Americans communicate and with whom, if not the actual content of those
communications. As Barton Gellman, Pulitzer Prize–winning intelligence
reporter for the *Washington Post*, said during a recent panel discussion, it's
not that the NSA knows everything about everyone, but that "it *wants* to be
able to know anything about anybody."

Thirty years after 1984, Big Brother is here. He's everywhere. In many 7
cases, we've invited him in. So the question we have to ask now is, How does
this constant surveillance affect us and what, if anything, can we do about it?

"Get Over It."

There's no question our privacy has been eroded with the help of technology. 8
There's also little question that those most responsible aren't much inclined to
retreat. As Scott McNealy, cofounder of Sun Microsystems, famously said:
"You have zero privacy anyway. Get over it."

Privacy is an intangible asset. If we never think about it, we may not realize it's gone. Does it still matter? Elias Aboujaoude, a professor of psychiatry at Stanford University and the author of *Virtually You: The Dangerous Powers of the E-Personality*, insists that it does. "We cannot afford to just 'get over it,' for nothing short of our self-custody seems to be at stake," he says. "At its heart, this is about our psychological autonomy and the maintenance of some semblance of control over the various little details that make us us."

"Does it still matter?"   9

In the modern surveillance environment, with so much personal information accessible by others—especially those with whom we have not chosen to share that information—our sense of self is threatened, as is our ability to manage the impression others have of us, says Ian Brown, senior research fellow at the Oxford Internet Institute.   10

If people treat us differently based on what they have discovered online, if the volume of data available about us eradicates our ability to make a first impression on a date or a job interview, the result, Brown believes, is reduced trust, increased conformity, and even diminished civic participation. The impact can be especially powerful when we know that our information was collected and shared without our consent.   11

To be sure, we are responsible for much of this. We're active participants in creating our surveillance record. Along with all of the personal information we voluntarily, often eagerly, share on social networks and shopping sites—and few of us take advantage of software or strategies to limit our digital footprint—we collectively upload 144,000 hours of video footage a day to YouTube. And with tech enthusiasts trumpeting personal drones as the next hot item, we may soon be equipped to photograph ourselves and, just as easily, our neighbors, from above.   12

Most of us try to curate the public identities we broadcast—not only through the way we dress and speak in public, but also in how we portray ourselves on social-media platforms. The problem arises when we become conscious that uninvited observers are also tuning in. "The most fundamental impact surveillance has on identity," Brown says, "is that it reduces individuals' control over the information they disclose about their attributes in different social contexts, often to such powerful actors as the state or multinational corporations." When we discover that such entities—and third parties to which our information may be sold or shared—make decisions about us based on that data, our sense of self can be altered.   13

The Right to Be Forgotten

There are existential threats to our psyches in a world where nothing we do can be forgotten, believes Viktor Mayer-Schönberger, professor of Internet governance and regulation at the Oxford Internet Institute. His book, *Delete: The Virtue of Forgetting in the Digital Age*, relates the experiences of people whose lives were negatively affected because of information available about them online.   14

In 2006, for example, psychotherapist Andrew Feldmar drove from his   15
Vancouver home to pick up a friend flying in to Seattle. At the United States
border, which Feldmar had crossed scores of times, a guard decided to do an
Internet search on him. The query returned an article Feldmar had written for
an academic journal five years earlier, in which he revealed that he'd taken
LSD in the 1960s. The guard held Feldmar for four hours, fingerprinted him,
and asked him to sign a statement that he had taken drugs almost 40 years
earlier. He was barred from entry into the U.S.

Aboujaoude relates the story of "Rob," a nurse in a public hospital emer-   16
gency room chronically short on staff. His willingness to fill in when the ER
needed extra hands led to significant overtime pay. When a website published
an "exposé" of seemingly overpaid public employees, Rob's name and salary
were posted as an example. He was then hounded by hate mail—both paper
and electronic. People called his house, and his daughter was harassed at
school. Eventually the stress and constant criticism made him feel as if he were
becoming paranoid and led him to Aboujaoude as a therapy patient.

The ability to forget past events, Mayer-Schönberger says, or at least to let   17
them recede in our minds, is critical for decision making. Psychologists often
note that our ability to forget is a valuable safety valve. As we naturally forget
things over time, we can move on and make future choices without difficult or
embarrassing episodes clouding our outlook. But when our decisions are tan-
gled up in the perfect memory of the Internet—when we must factor in the
effect of our online footprint before every new step—"we may lose a fundamental human capacity: to live and act firmly in the present," he says.

The result can be demoralizing and even paranoia-inducing. Lacking the   18
power to control what, when, and with whom we share, Mayer-Schönberger
explains, our sense of self may be diminished, leading to self-doubt internally
and self-censorship externally, as we begin to fixate on what others will think
about every potentially public action and thought, now and in the future.

Under normal circumstances, the passage of time allows us to shape our nar-   19
rative, cutting out or minimizing less important (or more embarrassing) details to
form a more positive impression. When we can't put the past behind us, it can
affect our behavior and intrude on our judgment. Instead of making decisions
fully in the present, we make them while weighed down by every detail of our past.

The effects are not trivial. A range of people, from a long-reformed crimi-   20
nal seeking a fresh slate to a sober former college party girl in the job market,
can find that the omnipresence of public
records and posted photos permanently
holds them back. At its worst, these
weights can inhibit one's desire to
change. If we can never erase the record
of one mistake we made long ago, if we're
convinced it will only continue to hinder

> "With easily accessible digital reminders, bygones cannot be bygones."

our progress, what motivation do we have to become anyone different from
the person who made that mistake? For that matter, why bother moving

beyond conflicts with others if the sources of those disputes remain current online? With easily accessible digital reminders, bygones cannot be bygones. It's no accident that the most successful legal campaign yet against permanent digital records hinges on "the right to be forgotten."

A Spanish lawyer, Mario Costeja González, sued Google over search 21 results that prominently returned a long-ago news article detailing a government order that he sell his home to cover unpaid debts. The European Court of Justice ruled in his favor, asserting, based on an older legal concept allowing ex-convicts to object to the publication of information related to their crimes, that each of us has the right to be forgotten. Even if the information about the man's foreclosure is true, the court ruled, it is "irrelevant, or no longer relevant," and should be blocked from Google's (and other browsers') searches.

Google is now working to implement a means for European users to 22 request that certain information be removed from their searches, a process it is finding to be more complicated than many observers had imagined. No similar verdict has been handed down in the U.S., and privacy experts believe that Congress is unlikely to take up the issue anytime soon.

Do Cameras Make Us More Honorable, or Just Paranoid?

Trust is perennially strained in our workplaces, where more employees than ever 23 are being overseen via cameras, recorded phone calls, location tracking, and email monitoring. Studies dating back two decades have consistently found that employees who were aware that they were being surveilled found their working conditions more stressful and reported higher levels of anxiety, anger, and depression. More recent research indicates that, whatever productivity benefits management hopes to realize, increased surveillance on the office floor leads to poorer performance, tied to a feeling of loss of control as well as to lower job satisfaction.

Outside the workplace, we expect more freedom and wider opportunity 24 to defend our privacy. But even as we become more savvy about online tracking, we're beginning to realize just how little we can do about so-called "passive" surveillance—the cameras recording our movements as we go about our business—especially because so much of this observation is covert. The visual range of surveillance cameras has expanded even as their physical size has shrunk, and as satellites and drones become more accurate from increasing distances, social scientists have begun to explore how near-constant surveillance, at least in the public sphere, affects our behavior. The research so far identifies both concerns and potential benefits. We tend, for example, to be more cooperative and generous when we suspect someone is watching—a recent Dutch study found that people were more likely to intervene when witnessing a (staged) crime if they knew they were being watched, either by others or by a camera. But we don't become more generous of spirit. Pierrick Bourrat, a graduate student at the University of Sydney, and cognitive scientist Nicolas Baumard of the École Normale Supérieure in Paris, recently published a study on how we judge other people's bad behavior. They found that when subjects believed they were being watched, they rated others' actions more severely. A possible explanation: When we think we're being observed, we adjust our behavior to project an image of moral uprightness through harsher-than-usual judgment of others.

But adjusting our behavior in the presence of cameras to project an image aligned with presumed social norms can have a downside. The Oxford Internet Institute's Brown sees a cooling effect on public discourse, because when people think they're being watched, they may behave, consciously or not, in ways that comply with what they presume governmental or other observers want. That doesn't mean we trust the watchers. A recent Gallup poll found that only 12 percent of Americans have "a lot of trust" that the government will keep their personal information secure; we trust banks three times as much.

When Users Strike Back

What would happen if we really tried to root out all of the surveillance in our life and took action to erase ourselves from it? We think such knowledge would equal power, but it may just bring on paranoia. Pulitzer Prize–winning investigative journalist Julia Angwin tried for a year to prevent her life from being monitored. She used a disposable cell phone. She installed encryption software on her email accounts. She even developed a fake identity ("Ida Tarbell") to prevent her online and commercial activities from being tied to her true self.

Angwin detailed these efforts in her book, *Dragnet Nation,* which, while ultimately hopeful, relates a draining journey during which she lost trust in nearly every institution that holds her data. Even with her resources and single-mindedness, Angwin could achieve only partial success: Her past personal data, after all, were stored in bits and pieces by hundreds of brokers that traffic in information, and she had no means of turning back the clock.

The efforts also affected her worldview: "I wasn't happy with the toll that my countersurveillance techniques had taken on my psyche. The more I learned about who was watching me, the more paranoid I became. By the end of my experiment, I was refusing to have digital conversations with my close friends without encryption. I began using my fake name for increasingly trivial transactions; a friend was shocked when we took a yoga class together and I casually registered as Ida Tarbell."

The Next Level

Modern surveillance does have some clear benefits. Cameras in public spaces help the authorities detect crime and catch perpetrators, though they catch us in the dragnet as well. Cell phone tracking and networked late-model cars allow us to be found if we become lost or injured, and mapping apps are incredibly useful for directing us where we want to go. These features save lives—but all of them constantly transmit our location and generate a precisely detailed record of our movements. Our social media history helps providers put the people and content we prefer front and center when we log on, and our online searches and purchase records allow marketers to offer us discounts at the places we shop most, all the while collecting data on our personal preferences and quirks. Given the difficulty of completely avoiding the monitoring, it may be somewhat reassuring to acknowledge this tradeoff.

Laura Brandimarte of Carnegie Mellon University and her colleagues have 30
studied people's willingness to disclose personal information. They found that when entities give people more control over the publication of their information, people disclose more about themselves—even if it is also clear that the information will be accessed and seen by others more often than it currently is.

Their work demonstrates the concept of illusion of control. In many situa- 31
tions, we tend to overestimate the control we have over events, especially when we get cues that our actions matter. The risk to our private information comes not just from what we've shared but from how much of it is sold or made available to others. And yet when we feel that we have been given more control over our information's dissemination, our privacy concerns decrease and our disclosure increases, even though that apparent control does not actually diminish the possibility that our data will be shared. "The control people perceive over the publication of personal information makes them pay less attention to the lack of control they have over access by others," Brandimarte says.

In other words, we are simply not very sophisticated when it comes to 32
making choices about what to share.

When it comes to privacy-protection, the first issue for social-media users 33
to grapple with is inertia: According to a range of surveys of U.S. Facebook users, for example, as many as 25 percent have never checked or adjusted their privacy settings to impose even the most basic restriction on their postings: not making them public.

There is a growing availability of privacy fixes for homes, cell phones, and 34
computers. Whether they will be able to keep up with tracking mechanisms is unclear. But evidence suggests that even if they work as advertised, we may not be savvy enough to use them.

So we have limited options to protect our privacy, and few of us take 35
advantage even of those. What's the ultimate cost? Aboujaoude argues that our need for privacy and true autonomy is rooted in the concept of individuation, the process by which we develop and maintain an independent identity. It's a crucial journey that begins in childhood, as we learn to separate our own identity from that of our parents, and continues through adulthood.

Many psychologists emphasize that maintaining self-identity requires a 36
separation from others, and Aboujaoude believes that, in today's environment, control over personal information is a critical piece of the process. "You are a psychologically autonomous individual," he says, "if you have the option to keep your person to yourself and dole out the pieces as you see fit."

And who do we become if we don't have that option? We may soon find out. 37

I Married a P.I.

When we worry about who might be watching us, we tend to focus our con- 38
cern on Facebook, the NSA, or marketers. But we may want to consider our own partners as well.

Sue Simring, an associate professor at Columbia University's School of   39
Social Work and a psychotherapist with four decades of experience working
primarily with couples, says the ease with which people can now monitor each
other has radically changed her work. "It used to be that, unless you literally
discovered them [in flagrante], there was no way to know for sure that people
were having an affair," she says.

No more.   40

When spouses stray today, their digital trail inevitably provides clues for   41
the amateur sleuth with whom they share a bed. Simring describes one case in
which a man had carried on an affair for years while traveling for work. He
managed to keep it secret until a technical glitch started sending copies of his
text messages to his wife's iPad.

But the easy availability of tools to track a partner can cut both ways.   42
In the case of another couple that Simring worked with, the husband was
convinced that his wife was having an affair. Determined to catch her, he
undertook increasingly complex and invasive surveillance efforts, eventually monitoring all of her communications and installing spy cameras in
their home to catch her in the act. The more he surveilled, the more his
paranoia grew. It turned out that the wife was not having an affair, but
because of the trauma the husband's surveillance caused her, she ended the
marriage.

This essay was posted to the online newspaper *The Start* on February 27, 2015.

MY CREEPY INSTAGRAM
MAP KNOWS WHERE I LIVE

CRAIG DESSON

U.S. Congressman Aaron Schock's reputation took a hit this week when the   1
Associated Press used geo-location data from his Instagram account to show
how he was flying on private jets provided by campaign donors, expensed
massages, and bought Katy Perry tickets for his interns.

The reporters involved explained that "the AP extracted location data   2
associated with each image, then correlated it with flight records showing airport stopovers and expenses later billed for air travel against Schock's office
and campaign records."

To track somebody on Instagram the way AP did for the Schock story   3
isn't difficult. There is a program called Creepy that will create a Google map
showing where you've been, based on what you've shared on Instagram, Twitter,
and Flickr.

I ran Creepy on my own Instagram account and found it wouldn't be   4
hard for a stranger to figure out where I live in the Annex.

This is the map the program made about my account, and with a bit of 5 deductive logic it's clear I live just north of Bloor and Spadina.

The photos taken around Front St. are all interiors of offices, because that's 6 where I've worked for the past two and a half years. The photos taken along major streets such as King and Bloor portray me hanging out with friends.

Then there is the funny collection of dots north of Bloor in the Annex 7 that link to Instagram photos of an apartment's interior.

You don't need to be Sherlock Holmes to guess that's my home. 8

It's true that 20 years ago, a phonebook might have led a stranger to my 9 home address. But I would at least know that I had a listed number. The trouble with Instagram tracking is that most users have no idea their photo-sharing app is also building a detailed history of where they work and live.

If Aaron Schock, a congressman with paid communications people, 10 couldn't figure this out, then it's likely most members of the public have no idea this is going on.

USA Today posted this article to its website on March 27, 2014.

IS ONLINE DATING SAFE?

SHARON JAYSON

Change may be coming to the rapidly growing dating industry as concern 1 mounts about the privacy and safety of all online and mobile users.

Sen. Al Franken, D-Minn., introduced legislation Thursday requiring 2 companies to get customers' permission before collecting location data off their mobile devices and sharing it with others.

It's a move that would greatly affect dating websites and apps. As mobile dating proliferates, the focus no longer is just on daters leery of scams or sexual predators, but on keeping their locations confidential.

"This stuff is advancing at a faster and faster rate, and we've got to try and catch up," Franken says. "This is about Americans' right to privacy and one of the most private things is your location."

> "As mobile dating proliferates, the focus no longer is just on daters leery of scams or sexual predators, but on keeping their locations confidential."

3

4

Illinois, New York, New Jersey, and Texas have laws that require Internet 5 dating sites to disclose whether they conduct criminal background checks on users and to offer advice on keeping safe.

"I see more regulation about companies stating what kind of information 6 they actually use and more about their specific operation(s)," says analyst Jeremy Edwards, who authored a report on the industry last fall for IBIS-World, a Santa Monica, Calif.–based market research company. "I expect them to have to be more explicit in what they do with their data and what they require of users."

According to a Pew Research Center report in October, 11% of American 7 adults—and 38% of those currently "single and looking" for a partner—say they've used online dating sites or mobile dating apps.

"We entrust some incredibly sensitive information to online dating sites," 8 says Rainey Reitman of the San Francisco, Calif.–based Electronic Frontier Foundation, a nonprofit that advocates for user privacy amid technology development. "People don't realize how much information they're exposing even by doing something as slight as uploading a photograph."

He adds, "Many online apps are very cavalier about collecting that 9 information and perhaps exposing it in a way that would make you uncomfortable."

Dating services eHarmony, Match.com, and Spark Networks and 10 ChristianMingle signed an agreement in 2012 with the California attorney general's office to protect customers with online safety tools. These include companies checking subscribers against national sex offender registries and providing a rapid abuse reporting system for members.

However, cyberdating expert Julie Spira of Los Angeles says such reports 11 are sometimes little more than revenge.

"When people get reported, sometimes it's because they got jilted," she 12 says. "How do you quantify when someone feels rejected and pushes the report button, and when somebody really feels scared?"

Match.com, which has 1.9 million paid subscribers, has been screening all 13 subscribers against sexual offender registries since the summer of 2011, according to spokesman Matthew Traub. Earlier that year, a woman sued the dating site saying she was assaulted by someone she met through it.

Edwards believes dating sites are doing what they can to help users 14 be safe.

"It's difficult for these companies to do much else than provide information 15 and tips," he says. "Meeting someone through one of these websites does not present any greater risk than meeting someone in a bar or any other setting. There's no real added risk because you don't know who anyone is when you meet them for the first time."

⊘ EXERCISE 8.6

Read the blog post below and then answer the questions on page 327.

Read the blog post below and then answer the questions on page 327.

This article first appeared on Mashable.com on February 6, 2012.

SHOULD ATHLETES HAVE SOCIAL MEDIA PRIVACY? ONE BILL SAYS YES

SAM LAIRD

Should universities be allowed to force student athletes to have their Facebook 1
and Twitter accounts monitored by coaches and administrators?

No, says a bill recently introduced into the Maryland state legislature. 2

The bill would prohibit institutions "from requiring a student or an appli- 3
cant for admission to provide access to a personal account or service through
an electronic communications device"—by sharing usernames, passwords, or
unblocking private accounts, for example.

Introduced on Thursday, Mary- 4
land's Senate Bill 434 would apply to all
students but particularly impact college
sports. Student-athletes' social media
accounts are frequently monitored by
authority figures for instances of indecency or impropriety, especially in high-
profile sports like football and men's basketball.

> "Student-athletes' social media accounts are frequently monitored. . . ."

In one example, a top football recruit reportedly put his scholarship hopes 5
in jeopardy last month after a series of inappropriate tweets.

The bill's authors say that it is one of the first in the country to take on the 6
issue of student privacy in the social media age, according to the *New York Times*.

Bradley Shear is a Maryland lawyer whose work frequently involves sports 7
and social media. In a recent post to his blog, Shear explained his support for
Senate Bill 434 and a similar piece of legislation that would further extend students' right to privacy on social media.

"Schools that require their students to turn over their social media user 8
names and/or content are acting as though they are based in China and not in
the United States," Shear wrote.

But legally increasing student-athletes' option to social media privacy 9
could also help shield the schools themselves from potential lawsuits.

On his blog, Shear uses the example of Yardley Love, a former University 10
of Virginia women's lacrosse player who was allegedly murdered by her ex-
boyfriend, who played for the men's lacrosse team.

If the university was monitoring the lacrosse teams' social media accounts 11 and missed anything that could have indicated potential violence, it "may have had significant legal liability for negligent social media monitoring because it failed to protect Love," Shear wrote.

On the other hand, if the school was only monitoring the accounts of its 12 higher-profile football and basketball players, Shear wrote, then that could have been considered discrimination and the university "may have been sued for not monitoring the electronic content of all of its students."

Do you think universities should be allowed to force their athletes into 13 allowing coaches and administrators to monitor their Facebook and Twitter accounts?

Questions

1. What steps would you take to determine whether Laird's information is accurate?

2. How could you determine whether Laird is respected in his field?

3. Is Laird's blog written for an audience that is knowledgeable about his subject? How can you tell?

4. Do you think this blog post is a suitable research source? Why or why not?

5. This blog post was written in 2012. Do you think it is still relevant today? Why or why not?

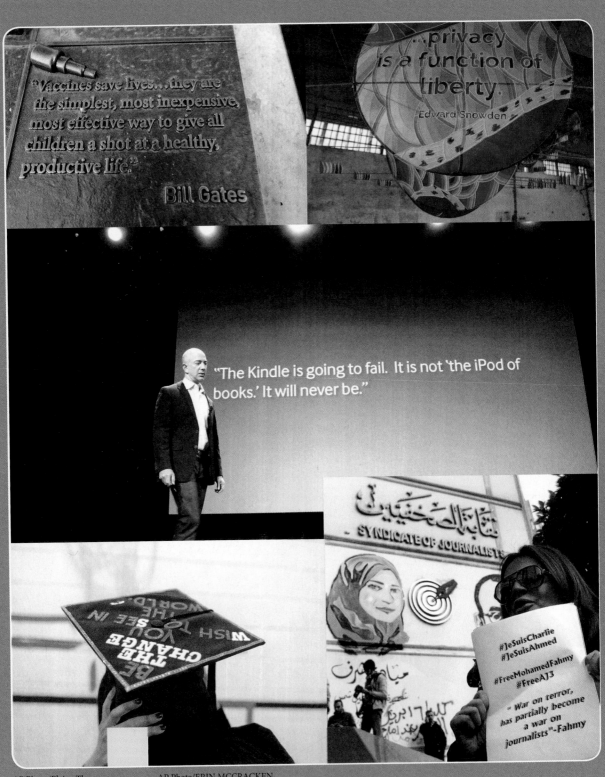

"Vaccines save lives...they are the simplest, most inexpensive, most effective way to give all children a shot at a healthy, productive life."

Bill Gates

...privacy is a function of liberty.

Edward Snowden

"The Kindle is going to fail. It is not 'the iPod of books.' It will never be."

SYNDICATE OF JOURNALISTS

#JeSuisCharlie
#JeSuisAhmed

#FreeMohamedFahmy
#FreeAJ3

" War on terror, has partially become a war on journalists"-Fahmy

BE THE CHANGE WISH YOU TO SEE IN THE WORLD

9

Summarizing, Paraphrasing, Quoting, and Synthesizing Sources

Is Technology a Serious Threat to Our Privacy? (continued)

In Chapter 8, you learned how to evaluate sources for an essay about the dangers of posting personal information online. In this chapter, you will learn how to take notes from various sources that address this issue.

As you saw in Chapter 8, before you can decide which material to use to support your arguments, you need to evaluate a variety of potential sources. After you decide which sources you will use, you can begin thinking about where you might use each source and about how to integrate information from the sources you have chosen into your essay in the form of *summary*, *paraphrase*, and *quotation*. When you actually write your argument, you will *synthesize* the sources into your paper, blending them with your own ideas and interpretations (as the student writer did when she wrote the MLA research paper in Chapter 10).

Summarizing Sources

A **summary** restates the main idea of a passage (or even of an entire book or article) in concise terms. Because a summary does not cover the examples or explanations in the source, and because it omits the original source's rhetorical strategies and stylistic characteristics, it is always much shorter than the original. Usually, in fact, it consists of just a sentence or two.

WHEN TO SUMMARIZE

Summarize when you want to give readers a general sense of a passage's main idea or a source's position on an issue.

When you summarize information, you do not include your own opinions, but you do use your own words and phrasing, not those of your source. If you want to use a particularly distinctive word or phrase from your source, you may do so—but you must always place such words in quotation marks and **document** them. If you do not, you will be committing **plagiarism**. (See Chapter 10 for information on documenting sources; see Chapter 11 for information on using sources responsibly.)

The following paragraph appeared in a newspaper opinion essay.

ORIGINAL SOURCE

When everyone has a blog, a MySpace page, or Facebook entry, everyone is a publisher. When everyone has a cellphone with a camera in it, everyone is a paparazzo. When everyone can upload video on YouTube, everyone is a filmmaker. When everyone is a publisher, paparazzo, or filmmaker, everyone else is a public figure. We're all public figures now. The blogosphere has made the global discussion so much richer—and each of us so much more transparent. ("The Whole World Is Watching," Thomas L. Friedman, *New York Times*, June 27, 2007, p. 23)

The following effective summary conveys a general but accurate sense of the original paragraph without using the source's phrasing or including the writer's own opinions. (One distinctive and hard-to-reword phrase is placed in quotation marks.) Parenthetical documentation indicates the source of the material.

EFFECTIVE SUMMARY

The popularity of blogs, social-networking sites, cell phone cameras, and YouTube has enhanced the "global discussion" but made it very hard for people to remain anonymous (Friedman 23).

Notice that this one-sentence summary is much shorter than the original passage and that it does not include all the original's examples. Still, it accurately communicates a general sense of the source's main idea.

The following summary is not acceptable. Not only does it express the student writer's opinion, but it also uses the source's exact words without putting them in quotation marks or providing documentation. (This constitutes plagiarism.)

UNACCEPTABLE SUMMARY

It seems to me that blogs, social-networking sites, cell phone cameras, and YouTube are everywhere, and what this means is that we're all public figures now.

SUMMARIZING SOURCES

Do

- Convey the main idea of the original passage.

- Be concise.

- Use your own original words and phrasing.

- Place any words borrowed from your source in quotation marks.

- Include documentation.

Do not

- Include your own analysis or opinions.

- Include digressions.

- Argue with your source.

- Use your source's syntax or phrasing (unless you are quoting).

⊙ EXERCISE 9.1

Write a two-sentence summary of the following passage. Then, edit your summary so that it is only one sentence long. Be sure your summary conveys the main idea of the original passage and includes proper documentation.

We're living at a time when attention is the new currency: with hundreds of TV channels, billions of Web sites, podcasts, radio shows, music downloads, and social networking, our attention is more fragmented than ever before.

Those who insert themselves into as many channels as possible look set to capture the most value. They'll be the richest, the most successful, the most connected, capable, and influential among us. We're all publishers now, and the more we publish, the more valuable connections we'll make.

Twitter, Facebook, Flickr, Foursquare, Fitbit, and the SenseCam give us a simple choice: participate or fade into a lonely obscurity. (Pete Cashmore, "Privacy Is Dead, and Social Media Hold Smoking Gun," *CNN.com*, October 28, 2009)

Paraphrasing Sources

A **paraphrase** is different from a summary. While a summary gives a general overview of the original, a paraphrase presents the source's ideas in detail, including its main idea, its key supporting points, and perhaps even its examples. For this reason, a paraphrase is longer than a summary. In fact, it may be as long as the original.

WHEN TO PARAPHRASE

Paraphrase when you want to communicate the key points discussed in a source—particularly a complex or complicated passage—in clear, accessible language.

Like a summary, a paraphrase uses your own words and phrasing, not the language and syntax of the original. Any words or phrases from your source must be placed in quotation marks. When you paraphrase, you may not always follow the order of the original source's ideas, but you should try to convey the writer's emphasis and most important points.

The following paragraph is from an editorial that appeared in a student newspaper.

ORIGINAL SOURCE

Additionally, as graduates retain their Facebook accounts, employers are increasingly able to use Facebook as an evaluation tool when making hiring decisions. Just as companies sometimes incorporate social functions into their interview process to see if potential hires can handle themselves responsibly, they may also check out a student's Facebook account to see how the student chooses to present him or herself. This may seem shady and underhanded, but one must understand that social networks are not anonymous; whatever one chooses to post will be available to all. Even if someone goes to great pains to keep an employer-friendly profile, his or her friends may still tag pictures of him or her which will be available to whoever wants to see them. Not only can unexpected Facebook members get information by viewing one's profile, but a user's personal information can also leak out by merely registering for the service. Both the user agreement and the privacy policy indicate that Facebook can give information to third parties and can supplement its data with information from newspapers, blogs, and instant messages. ("Beware What You Post on Facebook," *The Tiger*, Clemson University, August 4, 2006)

The following paraphrase reflects the original paragraph's emphasis and clearly communicates its key points.

EFFECTIVE PARAPHRASE

Because students keep their accounts at social-networking sites after they graduate, potential employers can use the information they find there to help them evaluate candidates' qualifications. This process is comparable to the way a company might evaluate an applicant in person in a social situation. Some people may see the practice of employers checking applicants' Facebook pages as "shady and underhanded," but these sites are not intended to be anonymous or private. For example, a person may try to maintain a profile that will be appropriate for employers, but friends may post inappropriate pictures. Also, people can reveal personal information not only in profiles but also simply by registering with Facebook. Finally, as Facebook states in its membership information, it can supply information to others as well as provide data from other sources. ("Beware")

Notice that this paraphrase includes many of the details presented in the original passage and quotes a distinctive phrase, but its style and sentence structure are different from those of the original.

The following paraphrase is not acceptable because its phrasing and sentence structure are too close to the original. It also borrows words and phrases from the source without attribution or documentation.

UNACCEPTABLE PARAPHRASE

As more and more college graduates keep their Facebook accounts, employers are increasingly able to use them as evaluation tools when they decide whom to hire. Companies sometimes set up social functions during the interview process to see how potential hires handle themselves; in the same way, they can consult a Facebook page to see how an applicant presents himself or herself. This may seem underhanded, but after all, Facebook is not anonymous; its information is available to all. Many people try to keep their profiles employer friendly, but their friends sometimes tag pictures of them that employers will be able to see. Besides, students' personal information is available not just on their profiles but also in the form they fill out when they register. Finally, according to their user agreement and their privacy policy, Facebook can give information to third parties and also add data from other sources.

PARAPHRASING SOURCES

Do

- Convey the source's ideas fully and accurately.
- Use your own words and phrasing.
- Convey the emphasis of the original.
- Simplify and clarify complex language and syntax.
- Put any words borrowed from the source in quotation marks.
- Include documentation.

Do not

- Use the exact words or phrasing of your source (unless you are quoting).
- Include your own analysis or opinions.
- Argue with or contradict your source.
- Wander from the topic of the source.

⊘ EXERCISE 9.2

Write a paraphrase of the passage you summarized in Exercise 9.1. How is your paraphrase different from your summary?

⊘ EXERCISE 9.3

The following paragraph is from the same Clemson University student newspaper article that was excerpted on pages 332–333. Read the paragraph, and then write a paraphrase that communicates its key ideas. Before you begin, circle any distinctive words and phrases that might be difficult to paraphrase, and consider whether you should quote them. Be sure to include documentation.

> All these factors make clear the importance of two principles: Responsibility and caveat emptor. First, people should be responsible about how they portray themselves and their friends, and employers, authorities, and the owners must approach this information responsibly and fairly. Second, "let the buyer beware" applies to all parties involved. Facebook users need to understand the potential consequences of the information they share, and outside viewers need to understand that the material on Facebook is often only a humorous, lighthearted presentation of one aspect of a person. Facebook is an incredibly valuable communications tool that will link the college generation more tightly than any before it, but users have to understand that, like anything good in life, they have to be aware of the downsides.

Quoting Sources

When you **quote** words from a source, you need to quote accurately—that is, every word and every punctuation mark in your quotation must match the source *exactly*. You also need to be sure that your quotation conveys the meaning its author intended and that you are not distorting the meaning by **quoting out of context** or by omitting an essential part of the passage you are quoting.

WHEN TO QUOTE

Quote a source's words only in the following situations:

- Quote when your source's words are distinctive or memorable.

- Quote when your source's words are so direct and concise that a paraphrase would be awkward or wordy.

- Quote when your source's words add authority or credibility to your argument (for example, when your source is a well-known expert on your topic).

- Quote an opposing point when you will go on to refute it.

Remember, quoting from a source adds interest to your paper—but only when the writer's words are compelling. Too many quotations—especially long quotations—distract readers and make it difficult for them to follow your discussion. Quote only when you must. If you include too many quotations, your paper will be a patchwork of other people's words, not an original, unified whole.

QUOTING SOURCES

Do

- Enclose borrowed words in quotation marks.
- Quote accurately.
- Include documentation.

Do not

- Quote out of context.
- Distort the source's meaning.
- Include too many quotations.

⊘ EXERCISE 9.4

Read the following paragraphs from a newspaper column that appeared in the *Calgary Herald*. (The full text of this column appears in Exercise 9.5.) If you were going to use these paragraphs as source material for an argumentative essay, which particular words or phrases do you think you might want to quote? Why?

> How do users not know that a server somewhere is recording where you are, what you ate for lunch, how often you post photos of your puppy, what you bought at the supermarket for dinner, the route you drove home, and what movie you watched before you went to bed?
>
> So why do we act so surprised and shocked about the invasion of the privacy we so willingly relinquish, and the personal information we forfeit that allows its captors to sell us products, convict us in court, get us fired, or produce more of the same banality that keeps us logging on?
>
> We, all of us, are digital captives. (Shelley Fralic, "Don't Fall for the Myths about Online Privacy," *Calgary Herald*, October 17, 2015.)

⊘ EXERCISE 9.5

Read the newspaper column that follows, and highlight it to identify its most important ideas. (For information on highlighting, see Chapter 2.) Then, write a summary of one paragraph and a paraphrase of another paragraph. Assume that this column is a source for an essay you are writing on the topic, "Is Technology a Serious Threat to Our Privacy?" Be sure to include documentation.

This column is from the *Calgary Herald*, where it appeared on October 17, 2015.

DON'T FALL FOR THE MYTHS ABOUT ONLINE PRIVACY

SHELLEY FRALIC

If you are a Facebooker—and there are 1.5 billion of us on the planet, so chances are about one in five that you are—you will have noticed yet another round of posts that suggest in quasi-legalese that you can somehow block the social network's invasion of your privacy. 1

This latest hoax cautions that Facebook will now charge $5.99 to keep privacy settings private, and the copyright protection disclaimers making the 2 rounds this week typically begin like this: "As of date-and-time here, I do not give Facebook or any entities associated with Facebook permission to use my pictures, information, or posts, both past and future. By this statement, I give notice to Facebook it is strictly forbidden to disclose, copy, distribute, or take any other action against me based on this profile and/or its contents. The content of this profile is private and confidential information."

Well, no, it's not.   3

This is a new-age version of an old story, oft-told. No one reads the   4
fine print. Not on contracts, not on insurance policies, and not on social media sites that are willingly and globally embraced by perpetually plugged-in gossipmongers, lonely hearts, news junkies, inveterate sharers, and selfie addicts.

Facebook's fine print, like that of many Internet portals, is specific and   5
offers users a variety of self-selected "privacy" options.

But to think that any interaction with it, and its ilk, is truly private is   6
beyond absurd.

How can there still be people out there who still don't get that Netflix and   7
Facebook, Instagram and Twitter, Google and Tinder and pretty much every keystroke or communication we register on a smartphone or laptop, not to mention a loyalty card and the GPS in your car, are constantly tracking and sifting and collating everything we do?

How do users not know that a server somewhere is recording where you   8
are, what you ate for lunch, how often you post photos of your puppy, what you bought at the supermarket for dinner, the route you drove home, and what movie you watched before you went to bed?

So why do we act so surprised and shocked about the invasion of the pri-   9
vacy we so willingly relinquish, and the personal information we forfeit that allows its captors to sell us products, convict us in court, get us fired, or produce more of the same banality that keeps us logging on?

We, all of us, are digital captives.   10

But do we have to be so stupid about it?   11

And the bigger question is this: If we, the adults who should know better,   12
don't get it, what are we teaching our kids about the impact and repercussions of their online lives? What are they learning about the voluntary and wholesale abandonment of their privacy? What are we teaching them about "sharing" with strangers?

Worried about future generations not reading books or learning how to   13
spell properly or write in cursive? Worry more, folks, that Internet ignorance is the new illiteracy.

Meantime, when another Facebook disclaimer pops up with a plea to   14
share, consider this clever post from a user who actually read the fine print:

"I hereby give my permission to the police, the NSA, the FBI and CIA,   15
the Swiss Guard, the Priory of Scion, the inhabitants of Middle Earth,

Agents Mulder and Scully, the Goonies, ALL the Storm Troopers and Darth Vader, the Mad Hatter, Chuck Norris, S.H.I.E.L.D., The Avengers, The Illuminati . . . to view all the amazing and interesting things I publish on Facebook. I'm aware that my privacy ended the very day that I created a profile on Facebook."

Yes, it did. 16

Working Source Material into Your Argument

When you use source material in an argumentative essay, your goal is to integrate the material smoothly into your discussion, blending summary, paraphrase, and quotation with your own ideas.

To help readers follow your discussion, you need to indicate the source of each piece of information clearly and distinguish your own ideas from those of your sources. Never simply drop source material into your discussion. Whenever possible, introduce quotations, paraphrases, and summaries with an **identifying tag** (sometimes called a *signal phrase*), a phrase that identifies the source, and always follow them with documentation. This practice helps readers identify the boundaries between your own ideas and those of your sources.

It is also important that you include clues to help readers understand why you are using a particular source and what the exact relationship is between your source material and your own ideas. For example, you may be using a source to support a point you are making or to disagree with another source.

Using Identifying Tags

Using identifying tags to introduce your summaries, paraphrases, or quotations will help you to accomplish the goals discussed above (and help you to avoid accidental plagiarism).

> **SUMMARY WITH IDENTIFYING TAG**
> <u>According to Thomas L. Friedman</u>, the popularity of blogs, social-networking sites, cell phone cameras, and YouTube has enhanced the "global discussion" but made it hard for people to remain anonymous (23).

Note that you do not always have to place the identifying tag at the beginning of the summarized, paraphrased, or quoted material. You can also place it in the middle or at the end:

IDENTIFYING TAG AT THE BEGINNING

<u>Thomas L. Friedman notes</u> that the popularity of blogs, social-networking sites, cell phone cameras, and YouTube has enhanced the "global discussion" but made it hard for people to remain anonymous (23).

IDENTIFYING TAG IN THE MIDDLE

The popularity of blogs, social-networking sites, cell phone cameras, and YouTube, <u>Thomas L. Friedman observes</u>, has enhanced the "global discussion" but made it hard for people to remain anonymous (23).

IDENTIFYING TAG AT THE END

The popularity of blogs, social-networking sites, cell phone cameras, and YouTube has enhanced the "global discussion" but made it hard for people to remain anonymous, <u>Thomas L. Friedman points out</u> (23).

TEMPLATES FOR USING IDENTIFYING TAGS

To avoid repeating phrases like *he says* in identifying tags, try using some of the following verbs to introduce your source material. (You can also use "According to . . . ," to introduce a source.)

For Summaries or Paraphrases

[Name of writer]	notes	acknowledges	proposes	that [summary or paraphrase].
The writer	suggests	believes	observes	
The article	explains	comments	warns	
The essay	reports	points out	predicts	
	implies	concludes	states	

For Quotations

As [name of writer]	notes,	acknowledges,	proposes,	" _____[quotation]_____ ."
As the writer	suggests,	believes,	observes,	
As the article	warns,	reports,	points out,	
As the essay	predicts,	implies,	concludes,	
	states,	explains,		

Working Quotations into Your Sentences

When you use quotations in your essays, you may need to edit them to provide context or to make them fit smoothly into your sentences. If you do edit a quotation, be careful not to distort the source's meaning.

Adding or Changing Words When you add or change words in a quotation, use **brackets** to indicate your edits.

ORIGINAL QUOTATION

"Twitter, Facebook, Flickr, FourSquare, Fitbit, and the SenseCam give us a simple choice: participate or fade into a lonely obscurity." (Cashmore)

WORDS ADDED FOR CLARIFICATION

As Cashmore observes, "Twitter, Flickr, FourSquare, Fitbit, and the SenseCam [as well as similar social-networking sites] give us a simple choice: participate or fade into a lonely obscurity."

ORIGINAL QUOTATION

"The blogosphere has made the global discussion so much richer—and each of us so much more transparent" (Friedman 23).

WORDS CHANGED TO MAKE VERB TENSE LOGICAL

As Thomas L. Friedman explains, increased access to cell phone cameras, YouTube, and the like continues to "[make] the global discussion so much richer—and each of us so much more transparent" (23).

Deleting Words When you delete words from a quotation, use **ellipses**—three spaced periods—to indicate your edits. However, never use ellipses to indicate a deletion at the beginning of a quotation.

ORIGINAL QUOTATION

"Just as companies sometimes incorporate social functions into their interview process to see if potential hires can handle themselves responsibly, they may also check out a student's Facebook account to see how the student chooses to present him or herself" ("Beware").

UNNECESSARY WORDS DELETED

"Just as companies sometimes incorporate social functions into their interview process, . . . they may also check out a student's Facebook account . . ." ("Beware").

DISTORTING QUOTATIONS

Be careful not to distort a source's meaning when you add, change, or delete words from a quotation. In the following example, the writer intentionally deletes material from the original quotation that would weaken his argument.

Original Quotation

"This incident is by no means an isolated one. Connecticut authorities are investigating reports that seven girls were sexually assaulted by older men they met on MySpace" ("Beware").

Distorted

"This incident is by no means an isolated one. [In fact,] seven girls were sexually assaulted by older men they met on MySpace" ("Beware").

⊛ EXERCISE 9.6

Look carefully at the quotations that accompany this chapter's opening images (p. 328). Select three quotations, and summarize each quotation in one sentence. Then, compose an original sentence that quotes each statement. Be sure to acknowledge each source in an identifying tag and to integrate the borrowed material smoothly into each sentence.

⊛ EXERCISE 9.7

Reread the summary you wrote for Exercise 9.1 and the paraphrase you wrote for Exercise 9.3. Add three different identifying tags to each, varying the verbs you use and the position of the tags. Then, check to make sure you have used correct parenthetical documentation. (If the author's name is included in the identifying tag, it should not also appear in the parenthetical citation.)

Synthesizing Sources

In a **synthesis**, you combine summary, paraphrase, and quotation from several sources with your own ideas to support an original conclusion. A synthesis sometimes identifies similarities and differences among ideas, indicating where sources agree and disagree and how they support or challenge one another's ideas. Transitional words and phrases identify points of similarity (*also, like, similarly*, and so on) or difference (*however, in contrast*, and so on). When you write a synthesis, you include identifying tags and parenthetical documentation to identify each piece of information you get from a source and to distinguish your sources' ideas from one another and from your own ideas.

The following effective synthesis is excerpted from the student paper in Chapter 10. Note how the synthesis blends information from three sources with the student's own ideas to support her point about how the Internet has affected people's concepts of "public" and "private."

EFFECTIVE SYNTHESIS

Student's original point

Paraphrase

Student's own ideas

Quotation

Student's evaluation of source

Quotation

Part of the problem is that the Internet has fundamentally altered our notions of "private" and "public" in ways that we are only just beginning to understand. As Shelley Fralic observes in "Don't Fall for the Myths about Online Privacy," Facebook's privacy options do not really protect its users' privacy. On sites like Facebook, people often reveal intimate details of their lives to hundreds—perhaps even thousands—of strangers. This situation is unprecedented and, at least for the foreseeable future, irreversible. As *New York Times* columnist Thomas L. Friedman observes, "When everyone has a blog, a MySpace page, or Facebook entry, everyone is a publisher. . . . When everyone is a publisher, paparazzo, or filmmaker, everyone else is a public figure." Given the public nature of the Internet, the suggestion that we should live our lives by the same rules we lived by twenty years ago simply does not make sense. As Friedman notes, in the Internet age, more and more of "what you say or do or write will end up as a digital fingerprint that never gets erased" (23).

Compare the effective synthesis above with the following unacceptable synthesis.

UNACCEPTABLE SYNTHESIS

"The sheer volume of personal information that people are publishing online—and the fact that some of it could remain visible permanently— is changing the nature of personal privacy." On sites like Facebook, people can reveal the most intimate details of their lives to millions of total strangers. This development is unprecedented and, at least for the foreseeable future, irreversible. "When everyone has a blog, a MySpace page, or Facebook entry, everyone is a publisher. . . . When everyone is a publisher, paparazzo, or filmmaker, everyone else is a public figure" (Friedman 23). Given the changes in our understanding of privacy and the essentially public nature of the Internet, the analogy that Hall makes between a MySpace post and a private conversation seems of limited use. In the Internet age, more and more of "what you say or do or write will end up as a digital fingerprint that never gets erased."

Unlike the effective synthesis, the unacceptable synthesis above does not begin with a topic sentence that states the point the source material in the paragraph will support. Instead, it opens with an out-of-context quotation whose source is not identified. This quotation could have been paraphrased—

its wording is not particularly memorable—and, more important, it should have been accompanied by documentation. (If source information is not provided, the writer is committing plagiarism even if the borrowed material is set in quotation marks.) The second quotation, although it includes parenthetical documentation (Friedman 23), is dropped into the paragraph without an identifying tag; the third quotation, also from the Friedman article, is not documented at all, making it appear to be from Hall. All in all, the paragraph is not a smoothly connected synthesis but a string of unconnected ideas. It does not use sources effectively and responsibly, and it does not cite them appropriately.

⊘ EXERCISE 9.8

Write a synthesis that builds on the paraphrase you wrote for Exercise 9.2. Add your own original ideas—examples and opinions—to the paraphrase, and also blend in information from one or two of the other sources that appear in this chapter. Use identifying tags and parenthetical documentation to introduce your sources and to distinguish your own ideas from ideas expressed in your sources.

Documenting Sources: MLA

When you are building an argument, you use sources for support. To acknowledge the material you borrow and to help readers evaluate your sources, you need to supply documentation. In other words, you need to tell readers where you found your information. If you use documentation responsibly, you will also avoid **plagiarism**, an ethical offense with serious consequences. (See Chapter 11 for more on plagiarism.)

WHY DOCUMENT SOURCES?

- To acknowledge the debt that you owe to your sources
- To demonstrate that you are familiar with the conventions of academic discourse
- To enable readers to judge the quality of your research
- To avoid plagiarism
- To make your argument more convincing

MLA documentation consists of two parts: **parenthetical references** in the text of your paper and a **works-cited list** at the end of the paper. (The references are keyed to the works-cited list.)

Using Parenthetical References

The basic parenthetical citation consists of the author's last name and a page number:

(Fielding 213)

If the author is referred to in the sentence, include only the page number in the parenthetical reference.

> According to environmental activist Brian Fielding, the number of species affected is much higher (213).

Here are some other situations you may encounter:

- When referring to a work by two authors, include both authors' names.

> (Stange and Hogarth 53)

- When citing a work with no listed author, include a short version of the title.

> ("Small Things" 21)

- When citing a source that is quoted in another source, indicate this by including the abbreviation *qtd. in.*

> According to Kevin Kelly, this narrow approach is typical of the "hive mind" (qtd. in Doctorow 168).

- When citing two or more works by the same author, include a short title after the author's name.

> (Anderson, *Long Tail* 47)

- If a source does not include page numbers, or if you are referring to the entire source rather than to a specific page, cite the author's name in the text of your paper rather than in a parenthetical reference.

You must document *all* information that is not **common knowledge**, whether you are summarizing, paraphrasing, or quoting. (See p. 374 for an explanation of common knowledge.) With direct quotations, include the parenthetical reference and a period *after* the closing quotation marks.

> According to Doctorow, this is "authorship without editorship. Or authorship fused with editorship" (166).

When quoting a passage of more than four lines, indent the entire passage half an inch from the left margin, and do not use quotation marks. Place the parenthetical reference *after* the final punctuation mark.

Doctorow points out that *Wikipedia*'s history pages can be extremely informative:

> This is a neat solution to the problem of authority—if you want to know what the fully rounded view of opinions on any controversial subject looks like, you need only consult its entry's history page for a blistering eyeful of thorough debate on the subject. (170)

Preparing the Works-Cited List

Start your works-cited list on a new page following the last page of your paper. Center the heading Works Cited at the top of the page. List entries alphabetically by the author's last name—or by the first word (other than an article such as *a* or *the*) of the title if an author is not given. Double-space within and between entries. Each entry should begin at the left-hand margin, with subsequent lines indented one-half inch. (This format can be automatically generated if you use the "hanging indent" option in your word processing program.)

Here are some additional guidelines:

- Italicize all book and periodical titles.

- Use a short version of a publisher's name (Penguin rather than Penguin Books), and abbreviate *University Press* (as in Princeton UP or U of Chicago P).

- If you are listing more than one work by the same author, include the author's name in the first entry, and substitute three unspaced hyphens followed by a period for the second and subsequent entries.

- Put quotation marks around the title of a periodical article or a section of an edited book or anthology, and provide the inclusive page numbers: 44–99. For page numbers larger than 99, give the last two digits of the second number if the first is the same: 147–69 (but 286–301).

When you have completed your list, double-check your parenthetical references to make sure they match the items in your works-cited list.

The following models illustrate the most common kinds of references.

Periodicals

For periodical articles found online or through a full-text database, see page 355.

Guidelines for Citing a Periodical Article

To cite a print article in MLA style, include the following:

1. Author, last name first
2. Title of the article, in quotation marks
3. Title of the periodical, in italics
4. Volume and issue numbers
5. Date or year of publication
6. Page number(s) of the article

   (See images on page 349.)

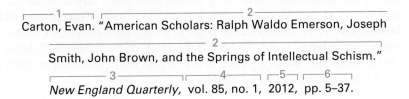

Carton, Evan. "American Scholars: Ralph Waldo Emerson, Joseph Smith, John Brown, and the Springs of Intellectual Schism." *New England Quarterly,* vol. 85, no. 1, 2012, pp. 5–37.

Journals

Journals are periodicals published for experts in a field. Cite both volume number and issue number when available. In cases where only an issue number is available, cite just the issue.

> Minkler, Lanse. "Economic Rights and Political Decision-Making."
> *Human Rights Quarterly*, vol. 31, no. 2, 2009, pp. 369–93.
> Picciotto, Joanna. "The Public Person and the Play of Fact."
> *Representations*, no. 105, 2009, pp. 85–132.

Magazines

Magazines are periodicals published for a general audience. Do not include a magazine's volume and issue number, but do include the date (day, month, and year for weekly publications; month and year for those published less frequently). If pages are not consecutive, give the first page followed by a plus sign.

> Aviv, Rachel. "The Death Treatment." *The New Yorker,* 22 June
> 2015, pp. 56–65.
> Rice, Andrew. "Mission from Africa." *The New York Times Magazine,*
> 12 Apr. 2009, pp. 30+.

Copyright Page

THE
NEW ENGLAND
QVARTERLY

A Historical Review of New England Life and Letters

Registered in the U.S. Patent and Trademark Office

EDITORS

Edmund S. Morgan   Robert L. Middlekauff
David Brion Davis   William M. Fowler Jr.
Andrew Delbanco   Robert D. Richardson
Bernard Bailyn   Daniel R. Coquillette
Louis Menand   Laura Dassow Walls
Mary Kelley   Richard D. Brown
Neil Harris   Michael Kammen
Nina Baym   Mary Loeffelholz

Editor
Linda Smith Rhoads

Editorial Assistant
Anna Kimball Williams

Volume LXXXV   Number 1
March 2012

Copyright 2012 by The New England Quarterly
ISSN 0028-4866

— Title of periodical

Volume and issue number

Date of publication

Title of article

Author

First Page of Article

✳+✳+✳+✳+✳+✳+✳+✳+✳+✳+✳+✳+✳+✳+✳+✳+✳+✳+✳+

American Scholars: Ralph Waldo Emerson,
Joseph Smith, John Brown, and the Springs
of Intellectual Schism

EVAN CARTON

Every man, woman, and child was more or less a theologian.
—Harriet Beecher Stowe

THE literary intellectual, the Christian evangelical, and the political radical are, according to our contemporary civic understanding, denizens of distinctly separate spheres, spheres bounded and policed, to the extent that they come into contact at all, by mutual distrust or disdain. I propose to advance a counter-claim (for which I will begin to muster evidence and assess implications): to wit, that the seemingly divergent cultural icons of the American scholar, prophet, and revolutionary in fact share a common milieu and moment of origin in the social, spiritual, and epistemological ferment of the early nineteenth century. Thus, I contend, the icons' apparently incommensurable vocations and commitments are better viewed as variations on the volatile "American synthesis" of scriptural, rational, and ideological authority that historian of religion Mark Noll describes in his magisterial *America's God* or, rather, as schismatic expressions of what political scientist Hugh Heclo calls the "mutual and tensioned embrace between the democratic and Christian faiths."[1]

[1]Mark Noll, *America's God: From Jonathan Edwards to Abraham Lincoln* (New York: Oxford University Press, 2002), p. 9; Hugh Heclo, *Christianity and American Democracy* (Cambridge: Harvard University Press, 2007), p. 5.

The New England Quarterly, vol. LXXXV, no. 1 (March 2012). © 2012 by The New England Quarterly. All rights reserved.

Page numbers

5

Newspapers

Include both the letter of the section and the page number. If an article continues on to a nonconsecutive page, give just the first page followed by a plus sign.

> Darlin, Damon. "Software That Monitors Your Work, Wherever You Are." *The New York Times*, 12 Apr. 2009, pp. B2+.

Editorial, Letter to the Editor, or Review

Include authors and titles where available as well as a descriptive label—for example Editorial, Letter, or Review. In the case of reviews, include the title and author of the work that is reviewed.

> Bernath, Dan. "Letter to the Editor." *The Washington Post*, 12 Apr. 2009, p. A16. Letter.
>
> Franklin, Nancy. "Whedon's World." Review of *Dollhouse*, directed by Joss Whedon. *The New Yorker*, 2 Mar. 2009, p. 45.
>
> "World Bank Responsibility." *The Wall Street Journal*, 28 Mar. 2009, p. A10. Editorial.

Political Cartoon or Comic Strip

Include the author and title (if available) of the cartoon or comic strip, followed by a descriptive label and publication information.

> Adams, Scott. "Dilbert." *The Chicago Tribune,* 10 Mar. 2012, p. C9. Comic strip.
>
> Pett, Joel. *Lexington Herald-Leader,* 30 Apr. 2012, p. A12. Cartoon.

Advertisement

Cite the name of the product or company that is advertised, followed by the descriptive label and the publication information.

> Maxwell House. *Rolling Stone,* 18 June 2015, p. 35. Advertisement.

Books

Guidelines for Citing a Book

To cite a book in MLA style, include the following:

1. Author, last name first

2. Title, in italics

3. Full publisher's name

4. Date of publication

```
  ┌───── 1 ─────┐  ┌────── 2 ──────┐  ┌───────── 3 ─────────┐  ┌─ 4 ─┐
```
Kahneman, Daniel. *Thinking, Fast and Slow*. Farrar, Straus and Grioux, 2011.

Copyright Page

Farrar, Straus and Giroux
18 West 18th Street, New York 10011

Date of
publication ——— Copyright © 2011 by Daniel Kahneman
All rights reserved
Printed in the United States of America
First edition, 2011

*Grateful acknowledgment is made for permission to reprint the following previously published material:
"Judgment Under Uncertainty: Heuristics and Biases" from* Science, New Series. Vol. 185, No. 4157, copyright
© 1974 by Amos Tversky and Daniel Kahneman. Reprinted by permission of Science. "Choices, Values, and
Frames" from The American Psychologist, copyright © 1983 by Daniel Kahneman and Amos Tversky. Reprinted
by permission of the American Psychological Association.

*Grateful acknowledgment is made for permission to reprint the following images: Image on page 19 courtesy of
Paul Ekman Group, LLC. Image on page 57 from "Cues of Being Watched Enhance Cooperation in a
Real-World Setting" by Melissa Bateson, Daniel Nettle, and Gilbert Roberts,* Biology Letters *(2006); reprinted
by permission of* Biology Letters. *Image on page 100 from Mind Sights by Roger N. Shepard (New York: W.H.
Freeman and Company, 1990); reprinted by permission of Henry Holt and Company. Image on page 300 from
"Human Amygdala Responsivity to Masked Fearful Eye Whites" by Paul J. Whalen et al.,* Science 306 (2004).
Reprinted by permission of Science.

Library of Congress Cataloging-in-Publication Data
Kahneman, Daniel, 1934–
    Thinking, fast and slow / Daniel Kahneman. — 1st ed.
        p.   cm.
    Includes bibliographical references and index.
    ISBN 978-0-374-27563-1 (alk. paper)
    1. Thought and thinking.   2. Decision making.   3. Intuition.   4. Reasoning.   1. Title.

BF441 .K238 2011
153.4'2—dc23

Designed by Abby Kagan

www.fsgbooks.com

1   3   5   7   9   10   8   6   4   2

Title Page

Title of
book ——— T H I N K I N G ,

F A S T   A N D   S L O W

Author ——— D A N I E L

K A H N E M A N

Publisher
—————
FARRAR, STRAUS AND GIROUX   NEW YORK

Book by One Author

List the author, last name first, followed by the title (italicized). Include the full publisher's name, abbreviated when called for, and end with the date of publication.

> Skinner, Quentin. *Forensic Shakespeare*. Oxford UP, 2014.

Book by Two Authors

List authors in the order in which they are listed on the book's title page. List the first author with last name first, but list the second author with first name first.

> Singer, Peter, and Jim Mason. *The Way We Eat: Why Our Food
> Choices Matter*. Rodale, 2006.

Book by Three or More Authors

List only the first author, last name first, followed by the abbreviation et al. ("and others").

> Gould, Harvey, et al. *Advanced Computer Simulation Methods*.
> Pearson Education, 2009.

Two or More Books by the Same Author

List the entries alphabetically by title. In each entry after the first, substitute three unspaced hyphens, followed by a period, for the author's last name.

> Friedman, Thomas L. *Hot, Flat, and Crowded: Why We Need a
> Green Revolution—and How It Can Renew America*. Farrar,
> Strauss and Giroux, 2008.
> ---. *The World Is Flat: A Brief History of the Twenty-First Century*.
> Farrar, Strauss and Giroux, 2005.

Edited Book

If your focus is on the *author,* include the name of the editor (or editors) after the title, preceded by the abbreviation Ed. (for "edited by"). If the book is an edited collection of essays by different authors, treat it as an anthology.

> Whitman, Walt. *The Portable Walt Whitman*. Edited by Michael
> Warner, Penguin Classics, 2004.

If your focus is on the *editor*, begin with the editor's name followed by editor or editors.

> Michael Warner, editor. *The Portable Walt Whitman*. Penguin
>   Classics, 2004.

Translation

> Bolaño, Roberto. *The Savage Detectives*. Translated by Natasha
>   Wimmer, Picador, 2008.

Revised Edition

> Smith, Steven S., et al., *The American Congress*. 4th ed., Cambridge
>   UP, 2006.

Anthology

Include the name of the editor (or editors) of the anthology, followed by editor or editors.

> Browning, John Edgar, and Caroline Joan S. Picart, editors.
>   *Speaking of Monsters*, Palgrave, 2012.

Work in an Anthology

> Malone, Dan. "Immigration, Terrorism, and Secret Prisons."
>   *Keeping Out the Other: Immigration Enforcement Today*,
>   edited by David C. Brotherton and Philip Kretsedemas,
>   Columbia UP, 2008, pp. 44–62.

More Than One Work in the Same Anthology

To avoid repeating the entire anthology entry, you may provide a cross-reference from individual essays to the entire anthology.

> Adelson, Glenn et al., editors. *Environment: An Interdisciplinary
>   Anthology*, Yale UP, 2008.
> Lesher, Molly. "Seeds of Change." Adelson, pp. 131–37.
> Marshall, Robert. "The Problem of the Wilderness." Adelson,
>   pp. 288–92.

Section or Chapter of a Book

Leavitt, Steven D., and Stephen J. Dubner. "Why Do Drug Dealers Still Live with Their Moms?" *Freakonomics: A Rogue Economist Explores the Hidden Side of Everything,* Morrow, 2006, pp. 49-78.

Introduction, Preface, Foreword, or Afterword

Christiano, Thomas, and John Christman. Introduction. *Contemporary Debates in Political Philosophy.* Edited by Thomas Christiano and John Christman, Wiley, 2009, pp. 1–20.

Multivolume Work

McNeil, Peter, editor. *Fashion: Critical and Primary Sources.* Berg Publishers, 2009. 4 vols.

Article in a Reference Work

A **reference work** is a book (print or electronic)—such as an encyclopedia, a dictionary, a bibliography, an almanac, or a handbook—that contains factual information. If the entries in a reference work are arranged alphabetically, do not include page numbers or volumes. When citing a familiar encyclopedia that publishes new editions regularly, include only the edition (if given) and year. If the article's author is given, include that as well. For less well-known reference encyclopedias, include publication information.

"Human Rights." *Encyclopedia Americana.* 2003 ed.

"Seagrass Beds." *Ocean: A Visual Encyclopedia.* DK Publishing, 2015.

> **NOTE**
> Keep in mind that many instructors do not consider encyclopedia articles acceptable research sources. Before including a citation for an encyclopedia article in your works-cited list, check with your instructor.

Audiovisual Sources

TV Show

"A Desperate Man." *NCIS,* written by Nicole Mirante-Matthews, directed by Leslie Libman, CBS, 10 Jan. 2012.

Film

> *The Tree of Life*. Directed by Terrence Malick, performances by Brad
> Pitt, Sean Penn, and Jessica Chastain, Fox Searchlight, 2011.

Internet Sources

Citing Internet sources can be problematic because they sometimes lack
basic information—for example, dates of publication or authors' names.
When citing Internet sources, include all the information you can find.

- For sites that are online editions of printed works, include as much of
  the original print information as is available, as well as the URL.

- For sites that exist only online, include (when available) the author,
  title, overall website title (if part of a larger project), the date it was last
  updated, and the URL.

- For works that are accessed through a library database, include the
  name of the database (in italics) and the URL or Digital Object Identifier (DOI). A DOI is a unique series of numbers assigned to electronic
  documents. The DOI remains the same regardless of where on the
  Internet a document is located.

For particularly long URLs (three lines or greater), you may use the
URL for the main website on which you found the content instead of the
URL for the specific page which you are referencing. However, your
instructor may not require a URL, so be sure to confirm their preference.
It is always a good idea, however, to keep a record of the URLs for yourself
in case you need to revisit your source.

If you type a URL into a works-cited entry that carries over to the next
line, make sure that you break it at an appropriate place—for example,
after a slash or a hyphen. If you paste a URL into a works-cited entry,
Word will do this for you.

Guidelines for Citing a Website

To cite a website in MLA style, follow these guidelines:

1. Author (if any)

2. Title (if any)

3. Name of website or sponsor

4. Date the site was last updated

5. DOI or URL

Author

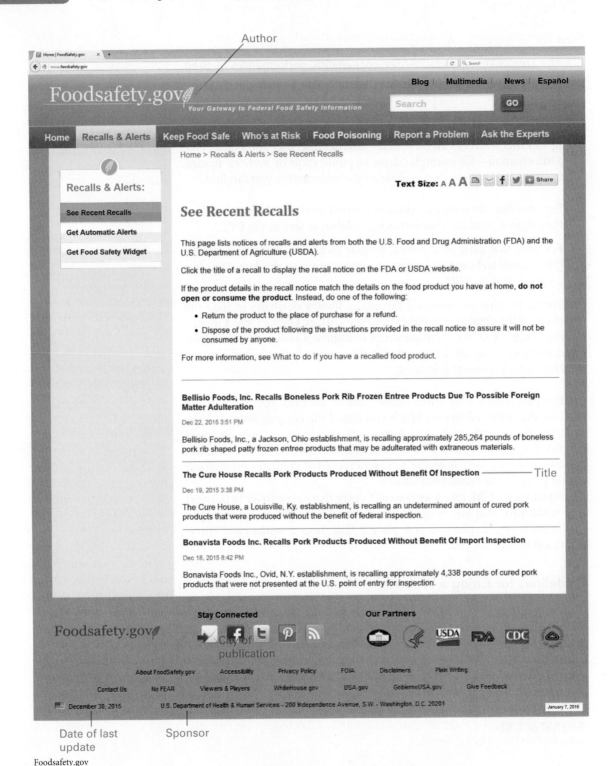

Foodsafety.gov

Blog | Multimedia | News | Español

Foodsafety.gov
Your Gateway to Federal Food Safety Information

Search [ ] GO

Home | Recalls & Alerts | Keep Food Safe | Who's at Risk | Food Poisoning | Report a Problem | Ask the Experts

Home > Recalls & Alerts > See Recent Recalls

Text Size: A A A

Recalls & Alerts:

See Recent Recalls

Get Automatic Alerts

Get Food Safety Widget

See Recent Recalls

This page lists notices of recalls and alerts from both the U.S. Food and Drug Administration (FDA) and the U.S. Department of Agriculture (USDA).

Click the title of a recall to display the recall notice on the FDA or USDA website.

If the product details in the recall notice match the details on the food product you have at home, **do not open or consume the product**. Instead, do one of the following:

- Return the product to the place of purchase for a refund.
- Dispose of the product following the instructions provided in the recall notice to assure it will not be consumed by anyone.

For more information, see What to do if you have a recalled food product.

Bellisio Foods, Inc. Recalls Boneless Pork Rib Frozen Entree Products Due To Possible Foreign Matter Adulteration

Dec 22, 2015 3:51 PM

Bellisio Foods, Inc., a Jackson, Ohio establishment, is recalling approximately 285,264 pounds of boneless pork rib shaped patty frozen entree products that may be adulterated with extraneous materials.

The Cure House Recalls Pork Products Produced Without Benefit Of Inspection ——— Title

Dec 19, 2015 3:38 PM

The Cure House, a Louisville, Ky. establishment, is recalling an undetermined amount of cured pork products that were produced without the benefit of federal inspection.

Bonavista Foods Inc. Recalls Pork Products Produced Without Benefit Of Import Inspection

Dec 18, 2015 8:42 PM

Bonavista Foods Inc., Ovid, N.Y. establishment, is recalling approximately 4,338 pounds of cured pork products that were not presented at the U.S. point of entry for inspection.

Foodsafety.gov

Stay Connected   **Our Partners**

City of publication

USDA FDA CDC

About FoodSafety.gov | Accessibility | Privacy Policy | FOIA | Disclaimers | Plain Writing

Contact Us | No FEAR | Viewers & Players | WhiteHouse.gov | USA.gov | GobiernoUSA.gov | Give Feedback

December 30, 2015   U.S. Department of Health & Human Services - 200 Independence Avenue, S.W. - Washington, D.C. 20201

January 7, 2016

Date of last update

Sponsor

Foodsafety.gov

<table>
<tr><td>┌──── 1 ────┐ ┌──────── 2 ────────┐</td></tr>
</table>

Foodsafety.gov. "The Cure House Recalls Pork Products without

┌──────── 3 ────────┐

Benefit of Inspection." US Dept of Health and Human

┌── 4 ──┐ ┌──────── 5 ────────┐

Services, 30 Dec. 2015. www.fsis.usda.gov/wps/wcm/connect

──────── 5 ────────

/FSIS-Content/internet/main/topics/recalls-and-public-health

──────── 5 ────────

-alerts/recall-case-archive/archive/2015/recall-148-2015-release.

Entire Website

Include (if available) the author, title of the website, date of last update, and the URL.

Document within a Website

"Uniform Impunity: Mexico's Misuse of Military Justice to Prosecute
Abuses in Counternarcotics and Public Security Operations."
Human Rights Watch, Apr. 2009, www.hrw.org/report/2009/04/29
/uniform-impunity/mexicos-misuse-military-justice-prosecute
-abuses-counternarcotics.

Online Video

Baggs, Amanda. "In My Language." *YouTube*, 14 Jan. 2007,
www.youtube.com/watch?v=JnyIM1hI2jc.

Blog Posts and Blog Comments

Caryl, Christian. "Burma: How Much Change?" *NYR Daily*, NYREV,
17 Nov. 2015, www.nybooks.com/daily/2015/11/17/burma
-election-how-much-change/.

Cimons, Marlene. "Why Cities Could Be the Key to Solving the
Climate Crisis." *Thinkprogress.org*, Center for American
Progress Action Fund, 10 Dec. 2015, thinkprogress.org
/climate/2015/12/10/3730938/cities-key-to-climate-crisis/.

Tweet

Begin with the author's real name, followed by the user name in parentheses. Include only the user name if the real name is unknown. Next, include the entire text of the tweet in quotation marks, followed by the date, the time, and the medium (Tweet).

Curiosity Rover. "Can you see me waving? How to spot #Mars in the night sky: https://youtu.be/hv8hVvJlcJQ." *Twitter*, 5 Nov. 2015, 11:00 a.m., twitter.com/marscuriosity/status /672859022911889408.

Podcast

Koenig, Sarah. "The Alibi." *Serial,* Chicago Public Radio, 3 Oct. 2014, serialpodcast.org/season-one/1/the-alibi.

Ogg, Erica. "Google Tries to Rehab Its Antitrust Image." *CNET News Daily Podcast*, CBS Interactive, 8 May 2009, www.cnet.com /news/cnet-news-daily-podcast-google-tries-to-rehab-its -antitrust-image/.

Online Book

Doctorow, Cory. *Content: Selected Essays on Technology, Creativity, Copyright, and the Future of the Future,* Tachyon, 2008. *Craphound.com.*

Part of an Online Book

Zittrain, Jonathan L. "The Lessons of *Wikipedia*." *The Future of the Internet and How to Stop It,* Yale UP, 2008. *futureoftheinternet.org.*

Article in an Online Scholarly Journal

Johnston, Rebecca. "Salvation or Destruction: Metaphors of the Internet." *First Monday*, vol. 14, no. 4, 2009, firstmonday.org/article/view/2370/2158.

Magazine Article Accessed Online

Marantz, Andrew. "What to Do When Your App Is Racist." *The New Yorker*, 29 Jul. 2015, www.newyorker.com/business/currency /what-to-do-when-your-app-is-racist.

Newspaper Article Accessed Online

Possley, Maurice, and Ken Armstrong. "The Verdict: Dishonor." *Chicago Tribune*, 11 Jan. 1999, www.chicagotribune.com/news /watchdog/chi-020103trial1-story.html.

Article from a Library Database

Hartley, Richard D. "Sentencing Reform and the War on Drugs: An
Analysis of Sentence Outcomes for Narcotics Offenders
Adjudicated in the US District Courts on the Southwest
Border." *Criminal Justice Policy Review,* vol. 19, no. 4, 2008,
pp. 414-37. *Sage Premier,* doi: 10.1177/1043986208323264.

Legal Case

When citing a court opinion, provide the plaintiffs' names, the legal
citation (volume, abbreviation of the source, page numbers), the name
of the court, the year of the decision, and any relevant information
about where you found it. In many cases, online versions of the opinions will include only the first page; in those cases, supply that page
number followed by a plus sign.

Miranda v. Arizona, 384 US 436+. Supreme Court of the US. 1966.
FindLaw, Thompson Reuters, caselaw.findlaw.com
/us-supreme-court/384/436.html.

Government Document

Include the government agency or body issuing the document, followed by
publication information.

United States, Department of Homeland Security, *Estimates of the
Unauthorized Immigrant Population Residing in the United
States, Office of Immigration Policy*, Feb. 2009, www.dhs.gov
/sites/default/files/publications/ois_ill_pe_2011_0.pdf.

 LaunchPad
macmillan learning
For more practice, see the LearningCurve on
Working with Sources (MLA) in the LaunchPad
for *Practical Argument*.

⬇ The following student research paper, "Should Data Posted on
Social-Networking Sites Be 'Fair Game' for Employers?" by Erin Blaine,
follows MLA documentation style as outlined in the preceding pages.

MLA PAPER GUIDELINES

- An MLA paper should have a one-inch margin all around and be double-spaced.

- Indent the first line of every paragraph. Number all pages, including the first, consecutively. Type your name, followed by the page number, in the upper right-hand corner.

- An MLA paper does not typically have a title page. Type the following information at the top of the paper, one inch from the left-hand margin:

    Name

    Instructor

    Course

    Date submitted

- Center the title of the paper. Capitalize all important words of the title, except prepositions, articles, coordinating conjunctions, and the *to* in infinitives—unless the word is the first or last word of the title. Titles should never be italicized, underlined, or followed by a period.

- Begin the **works-cited list** on a new numbered page, after the body of the paper. (See page 347 for a discussion of the works-cited list.)

- Citations should follow MLA documentation style.

NOTE

In the student essay that follows, note that the green annotations explain the student's choice of sources and the orange annotations highlight features of the student's use of documentation.

Blaine 1

Erin Blaine

Professor Adams

Humanities 101

4 March 2015

Should Data Posted on Social-Networking Sites

Be "Fair Game" for Employers?

The popularity of social-networking sites such as   1
Facebook and Twitter has increased dramatically over the last
several years, especially among college students and young
professionals. These sites provide valuable opportunities for
networking and for connecting socially. At the same time, however, potential employers, human resources professionals, and
even college admissions officers routinely use these sites to
evaluate applicants. Because it is so easy to access social-
networking sites and because they provide valuable information,
this trend is certain to continue. Some people are concerned
about this development, arguing that social-networking sites
should be off-limits to potential employers because they do not
have the context they need to evaluate information. As long as
applicants have freely posted information in a public forum,
however, there is no reason for an employer not to consult this
information during the hiring process.

The number of employers and universities using social-   2
networking sites to evaluate candidates is growing every year.
A recent survey found that 24 percent of college admissions
officers acknowledged visiting sites like Facebook to learn more
about applicants, and 12 percent said that the information they
found "negatively impacted the applicant's admissions chances"
("Online Behavior"). This practice also occurs in the business
world, where the numbers are even more striking. A study conducted by CareerBuilder found that 43 percent of employers use

This source and
the following
one supply
statistics that
support the
main point of
the paragraph.

Parenthetical
reference
identifies the
source, which is
included in the
works-cited list.

Blaine 2

Because the article has no listed author, a shortened version of the title is included in the parenthetical documentation.

Citations from Preston and Cammenga add credibility.

Parenthetical documentation containing *qtd. in* indicates a source quoted in another source.

Preston is summarized here to present an opposing viewpoint.

social-networking sites such as Facebook, Twitter, and LinkedIn to help them evaluate potential employees ("Number of Employers"). According to the *New York Times*, 75 percent of recruiters are required by their companies to research applicants online, and 70 percent of recruiters have rejected applicants because of information they found. The practice of checking social media is so common that some employers use outside companies, such as Social Intelligence Corp., to do Internet background checks on job candidates (Preston).

Not everyone is happy with this practice, though, and some have strong objections. Becca Bush, a college student in Chicago, argues that employers should not have the right to use social media to evaluate potential employees. "It's a violation of privacy," she says. "Twenty years ago, people still did the same things as now," but the information "wasn't as widespread" (qtd. in Cammenga). Marc S. Rotenberg, president of the Electronic Privacy Information Center, agrees, saying, "Employers should not be judging what people in their private lives do away from the workplace" (qtd. in Preston). Rotenberg goes on to say that privacy settings on sites like Facebook are often misunderstood. According to him, "People are led to believe that there is more limited disclosure than there actually is" (qtd. in Preston). Some people mistakenly think that looking at an applicant's Facebook page is illegal (Cammenga). Even though it is not, this practice can lead to discrimination, which *is* illegal. An online search can reveal characteristics that an applicant is not required to disclose to employers—for example, race, age, religion, sex, national origin, marital status, or disability (Preston).

Given the realities of the digital age, however, admissions committees and job recruiters are acting reasonably when they access social-networking sites. As a practical matter, it would be

Blaine 3

almost impossible to prevent employers from reviewing online sites as part of informal background and reference checks. Moreover, those who believe that it is unethical for recruiters to look at the online profiles of prospective job candidates seem willing to accept the benefits of social-networking sites but unwilling to acknowledge that these new technologies bring new responsibilities and liabilities. Finally, the problems associated with employers' use of social-networking sites would not be an issue in the first place if users of social-networking sites took full advantage of the available measures to protect themselves.

Part of the problem is that the Internet has fundamentally altered our notions of "private" and "public" in ways that we are only just beginning to understand. As Shelley Fralic observes in "Don't Fall for the Myths about Online Privacy," Facebook's privacy options do not really protect its users' privacy, and thinking they do "is beyond absurd" (1). On sites like Facebook, people can reveal intimate details of their lives to millions of strangers. This situation is unprecedented and, at least for the foreseeable future, irreversible. As *New York Times* columnist Thomas L. Friedman observes, "When everyone has a blog, a MySpace page, or Facebook entry, everyone is a publisher. . . . When everyone is a publisher, paparazzo, or filmmaker, everyone else is a public figure." Given the changes in our understanding of privacy and the public nature of the Internet, the suggestion that we should live our lives by the same rules we lived by twenty years ago simply does not make sense. As Friedman notes, in the Internet age, more and more of "what you say or do or write will end up as a digital fingerprint that never gets erased" (23).

5

Because the source and the author are named in an identifying tag, only the page numbers are needed parenthetically.

Ellipses indicate that words have been left out of a quotation.

Including a recognized authority, such as Friedman, adds credibility.

Blaine 4

Rather than relying on outdated notions of privacy,   6
students and job seekers should accept these new conditions
and take steps to protect themselves. Most college and career
counseling services have easy-to-follow recommendations for
how to maintain a positive online reputation. First on almost
everyone's list is the advice, "Adjust your privacy settings."
Northwestern University's Career Services says it simply:
"Use your settings wisely and employers will not have access
to the contents of your sites" ("Using Social Networking").
Understanding and employing these settings is a user's
responsibility; misunderstanding such protections is no excuse.
As Mariel Loveland suggests, those who want extra help can
hire an online reputation-management company such as
Reputation.com or Integrity Defenders or use services such as
those offered by Reppler. The "Reppler Image Score" enables
social-networking users to identify questionable material
"across different social networks" and to rate its "professional-
ism and consistency."

The most important way for people to protect themselves   7
against the possible misuse of personal information is for them
to take responsibility for the information they post online.
According to a recent article in *Education Week*, even middle
school students should keep their future college and career
plans in mind when they post information online ("Online
Behavior"). In preparing students to apply for college, many
high school counselors stress the "golden rule": "students
should never post anything online they wouldn't want their

Internet source includes no page number in the parenthetical documentation.

Distinctive key phrases are quoted directly.

Not every summary or paraphrase needs to include a quotation.

Blaine 5

parents to see" ("Online Behavior"). Students and job seekers
must realize that a commonsense approach to the Internet
requires that they develop good "digital grooming" habits
(Bond). For example, one self-described "cautious Internet
user" says that she "goes through the information on her
[Facebook] account every few weeks and deletes statuses, messages, and other things" (Bond). She understands that a potential employer coming across an applicant's membership in a
Facebook group such as "I Sold My Grandma for Crack-
Cocaine!" or a picture of a student posing with an empty liquor
bottle may not understand the tone, the context, or the joke.
Students should also be careful about "friends" who have
access to their online social networks, asking themselves whether
these people really know them and would have good things to
say about them if a prospective employer contacted them for a
reference. According to one high school principal, 75 percent of
the students at his school admitted to accepting a friend request
from someone they did not know ("Online Behavior"). Getting
students to consider the repercussions of this kind of choice is
central to many social-media education programs.

    Although social-networking sites have disadvantages, they
also have advantages. These sites provide an excellent opportunity for job seekers to connect with potential employers and to
get their names and résumés in circulation. For example, a job
seeker can search the LinkedIn networks of a company's executives or human resources staff for mutual connections. In
addition, a job seeker can post information calculated to appeal
to potential employers. Recruiters are just as likely to hire

8

Brackets
indicate that a
quotation has
been edited for
clarity.

Paraphrasing
provides
readers with the
key points of a
source.

Blaine 6

candidates based on social-media screening as they are to

reject them. A recent article reports the following:

> However, one third (33 percent) of employers who
>
> research candidates on social networking sites say
>
> they've found content that made them more likely
>
> to hire a candidate. What's more, nearly a quarter
>
> (23 percent) found content that directly led to them
>
> hiring the candidate, up from 19 percent last year.
>
> ("Number of Employers")

In today's job market, people should think of their networks as

extensions of themselves. They need to take an active role in

shaping the image they want to project to future employers.

As Thomas L. Friedman argues in his column, "The Whole   9

World Is Watching," access to information creates opportunities

as well as problems. Quoting Dov Seidman, Friedman main-

tains that the most important opportunity may be the one to

"out-behave your competition." In other words, just as the

Internet allows negative information to travel quickly, it also

allows positive information to spread. So even though students

and job seekers should be careful when posting information

online, they should not miss the opportunity to take advantage

of the many opportunities that social-networking sites offer.

A quotation of more than four lines of text is double-spaced, indented one inch from the left margin, and typed as a block, without quotation marks. Parenthetical documentation comes after the final punctuation.

Blaine 7

Works Cited

Bond, Michaelle. "Facebook Timeline a New Privacy Test." *USA Today*, 2 Nov. 2011, www.usatoday.com/tech/news/internetprivacy/story/2011-11-02/facebook-timeline-privacy/51047658/1.

Cammenga, Michelle. "Facebook Might Be the Reason You Don't Get That Job." *Hub Bub*, Loyola University Chicago's School of Communication, 23 Feb. 2012, blogs.luc.edu/hubbub/reporting-and-writing/employers-screen-facebook/.

Fralic, Shelley. "Don't Fall for the Myths about Online Privacy." *Calgary Herald*, 17 Oct. 2015, p. 1.

Friedman, Thomas L. "The Whole World Is Watching." *The New York Times,* 27 June 2007, p. A23.

Loveland, Mariel. "Reppler Launches 'Reppler Image Score,' Rates Social Network Profile Content for Potential Employers." *Scribbal*, 27 Sept. 2011, www.scribbal.com/reppler-launches-rates-social-network-profile-content-09-27-11/.

"Number of Employers Passing on Applicants Due to Social Media Posts Continues to Rise." *CareerBuilder*, 26 June 2014, www.careerbuilder.com/share/aboutus/pressreleasesdetail.aspx?sd=6%2F26%2F2014&id=pr829&ed=12%2F31%2F2014.

"Online Behavior Jeopardizing College Plans; Admissions Officers Checking Social-Networking Sites for Red Flags." *Education Week,* 14 Dec. 2011, p. 11. *Academic One File*, www.edweek.org/ew/articles/2011/12/08/14collegeadmit.h31.html.

Preston, Jennifer. "Social Media History Becomes a New Job Hurdle." *The New York Times*, 20 July 2011, www.nytimes.com/2011/07/21/technology/social-media-history-becomes-a-new-job-hurdle.html?_r=0.

"Using Social Networking in Your Employment Search." *University Career Services*, Northwestern University, 2011, www.northwestern.edu/careers/job-intern-prep/social-media-advice/index.html.

The works-cited list includes full information for all sources cited in the paper.

Be sure that your data comes from recent sources.

Tim Roberts/Getty Images

Using Sources Responsibly

Where Should We Draw the Line with Plagiarism?

In recent years, a number of high-profile plagiarism cases have put a spotlight on how much "borrowing" from other sources is acceptable. Some critics—and many colleges and universities—draw little distinction between intentional and unintentional plagiarism, arguing that any unattributed borrowing is theft. Others are more forgiving, accepting the fact that busy historians or scientists (or students) might not realize that a particular sentence in their notes was not their original idea or might accidentally incorporate a source's exact words (or its unique syntax or phrasing) into their own work without attribution.

In the age of the Internet, with its "cut-and-paste" culture, plagiarism has become easier to commit; however, with the development of plagiarism-detection software, it is also now much easier to detect. Still, some colleges and universities are uncomfortable with the idea of using such software, arguing that it establishes an atmosphere of distrust.

On college campuses, as in the professional world, questions like the following have arisen: What exactly constitutes plagiarism? How serious a matter is it? Is there a difference between intentional and unintentional plagiarism? Is plagiarizing a few sentences as bad as plagiarizing an entire paper? Why do people commit plagiarism? What should be done to prevent it? How should it be punished? What are its short- and long-term consequences?

These are some (although by no means all) of the questions that you might think about as you consider the sources at the end of this chapter. After reading these sources, you will be asked to write an argumentative essay that takes a position on the issue of what exactly constitutes plagiarism and how it should be dealt with.

Understanding Plagiarism

Plagiarism is the act of using the words or ideas of another person without attributing them to their rightful author—that is, presenting those borrowed words and ideas as if they are your own. When you plagiarize, you fail to use sources ethically or responsibly.

TWO DEFINITIONS OF PLAGIARISM

From *MLA Handbook* Eighth Edition (2016)

Merriam-Webster's Collegiate Dictionary defines plagiarizing as committing "literary theft." Plagiarism is presenting another person's ideas, information, expressions, or entire work as one's own. It is thus a kind of fraud: deceiving others to gain something of value. While plagiarism only sometimes has legal repercussions (e.g., when it involves copyright infringement—violating an authors' exclusive legal right to publication), it is always a serious moral and ethical offense.

From *Publication Manual of the American Psychological Association*, Sixth Edition (2009)

Researchers do not claim the words and ideas of another as their own; they give credit where credit is due (APA Ethics Code Standard 8.11, Plagiarism). Quotation marks should be used to indicate the exact words of another. *Each time* you paraphrase another author (i.e., summarize a passage or rearrange the order of a sentence and change some of the words), you need to credit the source in the text.

The key element of this principle is that authors do not present the work of another as if it were their own work. This can extend to ideas as well as written words. If authors model a study after one done by someone else, the originating author should be given credit. If the rationale for a study was suggested in the Discussion section of someone else's article, that person should be given credit. Given the free exchange of ideas, which is very important to the health of intellectual discourse, authors may not know where an idea for a study originated. If authors do know, however, they should acknowledge the source; this includes personal communications.

For many people, defining plagiarism is simple: it is not "borrowing" but stealing, and it should be dealt with severely. For others, it is a more slippery term, seen as considerably more serious if it is intentional than if it is accidental (for example, the result of careless research methods). Most colleges and universities have guidelines that define plagiarism strictly and have penalties in place for those who commit it. To avoid committing unintentional plagiarism, you need to understand exactly what it is and why it occurs. You also need to learn how to use sources responsibly and to understand what kind of information requires documentation and what kind does not.

Avoiding Unintentional Plagiarism

Even if you do not intentionally misuse the words or ideas of a source, you are still committing plagiarism if you present the work of others as your own. The most common errors that lead to unintentional plagiarism—and how to avoid them—are listed below.

COMMON ERROR	HOW TO AVOID IT
No source information is provided for borrowed material (including statistics).	Always include full parenthetical documentation and a works-cited list that make the source of your information clear to readers. (See Chapter 10.)
A source's ideas are presented as if they are your own original ideas.	Keep track of the sources you consult, and always keep full source information with your sources. Never cut and paste material from an electronic source directly into your paper.
The boundaries of borrowed material are unclear.	Be sure to use an identifying tag *before* and parenthetical documentation *after* borrowed material. (See Chapter 9.)
The language of paraphrases or summaries is still too close to that of the original source.	Be careful to use original phrasing and syntax when you write summaries and paraphrases. (See Chapter 9.)

(Continued)

COMMON ERROR	HOW TO AVOID IT
A friend's or tutor's words or ideas appear in your paper.	Any help you receive should be in the form of suggestions, not additions.
Material you wrote for another course is used in your paper.	Always get permission from *both* instructors if you want to reuse work you did for another course, and be sure the material you use is substantially revised.

To avoid unintentional plagiarism, you need to maintain control over your sources, keeping track of all the material you use so that you remember where you found each piece of information.

As you take notes, be careful to distinguish your sources' ideas from your own. If you are copying a source's words into your notes, put them in quotation marks. (If you are taking notes by hand, circle the quotation marks; if you are typing your notes, put the quotation marks in boldface.) If you photocopy material, write the full source information on the first page, and staple the pages together. When you download material from the Internet, be sure the URL appears on every page. Finally, never cut and paste material from a source directly into your paper.

INTERNET SOURCES AND PLAGIARISM

The Internet presents a particular challenge for students as they try to avoid plagiarism. Committing plagiarism (intentional or unintentional) with electronic sources is easy because it is simple to cut and paste material from online sources into a paper. However, inserting even a sentence or two from an Internet source (including a blog, an email, or a website) into a paper without quotation marks and documentation constitutes plagiarism.

It is also not acceptable to use a visual (such as a graph, chart, table, or photograph) found on the Internet without acknowledging its source. Finally, even if an Internet source does not identify its author, the words or ideas you find there are not your own original material, so you must identify their source.

As you draft your paper, be sure to quote your sources' words accurately (even punctuation must be reproduced exactly as it appears in the source). Be careful not to quote out of context, and be sure that you are presenting your sources' ideas accurately when you summarize or paraphrase. (For information on quoting, paraphrasing, and summarizing source material, see Chapter 9.)

INTENTIONAL PLAGIARISM

Deliberately plagiarizing from a source, handing in another student's paper as your own, or buying a paper from an Internet site is never acceptable. Such acts constitute serious violations of academic integrity. Creating your own original work is an important part of the educational experience, and misrepresenting someone else's work as your own undermines the goals of education.

Cartoon by Loos Diallo from Whitman Pioneer.

Knowing What to Document

Documentation is the practice of identifying borrowed material and providing the proper bibliographic information for each source. Different academic disciplines require different formats for documentation—for example, English uses MLA, and psychology uses APA. For this reason, you should be sure to check with your instructor to find out what documentation style he or she requires. (For information on MLA and APA documentation formats, see Chapter 10 and Appendix B, respectively.)

Regardless of the discipline, the following kinds of information should always be documented:

- Quotations from a source

- Summaries or paraphrases of a source's original ideas

- Opinions, judgments, and conclusions that are not your own

- Statistics from a source

- Visuals from a source

- Data from charts or graphs in a source

The following kinds of information, however, do not require documentation:

- **Common knowledge**—that is, factual information that can be found in several different sources (for example, a writer's date of birth, a scientific fact, or the location of a famous battle)

- Familiar quotations—anything from proverbs to frequently quoted lines from Shakespeare's plays—that you expect readers will recognize

- Your own original opinions, judgments, and conclusions

⊙ EXERCISE 11.1

Which of the following statements requires documentation, and why?

1. Doris Kearns Goodwin is a prize-winning historian.

2. Doris Kearns Goodwin's *The Fitzgeralds and the Kennedys* is a 900-page book with about 3,500 footnotes.

3. In 1994, Lynne McTaggart accused Goodwin of borrowing material from a book that McTaggart wrote.

4. My own review of the background suggests that Goodwin's plagiarism was unintentional.

5. Still, these accusations left Goodwin to face the "slings and arrows" of media criticism.

6. As Goodwin explains, "The more intensive and far-reaching a historian's research, the greater the difficulty of citation."

7. In her defense, Goodwin argued that the more research a historian does, the harder it is to keep track of sources.

8. Some people still remain convinced that Goodwin committed plagiarism.

9. Goodwin believes that her careful research methods, which she has described in exhaustive detail, should have prevented accidental plagiarism.

10. Some of Goodwin's critics have concluded that her reputation as a historian was hurt by the plagiarism charges.

⊘ EXERCISE 11.2

Assume you are using the following editorial as a source. Identify two pieces of information you would need to document (for example, statistics). Then, identify two pieces of information you would *not* need to document (for example, common knowledge).

This unsigned newspaper editorial appeared on August 11, 2006.

CHEATERS NEVER WIN
AUSTIN AMERICAN-STATESMAN

We live in the era of cut and paste, thanks to the Internet, which provides students with countless materials to plagiarize. 1

If you think that's an exaggeration, do an Internet search of "free term papers." You'll find cheathouse.com, Cheater.com, Schoolsucks.com, echeat .com, and Free Essay Network (freeessay.com) among the 603 million results that turn up. 2

One site, 24hourtermpapers.com, even boasts of providing "custom term papers" within 24 hours (at $23.95 per page), targeting college students who put off writing papers until the 11th hour. A disclaimer warns that "these term papers are to be used for research purposes only. Use of these papers for any other purpose is not the responsibility of 24 Hour Term Papers." Funny that they say that, because the site provides the student with a nice package to hand directly to the professor: All term papers are "sent within the due date," with a bibliography page thrown in for no extra charge. 3

A student who pays such a steep price for a term paper is not likely to use it only as a resource. One of the perks of being a student today is unlimited access to a slew of research tools, from the library to an online research database the institution pays for the student to use. 4

Student Judicial Services at the University of Texas defines plagiarism as "representing as your own work any material that was obtained from another 5 source, regardless of how or where you acquired it." This includes borrowing ideas or even structure. And "by merely changing a few words or rearranging several words or sentences, you are not paraphrasing. Making minor revisions to borrowed text amounts to plagiarism," the Web site warns.

But those warnings go unheeded by many. The Center for Academic 6 Integrity found last year that more than 70 percent of college students admitted to having cheated at least once, more than 60 percent admitted to plagiarizing, and nearly 40 percent said they have plagiarized from the Internet.

Strict disciplinary action should follow students who are caught trying to 7 claim someone else's work as their own. The more it goes unnoticed, the easier it is for students to keep stealing. Educators should devote time and attention to properly educating students on what plagiarism is and why it's stupid to do it.

In the end, the plagiarizer has the most to lose, whether he or she gets 8 caught or not. Many of the online papers are not worthy of copying, especially if a student wants to excel in college. By stealing someone else's work and labeling it as their own, students forgo the opportunity to learn how to research, develop ideas, and translate them into quality writing. Not to mention tarnishing a reputation, if the student gets caught.

> "In the end, the plagiarizer has the most to lose, whether he or she gets caught or not."

Cheathouse.com and other sites like it might get students a passing grade 9 in a course, but it only puts them a step behind everyone else who is developing the skills needed to thrive in the workplace. Employers won't be as forgiving as teachers or disciplinary committees. The day will come when the "I'm a student. I'm still learning" excuse will fall on deaf ears.

Revising to Eliminate Plagiarism

As you revise your papers, scrutinize your work carefully to be sure you have not inadvertently committed plagiarism.

The following paragraph (from page 28 of *Hot, Flat, and Crowded* by Thomas L. Friedman) and the four guidelines that follow it will help you to understand the situations in which accidental plagiarism is most likely to occur.

> So if you think the world feels crowded now, just wait a few decades. In 1800, London was the world's largest city with one million people. By 1960, there were 111 cities with more than one million people. By 1995 there were 280, and today there are over 300, according to

UN Population Fund statistics. The number of megacities (with ten million or more inhabitants) in the world has climbed from 5 in 1975 to 14 in 1995 and is expected to reach 26 cities by 2015, according to the UN. Needless to say, these exploding populations are rapidly overwhelming infrastructure in these megacities—nineteen million people in Mumbai alone—as well as driving loss of arable land, deforestation, overfishing, water shortages, and air and water pollution.

1. **Be sure you have identified your source and provided appropriate documentation.**

PLAGIARISM
The world is becoming more and more crowded, and some twenty-six cities are expected to have populations of over 10 million by 2015.

This student writer does not quote directly from Friedman's discussion, but her summary of his comments does not represent her original ideas and therefore needs to be documented.

The following correct use of source material includes both an **identifying tag** (a phrase that identifies Friedman as the source of the ideas) and a page number that directs readers to the exact location of the material the student is summarizing. (Full source information is provided in the works-cited list.)

CORRECT
According to Thomas L. Friedman, the world is becoming more and more crowded, and twenty-six cities are expected to have populations of over 10 million by 2015 (28).

2. **Be sure you have placed quotation marks around borrowed words.**

PLAGIARISM
According to Thomas L. Friedman, the exploding populations of megacities around the world are overwhelming their infrastructure (28).

Although the passage above provides parenthetical documentation and includes an identifying tag indicating the source of its ideas, it uses Friedman's exact words without placing them in quotation marks.

To avoid committing plagiarism, the writer needs to either place quotation marks around Friedman's words or paraphrase his comments.

CORRECT (BORROWED WORDS IN QUOTATION MARKS)
According to Thomas L. Friedman, the "exploding populations" of large cities around the world are "rapidly overwhelming infrastructure in these megacities" (28).

CORRECT (BORROWED WORDS PARAPHRASED)
According to Thomas L. Friedman, the rapid rise in population of large cities around the world poses a serious threat to their ability to function (28).

3. **Be sure you have indicated the boundaries of the borrowed material.**

PLAGIARISM
The world is becoming more and more crowded, and this will lead to serious problems in the future. Soon, as many as twenty-six of the world's cities will have populations over 10 million. It is clear that "these exploding populations are rapidly overwhelming infrastructure in these megacities" (Friedman 28).

In the passage above, the student correctly places Friedman's words in quotation marks and includes appropriate parenthetical documentation. However, she does not indicate that other ideas in the passage, although not quoted directly, are also Friedman's.

To avoid committing plagiarism, the student needs to use identifying tags to indicate the boundaries of the borrowed material, which goes beyond the quoted words.

CORRECT
According to Thomas L. Friedman, the world is becoming more and more crowded, and this will lead to serious problems in the future. Soon, Friedman predicts, as many as twenty-six of the world's cities will have populations of over 10 million, and this rise in population will put a serious strain on the cities' resources, "rapidly overwhelming infrastructure in these megacities" (28).

4. **Be sure you have used your own phrasing and syntax.**

PLAGIARISM
If you feel crowded now, Thomas L. Friedman says, just wait twenty or thirty years. In 1800, London, with a million inhabitants, was the largest city in the world; over 111 cities had more than a million people by 1960. Thirty-five years later, there were 280; today, according to statistics provided by the UN Population Fund, there are more than 300. There were only five megacities (10 million people or more) in 1975 and fourteen in 1995. However, by 2015, the United Nations predicts, there might be twenty-six. These rapidly growing populations threaten to overwhelm the infrastructure of the megacities (Mumbai alone has 19 million people), destroying arable land, the forests, and fishing and causing water shortages and water and air pollution (28).

The student who wrote the paragraph on the preceding page does provide an identifying tag and parenthetical documentation to identify the source of her ideas. However, her paragraph's phrasing and syntax are almost identical to Friedman's.

In the following paragraph, the writer correctly paraphrases and summarizes Friedman's ideas, quoting a few distinctive passages. (See Chapter 9 for information on paraphrase and summary.)

CORRECT

As Thomas L. Friedman warns, the world has been growing more and more crowded and is likely to grow still more crowded in the years to come. Relying on UN population data, Friedman estimates that there will be some twenty more "megacities" (those with more than 10 million people) in 2015 than there were in 1975. (In 1800, in contrast, only one city in the world—London—had a million inhabitants.) Obviously, this is an alarming trend. Friedman believes that these rapidly growing populations are "overwhelming infrastructure in these megacities" and are bound to strain resources, leading to "loss of arable land, deforestation, [and] overfishing" and creating not only air and water pollution but water shortages as well (28).

> **NOTE**
>
> Do not forget to document statistics that you get from a source. For example, Thomas L. Friedman's statistics about the threat of rising population are the result of his original research, so you need to document them.

⊖ EXERCISE 11.3

The following student paragraph synthesizes information from two different sources (which appear on pp. 380–381, following the student paragraph), but the student writer has not used sources responsibly. (For information on synthesis, see Chapter 9.) Read the sources and the paragraph, and then make the following changes:

- Insert quotation marks where the student has quoted a source's words.

- Edit paraphrased and summarized material if necessary so that its syntax and phrasing are not too close to those of a source.

- Add parenthetical documentation where necessary to acknowledge the use of a source's words or original ideas.

- Add identifying tags where necessary to clarify the scope of the borrowed material or to differentiate material from the two sources.

- Check every quoted passage once more to see if the quotation adds something vital to the paragraph. If it does not, summarize or paraphrase the source's words instead.

STUDENT PARAGRAPH

In recent years, psychologists have focused on the idea that girls (unlike boys) face a crisis of self-esteem as they approach adolescence. Both Carol Gilligan and Mary Pipher did research to support this idea, showing how girls lose their self-confidence in adolescence because of sexist cultural expectations. Women's groups have expressed concern that the school system favors boys and is biased against girls. In fact, boys are often regarded not just as classroom favorites but also as bullies who represent obstacles on the path to gender justice for girls. Recently, however, this impression that boys are somehow privileged while girls are shortchanged is being challenged.

Source 1

That boys are in disrepute is not accidental. For many years women's groups have complained that boys benefit from a school system that favors them and is biased against girls. "Schools shortchange girls," declares the American Association of University Women. . . . A stream of books and pamphlets cite research showing not only that boys are classroom favorites but also that they are given to schoolyard violence and sexual harassment.

In the view that has prevailed in American education over the past decade, boys are resented, both as the unfairly privileged sex and as obstacles on the path to gender justice for girls. This perspective is promoted in schools of education, and many a teacher now feels that girls need and deserve special indemnifying consideration. "It is really clear that boys are Number One in this society and in most of the world," says Patricia O'Reilly, a professor of education and the director of the Gender Equity Center, at the University of Cincinnati.

The idea that schools and society grind girls down has given rise to an array of laws and policies intended to curtail the advantage boys have and to redress the harm done to girls. That girls are treated as the second sex in school and consequently suffer, that boys are accorded privileges and consequently benefit—these are things everyone is presumed to know. But they are not true.

—CHRISTINA HOFF SOMMERS, "THE WAR AGAINST BOYS"

Source 2

Girls face an inevitable crisis of self-esteem as they approach adolescence. They are in danger of losing their voices, drowning, and facing a devastating dip in self-regard that boys don't experience. This is the picture that Carol Gilligan presented on the basis of her research at the Emma Willard School, a private girls' school in Troy, N.Y. While Gilligan did not refer to genes in her analysis of girls' vulnerability, she did cite both the "wall of Western culture" and deep early childhood socialization as reasons.

Her theme was echoed in 1994 by the clinical psychologist Mary Pipher's surprise best seller, *Reviving Ophelia* (Putnam, 1994), which spent three years on the *New York Times* best-seller list. Drawing on case studies rather than systematic research, Pipher observed how naturally outgoing, confident girls get worn down by sexist cultural expectations. Gilligan's and Pipher's ideas have also been supported by a widely cited study in 1990 by the American Association of University Women. That report, published in 1991, claimed that teenage girls experience a "free-fall in self-esteem from which some will never recover."

The idea that girls have low self-esteem has by now become part of the academic canon as well as fodder for the popular media. But is it true? No.

—ROSALIND C. BARNETT AND CARYL RIVERS, "MEN ARE FROM EARTH, AND SO ARE WOMEN. IT'S FAULTY RESEARCH THAT SETS THEM APART"

Where Should We Draw the Line with Plagiarism?

Tim Roberts/Getty Images

Reread the At Issue box on page 369. Then, read the sources on the following pages. As you read these sources, you will be asked to answer questions and to complete some activities. This work will help you to understand the content and structure of the material you read. When you have read the sources, you will be ready to write an argumentative essay in which you take a position on the topic, "Where Should We Draw the Line with Plagiarism?"

SOURCES

In this *Slate* article, Shafer accuses a *New York Times* reporter of plagiarism. As evidence, he presents the opening paragraphs from the source (a *Bloomberg News* story), the accused reporter's *New York Times* article, and—for contrast—two other newspaper articles that report the same story without relying heavily on the original source.

This article appeared in *Slate* on March 5, 2008.

SIDEBAR:° COMPARING THE COPY

JACK SHAFER

A short news story printed alongside a longer related article

How different can four news stories generated by the same assignment be? Compare the opening paragraphs of these pieces about the 2005 mad cow disease conference call: the *Bloomberg News* version; the *New York Times* version,

> "How different can four news stories generated by the same assignment be?"

1

which lifts passages from *Bloomberg* without attribution; and the starkly different pieces run by the globeandmail.com and the *Omaha World-Herald*.

Opening paragraphs from the July 15, 2005, *Bloomberg News* story by Daniel Goldstein:

The U.S. plans to resume imports of Canadian cattle, after an appellate court cleared the way to end a ban imposed two years ago because of mad-cow disease.° Cattle prices fell and shares of beef producer Tyson Foods Inc. surged.

2

A brain disease that can be transmitted to humans through consumption of contaminated beef

The first shipments from Canada may arrive at U.S. slaughterhouses in days, U.S. Agriculture Secretary Mike Johanns said today in a conference call. "If things go well, it could very well be next week." USDA and Canadian officials are coordinating how to certify animals for shipment, he said.

3

A U.S. appellate court° yesterday ruled in favor of the government, which argued Canadian cattle under 30 months of age don't pose a risk of mad-cow disease. Tyson's beef business had a loss of $19 million in the quarter ended April 2, as the lack of available cattle boosted costs and led to plant closings. Canada before the ban supplied about 5 percent of U.S. beef.

4

A higher court that hears appeals of rulings that were made by a lower court

Opening paragraphs from the July 16, 2005, *New York Times* story by Alexei Barrionuevo:

The United States Agriculture Department said on Friday that it planned to resume imports of Canadian cattle within days, after an appellate court lifted a two-year-old injunction imposed because of mad cow disease.

5

383

The first shipments from Canada could arrive at American slaughter-houses as early as next week, Agriculture Secretary Mike Johanns said in a conference call with reporters. Officials in Canada and the United States are coordinating how to certify the animals for shipment, he said. 6

"We want to make sure everything is in place," he said. "If things go well, it could very well be next week." 7

The news sent shares of the beef producer Tyson Foods and McDonald's restaurants surging. Cattle prices fell. Shares of Tyson rose 7.5 percent in early trading, and closed at $19.47 a share, a 5 percent increase, while McDonald's closed at $30.99 a share, up 4.7 percent. 8

Tyson's beef business recorded a loss of $19 million in the quarter ended April 2. The company was hurt by the ban on cattle from Canada, which increased costs and led to temporary plant closings. Before the ban, Canada supplied about 5 percent of the nation's beef. 9

A United States appeals court ruled on Thursday in favor of the government, which had argued that Canadian cows under 30 months of age did not pose a risk of bovine spongiform encephalopathy, or mad cow disease. 10

Opening paragraphs from the July 15 globeandmail.com story by Terry Weber, time stamped 12:28 p.m.:

The United States is taking immediate steps to reopen the border to Canadian cattle imports, Agriculture Secretary Mike Johanns said Friday. 11

During a webcast, Mr. Johanns said that Washington has been in touch with Ottawa and that the two sides are now going through the logistical steps necessary to resume trade of live cattle for the first time since May, 2003. 12

"Our hope is we're talking about days and not weeks," he said. "If things go well, it could very well be next week, but we have not set a specific date." 13

Late Thursday, a three-member U.S. appeal court panel in Seattle overturned a temporary injunction issued by Montana Judge Richard Cebull halting the U.S. Department of Agriculture's March plan to reopen the border. 14

Judge Cebull had sided with U.S. ranchers group R-Calf in its argument that reopening the border exposed U.S. ranchers and consumers to unnecessary risks from mad-cow disease. The USDA had been planning to ease restrictions by allowing cattle younger than 30 months to be imported. 15

Mr. Johanns noted that Canadian officials had already anticipated the ruling and taken steps to meet U.S. requirements, should Thursday's favor reopening the border. 16

"It [the reopening] could be as early as next week, but we want to make sure everything is in place," he said. 17

Those requirements, he said, including ensuring that animals being imported into the U.S. meet minimal-risk rule criteria, getting documents to U.S. customs to confirm the shipments are appropriate for entry. 18

Opening paragraphs from the July 15 *Omaha World-Herald* **story by Chris Clayton:**

Canadian cattle could start arriving at U.S. feedlots and meatpacking plants as early as next week, U.S. Agriculture Secretary Mike Johanns said Friday. 19

Thursday's unanimous decision by the 9th U.S. Circuit Court of Appeals lifting a lower court's injunction gives U.S. and Canadian officials a nearly two-week window to begin shipping live cattle from Canada before another court hearing, scheduled late this month in Montana. 20

No date has been set, but Johanns said he will move as "expeditiously as possible" to begin importing Canadian cattle once officials work out the ground rules. Canadian and USDA officials anticipated the requirements would be in place at whatever time the legal issues were resolved. 21

"Our hope is we are talking about days, not weeks," Johanns said. "It could be as early as next week, but we want to make sure everything is in place. . . . If things go well, it could very well be next week, but we haven't set a specific date" [*ellipsis in the original*]. 22

Johanns has lamented the closed border since becoming agriculture secretary in late January, saying that it hurts U.S. cattle feeders and meatpackers because the United States continued to import boxed beef from Canada. 23

Higher cattle prices because of tight supplies caused meatpackers to scale back production at U.S. facilities. Industry officials claim to have lost as many as 8,000 meatpacking jobs because of the closed border. 24

"I'm just worried that many of those jobs were impacted in a very permanent way," Johanns said. "My hope is that restructuring now will be abated and this industry can start getting back to a normal flow of commerce here." 25

About 1 million cattle were imported from Canada in the year before the border closed in May 2003 when Canada reported its first case of mad-cow disease, or bovine spongiform encephalopathy. 26

⊙ AT ISSUE: SOURCES FOR UNDERSTANDING PLAGIARISM

1. Identify the passages in the *New York Times* story that you think are too close to the original *Bloomberg News* story.

2. Identify passages in the other two excerpts that convey the same information as the *Times* story (paraphrased or summarized).

3. In his introduction, Shafer says that the passages from the Toronto *Globe and Mail* and the *Omaha World-Herald* are "starkly different" from the *Bloomberg News* story. Do you agree?

4. Can you identify any passages in the *Globe and Mail* or *Omaha World-Herald* excerpts that you believe are too close to the original source?

5. On the basis of what you see here, do you agree with Shafer that the *New York Times* reporter is guilty of plagiarism? Explain your conclusion.

This essay appeared in the *Washington Post* on September 3, 2004.

HOW TO FIGHT COLLEGE CHEATING

LAWRENCE M. HINMAN

Recent studies have shown that a steadily growing number of students cheat or 1 plagiarize in college—and the data from high schools suggest that this number will continue to rise. A study by Don McCabe of Rutgers University showed that 74 percent of high school students admitted to one or more instances of serious cheating on tests. Even more disturbing is the way that many students define cheating and plagiarism. For example, they believe that cutting and pasting a few sentences from various Web sources without attribution is not plagiarism.

Before the Web, students certainly plagiarized—but they had to plan 2 ahead to do so. Fraternities and sororities often had files of term papers, and some high-tech term-paper firms could fax papers to students. Overall, however, plagiarism required forethought.

Online term-paper sites changed all that. Overnight, students could order 3 a term paper, print it out, and have it ready for class in the morning—and still get a good night's sleep. All they needed was a charge card and an Internet connection.

One response to the increase in cheating has been to fight technology with 4 more technology. Plagiarism-checking sites provide a service to screen student papers. They offer a color-coded report on papers and the original sources from which the students might have copied. Colleges qualify for volume discounts, which encourages professors to submit whole classes' worth of papers—the academic equivalent of mandatory urine testing for athletes.

The technological battle between term-paper mills and anti-plagiarism services will undoubtedly continue to escalate, with each side constructing more elaborate countermeasures to outwit the other. The cost of both plagiarism and its detection will also undoubtedly continue to spiral. 5

> "The cost of both plagiarism and its detection will also undoubtedly continue to spiral."

But there is another way. Our first and 6 most important line of defense against academic dishonesty is simply good teaching. Cheating and plagiarism often arise in a vacuum created by routine, lack of interest, and overwork. Professors who give the same assignment every semester, fail to guide students in the development of their projects, and have little interest in what the students have to say contribute to the academic environment in which much cheating and plagiarism occurs.

Consider, by way of contrast, professors who know their students and 7 who give assignments that require regular, continuing interaction with them about their projects—and who require students to produce work that is a meaningful development of their own interests. These professors create an environment in which cheating and plagiarism are far less likely to occur. In this context, any plagiarism would usually be immediately evident to the professor, who would see it as inconsistent with the rest of the student's work. A strong, meaningful curriculum taught by committed professors is the first and most important defense against academic dishonesty.

The second remedy is to encourage the development of integrity in our stu- 8
dents. A sense of responsibility about one's intellectual development would preclude cheating and plagiarizing as inconsistent with one's identity. It is precisely this sense of individual integrity that schools with honor codes seek to promote.

Third, we must encourage our students to perceive the dishonesty of their 9
classmates as something that causes harm to the many students who play by the rules. The argument that cheaters hurt only themselves is false. Cheaters do hurt other people, and they do so to help themselves. Students cheat because it works. They get better grades and more advantages with less effort. Honest students lose grades, scholarships, recommendations, and admission to advanced programs. Honest students must create enough peer pressure to dissuade potential cheaters. Ultimately, students must be willing to step forward and confront those who engage in academic dishonesty.

Addressing these issues is not a luxury that can be postponed until a more 10
convenient time. It is a short step from dishonesty in schools and colleges to dishonesty in business. It is doubtful that students who fail to develop habits of integrity and honesty while still in an academic setting are likely to do so once they are out in the "real" world. Nor is it likely that adults will stand up against the dishonesty of others, particularly fellow workers and superiors, if they do not develop the habit of doing so while still in school.

⊘ AT ISSUE: SOURCES FOR UNDERSTANDING PLAGIARISM

1. In the first five paragraphs of this essay, Hinman provides background on how plagiarism by students has been changed by the Internet. Summarize the plagiarism situation before and after the development of the Internet.

2. The essay's thesis is stated in paragraph 6. Restate this thesis in your own words.

3. Does Hinman view plagiarism-detection sites as a solution to the problem of college cheating? What are the limitations of such sites?

4. According to Hinman, what steps can "committed professors" (para. 7) take to eliminate academic dishonesty?

5. In paragraphs 8 and 9, Hinman suggests two additional solutions to the problem of plagiarism. What solutions does he propose? Given what you know about college students, do you think Hinman's suggestions are realistic? Explain.

6. Hinman does not address arguments that challenge his recommendations. What opposing arguments might he have presented? How would you refute these opposing arguments?

7. This essay was published more than ten years ago. Do you think Hinman's observations and recommendations are still valid? Why or why not?

This article is from the August 1, 2010, edition of the *New York Times*.

PLAGIARISM LINES BLUR FOR STUDENTS IN DIGITAL AGE

TRIP GABRIEL

At Rhode Island College, a freshman copied and pasted from a Web site's fre- 1 quently asked questions page about homelessness—and did not think he needed to credit a source in his assignment because the page did not include author information.

At DePaul University, the tip-off to one student's copying was the purple 2 shade of several paragraphs he had lifted from the Web; when confronted by a writing tutor his professor had sent him to, he was not defensive—he just wanted to know how to change purple text to black.

And at the University of Maryland, a student reprimanded for copying 3 from *Wikipedia* in a paper on the Great Depression said he thought its entries—unsigned and collectively written—did not need to be credited since they counted, essentially, as common knowledge.

Professors used to deal with plagiarism by admonishing students to give 4 credit to others and to follow the style guide for citations, and pretty much left it at that.

But these cases—typical ones, according to writing tutors and officials 5 responsible for discipline at the three schools who described the plagiarism— suggest that many students simply do not grasp that using words they did not write is a serious misdeed.

It is a disconnect that is growing in the Internet age as concepts of intel- 6 lectual property, copyright, and originality are under assault in the unbridled exchange of online information, say educators who study plagiarism.

Digital technology makes copying and pasting easy, of course. But that is 7 the least of it. The Internet may also be redefining how students—who came of age with music file-sharing, *Wikipedia*, and Web-linking—understand the concept of authorship and the singularity of any text or image.

"Now we have a whole generation of students who've grown up with 8 information that just seems to be hanging out there in cyberspace and doesn't seem to have an author," said Teresa Fishman, director of the Center for Academic Integrity at Clemson University. "It's possible to believe this information is just out there for anyone to take."

Professors who have studied plagiarism do not try to excuse it—many are 9 champions of academic honesty on their campuses—but rather try to understand why it is so widespread.

In surveys from 2006 to 2010 by Donald L. McCabe, a co-founder of the 10 Center for Academic Integrity and a business professor at Rutgers University, about 40 percent of 14,000 undergraduates admitted to copying a few sentences in written assignments.

Perhaps more significant, the number who believed that copying from the 11 Web constitutes "serious cheating" is declining—to 29 percent on average in recent surveys from 34 percent earlier in the decade.

Sarah Brookover, a senior at the Rutgers campus in Camden, N.J., said 12 many of her classmates blithely cut and paste without attribution.

"This generation has always existed in a world where media and intellec- 13 tual property don't have the same gravity," said Ms. Brookover, who at 31 is older than most undergraduates. "When you're sitting at your computer, it's the same machine you've downloaded music with, possibly illegally, the same machine you streamed videos for free that showed on HBO last night."

Ms. Brookover, who works at the campus library, has pondered the differ- 14 ences between researching in the stacks and online. "Because you're not walking into a library, you're not physically holding the article, which takes you closer to 'this doesn't belong to me,'" she said. Online, "everything can belong to you really easily."

> "Online, 'everything can belong to you really easily.'"

A University of Notre Dame anthropologist, Susan D. Blum, disturbed by 15 the high rates of reported plagiarism, set out to understand how students view authorship and the written word, or "texts" in Ms. Blum's academic language.

She conducted her ethnographic research among 234 Notre Dame under- 16 graduates. "Today's students stand at the crossroads of a new way of conceiving texts and the people who create them and who quote them," she wrote last year in the book *My Word! Plagiarism and College Culture*, published by Cornell University Press.

Ms. Blum argued that student writing exhibits some of the same qualities 17 of pastiche that drive other creative endeavors today—TV shows that constantly reference other shows or rap music that samples from earlier songs.

In an interview, she said the idea of an author whose singular effort cre- 18 ates an original work is rooted in Enlightenment ideas of the individual. It is buttressed by the Western concept of intellectual property rights as secured by copyright law. But both traditions are being challenged. "Our notion of authorship and originality was born, it flourished, and it may be waning," Ms. Blum said.

She contends that undergraduates are less interested in cultivating a 19 unique and authentic identity—as their 1960s counterparts were—than in trying on many different personas, which the Web enables with social networking.

"If you are not so worried about presenting yourself as absolutely unique, 20 then it's O.K. if you say other people's words, it's O.K. if you say things you don't believe, it's O.K. if you write papers you couldn't care less about because they accomplish the task, which is turning something in and getting a grade," Ms. Blum said, voicing student attitudes. "And it's O.K. if you put words out there without getting any credit."

The notion that there might be a new model young person, who freely 21 borrows from the vortex of information to mash up a new creative work, fueled a brief brouhaha earlier this year with Helene Hegemann, a German teenager whose best-selling novel about Berlin club life turned out to include passages lifted from others.

Instead of offering an abject apology, Ms. Hegemann insisted, "There's no 22 such thing as originality anyway, just authenticity." A few critics rose to her defense, and the book remained a finalist for a fiction prize (but did not win).

That theory does not wash with Sarah Wilensky, a senior at Indiana Uni- 23 versity, who said that relaxing plagiarism standards "does not foster creativity, it fosters laziness."

"You're not coming up with new ideas if you're grabbing and mixing and 24 matching," said Ms. Wilensky, who took aim at Ms. Hegemann in a column in her student newspaper headlined "Generation Plagiarism."

"It may be increasingly accepted, but there are still plenty of creative 25 people—authors and artists and scholars—who are doing original work," Ms. Wilensky said in an interview. "It's kind of an insult that that ideal is gone, and now we're left only to make collages of the work of previous generations."

In the view of Ms. Wilensky, whose writing skills earned her the role of 26 informal editor of other students' papers in her freshman dorm, plagiarism has nothing to do with trendy academic theories.

The main reason it occurs, she said, is because students leave high school 27 unprepared for the intellectual rigors of college writing.

"If you're taught how to closely read sources and synthesize them into your 28 own original argument in middle and high school, you're not going to be tempted to plagiarize in college, and you certainly won't do so unknowingly," she said.

At the University of California, Davis, of the 196 plagiarism cases referred 29 to the disciplinary office last year, a majority did not involve students ignorant of the need to credit the writing of others.

Many times, said Donald J. Dudley, who oversees the discipline office on 30 the campus of 32,000, it was students who intentionally copied—knowing it was wrong—who were "unwilling to engage the writing process."

"Writing is difficult, and doing it well takes time and practice," he said. 31

And then there was a case that had nothing to do with a younger genera- 32 tion's evolving view of authorship. A student accused of plagiarism came to Mr. Dudley's office with her parents, and the father admitted that he was the one responsible for the plagiarism. The wife assured Mr. Dudley that it would not happen again.

⊘ AT ISSUE: SOURCES FOR UNDERSTANDING PLAGIARISM

1. Gabriel begins inductively, presenting three paragraphs of evidence before he states his thesis. Is this the best strategy, or should these examples appear later in his discussion? Explain.

2. In paragraph 5, Gabriel notes that "many students simply do not grasp that using words they did not write is a serious misdeed." Is this his thesis statement? Does he take a position, or is he just presenting information?

3. Why, according to Gabriel, is plagiarism so widespread? Do you think the reasons he cites in any way excuse plagiarism—at least accidental plagiarism? Does Gabriel seem to think they do?

4. What is *pastiche* (para. 17)? What is a collage (25)? How does the concept of pastiche or collage apply to plagiarism? Do you see the use of pastiche in TV shows or popular music (17) as different from its use in academic writing? Why or why not?

5. Summarize Sarah Wilensky's views (23–28) on the issue Gabriel discusses. Do you agree with her? Do you agree with Helene Hegemann's statement, "There's no such thing as originality anyway, just authenticity" (22)?

6. Do you think the anecdote in paragraph 32 is a strong ending for this article? Does the paragraph need a more forceful concluding statement? Explain.

This essay appeared on the *New Yorker*'s "Book Bench" blog on August 4, 2010.

TOO HARD *NOT* TO CHEAT IN THE INTERNET AGE?

ELIZABETH MINKEL

A deeply troubling article sat atop the *New York Times'* most-emailed list 1 yesterday (no, not the one about catching horrible diseases at the gym). "Plagiarism Lines Blur for Students in Digital Age," the headline proclaimed, pinpointing a problem, weaving a theory, and excusing youthful copycats in one fell swoop. The story here is that a large number of college students today are acting as college students always have—baldly lifting whole passages for their term papers from other sources. But it's the Digital Age now, and between unverifiable, unattributed information sitting around online and the general ease with which young people obtain, alter, and share creative content on the Internet, students can't seem to figure out that cheating on a paper is wrong. In fact, a lot of them can't even tell that they're cheating, and the Internet is to blame.

Really? When I was in college (I graduated three years ago), I was well 2 aware of the necessity of avoiding minefields of unattributed—and often incorrect—information on the Web. *Wikipedia* was never an acceptable source, perhaps because my professors knew they'd get students like the one from the University of Maryland who, when "reprimanded for copying from *Wikipedia* . . . said he thought its entries—unsigned and collectively written—did not need to be credited since they counted, essentially, as common knowledge." There are probably only two types of people pulling these excuses: the crafty, using the Digital Age argument to their advantage, and the completely clueless, who, like plenty in preceding generations, just don't understand the concept of plagiarism. The *Times* asked current students to weigh in (helpfully labelling them "Generation Plagiarism"), and one wrote:

"I never 'copy and paste' but I will take information from the Internet and 3 change out a few words then put it in my paper. So far, I have not encountered any problems with this. Thought [*sic*] the information/words are technically mine because of a few undetectable word swaps, I still consider the information to be that of someone else."

The student goes on to say that, "In the digital age, plagiarism isn't and shouldn't be as big of a deal as it used to be when people used books for research." The response leaves me just as confused as I believe he is,

> "I'm pretty convinced that he'd still be fuzzy on plagiarism if he'd lived back when people actually used books." 4

but I'm pretty convinced that he'd still be fuzzy on plagiarism if he'd lived back when people actually used books. But what I've found most frustrating in the ensuing debate is the assertion that these students are a part of some new *Reality Hunger*–type wave of open-source everything—if every song is sampled, why shouldn't writers do the same? The question is interesting, complicated, and divisive, but it has little bearing on a Psych 101 paper.

Excusing plagiarism as some sort of modern-day academic mash-up 5 won't teach students anything more than how to lie and get away with it. We should be teaching students how to produce original work—and that there's plenty of original thinking across the Internet—and leave the plagiarizing to the politicians.

⊘ AT ISSUE: SOURCES FOR UNDERSTANDING PLAGIARISM

1. Minkel's essay is a refutation of Trip Gabriel's article (p. 389), whose headline she accuses of "pinpointing a problem, weaving a theory, and excusing youthful copycats in one fell swoop" (para.1). Do you agree that Gabriel's article excuses plagiarism, or do you think it simply identifies a problem? Explain.

2. In paragraph 1, Minkel summarizes Gabriel's article. Is this a fair and accurate summary?

3. When Minkel quotes the student in paragraphs 3 and 4, is she setting up a **straw man**? Why or why not?

4. How would you characterize Minkel's tone? For example, is she angry? Frustrated? Condescending? Annoyed? Is this tone appropriate for her audience? (Note that this essay first appeared in the *New Yorker*, a magazine likely to be read by educated readers.)

5. In paragraph 2, Minkel identifies herself as a recent college graduate. Why? Is she appealing here to *ethos*, *pathos*, or *logos*?

6. Evaluate Minkel's last paragraph, particularly her concluding statement. Does this paragraph accurately express her reasons for criticizing Gabriel's article? What, if anything, do you think she should add to her conclusion? Why?

This essay appeared in *Newsday* on May 18, 2003.

THE TRUTH ABOUT PLAGIARISM

RICHARD A. POSNER

Plagiarism is considered by most writers, teachers, journalists, scholars, and even 1
members of the general public to be the capital intellectual crime. Being caught
out in plagiarism can blast a politician's career, earn a college student expulsion,
and destroy a writer's, scholar's, or journalist's reputation. In recent days, for example, the *New York Times* has referred to "widespread fabrication and plagiarism"
by reporter Jayson Blair as "a low point in the 152-year history of the newspaper."

In James Hynes' splendid satiric novella of plagiarism, *Casting the Runes*, 2
the plagiarist, having by black magic murdered one of the historians whom he
plagiarized and tried to murder a second, is himself killed by the very same
black magic, deployed by the widow of his murder victim.

There is a danger of overkill. Plagiarism can be a form of fraud, but it is no 3
accident that, unlike real theft, it is not a crime. If a
thief steals your car, you are out the market value
of the car, but if a writer copies material from a
book you wrote, you don't have to replace the
book. At worst, the undetected plagiarist obtains a
reputation that he does not deserve (that is the ele-
ment of fraud in plagiarism). The real victim of his fraud is not the person
whose work he copies, but those of his competitors who scruple to enhance
their own reputations by such means.

> "There is a
> danger of
> overkill."

The most serious plagiarisms are by students and professors, whose 4
undetected plagiarisms disrupt the system of student and scholarly evaluation.
The least serious are those that earned the late Stephen Ambrose and Doris
Kearns Goodwin such obloquy° last year. Popular historians, they jazzed up their
books with vivid passages copied from previous historians without quotation
marks, though with footnote attributions that made their "crime" easy to detect.

Abusive language

(One reason that plagiarism, like littering, is punished heavily, even 5
though an individual act of plagiarism usually does little or no harm, is that it
is normally very difficult to detect—but not in the case of Ambrose and Goodwin.) Competing popular historians might have been injured, but I'm not
aware of anyone actually claiming this.

Confusion of plagiarism with theft is one reason plagiarism engenders 6
indignation; another is a confusion of it with copyright infringement. Wholesale copying of copyrighted material is an infringement of a property right,
and legal remedies are available to the copyright holder. But the copying of
brief passages, even from copyrighted materials, is permissible under the doctrine of "fair use," while wholesale copying from material that is in the public
domain—material that never was copyrighted, or on which the copyright has
expired—presents no copyright issue at all.

Plagiarism of work in the public domain is more common than otherwise. 7 Consider a few examples: *West Side Story* is a thinly veiled copy (with music added) of *Romeo and Juliet*, which in turn plagiarized Arthur Brooke's *The Tragicall Historye of Romeo and Juliet*, published in 1562, which in turn copied from several earlier Romeo and Juliets, all of which were copies of Ovid's story of Pyramus and Thisbe.

Paradise Lost plagiarizes the book of Genesis in the Old Testament. Classical 8 musicians plagiarize folk melodies (think only of Dvorak, Bartok, and Copland) and often "quote" (as musicians say) from earlier classical works. Edouard Manet's most famous painting, *Déjeuner sur l'herbe*, copies earlier paintings by Raphael, Titian, and Courbet, and *My Fair Lady* plagiarized Shaw's play *Pygmalion*, while Woody Allen's movie *Play It Again, Sam* "quotes" a famous scene from *Casablanca*. Countless movies are based on books, such as *The Thirty-Nine Steps* on John Buchan's novel of that name or *For Whom the Bell Tolls* on Hemingway's novel.

Many of these "plagiarisms" were authorized, and perhaps none was 9 deceptive; they are what Christopher Ricks in his excellent book *Allusions to the Poets* helpfully terms *allusion* rather than *plagiarism*. But what they show is that copying with variations is an important form of creativity, and this should make us prudent and measured in our condemnations of plagiarism.

Especially when the term is extended from literal copying to the copying 10 of ideas. Another phrase for copying an idea, as distinct from the form in which it is expressed, is dissemination of ideas. If one needs a license to repeat another person's idea, or if one risks ostracism by one's professional community for failing to credit an idea to its originator, who may be forgotten or unknown, the dissemination of ideas is impeded.

I have heard authors of history textbooks criticized for failing to document 11 their borrowing of ideas from previous historians. This is an absurd criticism. The author of a textbook makes no claim to originality; rather the contrary— the most reliable, if not necessarily the most exciting, textbook is one that confines itself to ideas already well accepted, not at all novel.

It would be better if the term *plagiarism* were confined to literal copying, 12 and moreover literal copying that is not merely unacknowledged but deceptive. Failing to give credit where credit is due should be regarded as a lesser, indeed usually merely venial, offense.

The concept of plagiarism has expanded, and the sanctions for it, though 13 they remain informal rather than legal, have become more severe, in tandem with the rise of individualism. Journal articles are no longer published anonymously, and ghostwriters demand that their contributions be acknowledged.

Replaceable

Individualism and a cult of originality go hand in hand. Each of us sup- 14 poses that our contribution to society is unique rather than fungible° and so deserves public recognition, which plagiarism clouds.

This is a modern view. We should be aware that the high value placed on 15 originality is a specific cultural, and even field-specific, phenomenon, rather than an aspect of the universal moral law.

Judges, who try to conceal rather than to flaunt their originality, far 16 from crediting their predecessors with original thinking like to pretend that there is no original thinking in law, that judges are just a transmission belt for rules and principles laid down by the framers of statutes or the Constitution.

Resorting to plagiarism to obtain a good grade or a promotion is fraud 17 and should be punished, though it should not be confused with "theft." But I think the zeal to punish plagiarism reflects less a concern with the real injuries that it occasionally inflicts than with a desire on the part of leaders of professional communities, such as journalists and historians, to enhance their profession's reputation.

Journalists (like politicians) have a bad reputation for truthfulness, and 18 historians, in this "postmodernist"° era, are suspected of having embraced an extreme form of relativism and of having lost their regard for facts. Both groups hope by taking a very hard line against plagiarism and fabrication to reassure the public that they are serious diggers after truth whose efforts, a form of "sweat equity," deserve protection against copycats.

Postmodernism is a school of criticism that denies concepts such as scientific certainty and absolute truth.

Their anxieties are understandable; but the rest of us will do well to keep 19 the matter in perspective, realizing that the term *plagiarism* is used loosely and often too broadly; that much plagiarism is harmless and (when the term is defined broadly) that some has social value.

⊘ AT ISSUE: SOURCES FOR UNDERSTANDING PLAGIARISM

1. According to Posner, how do most people define *plagiarism*? How is the definition he proposes different from theirs? Do you think this definition is too broad? Too narrow?

2. Why does Posner believe that the plagiarisms committed by students and professors are the most serious? Can you think of an argument against this position?

3. How do the examples Posner cites in paragraphs 7 and 8 strengthen his argument? Do you agree that the examples he gives here constitute plagiarism? Why or why not?

4. Explain the connection the author makes in paragraph 16 between judges and plagiarism. (Note that Posner himself is a federal judge.)

5. Why, according to Posner, do journalists and historians think plagiarism should be punished severely?

6. According to Posner, "the truth about plagiarism" is that "much plagiarism is harmless and (when the term is defined broadly) that some has social value" (para. 19). Does the evidence he presents in this essay support this conclusion? What connection do you see between this position and his comments about the rise of individualism and the "cult of originality" in paragraphs 13–15?

This article first appeared on July 25, 2014, on Politico.com.

PLAGIARISM AND BUZZFEED'S ACHILLES' HEEL

DYLAN BYERS

In 2013, the satirical website *The Onion* wrote an article titled "BuzzFeed Writer Resigns in Disgrace after Plagiarizing '10 Llamas Who Wish They Were Models.'" It appealed to reporters because it was a clever knock on the state of digital journalism—and because it resonated with a widely held perception about BuzzFeed. 1

High-profile plagiarism cases are always met with a certain amount of schadenfreude from the media's chattering classes, as well as calls for the defendant's head, but the response to BuzzFeed editor Benny Johnson's serial plagiarism has been especially intense. 2

There's a reason for that: In the eyes of many journalists, BuzzFeed is constantly walking a fine line between aggregation, or "curation," and theft. Go to BuzzFeed.com and click on any one of its lists. In very fine print, buried below each photo, there will be a link to another site—usually Reddit—which is where the photograph came from. 3

Is this plagiarism? Of course not. Does it feel a little seedy? Yeah, a bit. 4

In 2012, as BuzzFeed was growing into the Internet sensation it is today, *Slate*'s Farhad Manjoo (now with the *New York Times*) wrote a lengthy post explaining "the secret to BuzzFeed's monster online success." 5

"How does this one site come up with so many simple ideas that people want to spread far and wide? What's their secret?" he wrote. "The answer, in short, is that BuzzFeed's staff finds stuff elsewhere on the Web, most often at Reddit. They polish and repackage what they find. And often—and, from what I can tell, deliberately—their posts are hard to trace back to the original source material." 6

Because BuzzFeed is so popular, Manjoo wrote, its "pilfered" lists all but eclipse the original sources of content: "Once you understand how central Reddit is to BuzzFeed, it's like spotting the wizard behind the curtain. Whenever you see a popular BuzzFeed post, search Reddit, and all will be revealed." 7

Jonah Peretti, BuzzFeed's founder, told Manjoo that there was "nothing wrong" with picking up other people's content "because few things on the Web are really original." 8

Gawker's Adrian Chen (now with the *New Inquiry*) also wrote an extensive analysis of BuzzFeed's "plagiarism problem" in 2012. 9

"BuzzFeed has built a lucrative business on organizing the internet's confusing spectacle into listicles easily comprehended by even the most numbed office workers," Chen wrote. "But the site's approach to all content as building blocks for viral lists puts it in an awkward position in relation to internet etiquette and journalistic ethics." 10

"For example," Chen wrote, "the BuzzFeed listicle '21 Pictures That Will 11
Restore Your Faith in Humanity,' appears to be an almost exact replica of a
couple of posts on an obscure site called Nedhardy . . . BuzzFeed slapped
together many of the same pictures, presented it as an original idea, and it
went Avian-Flu-level-viral, ending up with more than seven million page
views."

Is *this* plagiarism? It's certainly closer to it. Somehow, the Internet came 12
to accept it: The *New York Times* reported, Huffington Post aggregated,
BuzzFeed curated. Maybe "repackaging funny things found on Reddit is just
how the Internet works these days," Chen wrote.

Text, of course, was a different story. You couldn't publish someone else's 13
articles or *Wikipedia* entries and just throw a link to the original source at the
bottom. When BuzzFeed reporters wrote, they were subject to the same rules
as everyone else. Sure you could draw facts from elsewhere—everyone does
—but you had to write it in your own language.

At some point, Johnson probably got lazy and started inserting text into 14
his posts the same way he had been inserting photographs—by pressing
Ctrl+C and Ctrl+V. His mistake was that he forgot to put quote marks around
it and add "according to."

It didn't help reporters' perception of BuzzFeed that, when the first 15
instances of plagiarism were brought to editor-in-chief Ben Smith's attention,
he called them "serious failures" of attribution, rather than "plagiarism," and
simply "corrected" the posts.

"Ben, you can't 'correct' articles that were clearly plagiarized. I know you 16
know this!" Gawker's J. K. Trotter wrote on Twitter.

BuzzFeed is currently conducting an internal review of Johnson's work 17
before deciding on how to proceed. Whatever Johnson's fate, his plagiarism is
one more instance in which the public spotted the
wizard behind BuzzFeed's curtain. And the wizard
seems a little seedy.

> "Meanwhile, *The Onion*'s satire has become reality."

Meanwhile, *The Onion*'s satire has become 18
reality.

"Journalism today," one *Bloomberg News* 19
journalist tweeted: "accused of plagiarism 'for an article it did about former
President George H. W. Bush's socks.'"

Update (July 26) 20

Late Friday evening Smith announced Johnson had been fired after an 21
internal review found 40 instances of plagiarism.

⤷ AT ISSUE: SOURCES FOR UNDERSTANDING PLAGIARISM

1. Do you consider the material typically posted on BuzzFeed to be plagiarized? Explain. (If you are not familiar with BuzzFeed, visit the site
   and read a few posts.)

2. What does "Achilles' heel" mean? In what sense does plagiarism constitute BuzzFeed's Achilles' heel?

3. Why does Byers begin and end his discussion with paragraphs about *The Onion* (para. 1, 18–19)? Is this an effective strategy? Why or why not?

4. In paragraph 3, Byers says that many journalists believe that "BuzzFeed is constantly walking a fine line between aggregation, or 'curation,' and theft." What distinction is he making here? Do you see a difference between BuzzFeed's "aggregation" or "curation" and outright theft? Does Byers?

5. Byers quotes Farhad Manjoo, Adrian Chen, and others. What positions do his sources take on the issue of BuzzFeed and plagiarism?

6. Do you think it matters that Benny Johnson's "repackaging" of material from other sources was done deliberately rather than accidentally? Why or why not?

7. An update to this article notes that Johnson was fired from BuzzFeed "after an internal review found 40 instances of plagiarism." Do you think this punishment was justified? Why or why not?

8. Does Byers take a position on the issue of BuzzFeed and plagiarism? If so, what is that position? Do you see this essay as an argument? Which of the four elements of an argumentative essay are present here? Which are absent?

This summary was posted on July 24, 2014, on the WriteCheck.com blog.

OK OR NOT?

K. BALIBALOS AND J. GOPALAKRISHNAN

OK or not? This is an age-old question on plagiarism that arises during the 1
writing process, whether from researching a topic, incorporating and paraphrasing sources, or supporting arguments within a paper. Students commonly
find themselves in situations in which ethical questions are raised, and, all too
often, students wonder whether the decisions they made were the right ones.

This new poll series brings to light common scenarios—specifically 2
focused on plagiarism and perhaps a few examples on other forms of academic misconduct—and helps students better think critically about situations
in order to make ethical choices. All polls can be found on the WriteCheck
page on Facebook.

POLL QUESTION #1
**"OK or not? You and a partner collaborate on a paper by sharing notes and
paraphrasing the same ideas."**

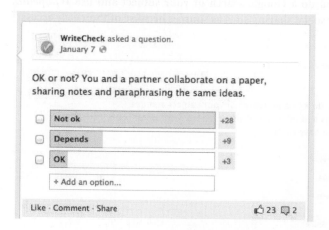

We started off the series by asking about collaboration because collaborating with 3
peers is a common thing to do among students. Students "collaborate" to
complete schoolwork and to help their friends in need. But collaborating with
peers can sometimes cross ethical boundaries. For example, in this question,
has the student copied-and-pasted the other student's work? The question
doesn't really get into that concern, but we do know that the students shared
the same ideas by "paraphrasing." This is where the question gets tricky. If

done properly, meaning the student wrote the idea in his/her own words and included citations, then paraphrasing is acceptable. Plagiarism is, by definition, the taking of another person's work or ideas.

The Results

The majority of respondents (28) chose "not OK" in response to student collaboration on a paper. However, two viewers who weighed in had a different perspective. 4

English Instructor, Beth Calvano, made the following comment: "If the paper is supposed to be individual, this scenario is not okay. If, according to plagiarism rules, it is not acceptable to use another person's ideas without citing that individual, collaborating in this way is not ethical. Your paper should consist of your own notes and original ideas." 5

Facebook fan Quenna Corchado agreed with Calvano, adding: "I think it's okay if they are citing. It doesn't matter if they are using the same sources as long as they cite it. They are helping each other out, so it makes sense that they are using the same notes and paraphrasing the same thing. What is important is to cite everything accordingly, which doesn't make it plagiarism." 6

Overall, it can be concluded from these responses that it is "OK" to share notes and paraphrase the same idea with proper attribution, unless the assignment is supposed to be done individually. 7

POLL QUESTION #2

"OK or not? You do a Google search of your subject and use *Wikipedia*, blogs, and other social sharing sites as sources because of their easy access."

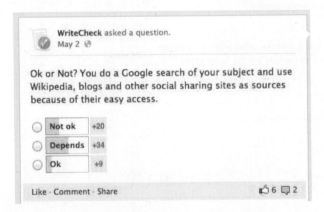

This situation resonates with students because of the amount of free, available information due in part to the mass connectivity of the digital age. Nowadays, *Wikipedia* is synonymous with accessibility and reader-friendly information since it provides accurate information on nearly every topic one might be researching. The number of blogs on the internet grows exponentially by the day since anyone has the ability to create a blog and share their thoughts. And, of course, social sites are a normal part of millions of people's lives. However, 8 just because information is available on the web doesn't mean that it's reputable to use as a source in your academic paper.

The Results

Based on 34 respondents, "depends" was the top answer, followed by "not 9 OK" (20 respondents).

To provide some insight, Jason Chu from Plagiarism.org weighed in with 10 the following comment: "It's OK to use Google search, *Wikipedia*, and social sharing sites as the starting point for doing research for a paper. But you should NOT rely on these sources alone. In fact, *Wikipedia* entries typically list references that are great to use in your research in support of your paper. But, by and large, sources that rely heavily on crowd-sourced or shared content—like *Wikipedia* or Yahoo! Answers—do not carry the same authority as a peer-reviewed journal article, for example."

Jessica from WriteCheck argued that it was "not OK," citing educator 11 insight that social sites should never be cited in research papers. Academic writing requires looking at primary or secondary sources, which are typically presented in academic journals, whereas *Wikipedia* is written for the general public.

Overall, it can be concluded that the answer is "depends." Social sites like 12 *Wikipedia* can be used as a starting point for research papers, but adding academic credibility to your sources will result in a more thorough and scholarly research paper.

POLL QUESTION #3
"OK or not? You get 2 assignments with enough overlap to submit the same paper to both."

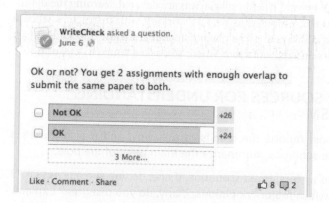

The most recent poll was inspired by a recent article on the *Ethicist*, a blog on 13 the *New York Times*, entitled, "Can I Use the Same Paper for Multiple College Courses?" Some readers see it as a stroke of genius, while others view it as the mark of laziness. Some suggest that it is cheating, while others opine that you are only cheating yourself. *International Business Times* writer James DiGioia disagreed with *The Ethicist* in his article, "*The Ethicist* Is Wrong: Self-Plagiarism Is Cheating." Given those different opinions, we wanted to see what our WriteCheck community thought. "Is it OK to submit one paper for two assignments?"

The Results

The results were evenly split among the poll respondents between "not OK" 14 and "OK." *The Ethicist* describes why this situation is tricky, explaining that emotionally, our hearts cry that "this *must* be unethical, somehow," but aside from these emotions, he argued that there were no grounds that inherently make submitting papers to multiple assignments unethical.

Unlike James DiGioia, Jason Chu of Plagiarism.org agreed somewhere in 15 the middle, saying: "OK — if instructor approval is received. Not OK otherwise."

In summary, although debatable, it could be concluded that submitting a 16 paper to multiple assignments is "OK" with approval from both instructors. Otherwise, it may be a violation of university-wide academic integrity codes and generally accepted principles that assignments are unique to a class.

Conclusion

These three scenarios are real-life situations that students may face at one 17 point in their academic journeys. Some scenarios may appear more straightforward than others, however, no plagiarism allegation is simple. Self-plagiarism, for example, may make more sense in a professional or scholarly environment because of copyright issues. Self-plagiarism is a gray area, and a relatively new term within academia, and is still to be explored. *Wikipedia* also is a newly introduced site, becoming popular only within the last decade.

While definitions and rules of plagiarism are debated, learning the defini- 18 tions and how to cite properly, as well as working with instructors when a question arises are all ways to avoid plagiarism and academic misconduct.

Have you encountered situations where you asked yourself "OK or not?" 19

○ AT ISSUE: SOURCES FOR UNDERSTANDING PLAGIARISM

1. This blog post reports the results of a survey, and it also makes a point. In one sentence, summarize the main point of the post.

2. Which of the writers' three scenarios, if any, do you see as "not OK"? Why? With which majority opinions, if any, do you disagree? Explain.

3. For what purpose did the writers design this poll? Where do they state this purpose?

4. Who is the intended audience for the three poll questions? Is this the same audience as the one the writers expected to read the results of the poll? How can you tell?

5. In poll question #2, what conclusions do the writers draw about the use of *Wikipedia*? What problems does this site, as well as "blogs and other social sharing sites," present for college students?

6. Do you think the writers' conclusion takes a strong enough stand on the issue discussed? Is this post actually an argument? Why or why not?

This essay originally appeared in the *Los Angeles Times* on June 17, 2012.

ESSAY MILLS: A COARSE LESSON IN CHEATING

DAN ARIELY

Sometimes as I decide what kind of papers to assign to my students, I worry about essay mills, companies whose sole purpose is to generate essays for high school and college students (in exchange for a fee, of course). 1

The mills claim that the papers are meant to be used as reference material to help students write their own, original papers. But with names such as echeat.com, it's pretty clear what their real purpose is. 2

Professors in general are concerned about essay mills and their effect on learning, but not knowing exactly what they provide, I wasn't sure how concerned to be. So together with my lab manager Aline Grüneisen, I decided to check the services out. We ordered a typical college term paper from four different essay mills. The topic of the paper? Cheating. 3

Here is the prompt we gave the four essay mills: 4

"When and why do people cheat? Consider the social circumstances involved in dishonesty, and provide a thoughtful response to the topic of cheating. Address various forms of cheating (personal, at work, etc.) and how each of these can be rationalized by a social culture of cheating." 5

We requested a term paper for a university-level social psychology class, 12 pages long, using 15 sources (cited and referenced in a bibliography). The paper was to conform to American Psychological Assn. style guidelines and needed to be completed in the next two weeks. All four of the essay mills agreed to provide such a paper, charging us in advance, between $150 and $216 for the paper. 6

Right on schedule, the essays came, and I have to say that, to some degree, they allayed my fears that students can rely on the services to get good grades. What we got back from the mills can best be described as gibberish. A few of the papers attempted to mimic APA style, but none achieved it without glaring errors. Citations were sloppy. Reference lists contained outdated and unknown sources, including blog posts. Some of the links to reference material were broken. 7

> "What we got back from the mills can best be described as gibberish."

And the writing quality? Awful. The authors of all four papers seemed to have a very tenuous grasp of the English language, not to mention how to format an essay. Paragraphs jumped bluntly from one topic to another, often simply listing various forms of cheating or providing a long stream of examples that were never explained or connected to the "thesis" of the paper. 8

406

One paper contained this paragraph: "Cheating by healers. Healing is different. There is harmless healing, when healers-cheaters and wizards offer omens, lapels, damage to withdraw, the husband-wife back and stuff. We read in the newspaper and just smile. But these days fewer people believe in wizards." 9

This comes from another: "If the large allowance of study undertook on scholar betraying is any suggestion of academia and professors' powerful yearn to decrease scholar betraying, it appeared expected these mind-set would component into the creation of their school room guidelines." 10

And finally, these gems: 11

"By trusting blindfold only in stable love, loyalty, responsibility and honesty the partners assimilate with the credulous and naive persons of the past." 12

"Women have a much greater necessity to feel special." 13

"The future generation must learn for historical mistakes and develop the sense of pride and responsibility for its actions." 14

It's hard to believe that students purchasing such papers would ever do so again. 15

And the story does not end there. We submitted the four essays to WriteCheck.com, a website that inspects papers for plagiarism, and found that two of the papers were 35% to 39% copied from existing works. We decided to take action on the two papers with substantial plagiarizing and contacted the essay mills requesting our money back. Despite the solid proof we provided to them, the companies insisted they did not plagiarize. One company even threatened to expose us by calling the dean and saying we had purchased the paper. 16

It's comforting in a way that the technological revolution has not yet solved students' problems. They still have no other option but to actually work on their papers (or maybe cheat in the old-fashioned way and copy from friends). But I do worry about the existence of essay mills and the signal that they send to our students. 17

As for our refund, we are still waiting. 18

⊘ AT ISSUE: SOURCES FOR UNDERSTANDING PLAGIARISM

1. Consider the title of this essay. What does the word *coarse* mean? What does it suggest in this context?

2. What is an essay mill? Look up the word *mill*. Which of the definitions provided applies to the word as it is used in the phrase *essay mill*?

3. Why does Ariely decide to investigate the services provided by essay mills? What does he want to find out? Is he successful?

4. What does Ariely conclude about the four companies he surveys? Does he provide enough evidence to support his conclusion? If not, what kind of evidence should he add?

407

5. In paragraph 15, Ariely says, "It's hard to believe that students purchasing such papers would ever do so again." Given the evidence Ariely presents, how do you explain the continued popularity of essay mills?

6. What information does Ariely provide in his conclusion? Do you think he is departing from his essay's central focus here, or do you think the concluding paragraph is an appropriate and effective summary of his ideas? Explain.

TERM PAPERS FOR SALE ADVERTISEMENT (WEB PAGE)

⊃ AT ISSUE: SOURCES FOR UNDERSTANDING PLAGIARISM

1. The Web page above is from a site that offers papers for sale to students. What argument does this Web page make? What counter-argument could you present?

2. Identify appeals to *logos*, *pathos*, and *ethos* on the TermPaperWriter .org page. Which appeal dominates?

3. Study the images of students on the page. What message do these images convey?

4. Unlike the TermPaperWriter.org page, many other sites that offer papers for sale include errors in grammar, spelling, and punctuation. Search the Web for some other sites that offer papers for sale. What errors can you find? Do such errors weaken the message of these ads, or are they irrelevant?

5. One site promises its papers are "100% plagiarism free." Does this promise make sense? Explain.

TEMPLATE FOR WRITING AN ARGUMENT ABOUT PLAGIARISM

Write a one-paragraph argument in which you take a position on where to draw the line with plagiarism. Follow the template below, filling in the blanks to create your argument.

> To many people, plagiarism is theft; to others, however, it is not that simple. For example, some define *plagiarism* as _____
> _____ ; others see it as _____
> _____. Another thing to consider is
> _____
> _____. In addition, _____
> _____. Despite these differences of opinion,
> plagiarism is often dealt with harshly and can ruin careers and reputations. All things considered,
> _____
> _____.

➲ EXERCISE 11.4

Discuss your feelings about plagiarism with two or three of your class-mates. Consider how you define *plagiarism*, what you believe causes it, whether there are degrees of dishonesty, and so on, but focus on the *effects* of plagiarism—on those who commit it and on those who are its victims. Then, write a paragraph that summarizes the key points of your discussion.

➲ EXERCISE 11.5

Write an argumentative essay on the topic, "Where Should We Draw the Line with Plagiarism?" Begin by defining what you mean by *plagiarism*, and then narrow your discussion down to a particular group—for example, high school or college students, historians, scientists, or journalists. Cite the sources on pages 383–409, and be sure to document the sources you use and to include a works-cited page. (See Chapter 10 for information on documenting sources.)

➲ EXERCISE 11.6

Review the four pillars of argument discussed in Chapter 1. Does your essay include all four elements of an effective argument? Add anything that is missing. Then, label the elements of your argument.

⊙ WRITING ASSIGNMENTS: USING SOURCES RESPONSIBLY

1. Write an argument in which you take a position on who (or what) is to blame for plagiarism among college students. Is plagiarism always the student's fault, or are other people (or other factors) at least partly to blame?

2. Write an essay in which you argue that an honor code will (or will not) eliminate (or at least reduce) plagiarism and other kinds of academic dishonesty at your school.

3. Reread the essays by Posner and Balibalos and Gopalakrishnan in this chapter. Then, write an argument in which you argue that only intentional plagiarism should be punished.

4. Do you consider student plagiarism a victimless crime that is best left unpunished? If so, why? If not, how does it affect its victims—for example, the student who plagiarizes, the instructor, the other students in the class, and the school?

Strategies for Argument

Part 5: Strategies for Argument

In Chapter 1, you were introduced to the four pillars of argument—*thesis statement*, *evidence*, *refutation*, and *concluding statement*—the basic building blocks of an effective argumentative essay. The chapters that follow expand this discussion by illustrating and explaining different types of arguments.

Different purposes call for different argumentative strategies:

- If you want to argue that something is (or is not) consistent with a particular definition, you can write a **definition argument**: "Is *Wikipedia* a legitimate research source?" **See Chapter 12.**

- If you want your argument to take a stand on the causes or effects of an event or situation, you can write a **cause-and-effect argument**: "Should vaccination be required for all children?" **See Chapter 13.**

- If you want your argument to take a stand on the quality or worth of something, you can write an **evaluation argument**: "Do the benefits of fracking outweigh the environmental risks?" **See Chapter 14.**

- If you want your argument to recommend a solution to a problem, you can write a **proposal argument**: "Should the government do more to relieve the student-loan burden?" **See Chapter 15.**

- If your purpose is to recommend a course of action because it is good or right (or argue against something because it is bad or wrong), you can write an **ethical argument**: "How far should schools go to keep students safe?" **See Chapter 16.**

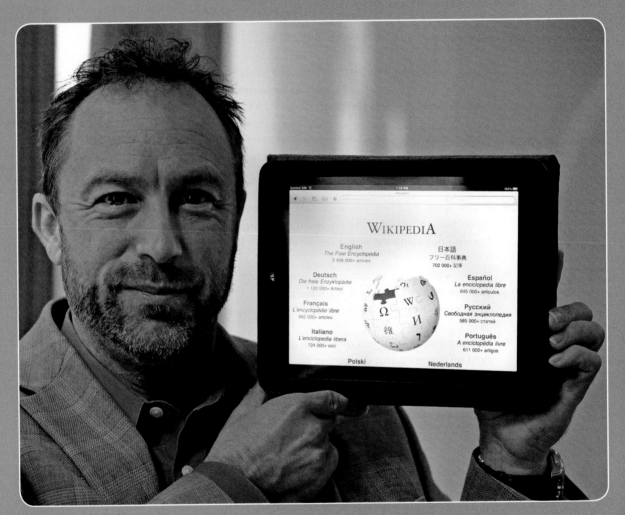

12 Definition Arguments

Is *Wikipedia* a Legitimate Research Source?

Wikipedia—the open-source online encyclopedia—is probably the most frequently used reference source on the planet. Currently, there are over 5 million articles in the English *Wikipedia*, and the number increases at a rate of 750 articles a day. The use of this encyclopedia is not without controversy, however. Because anyone can write and edit entries, articles can—and do—contain errors. Over time, many errors get corrected, but some do not, perhaps because no one person or group is responsible for quality control. As a result, many college instructors question the reliability of *Wikipedia* as a research source. In fact, academic departments at many schools—for example, the history department at Middlebury College—have banned students from citing *Wikipedia* as a source. According to Don Wyatt, chair of the department, "Even though *Wikipedia* may have some value, particularly in leading students to citable sources, it is not itself an appropriate source for citation." Others disagree, pointing out that *Wikipedia* contains no more (and in some cases fewer) factual errors than traditional encyclopedias.

Later in this chapter, you will be asked to think more about this issue. You will be given several research sources to consider and asked to write a definition argument that takes a position on whether *Wikipedia* should be considered a legitimate research source.

What Is a Definition Argument?

When your argument depends on the meaning of a key term, it makes sense to structure your essay as a **definition argument**. In this type of essay, you will argue that something fits (or does not fit) the definition of a particular class of items. For example, to argue that *Wikipedia* is a legitimate research source, you have to define *legitimate research source* and then show that *Wikipedia* fits this definition.

Many arguments focus on definition. In fact, you encounter them so often that you probably do not recognize them for what they are. For example, consider the following questions:

- Is spanking child abuse?

- Should offensive speech be banned on campus?

- Should the rich pay more taxes than others?

- Are electric cars harmful to the environment?

- Is cheerleading a sport?

- Is *Wikipedia* a legitimate research source?

You cannot answer these questions without providing definitions. In fact, if you were writing an argumentative essay in response to one of these questions, much of your essay would be devoted to defining and discussing a key term.

QUESTION	KEY TERM TO BE DEFINED
Is spanking child abuse?	*child abuse*
Should offensive speech be banned on campus?	*offensive speech*
Should the rich pay more taxes than others?	*rich*
Are electric cars harmful to the environment?	*harmful*
Is cheerleading a sport?	*sport*
Is *Wikipedia* a legitimate research source?	*legitimate research source*

Many contemporary social and legal disputes involve definition arguments. For example, did a coworker's actions constitute *sexual harassment*? Is an individual trying to enter the United States an *undocumented worker* or an *illegal alien*? Is a person guilty of *murder* or of *manslaughter*? Did the CIA engage in *torture* or in *aggressive questioning*? Was the magazine cover *satirical* or *racist*? Is the punishment *just*, or is it *cruel and unusual*? The answers to these and many other questions hinge on definitions of key terms.

The last public hanging in the United States (Owensboro, Kentucky, August 14, 1936)

AP Photo

Keep in mind, however, that definitions can change as our thinking about certain issues changes. For example, fifty years ago the word *family* generally referred to one or more children living with two heterosexual married parents. Now, the term can refer to a wide variety of situations—children living with single parents, gay and lesbian couples, and unmarried heterosexual couples, for example. Our definition of what constitutes *cruel and unusual punishment* has also changed. Public hanging, a common method of execution for hundreds of years, is now considered barbaric.

Developing Definitions

Definitions explain terms that are unfamiliar to an audience. To make your definitions as clear as possible, avoid making them *too narrow, too broad,* or *circular.*

A definition that is **too narrow** leaves out information that is necessary for understanding a particular word or term. For example, if you define an *apple* as "a red fruit," your definition is too narrow since some apples are not red. To be accurate (and useful), your definition needs to be more inclusive and acknowledge the fact that apples can be red, green, or yellow: an apple is the round edible fruit of a tree of the rose family, which typically has thin red, yellow, or green skin.

A definition that is **too broad** includes things that should not be part of the definition. If, for example, you define *chair* as "something that people sit on," your definition includes things that are not chairs—stools, park benches, and even tree stumps. To be accurate, your definition needs to be much more specific: "A chair is a piece of furniture that has a seat, legs, arms, and a back and is designed to accommodate one person."

A **circular definition** includes the word being defined as part of the definition. For example, if you define *patriotism* as "the quality of being patriotic," your definition is circular. For the definition to work, you have to provide new information that enables readers to understand the term: "*Patriotism* is a belief characterized by love and support for one's country, especially its values and beliefs."

NOTE

Sometimes you can clarify a definition by explaining how one term is different from another similar term. For example, consider the following definition:

> *Patriotism* is different from *nationalism* because *patriotism* focuses on love for a country while *nationalism* assumes the superiority of one country over another.

The success of a definition argument depends on your ability to define a term so that readers (even those who do not agree with your position) will see its validity. For this reason, the rhetorical strategies you use to develop your definitions are important.

Dictionary Definitions (Formal Definitions)

When most people think of definitions, they think of the formal definitions they find in a dictionary. Typically, a formal **dictionary definition** has three parts: the term to be defined, the general class to which the term belongs, and the qualities that differentiate the term from other items in the same class.

TERM	CLASS	DIFFERENTIATION
dog	a domesticated mammal	that has a snout, a keen sense of smell, and a barking voice
naturalism	a literary movement	whose followers believed that writers should treat their characters' lives with scientific objectivity

⊝ EXERCISE 12.1

Write a one-sentence formal definition of each of the following words. Then, look each word up in a dictionary, and compare your definitions to the ones you found there.

Terrorism	Marriage
App	Blog
Tablet	Fairness

Extended Definitions

Although a definition argument may include a short dictionary definition, a brief definition is usually not enough to define a complex or abstract term. For example, if you were arguing that *Wikipedia* is a *legitimate research source*, you would have to include an **extended definition**, explaining to readers in some detail what you mean by this term and perhaps giving examples of other research sources that fit your definition.

Examples are often used to develop an extended definition in an argumentative essay. For instance, you could give examples to make the case that a particular baseball player, despite his struggles with substance abuse, is a great athlete. You could define *great athlete* solely in terms of athletic prowess, presenting several examples of other talented athletes and then showing that the baseball player you are discussing possesses the same qualities.

For your examples to be effective, they have to be relevant to your argument. Your examples also have to represent (or at least suggest) the full range of opinion concerning your subject. Finally, you have to make sure that your readers will accept your examples as typical, not unusual. For example, in the Declaration of Independence, Thomas Jefferson presented twenty-five paragraphs of examples to support his extended definition of the king's tyranny. With these examples, he hoped to convince the world that the colonists were justified in breaking away from England.

Writing the Declaration of Independence, 1776 by Jean Leon Gerome Ferris (Virginia Historical Society)

Virginia Historical Society, Richmond, Va. USA/Bridgeman Images

To accomplish his goal, Jefferson made sure that his examples supported his position, that they represented the full range of abuses, and that they were not unusual or atypical.

⊖ EXERCISE 12.2

Choose one of the terms you defined in Exercise 12.1, and write a paragraph-length definition argument that takes a position related to that term. Make sure you include two or three examples in your definition.

Operational Definitions

Whereas a dictionary definition tells what a term means, an **operational definition** defines something by telling how it acts or how it works. Thus, an operational definition transforms an abstract concept into something concrete, observable, and possibly measurable. Children instinctively understand the concept of operational definitions. When a parent tells them to *behave*, they know what the components of this operational definition are: clean up your room, obey your parents, come home on time, and do your homework. Researchers in the natural and social sciences must constantly come up with operational definitions. For example, if they want to study the effects of childhood obesity, they have to construct an operational definition of *obese*. Without such a definition, they will not be able to measure the various factors that make a person obese. For example, at what point does a child become obese? Does he or she have to be 10 percent above normal weight? More? Before researchers can carry out their study, they must agree on an operational (or working) definition.

Structuring a Definition Argument

In general terms, a definition argument can be structured as follows:

- **Introduction:** Establishes a context for the argument by explaining the need for defining the term; presents the essay's thesis

- **Evidence (first point in support of thesis):** Provides a short definition of the term as well as an extended definition (if necessary)

- **Evidence (second point in support of thesis):** Shows how the term does or does not fit the definition

- **Refutation of opposing arguments:** Addresses questions about or objections to the definition; considers and rejects other possible meanings (if any)

- **Conclusion:** Reinforces the main point of the argument; includes a strong concluding statement

⚡ The following student essay includes all the elements of a definition argument. The student who wrote this essay is trying to convince his university that he is a nontraditional student and is therefore entitled to the benefits such students receive.

WHY I AM A NONTRADITIONAL STUDENT
ADAM KENNEDY

Ever since I started college, I have had difficulty getting the extra   1
help I need to succeed. My final disappointment came last week when
my adviser told me that I could not take advantage of the programs the
school offers to nontraditional students. She told me that because I am
not old enough, I simply do not qualify. This is confusing to me because
I am anything but a "traditional" student. In fact, I am one of the most
nontraditional students I know. In spite of my age—I am twenty-two—
I have had experiences that separate me from most other students my
age. The problem is that the school's definition of the term *nontraditional*   Thesis statement
is so narrow that it excludes people like me who should be able to qualify.

According to researchers, the term *nontraditional student* is difficult to   2
define. Studies show that a broad operational definition that acknowledges   Evidence: Operational
many factors is preferable to one that focuses on age alone. For example,   definition of
the National Center for Educational Statistics bases its definition on   *nontraditional student*
whether or not a student has any of the following seven characteristics:

- Did not enter college right after high school
- Is a part-time student
- Does not depend on parents for money
- Has a full-time job
- Has children or a spouse
- Is a single parent
- Has a GED instead of a high school diploma (Kim et al. 405–6)

Many colleges use similar, or even broader, criteria to define   3
nontraditional student. For example, the University of Arkansas provides

Evidence: Other
schools' definitions of
nontraditional student

special services for older students as well as for students with other
work- or family-related responsibilities. In fact, the school has a special
department—Non-Traditional Student Services—to meet these
students' needs. The university website says that a nontraditional
student is someone who meets just one of the criteria listed above
("Non-Traditional Student Programs"). In addition, the university
recognizes other factors, like whether the student is a veteran, an active
member of the military, or the first in his or her family to go to college
("Non-Traditional Student Programs").

Evidence: Our
school's definition of
nontraditional student

According to the criteria from the National Center for Educational
Statistics (listed above), I would have no problem qualifying as a nontraditional student at the University of Arkansas. Our school, however, has
a much narrower definition of the term. When I went to Non-Traditional
Student Services, I was told that my case did not fit the definition that
the school had established. Here, a nontraditional student is someone
who is twenty-five or older, period. The person I spoke to said that the
school's intention is to give special help to older students. I was then
told that I could appeal and try to convince the dean of Non-Traditional
Student Services that I do not fit the definition of a traditional student.

4

By any measure, I am not a "traditional student." After getting
married at seventeen, I dropped out of high school and got a full-time
job. Soon, my wife and I began to resent our situation. She was still a
high school student and missed being able to go out with her friends
whenever she wanted to. I hated my job and missed being a student.
Before long, we decided it was best to end our marriage. Instead of going
back to high school, however, I enlisted in the Army National Guard. After
two years, I had completed a tour in Iraq and earned my GED. As soon as
I was discharged from active duty, I enrolled in college—all this before
I turned twenty-one.

5

Evidence: How writer
fits the definition of
nontraditional student

Refutation of opposing
argument

I can see how someone could say that I am too young to be
considered a nontraditional student. However, I believe that my life
experiences should qualify me for this program. My marriage and divorce,
time in the army, and reentry issues make me very different from the
average first-year student. The special resources available to students who
qualify for this program—tutors, financial aid, special advising, support
groups, and subsidized housing—would make my adjustment to college a

6

lot easier. I am only four years older than the average first-year students, but I am nothing like them. The focus on age to define *nontraditional* ignores the fact that students younger than twenty-five may have followed unconventional paths to college. Life experience, not age, should be the main factor in determining whether a student is nontraditional.

The university should expand the definition of *nontraditional* to include younger students who have followed unconventional career paths and have postponed college. Even though these students may be younger than twenty-five, they face challenges similar to those faced by older students. Students like me are returning to school in increasing numbers. Our situation is different from that of others our age, and that is exactly why we need all the help we can get.   *Concluding statement*

7

Works Cited

Kim, Karen A., et al. "Redefining Nontraditional Students: Exploring the
    Self-Perceptions of Community College Students." *Community
    College Journal of Research and Practice,* vol. 34, 2009–2010,
    pp. 402–422. *Academic Search Complete,* web.b.ebscohost.com
    .ezproxy.bpl.org/.

"Non-Traditional Student Programs." Office of Campus Life. *University of
    Arkansas at Little Rock*, 2012, ualr.edu/campuslife/ntsp/.

GRAMMAR IN CONTEXT

Avoiding *Is Where* and *Is When*

In a formal definition, you may find yourself using the phrase *is where* or *is when*. If so, your definition is incomplete because it omits the term's class. The use of *is where* or *is when* signals that you are giving an example of the term, not a definition. You can avoid this problem by making sure that the verb *be* in your definition is always followed by a noun.

INCORRECT   The university website says that a nontraditional student
is when you live off campus, commute from home, have
children, are a veteran, or are over the age of twenty-five.

CORRECT   The university website says that a nontraditional student is
someone who lives off campus, commutes from home,
has children, is a veteran, or is over the age of twenty-five.

⊖ **EXERCISE 12.3**

The following essay, "Athlete vs. Role Model" by Ej Garr, includes the basic elements of a definition argument. Read the essay, and then answer the questions that follow it, consulting the outline on page 422 if necessary.

This blog post first appeared on August 31, 2014, in the Lifestyle section of newshub.com.

ATHLETE VS. ROLE MODEL

EJ GARR

Expectations of professional athletes have become such a touchy subject over 1 the years, and deciphering what defines a role model has become an even darker subject.

Kids who are into sports tend to look up to a favorite player or team and 2 find someone they say they want to be like when they grow up. Unfortunately, athletes today are not what they were decades ago when a paycheck was not the sole reason they wanted an athletic career.

Take Roger Staubach or Bart Starr for example. Both have multiple Super 3 Bowl titles. Both had tremendous NFL careers, and both conducted themselves in public with class and dignity. They deserved every accolade they received, both personally and professionally. Starr and his wife co-founded the Rawhide Boys Ranch, which helps kids who are in need of proper direction and might not have the family resources that can make a kid's life easier.

Roger Staubach was a class act, served in our Navy, and is a Vietnam vet. 4 These are just two examples of players who gained role model status because of how they acted and what they contributed, not simply because they played in the NFL, earned a big paycheck. People rooted for them and looked up to them. Kids wanted to be like them. There were absolutely no discouraging words said about them from anyone who has ever met them. They had class, caring, and concern for other people, both on the field and off.

It is easy for kids, who hear about their favorite athlete who signed a 5 multi-million dollar contract, to say to themselves, "I wish I could do that." Do what? Become a pro or make lots of money? What about becoming a better person? What about giving back?

Many athletes do not think about how to be a better role model to those 6 kids that look up them, how to make their community better, or what they can "give back" to the less fortunate.

Think back to Pete Rose, who was an amazing ballplayer when he was on 7 the field, but all he is known for today is gambling when he became a manager and being banned for life from baseball and the Hall of Fame. Pete Rose was a role model for every kid in his generation when he played baseball. Ran hard to first on a simple walk and gave every ounce of his being to the game. Then, that all went out the window and the role model moniker was gone faster than you could shake your head at what he did. He didn't think of those kids who looked up to him.

Then there's Ray Rice, who was on the cusp of being a role model with a 8 Super Bowl trophy in tow with the Baltimore Ravens. Kids looked up to him. Instead, he was caught on video dragging his unconscious wife out of an elevator after she "accidentally" put her face in front of his fist.

And who can ever forget Michael Vick, who went to prison on dog 9 fighting charges and arranging a death sentence for animals. It has been documented that he even placed a bet or two on those fights! Just recently, although not as criminally serious, USC's Josh Shaw lied about an injury that he claimed to receive when he rescued his nephew. He finally admitted he fabricated the story and all the facts are not out yet, but he went from a potential role model to a hero and then to a zero in record time. These guys sure aren't thinking about the kids who look up to them and want to be like them.

These days, sports newscasts are chock-filled with reports of pro ath- 10 letes using performance enhancing drugs. Over the years there's been Lance Armstrong, Alex Rodriguez, Jose Canseco, Shawne Merriman, Barry Bonds, and even gold medalist Marion Jones. It is well-documented that Alex Rodriguez spent a lot of money buying performance enhancing drugs, rather than becoming a hard-working baseball player and using his money for good. Alex Rodriguez is only worried about Alex Rodriguez. That, unfortunately, is the ego that many athletes have today. I am me, you are you, and I can do what I want. And who cares if you're watching what I'm doing and looking up to me.

No sir! Athletes like this are arrogant and act like idiots, carrying guns, 11 hitting spouses, and taking drugs which are all, by the way . . . ILLEGAL in this country! Our world needs more role models like Staubach and Starr and less arrogant athletes who think society owes them something simply because they make big money and live in a big house and drive a nice car.

Professional athletes are not born role models. They are getting paid to 12 play a game. That far from constitutes the making of a role model. Perhaps this mentality of being better than anyone else starts at the college level. Even the NCAA has acknowledged that bringing in athletes to fill the stands is more important than making sure they get a quality education, because 75% of the athletes who play in college basketball or

"Will that make kids look up to you?"

football are simply there to play their two years and move on to collect a big fat paycheck in the pros. Are they taught anything about giving back and setting a positive example?

A role model comes not from being an athlete and collecting that big pay- 13
check, but for what you do with and in your life. Throw a football and score
three touchdowns today? Hey, good for you man. You will make the headlines, be highlighted on ESPN, and the press will come calling. Will that make
kids look up to you? Sure it will, you won the game and had a great day, good
for you. But you're not a role model.

Do you know why Derek Jeter, Drew Brees, and Tom Brady are true 14
role models? It's about how they carry themselves on and off the field. It's
about how Jeter, during his rookie year in 1996, achieved his goal of establishing the Turn 2 Foundation, where he gives back and helps kids who are
less fortunate. That is a role model! And Drew Brees is a great family man
who gives of his time. Here, let me break it down for you. "Brittany and
Drew Brees, and the Brees Dream Foundation, have collectively committed
and/or contributed just over $20,000,000 to charitable causes and academic
institutions in the New Orleans, San Diego and West Lafayette/Purdue
communities."

He didn't buy his way into being a role model. He simply cares about the 15
people who he knows have supported him in his career.

Tom Brady has a beautiful supermodel wife and many guys are saying, "I 16
wish I was Tom Brady so I could be married to a supermodel and win Super
Bowls." That doesn't make him a role model. It's because he is a class act who
does a ton for the Boys and Girls Clubs of America and gives his time and
money to help others.

I have the pleasure of hosting a radio show called *Sports Palooza Radio* 17
on Blogtalkradio. My wife and I interview professional athletes every
Thursday on our two-hour show. Do you know what one of the biggest
things is that we look for when we are booking guests? It's what the athlete
does to make someone else's life a bit easier. Not everyone has it easy and
gets spoon fed money and material things in life. That's who kids should be
looking up to.

There are former NFLers Dennis McKinnon and Lem Barney, who work 18
tirelessly with Gridiron Greats to help former football players. There's former
New York Mets Ed Hearn, who is fighting his own health battle, but works
with the NephCure Foundation and his own Bottom of the 9th Foundation.
There's Roy Smalley, who is president of the Pitch in for Baseball foundation,
an organization that collects baseball gear for children who don't have access
to others. NFLer Calais Campbell has his own foundation and works hard to
help others as well. There are so many other positive examples of athletes
doing good things, but they aren't making the headlines. Those athletes are
role models.

And then there's Donald Driver. He didn't start out as role model 19
material. In his book, *Driven*, he tells the story of his rough childhood
where he sold drugs to make money and carried guns. But he cleaned up
his act and became a stellar NFL superstar, carrying himself with class and

dignity. He is founder of the Donald Driver Foundation and the recipient of the 2013 AMVETS Humanitarian of the Year. If a kid looks up to him it's because he shows them how to overcome and persevere. That's a role model.

Don't expect the athletes of today to be instant role models. Instantly 20 famous? Maybe that is a better description, but an athlete needs to earn the role model status. That honor is not bestowed on you because you cashed a nice paycheck for playing a game!

Identifying the Elements of a Definition Argument

1. In your own words, summarize the essay's thesis.

2. This essay does not include a formal definition of *role model*. Why not? Following the template below, write your own one-sentence definition of *role model*.

    A *role model* is a _____ who _____
    _____

    _____ .

3. Throughout this essay, Garr gives examples of athletes who are and who are not role models. What does he accomplish with this strategy?

4. In paragraph 16, Garr discusses why Tom Brady, quarterback for the NFL's New England Patriots, is a role model. Since this article was written, Brady was accused of deflating footballs during the 2015 Super Bowl to give his team an unfair advantage. Although Brady denied the charges, the NFL gave him a four-game suspension. Does this scandal disqualify him from being a role model? Does Brady's scandal rise to the level of those involving Pete Rose, Ray Rice, and Michael Vick? Why or why not?

5. Where in the essay does Garr define the term *role model* by telling what it is not? What does Garr accomplish with this strategy?

6. Where does Garr introduce possible objections to his idea of a role model? Does he refute these objections convincingly? If not, how should he have addressed them?

7. In paragraph 17, Garr says that he and his wife host a radio show. Why does he mention this fact?

Tom Brady, a quarterback for the New England Patriots.

Maddie Meyer/Getty Images

➔ EXERCISE 12.4

According to former First Lady Eleanor Roosevelt, "We gain strength, and courage, and confidence by each experience in which we really stop to look fear in the face. . . . We must do that which we think we cannot." Each of the two pictures on the facing page presents a visual definition of *courage*. Study the pictures, and then write a paragraph in which you argue that they are (or are not) consistent with Roosevelt's concept of courage.

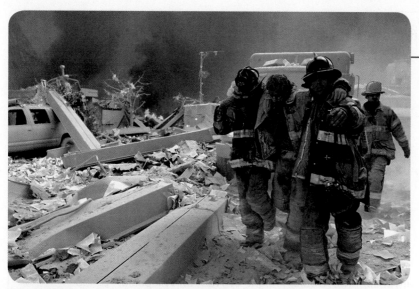

Firefighters at Ground Zero after the World Trade Center terrorist attacks on September 11, 2001, in New York City

New York Daily News Archive/Getty Images

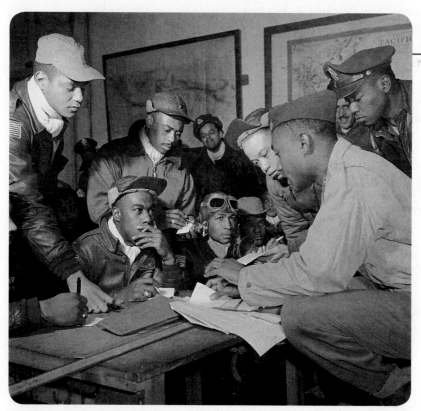

The Tuskegee Airmen, a group of African-American men who overcame tremendous odds to become U.S. Army pilots during World War II

Toni Frissell Collection, Library of Congress

Is *Wikipedia* a Legitimate Research Source?

Go back to page 417 and reread the At Issue box, which gives some background on the question of whether *Wikipedia* is a legitimate research source. As the following sources illustrate, this question suggests a variety of possible responses.

As you read the sources that follow, you will be asked to answer some questions and to complete some simple activities. This work will help you understand both the content and the structure of the sources. When you are finished, you will be ready to write a **definition argument** on the topic, "Is *Wikipedia* a Legitimate Research Source?"

© Fabian Bimmer/dpa/Corbis

SOURCES

This essay was published on February 12, 2012, in the *Chronicle Review*.

THE "UNDUE WEIGHT" OF TRUTH ON *WIKIPEDIA*

TIMOTHY MESSER-KRUSE

For the past 10 years I've immersed myself in the details of one of the most 1
famous events in American labor history, the Haymarket riot and trial of 1886.
Along the way I've written two books and a couple of articles about the episode. In some circles that affords me a presumption of expertise on the subject. Not, however, on *Wikipedia*.

The bomb thrown during an anarchist rally in Chicago sparked America's 2
first Red Scare, a high-profile show trial, and a worldwide clemency movement for the seven condemned men. Today the martyrs' graves are a national
historic site, the location of the bombing is marked by a public sculpture, and
the event is recounted in most American history textbooks. Its *Wikipedia*
entry is detailed and elaborate.

A couple of years ago, on a slow day at the office, I decided to experiment 3
with editing one particularly misleading assertion chiseled into the *Wikipedia*
article. The description of the trial stated, "The prosecution, led by Julius
Grinnell, did not offer evidence connecting any of the defendants with the
bombing. . . ."

Coincidentally, that is the claim that initially hooked me on the topic. In 4
2001 I was teaching a labor-history course, and our textbook contained nearly
the same wording that appeared on *Wikipedia*. One of my students raised her
hand: "If the trial went on for six weeks and no evidence was presented, what
did they talk about all those days?" I've been working to answer her question
ever since.

I have not resolved all the mysteries that surround the bombing, but I 5
have dug deeply enough to be sure that the claim that the trial was bereft of
evidence is flatly wrong. One hundred and eighteen witnesses were called to
testify, many of them unindicted coconspirators who detailed secret meetings
where plans to attack police stations were mapped out, coded messages were
placed in radical newspapers, and bombs were assembled in one of the defendants' rooms.

In what was one of the first uses of forensic chemistry in an American 6
courtroom, the city's foremost chemists showed that the metallurgical profile
of a bomb found in one of the anarchists' homes was unlike any commercial
metal but was similar in composition to a piece of shrapnel cut from the body
of a slain police officer. So overwhelming was the evidence against one of the
defendants that his lawyers even admitted that their client spent the afternoon
before the Haymarket rally building bombs, arguing that he was acting in self-
defense.

So I removed the line about there being "no evidence" and provided a full 7 explanation in *Wikipedia*'s behind-the-scenes editing log. Within minutes my changes were reversed. The explanation: "You must provide reliable sources for your assertions to make changes along these lines to the article."

That was curious, as I had cited the documents that proved my point, 8 including verbatim testimony from the trial published online by the Library of Congress. I also noted one of my own peer-reviewed articles. One of the people who had assumed the role of keeper of this bit of history for *Wikipedia* quoted the Web site's "undue weight" policy, which states that "articles should not give minority views as much or as detailed a description as more popular views." He then scolded me. "You should not delete information supported by the majority of sources to replace it with a minority view."

> "'You should not delete information supported by the majority of sources to replace it with a minority view.'"

The "undue weight" policy posed a problem. Scholars have been publish- 9 ing the same ideas about the Haymarket case for more than a century. The last published bibliography of titles on the subject has 1,530 entries.

"Explain to me, then, how a 'minority' source with facts on its side would 10 ever appear against a wrong 'majority' one?" I asked the Wiki-gatekeeper. He responded, "You're more than welcome to discuss reliable sources here, that's what the talk page is for. However, you might want to have a quick look at *Wikipedia*'s civility policy."

I tried to edit the page again. Within 10 seconds I was informed that my 11 citations to the primary documents were insufficient, as *Wikipedia* requires its contributors to rely on secondary sources, or, as my critic informed me, "published books." Another editor cheerfully tutored me in what this means: "*Wikipedia* is not 'truth,' *Wikipedia* is 'verifiability' of reliable sources. Hence, if most secondary sources which are taken as reliable happen to repeat a flawed account or description of something, *Wikipedia* will echo that."

Tempted to win simply through sheer tenacity, I edited the page again. 12 My triumph was even more fleeting than before. Within seconds the page was changed back. The reason: "reverting possible vandalism." Fearing that I would forever have to wear the scarlet letter of *Wikipedia* vandal, I relented but noted with some consolation that in the wake of my protest, the editors made a slight gesture of reconciliation—they added the word "credible" so that it now read, "The prosecution, led by Julius Grinnell, did not offer credible evidence connecting any of the defendants with the bombing. . . ." Though that was still inaccurate, I decided not to attempt to correct the entry again until I could clear the hurdles my anonymous interlocutors had set before me.

So I waited two years, until my book on the trial was published. "Now, at 13 last, I have a proper *Wikipedia* leg to stand on," I thought as I opened the page and found at least a dozen statements that were factual errors, including some that contradicted their own cited sources. I found myself hesitant to write, eerily aware that the self-deputized protectors of the page were reading over my shoulder, itching to revert my edits and tutor me in Wiki-decorum. I made a small edit, testing the waters.

My improvement lasted five minutes before a Wiki-cop scolded me, "I hope you will familiarize yourself with some of *Wikipedia*'s policies, such as verifiability and undue weight. If all historians save one say that the sky was green in 1888, our policies require that we write 'Most historians write that the sky was green, but one says the sky was blue.' . . . As individual editors, we're not in the business of weighing claims, just reporting what reliable sources write." 14

I guess this gives me a glimmer of hope that someday, perhaps before another century goes by, enough of my fellow scholars will adopt my views that I can change that *Wikipedia* entry. Until then I will have to continue to shout that the sky was blue. 15

⊘ AT ISSUE: SOURCES FOR DEVELOPING A DEFINITION ARGUMENT

1. Throughout most of his essay, Messer-Kruse makes an appeal to *ethos*. What is this appeal? How does it strengthen his argument?

2. What misconception in the "Haymarket Affair" entry did Messer-Kruse try to correct? What changes did he make? What documents did he cite to support these changes?

3. What is *Wikipedia*'s "undue weight" policy? How did this policy cause the *Wikipedia* gatekeeper to reject Messer-Kruse's changes? What did the editor mean when he said, "*Wikipedia* is not 'truth,' *Wikipedia* is 'verifiability' of reliable sources" (para. 11)?

4. Do you think that Messer-Kruse's complaints about *Wikipedia* have merit, or do you think that the *Wikipedia* editors were right to reject his changes? Explain.

5. In a response to Messer-Kruse's article, one person posted the following:

   On the Internet, no one knows that your [*sic*] a professor. If you're used to deferential treatment, at your home institution, you'll be treated like anyone else in the Wide Open Internet. This skepticism is a good thing—after all, some prankster could easily create an account using your name and pretend to be you.

   Do you think this statement points out *Wikipedia*'s strengths or its weaknesses? Explain.

6. How do you think Randall Stross (p. 453) would respond to Messer-Kruse's essay?

435

This post first appeared on Michael Martinez's blog, SEO Theory, on June 22, 2014.

WHY CITATIONS DO NOT MAKE *WIKIPEDIA* AND SIMILAR SITES CREDIBLE

MICHAEL MARTINEZ

If you search Twitter for word combinations like "*Wikipedia* credible" you may find people arguing back and forth about how credible the site is as a source of information. I even found a Tweet where someone wrote: "I hate when people say *Wikipedia* isn't a credible source. You click on the links on the page which lead to credible sources." That's very true. Many (though not all) *Wikipedia* articles link out to "credible sources" but there are several reasons why providing citations doesn't make you instantly credible. This is true for everyone; it's not something that is peculiar to *Wikipedia*. 1

And then there are reasons why *Wikipedia* is not and never can be a credible source of information. So let me deal with these two very different explanations separately. But first, let's talk about credibility. 2

> "But first, let's talk about credibility."

Credible Information Is Not Always Reliable

History is filled with grave mistakes that were committed on the basis of credible information. The interpretations of the credible information may not always be universally supported; and not everyone will agree that information is credible. Nonetheless, information may be presented as credible by a credible (or authoritative) person. 3

For example, during World War II both the Axis and the Allies used extensive networks of spies supported by intelligence agencies with all the latest technology and encryption/decryption skills to study each other's forces and strategies, report back, and analyze enemy intentions. Knowing that both sides were doing this, both sides in the war resorted to disseminating false information. 4

As it turns out the Allies proved to be more successful during critical operations. The United States' use of Navajo "Wind-talkers" confounded Japanese intelligence. While preparing for the D-Day invasion of northern France General Eisenhower deployed a false army under the command of General Patton to mislead the Germans about Allied intentions. In at least one airdrop operation dummies on parachutes were dropped out of plans to fool German gunners and inflate the numbers of attacking soldiers being reported to headquarters. 5

The Axis soldiers and spies charged with collecting and reporting this information were generally credible sources of information. They just didn't pass on reliable information. Credibility doesn't make you accurate or correct. 6

To be credible, a source is convincing. It may be convincing on the basis of past interaction (such as an undercover police officer who has conducted 7 numerous successful investigations). It may be convincing on the basis of logic (organizing facts in as complete and supportable manner as possible). It may also be convincing due to a lack of alternative or contradictory information.

In many UFO investigations police officers are often deemed to be highly 8 credible sources of information. However, police witnesses do not always recognize what they are describing. In fact, we don't investigate Unidentified Flying Objects unless we have reason to believe they are hostile. So just because a police officer credibly reports a UFO doesn't mean that any claims of extraterrestrial visitation on the basis of that report are valid.

Credibility in reporting source does not necessarily confer validity upon 9 any conclusions drawn on the basis of the reported information. Hence, credibility of source in itself is not a persuasive argument for believing something. And that is especially true when you need to establish provable facts. So being credible is no guarantee of being a reliable source of good or useful information.

Why Providing Citations Is Not Enough to Make You Reliable

Whether you write a huge long article or a very short quote, if you are relaying 10 information you found elsewhere on the Web it is courteous to provide a citation of your source. Pointing people to your source discredits any allegation that you made up what you are sharing.

Nonetheless, even if you publish 1,000,000 articles that all include cita- 11 tions for sources, your credibility depends on more than the credibility of your sources. If your credible sources are wrong, for example, then your use of those sources undermines your credibility. And credible sources can be very, very wrong.

Here is an article from 2005 that was published in the Harvard [Men's 12 Health Watch]: "Help for Your Cholesterol When the Statins Won't Do." The article includes the following information:

> . . . 3%–4% of people [. . .] don't do well with a statin drug. In a few cases, the drugs simply don't work, but more often the reason is a side effect. The most common statin toxicity is liver inflammation. Most patients with the problem don't even know they have it, but some develop abdominal distress, loss of appetite, or other symptoms. Even without these complaints, liver enzyme abnormalities, such as high *aminotransferase* levels, show up in the blood tests of 1%–2% of people taking a statin drug. The other major side effect is muscle inflammation, which can be silent or cause cramps, fatigue, or heavy, aching muscles.

At the time this article was published the information was deemed highly credible, even correct, based on the science available at the time. Unfortunately for millions of statin patients worldwide, the research was highly flawed. We now know that 37.5% of clinical trial patients could not tolerate statins.

Also, based on patient feedback over the past 9 years, most medical 13 resources now show that muscle problems are the most common side effect. When the Harvard [Men's Health Watch] publishes horribly wrong information about a widely used class of medicines, people should sit up and take notice.

To their credit, doctors at Harvard University have come out this year in strong opposition to the use of statins for patients who have not had a cardio-vascular event. Recent research shows very convincingly that there is 0 benefit for 80% of people with high cholesterol from taking statins. Only people who have already suffered a heart attack or other CVE may benefit from use of statins.

Credible information can therefore be wrong enough that even citing it is 14 not useful. Basing any article on a citation of a credible source that has been discredited in topical context means you are reporting wrong information, and therefore your article is not credible. So what if the 2005 article was once deemed correct? We now know it to be wrong; therefore using it as a source of information for any current survey of medical practice is inappropriate.

You can provide all the citations to credible sources you wish, but if they 15 are wrong then your own credibility may not suffer because you use credible sources but your information is unreliable.

The key takeaway here is that just because information is credible does 16 not mean it is accurate, correct, or reliable.

Why Accurate Citations Do Not Make You Reliable

So let's say you go the extra mile and do your research so well that you not 17 only compile credible sources of information you also find independent con-firmation of the claims those sources make. Your sources' credibility is impec-cable and the information they present does not appear to be contradicted by any other credible points of view. There are still potential pitfalls you have to overcome.

Less Credible Sources May Be More Correct Sometimes people who are 18 hard to believe really do get the facts straight. Maybe they are being intuitive. Maybe they lack any scientific proof. Maybe there is no way to confirm what they are saying. These deficiencies in support context do not make a view-point wrong any more than hundreds of supporting contexts make a view-point right.

The Correct Information May Not Yet Be Known Sometimes everyone 19 latches on to the same plausible explanation for lack of anything better. This even happens in science, especially in theoretical science where independent observations and experiments have not yet shown a theory to be true (or as true as we can confirm it to be given our current state of knowledge). Scien-tists will tell you that Einstein's Theory of General Relativity is true because it has been proven so by many experiments. They'll also point out that we have spent billions of dollars on experiments that attempt to prove the theory false. Although no one expects that to happen we would be practicing poor science by neglecting to attack and challenge the theory from every conceivable angle.

We may never fully know if Einstein was wrong. 20

Truth is not democratically determined. It doesn't matter how many 21 sources report the same information, even if they all arrived at their conclu-sions independently of each other. They can still be wrong. They may be wrong. In any given topic you have to allow for the possibility that some new verifiable evidence will eventually turn the entire world upside down.

Credible Sources May Be Corrupt Whether you are dealing with a police 22 officer who has turned to crime, a scientist who is falsifying data, or a reporter who just makes up a false story sometimes your credible source is actively trying to deceive you. You can't trust anyone. Literally.

Credible Sources May Have Been Deceived As noted above, credible 23 sources of information were misled by counter-intelligence operations during World War II. More recently, former U.S. Secretary of State Colin Powell presented the U.S.'s case for invading Iraq to the United Nations. His argument was based on two points: Saddam Hussein refused to allow UN Weapons Inspectors back into Iraq to verify that all his weapons of mass destruction (and the capability to make more) had been destroyed; and the U.S. had intelligence that led government analysts to conclude there was a high probability that Saddam Hussein was hiding something (probably Weapons of Mass Destruction).

Secretary Powell was viewed by everyone as a very credible, sincere man 24 who would not intentionally mislead anyone. He was a very credible source. He just didn't have very good information. After we invaded Iraq our forces did find several hundred chemical warheads that had been falsely reported as destroyed years before. WMD experts dismissed these warheads as being so old their chemicals would be inert. The military destroyed the warheads with all safety protocols just in case.

So as it turned out Saddam Hussein did not have a functioning WMD 25 program or even a viable cache of weapons. But no one knew that at the time because some of the intelligence given to Secretary Powell was false. Someone lied and the lies were passed on.

> "Someone lied and the lies were passed on."

The key takeaway here is that lies often get fed into the information chain 26 and they are passed around. Viral propaganda theory tells us that it doesn't matter if information is true or false: people will accept it if the source is credible, and once they believe a certain point of view it becomes next to impossible to change their minds.

Why Your Beliefs May Make You Unreliable

You may have the most credible sources of information to hand. You may 27 have eliminated all relevant doubt. You may have clear-cut scientific proof that shows no one has lied in the chain of information leading up to your own presentation. And yet your own article may be unreliable. Why? Because you believe.

As I pointed out above, viral propaganda theory shows us that people are 28 reluctant to change their minds. Just because I come along and point out all the fallacies of the viewpoint that you believe to be true doesn't mean you're going to question what you have believed again. You have already questioned that viewpoint and challenged it according to your prior knowledge and beliefs and it has passed all your tests.

To change your mind now would be to admit you were wrong and most 29 people hate to admit they are wrong. In fact, recent research suggests that people don't easily stop believing false information. Conviction is most likely a hard-wired trait in our behavior. My guess is that we need it in order to survive challenging times. If you don't believe you'll "get through this" then you may give up and die.

But if that is correct then conviction (or self-imposed belief) is irrational 30 and irrational behavior cannot easily be changed. The same factors that contribute to stubbornness when you're trying to survive also contribute to your pig-headedness when you're flat out wrong.

So when you prepare an article on any topic (and this is equally true of me), 31 you will write to support your belief and to undermine any doubts or challenges to your belief. You may have persuasive arguments to shoot down all objections to the points you make but it is easy to find examples of compelling arguments that rely in part on errors of omission. Intentionally (or even subconsciously) omitting relevant information changes the degree of completeness of your argument. In fact, errors of omission are often used to strengthen arguments.

Omitting inconvenient facts and points of view makes you an unreliable 32 source of information, even if the omissions make your arguments more persuasive and compelling. You may omit something merely because you couldn't think of everything you should have mentioned, or because you sincerely believe what you are omitting is not worthy of inclusion. Nonetheless, you can easily paint an incomplete (and therefore inaccurate) picture.

But many people turn to errors of omission as a way of winning arguments. 33 If they present only the facts that support their own points of view they can score points and change minds. It's easier to win people to your cause by omitting relevant information than by pointing out that the other guy left something out.

You may also lend more credence to sources you trust than to sources you 34 trust less. Hence, you introduce a bias into your presentation by saying things like "Dubious Dave has shown conclusively that frogs leap 15 feet backwards" and "Scientific Sam argues with Dubious Dave but has yet to provide a compelling argument" and "Silly Sally has challenged Scientific Sam several times."

The key takeaway here is that people favor the viewpoint they believe and 35 tend to treat opposing viewpoints unfairly. To do otherwise might force them to admit they were wrong.

And So *Wikipedia* Introduces More Problems

In addition to all the problems listed above, *Wikipedia* has its own peculiar set 36 of issues that make its well-cited articles unreliable.

Poor writing is the worst aspect of *Wikipedia*. The English-language 37 Website's content is a spaghetti-weave of mismatched idiom, much of it written by non-native English writers. But even among the native English writers there are regional variations in word choices and colloquial expressions.

Poor internal annotation is another grave problem with *Wikipedia*. It 38 provides no mechanism for explaining idiomatic expressions, unless those expressions are notable enough to have their own articles (but even then many marked up articles do not exist and so explanations are lacking). Use of unexplained idiom makes it hard for the average reader to understand what a given contributor is trying to say or whether other contributors agree with him.

Wikipedia's conflict resolution system always favors the biased reverter. 39 Whenever someone tries to correct a *Wikipedia* article, the first person to revert that change will win any reversion war because *Wikipedia* rules don't allow the person who made the change to make the last reversion. All disputes must be left up to the community to decide, and there you are asking incompetent people to decide between two opposing points of view, one of which almost certainly has more experience in *Wikipedia*'s in-site debates than the other.

Wikipedia's rules for citation also don't require that a proper context be 40 provided. For example, you could write "Michael Martinez says that SEO is not all about links" or you could write "Michael Martinez opposes link-based SEO strategies" and then provide a numbered citation that links to an SEO Theory article like "How Best to Use Links for SEO" (where I do in fact say "SEO is not all about links" but go on to show you how to use links in all sorts of SEO).

In this example you can write something completely misleading simply 41 by omitting proper context: "Martinez disagrees with SEOs who rely on links." Most readers will not check the citation so they will never know that I actually show people how to use links in SEO.

Wikipedia further instructs contributors not to use blogs as credible 42 sources. Many articles use blogs anyway but sometimes blogs are the only sources of information on a topic. Worse, many news articles cite very unreliable people as sources of information (for many of the reasons given above). In the world of ignorant people the self-confident man is king, no matter how wrong he is. We see that in Internet marketing all the time, not to mention politics and government.

Finally, *Wikipedia*'s content may change at any given time. How credible 43 would you think your neighbor if this morning he tells you it's June 2 and in the afternoon says June 3 and in the evening changes his mind back to June 2? Would you want to be treated by a doctor who says today, "You have high cholesterol," tomorrow "your cholesterol is fine," and two weeks from today says "dubious studies suggest that statistically your cholesterol will fall somewhere inside the marginal zone because you eat butter"?

Wikipedia, other Wiki sites, and indeed all crowd-sourced Websites are 44 fundamentally and inherently UNcredible. They lack credibility because they can be changed, not because of whatever they say today.

A credible source of information is consistent. An incredible source of 45 information is unpredictable.

441

A credible source of information may be reliable or it may be unreliable. 46

In fact, it doesn't matter how credible *Wikipedia* seems to you or me, 47 it is truly an unreliable source of information simply because there is no way that any of us can ensure that its information is accurate, reliable, correct, or complete.

All the citations in the world won't change that. 48

⊘ AT ISSUE: SOURCES FOR DEVELOPING A DEFINITION ARGUMENT

1. Martinez devotes most of his essay to defining *credibility*. Should he have spent more time discussing *Wikipedia*? Why or why not?

2. What does Martinez mean when he says "just because information is credible does not mean it is accurate, correct, or reliable" (para. 16)? What distinction does he make between credible information and reliable information?

3. What specific objections does Martinez have to *Wikipedia*? Why does he think that the problems he mentions make *Wikipedia* (and all crowd-sourced sites) an unreliable source of information?

4. Is Martinez's essay organized deductively or inductively? What are the advantages and disadvantages of this organization?

5. Given Martinez's guidelines, what kind of information in an encyclopedia entry is credible? What kind of information can never be credible?

6. Martinez does not address opposing arguments. Would his argument have been stronger had he done so? Explain.

Morris's article appeared online at DailyDot.com on January 1, 2013.

AFTER A HALF-DECADE, MASSIVE *WIKIPEDIA* HOAX FINALLY EXPOSED

KEVIN MORRIS

Up until a week ago, here is something you could have learned from *Wikipedia*: 1

From 1640 to 1641 the might of colonial Portugal clashed with India's 2 massive Maratha Empire in an undeclared war that would later be known as the Bicholim Conflict. Named after the northern Indian region where most of the fighting took place, the conflict ended with a peace treaty that would later help cement Goa as an independent Indian state.

Except none of this ever actually happened. The Bicholim Conflict is a fig-ment of a creative Wikipedian's imagina-tion. It's a huge, laborious, 4,500 word hoax. And it fooled *Wikipedia* editors for more than 5 years. 3

> "Except none of this ever actually happened."

But even exposed and deleted, *Wikipedia*'s influence over the Web is such 4 that the Bicholim Conflict continues to persist, like a resilient parasite.

The perpetrator of the hoax is a mystery. *Wikipedia* admins deleted the 5 edit history along with the article. Users of the Wikipediocracy forum have pinned down a likely suspect, however, a Wikipedian who went by the handle "A-b-a-a-a-a-a-b-a." He or she authored a big chunk of the article's text, and also nominated it for "Featured Article" standing in October 2007, writing:

> I'm nominating this article for featured article because after much work I believe it has reached its maximum potential. It is not a very huge event and doesn't have more than a few chapters in literature based on it but I've still created the article to quite a good size.

"Featured Article" status is a bit of a badge of honor on *Wikipedia*, a recogni-tion bestowed to only the highest quality pieces on the site. Out of more than 4 million English *Wikipedia* articles, only 3,772 are "featured." Thankfully the Bicholim Conflict didn't pass muster—editors who reviewed it cited an over-reliance on a few weak sources, never realizing that those sources never existed in the first place.

And the Bicholim Conflict was still labeled a "Good Article," a status it 6 had received just two months after being created in July, 2007. That status is a step down from featured, but still a designation given to less than 1 percent of all English-language articles on the site.

Enter Wikipedian-detective ShelfSkewed, who decided in late December, 7 for no apparent reason, to delve into the article's sources. What he found was pretty amazing: None of the books used as source material in the article appeared to exist.

On Dec. 29, 2012, ShelfSkewed nominated the whole thing for deletion: 8

> After careful consideration and some research, I have come to the conclu-
> sion that this article is a hoax—a clever and elaborate hoax, but a hoax
> nonetheless. An online search for "Bicholim conflict" or for many of the
> article's purported sources produces only results that can be traced back
> to the article itself. Take, for example, one of the article's major sources:
> Thompson, Mark, Mistrust between states, Oxford University Press, Lon-
> don 1996. No record at WorldCat. No mention at the [Oxford University
> Press] site. No used listings at Alibris or ABE. I can find no evidence any-
> where that this book exists.

He or she added: "Ridiculous."

Six other editors agreed. And with that, the five-and-a-half-year lie was   9
finally snuffed out of existence.

A half-decade sounds like a long time. But while impressive, seven other   10
Wikipedia hoaxes have actually lived longer. These include an article on a supposed torture device called "Crocodile Shears" (which persisted for six years
and four months) and one on Chen Fang, a Harvard University student who,
intent to demonstrate the limitations of *Wikipedia,* named himself the mayor
of a small Chinese town. It took more than seven years for *Wikipedia* editors
to finally strip Chen of that mayorship.

And then there's the case of Gaius Flavius Antoninus, whose *Wikipedia*   11
page described him as a perpetrator in one of the most famous events in
history—the assassination of Julius Caesar. "He was later murdered by a male
prostitute hired by Mark Antony," the *Wikipedia* entry told us. Antoninus,
like the Bicholim Conflict, never existed. The hoax evaded *Wikipedia*'s legions
of volunteers for more than eight years, until it was finally uncovered in July,
2012, and similarly purged from existence.

Except, not really. While *Wikipedia* editors do their best to battle the   12
army of trolls and vandals who disrupt the millions of articles on the site, the
scams continue to live on elsewhere. There is a small club of *Wikipedia* copy-
cat sites on the Internet, which scrape, copy, and paste the encyclopedia's content en masse to their own sites, then plaster it with ads (copying *Wikipedia*
content is legal under its Creative Commons license).

So while the Bicholim Conflict is now dead on *Wikipedia,* it still persists   13
on the "New World Encyclopedia" and "Encyclo."

And for just $20, you can buy a hard copy.   14

⊘ AT ISSUE: SOURCES FOR DEVELOPING A DEFINITION ARGUMENT

1. What is the Bicholim Conflict? Why, according to Morris, does the
   problem regarding this conflict continue to exist?

2. What does Morris mean when he says, "'Featured Article' status is a bit of a badge of honor on *Wikipedia*" (para. 5)? What is the difference between a "Featured Article" and a "Good Article"?

3. What is Morris's thesis? Restate it in your own words.

4. Morris points out that in addition to the Bicholim Conflict, which took five and a half years to remove, "seven other *Wikipedia* hoaxes have actually lasted longer" (10). Are these eight examples enough to support Morris's thesis? Explain.

5. All the hoaxes that Morris discusses were eventually discovered. Does this fact undermine his thesis? Why or why not?

6. Do you think this essay is an argument? Explain.

This article appeared online on December 1, 2014, on Skeptoid.com, a site for critically analyzing popular culture.

STOP *WIKIPEDIA* SHAMING

ALISON HUDSON

Wikipedia has gotten a bogeyman reputation for inaccuracy. "I read it on *Wikipedia*" has become a punchline for obviously incorrect information, and any reference to *Wikipedia* in an article has a tendency to draw derisive comments that essentially dismiss the entire article due to the addition of a link. I've come to think of it as "*Wikipedia* shaming"—deriding and discrediting an article because it happens to reference or link to *Wikipedia* at some point, regardless of the quality of the information presented both in the *Wikipedia* link and in the original article. Such views are themselves inaccurate and ill-informed. *Wikipedia*'s reputation for unreliability is itself an unreliable position to take.

I am a college English instructor, and I've found it to be a common trope in education that *Wikipedia* is a useless resource. Every college I have ever worked for had some sort of general academic policy on *Wikipedia*, mostly "do not let your students reference *Wikipedia* in their papers." You can also find examples of such policies online. The reason usually given is that "*Wikipedia* is non-scholarly and unreliable."

They're half right; *Wikipedia* is non-scholarly, for sure. But then again, so are a lot of resources people trust. "Non-scholarly" is not a synonym for "not reliable." "Non-scholarly" simply means "wasn't written by a credited expert in the field and published in a peer-reviewed journal with complete references." Despite the fact that many field experts do spend time reading and editing in *Wikipedia* and *Wikipedia* articles do strive for complete references, it's not a scholarly source.

Where I dissent from the popular view of *Wikipedia* is in its reputation for unreliability. A 2005 study by *Nature* found that *Wikipedia*'s accuracy was comparable to the *Encyclopaedia Britannica* (though the writing style was considered inferior). A University of Oxford/Epic e-learning follow-up study released in 2012 (yes, with some support from the Wikimedia Foundation) found that *Wikipedia* held its own against a variety of reference works. A 2014 study of drug information on *Wikipedia* found that its drug-related information was 99.7% accurate compared to pharmacological textbooks. If you want a more comprehensive listing of reliability studies on *Wikipedia*, there's one place you can go: *Wikipedia*, which doesn't shy away from reporting on the good and bad of its own content.

"But what about that story I heard about the kid who wrote a fake entry and it stayed up for, like, four years?" Yes, that is one of the weaknesses on the model, and one of the reasons I just called it "non-scholarly." You know who keeps a running list of acknowledged *Wikipedia* hoaxes? *Wikipedia* does.

And you'll notice that most of the longstanding ones were able to survive mostly because they were small, unimportant topics that people weren't likely to be referencing anyway—a made-up but otherwise historically unimportant supposed assassin of Julius Caesar, or someone claiming they were the mayor of a small Chinese town. Vandalism happens, but it's usually caught fairly quickly and reverted; and the vandals are usually blocked and banned.

Time is also a factor in *Wikipedia*'s reliability. *Wikipedia* has gotten consistently better since its inception more than a decade ago. Unlike a journal article, a blog post, or the *Encyclopaedia Britannica, Wikipedia* is constantly being updated. That's the very nature of the wiki model—allowing the collected knowledge of the world to accrete in one place. *Wikipedia* also has the Wikimedia Foundation behind it actively looking for ways to improve the information on the site, as well as an entire process of editorial control. The days of "you can write anything you want on *Wikipedia*" are long gone.

> "The days of 'you can write anything you want on *Wikipedia*' are long gone."

It is for all these reasons that I *do* reference *Wikipedia* in my blog posts and I will continue to do so in the future. When I do, it's usually for the purpose of **general information**, which is exactly what *Wikipedia* is good for. If someone doesn't know what ascorbic acid is, it's much more practical, from a get-the-basics-and-get-back-to-reading perspective, to just link the reader to *Wikipedia* where they can read the first paragraph or two, get the idea, and then return to the original article.

Wikipedia is also a good source of **links to other resources**. One thing I often point out to students in my college courses is that "*Wikipedia* has more, better citations than your last essay did." For example, consider the following passage from *Wikipedia*'s entry on aspartame:

> The safety of aspartame has been studied extensively since its discovery with research that includes animal studies, clinical and epidemiological research, and postmarketing surveillance,[38] with aspartame being one of the most rigorously tested food ingredients to date.[39] Peer-reviewed comprehensive review articles and independent reviews by governmental regulatory bodies have analyzed the published research on the safety of aspartame and have found aspartame is safe for consumption at current levels.[8][38][40][41] Aspartame has been deemed safe for human consumption by over 100 regulatory agencies in their respective countries,[41] including the UK Food Standards Agency,[42] the European Food Safety Authority (EFSA)[43], and Health Canada.[44]

That passage has ten references to eight different sources, many of them the official statements of various government agencies; it also comes from an entry with eighty-five different referenced works. I wish the typical student essay or Internet comment post were so thoroughly sourced!

It's because of these two views that I often actually tell my students to **start with *Wikipedia*** when they conduct research. Many times students, like your typical Internet commenter, know a little bit about a topic but not nearly enough to go on at length. In fact, in some classes I will actually assign the *Wikipedia* article as a reading assignment and then have them answer some pointed questions based on the information found there. They're going to read it anyways; I might as well acknowledge the fact and make sure everyone's got the basics down before they begin the real research. [It also reminds them that I read *Wikipedia*, too, which usually dissuades at least a few attempts at lazy *Wikipedia* plagiarism.]

Of course, I also tell my students to **verify information in a second source**, because I'm aware that any single source of information may be flawed. That's not my stance just on *Wikipedia*, but on any important fact. Starting with *Wikipedia* is fine; but ending with *Wikipedia* is a lazy way to do research.

By the sheer power of its size, *Wikipedia* actually does what the *wiki* concept intends to do: it harnesses the collective knowledge of the Internet and distills it into digestible form. Sure, there are weaknesses in the model, but there's weaknesses in every model. There is no shame in making a general reference to *Wikipedia*, and there is *certainly* no shame in mining *Wikipedia*'s references for other sources. So please, stop *Wikipedia* shaming authors who toss an informational link to *Wikipedia* into their posts. It makes you look petulant and clearly indicates that you didn't even bother to read the referenced passage and/or you want to avoid the point being made.

And before you respond to this article with "But look! Here's an error I found in *Wikipedia*!" consider this: you found an error on *Wikipedia*? Good! You're supposed to. If you're smart enough to notice it, though, you're smart enough to correct it, so why not make your own little contribution to the collected knowledge of the Internet community. Just be ready to credit a source; unlike most discussion forums or comments sections, *Wikipedia* demands citation.

⊙ AT ISSUE: SOURCES FOR DEVELOPING A DEFINITION ARGUMENT

1. Hudson begins her essay discussing the major arguments against *Wikipedia*. Why does she begin this way? Is this an effective strategy?

2. What is "*Wikipedia* shaming"?

3. Explain the difference between the terms *non-scholarly* and *not reliable*. Why does Hudson disagree with the generally held view that

Wikipedia is not a reliable source? What evidence does she present to support this position?

4. According to Hudson, what are the strengths of *Wikipedia*?

5. At what point does Hudson address opposing arguments? How effectively does she refute them?

6. In paragraph 7, Hudson notes that she refers to *Wikipedia* in her blog posts. Why does she mention this? Do you agree with her rationale for doing so? Why or why not?

Wikipediocracy.com, a site dedicated to exploring issues related to *Wikipedia*, posted this article on February 16, 2014.

DEBUNKING THE "ACCURATE AS BRITANNICA" MYTH

ANDREAS KOLBE

A factoid regularly cited in the press to this day is that a 2005 study by *Nature* 1 found *Wikipedia* to be almost as reliable as *Britannica*. While the study's (if that is the right word—it wasn't a peer-reviewed study, but a news story) methodology and conclusions were disputed by *Britannica*, the result of the *Nature* comparison has become part of received knowledge for much of the media. As the saying goes, a lie told often enough becomes the truth.

> "As the saying goes, a lie told often enough becomes the truth."

A Meme Is Born

The problems really began as soon as the *Nature* piece was published. Many 2 news outlets failed to mention that in its survey, *Nature* looked at hard science topics only—subjects like physics, chemistry, biology, astronomy and paleontology—despite the fact that *Nature* clearly said so, in the very first line of its piece. The following headline and lead from CNET will serve as an example:

Study: **Wikipedia** *as accurate as* **Britannica.**

Wikipedia *is about as good a source of accurate information as* Britannica, *the venerable standard-bearer of facts about the world around us, according to a study published this week in the journal* Nature.

Few observers were astute enough to note, as the *Register*'s Andrew Orlowski did, that restricting the comparison to hard science articles was what "gave the free-for-all web site a fighting chance—as it excluded the rambling garbage and self-indulgence that constitute much of the wannabe encyclopedia's social science and culture entries." Another notable exception was Bill Thompson, writing for the BBC, who noted *Wikipedia*'s problems in "contentious areas such as politics, religion or biography," and how easily *Wikipedia* can "be undermined through malice or ignorance thanks to its open architecture."

Nicholas Carr put it this way: in limiting itself to topics like the "kinetic 3 isotope effect" or "Meliaceae," which no one without some specialized understanding of the subject matter would even be aware of, the *Nature* survey played to *Wikipedia*'s strengths. Carr also established that the *Nature* "study" was not actually an expert-written research article of the type that built the reputation of *Nature*, but a non-peer-reviewed piece of news journalism (a fact he confirmed with the piece's author, Jim Giles).

Another fact that is largely forgotten today: the *Nature* survey found that 4
many *Wikipedia* entries were "poorly structured and confusing" and gave
undue prominence to controversial theories. Both of these failings are a result
of *Wikipedia*'s crowdsourcing method—one editor adding a sentence here,
another adding a sentence there. The study's highly publicized count of "inaccuracies," which led to the "*Wikipedia* is as accurate as *Britannica*" meme,
did not reflect that. While the count penalized *Britannica* for alleged omissions—which *Britannica* contested—it imposed no penalty on *Wikipedia* for
meandering off topic.

In effect, it considered a sprawling, badly organized jumble of facts to be 5
as valuable as a masterfully written and easy-to-understand introduction to a
topic by a world-renowned scholar. The results are not the same. Even so,
Nature found that *Wikipedia* contained about a third more inaccuracies than
Britannica. (This doesn't stop some writers going the whole hog and claiming
that *Nature* found *Wikipedia* to be more reliable than *Britannica*. It's stunning, really, how memes morph on the internet.)

**The Reality: A Site Riddled with Hoaxes, Vandalism, PR Manipulation,
and Anonymous Defamation**

Another point that was lost is that *Wikipedia*'s quality is very uneven. *Wikipe-* 6
dia articles on more obscure topics are often lacking in basic literacy. In the
worst case, the information they contain may be entirely made up, or so self-
serving to the interests of some anonymous *Wikipedia* author as to make a
mockery of *Wikipedia*'s vaunted concept of a "neutral point of view."

Saying that *Wikipedia* is "as reliable as *Britannica*" implies that this is so 7
for any article in *Wikipedia*. And that just ain't so. Some of *Wikipedia*'s articles are indeed reliable. The problem is that you never know whether the article you are looking at is one of them.

Wikipedia contains hoaxes and vandalism. It contains malicious defama- 8
tion and anonymous hatchet jobs authored by people who are in conflict with
the person they are writing about, or sim-
ply jealous of their success. It contains
barely disguised advertising—entries on
people and companies written by their
subjects, or their PR agents. It contains articles on politics and history that
have been meddled with by political extremists. *Wikipedia* entries are protean
edifices: they may say one thing today and a completely different thing tomorrow. Those are all problems conventional reference works like *Britannica*
never had. Is this progress?

> "*Wikipedia* contains
> hoaxes and vandalism."

What reference works like *Britannica* do have are editors in the tradi- 9
tional sense of the word—experts in their fields, who ensure that what is published meets academic standards. *Wikipedia* has editors, too, but in Jimmy
Wales' online encyclopedia the word means something entirely different: it is
applied to any anonymous person with an internet connection who clicks
"Edit" on a *Wikipedia* page—whether it's a schoolchild, a mentally disturbed

person, a political activist, a knowledgeable amateur, or an actual scholar. *Wikipedia* has all of them. But academics venturing into the "encyclopedia anyone can edit" (allegedly) often find it a very time-consuming and frustrating experience, punctuated by interminable arguments with young men who may only have a very superficial understanding of the academic's area of expertise, but unlimited time to spend on *Wikipedia*, familiarity with the site's arcane and self-contradictory policies and guidelines, and wiki-friends to back them up. Many a distinguished academic lacks the time and patience to engage with them, and has been blocked from further participation for "incivility." It's not the same as talking to your editor at a university press!

Horses for Courses

Wikipedia is free. It's understandable that people don't like to look a gift horse   10
in the mouth. But no one should fool themselves into thinking that the nag they got for free is an Arabian racehorse.

⊘ AT ISSUE: SOURCES FOR DEVELOPING A DEFINITION ARGUMENT

1. What does Kolbe mean in paragraph 1 when he says, "[A] lie told often enough becomes the truth"? What lie does Kolbe address in his essay?

2. What point does Kolbe concede in paragraph 7? How does he go on to refute this point?

3. According to Kolbe, what is the major strength of *Britannica*?

4. Kolbe clearly does not consider *Wikipedia* a source of reliable information. Why not? Do any of his arguments seem unfair or biased? Explain.

5. What point does Kolbe make in his conclusion? Why does he focus on the fact that *Wikipedia* is free?

The *New York Times* published this essay on March 12, 2006.

ANONYMOUS SOURCE IS NOT THE SAME AS OPEN SOURCE

RANDALL STROSS

Wikipedia, the free online encyclopedia, currently serves up the following: 1
Five billion pages a month. More than 120 languages. In excess of one million
English-language articles. And a single nagging epistemological° question:
Can an article be judged as credible without knowing its author?

Concerning the nature of knowledge

Wikipedia says yes, but I am unconvinced. 2

Dispensing with experts, the Wikipedians invite anyone to pitch in, writ- 3
ing an article or editing someone else's. No expertise is required, nor even a
name. Sound inviting? You can start immediately. The system rests upon the
belief that a collectivity of unknown but enthusiastic individuals, by dint of
sheer mass rather than possession of conventional credentials,° can serve in
the supervisory role of editor. Anyone with an interest in a topic can root out
inaccuracies and add new material.

Qualifications such as a degree in a field

At first glance, this sounds straightforward. But disagreements arise all the 4
time about what is a problematic passage or an encyclopedia-worthy topic, or
even whether a putative correction improves or detracts from the original version.

The egalitarian nature of a system that accords equal votes to everyone in 5
the "community"—middle-school student and Nobel laureate alike—has difficulty resolving intellectual disagreements.

Wikipedia's reputation and internal editorial process would benefit by 6
having a single authority vouch for the quality of a given article. In the jargon
of library and information science, lay readers rely upon "secondary epistemic
criteria," clues to the credibility of information when they do not have the
expertise to judge the content.

Once upon a time, *Encyclopaedia Britannica* recruited Einstein, Freud, 7
Curie, Mencken, and even Houdini as contributors. The names helped the encyclopedia bolster its credibility. *Wikipe-
dia*, by contrast, provides almost no
clues for the typical article by which
reliability can be appraised. A list of
edits provides only screen names or, in
the case of the anonymous editors,
numerical Internet Protocol addresses.

> "What does *Wikipedia*'s
> system offer in place of
> an expert authority?"

Wasn't yesterday's practice of attaching "Albert Einstein" to an article on
"Space-Time" a bit more helpful than today's "71.240.205.101"?

What does *Wikipedia*'s system offer in place of an expert authority willing 8
to place his or her professional reputation on the line with a signature attached
to an article?

When I asked Jimmy Wales, the founder of *Wikipedia*, last week, he 9
discounted the importance of individual contributors to *Britannica*. "When
people trust an article in *Britannica*," he said, "it's not who wrote it, it's the
process." There, a few editors review a piece and then editing ceases. By contrast, *Wikipedia* is built with unending scrutiny and ceaseless editing.

He predicts that in the future, it will be *Britannica*'s process that will 10
seem strange: "People will say, 'This was written by one person?
Then looked at by only two or three other people? How can I trust that
process?'"

The Wikipedian hive is capable of impressive feats. The English-language 11
collection recently added its millionth article, for example. It was about the
Jordanhill railway station, in Glasgow. The original version, a few paragraphs,
appeared to say all that a lay reader would ever wish to know about it. But the
hive descended and in a week, more than 640 edits were logged.

If every topic could be addressed like this, without recourse to specialized 12
learning—and without the heated disputes called flame wars—the anonymous
hive could be trusted to produce work of high quality. But the Jordanhill station is an exception.

Biographical entries, for example, are often accompanied by controversy. 13
Several recent events have shown how anyone can tamper with someone else's
entry. Congressional staff members have been unmasked burnishing articles
about their employers and vandalizing those of political rivals. (Sample addition: "He likes to beat his wife and children.")

Mr. Wales himself ignored the encyclopedia's guidelines about "Dealing 14
with Articles about Yourself" and altered his own *Wikipedia* biography; when
other editors undid them, he reapplied his changes. The incidents, even if few
in number, do not help *Wikipedia* establish the legitimacy of a process that is
reluctant to say no to anyone.

It should be noted that Mr. Wales is a full-time volunteer, and that nei- 15
ther he nor the thousands of fellow volunteer editors has a pecuniary interest
in this nonprofit project. He also deserves accolades for keeping *Wikipedia*
operating without the intrusion of advertising, at least so far.

Most winningly, he has overseen a system that is gleefully candid in its 16
public self-examination. If you're seeking a well-organized list of criticisms of
Wikipedia, you won't find a better place than *Wikipedia*'s coverage of itself.
Wikipedia also provides a taxonomy of no fewer than 23 different forms of
vandalism that strike it.

It is easy to forget how quickly *Wikipedia* has grown; it began only in 17
2001. With the passage of a little more time, Mr. Wales and his associates may
come around to the idea that identifying one person as a given article's super-
vising editor would enhance the encyclopedia's reputation.

Mr. Wales has already responded to recent negative articles about 18
vandalism at the site with announcements of modest reforms. Anonymous
visitors are no longer permitted to create pages, though they still may edit
existing ones.

To curb what Mr. Wales calls "drive-by pranks" that are concentrated on 19
particular articles, he has instituted a policy of "semi-protection." In these
cases, a user must have registered at least four days before being permitted to
make changes to the protected article. "If someone really wants to write
'George Bush is a poopy head,' you've got to wait four days," he said.

When asked what problems on the site he viewed as most pressing, 20
Mr. Wales said he was concerned with passing along the Wikipedian culture
to newcomers. He sounded wistful when he spoke of the days not so long ago
when he could visit an article that was the subject of a flame war and would
know at least some participants—and whether they could resolve the dispute
tactfully.

As the project has grown, he has found that he no longer necessarily 21
knows anyone in a group. When a dispute flared recently over an article
related to a new dog breed, he looked at the discussion and asked himself in
frustration, "Who are these people?"

Isn't this precisely the question all users are bound to ask about contributors? 22

By wide agreement, the print encyclopedia in the English world reached 23
its apogee in 1911, with the completion of *Encyclopaedia Britannica*'s 11th
edition. (For the fullest tribute, turn to *Wikipedia*.) But the *Wikipedia* experiment need not be pushed back in time toward that model. It need only be
pushed forward, so it can catch up to others with more experience in online
collaboration: the open-source software movement.

Wikipedia and open-source projects like Linux are similarly noncommer- 24
cial, intellectual enterprises, mobilizing volunteers who will probably never
meet one another in person. But even though Wikipedians like to position
their project under the open-source umbrella, the differences are wide.

Jeff Bates, a vice president of the Open Source Technology Group who 25
oversees SourceForge.net, the host of more than 80,000 active open-source
projects, said, "It makes me grind my teeth to hear *Wikipedia* compared to
open source." In every open-source project, he said, there is "a benevolent dictator" who ultimately takes responsibility, even though the code is contributed
by many. Good stuff results only if "someone puts their name on it."

Wikipedia has good stuff, too. These have been designated "featured arti- 26
cles." But it will be a long while before all one-million-and-counting entries
have been carefully double-checked and buffed to a high shine. Only 923 have
been granted "featured" status, and the consensus-building process is presently capable of adding only about one a day.

Mr. Wales is not happy with this pace and seems open to looking again at 27
the open-source software model for ideas. Software development that relies on
scattered volunteers is a two-step process: first, a liberal policy encourages the
contributions of many, then a restrictive policy follows to stabilize the code in
preparation for release. *Wikipedia*, he said, has "half the model."

There's no question that *Wikipedia* volunteers can address many more 28
topics than the lumbering, for-profit incumbents like *Britannica* and *World
Book*, and can update entries swiftly. Still, anonymity blocks credibility.

One thing that Wikipedians have exactly right is that the current form of the encyclopedia is a beta test. The quality level that would permit speaking of Version 1.0 is still in the future.

⟡ AT ISSUE: SOURCES FOR DEVELOPING A DEFINITION ARGUMENT

1. In paragraph 3, Stross presents the *Wikipedia* philosophy. In your own words, summarize this philosophy.

2. At what points in his essay does Stross refute the *Wikipedia* philosophy? What aspects of this philosophy does he seem to disagree with most?

3. Do you think Stross should have provided formal definitions of the terms *anonymous source* and *open source*? Why or why not?

4. Where in the essay does Stross acknowledge *Wikipedia*'s strengths? Do you think that the encyclopedia's strengths outweigh its weaknesses? Explain.

5. Do you agree with Jimmy Wales, founder of *Wikipedia*, that in the future, *Britannica*'s process "will seem strange" (para. 10)? Why or why not?

6. What does Stross mean when he says, "Version 1.0 is still in the future" (28)?

WIKIPEDIA: ABOUT
WIKIPEDIA

From *Wikipedia*, the free encyclopedia   1

A general introduction for visitors to *Wikipedia*. The project also has an   2
encyclopedia article about itself, *Wikipedia*, and some introductions for aspiring contributors.

For *Wikipedia*'s formal organi- 3
zational structure, see *Wikipedia*:
Formal organization.

Wikipedia (◄ᵈ/ˌwɪkɨˈpiːdi.ə/ or   4
◄ᵈ/ˌwɪkiˈpiːdi.ə/ *WIK-i-PEE-dee-ə*) is a
multilingual, web-based, free-content
encyclopedia project based on an
openly editable model. The name
Wikipedia is a portmanteau of
the words *wiki* (a technology for
creating collaborative websites, from
the Hawaiian word *wiki*, meaning
"quick") and *encyclopedia*. *Wikipedia*'s articles provide links to guide
the user to related pages with additional information.

> ### English *Wikipedia* right now
>
> *Wikipedia* is running MediaWiki version 1.18wmf1 (r109351).
>
> It has 3,859,117 content articles, and 26,106,710 pages in total.
>
> There have been 513,565,315 edits.
>
> There are 797,211 uploaded files.
>
> There are 16,163,858 registered users, including 1,507 administrators.
>
> This information is correct as of 18:50, 30 January 2012 (UTC).

Wikipedia is written collaboratively by largely anonymous Internet 5
volunteers who write without pay. Anyone with Internet access can write
and make changes to *Wikipedia* articles (except in certain cases where editing is restricted to prevent disruption or vandalism). Users can contribute
anonymously, under a pseudonym, or with their real identity, if they
choose.

The fundamental principles by which *Wikipedia* operates are the five pil- 6
lars. The *Wikipedia* community has developed many policies and guidelines
to improve the encyclopedia; however, it is not a formal requirement to be
familiar with them before contributing.

Since its creation in 2001, *Wikipedia* has grown rapidly into one of the larg- 7
est reference websites, attracting 400 million unique visitors monthly as of
March 2011 according to ComScore. There are more than 82,000 active contributors (http://en.wikipedia.org/wikistats/EN/TablesWikipediansEditsGt5
.htm) working on more than 19,000,000 articles in more than 270 languages. As
of today, there are 3,859,117 articles in English. Every day, hundreds of thousands of visitors from around the world collectively make tens of thousands of

edits and create thousands of new articles to augment the knowledge held by the *Wikipedia* encyclopedia. (See also *Wikipedia*: Statistics.)

People of all ages, cultures, and backgrounds can add or edit article 8 prose, references, images, and other media here. What is contributed is more important than the expertise or qualifications of the contributor. What will remain depends upon whether it fits within *Wikipedia*'s policies, including being verifiable against a published reliable source, so excluding editors' opinions and beliefs and unreviewed research, and is free of copyright restrictions and contentious material about living people. Contributions cannot damage *Wikipedia* because the software allows easy reversal of mistakes and many experienced editors are watching to help ensure that edits are cumulative improvements. Begin by simply clicking the *edit* link at the top of any editable page!

Wikipedia is a live collaboration differing from paper-based reference 9 sources in important ways. Unlike printed encyclopedias, *Wikipedia* is continually created and updated, with articles on historic events appearing within minutes, rather than months or years. Older articles tend to grow more comprehensive and balanced; newer articles may contain misinformation, unencyclopedic content, or vandalism. Awareness of this aids obtaining valid information and avoiding recently added misinformation (see Researching with *Wikipedia*).

This Web page was accessed on April 24, 2012.

ABOUT THE *IEP*

INTERNET ENCYCLOPEDIA OF PHILOSOPHY

The *Internet Encyclopedia of Philosophy* (*IEP*) (ISSN 2161-0002) was founded 1 in 1995 as a non-profit organization to provide open access to detailed, scholarly information on key topics and philosophers in all areas of philosophy. The *Encyclopedia* receives no funding, and operates through the volunteer work of the editors, which consists of editors, authors, volunteers, and technical advisers. At present the *IEP* is visited by over 500,000 persons per month.

Most of the articles in the *IEP* are original contributions by specialized 2 philosophers; these are identifiable by the author's name at the foot of the article. Others are temporary, or "proto articles," and have largely been adapted from older sources. They are identifiable by the inclusion of the initials "*IEP*" at the close and will in time be replaced by original articles.

Statement of Purpose

The purpose of the *IEP* is to provide detailed, scholarly information on key 3 topics and philosophers in all areas of philosophy. The *Encyclopedia* is free of charge and available to all users of the Internet world-wide. The present staff of 25 editors and approximately 300 authors hold doctorate degrees and are professors at colleges and universities around the world, most notably from the United States, Great Britain, and

> "The purpose of the *IEP* is to provide detailed, scholarly information on key topics and philosophers in all areas of philosophy."

Australia. The submission and review process of articles is the same as that with printed philosophy journals, books, and reference works. The authors are specialists in the areas in which they write and are frequently leading authorities. Submissions are peer reviewed by specialists according to strict criteria.

Scholarly Standards

Our peer review process is rigorous and meets high academic standards. 4 Authors submit their articles to a specific *IEP* area editor, who reads through the article and makes an initial judgment about its overall quality. Many submissions are rejected at this stage. The area editor then sends the promising submission to qualified referees. Usually there are two referees per article. The area editor evaluates the reviews from the referees, makes a decision whether to publish, and sends a recommendation to the author. Most submissions are then revised, in either their form or substance. In some cases more rounds of revision are required, and we sometimes must reject entries because of inadequate revision. More commonly, any problems with entries are fixed with revision—as one might expect when well-qualified people are recruited to write entries. This is a common pattern for scholarly journal articles and reference works.

Consequently, the quality of our articles is at the same level as that of the 5 best multi-volume encyclopedias of philosophy which appear in print. However, an article published in our *Encyclopedia* surveys its field and so is not equivalent to a journal article that advances the field. Nevertheless, it is also the case that journals from time to time publish or commission review articles that do not necessarily have this function and that *IEP* articles can be considered as comparable to such review articles. For additional information, please contact the general editors.

Citing Entries

Here is a suggested way to cite our articles in your own writing: 6

> "Naturalistic Epistemology," by Chase B. Wrenn, *The Internet Encyclopedia of Philosophy*, ISSN 2161-0002, http://www.iep.utm.edu/, today's date.

As the *Encyclopedia* is regularly updated, we archive earlier versions for 7 our own records; earlier versions are publicly available at archive.org. Teachers and scholars with special needs—such as authenticating quotations and detecting plagiarism—may be provided copies of an earlier version of an article upon request to the General Editor.

⊘ AT ISSUE: SOURCES FOR DEVELOPING A DEFINITION ARGUMENT

1. According to the "About" sections of these two online encyclopedias, how is *The Internet Encyclopedia of Philosophy* different from *Wikipedia*? Do you think both encyclopedias are aimed at the same audience?

2. Who is able to add to or edit *Wikipedia* articles? Who is able to make changes to *The Internet Encyclopedia of Philosophy*? Who is *not* able to make changes?

3. How do the editors of each online encyclopedia try to maintain the quality of their articles? Which encyclopedia do you think is more successful at doing this?

4. Both *Wikipedia* and *The Internet Encyclopedia of Philosophy* give users access to earlier versions of articles. Why do they do this? What can users gain by looking at these earlier versions?

5. In your opinion, which is the more reliable source, *The Internet Encyclopedia of Philosophy* or *Wikipedia*? Why?

This essay was published in the *Middlebury Campus*, the student weekly newspaper of Middlebury College, on April 11, 2007.

WIKIPHOBIA: THE LATEST IN OPEN SOURCE

NEIL WATERS

It seemed like a no-brainer. Several students in one of my classes included 1
the same erroneous information in final examination essays. Google whisked
me immediately to *Wikipedia*, where I found the source of the erroneous
information in under a minute. To prevent recurrences of the problem, I
wrote a policy for consideration by the history department, in less than two
minutes:

> 1) Students are responsible for the accuracy of information they provide,
> and they cannot point to *Wikipedia* or any similar source that may appear
> in the future to escape the consequences of errors. 2) *Wikipedia* is not an
> acceptable citation, even though it may lead one to a citable source.

I brought up this modest policy proposal, suitably framed in whereases 2
and be it resolved, at the next meeting of the department, and it was passed
within about three minutes, and we moved on to more pressing business. And
that, I thought, was that—a good six minutes' worth of work, culminating in
clear guidelines for the future. Some colleagues felt I was belaboring the obvious, and they were right. The history department always has held students
responsible for accuracy, and does not consider general encyclopedias of the
bound variety to be acceptable for citation either. But *Wikipedia* seemed worth
mentioning by name because it is omnipresent and because its "open-source"
method of compilation makes it a different animal from, say, the *Encyclopaedia
Britannica*.

The *Campus* published an article on the departmental policy, and the 3
rest, as they say, is history. Alerted by the online version of the *Campus* Tim
Johnson of the *Burlington Free Press* interviewed me and a spokesman for
Wikipedia who agreed with the history department's position, and published
an article. Several college newspapers followed suit, and then Noam Cohen
of the *New York Times* interviewed Don Wyatt, chair of the history department, and me, and published the story. Within a day it received more online
"hits" than any other *New York Times* feature. Another interview followed
with the *Asahi Shimbun* in Tokyo, and additional articles appeared in *El Pais*
in Spain, the *Guardian* in England, and then in literally hundreds of newspapers in the U.S. and abroad. Along with other members of the history
department, I found myself giving interviews almost daily—to radio
stations, newspaper reporters, inquisitive high school students, WCAX television news in Burlington, and even to the *NBC Nightly News*, which sent

correspondent Lisa Daniels to Middlebury to interview me and students in my History of Modern Japan class. A stream of phone calls and e-mails from a wide range of people, from *Wikipedia* disciples to besieged librarians who felt free at last to express their *Wikipedia* misgivings, continues to the present. Somehow the modest policy adoption by the history department at Middlebury College hit a nerve.

Why this overwhelming spate of interest? I can think of three reasons 4 immediately: 1) Timing. *Wikipedia* has existed since 2001, but it has expanded exponentially, and reached a critical mass in the last couple of years. With over 1.6 million entries in its English language edition, *Wikipedia* has something to say about almost everything. Its popularity has soared with its comprehensiveness and ease of use, and its ease of use in turn has been enhanced by popularity-driven algorithms; Google lists a *Wikipedia* article in first or second place more often than not. 2) Passion. There is something exciting about the growth and development of an entity to which anyone can contribute.

At its best, *Wikipedia* works wonders. Anonymous editors actually 5 improve entries over time, including new material, editing away mistakes, polishing the writing. Accordingly, some of *Wikipedia*'s defenders approach their task with near-religious zeal. But *Wikipedia* at its worst excites similarly intense passions, because anonymous, non-accountable editors can include, through ignorance or malice, misinformation that may or may not get "fixed." Further, thousands of high school teachers as well as college professors who try mightily to induce a measure of critical thinking in their students' approach to sources for research grow quietly furious because the very ubiquity of *Wikipedia* tempts people to use it in lieu of other, more reliable sources of information. 3) Scandals. The *Wikipedia* entry for John Seigenthaler, Sr., in 2004 contained spurious accusations that he was a suspect in the assassinations of both John F. Kennedy and Robert Kennedy. The entry was unaltered for four months (thereafter authors of new entries, but not editors of existing entries, had to register their names with *Wikipedia*). A *Wikipedia* "policeman" turned out to have bogus credentials. Sinbad was declared dead (he has since risen again). All this keeps the pot boiling.

In the final analysis, *Wikipedia*'s greatest strength is also its greatest 6 weakness. Anonymous, unaccountable, unpaid, often non-expert yet passionate editors built *Wikipedia*, but their anonymity and lack of accountability assures that *Wikipedia* cannot be considered an authoritative source. And yet it is frequently used as if it were, *Wikipedia*'s own disclaimers notwithstanding. College professors and high school teachers alike

> "In the final analysis, *Wikipedia*'s greatest strength is also its greatest weakness."

need to remember that the impressive computer acumen of their students does not automatically translate into impressive levels of critical thought, particularly when it comes to evaluating the reliability of the new tools at their disposal, and of the information those tools provide. The Internet has opened up new highways of information, but we need to know how to spot the potholes.

⊙ AT ISSUE: SOURCES FOR DEVELOPING A DEFINITION ARGUMENT

1. In paragraph 1, Waters, who teaches at Middlebury, lists the two policies he proposed to the history department. Do you think these policies make sense? Are they fair? Explain.

2. Why do you think Waters's "modest policy proposal" (para. 2) attracted so much interest not only on campus but also around the world?

3. Do you think Waters oversimplifies the issue of using *Wikipedia* as a source? What additional points could he have discussed?

4. Where does Waters acknowledge the arguments in favor of using *Wikipedia* as a research source? How does he refute these arguments?

5. Summarize Waters's reasons for concluding that *Wikipedia* is not an acceptable research source. Does he convince you?

6. How do you suppose Waters would respond to Alison Hudson's essay "Stop *Wikipedia* Shaming" (p. 446)?

TEMPLATE FOR WRITING A DEFINITION ARGUMENT

Write a one-paragraph definition argument in which you take a position on the topic, "Is *Wikipedia* a Legitimate Research Source?" Follow the template below, filling in the blanks to create your argument.

> Many people are questioning the use of *Wikipedia* as a legitimate research source. A *legitimate source* can be defined as a source that _____
> _____
> _____.
> According to this definition, *Wikipedia* _____
> _____
> _____. Not everyone agrees, however. Some people say that
> *Wikipedia* _____
> _____
> _____
> _____. Others say that _____
> _____
> _____.
> Although these points make sense, it is clear that _____
> _____
> _____
> _____. In conclusion, *Wikipedia* _____
> _____
> _____
> _____.

⊛ EXERCISE 12.5

Ask two or three of your instructors whether they consider *Wikipedia* a legitimate research source. Then, revise the draft of the paragraph you wrote in the template so that it includes your instructors' opinions.

➲ EXERCISE 12.6

Write a definition argument on the topic, "Is *Wikipedia* a Legitimate Research Source?" Make sure that you define the term *legitimate research source* and that you give examples to develop your definition. (If you like, you may incorporate the material you developed in the template and Exercise 12.5.) You can refer to the At Issue readings on pages 433–463 to find sources to support your position. Be sure to document the sources you use and to include a works-cited page. (See Chapter 10 for information on documenting sources.)

➲ EXERCISE 12.7

Review the four pillars of argument discussed in Chapter 1. Does your essay include all four elements of an effective argument? Add anything that is missing. Then, label the key elements of your essay.

➲ WRITING ASSIGNMENTS: DEFINITION ARGUMENTS

1. On most campuses, instructors have the right to pursue, teach, and discuss ideas without restriction. This principle is called *academic freedom*. Do you think that instructors should have academic freedom, or do you believe that this principle should be restricted? For example, are there any subjects or ideas an instructor should *not* be allowed to discuss? Write a definition argument in which you define *academic freedom* and take a position on this issue. For sources to incorporate into your argument, see Chapter 5.

2. Many colleges require students to perform community service before they graduate. Do you think that college students should have to do community service? Before you begin your argument, find a definition of the term *community service*. Be sure your argument focuses on the definition of this term.

3. Take detailed notes about the food and service in your campus cafeteria. Then, write an argumentative essay in which you rate the cafeteria as *excellent*, *good*, *bad*, or *poor*. Keep in mind that you are presenting *operational definitions* of these terms (see p. 422) and that you will have to explain the factors you examined to form your assessment.

Cause-and-Effect Arguments

Should Vaccination Be Required for All Children?

The debate over mandatory vaccination goes back to 1902, when a Massachusetts man refused to receive a smallpox vaccine, claiming that he had had bad reactions to previous vaccines. His case eventually made its way to the Supreme Court, which ruled that he was required to receive the preventative treatment for the sake of the common good. In the hundred-plus years since that ruling, the number of vaccines available has multiplied, and the debate has grown more and more intense.

Supporters of stricter regulations agree with the Centers for Disease Control, which calls mass vaccination one of the "10 great public health achievements" of the last century, citing the eradication of several deadly diseases, such as polio and smallpox, in the United States. Studies show that in order for a community to achieve this benefit, 95 percent of individuals in the community must be vaccinated. This level of resistance to disease is referred to as "herd immunity." Supporters of mandatory

vaccination fear that if enough parents fail to vaccinate their children, herd immunity will not be achieved and preventable diseases will reemerge and spread, putting the health of the community in danger. (At particular risk are those who cannot receive vaccinations, such as the immune-compromised, infants, and those who are allergic to the components of the vaccine.)

Those who oppose mandatory vaccination often cite religious or philosophical objections. For example, members of the Christian Science church abstain from medical intervention entirely. Other opponents object to the frequency of vaccinations in the prescribed course of immunizations, claiming that what started out as a few essential vaccines in the first part of the twentieth century has grown into an unnecessarily aggressive course of treatment. They believe that not enough research has been done on the effects of these frequent vaccinations on young children, and they want the option

(continued)

(*continued*)

to slow the standard vaccination schedule—or to abstain entirely. Some have been concerned that vaccines were responsible for the rise in autism rates, but this theory has been discredited. Still, opponents of mandatory vaccination claim that not enough is known about how the vaccines work when administered together, that there is too much protection of vaccine manufacturers by the government, and that vaccine regulations infringe upon parents' ability to decide what is best for their children.

Recently, the vaccination debate has been centered in California, where a policy of granting exemptions from vaccination for personal as well as religious reasons has led to a steady increase in the number of unvaccinated children. In response to this situation, which attracted national attention following a measles epidemic among children who visited Disneyland, a state law allowing only medical (not personal or religious) exemptions from vaccination for schoolchildren was passed in 2015.

Clearly, there is much more to learn about the causes of disease outbreaks and about the possible negative effects of vaccinations. Do the benefits of vaccination outweigh the possible risks? Should parents be allowed to refuse vaccinations for their children—and if so, for what reasons? Should individual school districts continue to require that all schoolchildren be vaccinated? And, given these questions, should government have the right to mandate the vaccination of all children? These are some of the questions you should think about as you read the research sources that appear later in this chapter. After reading these sources, you will be asked to write a **cause-and-effect argument** that takes a position on the vaccination debate.

What Is a Cause-and-Effect Argument?

Cause-and-effect arguments attempt to find causes (Why don't more Americans vote?) or identify possible effects (Does movie violence cause societal violence?). A cause-and-effect argument identifies the causes of an event or situation and takes a stand on what actually caused it. Alternatively, a cause-and-effect argument can focus on effects, taking a position on what a likely outcome is, has been, or will be.

Many of the arguments that you read and discuss examine causes and effects. In an essay on one of the topics listed below, you would search for the causes of an event or a situation, examining a number of different possible causes before concluding that a particular cause was the most likely one. You also could consider the possible outcomes or results of a given event or situation and conclude that one possible effect would most likely occur:

- Are designated bicycle lanes really safer for cyclists?

- Is fast food making Americans fat?

- Is human activity responsible for climate change?

- Do mandatory minimum sentences discourage crime?
- Do charter schools improve students' academic performance?
- Does profiling decrease the likelihood of a terrorist attack?

⊙ EXERCISE 13.1

Each of the following visuals takes a stand on an issue related to public health and safety. Look at the visuals, and consider the causes and effects you might discuss if you were writing a cause-and-effect argument, developing the position each one takes. List as many possible causes and effects as you can.

Advertisement promoting gun safety

NoDerog/iStock/Getty Images

Surgeon general's warnings

© James Leynse/Corbis

Public-service ad
cautioning against
driving after drinking
alcohol

Courtesy of the Advertising Council. Used with permission.

⊖ EXERCISE 13.2

Bumper-sticker slogans frequently make cause-and-effect arguments that suggest the consequences of ignoring the message or the positive results of following the slogan's advice. Choose three of the bumper stickers pictured on the facing page, and explain the cause-and-effect argument each slogan makes.

Bumper stickers

© Phil Schermeister/Corbis

Understanding Cause-and-Effect Relationships

Before you can write a cause-and-effect argument, you need to understand the nature of cause-and-effect relationships, some of which can be very complex. For one thing, a single event or situation can have many possible results, and not all of these will be equally significant. In the same way, identifying causes can be particularly challenging because an event or situation can have more than one cause. For example, many factors might explain why more Americans do not vote. (The diagram below illustrates some possible causes.)

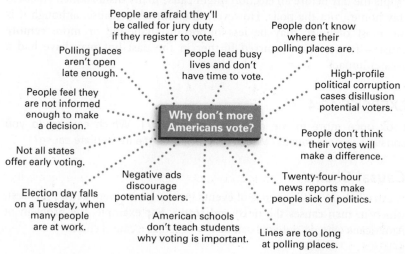

Main and Contributory Causes

In a cause-and-effect argument, your focus is on identifying the cause you believe is the most important and presenting arguments to convince readers *why* it is the most important (and why other causes are not as important).

The most important cause is the **main cause**; the less important causes are **contributory causes**. Typically, you will present the main cause as your key argument in support of your thesis, and you will identify the contributory causes elsewhere in your argument. (You may also identify factors that are *not* causes and explain why they are not.)

Identifying the main cause is not always easy; the most important cause may not always be the most obvious one. However, you need to figure out which cause is most important so you can structure and support your essay with this emphasis in mind.

⊘ EXERCISE 13.3

Look at the diagram on page 471. Which causes do you see as the most and least important? Why? Do you think that any of the factors presented in the diagram are not really causes? Can you suggest any additional causes? If you were writing a cause-and-effect argument taking a position on the topic of why many Americans do not vote, which cause would you focus on? What kind of evidence would you use to support your argument?

Immediate and Remote Causes

As mentioned earlier, identifying the main cause of a particular effect can be difficult because the most important cause is not necessarily the most obvious one. Usually, the most obvious cause is the **immediate cause**—the one that occurs right before an event. For example, a political scandal that erupts the day before an election might cause many disillusioned voters to stay home from the polls. However, this immediate cause, although it is the most obvious, may be less important than one or more **remote causes**—factors that occurred further in the past but may have had a greater impact.

⊘ EXERCISE 13.4

Look once more at the diagram on page 471. Which causes do you consider remote causes? Which one might be the immediate cause?

Causal Chains

A **causal chain** is a sequence of events in which one event causes the next, which in turn causes the next, and so on. For example, the problem of Americans who do not vote can be presented as a causal chain.

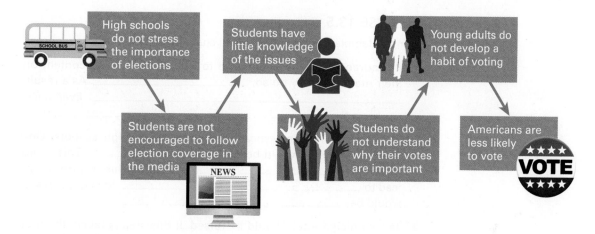

When you write a cause-and-effect argument, you can organize your essay as a causal chain, as the following outline illustrates.

Thesis statement: Because they do not encourage students to see voting as a civic duty, U.S. high schools are at least partly to blame for the low turnout in many elections.

- High schools do not stress the importance of elections.
- As a result, students do not follow election coverage in the media.
- Because they do not follow election coverage, students have little knowledge of the issues.
- With little knowledge of the issues, students do not understand that it is important to vote.
- Because they do not see voting as important, young adults do not develop a habit of regular voting.
- As a result, American adults are less likely to vote.

KEY WORDS FOR CAUSE-AND-EFFECT ARGUMENTS

When you write cause-and-effect arguments, choose verbs that indicate causal connections:

bring about	create	lead to	encourage
influence	contribute to	originate in	cause

Be sure to use transitional words and phrases such as *consequently* and *as a result* to help readers follow your argument. You should also try to repeat words like *cause*, *effect*, *outcome*, and *result* to help identify individual causes and effects.

⊘ **EXERCISE 13.5**

Fill in the templates to create a causal chain for each of these sequences:

1. Restaurants should be required to list fat and calorie content on their menus. If they do so, _____. As a result, _____. Eventually, _____.

2. Abstinence programs should be instituted in high schools. One immediate result would be _____. This could bring about _____. This in turn might lead to _____. Ideally, the result would be _____.

3. Taxes on cigarettes should be raised. If this step is taken, the first result would be _____. This might encourage _____. In a few years' time, the outcome might be _____.

Post Hoc Reasoning

Post hoc reasoning is the incorrect assumption that because an event precedes another event, it has caused that event. For example, you may notice that few of your friends voted in a recent election, and you may realize that many of your friends had previously decided to become science majors. This does not mean, of course, that their decision to choose careers in science has made them nonvoters. In fact, a scientist can be very interested in electoral politics. As you develop your cause-and-effect argument, be careful not to assume that every event that precedes another event has somehow caused it. (For information on avoiding **post hoc fallacies**, see Chapter 5.)

⊘ **EXERCISE 13.6**

The following excerpt from a humorous essay takes a lighthearted look at the concept of post hoc reasoning. Identify the cause and the effect discussed in each paragraph. Then, list several more plausible causes for each effect.

This essay appeared in the *New York Times* on January 13, 2008.

THE CHICKEN SOUP CHRONICLES

NORA EPHRON

The other day I felt a cold coming on. So I decided to have chicken soup to ward off the cold. Nonetheless I got the cold. This happens all the time: you think you're   1 getting a cold; you have chicken soup; you get the cold anyway. So: is it possible that chicken soup gives you a cold?

> "So: is it possible that chicken soup gives you a cold?"

I will confess a bias: I've never understood the religious fervor that surrounds breast-feeding. There are fanatics out there who believe you should breast-feed your child until he or she is old enough to unbutton your blouse. Their success in conning a huge number of women into believing this is one of the truly grim things about modern life. Anyway, one of the main reasons given for breast-feeding is that breast-fed children are less prone to allergies. But children today are far more allergic than they were when I was growing up, when far fewer women breast-fed their children. I mean, what is it with all these children dropping dead from sniffing a peanut? This is new, friends, it's brand-new new, and don't believe anyone who says otherwise. So: is it possible that breast-feeding causes allergies?

It's much easier to write a screenplay on a computer than on a typewriter. Years ago, when you wrote a screenplay on a typewriter, you had to retype the entire page just to make the smallest change; now, on the computer, you can make large and small changes effortlessly, you can fiddle with dialogue, you can change names and places with a keystroke. And yet movies are nowhere near as good as they used to be. In 1939, when screenwriters were practically still using quill pens, the following movies were among those nominated for best picture: *Gone with the Wind, The Wizard of Oz, Mr. Smith Goes to Washington, Wuthering Heights,* and *Stagecoach,* and that's not even the whole list. So: is it possible that computers are responsible for the decline of movies?

There is way too much hand-washing going on. Someone told me the other day that the act of washing your hands is supposed to last as long as it takes to sing the song "Happy Birthday." I'm not big on hand-washing to begin with; I don't even like to wash fruit, if you must know. But my own prejudices aside, all this washing-of-hands and use of Purell before picking up infants cannot be good. (By the way, I'm not talking about hand-washing in hospitals, I'm talking about everyday, run-of-the-mill hand-washing.) It can't possibly make sense to keep babies so removed from germs that they never develop an immunity to them. Of course, this isn't my original theory—I read it somewhere a few weeks ago, although I can't remember where. The *New York Times*? The *Wall Street Journal*? Who knows? Not me, that's for sure. So: is it possible that reading about hand-washing leads to memory loss?

Structuring a Cause-and-Effect Argument

Generally speaking, a cause-and-effect argument can be structured in the following way:

- **Introduction:** Establishes a context for the argument by explaining the need to examine causes or to consider effects; states the essay's thesis

- **Evidence (first point in support of thesis):** Discusses less important causes or effects

- **Evidence (second point in support of thesis):** Discusses major causes or effects

- **Refutation of opposing arguments:** Considers and rejects other possible causes or effects

- **Conclusion:** Reinforces the argument's main point; includes a strong concluding statement

Other organizational patterns are also possible. For example, you might decide to refute opposing arguments *before* you have discussed arguments in support of your thesis. You might also include a background paragraph (as the student writer whose essay begins below does). Finally, you might decide to organize your essay as a **causal chain** (see pp. 472–473).

The following student essay illustrates one possible structure for a cause-and-effect argument. (Note, for example, that the refutation of opposing arguments precedes the evidence.) The student writer argues that, contrary to popular opinion, texting is not causing damage to the English language but is a creative force with the power to enrich and expand the language.

TEXTING: A BOON, NOT A THREAT, TO LANGUAGE

KRISTINA MIALKI

Certain technological developments of the last two decades have a lot of 1
people worrying about the state of the English language. Emailing, blogging, instant-messaging, tweeting, and texting are introducing new ways of writing and communicating, and the fear is that these technologies will encourage a sloppy, casual form of written English that will eventually replace "proper" English altogether. Texting, in particular, has people concerned because it encourages the use of a specialized, nonstandard form of English. However,

Thesis statement   the effects of this new "textese" are misunderstood. Texting is not destroying the English language; in fact, it is keeping the language alive.

Background   Texting has become extremely popular because sending text mes- 2
sages is instant, mobile, and silent. To make texting more efficient, texters have developed a shorthand—an abbreviated form of English that

uses numbers and symbols in addition to letters. In textese, common phrases such as "see you later" or "talk to you later" become "cul8r" and "ttyl." Feelings and phrases are also expressed with emoticons, such as ":-o" (meaning "alarmed") or ">:-<" (meaning "angry"). Today, texting is the preferred method of communication for millions of people—especially young people, who are the most enthusiastic users of this technology. Not surprisingly, unwarranted fears that texting will destroy the language often focus on this group.

Some people say texting will destroy the English language because it encourages the use of an overly simplified form of written English that does not follow standard rules of spelling, grammar, and punctuation. The implication is that people who text, particularly children and teens, will not learn standard written English. However, there is no evidence that texting is having or will have this effect. In fact, Australian researchers Nenagh Kemp and Catherine Bushnell at the University of Tasmania recently found just the opposite to be true. They demonstrated that students who were good at texting were also strong in reading, writing, and spelling (Rock). If, in fact, young people's language skills are weakening, researchers should look for the real cause for this decline rather than incorrectly blaming texting.

3 Refutation of opposing argument

Despite what its critics charge, texting is a valuable way of communicating that actually encourages more writing and reading. Texters often spend hours each day engaged with language. This is time that would otherwise probably be spent on the phone, not reading or writing. Textese may not be standard written English, but it is a rich and inventive form of communication, a creative modification of English for a particular purpose. For this reason, standard English is not in danger of being destroyed or replaced by textese. Just as most young people know not to talk to their teachers the way they talk to their friends, they know not to write essays the way they write text messages. Texting simply broadens young people's exposure to the written word.

4 Evidence: First point in support of thesis

Another reason texting is valuable is that it encourages creative use of language. These messages are typically quick and brief, so the need for new and clever abbreviations is constant. Texters are continually playing with words and coming up with new ways of expressing themselves. Texting does not, as some fear, encourage sloppy, thoughtless, or careless writing. On the contrary, it rewards ingenuity and precision. One ongoing study by Canadian researchers aims to prove this point. They have already been able

5 Evidence: Second point in support of thesis

to demonstrate that texters are "creative and efficient at communicating" and use "novel forms of communications" (Shaw). Nenagh Kemp has also observed how texting encourages word play. Kemp maintains that texting shows "language is fluid and flourishing, rather than in a sad state of decline" (Rock). In other words, researchers recognize that texting is not damaging the English language but actually enriching it and keeping it alive.

According to *Business Insider*, eighteen- to twenty-four-year-olds now send 2,022 texts per month and receive 1,831 texts (Cocotas). That averages out to around 67 texts per day. The exceptional popularity of texting and its fast growth over the last fifteen years explain why it is attracting attention. It is not, however, the threat that some believe it to be. It is neither destroying the language nor deadening people's thoughts and feelings. It is a lively, original, and creative way for people to play with words and stay connected. 6

Concluding statement

Works Cited

Cocotas, Alex. "Chart of the Day: Kids Send a Mind Boggling Number of Texts Every Month." *Business Insider*, 22 Mar. 2013, www.businessinsider.com/chart-of-the-day-number-of-texts-sent-2013-3.

Rock, Margaret. "Texting May Improve Literacy." *Mobiledia*, Mashable, 12 Sept. 2011, mashable.com/2011/09/12/texting-improves-literacy/#sCYnNT6VB8qL.

Shaw, Gillian. "Researchers Study Text Messages as Language Form." *Vancouver Sun*, 18 Jan. 2012, www.vancouversun.com/life/researchers+study+text+messages+language+form/6010501/story.html.

GRAMMAR IN CONTEXT

Avoiding "The Reason Is Because"

When you write a **cause-and-effect argument**, you connect causes to effects. In the process, you might be tempted to use the ungrammatical phrase *the reason is because*. However, the word *because* means "for the reason that"; therefore, it is redundant to say "the reason is because" (which actually means "the reason is for the reason that"). Instead, use the grammatical phrase "the reason is *that*."

INCORRECT Another <u>reason</u> texting is so valuable <u>is because</u> it encourages creative use of language.

CORRECT Another <u>reason</u> texting is so valuable <u>is that</u> it encourages creative use of language.

⊙ EXERCISE 13.7

The following essay, "Should the World of Toys Be Gender-Free?" by Peggy Orenstein, is a cause-and-effect argument. Read the essay carefully, and then answer the questions that follow it, consulting the outline on pages 475–476 if necessary.

This opinion column is from the December 29, 2011, *New York Times*.

SHOULD THE WORLD OF TOYS BE GENDER-FREE?

PEGGY ORENSTEIN

Now that the wrapping paper and the infernal clamshell packaging have been 1 relegated to the curb and the paying off of holiday bills has begun, the toy industry is gearing up—for Christmas 2012. And its early offerings have ignited a new debate over nature, nurture, toys, and sex.

Hamleys, which is London's 251-year-old version of F.A.O. Schwarz, 2 recently dismantled its pink "girls" and blue "boys" sections in favor of a gender-neutral store with red-and-white signage. Rather than floors dedicated to Barbie dolls and action figures, merchandise is now organized by types (Soft Toys) and interests (Outdoor).

That free-to-be gesture was offset by Lego, whose Friends collection, 3 aimed at girls, will hit stores this month with the goal of becoming a holiday must-have by the fall. Set in fictive Heartlake City (and supported by a $40 million marketing campaign), the line features new, pastel-colored blocks that allow a budding Kardashian, among other things, to build herself a cafe or a beauty salon. Its tasty-sounding "ladyfig" characters are also taller and curvier than the typical Legoland denizen.

So who has it right? Should gen- 4 der be systematically expunged from playthings? Or is Lego merely being realistic, earnestly meeting girls half-way in an attempt to stoke their interest in engineering?

> "Should gender be systematically expunged from playthings?"

Among the "10 characteristics for Lego" described in 1963 by a son of the 5 founder was that it was "for girls and for boys," as *Bloomberg Businessweek* reported. But the new Friends collection, Lego says, was based on months of anthropological research revealing that—gasp!—the sexes play differently.

While as toddlers they interact similarly with the company's Duplo blocks, 6 by preschool girls prefer playthings that are pretty, exude "harmony," and allow them to tell a story. They may enjoy building, but they favor role play.

So it's bye-bye Bionicles, hello princesses. In order to be gender-fair, today's executives insist, they have to be gender-specific.

As any developmental psychologist will tell you, those observations are, to 7 a degree, correct. Toy choice among young children is the Big Kahuna of sex differences, one of the largest across the life span. It transcends not only culture but species: in two separate studies of primates, in 2002 and 2008, researchers found that males gravitated toward stereotypically masculine toys (like cars and balls) while females went ape for dolls. Both sexes, incidentally, appreciated stuffed animals and books.

Human boys and girls not only tend to play differently from one 8 another—with girls typically clustering in pairs or trios, chatting together more than boys, and playing more cooperatively—but, when given a choice, usually prefer hanging with their own kind.

Score one for Lego, right? Not so fast. Preschoolers may be the self- 9 appointed chiefs of the gender police, eager to enforce and embrace the most rigid views. Yet, according to Lise Eliot, a neuroscientist and the author of *Pink Brain, Blue Brain*, that's also the age when their brains are most malleable, most open to influence on the abilities and roles that traditionally go with their sex.

Every experience, every interaction, every activity—when they laugh, cry, 10 learn, play—strengthens some neural circuits at the expense of others, and the younger the child the greater the effect. Consider: boys from more egalitarian homes are more nurturing toward babies. Meanwhile, in a study of more than 5,000 3-year-olds, girls with older brothers had stronger spatial skills than both girls and boys with older sisters.

At issue, then, is not nature or nurture but how nurture becomes 11 nature: the environment in which children play and grow can encourage a range of aptitudes or foreclose them. So blithely indulging—let alone exploiting—stereotypically gendered play patterns may have a more negative long-term impact on kids' potential than parents imagine. And promoting, without forcing, cross-sex friendships as well as a breadth of play styles may be more beneficial. There is even evidence that children who have opposite-sex friendships during their early years have healthier romantic relationships as teenagers.

Traditionally, toys were intended to communicate parental values and 12 expectations, to train children for their future adult roles. Today's boys and girls will eventually be one another's professional peers, employers, employees, romantic partners, co-parents. How can they develop skills for such collaborations from toys that increasingly emphasize, reinforce, or even create, gender differences? What do girls learn about who they should be from Lego kits with beauty parlors or the flood of "girl friendly" science kits that run the gamut from "beauty spa lab" to "perfume factory"?

The rebellion against such gender apartheid may have begun. Consider 13 the latest cute-kid video to go viral on YouTube: "Riley on Marketing" shows a little girl in front of a wall of pink packaging, asking, "Why do all the girls have to buy pink stuff and all the boys have to buy different-color stuff?" It has been viewed more than 2.4 million times.

Perhaps, then, Hamleys is on to something, though it will doubtless meet 14 with resistance—even rejection—from both its pint-size customers and multi-national vendors. As for me, I'm trying to track down a poster of a 1981 ad for a Lego "universal" building set to give to my daughter. In it, a freckle-faced girl with copper-colored braids, baggy jeans, a T-shirt, and sneakers proudly holds out a jumbly, multi-hued Lego creation. Beneath it, a tag line reads, "What it is is beautiful."

Identifying the Elements of a Cause-and-Effect Argument

1. Where does Orenstein answer the question her title asks? How would you answer this question?

2. Orenstein's discussion of toys is based on the assumption that the world would be a better place if children were raised in a gender-neutral environment, but she does not offer any evidence to support this implied idea. Should she have? Is she **begging the question**?

3. In paragraph 7, Orenstein reports on two studies of primates. What conclusion does this evidence support? What conclusion does Lise Eliot's research (para. 9) support?

4. How do you react to Orenstein's use of the term *gender apartheid* (13)? What does this term mean? What connotations does it have? Given these connotations, do you think her use of this term is appropriate? Why or why not?

5. According to Orenstein, what effects do stereotyped toys have on children? Does she support her claims?

6. Orenstein's thesis seems to leave no room for compromise. Given the possibility that some of her readers might disagree with her, should she have softened her position? What compromise position might she have proposed?

7. This essay traces a causal chain. The first link in this chain is the "anthropological research revealing that . . . the sexes play differently" (5). Complete the causal chain by filling in the template below.

Anthropological research ─────────────────────────⟶

────────────────────────────────────⟶

────────────────────────────────────⟶

────────────────────────────────────⟶

Should Vaccination Be Required for All Children?

AP Photo/Damian Dovarganes

Reread the At Issue box on pages 467–468. Then, read the sources on the pages that follow.

As you read each of these sources, you will be asked to respond to a series of questions and complete some simple activities. This work will help you to understand the content and structure of the material you read. When you are finished, you will be prepared to write a **cause-and-effect argument** in which you take a position on the topic, "Should Vaccination Be Required for All Children?"

SOURCES

 Clyde Haberman, "A Discredited Vaccine Study's Continuing Impact on Public Health," p. 483

 Janet D. Stemwedel, "Saying No to Vaccines," p. 486

 Mahesh Vidula, "Individual Rights vs. Public Health: The Vaccination Debate," p. 491

 Ben Carson, "Vaccinations Are for the Good of the Nation," p. 502

 Russell Saunders, "Pediatrician: Vaccinate Your Kids—or Get Out of My Office," p. 504

 Jeffrey Singer, "Vaccination and Free Will," p. 507

 Jenny McCarthy, "The Gray Area on Vaccines," p. 510

 "Facts about the Measles" (graphics), p. 512

This story first appeared in the *New York Times* on February 1, 2015.

A DISCREDITED VACCINE STUDY'S CONTINUING IMPACT ON PUBLIC HEALTH

CLYDE HABERMAN

In the churning over the refusal of some parents to immunize their children against certain diseases, a venerable Latin phrase may prove useful: Post hoc, ergo propter hoc. It means, "After this, therefore because of this." In plainer language: Event B follows Event A, so B must be the direct result of A. It is a classic fallacy in logic.

It is also a trap into which many Americans have fallen. That is the consensus among health professionals trying to contain recent spurts of infectious diseases that they had believed were forever in the country's rearview mirror. They worry that too many people are not getting their children vaccinated, out of a conviction that inoculations are risky.

Some parents feel certain that vaccines can lead to autism, if only because there have been instances when a child got a shot and then became autistic. Post hoc, ergo propter hoc. Making that connection between the two events, most health experts say, is as fallacious in the world of medicine as it is in the field of logic.

An outbreak of measles several weeks ago at Disneyland in Southern California focused minds and deepened concerns. It was as if the amusement park had become the tragic kingdom. Dozens of measles cases have spread across California. Arizona and other nearby states reported their own eruptions of this nasty illness, which officialdom had pronounced essentially eradicated in this country as recently as 2000.

But it is back. In 2014, there were 644 cases in 27 states, according to the Centers for Disease Control and Prevention. Should the pace set in January continue, the numbers could go

> "If the past is a guide, one or two of every 1,000 infected people will not survive."

still higher in 2015. While no one is known to have died in the new outbreaks, the lethal possibilities cannot be shrugged off. If the past is a guide, one or two of every 1,000 infected people will not survive.

To explore how matters reached this pass, *Retro Report*, a series of video documentaries studying major news stories of the past and their consequences, offers this special episode. It turns on a seminal moment in anti-vaccination resistance. This was an announcement in 1998 by a British doctor who said he had found a relationship between the M.M.R. vaccine—measles, mumps, rubella—and the onset of autism.

Typically, the M.M.R. shot is given to infants at about 12 months and again at age 5 or 6. This doctor, Andrew Wakefield, wrote that his study of 12 children showed that the three vaccines taken together could alter immune systems, causing intestinal woes that then reach, and damage, the brain. In fairly short order, his findings were widely rejected as—not to put too fine a point on it—bunk. Dozens of epidemiological studies found no merit to his work, which was based on a tiny sample. The *British Medical Journal* went so far as to call his research "fraudulent." The British journal *Lancet*, which originally published Dr. Wakefield's paper, retracted it. The British medical authorities stripped him of his license.

Nonetheless, despite his being held in disgrace, the vaccine-autism link has continued to be accepted on faith by some. Among the more prominently outspoken is Jenny McCarthy, a former television host and Playboy Playmate, who has linked her son's autism to his vaccination: He got the shot, and then he was not O.K. Post hoc, etc.

Steadily, as time passed, clusters of resistance to inoculation bubbled up. While the nationwide rate of vaccination against childhood diseases has stayed at 90 percent or higher, the percentage in some parts of the country has fallen well below that mark. Often enough, these are places whose residents tend to be well off and well educated, with parents seeking exemptions from vaccinations for religious or other personal reasons.

At the heart of the matter is a concept known as herd immunity. It means that the overall national rate of vaccination is not the only significant gauge. The rate in each community must also be kept high to ensure that pretty much everyone will be protected against sudden disease, including those who have not been immunized. A solid display of herd immunity reduces the likelihood in a given city or town that an infected person will even brush up against, let alone endanger, someone who could be vulnerable, like a 9-year-old whose parents rejected inoculations, or a baby too young for the M.M.R. shot. Health professionals say that a vaccination rate of about 95 percent is needed to effectively protect a community. Fall much below that level and trouble can begin.

Mass vaccinations have been described by the C.D.C. as among the "10 great public health achievements" of the 20th century, one that had prevented tens of thousands of deaths in the United States. Yet diseases once presumed to have been kept reasonably in check are bouncing back. Whooping cough is one example. Measles draws especially close attention because it is highly infectious. Someone who has it can sneeze in a room, and the virus will linger in the air for two hours. Any unvaccinated person who enters that room risks becoming infected and, of course, can then spread it further. Disneyland proved a case in point. The measles outbreak there showed that it is indeed a small world, after all.

What motivates vaccine-averse parents? One factor may be the very success of the vaccines. Several generations of Americans lack their parents' and grandparents' visceral fear of polio, for example. For those people, "you might as well be protecting against aliens—these are things they've never seen," said Seth Mnookin, who teaches science writing at the Massachusetts Institute of

Technology and is the author of *The Panic Virus*, a 2011 book on vaccinations and their opponents.

Mr. Mnookin, interviewed by *Retro Report*, said skepticism about inocu- 13
lations is "one of those issues that seem to grab people across the political spectrum." It goes arm in arm with a pervasive mistrust of many national institutions: the government that says vaccinations are essential, news organizations that echo the point, pharmaceutical companies that make money on vaccines, scientists who have hardly been shown to be error-free.

Then, too, Mr. Mnookin said, scientists don't always do themselves favors 14
in their choice of language. They tend to shun absolutes, and lean more toward constructions on the order of: There is no vaccine-autism link "to the best of our knowledge" or "as far as we know." Those sorts of qualifiers leave room for doubters to question how much the lab guys do, in fact, know.

Thus far, the Disneyland measles outbreak has failed to deter the more 15
fervent anti-vaccine skeptics. "Hype." That is how the flurry of concern in California and elsewhere was described by Barbara Loe Fisher, president of the National Vaccine Information Center, an organization that takes a dim view of vaccinations. The hype, Ms. Fisher said in a Jan. 28 post on her group's website, "has more to do with covering up vaccine failures and propping up the dissolving myth of vaccine acquired herd immunity than it does about protecting the public health." Clearly, she remained untroubled that most health professionals regard her views as belonging somewhere in Fantasyland.

⤵ AT ISSUE: SOURCES FOR DEVELOPING A CAUSE-AND-EFFECT ARGUMENT

1. What is the discredited vaccine study mentioned in the title? In general terms, what "impact on public health" has this study had?

2. Why does Haberman begin his essay by discussing the **post hoc fallacy**? Define this fallacy. How does it apply to the vaccination debate?

3. In paragraph 9, Haberman cites the steady rise of "resistance to inoculation." What has caused this rise? What has been the result of this resistance?

4. What is *herd immunity*? Why is it of central importance in the vaccination debate?

5. In paragraph 12, Haberman asks, "What motivates vaccine-averse parents?" How does he answer this question? Do you agree with him? Explain.

6. Why does Haberman quote Barbara Loe Fisher in his conclusion? Is he creating a **straw man** here? Why or why not?

Stemwedel's argument appeared in *Scientific American* in June 2013.

SAYING NO TO VACCINES

JANET D. STEMWEDEL

At my last visit to urgent care with one of my kids, the doctor who saw us mentioned that there is currently an epidemic of pertussis (whooping cough) in California, one that presents serious danger for the very young children (among others) hanging out in the waiting area. We double-checked that both my kids are current on their pertussis vaccinations (they are). I checked that I was current on my own pertussis vaccination back in December when I got my flu shot. 1

Sharing a world with vulnerable little kids, it's just the responsible thing to do. 2

You're already on the Internet reading about science and health, so it will probably come as no surprise to you that California's pertussis epidemic is a result of the downturn in vaccination in recent years, nor that this downturn has been driven in large part by parents worried that childhood vaccinations might lead to their kids getting autism, or asthma, or some other chronic disease. Never mind that study after study has failed to uncover evidence of such a link; these parents are weighing the risks and benefits (at least as they understand them) of vaccinating or opting out and trying to make the best decision they can for their children. 3

The problem is that the other children with which their children are sharing a world get ignored in the calculation. 4

Of course, parents are accountable to the kids they are raising. They have a duty to do what is best for them, as well as they can determine what that is. They probably also have a duty to put some effort into making a sensible determination of what's best for their kids (which may involve seeking out expert advice, and evaluating who has the expertise to be offering trustworthy advice). 5

But parents and kids are also part of a community, and arguably they are accountable to other members of that community. I'd argue that members of a community may have an obligation to share relevant information with each other—and, to avoid spreading misinformation, not to represent themselves as experts when they are not. Moreover, **when parents make choices with the potential to impact not only themselves and their kids but also other members of the community, they have a duty to do what is necessary to minimize bad impacts on others.** Among other things, this might mean keeping your unvaccinated-by-choice kids isolated from kids who haven't been vaccinated because of their age, because of compromised immune function, or because they are allergic to a vaccine ingredient. **If you're not willing to do your part for herd immunity, you need to take responsibility for staying out of the herd.** 6

Otherwise, you are a free-rider on the sacrifices of the other members of the community, and you are breaking trust with them. 7

I know from experience that this claim upsets non-vaccinating parents a lot. They imagine that I am declaring them bad people, guilty of making a conscious choice to hurt others. I am not. However, I do think they are making a choice that 8 has the potential to cause great harm to others. If I didn't think that pointing out the potential consequences might be valuable to these non-vaccinating parents, at least in helping them understand more fully what they're choosing, I wouldn't bother.

So here, let's take a careful look at my claim that vaccination refuseniks 9 are free-riders.

First, what's a free-rider? 10

In the simplest terms, a free-rider is someone who accepts a benefit with- 11 out paying for it. The free-rider is able to partake of this benefit because others have assumed the costs necessary to bring it about. But if *no one* was willing to assume those costs (or indeed, in some cases, if there is not a critical mass of people assuming those costs), then that benefit would not be available, either.

Thus, when I claim that people who opt out of vaccination are free-riders 12 on society, what I'm saying is that they are receiving benefits for which they haven't paid their fair share—and that they receive these benefits only because other members of society have assumed the costs by being vaccinated.

Before we go any further, let's acknowledge that people who choose to 13 vaccinate and those who do not probably have very different understandings of the risks and benefits, and especially of their magnitudes and likelihoods. Ideally, we'd be starting this discussion about the ethics of opting out of vac- cination with some agreement about what the likely outcomes are, what the unlikely outcomes are, what the unfortunate-but-tolerable outcomes are, and what the to-be-avoided-at-all-costs outcomes are.

That's not likely to happen. People don't even accept the same facts 14 (regardless of scientific consensus), let alone the same weightings of them in decision making.

But ethical decision making is supposed to help us get along even in a world 15 where people have different values and interests than our own. So, plausibly, we can talk about whether certain kinds of choices fit the pattern of free-riding even if we can't come to agreement on probabilities and a hierarchy of really bad outcomes.

So, let's say all the folks in my community are vaccinated against measles 16 except me. Within this community (assuming I'm not wandering off to exotic and unvaccinated lands, and that people from exotic and unvaccinated lands don't come wandering through), my chances of getting measles are extremely low. Indeed, they are as low as they are *because* everyone else in the commu- nity has been vaccinated against measles—none of my neighbors can serve as a host where the virus can hang out and then get transmitted to me. (By the way, the NIH has a nifty Disease Transmission Simulator that you can play around with to get a feel for how infectious diseases and populations whose members have differing levels of immunity interact.)

I get a benefit (freedom from measles) that I didn't pay for. The other 17 folks in my community who got the vaccine paid for it.

In fact, it usually doesn't require that *everyone else* in the community be vac- 18 cinated against measles for me to be reasonably safe from it. Owing to "herd immunity," measles is unlikely to run through the community if the people with- out immunity are relatively few and well interspersed with the vaccinated people. This is a good thing, since babies in the U.S. don't get their first vaccination against measles until 12 months, and some people are unable to get vaccinated even if they're willing to bear the cost (e.g., because they have compromised immune systems or are allergic to an ingredient of the vaccine). And, in other cases, people may get vaccinated but the vaccines might not be fully effective—if exposed, they might still get the disease. Herd immunity tends to protect these folks from the disease—at least as long as enough of the herd is vaccinated.

19 If too few members of the herd are vaccinated, even some of those who have borne the costs of being vaccinated (because even very good vaccines can't deliver 100 percent protection to 100 percent of the people who get them), or who would bear those costs were they able (owing to their age or health or access to medical care), may miss out on the benefit. Too many free-riders can spoil things even for those who are paying their fair share.

20 A standard reply from non-vaccinating parents is that their unvaccinated kids are not free-riders on the vaccinated mass of society because they actually get diseases like chicken pox, pertussis, and measles (and are not counting on avoiding the other diseases against which people are routinely vaccinated). In other words, they argue, they didn't pay the cost, but they didn't get the benefit, either.

21 Does this argument work?

22 I'm not convinced that it does. First off, even though unvaccinated kids may get a number of diseases that their vaccinated neighbors do not, it is still unlikely that they will catch *everything* against which we routinely vaccinate. By opting out of vaccination but living in the midst of a herd that is mostly vaccinated, non-vaccinating parents significantly reduce the chances of their kids getting many diseases compared to what the chances would be if they lived in a completely unvaccinated herd. That statistical reduction in disease is a benefit, and the people who got vaccinated are the ones paying for it.

23 Now, one might reply that unvaccinated kids are actually incurring harm from their vaccinated neighbors, for example if they contract measles from a recently vaccinated kid shedding the live virus from the vaccine. However, the measles virus in the MMR vaccine is an attenuated virus—which is to say, it's quite likely that unvaccinated kids contacting measles from vaccinated kids will have a milder bout of measles than they might have if they had been exposed to a full-strength measles virus out in the wild. A milder case of measles is a benefit, at least when the alternative is a severe case of measles. Again, it's a benefit that is available because other people bore the cost of being vaccinated.

24 Indeed, even if they were to catch *every single disease against which we vaccinate*, unvaccinated kids would still reap further benefits by living in a society with a high vaccination rate. The fact that most members of society are vaccinated means

> "Those who opt out of vaccinating are taking that benefit for free."

that there is much less chance that epidemic diseases will shut down schools, industries, or government offices, much more chance that hospitals and medical offices will not be completely overwhelmed when outbreaks happen, much more chance that economic productivity will not be crippled and that people will be able to work and pay the taxes that support all manner of public services we take for granted. The people who vaccinate are assuming the costs that bring us a largely epidemic-free way of life. Those who opt out of vaccinating are taking that benefit for free.

I understand that the decision not to vaccinate is often driven by concerns 25 about what costs those who receive the vaccines might bear, and whether those costs might be worse than the benefits secured by vaccination. Set aside for the moment the issue of whether these concerns are well grounded in fact. Instead, let's look at the parallel we might draw: If I vaccinate my kids, no matter what your views about the etiology of autism and asthma, you are not going to claim that my kids getting their shots raise your kids' odds of getting autism or asthma. But if you don't vaccinate your kids, even if I vaccinate mine, your decision does raise my kids' chance of catching preventable infectious diseases. My decision to vaccinate doesn't hurt you (and probably helps you in the ways discussed above). Your decision not to vaccinate could well hurt me.

The asymmetry of these choices is pretty unavoidable. 26

Here, it's possible that a non-vaccinating parent might reply by saying 27 that it ought to be possible for her to prioritize protecting her kids from whatever harms vaccination might bring to them without being accused of violating a social contract.

The herd immunity thing works for us because of an implicit social con- 28 tract of sorts: those who are medically able to be vaccinated get vaccinated. Obviously, this is a social contract that views the potential harms of the diseases as more significant than the potential harms of vaccination. I would argue that under such a social contract, we as a society have an obligation to take care of those who end up paying a higher cost to achieve the shared benefit.

But if a significant number of people disagree, and think the potential 29 harms of vaccination outweigh the potential harms of the diseases, shouldn't they be able to opt out of this social contract?

The only way to do this without being a free-rider is to opt out of the herd 30 altogether—or to ensure that your actions do not bring additional costs to the folks who are abiding by the social contract. If you're planning on getting those diseases naturally, this would mean taking responsibility for keeping the germs contained and away from the herd (which, after all, contains members who are vulnerable owing to age, medical reasons they could not be vaccinated, or the chance of less than complete immunity from the vaccines). No work, no school, no supermarkets, no playgrounds, no municipal swimming pools, no doctor's office waiting rooms, *nothing* while you might be able to transmit the germs. The whole time you're able to transmit the germs, you need to isolate yourself from the members of society whose default assumption is vaccination. Otherwise, you endanger members of the herd who bore the costs of achieving herd immunity while reaping benefits (of generally disease-free work, school, supermarkets, playgrounds, municipal swimming pools, doctor's office waiting rooms, and so forth, for which you opted out of paying your fair share).

Since you'll generally be able to transmit these diseases before the first 31 symptoms appear—even before you know for sure that you're infected—you will not be able to take regular contact with the vaccinators for granted.

And if you're traveling to someplace where the diseases whose vaccines 32
you're opting out of are endemic, you have a duty not to bring the germs
back with you to the herd of vaccinators. Does this mean quarantining yourself for some minimum number of days before your return? It probably
does. Would this be a terrible inconvenience for you? Probably so, but the
10-month-old who catches the measles you bring back might also be terribly
inconvenienced. Or worse.

Here, I don't think I'm alone in judging the harm of a vaccine refusenik 33
giving an infant pertussis as worse than the harm in making a vaccine refusenik feel bad about violating a social contract.

An alternative, one which would admittedly require some serious logisti- 34
cal work, might be to join a geographically isolated herd of other people opting out of vaccination, and to commit to staying isolated from the vaccinated
herd. Indeed, if the unvaccinated herd showed a lower incidence of asthma
and autism after a few generations, perhaps the choices of the members of the
non-vaccinating herd would be vindicated.

In the meantime, however, opting out of vaccines but sharing a society with 35
those who get vaccinated is taking advantage of benefits that others have paid for
and even threatening those benefits. Like it or not, that makes you a free-rider.

⟳ ISSUE: SOURCES FOR DEVELOPING A CAUSE-AND-EFFECT ARGUMENT

1. Stemwedel's argument in paragraph 13 includes the word *ethics*. Is she appealing strictly to *ethos* in this essay, or does she also appeal to *logos* and *pathos*? For example, what appeal is she using in the first two paragraphs by presenting herself as a responsible parent?

2. Throughout this essay—for example, in paragraph 7 and in the conclusion—Stemwedel uses the term *free-rider*. According to Stermwedel, what does this term mean? What are the connotations of this term? How does she apply this term to the vaccination debate?

3. In paragraph 6, Stemwedel says, "If you're not willing to do your part for herd immunity, you need to take responsibility for staying out of the herd." Does offering parents this option undercut her strong posi-tion in favor of universal vaccination? Could she be accused of com-mitting the **either/or fallacy**? Explain.

4. Why does Stemwedel call herd immunity "an implicit social contract of sorts" (para. 28)?

5. According to Stemwedel, how do "non-vaccinating parents" (20) defend themselves against the charge of being free-riders? How does Stemwedel refute their arguments?

Vidula's argument was posted online at MIT.edu in a collection of writing about medicine and technology.

INDIVIDUAL RIGHTS VS. PUBLIC HEALTH: THE VACCINATION DEBATE

MAHESH VIDULA

A pediatrician enters Examination Room B, ready for a routine check-up with a 1 two-month-old infant. He greets the mother, and begins to discuss the next step in infant care: receiving the required vaccinations. As he starts to ask the mother to schedule an appointment with the receptionist, she interrupts, "Sorry, doctor. My child will not be immunized."

The Centers for Disease Control (CDC) defines vaccination as the injec- 2 tion of weak disease-causing agents that help the body develop immunity against specific infectious diseases (CDC, How Vaccines Prevent Disease 2009). Scientists hope that "through vaccination, children develop immunity without suffering from the actual diseases that vaccines prevent" (CDC, How Vaccines Prevent Disease 2009). States often require that children receive vaccinations against particularly dangerous diseases, such as polio, varicella (chicken pox), diphtheria/tetanus/pertussis (DTP), Haemophilus influenza B (Hib), and measles/mumps/rubella (MMR) (Goodman 2007: 266). In the U.S., unvaccinated children may suffer severe consequences, such as being prevented from attending schools, camps, sports, and other organized group activities (Park 2008). While proponents of mandatory vaccinations believe that these procedures are absolutely necessary for maintaining public health, opponents argue that compulsory immunizations infringe on the rights of individuals to control their own bodies and the bodies of their minor children.

The controversy surrounding compulsory vaccinations in the United 3 States is not new. In 1809, Massachusetts passed a law that "granted city boards of health the authority to require vaccination 'when necessary for public health or safety'" (Mariner 2005: 582). When the state required all residents to receive a smallpox vaccine in 1902, 46-year-old Henning Jacobson declined the vaccine, claiming that he had suffered "bad reactions to earlier vaccines" (Mariner 2005: 582). Due to his refusal of the vaccine, he was fined five dollars by the state. After an unsuccessful challenge to the fine in the Massachusetts State Supreme Judicial Court, he appealed in 1905 to the United States Supreme Court in the famous case, *Jacobson v. Massachusetts* (Mariner 2005: 582). Despite Jacobson's argument that compulsory immunization violated his Fourteenth Amendment right to personal liberty, the Supreme Court ruled against him (Jacobson v. Massachusetts, Oyez Project). According to the 1905 Supreme Court ruling, the state had the right to mandate the smallpox vaccine since "[the] safety and the health of the people of Massachusetts are for that Commonwealth to guard and protect" (*Jacobson v. Massachusetts*, LSU Law Center).

Similar to the Supreme Court decision in *Jacobson v. Massachusetts*, contemporary advocates for mandatory vaccinations contend that immunizations are necessary to maintain public health. For one, vaccinations have effectively curbed the spread of several deadly infectious diseases in the United States and around the world. For instance, before the development of the poliomyelitis vaccine by Jonas Salk in the 1950s, "13,000 to 20,000 cases of paralytic polio were reported each year" (CDC 2007). Poliomyelitis is a highly contagious and dangerous viral infection; children under five are most commonly affected. Since the polio virus affects the nervous system, some children who contract the disease become paralyzed and may even lose breathing ability (WHO: Poliomyelitis). In the early to mid 20th century, some children with polio had to use an iron lung, a machine to pump air into their lungs, to breathe. In the 1930s, these devices often cost as much as a home (National Museum of American History, The Iron Lung). However, by 1964, the widespread use of the polio vaccine essentially eradicated the disease in America (Health and Human Services). As described by science journalist Alan Dove, "The benefit to the United States alone for [the polio vaccine] runs into the trillions of dollars. The social impact has been incalculable. The crutches, wheelchairs, and iron lungs of polio victims have at last been banished from children's and parents' nightmares" (PICO).

Other dangerous infectious diseases virtually eliminated in America by vaccinations include diphtheria and pertussis. Both diphtheria and pertussis can cause severe breathing complications in children (CDC Diphtheria). Over

"Following the distribution of vaccines for these diseases, the number of reported disease events fell dramatically."

206,000 people were reported to have diphtheria in 1921, and there were 150,000–260,000 cases of pertussis per year (CDC 2007). Following the distribution of vaccines for these diseases, the number of reported disease events fell dramatically, and scientists believe that the immunizations directly lowered the incidence of disease (CDC 2007). For instance, recent studies report that there are currently 97.56 percent fewer pertussis cases in the United States, than would be expected without mass immunization, due to compulsory vaccination programs (Health and Human Services). Moreover, as the CDC argues, "[those] same germs exist today, but babies are now protected by vaccines, [and so] we do not see these diseases as often" (CDC, How Vaccines Prevent Disease 2009). For these reasons, supporters of mandatory vaccinations argue that immunizations in the United States have been very effective. After noting the large impact of vaccinations on American public health, philanthropists such as Bill and Melinda Gates have begun funding vaccine research and distribution to improve the quality of health in third world countries (Gates Foundation).

In addition, advocates of compulsory vaccinations believe that through immunization, a person not only avoids contracting the disease himself, but also prevents spreading the illness to others (Why Immunize 2009). According to a study by Salmon et al. from 1985 to 1992 in the United States, the incidence of measles increased by 35 times in children without the vaccination (Omer et al. 2009: 1983). Additional studies showed that unvaccinated children had a higher risk for developing mumps and pertussis as well (Omer et al. 2009: 1983). While aiming to identify the reasons for lower rates of disease in some communities, researchers found that "[school] immunization laws have had a remarkable impact on vaccine-preventable diseases in the United States" (Orenstein and Hinman 1999: S19).

Although proponents believe that vaccines are important in ensuring personal safety, they also support the necessity of immunizations for preserving the health of the community. In an interview with *USA Today*, Dr. Lance Rodewald, Director of the CDC Immunization Services Division, suggested that receiving vaccinations is a social responsibility, since an unvaccinated sick person can infect many more people (Leblanc 2007). As Dr. Rodewald stated, "When you choose not to get a vaccine, you're not just making a choice for yourself, you're making a choice for the person sitting next to you" (Leblanc 2007). Moreover, several studies indicate that disease incidence rises in communities "when there is geographic aggregation of persons refusing vaccination" (Omer et al. 2009: 1983). For example, in a 1987 measles outbreak at a Colorado school, unvaccinated children infected 11 percent of vaccinated students (Feikin et al. 2000: 3148). Supporters also encourage healthy children to receive vaccinations, to protect other children unable to be vaccinated due to health conditions or young age (Omer et al. 2009: 1984). Some children may fail to respond to vaccines due to weak immune systems, and therefore rely on "other parents to keep germs out of circulation by vaccinating their kids" (Szabo 2010). As a result, supporters of compulsory immunizations believe that parents of healthy children have a moral responsibility to have their offspring vaccinated (Szabo 2010).

According to mandatory immunization advocates, vaccines also prevent disease outbreaks for future generations. For example, the CDC argues that if vaccinations ceased, "[diseases] that are almost unknown would stage a comeback [and before] long we would see epidemics of diseases that are nearly under control today" (CDC, Why Immunize 2009). In August 2008, the *New York Times* reported 131 cases of measles from January 2008 to July 2008 in the United States; the majority of infected patients had not received the measles (MMR) vaccination (Harris 2008). Besides gathering data on infectious disease incidence, the CDC has also projected the number of cases of certain diseases expected if vaccinations were discontinued. For instance, the CDC predicted that if people did not receive the MMR vaccination, 2.7 million individuals around the world would die of measles every year (CDC 2007). Moreover, advocates argue that compulsory vaccinations may eradicate diseases for future generations. Drawing from the success of the smallpox vaccine, which eliminated the smallpox virus and made it unnecessary for future generations to receive the vaccine, the CDC contends that other diseases may similarly be eradicated if immunizations continue. The CDC states, "If we keep vaccinating now, parents in the future may be able to trust that diseases like polio and meningitis won't infect, cripple, or kill children" (Why Immunize 2009). Due to the significant global health benefits of immunization, public health officials such as immunologist Anthony Fauci argue that any small risks associated with vaccinations are "acceptable" (*Frontline: The Vaccine War*). In the 2010 public television documentary, *Frontline: The Vaccine War*, Fauci addresses the risks of vaccination:

> What is the risk of injecting something into someone's arm? The risk is that a certain proportion of people will get swelling and a little bit of pain, lasting from an hour to a day. That is a very acceptable risk. A very, very, very small percentage of people will get an allergic reaction. . . . And then there's a subset of a very, very, very, very small percentage of those who actually can get a serious reaction. But if you look at that, the risk of that is so minisculely small as to be completely outweighed by the benefit.

Overall, immunization supporters believe that compulsory vaccinations 9 are justified, since they protect the public health in the present and future, and tend to have acceptable risks.

Although proponents tout the efficacy and need of vaccinations in the 10 United States and other countries, opponents argue against compulsory immunization for a variety of reasons including harmful side effects, individual liberty, and religious freedom. Compared to all the other reasons for avoiding immunization, "the most frequent reason for nonvaccination, stated by 69 percent of the parents, was a concern that the vaccine might cause harm" (Omer et al. 2009: 1985). It is widely known that vaccines have possible side effects, which are published by the CDC. For instance, a reaction to the varicella vaccine can range from a rash to severe infection (CDC 2010). Freed et al. found in 2010 that despite reassurances from the CDC and FDA that vaccines "undergo a rigorous review of laboratory and clinical data to ensure the safety, efficacy, purity, and potency" (FDA 2009), some parents continue to believe that vaccinations have strong potential to hurt their children (Freed et al. 2010: 654). Although no strong scientific evidence exists to support these claims, some people also fear that vaccinations may predispose children to Type 1 diabetes (Levitsky 2004: 1382).

The most prevalent concern among some contemporary American par- 11 ents is whether vaccinations will result in autism (Freed et al. 2010: 657). The fear that vaccinations cause autism in some children gained prominence in 1998 when British researcher Dr. Andrew Wakefield published an article in *The Lancet* that suggested a link between autism and the MMR vaccine (Harrell 2010). Moreover, research groups found that several vaccines contained thimerosal, a mercury compound used to preserve vaccines (Park 2008). Since at high exposures, mercury may "cause neurologic damage, the presence of organic mercury in several common vaccines aroused particular concern" (Levitsky 2004: 1381). For instance, the National Autism Association urged the CDC to remove thimerosal from vaccines, and suggested that it contributed to the rise in autism cases since "at the same time that the incidence of autism was growing, the number of childhood vaccines containing thimerosal was growing" (National Autism Association). Although *The Lancet* later retracted Wakefield's article due to his unethical scientific method, and several later studies showed no link between autism and the MMR vaccine or thimerosal (Harrell 2010), a study by Freed et al. in 2010 reported that "[more than] 1 in 5 [parents], continue to believe that some vaccines cause autism in otherwise healthy children" (2010: 657). In his *Time* article, journalist Karl Taro Greenfield suggests that parents may continue to believe that autism is caused by vaccinations due to their distrust in scientific research and reliance on their emotions (2010). When a prominent anti-vaccination activist was asked about the lack of scientific proof linking vaccinations to autism, she replied, "My science is [my son]. He's at home. That's my science" (Greenfield 2010).

However, some parents opposing vaccinations do have faith in science, but 12 believe that the research is misguided or incomplete. In *Frontline: The Vaccine War*, parents express their frustration towards research groups that claim that autism is not linked to the MMR vaccine or thimerosal. They believe that some psychological transformation occurred in their children after receiving the vaccine, and yearn for a scientific understanding of why their children suffered. As one parent expressed, "My kid got six vaccines in one day, and he regressed. You don't have any science that can show me the regression wasn't triggered by the six vaccines. . . . We need to ask the question as to why the regression took place" (*Frontline: The Vaccine War*). In their view, epidemiological studies do not prove the safety of vaccines. Instead, these parents encourage scientists to investigate the physiological effects of receiving the vaccine load. In the documentary, one parent declared, "You have to do bench science. You have to look at the human body and what occurs in terms of changes in immune function, brain function. You can't just do epidemiology where you're comparing groups of children against each other" (*Frontline: The Vaccine War*). Therefore, before completely dismissing the possibility that vaccines can lead to negative side effects, some parents ask for more thorough scientific studies that analyze other vaccines, ingredients, and other risk factors that may predispose a child to a vaccine reaction (*Frontline: The Vaccine War*).

Parents may also distrust the integrity of a state mandate, which can lead 13 to their opposition to a particular vaccination. Gardasil, a vaccine created by Merck, prevents cervical cancer by targeting the human papillomavirus (HPV) (Savage 2007: 666). In 2007, Republican Governor of Texas Rick Perry mandated that all girls entering sixth grade must be vaccinated with Gardasil (Peterson 2/2/2007). In his plan, uninsured girls between ages nine and eighteen would receive free vaccinations, and Medicaid would cover women between 19 and 21 (Peterson 2/2/2007). However, due to the incensed debate that followed this decision, and the state's overall rejection of this idea, Perry's order was vetoed and revoked on April 25, 2007 (Blumenthal 4/26/07).

A major source of opposition to the mandatory HPV vaccination resulted 14 from the link between the Texas government and Merck, which drew suspicion around the motivation for the executive order. According to internal documents, Merck donated $5,000 to Rick Perry and another $5,000 to eight lawmakers on the same day the chief of staff held a meeting to discuss whether to mandate the HPV vaccine (Peterson 2/21/07). Merck had also previously made a $6,000 donation to the governor's reelection campaign (Peterson 2/2/07). Therefore, the financial connection between the Texas government and Merck gave some Texans the idea that the vaccination mandate was not in the interest of safeguarding women's health, but rather for improving Merck's financial situation.

Furthermore, some people may follow certain religions that oppose vaccination mandates. People seeking religious exemption from vaccinations argue that "the free-exercise clause of the First Amendment mandates state accommodation for members of religious groups who object to the vaccinations on religious grounds" (First Amendment Center). For instance, Christian Scientists prefer spiritual healing to Western medicine, and therefore do not completely support vaccinations (DeLacy Lecture). The founder of Christian Science, Mary Baker Eddy, wrote in 1896, "A calm, Christian state of mind is a better preventive of contagion than a drug, or than any other possible sanative method; and the 'perfect Love' that 'casteth out fear' is a sure defense" (Eddy, "Contagion"). Therefore, rather than relying on medications or vaccinations, Christian Scientists prefer "watching [their thoughts], guarding against influences that would pull [them] down, and daily taking time for silent, sacred moments alone with God" (DeLacy Lecture) while fighting diseases. Since vaccinations are against their religious beliefs, Christian Scientists often file for religious exemptions from compulsory immunizations.

> "Since vaccinations are against their religious beliefs, Christian Scientists often file for religious exemptions from compulsory immunizations."

15

However, this refusal of vaccinations has had negative repercussions for some Christian Scientists. In 1989, 15 Christian Scientists in Boston were infected with measles, after a "worshiper carrying the virus attended Sunday school services at the Christian Science campus" (Smith 2006). In 2006, a Boston Christian Scientist also contracted measles (Smith 2006). In both cases, to control the spread of measles, the Massachusetts Department of Public Health asked the infected Christian Scientists to remain isolated from the public, and to refrain from interacting with uninfected people (Smith 2006). In an interview with the *Boston Globe*, Boston's Chief Medical Officer Dr. Alfred DeMaria commented that Christian Scientists tend to comply with quarantines, since "[they] see it as the other side of the coin for not being vaccinated" (Smith 2006).

16

Additionally, some opponents of compulsory vaccinations cite "herd immunity" as a reason to avoid immunizations. The concept of "herd immunity" is that if many people are vaccinated in a community, those not vaccinated will still enjoy protection since "the disease has little opportunity for

17

an outbreak" (CDC Glossary). With regard to childhood vaccinations, some parents believe that "if everyone else is protected, then so is [their] child so why take even the minute risk of any vaccine side effect" (Calandrillo 2004: 361). Therefore, it is clear that some opponents of mandatory vaccinations believe that they can "take advantage of the benefit created by the participation of others in the vaccination program while refusing to participate and share equitably in the risks and obligations of the program" (Diekema 2009: 92). However, proponents often argue that herd immunity is falling due to the increasing numbers of people failing to receive vaccinations (Calandrillo 2004: 361).

Finally, opponents of compulsory immunizations do not believe it is their 18 social responsibility to protect the public health, and they instead value their individual and family rights. After understanding the possible severe effects of vaccinations on their children, some parents refuse to take the risks associated with immunization. In their view, protecting the lives of their children holds greater importance than maintaining the health of the community. For example, a suburban Chicago mother, who declined vaccinations for her two daughters, asserts:

> I don't care about maintaining herd immunity, or protecting the health of the other sick children in the neighborhood. It's not about them, it's about my children. Who will protect my children if they develop some disability after receiving the vaccinations? . . . The only person who can protect them is me, and I am doing that by making sure they don't get any problems from vaccinations. . . . I can make this choice for my children (Personal interview 3/25/10).

Similarly, other anti-vaccination parents believe that it is unreasonable to 19 expect parents to risk their children's lives for the sake of public health (*Frontline: The Vaccine War*). In *The Vaccine War*, one parent states, "Physicians have to get over the idea that they can tell people what to do and people are going to do it without questioning." The fuel for this belief may be that parents desire to be the decision makers for their children, instead of having the government impose rules. If they succumb to the government's every request, even those that could potentially harm their children's health, some parents believe that they may slowly lose control over their children. As the suburban Chicago mother emphasizes, "What right does the government have over my children? I gave birth to them; no one else did. I have the right to choose what's best for them. . . . Soon, the government may ask me to talk to my kids in a certain way or feed them only some foods. These are my children, and I make the choices" (Personal interview 3/25/10).

The controversy surrounding compulsory vaccinations involves a wide 20 variety of individuals, with different personal beliefs. Proponents of mandatory vaccinations focus on disease statistics, which demonstrate the need of immunizations in maintaining public health. However, opponents argue against these measures since they value their own personal liberty and children's safety over public health, and they strive to protect their offspring by avoiding required vaccinations. From these two different perspectives, one primarily appealing to facts and the other largely to emotions, it is important to recognize the larger issue at hand. The debate regarding mandatory immunizations reflects the underlying conflict of individual rights versus the public good. Proponents of compulsory vaccinations may believe that improving and maintaining public health holds greater importance than preserving a person's individual right to control his body. On the other hand, opponents may fear a growing lack of control over their bodies and the bodies of their minor children. They may reasonably imagine a future society, where people no longer have the right to decide how they wish to treat their bodies. As the compulsory immunization controversy continues, pediatricians should no longer assume parental consensus that children will automatically receive vaccinations.

Works Cited

Blumenthal, Ralph. "Texas Legislators Block Shots for Girls against Cancer Virus." *The New York Times* 26 Apr. 2007. Web. 02 May 2010. <http://www.nytimes.com/2007/04/26/us/26texas.html?ref=health>.

Calandrillo, S. P. "Vanishing Vaccinations: Why Are So Many Americans Opting Out of Vaccinating Their Children?" *University of Michigan Journal of Law Reform* 2004; 37: 353–440.

"CDC National Vaccine Program Office: Glossary." *United States Department of Health and Human Services.* Web. 02 May 2010. <http://www.hhs .gov/nvpo/glossary1.htm>.

"CDC National Vaccine Program Office: The Effectiveness of Immunizations." *United States Department of Health and Human Services.* Web. 02 May 2010. <http://www.hhs.gov/nvpo/concepts/intro6.htm>.

"CDC — Vaccine History — Vaccine Safety." *Centers for Disease Control and Prevention.* 15 Jan. 2010. Web. 02 May 2010. <http://www.cdc .gov/vaccinesafety/Vaccine_Monitoring/history.html>.

DeLacy, Marceil. "Contagion Unmasked." Lecture. *Christian Science.* Web. 02 May 2010. <http://christianscience.com/>.

Diekema, D. S. "Choices Should Have Consequences: Failure to Vaccinate, Harm to Others, and Civil Liability." *Michigan Law Review First Impressions* 2009; 107: 0–94.

"Diphtheria." *Centers for Disease Control and Prevention.* 6 Oct. 2005. Web. 02 May 2010. <http://www.cdc.gov/ncidod/dbmd/diseaseinfo /diptheria_t.htm>.

Dove, Alan. "PICO-History." *Columbia University*. Web. 02 May 2010.
    <http://microbiology.columbia.edu/pico/Chapters/History.html>.

Eddy, Mary Baker. "Contagion" (1896). Web. 10 July 2010. <http://www
    .endtime.org/library/mbe/contagion.html>.

Feikin, D. R., Lezotte, D. C., Hamman, R. F., Salmon, D. A., Chen, R. T., Hoff-
    man, R. E. "Individual and Community Risks of Measles and Pertus-
    sis Associated with Personal Exemptions to Immunization." *JAMA* 2000;
    284: 3145–3150.

Freed, G. L., Clark, S. J., Butchart, A. T., Singer, D. C., Davis, M. M. "Parental
    Vaccine Safety Concerns in 2009." *Pediatrics* 2010; 125: 654–659.

Frontline: The Vaccine War. PBS, 27 Apr. 2010. Directed by Jon Palfreman.
    Web. 10 July 2010. < http://www.pbs.org/wgbh/pages/frontline
    /vaccines/view/>.

Goodman, Richard A. "Vaccination Mandates: The Public Health Imperative
    and Individual Rights." *Law in Public Health Practice*. New York:
    Oxford UP, 2007. Print.

Greenfield, Karl T. "The Autism Vaccine Debate: Who's Afraid of Jenny
    McCarthy?" *Time*. 25 Feb. 2010. Web. 02 May 2010. <http://www.time
    .com/time/nation/article/0,8599,1967796-1,00.html>.

Harrell, Eben. "Doctor in MMR-Autism Scare Ruled Unethical." *Time*. 29
    Jan. 2010. Web. 02 May 2010. <http://www.time.com/time/health
    /article/0,8599,1957656,00.html>.

Harris, Gardiner. "Measles Cases Grow in Number, and Officials Blame
    Parents' Fear of Autism." *The New York Times*. 21 Aug. 2008. Web.
    02 May 2010. <http://www.nytimes.com/2008/08/22/health
    /research/22measles.html?_r=2&fta=y>.

"*Jacobson v. Commonwealth of Massachusetts*, 197 U.S. 11 (1905)." *LSU Law
    Center*. 1998. Web. 02 May 2010. <http://biotech.law.lsu
    .edu/cases/vaccines/Jacobson_v_Massachusetts.htm>.

"*Jacobson v. Massachusetts*, U.S. Supreme Court Case Summary & Oral
    Argument." *The Oyez Project / Build 6*. Web. 02 May 2010. <http://
    www.oyez.org/cases/1901-1939/1904/1904_70>.

Leblanc, Steve. "Parents Use Religion to Avoid Vaccines." *USAToday.com*.
    18 Oct. 2007. Web. 02 May 2010. <http://www.usatoday.com/news
    /nation/2007-10-17-19819928_x.htm>.

Levitsky, L. L. "Childhood Vaccinations and Chronic Illness." *New England Journal of Medicine* 2004; 350: 1380–1382.

Mariner, W. K., Annas, G. J., Glantz, L. H. "*Jacobson v Massachusetts*: It's Not Your Great-Great-Grandfather's Public Health Law." *Am J Public Health* 2005; 95: 581–590.

"NMAH: The Iron Lung and Other Equipment." *National Museum of American History*. Web. 02 May 2010. <http://americanhistory.si .edu/polio/howpolio/ironlung.htm>.

Omer, S. B., Salmon, D. A., Orenstein, W. A., deHart, M. P., Halsey, N. "Vaccine Refusal, Mandatory Immunization, and the Risks of Vaccine-Preventable Diseases." *New England Journal of Medicine* 2009; 360: 1981–1988.

Orenstein, W. A., Hinman, A. R. "The Immunization System in the United States — the Role of School Immunization Laws." *Vaccine* 1999; 17: S19–S24.

Park, Alice. "How Safe Are Vaccines?" *Time*. 21 May 2008. Web. 02 May 2010. <http://www.time.com/time/health/article/0,8599,1808438-2,00.html>.

Peterson, Liz A. "Texas Gov. Orders Anti-Cancer Vaccine." *The Washington Post* 2 Feb. 2007. Web. 02 May 2010. <http://www.washingtonpost .com/wp-dyn/content/article/2007/02/02/AR2007020201528.html>.

Peterson, Liz A. "Vaccine Meeting, Merck Donation Coincide." *The Washington Post* 21 Feb. 2007. Web. 02 May 2010. <http://www.washingtonpost .com/wp-dyn/content/article/2007/02/21/AR2007022102025.html>.

"Religious Liberty in Public Life — Free-Exercise Clause Topic." *First Amendment Center Online*. Web. 02 May 2010. <http://www .firstamendmentcenter.org/rel_liberty/free_exercise/..%5C..%5C /rel_liberty/free_exercise/topic.aspx?topic=vaccination>.

Savage, Liz. "Proposed HPV Vaccine Mandates Rile Health Experts across the Country." *Journal of the National Cancer Institute* 2007; 99: 665–666.

Smith, Stephen. "Measles Spread to Christian Scientist." *The Boston Globe* 3 June 2006. Web. 02 May 2010. <http://www.boston.com/news/local /articles/2006/06/03/measles_spreads_to_christian_scientist/>.

Szabo, Liz. "Missed Vaccines Weaken 'Herd Immunity' in Children." *USAToday.com*. 6 Jan. 2010. Web. 02 May 2010. <http://www .usatoday.com/news/health/2010-01-06-childhoodvaccines 06_CV_N.htm>.

"Vaccines." Bill and Melinda Gates Foundation. Web. 02 May 2010.
<http://www.gatesfoundation.org/vaccines/pages/default.aspx>.

"Vaccines." U. S. Food and Drug Administration. Web. 02 May 2010.
<http://www.fda.gov/BiologicsBloodVaccines/Vaccines/default.htm>.

"Vaccines: Vac-Gen/How Vaccines Prevent Disease." Centers for Disease
Control and Prevention. 7 Aug. 2009. Web. 02 May 2010. <http://
www.cdc.gov/vaccines/vac-gen/howvpd.htm>.

"Vaccines: Vac-Gen/What Would Happen If We Stopped Vaccinations."
Centers for Disease Control and Prevention. 12 June 2007. Web. 02 May
2010. <http://www.cdc.gov/vaccines/vac-gen/whatifstop.htm#intro>.

"Vaccines: Vac-Gen/Why Immunize?" Centers for Disease Control and
Prevention. 6 Aug. 2009. Web. 02 May 2010. <http://www.cdc.gov
/vaccines/vac-gen/why.htm>.

"What Causes Autism." National Autism Association. Web. 02 May 2010.
<http://www.nationalautismassociation.org/thimerosal.php>.

"WHO: Poliomyelitis." *World Health Organization.* Jan. 2008. Web. 02 May
2010. <http://www.who.int/mediacentre/factsheets/fs114/en/index.html>.

⊙ AT ISSUE: SOURCES FOR DEVELOPING A CAUSE-AND-EFFECT ARGUMENT

1. Does Vidula take a position on the issue of mandatory vaccination, or is his purpose in this essay simply to provide a context for the debate—for example, by presenting historical background and discussing religious objections to vaccination? Explain.

2. What kind of audience is Vidula addressing? For example, is he writing for parents? For medical professionals? How can you tell?

3. Vidula cites many experts and includes a lengthy works-cited list. What appeal is he making by using these strategies in his essay?

4. What positive results of mandatory vaccination laws does Vidula identify?

5. List the arguments against compulsory immunization. How does Vidula address these arguments? Does he dismiss them all, or does he believe some have merit? Do you see the writer as tolerant of those who oppose mandatory vaccination?

This piece was posted on February 11, 2015, to the online version of *National Review*.

VACCINATIONS ARE FOR THE GOOD OF THE NATION

BEN CARSON

There has been much debate recently over vaccination mandates, particularly in response to the measles outbreak currently taking place throughout the country.

At this juncture, there have been 102 confirmed measles cases in the U.S. during 2015, with 59 of them linked to a December 2014 visit to the Disneyland theme park in Southern California. (It is important to note that 11 of the cases associated with Disneyland were detected last year and, consequently, fall within the 2014 measles count.) This large outbreak has spread to at least a half-dozen other states, and the Centers for Disease Control and Prevention is currently requesting that all health care professionals "consider measles when evaluating patients with febrile rash and ask about a patient's vaccine status, recent travel history and contact with individuals who have febrile rash illness."

One must understand that there is no specific antiviral therapy for measles and that 90 percent of those who are not vaccinated will contract measles if they are indeed exposed to the virus. This explains why Arizona health officials are monitoring more than 1,000 people after potential exposure to measles. These are pretty staggering numbers that should concern not only parents and children, but also the general populace.

I have been asked many times throughout the past week for my thoughts concerning the issue of vaccines. The important thing is to make sure the public understands that there is no substantial risk from vaccines and that the benefits are very significant. Although I strongly believe in individual rights and the rights of parents to raise their children as they see fit, I also recognize that public health and public safety are extremely important in our society. Certain communicable diseases have been largely eradicated by immunization policies in this country. We should not allow those diseases to return by forgoing safety immunization programs for philosophical, religious, or other reasons when we have the means to eradicate them.

Obviously, there are exceptional situations to virtually everything, and we must have a mechanism whereby those can be heard. Nevertheless, there is public policy and health policy

> "We already have policies in place at schools that require immunization records—this is a positive thing."

that we must pay attention to regarding this matter. We already have policies in place at schools that require immunization records—this is a positive thing. Studies have shown over the course of time that the risk-benefit ratio for vaccination is grossly in favor of being vaccinated as opposed to not.

There is no question that immunizations have been effective in eliminat- 6 ing diseases such as smallpox, which was devastating and lethal. When you have diseases that have been demonstrably curtailed or eradicated by immunization, why would you even think about not doing it? Certain people have discussed the possibility of potential health risks from vaccinations. I am not aware of scientific evidence of a direct correlation. I think there probably are people who may make a correlation where one does not exist, and that fear subsequently ignites, catches fire, and spreads. But it is important to educate the public about what evidence actually exists.

I am very much in favor of parental rights for certain types of things. I am 7 in favor of you and me having the freedom to drive a car. But do we have a right to drive without wearing our seatbelts? Do we have a right to text while we are driving? Studies have demonstrated that those are dangerous things to do, so it becomes a public-safety issue. You have to be able to distinguish our rights versus the rights of the society in which we live, because we are all in this thing together. We have to be cognizant of the other people around us, and we must always bear in mind the safety of the population. That is key, and that is one of the responsibilities of government.

I am a small-government person, and I greatly oppose government intrusion 8 into everything. Still, it is essential that we distinguish between those things that are important and those things that are just intruding upon our basic privacy. Whether to participate in childhood immunizations would be an individual choice if individuals were the only ones affected, but our children are part of our larger community. None of us lives in isolation. Your decision does not affect only you— it also affects your fellow Americans.

⊘ AT ISSUE: SOURCES FOR DEVELOPING A CAUSE-AND-EFFECT ARGUMENT

1. Carson's title presents a strong thesis in favor of compulsory vaccination. Does Carson also state this thesis in the body of his essay? If so, where? If not, should he?

2. What is Carson's opinion of those who request exemption from vaccination for religious reasons?

3. Carson is careful to stress the importance of "individual rights" (para. 4) and "parental rights" (7). Why does he do this? How do you think he expects his audience—readers of the conservative *National Review*—to react to this strategy? How do you know?

4. In paragraph 7, Carson draws analogies between mandatory vaccination laws and other public-safety laws. How convincing are these arguments? What other public-safety or public-health laws do you see as analogous to mandatory vaccination? Why?

TheDailyBeast.com posted this article on January 30, 2014.

PEDIATRICIAN: VACCINATE YOUR KIDS— OR GET OUT OF MY OFFICE

RUSSELL SAUNDERS

1 If you won't trust your doctors on vaccinating your kids, will you ever really trust them at all?

2 If there is an issue more controversial and fraught with anger and frustration for pediatricians than the question of vaccine safety, I can't think of it.

3 Few topics are more apt to send my blood pressure skyrocketing than this. When the United Kingdom looks like sub-Saharan Africa in terms of wholly preventable disease outbreaks, something has gone terribly, tragically wrong.

4 No contemporary phenomenon confounds and confuses me more than seemingly sensible people turning down one of the most unambiguously helpful interventions in the history of modern medicine.

5 Yet they do.

6 When parents of prospective patients come to visit my office to meet our providers and to decide if we're the right practice for them, there are lots of things I make sure they know. I talk about the hospitals we're affiliated with. I tell them when we're open and how after-hours calls are handled. On my end, I like to know a bit about the child's medical history, or if there are special concerns that expecting parents might have.

7 And then this: *I always ask if the children are vaccinated*, or if the parents intend to vaccinate once the child is born. If the answer is no, I politely and respectfully tell them we won't be the right fit. We don't accept patients whose parents won't vaccinate them.

> "We don't accept patients whose parents won't vaccinate them."

8 It's not simply that we think these beliefs are wrong. Declining vaccines is, at best, misguided. But of course those inclined to refuse them don't agree with me, and I'm not going to try to change their minds. I've had too many of that kind of conversation over the years to hold out hope that anything I can say will sway them.

9 Which is *precisely* the problem.

10 There are few questions I can think of that have been asked and answered more thoroughly than the one about the safety and effectiveness of vaccines.

11 The measles-mumps-rubella vaccine does not cause autism.

12 The HPV vaccine is safe.

13 There is no threat to public health from thimerosal.

14 I can say all of this without hesitation because these concerns have been investigated and found to be groundless. But no amount of data seems sufficient to convince people who hold contrary beliefs.

So then, if the entire apparatus of medical science has bent itself to the   15
task of reassuring the public about the safety of vaccines and still comes up
short in vaccine refusers' estimation, how can I possibly rely on that apparatus
to undergird conversations about other potentially fraught topics? If a conclusion as sound as the importance of immunizing your kids is suspect to them,
what other conclusions may I rely upon?

The physician-patient relationship, like so many other human relation-   16
ships, requires an element of trust. I certainly neither want nor expect a return
to the paternalistic "doctor knows best" mindset of bygone years, but I do
need to know that patients' parents respect my training and expertise. Refusing an intervention I desperately want all children to receive makes that
respect untenably dubious.

There will be times when parents and I may not see eye to eye, but not   17
where I'm using the best evidence at hand to support my recommendations.
Maybe they'll want a test I think is useless, or want to use a supplement shown
to be harmful. Perhaps it will be a referral for an intervention shown to have
no benefit. If I can't hope to persuade them by making reference to the available research, what can I expect to be for them other than a rubber stamp for
their ideas? If medical science can't answer the meritless qualms they have
about vaccines, when can I use it at all?

I have no doubt that these parents love their children immensely and are   18
making what they believe to be the best decisions for them. I don't dispute
that. But any potential partnership we might create in caring for them together
would rely on their belief that I have something other than a signature on an
order form or prescription pad to offer.

They must believe I have a perspective worth understanding.   19

I often wonder why a parent who believes vaccines are harmful would want   20
to bring their children to a medical doctor at all. After all, for immunizations to
be as malign as their detractors claim, my colleagues and I would have to be
staggeringly incompetent, negligent, or malicious to keep administering them.

If vaccines caused the harms Jenny McCarthy and her ilk claim they do,   21
then my persistence in giving them must say something horrifying about me.
Why would you then want to bring your children to me when you're worried
about their illnesses? As a parent myself, I wouldn't trust my children's care to
someone I secretly thought was a fool or a monster.

It's not merely that I don't want to have to worry that the two-week-old   22
infant in my waiting room is getting exposed to a potentially fatal case of pertussis if these parents bring their children in with a bad cough. It's not just that
I don't want their kid to be the first case of epiglottitis I've ever seen in my
career. Those are reasons enough, to be sure. But they're not all.

What breaks the deal is that I would never truly believe that these parents   23
trust me. Giving kids vaccines is the absolute, unambiguous standard of care,
as easy an answer as I will ever be able to offer.

If they don't trust me about that, how can I hope they would if the ques-   24
tions ever got harder?

⊃ AT ISSUE: SOURCES FOR DEVELOPING A CAUSE-AND-EFFECT ARGUMENT

1. Like Ben Carson (p. 502) and Jeffrey Singer (p. 507), Saunders is a medical doctor. How does his professional experience influence the type of argument he makes?

2. In one sentence, paraphrase Saunders's thesis. Does this thesis appear in the essay? If so, where? If not, does its absence weaken Saunders's argument? Why or why not?

3. Saunders says that the issue under discussion makes his blood pressure rise and notes that the issue "confounds and confuses" him (paras. 3 and 4). Where else do his emotions come through? Do these emotional statements increase or decrease his credibility? Explain.

4. Why won't Saunders "accept patients whose parents won't vaccinate them" (7)? Do you agree with his position?

5. In paragraph 16, Saunders says, "The physician-patient relationship, like so many other human relationships, requires an element of trust." Where else does he discuss trust? Why does he see trust as central to the vaccination debate?

6. Discussing those who oppose mandatory vaccination, Saunders says, "I have no doubt that these parents love their children immensely and are making what they believe to be the best decisions for them" (18). Why does he make this concession?

Reason.com published Jeffrey Singer's position on vaccines on March 25, 2014.

VACCINATION AND FREE WILL

JEFFREY SINGER

In Steven Spielberg's 2002 sci-fi film *Minority Report*, a special police agency called PreCrime nabs suspects before they ever commit an offense. No trial is necessary because the crime is seen as an infallible prediction of the future and thus a matter of fact. The movie challenges viewers to consider the tension between technological determinism and free will, between the rights of an individual and the health of a community. It's a useful metaphor for the argument against coercive vaccination. 1

Some argue that mandatory mass vaccination is an act of communal self-defense, and thus completely compatible with the principles underpinning a free society. Unless people are forcibly immunized, they will endanger the life and health of innocent bystanders, goes the argument. But such a position requires a level of precognition we haven't yet attained. 2

Not everyone who is vaccinated against a microbe develops immunity to that microbe. Conversely, some unvaccinated people never become infected. Some people have inborn "natural" immunity against certain viruses and other microorganisms. Central Africans born with the sickle-cell trait provide a classic example of such inborn immunity: Their sickle-shaped red blood cells are inhospitable to the mosquito-borne parasite that causes malaria. Other people are just lucky and never get exposed to a contagious microbe. 3

> "Not everyone who is vaccinated against a microbe develops immunity to that microbe."

Just like not every pregnant woman who drinks alcohol or smokes tobacco passes on a malady or disability to her newborn baby, not every pregnant woman infected with a virus or other microbe passes on the infection to her fetus—nor are all such babies born with birth defects. 4

A free society demands adherence to the non-aggression principle. No person should initiate force against another, and should only use force in retaliation or self-defense. Forcibly injecting substances—attenuated microbes or otherwise—into someone else's body cannot be justified as an act of self-defense, because there is no way to determine with certainty that the person will ever be responsible for disease transmission. 5

Ronald Bailey suggests that the choice to remain unvaccinated is analogous to "walking down a street randomly swinging your fists without warning." But this is a poor analogy. Such a person is engaging in a deliberate action, as opposed to choosing inaction. And, unlike those prevented from opting out of vaccination, the fist-swinger incurs no threat to life or limb when prohibited from throwing his punches. 6

If someone chooses the inaction of non-vaccination based upon the 7 belief—right or wrong—that the vaccination is harmful or even life threatening, then coercive vaccination in this context is clearly a case of aggression. For it to be otherwise requires certainty that those beliefs are wrong. And certainty in this case is not possible. How can you be sure, for example, that a child won't have an adverse or even fatal reaction to a vaccine? And how can defending forced immunization as self-defense be justified when it can never be shown with certainty that the non-vaccinated person would have been responsible for another person's harm?

Then there is the matter of "herd immunity." The phenomenon of herd 8 immunity allows many unvaccinated people to avoid disease because they free ride off the significant portion of the population that is immunized. Economists point out that free riding is an unavoidable fact of life: People free ride when they purchase a new, improved, and cheaper product that was "pre-tested" on more affluent people who wanted to be the first to own it; people free ride when they use word-of-mouth reviews to decide whether to buy goods or services, or to see a film; those who choose not to carry concealed weapons free ride a degree of personal safety off the small percentage of the public that does.

So here is a way of thinking about it: As long as the person who is *being* 9 free-ridden is still getting desired value for an acceptable price, and is not being harmed by the free riding, it really shouldn't matter. Achieving a society without free riders is not only unnecessary, it is impossible.

Perhaps allowing a certain number of free riders could mitigate the disrup- 10 tion to liberty caused by mandatory vaccination programs. But then, how many free riders should be allowed? I don't think that question can be answered with any degree of certainty. And what criteria would be used to decide who gets to ride free? An objective answer to this question appears equally elusive. Finally, how can the population be monitored to make sure the proportion of free riders is maintained at the right level without unreasonably infringing on civil liberties and privacy rights? The task would be titanic. I think the only practical solution—and the solution that is in the best interest of liberty—is to just accept the free riding of the current regime as a fact of reality, and focus instead on persuading people about the benefits of vaccination.

Most states coax, but don't coerce, vaccination of children in the public 11 school system. Two of the 50 states, Mississippi and West Virginia, are indeed coercive. But the remaining 48 allow parents to opt out for religious reasons, and 19 allow for some kind of philosophical objection. Some states require parents to read about the risks of opting out before exempting their children. Some require them to acknowledge in writing that, in the event of a major school outbreak of a contagious disease for which their child has not received immunization, he or she will be held out of school until the outbreak clears.

Private schools' requiring vaccination of children as a precondition for 12 admission is not coercive, since private education is a voluntary transaction. But even with the government school monopoly in existence today, immunization policy in at least 19 states is compatible with the non-aggression principle.

As a medical doctor I am a strong advocate of vaccination against communicable and infectious diseases. I am irritated by the hysteria and pseudo-science behind much of the anti-vaccination literature and rhetoric. In my perfect world, everyone would agree with me and voluntarily get vaccinated against the gamut of nasty diseases for which we have vaccines. (In my perfect world, pregnant women also wouldn't smoke tobacco or drink alcohol until after delivery.) 13

But free societies are sometimes messy. To live in a free society, one must be willing to tolerate people who make bad decisions and bad choices, as long as they don't directly infringe on the rights of others. 14

A strong argument can be made that it is self-defense to quarantine people who are infected with a disease-producing organism and are objectively threatening the contamination of others. But in such a case, the use of force against the disease carrier is based upon evidence that the carrier is contagious and may infect others. 15

Any mass immunization program that uses compulsion rather than persuasion will, on balance, do more harm to the well being of a free people than any good it was intended to convey. 16

⊃ AT ISSUE: SOURCES FOR DEVELOPING A CAUSE-AND-EFFECT ARGUMENT

1. What is Singer's position on mandatory vaccination? What part does he believe "free will" plays in the vaccination debate?

2. In paragraph 1, Singer uses the term *coercive vaccination*; elsewhere, he uses other language with negative connotations, such as *forced immunization* (para. 7). What other negative terms does he use in place of the neutral "mandatory vaccination"? Does his use of such terms strengthen or weaken his argument? Explain.

3. How does Singer refute the "herd immunity" and "free-rider" arguments commonly advanced by supporters of mandatory vaccination? How does he refute Ronald Bailey's argument by analogy (6)? Are these refutations convincing? Why or why not?

4. Where in this essay does Singer make statements to show that he is a reasonable person? Given his likely audience, are such statements necessary? Explain.

5. In paragraph 14, Singer says, "[F]ree societies are sometimes messy." What does he mean? How does this characterization support the position he takes in this essay?

6. Reread Singer's last paragraph. Then, write a one-sentence paraphrase of this paragraph that could serve as this essay's thesis statement.

The *Chicago Sun-Times* ran this piece on May 14, 2014.

THE GRAY AREA ON VACCINES

JENNY MCCARTHY

I am not "anti-vaccine." This is not a change in my stance nor is it a new 1 position that I have recently adopted. For years, I have repeatedly stated that I am, in fact, "pro-vaccine" and for years I have been wrongly branded as "anti-vaccine."

My beautiful son, Evan, inspired this mother to question the "one size fits 2 all" philosophy of the recommended vaccine schedule. I embarked on this quest not only for myself and my family, but for countless parents who shared my desire for knowledge that could lead to options and alternate schedules, but never to eliminate the vaccines.

Blatantly inaccurate blog posts about my position have been accepted as 3 truth by the public at large as well as media outlets (legitimate and otherwise), who have taken those false stories and repeatedly turned them into headlines. What happened to critical thinking? What happened to asking questions because every child is different?

For my child, I asked for a schedule that would allow one shot per visit 4 instead of the multiple shots they were and still are giving infants.

I am passionate about important conversations on how we can improve health care for our children and generations to come. This is an extremely important discussion and I am dumbfounded that these conversations are discounted and negated because the answers are not black or white. Again I ask, what happened to critical thinking? 5

> "Again I ask, what happened to critical thinking?"

A recent column by a blogger named Nancy Colasurdo states: 6

> Here's how it goes in this country, like everything else—black or white. Those are your choices. You either fall in line with 40-plus vaccines your doctor recommends on his or her schedule or you're a wack-job "anti-vaxxer." Heaven forbid you think the gray zone is an intelligent place to reside and you express doubt or fear or maybe want to spread the vaccines out a bit on this tiny person you've brought into the world.

Her words echo and articulate my concern with inflexible thinking. This 7 is the real view I, Jenny McCarthy, hold. The gray one!

This is what I have said: 8

"People have the misconception that we want to eliminate vaccines," I 9 told *Time* magazine science editor Jeffrey Kluger in 2009. "Please understand that we are not an anti-vaccine group. We are demanding safe vaccines. We want to reduce the schedule and reduce the toxins."

This is what I believe: 10

I believe in the importance of a vaccine program and I believe parents 11
have the right to choose one poke per visit. I've never told anyone to not vaccinate. Should a child with the flu receive six vaccines in one doctor visit?
Should a child with a compromised immune system be treated the same way
as a robust, healthy child? Shouldn't a child with a family history of vaccine
reactions have a different plan? Or at least the right to ask questions?

I will continue to say what I have always said: "One size does not fit all." 12
God help us all if gray is no longer an option.

⊘ AT ISSUE: SOURCES FOR DEVELOPING A CAUSE-AND-EFFECT ARGUMENT

1. Why does McCarthy open her argument with the statement, "I am not 'anti-vaccine'"? Why does she think this statement is necessary? After reading this essay, do you conclude that her opening statement is true?

2. Do McCarthy's references to her son add to or detract from her credibility? Does quoting Nancy Colasurdo (para. 6) strengthen her argument? Why or why not?

3. In what sense, if any, is this essay a refutation? If it is, what argument does it refute?

4. What is the "gray area" to which McCarthy refers? What is the "'one size fits all' philosophy" (2)? How are these two concepts central to her argument?

5. In paragraph 3, McCarthy asks, "What happened to critical thinking?" What does she mean here (and in paragraph 5) by *critical thinking*? Why does she ask this question?

6. What modifications in the current childhood vaccination schedule does McCarthy propose? Do you think her suggestions are reasonable? Feasible? Why or why not?

Facts about the Measles

AN OUTBREAK

If no one has any immunity to a virus, one person who was infected could spread the virus to twelve to eighteen other people. A single infection could quickly become an epidemic.

HERD EFFECT

People who have been vaccinated remove themselves as a potential source for the virus—they are not able to give it to anyone else. This reduces the risk of infection for people who have not received vaccines. This slowing of the spread of the virus is called the herd effect.

HERD IMMUNITY

Herd immunity is the threshold needed to end an outbreak quickly. It has been discovered that this occurs when one person with a virus infects (on average) fewer than one other person. In a society where the majority of people are inoculated, the virus has nowhere to travel. Few people become infected, and so even those without the virus are often protected because they come into contact with so few potential carriers.

TEMPLATE FOR WRITING A CAUSE-AND-EFFECT ARGUMENT

Write a one-paragraph cause-and-effect argument in which you take a position on whether vaccination should be required for all children. Follow the template below, filling in the blanks to create your argument.

Although vaccination against life-threatening diseases saves many lives, some people believe that it has negative consequences as well. These people support exemptions from vaccination only for medical reasons. One positive result of widespread vaccination has been _____ _____. Another positive outcome has been _____ _____ _____ _____. Despite these encouraging results, many parents believe that vaccines pose dangers for their children. For example, they believe _____ _____ _____. Others object because _____ _____ _____. These parents suggest _____ _____ _____. Granted, _____ _____ _____. Still, _____ _____ _____.

All things considered, the government (should/should not) require all children to be vaccinated.

⊘ EXERCISE 13.8

Working with two or three of your classmates, discuss your feelings about mandatory vaccination. Do you believe exemptions should be granted only for medical reasons or for personal or religious reasons as well? Write a paragraph that summarizes your group's conclusions.

⊘ EXERCISE 13.9

Write a cause-and-effect argument on the topic, "Should Vaccination Be Required for All Children?" Begin by considering all possible problems associated with the increase in unvaccinated children and with mandatory vaccination. Then, consider whether stricter requirements and fewer exemptions are indicated—and whether such changes would have a positive effect on these problems. (If you like you may incorporate material you developed for Exercise 13.8 and the templated argument into your essay.) Cite the readings on pages 483–512 where necessary, and be sure to document the sources you use and to include a works-cited page. (See Chapter 10 for information on documenting sources.)

⊘ EXERCISE 13.10

Review the four pillars of argument discussed in Chapter 1. Does your essay include all four elements of an effective argument? Add anything that is missing. Then, label the key elements of your essay.

⊘ WRITING ASSIGNMENTS: CAUSE-AND-EFFECT ARGUMENTS

1. What could your school do to encourage students to adopt healthier lifestyles? Write an editorial for your college newspaper in the form of a cause-and-effect argument. In your editorial, take one of these two positions:

   ■ If the university takes steps to encourage healthier lifestyles, students will benefit greatly.

   ■ If the university does not take steps to encourage students to adopt healthier lifestyles, the consequences could be serious.

2. Look at pictures of female celebrities online, and consider the likely effects of these images on teenage girls. Then, write an essay arguing for or against the charge that images such as these help to encourage poor self-esteem, risky behavior, or eating disorders. Include some of

the images in your essay, and analyze the impact of their visual elements as well as the effect of the words in the accompanying articles or captions.

3. In recent years, young children's lives have become more and more structured. Instead of the free play that their parents enjoyed, many of today's children are busy with scheduled sports, lessons, and play dates. Write an essay structured as a causal chain that traces the probable causes of this change as well as its likely effects on children and on their families. In your thesis statement, indicate whether you consider the effects positive or negative.

14

Evaluation Arguments

Do the Benefits of Fracking Outweigh the Environmental Risks?

For years, Americans have dreamed of a time when the United States would be energy independent—free from the influence of international organizations, such as OPEC, that control the world's energy supply. Enter hydraulic fracturing, or "fracking," an extraction process that enables us to access massive reserves of natural gas that up until now have been inaccessible. Fracking is a drilling technology that uses fluids pumped under pressure to fracture shale rock as far as a mile or more beneath Earth's surface and release natural gas. Proponents of fracking point out that not only has fracking been used safely for years in Canada and the United States, but it can also provide years of clean energy as well as reduce our dependence on foreign oil. Supporters also point out that since the fracking revolution began, natural gas prices have dropped nearly 47 percent.

Critics, however, have serious environmental concerns about fracturing layers of sedimentary rock in the Earth's crust. For example, shale beds typically exist far below the level of ground water, and the toxic chemicals used in fracking pollute the water supply. In fact, residents in some communities near drill sites have reported that methane and other chemicals have contaminated their drinking water. Some critics have even suggested that excessive fracking could inadvertently cause earthquakes. Those who share these concerns see fracking as a textbook example of corporate greed gone wild, of short-term thinking eclipsing reason in a misguided effort to satisfy our nation's insatiable demand for energy.

Later in this chapter, you will read essays that address the pros and cons of fracking, and you will be asked to write an **evaluation argument** that takes a position on this topic. What do you think? Do the benefits of fracking outweigh the environmental risks?

What Is an Evaluation Argument?

When you **evaluate**, you make a value judgment about something or someone—for example, a product, service, program, performance, work of literature or art, or candidate for public office.

Evaluation is part of your daily life: after all, before you make any decision, you need to evaluate your options. For example, you evaluate clothing and electronic equipment before you make a purchase, and you evaluate films, concerts, and TV shows before you decide how to spend your evening. Before you decide to go to a party, you evaluate its positive and negative qualities—who will be there, what music you are likely to hear, and what kind of food and drink will probably be on hand. You also evaluate your teachers, your classes, and even your friends.

When constructing an **evaluation argument**, you have several options: you can make a positive or negative judgment, you can assert that someone else's positive or negative judgment is not accurate or justified, or you can write a comparative evaluation, in which you demonstrate that one thing is (or is not) superior to another.

As a college student, you might read (or write) evaluation arguments based on topics such as the following:

- Is the college bookstore doing its best to serve students?

- Is a vegan diet really a practical option?

- Is *Moby-Dick* the great American novel?

- Is the SAT a valid testing instrument?

- Are portable e-book readers superior to print books?

- Are Crocs a marvel of comfort and design or just ugly shoes?

- Are hybrid cars worth the money?

- Is Taylor Swift the most important musical artist of her generation?

↪ EXERCISE 14.1

List ten additional topics that would be suitable for evaluation arguments.

MAKING EVALUATIONS

When you write an evaluation, you use terms such as the following to express judgments and indicate the relative merits of two items.

Superior/inferior	Important/trivial
Useful/useless	Original/trite
Efficient/inefficient	Innovative/predictable
Effective/ineffective	Interesting/dull
Successful/unsuccessful	Inspiring/depressing
Deserving/undeserving	Practical/impractical

➔ EXERCISE 14.2

Choose one word in each of the word pairs listed above, and use each word in a sentence that evaluates a service, program, or employee at your school.

IDENTIFYING BIAS

Everyone has biases, and these are likely to show up in evaluations, where strong opinions may overcome objectivity. As you read and write evaluation arguments, be on the lookout for evidence of bias:

- When you *read* evaluation arguments, carefully consider what the writer reveals (or actually states) about his or her values, beliefs, and opinions. Also be alert for evidence of bias in a writer's language and tone as well as in his or her choice of examples. (See "Detecting Bias in Your Sources" on pages 261–262 for more on this issue.)

- When you *write* evaluation arguments, focus on trying to make a fair assessment of your subject. Be particularly careful not to distort or slant evidence, quote out of context, or use unfair appeals or logical fallacies. (See "Being Fair" on pages 268–269 for more on how to avoid bias in your writing.)

Criteria for Evaluation

When you evaluate something, you cannot simply state that it is good or bad, useful or useless, valuable or worthless, or superior or inferior to something else: you need to explain *why* this is so. Before you can begin to develop a thesis and gather supporting evidence for your argument, you need to decide what **criteria for evaluation** you will use: to support a *positive* judgment, you need to show that something has value because it satisfies certain criteria; to support a *negative* judgment, you need to show that something lacks value because it does not satisfy those criteria.

To make any judgment, then, you need to select the specific criteria you will use to assess your subject. For example, in an evaluation of a college bookstore, will you base your assessment on the friendliness of its service? Its prices? The number of books it stocks? Its return policy? The efficiency or knowledge of the staff? Your answers to these questions will help you begin to plan your evaluation.

The criteria that you establish will help you decide how to evaluate a given subject. If, for example, your criteria for evaluating musical artists focus on these artists' impact on the music industry, the number of downloads of their music, the number of corporate sponsors they attract, and their concert revenue, you may be able to support the thesis that Taylor Swift is the most important musical artist of her generation. If, however, your main criterion for evaluation is the artist's influence on other contemporary performers, your case may be less compelling. Similarly, if you are judging health-care systems on the basis of how many individuals have medical coverage, you may be able to demonstrate that the Canadian system is superior to the U.S. system. If your criteria are referral time and government support for medical research, your evaluation argument might support a different position. Whatever criteria you decide on, a bookstore (or band or health-care system) that satisfies them will be seen as superior to one that does not.

Taylor Swift: The most important artist?

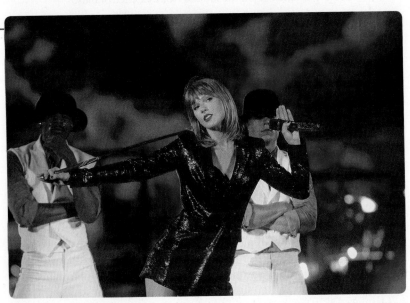

John Medina/Getty Images

Consider another example. Suppose you want to evaluate the government's Head Start program, which was established in 1964 to provide preschool education to children from low-income families. The program also provides medical coverage and social services to the children enrolled, and in recent years it has expanded to cover children of migrant workers and children in homeless families. On what basis would you evaluate this program? Would you evaluate only the children's educational progress or also consider the program's success in providing health care? In considering educational progress, would you focus on test scores or on students' performance in school? Would you measure long-term effects—for example, Head Start students' likelihood of attending college and their annual earnings as adults? Or would you focus on short-term results—for example, students' performance in elementary school? Finally, would you evaluate only the children or also their families? Depending on the criteria you select for your evaluation, the Head Start program could be considered a success or a failure—or something in between.

⊜ EXERCISE 14.3

Choose one of the topics you listed in Exercise 14.1, and list five possible criteria for an evaluation argument on that topic.

⊜ EXERCISE 14.4

By what criteria do you evaluate the textbooks for your college courses? Design? Content? Clarity? Comprehensiveness? Cost? Work with another student to decide on the most important criteria, and then write a paragraph in which you evaluate this textbook.

Structuring an Evaluation Argument

In general terms, an evaluation argument can be structured like this:

- **Introduction:** Establishes the criteria by which you will evaluate your subject; states the essay's thesis

- **Evidence (first point in support of thesis):** Supplies facts, opinions, and so on to support your evaluation in terms of one of the criteria you have established

- **Evidence (second point in support of thesis):** Supplies facts, opinions, and so on to support your evaluation in terms of one of the criteria you have established

- **Evidence (third point in support of thesis):** Supplies facts, opinions, and so on to support your evaluation in terms of one of the criteria you have established

- **Refutation of opposing arguments:** Presents others' evaluations and your arguments against them

- **Conclusion:** Reinforces the main point of the argument; includes a strong concluding statement

The following student essay includes all the elements of an evaluation argument. The student who wrote the essay was evaluating a popular website, RateMyProfessors.com.

EVALUATION OF A WEBSITE: RATEMYPROFESSORS.COM

KEVIN MURPHY

Since 1999, both students and professors have been writing, reading, defending, and criticizing the content on RateMyProfessors .com (RMP). With over 15 million student-written reviews and over 4 million visitors a month, RMP continues to be the most popular site of its kind ("About RateMYProfessors.com"). However, the fact that a website is popular does not mean that it is reliable. Certainly RMP may be interesting and entertaining (and even, as *New York Times* writer Virginia Heffernan recently wrote, "engrossing"), but is it useful? Will it help students to make informed decisions about the schools they choose to attend and the classes they choose to take? Are the ratings—as well as the site itself—trustworthy? Is the information about professors and schools comprehensive enough to be meaningful? No student wants to waste time in a course that is poorly taught by a teacher who lacks enthusiasm, knowledge, or objectivity. However, an evaluation of the reviews on RateMyProfessors.com suggests that the site is not trustworthy or comprehensive enough to help college students make the right choices about the courses they take.

Thesis statement

The first question to ask about the reviews on RMP is, "Who is writing them?" All reviews on the site are anonymous, and although anonymity protects the writers' privacy and may encourage them to offer

Evidence: First point in support of thesis

1

2

honest feedback, it is also a red flag. There is no guarantee that the reviews are written by students. In fact, anyone—even the professors themselves—can create RMP accounts and post reviews, and there is no way of knowing who is writing or what a writer's motivations and biases are. In addition, the percentage of students who actually write reviews is small. According to one recent survey, only 8 percent of students have ever written a review for an online professor-rating site; in other words, "a vocal minority" is running the show (Arden). Furthermore, the ratings for each individual professor vary greatly in number, quality, and currency. Even in the rare cases where a professor has hundreds of recent ratings, the score may represent the views of only a small percentage of that professor's students. This means that getting a representative sample is highly unlikely. Unless the website's managers institute rules and restrictions to ensure the legitimacy of the writer and the size of the sample, the RMP ratings will continue to be untrustworthy.

The second question to ask is, "Who controls RMP's content?" Although RMP posts "Site Guidelines" with a "Do" list and a "Do Not" list, these lists are merely suggestions. The RMP Site Moderation Team will remove obscene or unlawful posts, but it has no way to enforce other guidelines. For instance, one of the items on the "Do Not" list asks users not to "post a rating if you have not taken a class with the professor" ("Site Guidelines"). However, to sign up for an RMP account, a user does not have to identify his or her university or list the courses he or she has taken. The site asks only for a name, a birth date, and the right to share the user's personal information with its partner companies. This last question is a reminder that RMP is ultimately a commercial venture. The site is not owned by students or by their universities; it is owned by mtvU, a TV network that in turn is owned by media giant Viacom. The fact that each page of RMP content is surrounded on three sides by advertisements reminds users that the primary purpose of this site is to make money. When that fact is combined with the fact that the company has "the right to review, monitor, edit and/or screen any content you post," it indicates that RMP does not warrant students' trust ("Terms of Use"). A for-profit corporation, not the student reviewers, controls all of the information on the site and may modify content to increase traffic and impress advertisers.

3   Evidence: Second point in support of thesis

Evidence: Third point in support of thesis

The last question to ask is, "Does RMP offer students the right kind   4
of information—and enough in-depth information to give them a comprehensive understanding of a professor's effectiveness as a teacher?"
In fact, the site offers ratings in only four categories: "Helpfulness,"
"Clarity," "Easiness," and "Hotness." As one highly rated professor points out, "None of the dimensions [of RMP's rating system] directly addresses how much students felt they learned" (qtd. in Arden). Moreover, no category addresses the professor's knowledge of the subject matter. The ratings tend to focus attention on superficial qualities rather than on substance, apparently assuming that most students are looking for "easy A" classes taught by attractive, pleasant instructors. For students who are trying to make informed decisions about which classes to take, these criteria are inadequate. As one frustrated student user explains, "One of my professors had a really negative rating and comments, but he came to be one of my favorites. . . . his way of teaching matched me perfectly" (qtd. in Ross). The focus of RateMyProfessors.com is not on giving substantial feedback about teaching effectiveness or information about the educational value of a class. Perhaps these kinds of feedback do not attract advertisers; feedback about a professor's "Hotness"—the least important measure of effectiveness—apparently does.

Refutation of opposing arguments

Students who argue that RMP is a "useful resource" say that the site   5
helps them decide which professors to take and which to avoid (Davis).
For example, one community college student says that checking professors' scores on RMP "helps me choose a professor who will suit my needs" (qtd. in Davis). Committed RMP users also say that they are able to sift through the superficial comments and find useful information about professors' teaching styles. As one junior at Baruch College in New York City says, "It's all about perspective, and you need to be aware of this when you use the site" (qtd. in Ross). Users claim that they can read reviews and understand that "the same course materials may work really well with one group of students and less well with another" (McGrath) and that "even though [a particular student] doesn't seem to like the professor, it sounds like I might" (qtd. in Davis). This ability to read between the lines, however, does not change the fact that the information on RMP is neither verifiable nor comprehensive. RMP's reviews are anonymous, and some of them are almost certainly not written by students who have taken the professors' classes. Professors' "Overall Quality" scores, which so many students rely on, are based on ratings by these untrustworthy

reviewers. Furthermore, these "overall" ratings are based on only two factors: "Helpfulness" and "Clarity" ("Rating Categories"). A rating that is calculated on the basis of very limited information from questionable sources can hardly be a "useful resource." On balance, then, RMP does not give students the information they need to make informed decisions.

On RMP's homepage, the site managers encourage visitors to "join the fun!" ("About RateMyProfessors.com"). "Fun" is ultimately all users can hope to find at RMP. As Virginia Heffernan recommends, "Read it like a novel, watch it like MTV, study it like sociology. Just don't base any real decisions on it." Real students' honest and thorough reviews of professors are invaluable, but sites like RMP do not provide this kind of helpful feedback. When deciding between a commercial website and old-fashioned word of mouth, anyone who thinks that RMP offers more useful information should keep in mind who writes and controls the site's content. Because visitors to the site know almost nothing about the reviewers, they cannot know if their comments and ratings are trustworthy. Moreover, because they do know something about the site's owners, they should know enough to be wary of their motives. If students are looking for useful advice about which classes to take, they should look no further than their own campuses.

6

Concluding statement

Works Cited

"About RateMyProfessors.com." *Rate My Professors*, MTV Networks, 2011, ratemyprofessors.com.

Arden, Patrick. "Rate My Professors Has Some Academics Up in Arms." *Village Voice*, 26 Oct. 2011, www.villagevoice.com/arts/rate-my -professors-has-some-academics-up-in-arms-7165156.

Davis, Mandi. "Rate My Professor Gains Popularity with MCCC Students." *Agora*, Monroe County Community College, 7 Dec. 2011, www.mcccagora.com/news/view.php/509769/Rate-My-Professor -gains-popularity-with-.

Heffernan, Virginia. "The Prof Stuff." *The New York Times*, 11 Mar. 2010, www.nytimes.com/2010/03/14/magazine/14FOB-medium-t.html?_r=0.

McGrath, James F. "When My Son Discovered RateMyProfessors.com." *Inside Higher Ed*, 15 June 2015, www.insidehighered.com/ views/2015/06/15/essay-about-professor-who-learns-his-son-has -discovered-ratemyprofessorscom.

"Rating Categories." *Rate My Professors*, MTV Networks, 2011,
  ratemyprofessors.com.

Ross, Terrance. "Professor Evaluation Website Receives Mixed
  Reviews." *Ticker*, Baruch College, City U of New York, 12 Sept. 2011,
  ticker.baruchconnect.com/article/professor-evaluation-website
  -receives-mixed-reviews/.

"Site Guidelines." *Rate My Professors*, MTV Networks, 20 June 2011,
  ratemyprofessors.com.

"Terms of Use." *Rate My Professors*, MTV Networks, 20 June 2011,
  ratemyprofessors.com.

GRAMMAR IN CONTEXT

Comparatives and Superlatives

When you write an **evaluation argument**, you make judgments, and
these judgments often call for comparative analysis—for example,
arguing that one thing is better than another or the best of its kind.

When you compare two items or qualities, you use a **comparative** form:
bigger, better, more interesting, less realistic. When you compare three or
more items or qualities, you use a **superlative** form: *the biggest, the best, the
most interesting, the least realistic.* Be careful to use these forms appropriately.

- **Do not use the comparative when you are comparing more than two
things.**

  INCORRECT   Perhaps these kinds of feedback do not attract advertis-
                ers; comments about a professor's "Hotness"—<u>the less
                important measure</u> of effectiveness—apparently does.

  CORRECT   Perhaps these kinds of feedback do not attract advertis-
                ers; comments about a professor's "Hotness"—<u>the least
                important measure</u> of effectiveness—apparently does.

- **Do not use the superlative when you are comparing only two things.**

  INCORRECT   When deciding between a commercial website and old-
                fashioned word of mouth, anyone who thinks that RMP
                offers <u>the most useful information</u> should keep in mind
                who writes and controls the site's content.

  CORRECT   When deciding between a commercial website and old-
                fashioned word of mouth, anyone who thinks that RMP
                offers <u>more useful information</u> should keep in mind who
                writes and controls the site's content.

⊃ EXERCISE 14.5

The following commentary, "Nothing Pretty in Child Pageants," includes the basic elements of an evaluation argument. Read the essay, and then answer the questions that follow it, consulting the outline on pages 521–522 if necessary.

This article was published in the *Lexington Herald-Leader* on August 14, 2011.

NOTHING PRETTY IN CHILD PAGEANTS

VERNON R. WIEHE

Toddlers and Tiaras is a televised beauty pageant for very young children 1 which appears weekly ironically on The Learning Channel. The Web site for the show describes it this way: "On any given weekend, on stages across the country, little girls and boys parade around wearing makeup, false eyelashes, spray tans, and fake hair to be judged on their beauty, personality, and costumes. *Toddlers and Tiaras* follows families on their quest for sparkly crowns, big titles, and lots of cash."

A TV viewer will see the program's feeble attempts at Las Vegas–like 2 glamour and glitz in a rented hotel ballroom or school auditorium with primarily little girls in adult-like pageant attire parading in front of a small audience consisting largely of participants' families. The tots' attire includes makeup, hair extensions, and "flippers" to hide missing teeth. Mothers, often overweight, engage in silly antics coaching the children in every move of their routines with the hope of winning a trophy taller than the child, a rhinestone crown, the title of "Ultimate Grand Supreme," and possibly some cash.

The viewer will also be taken behind the scenes to witness temper tan- 3 trums from children resisting the role into which they are being put. On a recent show, a 2-year-old cried the entire time on stage; in another show, a mother literally dragged the child around the stage supposedly putting the child through her routine.

It raises questions for the viewer: Whose idea is this—the child's or the 4 adult's? Is participating in such pageants age-appropriate behavior for a small child? Might such participation even represent a potential danger for the child's emotional development?

The potential impact of child beauty pageants may be viewed in terms of 5 the fallacious arguments most frequently cited in support of this activity:

All Little Girls Like to Play Dress-Up at Some Time

Dress-up, a sign of a child identifying with or mimicking the mother, is sig- 6 nificantly different from organized child beauty pageants.

First, dress-up play generally is an activity engaged in by a young girl 7 alone or with a group of playmates at home rather than on a stage in front of an audience.

Second, competition, an important element in child beauty pageants, 8 ranks contestants, with one child becoming a winner and the others losers.

Third, dress-up involves little girls wearing their mothers' cast-off clothing 9 or cosmetics in a way the child perceives mother uses these objects. Participants in *Toddlers and Tiaras* spend hundreds and even thousands of dollars for costumes, cosmetics, and even beauty consultants.

Parents certainly have a right to spend their money on children as they 10 wish, but if this expenditure of money and effort is for the ultimate goal of the child winning the contest and the child fails to do so, what is the emotional cost to the child? What happens to the child's self-esteem?

Children's Beauty Pageants Teach Poise and Self-Confidence

Even if the pageants do foster the development of these attributes, the ques- 11 tion must be raised whether poise and self-confidence stemming from beauty pageants is age appropriate for the child. One of the most dangerous aspects of these pageants is the sexualization of young girls.

Sexualization occurs through little girls wearing adult women's clothing 12 in diminutive sizes, the use of makeup which often is applied by makeup consultants, spray tanning the body, the dying of hair and the use of hair extensions, and assuming provocative postures more appropriate for adult models.

The sexualization of young children sends a conflicting message to the 13 child and a dangerous message to adults. To the child, a message is given that sexuality—expressed in clothing, makeup, and certain postures—is appropriate and even something to exploit. The message to adults, especially pedophiles, is one condoning children as sexual objects. Research on child sexual abuse shows that the sexualization of children is a contributing factor to their sexual abuse.

Children Enjoy Participating in Beauty Pageants

While young children may express enjoyment in participating in pageants, 14 children are eager to please adults. Sleeping with their hair in curlers, having to sit quietly while their hair is being tinted or rolled, fake nails being applied, or their body being spray tanned hardly seems like activities very young girls would choose over having fun with friends in age-appropriate play. The negative reactions of many of the participants in *Toddlers and Tiaras* testify to this.

Participation in Beauty Pageants Is No Different from Participating in Athletic or Suzuki Music Education Programs

Children's athletic programs and music education programs teach skills 15 appropriate to the developmental stage of the child upon which the child can build later in life rather than emphasizing the beauty of the human body that can change significantly with time. In Suzuki recitals, for example, the unique contribution of each child is recognized and no child loses.

Do child beauty pageants constitute child abuse?

"Do child beauty pageants constitute child abuse?"

16

17

This question must be answered on an individual basis. Parents who force their children to participate in pageants, as well as in athletic and music education programs, can be emotionally and even physically abusive, if participation is meeting parental needs rather that the needs of the child.

The risk for such abuse to occur is perhaps greatest when children are not recognized for what they are—children—but rather are forced to assume miniature adult roles. 18

Play is an important factor in children's early development because, through play, they learn skills for adulthood. 19

After all, what is the rush to become an adult? 20

Identifying the Elements of an Evaluation Argument

1. Wiehe does not state his thesis directly. Write a thesis statement for this essay by filling in the template below. (Hint: Try answering the questions Wiehe asks in paragraph 4.)

    Because _____

    _____, beauty pageants

    are bad for children.

2. What criteria does Wiehe use to evaluate child beauty pageants? If he wanted to make the opposite case, what criteria might he use instead?

3. In his essay's boldface headings, Wiehe identifies four opposing arguments. Which of these opposing arguments do you think presents the strongest challenge to Wiehe's position? Why?

4. Do you think Wiehe expects his readers to have seen the program *Toddlers and Tiaras*? Does he expect them to have strong feelings about child beauty pageants? How can you tell?

5. After he has refuted arguments against his position, Wiehe (a professor emeritus of social work) begins a discussion of whether "child beauty pageants constitute child abuse" (para. 16). Should he have done more to prepare readers for this discussion? Explain.

6. Do you think Wiehe's concluding statement would have a greater impact if it were in the form of a statement rather than a question? Write a new sentence that could serve as a strong concluding statement for this essay.

Do the Benefits of Fracking Outweigh the Environmental Risks?

Education Images/Getty Images

Reread the At Issue box on page 517, which provides background on the question of whether the perceived advantages of fracking outweigh concerns about possible environmental damage. Then, read the sources on the pages that follow.

As you read these sources, you will be asked to respond to some questions and complete some activities. This work is designed to help you understand the content and structure of the selections. When you are finished, you will be ready to decide on the criteria you will use to write an **evaluation argument** on the topic, "Do the Benefits of Fracking Outweigh the Environmental Risks?"

SOURCES

Elizabeth Kolbert, "Burning Love," p. 531

Sean Lennon, "Destroying Precious Land for Gas," p. 534

Thomas L. Friedman, "Get It Right on Gas," p. 537

Scott McNally, "Water Contamination—Fracking Is Not the Problem," p. 540

Shale Gas Production Subcommittee, From *Shale Gas Production Subcommittee 90-Day Report*, p. 543
US Department of Energy

USA Today Editorial Board, "Fracking, with Care, Brings Big Benefits," p. 546

This article first appeared in the December 5, 2011, issue of the *New Yorker*.

BURNING LOVE

ELIZABETH KOLBERT

Americans have never met a hydrocarbon they didn't like. Oil, natural gas, 1
liquefied natural gas, tar-sands oil, coal-bed methane, and coal, which is,
mostly, carbon—the country loves them all, not wisely, but too well. To the
extent that the United States has an energy policy, it is perhaps best summed
up as: if you've got it, burn it.

America's latest hydrocarbon crush is shale gas. Shale gas has been around 2
for a long time—the Marcellus Shale, which underlies much of Pennsylvania
and western New York, dates back to the mid-Devonian period, almost four
hundred million years ago—and geologists have been aware of its potential as
a fuel source for many decades. But it wasn't until recently that, owing to
advances in drilling technology, extracting the gas became a lucrative proposition. The result has been what *National Geographic* has called "the great shale
gas rush." In the past ten months alone, some sixteen hundred new wells have
been drilled in Pennsylvania; it is projected that the total number in the state
could eventually grow to more than a hundred thousand. Nationally, shale-gas
production has increased by a factor of twelve in the past ten years.

Like many rushes before it, the shale-gas version has made some people 3
wealthy and others miserable. Landowners in shale-rich areas have received
thousands of dollars an acre in up-front payments for the right to drill under
their property, with the promise of thousands more to come in royalties. A
new term has been invented to describe them: "shaleionaires."

Meanwhile, some of their neighbors—who are, perhaps, also shaleionaires— 4
have watched their tap water turn brown and, on occasion, explode. Shale gas is
embedded in dense rock, so drillers use a mixture of water, sand, and chemicals
to open up fissures in the stone through which it can escape. (This is the process known as "hydraulic fracturing," or, more colloquially, "fracking.") In the
2005 energy bill, largely crafted by Vice-President Dick Cheney, fracking was
explicitly exempted from federal review under the Safe Drinking Water Act. As
a result of this dispensation, which has been dubbed the Halliburton Loophole,
drilling companies are under no obligation to make public which chemicals
they use. Likely candidates include such recognized or suspected carcinogens
as benzene and formaldehyde.

Shale gas is found deep underground; most of the Marcellus Shale sits a 5
mile or more beneath the surface, far below the level of groundwater. Industry officials argue that the depth of the formations makes it impossible
for fracking to pollute drinking-water supplies. "There have been over a
million wells hydraulically fractured in the history of the industry, and there
is not one—not one—reported case of a freshwater aquifer having ever been

contaminated," Rex Tillerson, the chairman and C.E.O. of ExxonMobil, declared at a congressional hearing last year.

Nevertheless, as the *Times* recently reported, contamination with fracking 6 fluid has occurred. (Details of contamination cases are difficult to get, because most of the records have been sealed in litigation.) And, just a few weeks ago, the Environmental Protection Agency reported that drinking water in Pavillion, Wyoming, contained a chemical that is commonly found in fracking fluid, although the agency has not yet determined whether fracking was the source. The E.P.A. is also investigating several cases of suspected contamination in the town of Dimock, Pennsylvania.

Shale gas itself presents another potential problem. A recent study by 7 researchers at Duke University showed that methane frequently leaks into drinking water near active fracking sites, which probably explains why some homeowners have been able to set their tap water on fire. Yet another possible source of contamination is so-called "flowback" water. Huge quantities of water are used in fracking, and as much as forty percent of it can come back up out of the gas wells, bringing with it corrosive salts, volatile organic compounds, and radioactive elements, such as radium. Citing public-health concerns, Pennsylvania recently asked drillers to stop taking flowback water to municipal treatment plants.

New York State currently has a moratorium on fracking permits, pending 8 the adoption of new regulations. Anxiety about New York City's drinking-water supply has prompted the state's Department of Environmental Conservation to recommend, in a set of draft rules, that the practice be prohibited in the city's upstate watershed. (The department is holding a hearing on the proposed regulations this week in Manhattan; a similar hearing, held earlier this month in Binghamton, drew nearly two thousand people.) There is also a moratorium on fracking in the Delaware River Basin, which spans parts of New York, New Jersey, Delaware, and Pennsylvania and is the source of drinking water for fifteen million people. The Delaware River Basin Commission, the body charged with protecting water quality in the region, was expected to lift that moratorium last week; however, the decision was put off after Delaware's governor, Jack Markell, a commission member, announced that he would vote against the move. "Once hydrofracturing begins in the basin, the proverbial 'faucet' cannot be turned off, with any damage to our freshwater supplies likely requiring generations of effort to clean up," Markell wrote in a letter explaining his decision.

Every kind of energy extraction, of course, poses risks. Mountaintop-removal 9 mining, as the name suggests, involves "removing" entire mountaintops, usually with explosives, to get at a layer of coal. Coal plants, meanwhile, produce almost twice the volume of greenhouse gases as natural-gas plants per unit of energy generated. In the end, the best case to be made for fracking is that much of what is already being done is probably even worse.

> "In the end, the best case to be made for fracking is that much of what is already being done is probably even worse."

The trouble with this sort of argument is that, in the absence of a rational 10
energy policy, there's no reason to substitute shale gas for coal. We can combust
them both! The way things now stand, there's nothing to prevent us from getting
wasted mountains *and* polluted drinking water, and a ruined climate to boot.

In the coming decades, ever-improving technologies will almost certainly 11
make new sources of hydrocarbons accessible. At some point, either we will
outgrow our infatuation or we will burn our way to a very dark place.

⊘ AT ISSUE: SOURCES FOR DEVELOPING AN EVALUATION ARGUMENT

1. Kolbert opens her essay with a provocative statement: "Americans have never met a hydrocarbon they didn't like" (para. 1). Is she attacking her readers? If so, for what purpose?

2. In paragraph 3, Kolbert notes that shale-gas drilling "has made some people wealthy and others miserable." How does she support this statement?

3. In presenting background on the development of fracking, Kolbert notes that it was "explicitly exempted from federal review under the Safe Drinking Water Act" (4). What do you see as the significance of this exemption?

4. How do you think Kolbert might have expected her readers to react to the following?

   - "Americans' latest hydrocarbon crush is shale gas" (2).

   - "A new term has been invented . . . 'shaleionaires'" (3).

   - "The way things now stand, there's nothing to prevent us from getting wasted mountains *and* polluted drinking water, and a ruined climate to boot" (10).

   Do these statements exhibit bias on Kolbert's part? If so, how? If not, explain why the statements are both fair and logical.

5. Kolbert takes a strong stand against fracking. Paraphrase her thesis by filling in the following template:

   Although it has made many individuals and businesses wealthy, fracking should be banned because _____

   _____.

6. Reread Kolbert's last sentence. Is she committing the **either/or fallacy** here? Explain.

This op-ed ran in the *New York Times* on August 27, 2012.

DESTROYING PRECIOUS LAND FOR GAS

SEAN LENNON

On the northern tip of Delaware County, N.Y., where the Catskill Mountains 1 curl up into little kitten hills, and Ouleout Creek slithers north into the Susquehanna River, there is a farm my parents bought before I was born. My earliest memories there are of skipping stones with my father and drinking unpasteurized milk. There are bald eagles and majestic pines, honeybees and raspberries. My mother even planted a ring of white birch trees around the property for protection.

A few months ago I was asked by a neighbor near our farm to attend a 2 town meeting at the local high school. Some gas companies at the meeting were trying very hard to sell us on a plan to tear through our wilderness and make room for a new pipeline: infrastructure for hydraulic fracturing. Most of the residents at the meeting, many of them organic farmers, were openly defiant. The gas companies didn't seem to care. They gave us the feeling that whether we liked it or not, they were going to fracture our little town.

In the late '70s, when Manhattanites like Andy Warhol and Bianca Jagger 3 were turning Montauk and East Hampton into an epicurean Shangri-La for the Studio 54 crowd, my parents, John Lennon and Yoko Ono, were looking to become amateur dairy farmers. My first introduction to a cow was being taught how to milk it by hand. I'll never forget the realization that fresh milk could be so much sweeter than what we bought in grocery stores. Although I was rarely able to persuade my schoolmates to leave Long Island for what seemed to them an unreasonably rural escapade, I was lucky enough to experience trout fishing instead of tennis lessons, swimming holes instead of swimming pools, and campfires instead of cable television.

Though my father died when I was 5, I have always felt lucky to live on 4 land he loved dearly; land in an area that is now on the verge of being destroyed. When the gas companies showed up in our backyard, I felt I needed to do some research. I looked into Pennsylvania, where hundreds of families have been left with ruined drinking water, toxic fumes in the air, industrialized landscapes, thousands of trucks and new roads crosshatching the wilderness, and a devastating and irreversible decline in property value.

Natural gas has been sold as clean energy. But when the gas comes from 5 fracturing bedrock with about five million gallons of toxic water per well, the word "clean" takes on a disturbingly Orwellian tone. Don't be fooled. Fracking for shale gas is in truth dirty energy. It inevitably leaks toxic chemicals into the air and water. Industry stud- ies show that 5 percent of wells can leak immediately, and 60 percent over 30 years. There is no such thing as pipes and con- crete that won't eventually break down. It releases a cocktail of chemicals from a menu of more than 600 toxic substances, climate-changing methane, radium, and, of course, uranium.

> "Fracking for shale gas is in truth dirty energy."

New York is lucky enough to have some of the best drinking water in the 6 world. The well water on my family's farm comes from the same watersheds that supply all the reservoirs in New York State. That means if our tap water gets dirty, so does New York City's.

Gas produced this way is not climate-friendly. Within the first 20 years, 7 methane escaping from within and around the wells, pipelines, and compres- sor stations is 105 times more powerful a greenhouse gas than carbon dioxide. With more than a tiny amount of methane leakage, this gas is as bad as coal is for the climate; and since over half the wells leak eventually, it is not a small amount. Even more important, shale gas contains one of the earth's largest carbon reserves, many times more than our atmosphere can absorb. Burning more than a small fraction of it will render the climate unlivable, raise the price of food, and make coastlines unstable for generations.

Mayor Michael R. Bloomberg, when speaking for "the voices in the 8 sensible center," seems to think the New York State Association of County Health Officials, the American Academy of Pediatrics, the New York State Nurses Association, and the Medical Society of the State of New York, not to mention Dr. Anthony R. Ingraffea's studies at Cornell University, are "loud voices at the extremes." The mayor's plan to "make sure that the gas is extracted carefully and in the right places" is akin to a smoker telling you, "Smoking lighter cigarettes in the right place at the right time makes it safe to smoke."

Few people are aware that America's Natural Gas Alliance has spent 9 $80 million in a publicity campaign that includes the services of Hill and Knowlton—the public relations firm that through most of the '50s and '60s told America that tobacco had no verifiable links to cancer. Natural gas is clean, and cigarettes are healthy—talk about disinformation. To try to counteract this, my mother and I have started a group called Artists Against Fracking.

My father could have chosen to live anywhere. I suspect he chose to live 10 here because being a New Yorker is not about class, race, or even nationality; it's about loving New York. Even the United States Geological Survey has said New York's draft plan fails to protect drinking water supplies, and has also acknowledged the likely link between hydraulic fracturing and recent earth- quakes in the Midwest. Surely the voice of the "sensible center" would ask to stop all hydraulic fracturing so that our water, our lives, and our planet could be protected and preserved for generations to come.

⊘ AT ISSUE: SOURCES FOR DEVELOPING AN EVALUATION ARGUMENT

1. Throughout this essay, Lennon is careful to establish himself as a resident of a rural area, a farmer, and someone who grew up swimming and fishing in an idyllic natural setting. Why does he do this? Does this information appeal to *logos*, *ethos*, or *pathos*? Explain.

2. Although Lennon mentions his parents in paragraphs 1 and 2, he doesn't identify them by name until paragraph 3. Why not? Is his readers' knowledge of who his parents were likely to add to, detract from, or not affect his credibility on the subject of fracking?

3. Why do you think Lennon tells readers in paragraph 4 that he "needed to do some research"? What did his research reveal?

4. Reread paragraph 8. Do you think Lennon is making an **ad hominem** attack on former New York City mayor Michael R. Bloomberg here? Why or why not?

5. What kind of evidence does Lennon present to support his position against fracking? Does he include enough evidence—as well as the right kind of evidence—to support his defense of the land he believes is threatened? Why or why not?

The *New York Times* ran this op-ed on August 4, 2012.

GET IT RIGHT ON GAS

THOMAS L. FRIEDMAN

We are in the midst of a natural gas revolution in America that is a potential 1
game changer for the economy, environment, and our national security—if we
do it right.

The enormous stores of natural gas that have been locked away 2
in shale deposits across America that we've now been able to tap into,
thanks to breakthroughs in seismic imaging, horizontal drilling,
and hydraulic fracturing, or
"fracking," are enabling us to
replace much dirtier coal with
cleaner gas as the largest source of
electricity generation in America.
And natural gas may soon be pow-

> "This is helping to lower our
> carbon emissions faster than
> expected and make us more
> energy secure."

ering cars, trucks, and ships as well. This is helping to lower our carbon
emissions faster than expected and make us more energy secure. And, if
prices stay low, it may enable America to bring back manufacturing that
migrated overseas. But, as the energy and climate expert Hal Harvey puts
it, there is just one big, hugely important question to be asked about this
natural gas bounty: "Will it be a transition to a clean energy future, or does
it defer a clean energy future?"

That is *the* question—because natural gas is still a fossil fuel. The good 3
news: It emits only half as much greenhouse gas as coal when combusted and,
therefore, contributes only half as much to global warming. The better news:
The recent glut has made it inexpensive to deploy. But there is a hidden, long-
term, cost: A sustained gas glut could undermine new investments in wind,
solar, nuclear, and energy efficiency systems—which have zero emissions—
and thus keep us addicted to fossil fuels for decades.

That would be reckless. This year's global extremes of droughts and 4
floods are totally consistent with models of disruptive, nonlinear climate
change. After record warm temperatures in the first half of this year, it
was no surprise to find last week that the Department of Agriculture has
now designated more than half of all U.S. counties—1,584 in 32 states—
as primary disaster areas where crops and grazing areas have been ravaged
by drought.

That is why on May 29 the British newspaper *The Guardian* quoted 5
Fatih Birol, the chief economist for the International Energy Agency, as saying
that "a golden age for gas is not necessarily a golden age for the climate"—if
natural gas ends up sinking renewables. Maria van der Hoeven, executive

director of the I.E.A., urged governments to keep in place subsidies and regulations to encourage investments in wind, solar, and other renewables "for years to come" so they remain competitive.

Moreover, while natural gas is cleaner than coal, extracting it can be very 6 dirty. We have to do this right. For instance, the carbon advantage can be undermined by leakage of uncombusted natural gas from wellheads and pipelines because methane—the primary component of natural gas—is an extremely powerful greenhouse gas, more powerful than carbon dioxide. The big oil companies can easily maintain high drilling standards, but a lot of fracking is done by mom-and-pop drillers that do not. The standards that can make fracking environmentally O.K. are not expensive, but the big drillers want to make sure that the little guys have to apply them, too, so everyone has the same cost basis.

On July 19, *Forbes* interviewed George Phydias Mitchell, who, in the 7 1990s, pioneered the use of fracking to break natural gas free from impermeable shale. According to *Forbes*, Mitchell argued that fracking needs to be regulated by the Department of Energy, not just states: "Because if they don't do it right, there could be trouble," he says. There's no excuse not to get it right. "There are good techniques to make it safe that should be followed properly," he says. But, the smaller, independent drillers, "are wild." "It's tough to control these independents. If they do something wrong and dangerous, they should punish them."

Adds Fred Krupp, the president of the Environmental Defense Fund who 8 has been working with the government and companies on drilling standards: "The economic and national security advantages of natural gas are obvious, but if you tour some of these areas of intensive development the environmental impacts are equally obvious." We need nationally accepted standards for controlling methane leakage, for controlling water used in fracking—where you get it, how you treat the polluted water that comes out from the fracking process, and how you protect aquifers—and for ensuring that communities have the right to say no to drilling. "The key message," said Krupp, "is you gotta get the rules right. States need real inspector capacity and compliance schemes where companies certify they have done it right and there are severe penalties if they perjure."

Energy companies who want to keep regulations lax need to understand 9 that a series of mishaps around natural gas will—justifiably—trigger an environmental backlash to stop it.

But we also need to get the economics right. We'll need more tax revenue 10 to reach a budget deal in January. Why not a carbon tax that raises enough money to help pay down the deficit and lower both personal income taxes and corporate taxes—and ensures that renewables remain competitive with natural gas? That would ensure this gas revolution transforms America, not just our electric grid.

⊙ AT ISSUE: SOURCES FOR DEVELOPING AN EVALUATION ARGUMENT

1. Friedman uses the terms *revolution* and *game changer* in his opening paragraph. Is this language appropriate here, or do you think Friedman is exaggerating or overstating his case?

2. Friedman does not consider fracking to be evil, nor does he see it as a solution to all of America's energy problems; his position falls somewhere in between these two extremes. State Friedman's position in one sentence. Assuming that this sentence could serve as the essay's thesis statement, where would you locate it? Why?

3. What experts does Friedman quote? Do they agree with one another, or do they have different views of fracking? Do they all agree with Friedman? Explain.

4. What criteria does Friedman use to evaluate fracking? Are these the same criteria used by other writers whose essays appear in this section?

5. According to Friedman, how should the United States "get it right on gas"? What "right" steps does he propose? Do you agree?

Scientific American published this argument as a guest post on its blog on January 25, 2012.

WATER CONTAMINATION— FRACKING IS NOT THE PROBLEM

SCOTT MCNALLY

With the current negative attention and controversy surrounding shale gas 1 drilling, the words *hydraulic fracturing* or *fracking* have become synonymous with something else: water contamination. But according to recent research out of MIT, the contamination of drinking water near natural gas wells is caused by something totally different. In fact, fracking has nothing to do with it.

Shale gas was long considered inaccessible and unprofitable because of 2 the low permeability of shale formations, but recent developments in horizontal drilling and multi-stage hydraulic fracturing have made shale gas production economically viable. As a result, shale gas drilling has increased dramatically and sparked debates on the safety and environmental impacts of hydraulic fracturing.

You may have seen the commercials supporting fracking that say, "clean 3 burning natural gas is the gateway to our low carbon future." You may have also seen the Academy Award Nominated documentary *Gasland*, which highlights some of the environmental risks and discusses contaminated aquifers. Some have even called for a ban on fracking. Unfortunately, in this debate, some of the facts have been clouded by misinformation, anecdotal evidence, and back and forth attempts to discredit those on both side of the argument.

So what is the truth? 4

Can drilling for natural gas contaminate drinking water? Yes. 5

Is hydraulic fracturing to blame? No. 6

Bottom line: water contamination 7 does happen, but not because of hydraulic fracturing. The MIT Future of Natural Gas Study, released in June 2011, examines the causes of 43 reported environmental incidents and finds that, "no incidents of direct invasion of shallow water zones by fracture fluids during the fracturing process have been recorded."

> "Bottom line: water contamination does happen, but not because of hydraulic fracturing."

So what causes the contamination? According to the study, "almost 8 50 percent [of the incidents were] the result of drilling operations . . . most frequently related to inadequate cementing of casing into wellbores." The table below is from the Future of Natural Gas Study and highlights the frequency and causes of incidents.

Type of Incident	Number Reported	Percentage of Total
Groundwater contamination by natural gas	20	47%
On-site surface spills	14	33%
Off-site disposal issues	4	9%
Water withdrawal issues	2	4%
Air quality	1	2%
Blowouts	2	4%

9   While the most common incident is groundwater contamination resulting from drilling operations, the study also states that, "Properly implemented cementing procedures should prevent this from occurring."

10   But, to be absolutely clear, hydraulic fracturing is not part of the drilling process. It is part of well completions, and is typically done several weeks after drilling has stopped. This is where much of the confusion sets in. You may have heard something like this before: "There has never been a documented case of the fractures in a shale gas production zone migrating upward to the water bearing zones. There are thousands of feet of impermeable rock separating the two, and the rock mechanics make it a physical impossibility."

11   That is true. However, that does not mean fracking fluid cannot get into the aquifer. So how does this happen? If fractures never reach the aquifers, then how does the fracking fluid get there?

12   It goes like this:

13   Sometimes, drillers have to drill through an aquifer to access a natural gas zone that is farther below. (By the way, an aquifer is an underground layer of water-bearing permeable rock. It is not an underground lake or cavern that is filled with water, like many people imagine.) If the act of drilling through the aquifer and cementing the walls of the hole is not done carefully, there is a higher chance that the cement casing can crack, leaking hydrocarbons and other fluids into the aquifer. If there is a casing leak near the water table, whatever is traveling up or down the well can leak into the aquifer. Since the fracking fluids have to travel through this pipe twice (once on the way down, once on the way back up), it can contaminate the water through the casing leak. In fact, whatever travels through that pipe can leak into the aquifer. Sometimes it is fracking fluid, but more commonly, it is methane, drilling mud, or produced formation water.

14   Aquifer contamination can happen whether you frac a well or not, and bad cementing and casing leaks are possible in any well—vertical, horizontal, fracked, or unfracked.

15   Now, there are significant environmental concerns related to gas drilling, but let's put them into context. 20,000 shale gas wells have been fracked

in the last ten years, and the Future of Natural Gas Study pulled 43 of the most widely reported environmental incidents, and not a single one was caused by fracking. Now, there were likely more than just 43 environmental incidents, indeed, the study mentions, "The data set does not purport to be comprehensive, but is intended to give a sense of the relative frequency of various types of incidents."

Regardless of the frequency of incidents, any spill or leak is unacceptable, 16 and the pressure should be on the drillers and operators to minimize the environmental impacts of natural gas production. But, the data show the vast majority of natural gas development projects are safe, and the existing environmental concerns are largely preventable.

⊙ AT ISSUE: SOURCES FOR DEVELOPING AN EVALUATION ARGUMENT

1. In your own words, restate McNally's position on the relationship between fracking and water contamination. If, as his title states, "fracking is not the problem," what *is* the problem?

2. In paragraph 3, McNally refers to pro-fracking commercials and to the documentary *Gasland*. Why? What does he hope to accomplish?

3. In paragraph 7, McNally supports his position by summarizing the results of an MIT study. Does he provide additional support? If so, what kind and where? Do you think he provides enough support?

4. Evaluate the table presented in paragraph 8. Is it helpful? Is it necessary? Explain your reasoning.

5. In paragraph 15, McNally acknowledges that there are "significant environmental concerns related to gas drilling." Does this statement undercut his argument? Why or why not?

The material below first appeared in a report by the Shale Gas Production Subcommittee for the U.S. Department of Energy in 2011.

FROM *SHALE GAS PRODUCTION SUBCOMMITTEE 90-DAY REPORT*

The Subcommittee believes that the U.S. shale gas resource has enormous 1 potential to provide economic and environmental benefits for the county. Shale gas is a widely distributed resource in North America that can be relatively cheaply produced, creating jobs across the country. Natural gas—if properly produced and transported—also offers climate change advantages because of its low carbon content compared to coal.

US Department of Energy

Domestic production of shale gas also has the potential over time to 2 reduce dependence on imported oil for the United States. International shale gas production will increase the diversity of supply for other nations. Both these developments offer important national security benefits.[1]

The development of shale gas in the United States has been very rapid. Natural 3 gas from all sources is one of America's major fuels, providing about 25 percent of total U.S. energy. Shale gas, in turn, was less than 2 percent of total

U.S. natural gas production in 2001. Today, it is approaching 30 percent.[2] But it was only around 2008 that the significance of shale gas began to be widely recognized. Since then, output has increased four-fold. It has brought new regions into the supply mix. Output from the Haynesville shale, mostly in Louisiana, for example, was negligible in 2008; today, the Haynesville shale alone produces 8 percent of total U.S. natural gas output. According to the U.S. Energy Information Administration (EIA), the rapid expansion of shale gas production is expected to continue in the future. The EIA projects shale gas to be 46 percent of domestic production by 2035. The following figure shows the stunning change.

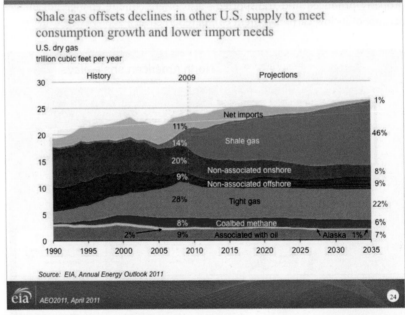

US Department of Energy

The economic significance is potentially very large. While estimates vary, 4 well over 200,000 jobs (direct, indirect, and induced) have been created over the last several years by the development of domestic production of shale gas, and tens of thousands more will be created in the future.[3] As late as 2007, before the impact of the shale gas revolution, it was assumed that the United States would be importing large amounts of liquefied natural gas from the Middle East and other areas. Today, the United States is essentially self-sufficient in natural gas, with the only notable imports being from Canada, and expected to remain so for many decades. The price of natural gas has fallen by more than a factor of two since 2008, benefiting consumers in the lower cost of home heating and electricity.

Endnotes

[1] The James Baker III Institute for Public Policy at Rice University has recently released a report on *Shale Gas and U.S. National Security*, available at: http://bakerinstitute.org/publications/EFpub-DOEShaleGas -07192011.pdf.

[2] As a share of total dry gas production in the "lower 48," shale gas was 6 percent in 2006, 8 percent in 2007, at which time its share began to grow rapidly—reaching 12 percent in 2008, 16 percent in 2009, and 24 percent in 2010. In June 2011, it reached 29 percent. Source: Energy Information Administration and Lippman Consulting.

[3] Timothy Considine, Robert W. Watson, and Nicholas B. Considine, "The Economy Opportunities of Shale Energy Development," Manhattan Institute, May 2011, Table 2, page 6.

⊘ AT ISSUE: SOURCES FOR DEVELOPING AN EVALUATION ARGUMENT

1. What position on fracking is taken by the authors of this report?

2. Do the visuals simply present information, or do they actually make an argument? Explain your reasoning.

3. This report was produced by a subcommittee for the U.S. Department of Energy. How do you think the affiliation of these writers might have influenced their *ethos*? How does their affiliation affect your response to the report?

This editorial was posted on July 5, 2015, at USAToday.com.

FRACKING, WITH CARE, BRINGS BIG BENEFITS

USA TODAY EDITORIAL BOARD

Fracking—the practice of cracking open underground oil and gas formations with water, sand, and chemicals—has rescued U.S. energy production from a dangerous decline. Any debate about banning it should take a hard look at what that would cost the nation and at facts that aren't always part of the discussion.

Those facts are spelled out in a recent report from the Environmental Protection Agency on fracking and groundwater. One of the harshest charges against fracking, often leveled with apocalyptic intensity by its foes, is that it indiscriminately contaminates vital drinking water supplies.

The EPA's timely report essentially said that's overblown.

The study identified many ways fracking *could* cause damage, but found little evidence that it had. Yes, there were instances of contaminated drinking water wells, but there was no evidence of "widespread, systemic" harm, and the number of problems that did occur "was small compared to the number of (fracked) wells."

> "The study identified many ways fracking *could* cause damage, but found little evidence that it had."

Presuming no follow-up investigations change these findings, the report adds to the solid case that fracking should continue, with careful oversight, and that bans in Maryland, New York, and other states are wrongheaded.

The EPA findings come as welcome news because it's hard to overstate the impact fracking has had on U.S. oil and gas production, which looked to be in irreversible decline in the 1980s. The decline raised fears that imports would soar, making the United States even more dependent than it already was on other nations.

Fracking now accounts for 56 percent of U.S. natural gas production and 48 percent of oil output, according to the Energy Information Administration. The boom has helped make America the world's No. 1 producer of oil and gas, and it has pushed the nation much closer to energy independence than almost anyone dared hope in the 1980s and 1990s.

Huge new natural gas supplies have helped lower prices, fuel a manufacturing turnaround, and displace much dirtier coal in electricity production, cutting air pollution and greenhouse gas emissions.

All that said, the EPA report does validate fears that fracking can be a serious hazard if done sloppily. Like conventional wells, fracked wells have to pass through groundwater on their way to oil and gas zones that can be a mile or more below the deepest groundwater. Wells must be secured with casing and cement that keep fracking fluids, oil, and gas from escaping into drinking water, but the EPA found scattered instances where inadequate casing or a bad cement job allowed natural gas and chemicals to get into groundwater.

Drilling for oil and gas is complicated and challenging, but safe drilling 10 and production practices have been known for decades. Drillers have learned that the price for sloppiness can be catastrophic, as with the Deepwater Horizon blowout in the Gulf of Mexico five years ago, which just cost BP a settlement for nearly $19 billion.

Ultimately, it's up to the industry to show that the considerable rewards 11 from fracking justify the sort of risks the EPA study identified. So far, that's what has happened.

⊘ AT ISSUE: SOURCES FOR WRITING AN EVALUATION ARGUMENT

1. This newspaper editorial begins with a definition of *fracking*. Is this an effective opening strategy? Why or why not?

2. The writers of this editorial take a stand against banning fracking, citing its benefits. What are those benefits? Do you agree with their position?

3. Where do the writers summarize arguments in favor of banning fracking? What are these arguments? Do the writers effectively refute them? Explain.

4. According to the writers, under what circumstances can fracking pose dangers? How might these dangers be minimized or eliminated?

5. What do the writers mean by "apocalyptic intensity" (para. 2)? What does their use of this phrase tell you about their view of those who are against fracking? Can you identify any other language that supports the writers' view of the anti-fracking community?

6. Do you find the editorial's brief conclusion to be sufficiently strong, or do you think the writers need to do more? Explain.

TEMPLATE FOR WRITING AN EVALUATION ARGUMENT

Write a one-paragraph evaluation argument in which you take a position on whether the benefits of fracking are worth the environmental risks. Follow the template below, filling in the blanks to create your argument.

Depending on the criteria used for evaluation, fracking can be seen in a largely positive or negative light. If it is judged on the basis of _____, it seems clear that it (is / is not) a valuable and necessary process. Some people say that _____ _____. They also point out that _____.

Others disagree with this position, claiming that _____ _____.

However, _____ _____.

All things considered, _____ _____.

➔ EXERCISE 14.6

In a group of three or four students, discuss your own opinions about the pros and cons of fracking. Is fracking really necessary? What benefits are associated with this process? What alternative scenarios are possible? What possible negative outcomes do you see? Write a paragraph that summarizes your group's conclusions.

➔ EXERCISE 14.7

Write an evaluation argument on the topic, "Do the Benefits of Fracking Outweigh the Environmental Risks?" Begin by establishing the criteria by which you will evaluate both benefits and risks. Then, consider how well fracking meets these criteria. (If you like, you may incorporate the material you developed in the template and Exercise 14.6 into your essay.) Cite the sources on pages 531–547, and be sure to document the sources you use and to include a works-cited page. (See Chapter 10 for information on documenting sources.)

➔ EXERCISE 14.8

Review the four pillars of argument discussed in Chapter 1. Does your essay include all four elements of an effective argument? Add anything that is missing. Then, label the key elements of your essay.

❍ WRITING ASSIGNMENTS: EVALUATION ARGUMENTS

1. As a college student, you have probably had to fill out course-evaluation forms. Now, you are going to write an evaluation of one of your courses in the form of an argumentative essay that takes a strong stand on the quality of the course. Before you begin, decide on the criteria by which you will evaluate it—for example, what practical skills it provided to prepare you for your future courses or employment, whether you enjoyed the course, or what you learned. (If you can download an evaluation form, you can use it to help you brainstorm.)

2. Write an evaluation argument challenging a popular position on the quality of a product or service that you know or use. For example, you can defend a campus service that most students criticize or criticize a popular restaurant or film. Be sure you establish your criteria for evaluation before you begin. (You do not have to use the same criteria used by those who have taken the opposite position.)

3. Write a comparative evaluation—an essay in which you argue that one thing is superior to another. You can compare two websites, two streaming services, two part-time jobs, or any other two subjects you feel confident you can write about. In your thesis, take the position that one of your two subjects is superior to the other. As you would with any evaluation, begin by deciding on the criteria you will use.

STUDENT DEBT has eclipsed $1 trillion

Student loan delinquencies are a national issue:
93% of student loans in 2012 were issued by the federal government*

$26,682**
the average
graduate debt

60%
of all college students
take out loans**

Who's Graduating?+

69%	62%	50%	39%
Asian/Pacific Islanders	White	Hispanic	Black

One in five
households have student debt.**

MassMutual has been providing college scholarships for

2,222   college students have been offered scholarships
from MassMutual to help them pay for college

$15,594,235   have been offered to students by
MassMutual to help pay for college

20 YEARS

surpassing both auto & home loans*

* Mitchell, Josh. Federal Student Lending Swells. The Wall Street Journal (Washington, D.C.), 28 Nov., 2012: A1.
** Pew Research Center. Tabulations of Survey of Consumer Finances Data (2012). A Record One-in-Five Households Now Owe Student Loan Debt. 26 Sept., 2012.
+ For first-time, full-time students (within 6 years) who began seeking a bachelor's degree in fall 2004. U.S. Department of Education, National Center for Education Statistics (2012), The Condition of Education 2012.

CRN201502-169297

15

Proposal Arguments

AT ISSUE

Should the Government Do More to Relieve the Student-Loan Burden?

In 2011, the protest movement called Occupy Wall Street began in New York City's Zuccotti Park. At first, the protestors' focus was on issues such as social and economic inequality, high unemployment, and lack of affordable health care. As the movement spread, other issues came to the forefront, including a demand for student-loan forgiveness. Perhaps in response to the wide attention attracted by the protests, President Barack Obama announced a program of student-loan relief. Acknowledging that student debt was excessive—it exceeded $1 trillion in 2012—the president reduced the maximum required payment on student loans from 15 percent to 10 percent of a borrower's annual income and instituted a policy of debt forgiveness after twenty years.

Currently, the student loan debt is over $1.2 trillion; needless to say, this is a cause for concern. According to some financial experts, student loans have created a financial bubble that will eventually burst and cause more damage than the housing bubble of 2008. Some critics point out that reforms to the current student-loan program do not address the root cause of

the problem—the ever-increasing cost of tuition. (For example, in academic year 2014, in-state tuition at public four-year colleges rose 2.9 percent, and tuition and fees at private non-profit four-year colleges rose 3.7 percent to $31,231 a year.) To address this problem, some critics have proposed a total restructuring of federal aid to colleges and universities, rewarding those schools that are able to reduce expenses and penalizing schools that are not. Those against government involvement in the student-loan program cite studies that suggest that most students receive enough financial aid to offset tuition; according to them, the situation is not as serious as activists would have us believe. Others say that students should not ask for debt forgiveness but should realize that like all borrowers, they have an obligation to live up to their end of the bargain and repay their loans.

Later in this chapter, you will be asked to think more about this issue. You will be given several sources to consider and asked to write a **proposal argument** that takes a position on whether the government should do more to relieve the student-loan burden.

Many college students apply for loans.

Kirby Hamilton/iStock/Getty Images

What Is a Proposal Argument?

When you write a **proposal argument**, you suggest a solution to a problem. The purpose of a proposal argument is to convince people that a problem exists and that your solution is both practical and worthwhile.

Proposal arguments are the most common form of argument. You see them every day on billboards and in advertisements, editorials, and letters to the editor. The problems proposal arguments address can be local:

- What steps should the community take to protect its historic buildings?
- How can the city promote the use of public transportation?
- What can the township do to help the homeless?
- What should be done to encourage recycling on campus?
- How can community health services be improved?

The problems addressed in proposal arguments can also be more global:

- Should the United States increase its military budget?
- What should be done to increase clean energy production?
- What is the best way to lower the federal deficit?
- What can countries do to protect themselves against terrorism?
- What should be done to decrease gun violence?

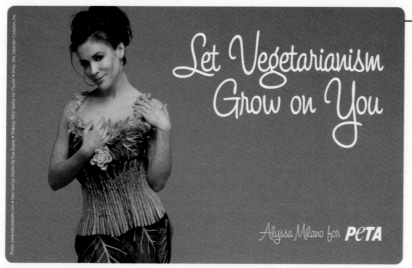

Many proposals try to influence behavior.

Image courtesy of People for the Ethical Treatment of Animals, www.peta.org

PROBLEM-SOLVING STRATEGIES

Because the purpose of a proposal argument is to solve a problem, you should begin by considering both the problem and its significance. By following a simple step-by-step process (alone or in a group), you can analyze the problem and develop effective strategies for solving it.

Identify the problem.

Explore the possible causes of the problem.

Brainstorm possible solutions.

Examine the advantages and disadvantages of each solution.

Select the best option.

Remember, problem solving is a process. If you solve the problem, you can begin to plan your proposal. If not, you should begin the process again, perhaps modifying the problem or its possible solutions.

Stating the Problem

When you write a proposal argument, you should begin by demonstrating that a problem exists. In some cases, readers will be familiar with the problem, so you will not have to explain it in great detail. For example, it would not take much to convince students at your university that tuition is high or that some classrooms are overcrowded. Most people also know about the need to provide health care to the uninsured and to reduce the rising level of student debt and are aware of other problems that have received a good deal of media attention.

Other, less familiar issues need more explanation—sometimes a great deal of explanation. In these cases, you should not assume that readers will accept (or even understand) the importance of the problem you are discussing. For example, why should readers care about the high dropout rate at a local high school? You can answer this question by demonstrating that this problem affects not only the students who drop out but others as well:

- Students who do not have high school diplomas earn substantially less than those who do.

- Studies show that high school dropouts are much more likely to live in poverty than students who complete high school.

- Taxpayers pay for the social services that dropouts often require.

- Federal, state, and local governments lose the taxes that dropouts would pay if they had better jobs.

When you explain the situation in this way, you show that a problem that appears to be limited to just a few individuals actually affects society as a whole.

How much background information you need to provide about a problem depends on how much your readers already know about it. In many cases, a direct statement of a problem is not enough: you need to explain the context of the problem and then discuss it with this context in mind. For example, you cannot simply say that the number of databases to which your college library subscribes needs to be increased. Why does it need to be increased? How many new databases should be added? Which ones? What benefits would result from increasing the number of databases? What will happen if the number is not increased? Without answers to these questions, readers will not be able to understand the full extent of the problem. (Statistics, examples, personal anecdotes, and even visuals can also help you demonstrate the importance of finding a solution to the problem.) By presenting the problem in detail, you draw readers into your discussion and motivate them to want to solve it.

Proposing a Solution

After you have established that a problem exists, you have to propose a solution. Sometimes the solution is self-evident, so that you do not need to explain it in much detail. For example, if you want to get a new computer for the college newspaper, you do not have to give a detailed account of how you intend to purchase it. On the other hand, if your problem is more complicated—for example, proposing that your school should sponsor a new student organization—you will have to go into more detail, possibly listing the steps that you will take to implement your plan as well as the costs associated with it.

Demonstrating That Your Solution Will Work

When you present a solution to a problem, you have to support it with **evidence**—facts, examples, and so on from your own experience and from research. You can also point to successful solutions that are similar to the one you are suggesting. For example, if you were proposing that the government should do more to relieve the student-loan burden, you could list the reasons why certain changes would be beneficial for many students. You might also point to student-friendly practices in other countries, such as Great Britain and Australia. Finally, you could use a visual, such as a chart or a graph, to help you support your position.

You also have to consider the consequences—both intended and unintended—of your proposal. Idealistic or otherwise unrealistic proposals almost always run into trouble when skeptical readers challenge them. If you think, for example, that the federal government should suspend taxes on hybrid cars to encourage clean energy, you should consider the effects of such a suspension. How much money would drivers actually save? How would the government make up the lost tax revenue? What programs would suffer because the government could no longer afford to fund them? In short, do the benefits of your proposal outweigh its negative effects?

Establishing Feasibility

Your solution not only has to make sense but also has to be **feasible**—that is, it has to be practical. Sometimes a problem can be solved, but the solution may be almost as bad as—or even worse than—the problem. For example, a city could drastically reduce crime by putting police on every street corner, installing video cameras at every intersection, and stopping and searching all

Advocacy groups frequently publish proposals.

Let the Sunshine In

As citizens we all have a right to know
what's going on in our government.

That's the foundation of our democracy –
Government of the people –
By the people –
And for the people.

We want our leaders to give us a government
that is open, transparent and accountable.

In this campaign season let's find out where
the candidates stand on open government.

Let the sunshine in –
Because it's your right to know.

It's Your Right to Know

SUNSHINE® WEEK
YOUR RIGHT TO KNOW

THE CREATIVE COALITION

RTNDF
ELECTRONIC JOURNALISM

ASNE
LEADING AMERICA'S NEWSROOMS

John S. and James L.
Knight Foundation
Writing the Story of Transformation

sunshineweek.org

cars that contain two or more people. These actions would certainly reduce crime, but most people would not want to live in a city that instituted such authoritarian policies.

Even if a solution is desirable, it still may not be feasible. For example, although expanded dining facilities might improve life on campus, the cost of a new student cafeteria would be high. If paying for it means that tuition would have to be increased, many students would find this proposal unacceptable. On the other hand, if you could demonstrate that the profits from the increase in food sales in the new cafeteria would offset its cost, then your proposal would be feasible.

Discussing Benefits

By presenting the benefits of your proposal, you can convince undecided readers that your plan has merit. How, for example, would students benefit from an expansion of campus parking facilities? Would student morale improve because students would get fewer parking citations? Would lateness to class decline because students would no longer have to spend time looking for a parking spot? Would the college earn more revenue from additional parking fees? Although not all proposals list benefits, many do. This information can help convince readers that your proposal has merit and is worth implementing.

An image of an overcrowded campus parking lot can help convince your audience to see the merits of a proposal to make more parking available.

Refuting Opposing Arguments

You should always assume that any proposal—no matter how strong—will be objectionable to some readers. Moreover, even sympathetic readers will have questions that they will want answered before they accept your ideas. That is why you should always anticipate and refute possible objections to your proposal. For example, if the federal government did more to relieve the student-loan burden, would some students try to take advantage of the program by borrowing more than they need? Would all students be eligible for help, even those from wealthy families? Would students who worked while attending school be eligible? If any objections are particularly strong, concede them: admit that they have merit, but point out their shortcomings. For instance, you could concede that some students might try to abuse the program, but you could then point out that only a small minority of students would do this and recommend steps that could be taken to address possible abuses.

➔ EXERCISE 15.1

List the evidence you could present to support each of these thesis statements for proposal arguments.

1. Because many Americans are obese, the government should require warning labels on all sugared cereals.

2. The United States should ban all gasoline-burning cars in ten years.

3. Candidates for president should be required to use only public funding for their campaigns.

4. Teachers should carry handguns to protect themselves and their students from violence.

5. To reduce prison overcrowding, states should release all nonviolent offenders.

⊘ EXERCISE 15.2

Review the proposals in Exercise 15.1, and list two problems that each one could create if implemented.

⊘ EXERCISE 15.3

Look at the following ad, which is designed to promote recycling. In what sense is it a proposal argument? For example, what problem does it identify?

An ad to encourage recycling

© Katvan Studios

What solution does it propose? What arguments does it present to support this solution? How does the image in the ad help to support the proposal?

⊙ EXERCISE 15.4

Read the following opinion column, "Teach Your Teachers Well" by Susan Engel. What problem does Engel discuss? How does she propose to solve this problem? What benefits does she expect her solution to have? Note that Engel does not refute possible objections to her proposal. What objections could she have mentioned? What evidence could she have added to strengthen her proposal?

This opinion column was published in the *New York Times* on November 2, 2009.

TEACH YOUR TEACHERS WELL

SUSAN ENGEL

Arne Duncan, the secretary of education, recently called for sweeping changes   1
to the way we select and train teachers. He's right. If we really want good schools, we need to create a critical mass of great teachers. And if we want smart, passionate people to become these great educators, we have to attract them with excellent programs and train them properly in the substance and practice of teaching.

Our best universities have, paradoxically, typically looked down   2
their noses at education, as if it were intellectually inferior. The result is that the strongest students are often in colleges that have no interest in education, while the most inspiring professors aren't working with students who want to teach. This means that comparatively weaker students in less intellectually rigorous programs are the ones preparing to become teachers.

So the first step is to get the best colleges to throw themselves into the fray. If education was a good enough topic for Plato, John Dewey, and William James, it should be good enough for 21st-century college professors.

> "If education was a good enough topic for Plato, John Dewey, and William James, it should be good enough for 21st-century college professors."   3

These new teacher programs should be selective, requiring a 3.5 undergrad- 4
uate grade point average and an intensive application process. But they should
also be free of charge, and admission should include a stipend for the first three
years of teaching in a public school.

Once we have a better pool of graduate students, we need to train them 5
differently from how we have in the past. Too often, teaching students spend
their time studying specific instructional programs and learning how to handle mechanics like making lesson plans. These skills, while useful, are not what
will transform a promising student into a good teacher.

First, future teachers should continue studying the subject they hope to 6
teach, with outstanding professors. It makes no sense at all to stop studying
the thing you want to teach at the very moment you begin to learn how.

Meanwhile, students should learn their craft the way a surgeon learns to 7
operate: by intense supervision in a real setting with expert mentors. Student-
teachers are usually observed only twice during a semester and then given a
written evaluation. But young teachers, like young doctors, should work side
by side with skilled mentors, getting plenty of feedback, having plenty of
opportunities to observe, and taking on greater and greater responsibility as
they improve.

Teacher training can also learn from family therapy programs. Therapists 8
spend a great deal of time watching videotapes of themselves in action, reflect-
ing on their sessions and discussing the most difficult moments with senior
therapists to explore other ways they might have responded. In much the same
way, young teachers need to record their daily encounters with their classrooms and then, with mentors and peers, have serious, open-minded conversations about what's working and what isn't.

Teachers must also learn far more about children: typically, teaching 9
students are provided with fairly static and superficial overviews of developmental stages but learn little about how to watch children, using
research and theory to understand what they are seeing. As James Comer,
a professor of child psychiatry at Yale, has argued for years, if we disregard
the developmental needs of our students, it's unlikely we'll succeed in
teaching them.

One more thing is required—give as many public schools as possible 10
the financial incentives to hire these newly prepared teachers in groups of
seven or more. This way, talented eager young teachers won't languish or
leave teaching because they felt bored, inept, isolated, or marginalized.
Instead, they will feel part of a robust community of promising professionals. They will struggle and learn together. Good teachers need good
colleagues.

To fix our schools, we need teaching programs that are as rich in 11
resources, interesting, high-reaching, and thoughtful as the young people we
want to attract to the profession. Show me a school where teachers are smart,
well-educated, skilled, and happy to be there, and I'll show you a group of children who are getting a good education.

◆ EXERCISE 15.5

Write a paragraph or two in which you argue for or against the recommendations Engel proposes in "Teach Your Teachers Well." Be sure to present a clear statement of the problems she is addressing as well as the strengths or weaknesses of her proposal.

Structuring a Proposal Argument

In general, a proposal argument can be structured in the following way:

- **Introduction:** Establishes the context of the proposal and presents the essay's thesis

- **Explanation of the problem:** Identifies the problem and explains why it needs to be solved

- **Explanation of the solution:** Proposes a solution and explains how it will solve the problem

- **Evidence in support of the solution:** Presents support for the proposed solution (this section is usually more than one paragraph)

- **Benefits of the solution:** Explains the positive results of the proposed course of action

- **Refutation of opposing arguments:** Addresses objections to the proposal

- **Conclusion:** Reinforces the main point of the proposal; includes a strong concluding statement

The following student essay contains all the elements of a proposal argument. The student who wrote this essay is trying to convince the college president that the school should adopt an **honor code**—a system of rules that defines acceptable conduct and establishes procedures for handling misconduct.

COLLEGES NEED HONOR CODES

MELISSA BURRELL

Today's college students are under a lot of pressure to do well in   1
school, to win tuition grants, to please teachers and family, and to
compete in the job market. As a result, the temptation to cheat is

greater than ever. At the same time, technology, particularly the Internet, has made cheating easier than ever. Colleges and universities have tried various strategies to combat this problem, from increasing punishments to using plagiarism-detection tools such as Turnitin .com. However, the most comprehensive and effective solution to the problem of academic dishonesty is an honor code, a campus-wide contract that spells out and enforces standards of honesty. To fight academic dishonesty, colleges should institute and actively maintain honor codes.

Although the exact number of students who cheat is impossible to determine, two out of three students in one recent survey admitted to cheating (Grasgreen). Some students cheat by plagiarizing entire papers or stealing answers to tests. Many other students commit so-called lesser offenses, such as collaborating with others when told to work alone, sharing test answers, cutting and pasting material from the Internet, or misrepresenting data. All of these acts are dishonest; all amount to cheating. Part of the problem, however, is that students are often unsure whether their decisions are or are not ethical (Balibalos and Gopalakrishnan para. 1). Because they are unclear about expectations and overwhelmed by the pressure to succeed, students can easily justify dishonest acts.

An honor code solves these problems by clearly presenting the rules and by establishing honesty, trust, and academic honor as shared values. According to recent research, "setting clear expectations, and repeating them early and often, is crucial" (Grasgreen). Schools with honor codes require *every* student to sign a pledge to uphold the honor code. Ideally, students write and manage the honor code themselves, with the help of faculty and administrators. According to Timothy M. Dodd, however, to be successful, the honor code must be more than a document; it must be a way of thinking. To accomplish this, all first-year students should receive copies of the school's honor code at orientation. At the beginning of each academic year, students should be required to reread the honor code and renew their pledge to uphold its values and rules. In addition, students and instructors need to discuss the honor code in class. (Some colleges

Thesis statement

Explanation of the problem: Cheating

Explanation of the solution: Institute honor code

2

3

post the honor code in every classroom.) In other words, Dodd believes that the honor code must be part of the fabric of the school. It should be present in students' minds, guiding their actions and informing their learning and teaching.

Studies show that serious cheating is 25 to 50 percent lower at schools with honor codes (Dodd). With an honor code in place, students cannot say that they do not know what constitutes cheating or that they do not understand what will happen to them if they cheat. Studies also show that in schools with a strong honor code, instructors are more likely to take action against cheaters. One study shows that instructors frequently do not confront students who cheat because they are not sure the university will back them up (Vandehey, Diekhoff, and LaBeff 469) and another suggests that students are more likely to cheat when they feel their instructor will be lenient (Hosny and Fatima 753). When a school has an honor code, however, instructors can be certain that both the students and the school will support their actions.

4 Evidence in support of the solution

When a school institutes an honor code, a number of positive results occur. First, an honor code creates a set of basic rules that students can follow. Students know in advance what is expected of them and what will happen if they commit an infraction. In addition, an honor code promotes honesty, placing more responsibility and power in the hands of students and encouraging them to act according to a higher standard. As a result, schools with honor codes often permit unsupervised exams that require students to monitor one other. Finally, according to Dodd, honor codes encourage students to act responsibly. They assume that students will not take unfair advantage of each other or undercut the academic community. As Dodd concludes, in schools with honor codes, plagiarism (and cheating in general) becomes a concern for everyone—students as well as instructors.

5 Benefits of the solution

Some people argue that plagiarism-detection tools such as Turnitin.com are more effective at preventing cheating than honor codes. However, these tools focus on catching individual acts of cheating, not on preventing a culture of cheating. When schools use these tools, they are telling students that their main concern is not to avoid

6 Refutation of opposing arguments

cheating but to avoid getting caught. As a result, these tools do not deal with the real problem: the decision to be dishonest. Rather than trusting students, schools that use plagiarism-detection tools assume that all students are cheating. Unlike plagiarism-detection tools, honor codes fight dishonesty by promoting a culture of integrity, fairness, and accountability. By assuming that most students are trustworthy and punishing only those who are not, schools with honor codes set high standards for students and encourage them to rise to the challenge.

Concluding statement

The only long-term, comprehensive solution to the problem of cheating is campus-wide honor codes. No solution will completely prevent dishonesty, but honor codes go a long way toward addressing the root causes of this problem. The goal of an honor code is to create a campus culture that values and rewards honesty and integrity. By encouraging students to do what is expected of them, honor codes help create a confident, empowered, and trustworthy student body.

7

Works Cited

Balibalos, K. and J. Gopalakrishnan. "'OK or Not?' A New Poll Series about Plagiarism." *WriteCheck*, 24 Jul. 2014, en.writecheck.com /blog/2013/07/24/ok-or-not-a-new-poll-series-about-plagiarism.

Dodd, Timothy M. "Honor Code 101: An Introduction to the Elements of Traditional Honor Codes, Modified Honor Codes and Academic Integrity Policies." *Center for Academic Integrity*, Clemson U, 2010, www.clemson.edu/ces/departments/mse/academics/honor-code.html.

Grasgreen, Allie. "Who Cheats, and How." *Inside Higher Ed,* 16 Mar. 2012, www.insidehighered.com/news/2012/03/16/arizona-survey -examines-student-cheating-faculty-responses.

Hosny, Manar and Shameem Fatima. "Attitude of Students towards Cheating and Plagiarism: University Case Study." *Journal of Applied Sciences,* vol. 14, no. 8, 2014, pp. 748–57.

Vandehey, Michael, et al. "College Cheating: A Twenty Year Follow-Up and the Addition of an Honor Code." *Journal of College Student Development*, vol. 48, no. 4, July/August 2007, pp. 468–80. *Academic OneFile*, go.galegroup.com/.

GRAMMAR IN CONTEXT

Will versus *Would*

Many people use the helping verbs *will* and *would* interchangeably. When you write a proposal, however, keep in mind that these words express different shades of meaning.

> *Will* expresses certainty. In a list of benefits, for example, *will* indicates the benefits that will definitely occur if the proposal is accepted.
>
>> First, an honor code will create a set of basic rules that students can follow.
>>
>> In addition, an honor code will promote honesty.
>
> *Would* expresses probability. In a refutation of an opposing argument, for example, *would* indicates that another solution could possibly be more effective than the one being proposed.
>
>> Some people argue that a plagiarism-detection tool such as Turnitin.com would be simpler and a more effective way of preventing cheating than an honor code.

⊙ EXERCISE 15.6

The following essay, "Self-Driving Cars Will Change the Rules of the Road" by Adam Cohen, includes the basic elements of a proposal argument. Read the essay, and answer the questions that follow it, consulting the outline on page 561 if necessary.

This opinion column appeared in *Time* on January 14, 2014.

SELF-DRIVING CARS WILL CHANGE THE RULES OF THE ROAD

ADAM COHEN

TIME

Not long ago, self-driving cars seemed like science fiction. But Google is now 1 operating so-called autonomous cars in California and Nevada, and last week at the annual Consumer Electronics Show in Las Vegas, Toyota and Audi unveiled prototypes for self-driving cars to sell to ordinary car buyers. (Google co-founder Sergey Brin said last year he expects his company to have them ready for the general public within five years.) In a report backing self-driving cars, the consulting firm KPMG and the Center for Automotive Research recently predicted that driving is "on the brink of a new technological revolution."

But as the momentum for self-driving cars grows, one question is get- 2
ting little attention: Should they even be legal? And if they are, how will the
laws of driving have to adapt? All
our rules about driving—from who   "Should they even be legal?"
pays for a speeding ticket to who is
liable for a crash—are based on having a human behind the wheel. That is
going to have to change.

There are some compelling reasons to support self-driving cars. Regular 3
cars are inefficient: the average commuter spends 250 hours a year behind the
wheel. They are dangerous. Car crashes are a leading cause of death for Americans
ages 4 to 34 and cost some $300 billion a year. In the first 300,000 miles,
Google reported that its cars had not had a single accident. Last August, one
got into a minor fender bender, but Google said it occurred while someone was
manually driving it.

After heavy lobbying and campaign contributions, Google persuaded 4
California and Nevada to enact laws legalizing self-driving cars. The California
law breezed through the state legislature—it passed 37-0 in the senate and 74-2 in
the assembly—and other states could soon follow. The Alliance of Automobile
Manufacturers, which represents big carmakers like GM and Toyota, opposed
the California law, fearing it would make it too easy for carmakers and individuals to modify cars to self-drive without the careful protections built in by Google.

That is a reasonable concern. If we are going to have self-driving cars, the 5
technical specifications should be quite precise. Just because your neighbor Jeb is
able to jerry-rig his car to drive itself using an old PC and some fishing tackle, that
does not mean he should be allowed to.

As self-driving cars become more common, there will be a flood of new 6
legal questions. If a self-driving car gets into an accident, the human who is
"co-piloting" may not be fully at fault—he may even be an injured party.
Whom should someone hit by a self-driving car be able to sue? The human in
the self-driving car or the car's manufacturer? New laws will have to be written
to sort all this out.

How involved—and how careful—are we going to expect the human 7
co-pilot to be? As a Stanford Law School report asks, "Must the 'drivers'
remain vigilant, their hands on the wheel and their eyes on the road? If not,
what are they allowed to do inside or outside, the vehicle?" Can the human
in the car drink? Text-message? Read a book? Not surprisingly, the insurance industry is particularly concerned and would like things to move
slowly. Insurance companies say all the rules of car insurance may need to
be rewritten, with less of the liability put on those operating cars and more
on those who manufacture them.

At the signing ceremony for California's self-driving-car law, Governor Jerry 8
Brown was asked who is responsible when a self-driving car runs a red light. He
answered: "I don't know—whoever owns the car, I would think. But we will
work that out. That will be the easiest thing to work out." Google's Brin joked,
"Self-driving cars don't run red lights."

Neither answer is sufficient. Self-driving cars should be legal—and they are   9
likely to start showing up faster and in greater numbers than people expect. But if
that is the case, we need to start thinking about the legal questions now. Given the
high stakes involved in putting self-guided, self-propelled, high-speed vehicles on
the road, "we will work that out" is not good enough.

Identifying the Elements of a Proposal Argument

1. What is the essay's thesis statement? How effective do you think it is?

2. Where in the essay does Cohen identify the problem he wants to solve?

3. According to Cohen, what are the specific problems that self-driving cars solve?

4. Where does Cohen present his solutions to the problems he identifies?

5. Where does Cohen discuss the benefits of his proposal? What other benefits could he have addressed?

6. Where does Cohen address possible arguments against his proposal? What other arguments might he have addressed? How would you refute each of these arguments?

7. Evaluate the essay's concluding statement.

Should the Government Do More to Relieve the Student-Loan Burden?

Courtesy of Massachusetts Mutual Life Insurance

Reread the At Issue box on page 551, which gives background on whether the government should do more to relieve the student-loan burden. Then, read the sources on the following pages.

As you read this material, you will be asked to answer questions and to complete some simple activities. This work will help you understand both the content and structure of the selections. When you are finished, you will be ready to write a **proposal argument** that makes a case for or against having the government do more to relieve the student-loan burden.

SOURCES

 SovereignDollar.com, "Student Debt Crisis Solution" (editorial cartoon), p. 569

 Richard Vedder, "Forgive Student Loans?," p. 570

 Kevin Carey, "The U.S. Should Adopt Income-Based Loans Now," p. 573

 Astra Taylor, "A Strike against Student Debt," p. 577

 Lee Siegel, "Why I Defaulted on My Student Loans," p. 580

 Sam Adolphsen, "Don't Blame the Government," p. 583

This editorial cartoon was adapted from an illustration in the *Atlantic Monthly*.

STUDENT DEBT CRISIS SOLUTION

⊙ AT ISSUE: SOURCES FOR DEVELOPING A PROPOSAL ARGUMENT

1. The editorial cartoon above shows Minerva, an ancient Roman goddess. Consult an encyclopedia to find out more about Minerva. Why do you think this mythical figure is used in this visual?

2. Why are Minerva's wrists chained? Why does she have a sign hanging from her neck? What point is the creator of this image trying to make?

3. How could you use this visual to support an argument about student loans? What position do you think it could support?

4. What argument does this editorial cartoon make?

The blog entry was posted to *National Review Online* on October 11, 2011.

FORGIVE STUDENT LOANS?

RICHARD VEDDER

As the Wall Street protests grow and expand beyond New York, growing 1
scrutiny of the nascent movement is warranted. What do these folks want?
Alongside their ranting about the inequality of incomes, the alleged inordi-
nate power of Wall Street and large corporations, the high level of unemployment, and the like, one policy goal ranks high with most protesters: the
forgiveness of student-loan debt. In an informal survey of over 50 protesters in New York last Tuesday, blogger and equity research analyst David
Maris found 93 percent of them advocated student-loan forgiveness. An
online petition drive advocating student-loan forgiveness has gathered an
impressive number of signatures (over 442,000). This is an issue that resonates with many Americans.

Economist Justin Wolfers recently opined that "this is the worst idea 2
ever." I think it is actually the second-worst idea ever—the worst was the creation of federally subsidized student loans in the first place. Under current
law, when the feds (who have basically taken over the student-loan industry)
make a loan, the size of the U.S. budget deficit rises, and the government borrows additional funds, very often from foreign investors. We are borrowing
from the Chinese to finance school attendance by a predominantly middle-
class group of Americans.

But that is the tip of the iceberg: Though the ostensible objective of the 3
loan program is to increase the proportion of adult Americans with college
degrees, over 40 percent of those pursuing a bachelor's degree fail to
receive one within six years. And default is a growing problem with
student loans.

Further, it's not clear that college imparts much of value to the average 4
student. The typical college student spends less than 30 hours a week, 32 weeks
a year, on all academic matters—class attendance, writing papers, studying for
exams, etc. They spend about half as much time on school as their parents
spend working. If Richard Arum and Josipa Roksa (authors of *Academically
Adrift*) are even roughly correct, today's students typically learn little in the
way of critical learning or writing skills while in school.

Moreover, the student-loan program has proven an ineffective way to 5
achieve one of its initial aims, a goal also of the Wall Street protesters: increasing
economic opportunity for the poor. In 1970, when federal student-loan and
-grant programs were in their infancy, about 12 percent of college graduates
came from the bottom one-fourth of the income distribution. While people
from all social classes are more likely to go to college today, the poor haven't
gained nearly as much ground as the rich have: With the nation awash in nearly
a trillion dollars in student-loan debt (more even than credit-card obligations),

the proportion of bachelor's-degree holders coming from the bottom one-fourth
of the income distribution has fallen to
around 7 percent.

"The sins of the loan
program are many. Let's
briefly mention just five."

The sins of the loan program are
many. Let's briefly mention just five.

First, artificially low interest rates are set by the federal government—
they are fixed by law rather than market forces. Low-interest-rate
mortgage loans resulting from loose Fed policies and the government-
sponsored enterprises Fannie Mae and Freddie Mac spurred the
housing bubble that caused the 2008 financial crisis. Arguably,
federal student financial assistance is creating a second bubble in
higher education.

Second, loan terms are invariant, with students with poor prospects of
graduating and getting good jobs often borrowing at the same
interest rates as those with excellent prospects (e.g., electrical-
engineering majors at MIT).

Third, the availability of cheap loans has almost certainly contributed to
the tuition explosion—college prices are going up even more than
health-care prices.

Fourth, at present the loans are made by a monopoly provider, the same
one that gave us such similar inefficient and costly monopolistic
behemoths as the U.S. Postal Service.

Fifth, the student-loan and associated Pell Grant programs spawned
the notorious FAFSA form that requires families to reveal all sorts
of financial information—information that colleges use to engage
in ruthless price discrimination via tuition discounting, charging
wildly different amounts to students depending on how much
their parents can afford to pay. It's a soak-the-rich scheme on
steroids.

Still, for good or ill, we have this unfortunate program. Wouldn't loan
forgiveness provide some stimulus to a moribund economy? The Wall Street
protesters argue that if debt-burdened young persons were free of this alba-
tross, they would start spending more on goods and services, stimulating
employment. Yet we demonstrated with stimulus packages in 2008 and 2009
(not to mention the 1930s, Japan in the 1990s, etc.) that giving people more
money to spend will not bring recovery. But even if it did, why should we
give a break to this particular group of individuals, who disproportionately
come from prosperous families to begin with? Why give them assistance while
those who have dutifully repaid their loans get none? An arguably more equitable and efficient method of stimulus would be to drop dollars out of air-
planes over low-income areas.

Moreover, this idea has ominous implications for the macro economy.
Who would take the loss from the unanticipated non-repayment of a

6

7

8

trillion dollars? If private financial institutions are liable for some of it, it could kill them, triggering another financial crisis. If the federal government shoulders the entire burden, we are adding a trillion or so more dollars in liabilities to a government already grievously overextended (upwards of $100 trillion in liabilities counting Medicare, Social Security, and the national debt), almost certainly leading to more debt downgrades, which could trigger investor panic. This idea is breathtaking in terms of its naïveté and stupidity.

The demonstrators say that selfish plutocrats are ruining our economy 9 and creating an unjust society. Rather, a group of predominantly rather spoiled and coddled young persons, long favored and subsidized by the American taxpayer, are complaining that society has not given them enough— they want the taxpayer to foot the bill for their years of limited learning and heavy partying while in college. Hopefully, this burst of dimwittery should not pass muster even in our often dysfunctional Congress.

⊘ AT ISSUE: SOURCES FOR DEVELOPING A PROPOSAL ARGUMENT

1. According to Vedder, forgiveness of student debt is "the second-worst idea ever" (para. 2). Why? What is the worst idea?

2. In paragraphs 3–6, Vedder examines the weaknesses of the federally subsidized student-loan program. List some of the weaknesses he identifies.

3. Why do you think Vedder waits until paragraph 7 to discuss debt forgiveness? Should he have discussed it sooner?

4. Summarize Vedder's primary objection to forgiving student debt. Do you agree with him? How would you refute his objection?

5. Throughout his essay, Vedder uses rather strong language to characterize those who disagree with him. For example, in paragraph 8, he calls the idea of forgiving student loans "breathtaking in terms of its naïveté and stupidity." In paragraph 9, he calls demonstrators "spoiled and coddled young persons" and labels Congress "dysfunctional." Does this language help or hurt Vedder's case? Would more neutral words and phrases have been more effective? Why or why not?

6. How would Vedder respond to Astra Taylor's solution to the student-loan crisis (p. 577)? Are there any points that Taylor makes with which Vedder might agree?

This commentary was published in the *Chronicle of Higher Education* on October 23, 2011.

THE U.S. SHOULD ADOPT INCOME-BASED LOANS NOW

KEVIN CAREY

A new generation of student debtors has seized the public stage. While the demands of the Occupy Wall Street movement are many, college lending reform is near the top of every list. Decades of greed, inattention, and failed policy have created a growing class of young men and women with few prospects of landing jobs good enough to bear the weight of their crushing college loans.

Some activists have called for wholesale student-loan forgiveness—a kind of 21st-century jubilee. That's unlikely. But there's something the federal government can do right now to help students caught by our terribly unjust higher-education financing system: End all federal student-loan defaults forever by moving to income-contingent loans.

The concept is simple. Right now, students pay back their loans on a fixed schedule, typically amortized over 10 years. Since people usually make less money early in their careers, their fixed monthly loan bill is hardest to manage in the first years after graduating (or not) from college. People unlucky enough to graduate during horrible recessions are even more likely to have bad jobs or no jobs and struggle paying back their loans. Not coincidentally, the U.S. Department of Education recently announced a sharp rise in loan defaults.

Under an income-contingent loan system, like those in Australia and Britain, students pay a fixed percentage of their income toward their loans. Payments are automatically deducted from their paychecks by the IRS, just like income-tax withholding. Self-employed workers pay in quarterly installments, just as they do with their taxes. If borrowers earn a lot, their payments rise accordingly, and their loans are retired quickly. If their income falls below a certain level—say, the poverty line—they pay nothing. After an extended time period of 20 or 30 years, any remaining debt is forgiven.

> "Under an income-contingent loan system, . . . students pay a fixed percentage of their income toward their loans."

In other words, nobody ever defaults on a federal student loan again. The whole concept of "default" is expunged from the system. No more collection agencies hounding people with 10 phone calls a night. No more ruined credit and dashed hopes of home-ownership. People who want to enter virtuous but lower-paid professions like social work and teaching won't be deterred by unmanageable debt.

And by calibrating interest and payment rates, the federal government 6
can make the program no more expensive than the current cost of subsidizing
loans and writing off unpaid debt. The only losers are the repo men.

The concept has been proven to work—Australia and Britain have used it 7
for years—and both liberals and conservatives have reason to get on board.
The Nobel Prize–winning economist Milton Friedman proposed the idea all
the way back in 1955.

Indeed, income-contingent loans are such a good idea, one might wonder 8
why they don't exist already. Historically, administrative complications have
been a major culprit. Until last year, the federal government managed most
student loans by paying private banks to act as lenders and then guaranteeing
their losses. The IRS would have had to maintain relationships with scores of
different lenders, relying on banks for notification of who owes how much and
disbursing money hither and yon. Income-contingent loans would have created a huge bureaucratic headache.

But in 2010, Congress abolished the old system, cutting out private banks. 9
Now the federal government originates all federal loans. The IRS would have
to deal with only one lender: the U.S. Department of Education. In other
words, there is a new opportunity to overhaul the way students repay their
college debt that didn't exist until this year.

It's true that students who pay over long periods of time will pay more 10
interest and that the taxpayers will bear the cost of partially forgiven loans. But
under the current system the federal government is already eating the cost of
defaulted loans, and low-income students who can't repay loans are often hit
with fines and penalties that dwarf the cost of extra interest.

When federal loans were first created, nobody imagined they would 11
become standard practice for financing college. As late as 1993, most undergraduates didn't borrow. Now, two-thirds take on debt, and most of those
loans are federal. The average debt load increased over 50 percent during
that time.

Nor is repayment an isolated problem. One recent study found that the 12
majority of American borrowers—56 percent—struggled with loan payments
in the first five years after college. In Britain, by contrast, 98 percent of borrowers are meeting their obligations.

Because student loans can almost never be discharged in bankruptcy, 13
defaulted loans can haunt students for a lifetime. Some senior citizens theoretically could have their Social Security checks garnished to make good on
old student debt. That is insane.

A similar-sounding federal program, called income-based repayment, 14
is now on the books and is scheduled to become somewhat more generous
starting in 2014. But the program is administratively complicated, involving
income-eligibility caps and requiring students to reapply every year. This points
to another major advantage of income-contingent loans: simplicity.

Even with the government as the sole source of federal loans, many 15
graduates still have to navigate a thicket of different rates, terms, lenders,

consolidation options, and schedules in order to meet their obligations. Some fall behind not because they're unwilling or unable to pay, but because they can't get the right check to the right place at the right time. An income-contingent system would remove all of that hassle, making repayment simple and automatic, and setting college graduates free to get on with the important business of starting their lives.

The student-loan system has grown into an out-of-control monster tearing at the fabric of civil society. In Chile, student anger over an inequitable, unaffordable, profit-oriented higher-education system led to nationwide protests and violent confrontation just months ago. Now the seeds of similar unrest are sprouting here. 16

Income-contingent loans won't solve the escalating college prices, state disinvestment in higher education, and overall economic weakness that are driving more students into debt. But they offer a simpler, fairer, more efficient, and more humane way of allowing students to repay loans that aren't disappearing from the higher-education landscape anytime soon. They could be put in place quickly at no extra cost to the taxpayer. In a dismal fiscal environment, there are few deals this good. 17

The students at the barricades are right to be angry. They didn't run the economy into the ditch. They didn't create the system in which a college degree is all but mandatory to pursue a good career, and loans are often unavoidable. But they have to live with it. Income-contingent loans are one way to give them the help they need. 18

⊘AT ISSUE: SOURCES FOR DEVELOPING A PROPOSAL ARGUMENT

1. Carey blames the current student-loan problem on years of "greed, inattention, and failed policy" (para. 1). Is he right to assume his readers will agree with him, or should he have provided evidence to support this statement? Explain.

2. In paragraph 2, Carey says that income-contingent loans would end "forever" all student-loan defaults. After reading Carey's explanation, how would you define *income-contingent loans*?

3. What evidence does Carey present to support his proposal? If income-contingent loans are such a good idea, why hasn't the government tried them before?

4. What kind of appeal does Carey make in paragraph 7? In your opinion, how effective is this appeal?

5. Where does Carey address arguments against his proposal? List these arguments. Which argument do you think presents the most effective challenge to Carey's position? Why?

6. In paragraph 16, Carey calls the student-loan system "an out-of-control monster tearing at the fabric of civil society." In paragraph 18, he says, "The students at the barricades are right to be angry." Do you think he is exaggerating, or is this strong language justified?

7. In paragraph 17, Carey lists problems that income-contingent loans will *not* solve. Does this paragraph undercut (or even contradict) his statement in paragraph 2 that income-contingent loans would end student-loan defaults? Explain.

Taylor's op-ed appeared on February 27, 2015, in the *New York Times*.

A STRIKE AGAINST STUDENT DEBT

ASTRA TAYLOR

This week a group of former students calling themselves the Corinthian 15 announced that they were committing a new kind of civil disobedience: a debt strike. They are refusing to make any more payments on their federal student loans.

Along with many others, they found themselves in significant debt after attending programs at the Corinthian Colleges, a collapsed chain of for-profit schools that the Consumer Financial Protection Bureau has accused of running a "predatory lending scheme." While the bureau has announced a plan to reduce some of the students' private loan debts, the strikers are demanding that the Department of Education use its authority to discharge their federal loans as well.

These 15 students are members of the Debt Collective, an organization that evolved out of a project I helped start in 2012 called the Rolling Jubilee. Until now, we have worked in the secondary debt market, using crowdfunded donations to buy portfolios of medical and educational debts for pennies on the dollar, just as debt collectors do.

Only, instead of collecting on them, we abolish them, operating under the belief that people shouldn't go into debt for getting sick or going to school. This week, we erased $13 million of "unpaid tuition receivables" belonging to 9,438 people associated with Everest College, a Corinthian subsidiary.

But this approach has its limits. Federal loans, for example, are guaranteed by the government, and debtors can be freed of them—via bankruptcy—only under exceedingly rare circumstances. That means they aren't sold at steep discounts and remain out of our reach. What's more, America's mountain of student debt is too immense for the Jubilee to make a significant dent in it.

Real change will require more organized actions like those taken by the Corinthian 15.

If anyone deserves debt relief—morally and legally—it's these students. For-profit colleges are notorious for targeting low-income minorities, single mothers, and veterans with high-pressure, misleading recruitment techniques. The schools slurp up about a quarter of all federal student aid money, more than $30 billion a year, while their students run up a lifetime of debt for a degree arguably worth no more than a high school diploma.

> "If anyone deserves debt relief—morally and legally—it's these students."

But for-profit schools aren't the only problem. Degrees earned from traditional colleges can also leave students unfairly burdened.

Today, a majority of outstanding student loans are in deferral, delinquency, or default. As state funding for education has plummeted, public colleges have raised tuition. Private university costs are skyrocketing, too, rising roughly 25 percent over the last decade. That's why every class of graduates is more in the red than the last.

Modest fixes are not enough. Consider the interest rate tweaks or income-based repayment plans offered by the Obama administration. They lighten the debt burden on some—but not everyone qualifies. They do nothing to address the $165 billion private loan market, where interest rates are often the most punishing, or how higher education is financed. 10

Americans now owe $1.2 trillion in student debt, a number predicted by the think tank Demos to climb to $2 trillion by 2025. What if more people from all types of educational institutions and with all kinds of debts followed the example of the Corinthian 15, and strategically refused to pay back their loans? This would transform the debts into leverage to demand better terms, or even a better way of funding higher education altogether. 11

The quickest fix would be a full-scale student debt cancellation. For students at predatory colleges like Corinthian, this could be done immediately by the Department of Education. For the broader population of students, it would most likely take an act of Congress. 12

Student debt cancellation would mean forgone revenue in the near term, but in the long term it could be an economic stimulus worth much more than the immediate cost. Money not spent paying off loans would be spent elsewhere. In that situation, lenders, debt collectors, servicers, guaranty agencies, asset-backed security investors, and others who profit from student loans would suffer the most from debt forgiveness. 13

We also need to bring back the option of a public, tuition-free college education once represented by institutions like the University of California, which charged only token fees. By the Rolling Jubilee's estimate, every public two- and four-year college and university in the United States could be made tuition-free by redirecting all current educational subsidies and tax exemptions straight to them and adding approximately $15 billion in annual spending. 14

This might sound like a lot, but it's a small price to pay to restore America's place on the long list of countries that provide tuition-free education. 15

To get there, more groups like the Corinthian 15 will have to show that they are willing to throw a wrench in the gears of the system by threatening to withhold payment on their debt. Everyone deserves a quality education. We need to come up with a better way to provide it than debt and default. 16

⊙ AT ISSUE: SOURCES FOR DEVELOPING A PROPOSAL ARGUMENT

1. Taylor begins her essay by discussing the Corinthian 15. How does this focus help her introduce the problem she wants to solve?

2. Paraphrase Taylor's thesis by filling in the following template.

    The Department of Education should solve the student debt crisis by

    _____

    _____ .

3. What two problems does Taylor discuss? Does she describe them in enough detail? Explain.

4. What solutions does Taylor offer? How feasible are these solutions?

5. At what points in her essay does Taylor address objections to her proposal? Does she address the most important objections? If not, what other objections should she have addressed?

6. Taylor uses three terms that might be unfamiliar to some readers.

    - *secondary debt market* (para. 3)

    - *crowdfunded donations* (3)

    - *unpaid tuition receivables* (4)

    Look up these terms, and then reread the paragraphs in which they appear. Do these terms help Taylor develop her argument, or could she have made her points without them?

7. What assumptions does Taylor assume are self-evident and need no proof? Do you agree? If not, what evidence should Taylor have included to support these assumptions?

The *New York Times* ran this article on June 6, 2015.

WHY I DEFAULTED ON MY STUDENT LOANS

LEE SIEGEL

One late summer afternoon when I was seventeen, I went with my mother 1 to the local bank, a long-defunct institution whose name I cannot remember, to apply for my first student loan. My mother co-signed. When we finished, the banker, a balding man in his late fifties, congratulated us, as if I had just won some kind of award rather than signed away my young life.

By the end of my sophomore year at a small private liberal arts college, my 2 mother and I had taken out a second loan, my father had declared bankruptcy, and my parents had divorced. My mother could no longer afford the tuition that the student loans weren't covering. I transferred to a state college in New Jersey, closer to home.

Years later, I found myself confronted with a choice that too many people 3 have had to and will have to face. I could give up what had become my vocation (in my case, being a writer) and take a job that I didn't want in order to repay the huge debt I had accumulated in college and graduate school. Or I could take what I had been led to believe was both the morally and legally reprehensible step of defaulting on my student loans, which was the only way I could survive without wasting my life in a job that had nothing to do with my particular usefulness to society.

I chose life. That is to say, I defaulted on my student loans. 4

As difficult as it has been, I've never looked back. The millions of young 5 people today, who collectively owe over $1 trillion in loans, may want to consider my example.

It struck me as absurd that one could amass crippling debt as a result, not 6 of drug addiction or reckless borrowing and spending, but of going to college. Having opened a new life to me beyond my modest origins, the education system was now going to call in its chits and prevent me from pursuing that new life, simply because I had the misfortune of coming from modest origins.

Am I a deadbeat? In the eyes of the law I am. Indifferent to the claim that 7 repaying student loans is the road to character? Yes. Blind to the reality of countless numbers of people struggling to repay their debts, no matter

> "Am I a deadbeat?"

their circumstances, many worse than mine? My heart goes out to them. To my mind, they have learned to live with a social arrangement that is legal, but not moral.

Maybe the problem was that I had reached beyond my lower-middle-class 8 origins and taken out loans to attend a small private college to begin with. Maybe I should have stayed at a store called The Wild Pair, where I once had a nice stable job selling shoes after dropping out of the state college because I thought I deserved better, and naïvely tried to turn myself into a professional reader and writer on my own, without a college degree. I'd probably be district manager by now.

Or maybe, after going back to school, I should have gone into finance, or 9 some other lucrative career. Self-disgust and lifelong unhappiness, destroying a precious young life—all this is a small price to pay for meeting your student loan obligations.

Some people will maintain that a bankrupt father, an impecunious back- 10 ground, and impractical dreams are just the luck of the draw. Someone with character would have paid off those loans and let the chips fall where they may. But I have found, after some decades on this earth, that the road to char-acter is often paved with family money and family connections, not to men-tion 14 percent effective tax rates on seven-figure incomes.

Moneyed stumbles never seem to have much consequence. Tax fraud, 11 insider trading, almost criminal nepotism—these won't knock you off the straight and narrow. But if you're poor and miss a child-support payment, or if you're middle class and default on your student loans, then God help you.

Forty years after I took out my first student loan, and thirty years after 12 getting my last, the Department of Education is still pursuing the unpaid bal-ance. My mother, who co-signed some of the loans, is dead. The banks that made them have all gone under. I doubt that anyone can even find the promis-sory notes. The accrued interest, combined with the collection agencies' opu-lent fees, is now several times the principal.

Even the Internal Revenue Service understands the irrationality of pursu- 13 ing someone with an unmanageable economic burden. It has a program called Offer in Compromise that allows struggling people who have fallen behind in their taxes to settle their tax debt.

The Department of Education makes it hard for you, and ugly. But it is 14 possible to survive the life of default. You might want to follow these steps: Get as many credit cards as you can before your credit is ruined. Find a stable housing situation. Pay your rent on time so that you have a good record in that area when you do have to move. Live with or marry someone with good credit (preferably someone who shares your desperate nihilism).

When the fateful day comes, and your credit looks like a war zone, don't be 15 afraid. The reported consequences of having no credit are scare talk, to some extent. The reliably predatory nature of American life guarantees that there will always be somebody to help you, from credit card companies charging strato-spheric interest rates to subprime loans for houses and cars. Our economic sys-tem ensures that so long as you are willing to sink deeper and deeper into debt, you will keep being enthusiastically invited to play the economic game.

I am sharply aware of the strongest objection to my lapse into default. If 16 everyone acted as I did, chaos would result. The entire structure of American higher education would change.

The collection agencies retained by the Department of Education would be 17 exposed as the greedy vultures that they are. The government would get out of the loan-making and the loan-enforcement business. Congress might even explore a special, universal education tax that would make higher education affordable.

There would be a national shaming of colleges and universities for charging 18 soaring tuition rates that are reaching lunatic levels. The rapacity of American colleges and universities is turning social mobility, the keystone of American freedom, into a commodified farce.

If people groaning under the weight of student loans simply said, "Enough," 19 then all the pieties about debt that have become absorbed into all the pieties about higher education might be brought into alignment with reality. Instead of guaranteeing loans, the government would have to guarantee a college education. There are a lot of people who could learn to live with that, too.

⊘ AT ISSUE: SOURCES FOR DEVELOPING A PROPOSAL ARGUMENT

1. In the first three paragraphs of his essay, Siegel discusses the reasons he decided to default on his student loans. How convincing are these reasons? Explain.

2. In paragraph 5, Siegel says, "As difficult as it has been, I've never looked back." Does his essay contradict this statement in any way?

3. Throughout his essay, Siegel discusses possible objections to his decision. For example, in paragraph 7, he admits that he is "a deadbeat." List all the objections he attempts to refute. How effectively does he refute them? For example, does he ever convince you that he is not a deadbeat?

4. What is Siegel's opinion of banks? Of colleges and universities? Of the Department of Education? Of American life? How do these opinions color his discussion?

5. Siegel's essay can be read as a proposal. Fill in the template below, paraphrasing Siegel's thesis statement and key points.

   Thesis Statement: _____.

   Explanation of the Problem: _____.

   Explanation of the Solution: _____.

   Benefits of the Solution: _____.

   Refutation of Opposing Arguments: _____.

6. How does the fact that Siegel is the author of five books and is now almost sixty years of age affect his credibility? Does this information make you more or less likely to see his call to action as reasonable?

This opinion piece was published online on May 1, 2012, at TheMaineWire.com.

DON'T BLAME THE GOVERNMENT

SAM ADOLPHSEN

I still remember the day. 1

I was sitting at my kitchen table, pen in hand, and I signed the dotted line to 2
borrow a significant amount of money to pay for my first year of college.

The funny thing was, despite what you might hear in the media these days, 3
no one was standing over my shoulder forcing me to. No government official
told me I had to borrow the money. It was my decision then and it's my debt
today. I weighed the price of borrowing against the value of a secondary degree,
and I chose education.

My decision, my responsibility. 4

That's not what you are hearing today from most of America's youth 5
though. There are rallies in the streets of Portland, and in cities across America,
with "Occupy" inspired students and graduates whining about their debt and
how they need a way out. Students that have borrowed too much, of their own
free will, for degrees that haven't led to a job, are now demanding a handout.

My generation is looking for a bailout. It doesn't matter that many of them 6
are in tough positions, loaded with debt, because they made poor choices. It
doesn't matter that borrowing money is a personal decision and requires personal responsibility. They want the easy way out.

Take the example of Stephanie, featured 7
in a recent story from the *Philadelphia Inquirer*
that re-ran in the *Portland Press Herald*. Stephanie, the story laments, owes over $100,000 in

> "They want the easy
> way out."

student loans. Poor Stephanie. Then we find out that, for one, Stephanie is in
law school (really, becoming a lawyer costs money? Who knew . . .) and even
worse, we find out that Stephanie, had a FREE RIDE to Rutgers, but instead
chose to borrow money to go to a smaller private school because she "fell in
love with it."

So Stephanie didn't have to take on student loan debt. She chose to. Why 8
should I feel sorry for her? Why should the government lower her interest rates
so taxpayers can help her pay those loans back? It's her debt. Not the taxpayers
of America.

Other decisions factor into this discussion as well. The *Press Herald* 9
ran another story a couple days ago, highlighting several students who carried student loan debt. One of the students was a Social Worker who owes
$97,000 in student loan debt. A cursory search of the Internet will tell you
that social workers don't earn enough to warrant that kind of debt. The
same goes for a Maine student who will owe more than $27,000 for his
degree in Philosophy.

Seriously, I know Walt Disney told my generation we can "be whatever   10
we want to be" if we "believe in ourselves" but borrowing $27,000 for a career
in philosophy . . . in Maine? That's a questionable decision at best, and it's not
the government's fault.

The government already stepped in quietly and took over the student   11
loan industry as part of Obamacare, and they already used taxpayer money to
lower interest rates on current government student loans to 3.4 percent. Now
those taxpayer subsidized interest rates are set to expire, and more than double, and the "gimme gimme" nation doesn't like it.

Naturally, those who want government to take care of them are calling for   12
the interest rates to be held at 3.4 percent, with the taxpayers chipping in for the
difference. But make no mistake, even if those rates are held, this won't be the end
of the discussion. Now that the government holds all student loans, they have the
opportunity to "bail out students" by forgiving loans. "Occupy" camps in a park
near you are already chanting to the beat of the "forgive all student loans" drum,
and you can expect that cry to get louder this summer. (It's warm so they can
start "occupying" again.)

Now don't get me wrong. I agree that college costs are too high. And that   13
IS partly government's fault. Consider the University of Maine, piling on
raises for their teachers, while simultaneously jacking up rates for students. In
just a few years, university salaries were up 29 percent overall while at the
same time tuition costs jumped 30 percent. That's unacceptable and it's a
problem that needs to be addressed.

It's also the government's fault that anybody considers a bailout a legitimate   14
solution to our problems. The bank bailouts and Obama's absolute boondoggle
"American Recovery Act" set the precedent and taught my generation that poor
decisions and failure can be fixed with a government check. Shame on them for
that, and shame on us for looking to government to bail out students now.

Ultimately, students and their parents make the decision to borrow   15
money for school. And it's their responsibility to pay it back. I'm tired of the
whining, I'm tired of the blame game, and I'm tired of people relying on government to bail them out.

It's your debt. Pay it yourself.   16

⊙ AT ISSUE: SOURCES FOR DEVELOPING
A PROPOSAL ARGUMENT

1. Adolphsen states his thesis in paragraph 4: "My decision, my respon-
    sibility." In your own words, write an alternate one-sentence thesis
    statement for this essay on the lines below.

Thesis Statement: _____

_____

_____.

Is your thesis more or less effective than Adolphsen's? Explain.

2. Adolphsen uses two examples to support his point that some people in his generation "want the easy way out" (para. 6). Are these examples enough to support his point? What other evidence could he have provided?

3. Could Adolphsen be accused of oversimplifying a complex issue? In other words, does he make **hasty or sweeping generalizations**? Does he **beg the question**? If so, where?

4. Where in his essay does Adolphsen concede a point to those who disagree with him? How effectively does he deal with this point?

5. How does Adolphsen characterize those who want student-debt relief? Are his characterizations fair? Accurate? Do these characterizations help or hurt his credibility? Explain.

6. In what sense is Adolphsen's essay a refutation of Lee Siegel's essay (p. 580)?

TEMPLATE FOR WRITING A PROPOSAL ARGUMENT

Write a one-paragraph proposal argument in which you consider the topic, "Should the Government Do More to Relieve the Student-Loan Burden?" Follow the template below, filling in the blanks to create your proposal.

The current federal student-loan program has some problems that must be addressed. For example, _____ _____. In order to address this situation, _____. First, _____ _____ _____. Second, _____ _____ _____ _____. Finally, _____ _____ _____.

Not everyone agrees that this is the way to solve these problems, however. Some say _____ _____ _____. Others point out that _____ _____. These objections make sense, but _____ _____ _____. All in all, _____ _____ _____ _____.

⊙ **EXERCISE 15.7**

Ask several of your instructors and your classmates whether they think the government should do more to relieve the student-loan burden. Then, add their responses to the paragraph you wrote using the template above.

⊙ EXERCISE 15.8

Write a proposal arguing that the government should do more to relieve the student-loan burden. Be sure to present examples from your own experience to support your arguments. (If you like, you may incorporate the material you developed for the template and for Exercise 15.7 into your essay.) Cite the readings on pages 569–585, and be sure to document your sources and include a works-cited page. (See Chapter 10 for information on documenting sources.)

⊙ EXERCISE 15.9

Review the four pillars of argument discussed in Chapter 1. Does your essay include all four elements of an effective argument? Add anything that is missing.

⊙WRITING ASSIGNMENTS: PROPOSAL ARGUMENTS

1. Each day, students at college cafeterias throw away hundreds of pounds of uneaten food. A number of colleges have found that by simply eliminating the use of trays, they can cut out much of this waste. At one college, for example, students who did not use trays wasted 14.4 percent less food for lunch and 47.1 percent less for dinner than those who did use trays. Write a proposal to your college or university in which you recommend eliminating trays from dining halls. Use your own experiences as well as information from your research and from interviews with other students to support your position. Be sure to address one or two arguments against your position.

2. Look around your campus, and find a service that you think should be improved. It could be the financial aid office, the student health services, or the writing center. Then, write an essay in which you identify the specific problem (or problems) and suggest a solution. If you wish, interview a few of your friends to get some information that you can use to support your proposal.

3. Assume that your college or university has just received a million-dollar donation from an anonymous benefactor. Your school has decided to solicit proposals from both students and faculty on ways to spend the money. Write a proposal to the president of your school in which you identify a good use for this windfall. Make sure you identify a problem, present a solution, and discuss the advantages of your proposal. If possible, address one or two arguments against your proposal—for example, that the money could be put to better use somewhere else.

Lawrence K. Ho/Getty Images

16

Ethical Arguments

How Far Should Schools Go to Keep Students Safe?

Unfortunately, it is no longer unusual to read reports of shootings, robberies, muggings, and even murders in schools—both urban and rural. In 2013 alone, more than two dozen shootings, which left eighteen people dead and many others injured, were reported at or near college campuses. But is this situation as bad as it seems? According to the Centers for Disease Control and Prevention (CDC), the vast majority of school-age children will never experience lethal violence at school. In addition, a number of studies suggest that college campuses experience less crime than society in general. Even so, the 2007 Virginia Tech massacre and the 2012 shooting at Sandy Hook Elementary have caused many people to worry that schools are no longer the safe environments they once were.

In response to pressure from parents, educators, students, and politicians, many public schools now require students to pass through metal detectors and teachers to lock classroom doors during school hours. Colleges have installed blue-light phones, card-access systems in dorms and labs, and surveillance cameras in parking garages and public areas. In addition, many colleges use text messages, automated phone calls, and emails to alert students and faculty to emergency situations.

Not everyone is happy about this emphasis on security, however. Some educators observe that public school buildings now look more like fortresses than places of learning. In addition, faculty members point out that colleges are supposed to promote free thought and that increased security undercuts this freedom by limiting access to campus and sanitizing the college experience. College students balk at having to wait in long lines to get into campus buildings as security guards examine and scan IDs. They also dislike having to register guests in advance and having to accompany them to dorm rooms. Students complain that colleges tell them they are adults but treat them like children.

Later in this chapter, you will be asked to think more about this issue. You will be given several research sources to consider and asked to write an **ethical argument** discussing how far schools should go to keep students safe.

What Is an Ethical Argument?

Ethics is the field of philosophy that studies the standards by which actions can be judged as right or wrong or good or bad. To make such judgments, we either measure actions against some standard (such as a moral rule like "Thou shall not kill") or consider them in terms of their consequences. Usually, making ethical judgments means examining abstract concepts such as *good, right, duty, obligation, virtue, honor,* and *choice*. **Applied ethics** is the field of philosophy that applies ethics to real-life issues, such as abortion, the death penalty, animal rights, and doctor-assisted suicide.

An **ethical argument** focuses on whether something should be done because it is good or right (or not done because it is bad or wrong). For example, consider the following questions:

- Should teenagers ever be tried as adults?
- Is torture ever justified?
- Should terrorists be tried in civilian courts?
- Is it right for the government to collect Americans' personal data?
- Is the death penalty ever justified?
- Do animals have rights?

Ethical arguments that try to answer questions like these usually begin with a clear statement that something is right or wrong and then go on to show how a religious, philosophical, or ethical principle supports this position. Consider how the last three questions on the list above can be examined in ethical arguments:

- **Is it right for the government to collect Americans' personal data?** You could begin your ethical argument by making the point that the government has a moral duty to protect its citizens. You could then go on to demonstrate that collecting personal data enables the United States government to accomplish this goal by addressing the threat of terrorism. You could end by saying that for this reason, the collection of personal data by the government is both moral and justified.

- **Is the death penalty ever justified?** You could begin your ethical argument by pointing out that because killing in any form is immoral, the death penalty is morally wrong. You could go on to demonstrate that despite its usefulness—it rids society of dangerous criminals—the death penalty hurts all of us. You could conclude by

Courtesy of National Association of Federal Credit Unions (NAFCU)

Respondents to a survey on WhiteHouse.gov said that they were concerned about how government agencies were collecting data about them.

saying that because the death penalty is so immoral, it has no place in a civilized society.

- **Do animals have rights?** You could begin your ethical argument by pointing out that like all thinking beings, animals have certain basic rights. You could go on to discuss the basic rights that all thinking beings have—for example, the right to respect, a safe environment, and a dignified death. You could conclude by saying that the inhumane treatment of animals should not be tolerated, whether those animals are pets, live in the wild, or are raised for food.

Stating an Ethical Principle

The most important part of an ethical argument is the **ethical principle**— a general statement about what is good or bad, right or wrong. It is the set of values that guides you to an ethically correct conclusion.

- **You can show that something is good or right** by establishing that it conforms to a particular moral law or will result in something good for society. For example, you could argue in favor of a policy restricting access to campus by saying that such a policy will reduce crime on campus or will result in a better educational experience for students.

- **You can show that something is bad or wrong** by demonstrating that it violates a moral law or will result in something bad for society. For example, you could argue against the use of torture by saying that respect for individual rights is one of the basic principles of American society and that by ignoring this principle we undermine our Constitution and our way of life.

Whenever possible, you should base your ethical argument on an ethical principle that is **self-evident**—one that needs no proof or explanation. (By doing so, you avoid having to establish the principle that is the basis for your essay.) Thomas Jefferson uses this strategy in the Declaration of Independence. When he says, "We hold these truths to be self-evident," he is saying that the ethical principle that supports the rest of his argument is so basic (and so widely accepted) that it requires no proof—in other words, that it is self-evident. If readers accept Jefferson's assertion, then the rest of his argument—that the thirteen original colonies owe no allegiance to England—will be much more convincing. (Remember, however, that the king of England, George III, would not have accepted Jefferson's assertion. For him, the ethical principle that is the foundation of the Declaration of Independence was not at all self-evident.)

Keep in mind that an ethical principle has to be self-evident to most of your readers—not just to those who agree with you or hold a particular set of religious or cultural beliefs. Using a religious doctrine as an ethical principle has its limitations, and doctrines that cut across religions and cultures are more suitable than those that do not. For example, every culture prohibits murder and theft. But some other doctrines—such as the Jehovah's Witness prohibition against blood transfusion or the Muslim dietary restrictions—are not universally accepted. In addition, an ethical principle must be stated so that it applies universally. For example, not all readers will find the statement, "As a Christian, I am against killing and therefore against the death penalty" convincing. A more effective statement would be, "Because it is morally wrong, the death penalty should be abolished" or "With few exceptions, taking the life of another person is never justified, and there should be no exception for the government."

Ethics versus Law

Generally speaking, an ethical argument deals with what is right and wrong, not necessarily with what is legal or illegal. In fact, there is a big difference between law and ethics. **Laws** are rules that govern a society and are enforced by its political and legal systems. **Ethics** are standards that determine how human conduct is judged.

Keep in mind that something that is legal is not necessarily ethical. As Socrates, St. Augustine, Henry David Thoreau, and Martin Luther King Jr. have all pointed out, there are just laws, and there are unjust laws. For example, when King wrote his famous "Letter from Birmingham Jail," segregation

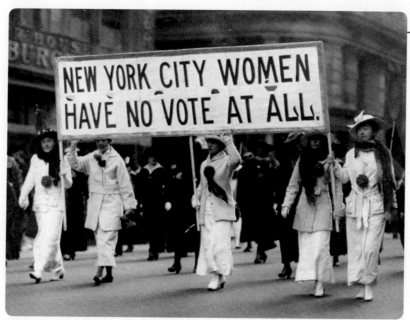

© Corbis

Women march for
the right to vote,
New York, 1913.

was legal in many Southern states. According to King, unjust laws—such as
those that institutionalized segregation—are out of harmony with both moral
law and natural law. As King wrote, "We should never forget that everything
Adolf Hitler did in Germany was 'legal.'" For King, the ultimate standard for
deciding what is just or unjust is morality, not legality.

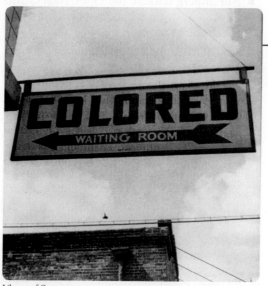

Library of Congress

For decades in
America, African
Americans were
treated unfairly due to
unjust laws.

German Jews being
sent to concentration
camps

© Bettmann/Corbis

There are many historical examples of laws that most people would
now consider unjust:

- **Laws against woman suffrage:** In the late eighteenth century, various
  states passed laws prohibiting women from voting.

- **Jim Crow laws:** In the mid-nineteenth century, laws were passed in the
  American South that restricted the rights of African Americans.

- **Nuremberg laws:** In the 1930s, Nazi Germany passed a series of laws
  that took away the rights of Jews living in Germany.

- **Apartheid laws:** Beginning in 1948, South Africa enacted laws that
  defined and enforced racial segregation. These laws stayed in effect
  until 1994, when Nelson Mandela was elected South Africa's first
  black president.

Today, virtually everyone would agree that these laws were wrong and
should never have been enacted. Still, many people obeyed these laws, with
disastrous consequences. These consequences illustrate the importance of
doing what is ethically right, not just what is legally right.

The difference between ethics and law can be seen in many everyday
situations. Although we have no legal obligation to stop a drunk friend
from driving, most people would agree that we should. In addition,
although motorists (or even doctors) have no legal obligation to help at the
scene of an accident, many people would say that it is the right thing to do.

An example of a person going beyond what is legally required occurred
in Lawrence, Massachusetts, in 1995, when fire destroyed Malden Mills, the
largest employer in town. Citing his religious principles, Aaron Feuerstein,

the owner of the mill and inventor of Polartec fleece, decided to rebuild in Lawrence rather than move his business overseas as many of his competitors had done. In addition, he decided that for sixty days, all employees would receive their full salaries—even though the mill was closed. Feuerstein was not required by law to do what he did, but he decided to do what he believed was both ethical and responsible.

Understanding Ethical Dilemmas

Life decisions tend to be somewhat messy, and it is often not easy to decide what is right or wrong or what is good or bad. In many real-life situations, people are faced with **dilemmas**—choices between alternatives that seem equally unfavorable. An **ethical dilemma** occurs when there is a conflict between two or more possible actions— each of which will have a similar consequence or outcome.

The classic ethical dilemma is the so-called lifeboat dilemma. In this hypothetical situation, a ship hits an iceberg, and survivors are crowded into a lifeboat. As a storm approaches, the captain realizes that he is faced with an ethical dilemma. If he does nothing, the overloaded boat will capsize, and all the people will drown. If he throws some of the passengers overboard, he will save those in the boat, but those he throws overboard will drown.

© Rick Friedman/Corbis

Aaron Feuerstein at Malden Mills

A scene from Alfred Hitchcock's *Lifeboat* (1944)

© Ray Tamarra/The NY Times/Everett Collection

© Cat's Collection/Corbis

In the 1982 film *Sophie's Choice,* a mother (played by Meryl Streep) is forced to make a terrible decision.

Another ethical dilemma occurs in William Styron's 1979 novel *Sophie's Choice.* The novel's narrator is fascinated by the story of Sophie, a woman who was arrested by the Nazis and sent along with her two children to the Auschwitz concentration camp. When she arrived, she was given a choice by a sadistic guard: one of her children would go to the gas chamber and one would be spared, but she had to choose which one. If she did not choose, both children would be murdered.

Ethical dilemmas are not just the stuff of fiction; people confront them every day. For example, an owner of a business who realizes that costs must be cut faces an ethical dilemma. If the owner takes no action, the business will fail, and all the employees will lose their jobs. If the owner lays off some employees, they will be hurt, but the business might be saved and so might the jobs of the remaining workers. A surgeon who has to separate conjoined twins who share a heart also faces an ethical dilemma. If the surgeon does nothing, both twins will die, but if the surgeon operates, one of the twins might live although the other will be sacrificed.

Often, the only way to resolve an ethical dilemma is to choose the lesser of two evils. Simple "right or wrong" or "good versus bad" prescriptions will not work in such cases. For example, killing may be morally, legally, and ethically wrong, but what if it is done in self-defense? Stealing is also wrong, but what if a person steals food to feed a hungry child? Although it may be tempting to apply clear ethical principles, you should be careful not to oversimplify the situations you are writing about.

⊙ EXERCISE 16.1

Consider the following topics for ethical arguments. Then, decide what ethical principle you could use for each argument. For example, if you were to argue against the legalization of marijuana, you could use the principle that getting high prevents people from making wise decisions as the basis for your argument. You could then demonstrate that society is harmed when large numbers of people smoke marijuana.

- The federal government should (or should not) legalize euthanasia.

- A student's race should (or should not) be a consideration in college admissions.

- Homeless people should (or should not) be forcibly removed from city streets.

- Everyone should (or should not) be required to sign an organ-donor card.

- A witness to academic cheating should (or should not) report the cheater.

⊙ EXERCISE 16.2

Make a list of some rules or laws that you think are unjust. Then, next to each item on your list, write down the ethical principle on which you based your conclusion.

⊙ EXERCISE 16.3

Look at the following two images. In what sense do they make ethical arguments? What ethical principle underlies each image?

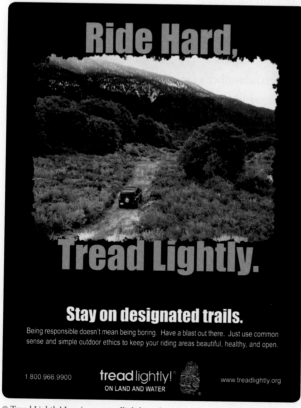

© Tread Lightly! Inc. (www.treadlightly.org)

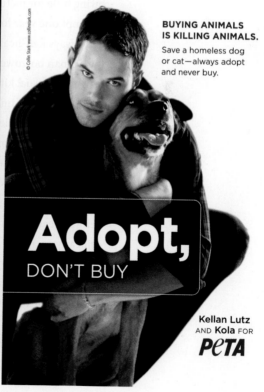

Courtesy of People for the Ethical Treatment of Animals, www.peta.org

⊘ **EXERCISE 16.4**

Read the following poem. What ethical dilemma does the poem present? Does the poem resolve this dilemma?

ETHICS

LINDA PASTAN

In ethics class so many years ago   1
our teacher asked this question every fall:
If there were a fire in a museum
which would you save, a Rembrandt painting
or an old woman who hadn't many   5
years left anyhow? Restless on hard chairs
caring little for pictures or old age
we'd opt one year for life, the next for art
and always half-heartedly. Sometimes
the woman borrowed my grandmother's face   10
leaving her usual kitchen to wander
some drafty, half imagined museum.
One year, feeling clever, I replied
why not let the woman decide herself?
Linda, the teacher would report, eschews   15
the burdens of responsibility.
This fall in a real museum I stand
before a real Rembrandt, old woman,
or nearly so, myself. The colors
within this frame are darker than autumn,   20
darker even than winter—the browns of earth,
though earth's most radiant elements burn
through the canvas. I know now that woman
and painting and season are almost one
and all beyond saving by children.   25

→ EXERCISE 16.5

How would you resolve the ethical dilemma that Pastan presents in her poem? Write a paragraph or two in which you discuss the dilemma as well as the ethical principle on which you based your conclusion.

Structuring an Ethical Argument

In general, an ethical argument can be structured in the following way.

- **Introduction:** Establishes the ethical principle and states the essay's thesis

- **Background:** Gives an overview of the situation

- **Ethical analysis:** Explains the ethical principle and analyzes the particular situation on the basis of this principle

- **Evidence:** Presents points that support the thesis

- **Refutation of opposing arguments:** Addresses arguments against the thesis

- **Conclusion:** Restates the ethical principle as well as the thesis; includes a strong concluding statement

  The following student essay contains all the elements of an ethical argument. The student takes the position that colleges should do more to help nontraditional students succeed.

ARE COLLEGES DOING ENOUGH FOR NONTRADITIONAL STUDENTS?

CHRIS MUÑOZ

Colleges and universities are experiencing an increase in the number of nontraditional students, and this number is projected to rise. Although these students enrich campus communities and provide new opportunities for learning, they also present challenges. Generally, nontraditional students are older, attend school part-time, and are self-supporting. With their years of life experience, they tend to have different educational goals from other students. Although many schools recognize that nontraditional students have unique needs, most schools

1

Ethical principle established

Thesis statement

ignore these needs and unfairly continue to focus on the "typical" student. As a result, nontraditional students frequently do not have the same access to educational opportunities as their younger counterparts. To solve this problem, universities need to do more to ensure equitable treatment of nontraditional students.

Background: Gives an overview of the situation

Most people's assumptions about who is enrolled in college are   2 out of date. According to the educational policy scholar Frederick Hess, only 15 percent of all undergraduates attend a four-year college and live on campus. In other words, so-called typical college students are in the minority. In fact, 38 percent of today's undergraduates are over age twenty-five, 37 percent attend part-time, 32 percent work full-time, and many are responsible for dependents. In addition, real-world responsibilities cause many nontraditional students to delay starting school, to take a break in the middle, or to drop out entirely. According to Alan Tripp, nearly two thirds of all nontraditional students drop out of college. Although some argue that schools already provide extra help, such as advising and tutoring, others point out that asking nontraditional students to adapt to an educational model that focuses on the traditional student is a form of discrimination against them. These people recommend that schools institute policies that reflect the growing number of nontraditional students on campus and address the challenges that these students face every day.

Ethical analysis: Presents the ethical principle and analyzes the situation on the basis of this principle

Most people would agree that diversity is highly valued on college   3 campuses. In fact, most universities go to great lengths to admit a diverse group of students—including nontraditional students. However, as Jacqueline Muhammad points out, universities do not serve these students well after they are enrolled. By asking nontraditional students to assimilate into the traditional university environment, colleges marginalize them, and this is not ethical. Evidence of this marginalization is not difficult to find. As one college student acknowledges, "These students have a lot to offer, but often they don't feel included" (qtd. in Muhammad). This lack of inclusion is seen in many areas of campus life, including access to classes and services, availability of relevant programs and courses, and use of fair and appropriate classroom practices. To be fair, a university should ensure that all of its students have equal access to a meaningful and fulfilling education. By maintaining policies and approaches that are not inclusive, colleges marginalize nontraditional students.

To ensure the fair treatment of nontraditional students, colleges need to remove the barriers those students face. One of the first barriers that nontraditional students face is difficulty gaining access to classes and student services. Academic schedules, including the academic calendar and class times, frequently exclude working adults and parents. As Frederick Hess explains, "A semester system . . . works well for 19-year-olds used to the rhythms of high school, but that's hugely frustrating for workers." In addition, unless classes and services are available in the evening, on weekends, or online, they are inaccessible to many students. As one professional advocate for nontraditional students explains, "Most nontraditional students have obligations during the day that make it difficult to access on-campus resources that are only open during business hours" (qtd. in Muhammad). This situation makes it difficult (and sometimes impossible) for nontraditional students to schedule required courses or to get extra help, such as tutoring. As long as these barriers to equal access exist, nontraditional students will always be "second-class citizens" in the university.

Schools also need to stop devaluing the kinds of programs in which nontraditional students tend to enroll. Research shows that the reasons older students want to continue their educations "indicate high motivation and commitment, but require accommodations to instruction" (Newman, Deyoe, and Seelow 107). Many are taking courses in order to return to work, change careers, or improve their chances for a promotion. According to Hess, although the greatest demand is for associate's degrees, over 50 percent of nontraditional students are seeking "subbaccalaureate" certification credentials. As Hess demonstrates, certification programs are considered to be marginal, even in community colleges. One reason for this situation is that most schools still judge their own worth by factors—such as academic ranking or grant money—that have little to do with teaching career skills. By devaluing practical training that certification programs offer, schools are undermining the educational experience that many nontraditional students want.

Finally, universities need to do more to encourage inclusive teaching approaches. According to Joshua L. Carreiro and Brian P. Kapitulik,

4 Evidence: First point in support of the thesis

5 Evidence: Second point in support of the thesis

6 Evidence: Third point in support of thesis

most educators assume their students are "traditional"—that they are recent high school graduates from middle-class backgrounds with little work experience (232). As a result, nontraditional students "are frequently mis-served by direct instruction due to financial, family, career, or learning style preferences" (Newman, Deyoe, and Seelow 107). Carreiro and Kapitulik conclude that these assumptions result in "an exclusive class-room environment" that excludes and marginalizes nontraditional students (246). One way of addressing this problem is for universities to expand online education offerings. Online courses enable nontraditional students to gradually assimilate into the college environment and to work at their own pace without fear of ridicule. Universities can also encourage instructors to develop new teaching approaches. If instructors want to be more inclusive, they can acknowledge diversity by engaging students in diverse ways of thinking and learning (Hermida). For example, they can ask students to relate course material to their own experiences, and they can bring in guest speakers from a variety of backgrounds. By acknowl-edging the needs of nontraditional students, instructors can provide a better education for all students.

Refutation of opposing arguments

Not everyone believes that colleges and universities need to change   7 their basic assumptions about education. They concede that nontraditional students might need extra support, but they say that these students are adults and should be able to fend for themselves. Students' commitments outside of school—for instance, children or a full-time job—should not be a concern for colleges and universities. If these students need help, they can get support from one another, or they can turn to student-led organiza-tions. Even those educators who are sympathetic to nontraditional stu-dents suggest that extra mentoring or advising is all that is necessary. However, the problems faced by these students need to be addressed, and according to Hermida, by ignoring institutional barriers and biases, col-leges and universities are essentially burying their heads in the sand (22). To be more welcoming to nontraditional students, universities must fun-damentally change some of the structures and practices that have tradi-tionally defined them. Ultimately, everyone—the schools, the communi-ties, and the students—will benefit from these adjustments.

According to Hermida, many of today's students are nontraditional   8 (20). Most of the current research suggests that inclusion is their most pressing concern. As this population continues to grow, say Newman, Deyoe, and Seelow, educators should focus on offering "clear objectives, direct ties to life experience, and multiple opportunities" for nontraditional students to engage in the college community (122). Giving preferential treatment to some students while ignoring the needs of others is ethically wrong, so schools need to work harder to end discrimination against this increasingly large group of learners.

Concluding statement

Works Cited

Carreiro, Joshua L., and Brian P. Kapitulik. "Budgets, Board Games, and Make Believe: The Challenge of Teaching Social Class Inequality with Nontraditional Students." *American Sociologist,* vol. 41, no. 3, Oct. 2010, pp. 232–48. *Academic Search Complete*, www.ebscohost.com/academic.

Hermida, Julian. "Inclusive Teaching: An Approach for Encouraging Nontraditional Student Success." *International Journal of Research and Review,* vol. 5, no. 1, Oct. 2010, pp. 19–30. *Academic Search Complete*, www.ebscohost.com/academic.

Hess, Frederick. "Old School: College's Most Important Trend Is the Rise of the Adult Student." *The Atlantic*, 28 Sept. 2011, www.theatlantic .com/business/archive/2011/09/old-school-colleges-most-important -trend-is-the-rise-of-the-adult-student/245823/.

Muhammad, Jacqueline. "New Coordinator to Address Nontraditional Student Needs." *Daily Egyptian*, Southern Illinois University, Carbondale, 8 Dec. 2011, archives.dailyegyptian.com/siu -2011/2011/12/8/new-coordinator-to-address-non-traditional -student-needs.html.

Newman, Dianna L., Meghan Morris Deyoe, and David Seelow. "Serving Nontraditional Students: Meeting Needs through an Online Writing Program." *Models for Improving and Optimizing Online and Blended Learning in Higher Education*, edited by Jared Keengwe and Joachim Jack Agamba, IGI Global, 2015, pp. 106–28.

Tripp, Alan. "Guest Post: Nontraditional Students Key to College Completion Goal." *Washington Post*, 25 Mar. 2011, www .washingtonpost.com/blogs/college-inc/post/guest-post-non -traditional-students-key-to-college-completion-goal/2011/03/25 /AFV8elXB_blog.html.

GRAMMAR IN CONTEXT

Subordination and Coordination

When you write an argumentative essay, you need to show readers the logical and sequential connections between your ideas. You do this by using *coordinating conjunctions* and *subordinating conjunctions*—words that join words, phrases, clauses, or entire sentences. Be sure to choose conjunctions that accurately express the relationship between the ideas they join.

Coordinating conjunctions—*and, but, for, nor, or, so,* and *yet*—join ideas of equal importance. In compound sentences, they describe the relationship between the ideas in the two independent clauses and show how these ideas are related.

- "Colleges and universities are experiencing an increase in the number of nontraditional students, and this number is projected to rise." (*And* indicates addition.) (para. 1)

- "These students have a lot to offer, but often they don't feel included." (*But* indicates contrast or contradiction.) (3)

Subordinating conjunctions—*after, although, because, if, so that, where,* and so on—join ideas of unequal importance. In complex sentences, they describe the relationship between the ideas in the dependent clause and the independent clause and show how these ideas are related.

- "Although these students enrich campus communities and provide new opportunities for learning, they also present challenges." (*Although* indicates a contrast.) (1)

- "Although many schools recognize that nontraditional students have unique needs, most schools ignore these needs and unfairly continue to focus on the 'typical' student." (*Although* indicates a contrast.) (1)

- "As long as these barriers to equal access exist, nontraditional students will always be 'second-class citizens' in the university." (*As long as* indicates a causal relationship.) (4)

- "If instructors want to be more inclusive, they can acknowledge diversity by engaging students in diverse ways of thinking and learning." (*If* indicates condition.) (6)

 LaunchPad macmillan learning

For more practice, see the LearningCurve on Coordination and Subordination in the LaunchPad for *Practical Argument*.

➲ EXERCISE 16.6

The following essay includes the basic elements of an ethical argument. Read the essay, and then answer the questions that follow it, consulting the outline on page 599 if necessary.

This essay was published in the *Wall Street Journal* on April 29, 2015.

MORE THAN "MORAL COMPLICITY" AT AUSCHWITZ

DANIEL SULEIMAN

On the opening day of his criminal trial in Lüneburg, Germany, on April 21   1 for complicity in the deaths of approximately 300,000 Jews, most of whom were Hungarian, former Waffen-SS officer Oskar Gröning conceded that he bears "moral" responsibility for the role he served at Auschwitz, the notorious concentration camp where he was stationed from 1942–44. But Mr. Gröning, who is 93, does not admit that he is guilty of crimes.

"It is without question that I am morally complicit in the murder of mil-   2 lions of Jews through my activities at Auschwitz," he told the court, according to the *Guardian*. "But as to the question whether I am criminally culpable, that's for you to decide."

Mr. Gröning's strategy of conceding one battle in an attempt to win a   3 more important one is a common criminal-defense tactic. Dzhokhar Tsarnaev, who was convicted by a jury on April 8 for his role in the Boston Marathon bombings, is trying something similar.

On the first day of the guilt phase of his trial, Tsarnaev's lawyer admitted   4 that Tsarnaev and his brother were responsible for the bombings and the murder of a university police officer. Why? Because by handing the government a victory in the guilt phase, Tsarnaev hopes to strengthen his argument, being made in the sentencing phase, that he should be spared the death penalty.[1]

Sometimes this strategy works. But sometimes it is merely all a defendant   5 has. Should Mr. Gröning's concession that he bears moral responsibility for the deaths at Auschwitz spare him a guilty verdict?

The short answer is no. There are clearly situations in which moral fail-   6 ings do not, and should not, equate with criminal guilt. Adultery is commonly considered a moral failure in the U.S., but Americans are no longer prosecuted for it. Doing nothing while a neighbor's house burns to the ground could result in feelings of moral guilt, but it is almost certainly not a crime. In an example closer to Mr. Gröning's situation, someone who refused to hide a friend or neighbor as the Jews were being rounded up in Budapest might feel

---

[1]Tsarnaev was found guilty and sentenced to death in 2015.

"morally complicit" in their subsequent deaths, but we would not consider him criminally responsible.

Let us assume the facts are as Mr. Gröning contends—that he collected 7 the belongings of incoming prisoners at Auschwitz, and witnessed atrocities, but that he did not personally participate in gassing innocent victims or, in his own horrifying example, beat to death an infant who had been left behind. We have no way of knowing whether these events occurred as he has told them, or if there were other instances in which Mr. Gröning directly participated in acts of murder. But it is indisputable, apparently even to Mr. Gröning himself, that he bears some moral responsibility for the deaths that occurred while he was at Auschwitz.

So is he also guilty of crimes? The camps were not his idea. He didn't, as 8 far as we know, deliver anyone to the gas chamber. Maybe he even privately came to reject Nazi ideology.

> "So is he also guilty of crimes?"

I recognize that my judgment might 9 be clouded by the fact that my mother, who was born in Budapest in 1939, could have been one of Oskar Gröning's victims, had she and her parents not survived the war under assumed identities. Or because other members of my family did perish in concentration camps, perhaps while Mr. Gröning looked on. Yet I am trained to examine legal questions analytically and, as a purely legal matter, I do not accept Mr. Gröning's argument, for it finds no support in common concepts of criminal law.

By way of example, every day across the U.S., defendants are indicted for 10 aiding and abetting others in the commission of their crimes, or serving as an accomplice, or participating with others in a criminal enterprise. These concepts are basic, and elastic. If I abhor bank robbery, but I nevertheless drive you to a local bank, where, dressed in a mask with a gun in your hand, you get out and rob the bank, you and I have both committed crimes. If I help route phone calls to a network of drug dealers, but never touch the stuff, I am still a criminal.

And if I strip Holocaust victims on their way to the gas chamber of their 11 last coins, because, as Mr. Gröning testified, "they didn't need it anymore," I am guilty. I am an accomplice to murder, a participant in a criminal enterprise. Caught up in activities of others' design, perhaps, but guilty nonetheless.

Ninety-three-year-old men are not ideal criminal defendants because 12 their frailty lends them a sympathetic sheen. Mr. Gröning, with his walker, hardly resembles the SS officer and money-counter he once was. But there is no statute of limitations on atrocity, and his concession of moral guilt should not confuse anyone into thinking that he does not also share criminal responsibility for what occurred at Auschwitz.

Identifying the Elements of an Ethical Argument

1. Look up the definition of *complicity*. What does Gröning mean when he says, "I am morally complicit in the murder of millions of Jews" (para. 2)?

2. What ethical principle does Suleiman apply in his essay? At what point in the essay does he state this principle? Why do you think he states it where he does?

3. What is the thesis of this essay? In your own words, write it on the lines in the template below.

   Despite his admission of moral guilt, _____

   _____

   _____.

4. According to Suleiman, what is the difference between *moral guilt* and *legal guilt*? Is it possible for a person to be morally complicit in murder but not criminally culpable? Explain.

5. Where in the essay does Suleiman discuss possible objections to his thesis? Where does he concede that he may be biased? How effectively does he address these issues?

6. What examples does Suleiman use to support his thesis? What other kinds of support could he have also used? Should he have used other support? Explain.

7. In his essay, Suleiman employs all three appeals—*logos*, *pathos*, and *ethos*. Locate examples of each. How effective is each appeal? Explain.

8. What ideas does Suleiman emphasize in his conclusion? Do you think that his conclusion is effective? Explain.

How Far Should Schools Go to Keep Students Safe?

Lawrence K. Ho/Getty Images

Go back to page 589, and reread the At Issue box, which gives background on how far schools should go to keep their students safe. Then, read the sources on the pages that follow.

As you read this source material, you will be asked to answer some questions and to complete some simple activities. This work will help you understand both the content and the structure of the selections. When you are finished, you will be ready to write an **ethical argument** that takes a position on the topic, "How Far Should Schools Go to Keep Students Safe?"

SOURCES

Brett A. Sokolow, "How Not to Respond to Virginia Tech — II," p. 609

Jesus M. Villahermosa Jr., "Guns Don't Belong in the Hands of Administrators, Professors, or Students," p. 613

Timothy Wheeler, "There's a Reason They Choose Schools," p. 616

Greg Hampikian, "When May I Shoot a Student?," p. 619

Todd C. Frankel, "Can We Invent Our Way Out of School Violence?," p. 622

Alan Schwarz, "A Bid for Guns on Campuses to Deter Rape," p. 625

Isothermal Community College, "Warning Signs: How You Can Help Prevent Campus Violence" (brochure), p. 629
Isothermal Community College

Amy Dion, "Gone but Not Forgotten" (poster), p. 633
© Amy Dion, Art Director, SIU

Inside Higher Ed published this essay on May 1, 2007.

HOW NOT TO RESPOND TO VIRGINIA TECH—II

BRETT A. SOKOLOW

If you believe the pundits and talking heads in the aftermath of the Virginia 1
Tech tragedy, every college and university should rush to set up text-message-based early warning systems, install loudspeakers throughout campus, perform criminal background checks on all incoming students, allow students to install their own locks on their residence hall room doors, and exclude from admission or expel students with serious mental health conditions. We should profile loners, establish lockdown protocols, and develop mass-shooting evacuation plans. We should even arm our students to the teeth. In the immediate aftermath, security experts and college and university officials have been quoted in newspapers and on TV with considering all of these remedies, and more, to be able to assure the public that WE ARE DOING SOMETHING.

Since when do we let the media dictate to us our best practices? Do we 2
need to do something? Do we need to be doing all or some of these things? Here's what I think. These are just my opinions, informed by what I have learned so far in the reportage on what happened at Virginia Tech. Because that coverage is inaccurate and incomplete, please consider these my thoughts so far, subject to revision as more facts come to light.

> "Since when do we let the media dictate to us our best practices?"

We should not be rushing to install text-message-based warning 3
systems. At the low cost of $1 per student per year, you might ask what the downside could be? Well, the real cost is the $1 per student that we don't spend on mental health support, where we really need to spend it. And, what do you get for your $1? A system that will send an emergency text to the cell phone number of every student who is registered with the service. If we acknowledge that many campuses still don't have the most current mailing address for some of our students who live off-campus, is it realistic to expect that students are going to universally supply us with their cell phone numbers? You could argue that students are flocking to sign up for this service on the campuses that currently provide it (less than 50 nationally), but that is driven by the panic of current events. Next fall, when the shock has worn off, apathy will inevitably return, and voluntary sign-up rates will drop. How about mandating that students participate? What about the costs of the bureaucracy we will need to collect and who will input this data? Who will track which students have yet to give us their numbers, remind them, and hound them to submit

the information? Who will update this database as students switch cell numbers mid-year, which many do? That's more than a full-time job, with implementation already costing more than the $1 per student. Some students want their privacy. They won't want administrators to have their cell number. Some students don't have cell phones. Many students do not have text services enabled on their phones. More added cost. Many professors instruct students to turn off their phones in classrooms.

Texting is useless. It's useless on the field for athletes, while students are swimming, sleeping, showering, etc. And, perhaps most dangerously, texting an alert may send that alert to a psychopath who is also signed-up for the system, telling him exactly what administrators know, what the emergency plan is, and where to go to effect the most harm. Would a text system create a legal duty that colleges and universities do not have, a duty of universal warning? What happens in a crisis if the system is overloaded, as were cellphone lines in Blacksburg? What happens if the data entry folks mistype a number, and a student who needs warning does not get one? We will be sued for negligence. We need to spend this time, money, and effort on the real problem: mental health. 4

We should consider installing loudspeakers throughout campus. This technology has potentially better coverage than text messages, with much less cost. Virginia Tech used such loudspeakers to good effect during the shootings. 5

We should not rush to perform criminal background checks (CBCs) on all incoming students. A North Carolina task force studied this issue after two 2004 campus shootings and decided that the advantages were not worth the disadvantages. You might catch a random dangerous applicant, but most students who enter with criminal backgrounds were minors when they committed their crimes, and their records may have been sealed or expunged. If your student population is largely of non-traditional age, CBCs may reveal more, but then you have to weigh the cost and the question of whether you are able to perform due diligence on screening the results of the checks if someone is red-flagged. How will you determine which students who have criminal histories are worthy of admission and which are not? And, there is always the reality that if you perform a check on all incoming students and the college across the street does not, the student with the criminal background will apply there and not to you. If you decide to check incoming students, what will you do about current students? Will you do a state-level check, or a 50-state and federal check? Will your admitted applicants be willing to wait the 30 days that it takes to get the results? Other colleges who admitted them are also waiting for an answer. The comprehensive check can cost $80 per student. We need to spend this time, money, and effort on the real problem: mental health. 6

We should not be considering whether to allow students to install their own locks on their dormitory room doors. Credit *Fox News Live* for this deplorably dumb idea. If we let students change their locks, residential life and campus law enforcement will not be able to key into student rooms when they overdose on alcohol or try to commit suicide. This idea would prevent us from 7 saving lives, rather than help to protect members of our community. The Virginia Tech killer could have shot through a lock, no matter whether it was the original or a retrofit. This is our property, and we need to have access to it. We need to focus our attention on the real issue: mental health.

Perhaps the most preposterous suggestion of all is that we need to relax 8 **our campus weapons bans so that armed members of our communities can defend themselves. We should not allow weapons on college campuses.** Imagine you are seated in Norris Hall, facing the whiteboard at the front of the room. The shooter enters from the back and begins shooting. What good is your gun going to do at this point? Many pro-gun advocates have talked about the deterrent and defense values of a well-armed student body, but none of them have mentioned the potential collateral criminal consequences of armed students: increases in armed robbery, muggings, escalation of interpersonal and relationship violence, etc. Virginia, like most states, cannot keep guns out of the hands of those with potentially lethal mental health crises. When we talk about arming students, we'd be arming them too. We need to focus our attention on the real issue: mental health.

We should establish lockdown protocols that are specific to the 9 **nature of the threat.** Lockdowns are an established mass-protection tactic. They can isolate perpetrators, insulate targets from threats, and restrict personal movement away from a dangerous line-of-fire. But, if lockdowns are just a random response, they have the potential to lock students in with a still-unidentified perpetrator. If not used correctly, they have the potential to lock students into facilities from which they need immediate egress for safety reasons. And, if not enforced when imposed, lockdowns expose us to the potential liability of not following our own policies. We should also establish protocols for judicious use of evacuations. When police at Virginia Tech herded students out of buildings and across the Drill Field, it was based on their assessment of a low risk that someone was going to open fire on students as they fled out into the open, and a high risk of leaving the occupants of certain buildings in situ, making evacuation from a zone of danger an appropriate escape method.

We should not exclude from admission or expel students with mental 10 **health conditions, unless they pose a substantial threat of harm to themselves or others.** Section 504 of the Rehabilitation Act prohibits colleges and universities from discrimination in admission against those with disabilities. It also prohibits colleges and universities from suspending or expelling disabled students, including those who are suicidal, unless the student is deemed to be a direct threat of substantial harm in an objective process based on the most current medical assessment available. Many colleges do provide health surveys to incoming students, and when those surveys disclose mental health conditions, we need to consider what appropriate follow-up should occur as a result. The Virginia Tech shooter was schizophrenic or mildly autistic, and identifying those disabilities early on and providing support, accommodation—and potentially intervention—is our issue.

We should consider means and mechanisms for early intervention with 11 students who exhibit behavioral issues, but we should not profile loners. At the University of South Carolina, the Behavioral Intervention Team makes many early catches of students whose behavior is threatening, disruptive, or potentially self-injurious. By working with faculty and staff at opening communication and support, the model is enhancing campus safety in a way that many other campuses are not. In the aftermath of what happened at Virginia Tech, I hope many campuses are considering a model designed to help raise flags for early screening and intervention. Many students are loners, isolated, withdrawn, pierced, tattooed, dyed, Wiccan, skate rats, fantasy gamers, or otherwise outside the "mainstream." This variety enlivens the richness of college campuses, and offers layers of culture that quilt the fabric of diverse communities. Their preferences and differences cannot and should not be cause for fearing them or suspecting them. But, when any member of the community starts a downward spiral along the continuum of violence, begins to lose contact with reality, goes off their medication regimen, threatens, disrupts, or otherwise gains our attention with unhealthy or dangerous patterns, we can't be bystanders any longer. Our willingness to intervene can make all the difference.

All of the pundits insist that random violence can't be predicted, but 12 many randomly violent people exhibit a pattern of detectable disintegration of self, often linked to suicide. People around them perceive it. We can all be better attuned to those patterns and our protocols for communicating our concerns to those who have the ability to address them. This will focus our attention on the real issue: mental health.

⬮ AT ISSUE: SOURCES FOR DEVELOPING AN ETHICAL ARGUMENT

1. Why does Sokolow begin his essay by discussing what "pundits and talking heads" think should be done to stop campus violence? Is this an effective opening strategy?

2. In paragraph 2, Sokolow says, "Here's what I think. These are just my opinions." Do these two statements undercut or enhance his credibility? Why do you suppose he includes them?

3. How does Sokolow propose to make campuses safer? Do you agree with his suggestions? Why or why not?

4. Is Sokolow's argument a refutation? If so, what arguments is he refuting?

5. In what sense is this essay an ethical argument?

6. In his concluding statement, Sokolow says that the real issue is "mental health." What does he mean? Do you agree?

This essay is from the April 18, 2008, issue of the *Chronicle of Higher Education*.

GUNS DON'T BELONG IN THE HANDS OF ADMINISTRATORS, PROFESSORS, OR STUDENTS

JESUS M. VILLAHERMOSA JR.

In the wake of the shootings at Virginia Tech and Northern Illinois University, a number of state legislatures are considering bills that would allow people to carry concealed weapons on college campuses. I recently spoke at a conference on higher-education law, sponsored by Stetson University and the National Association of Student Personnel Administrators, at which campus officials discussed the need to exempt colleges from laws that let private citizens carry firearms and to protect such exemptions where they exist. I agree that allowing guns on campuses will create problems, not solve them. 1

I have been a deputy sheriff for more than 26 years and was the first certified master defensive-tactics instructor for law-enforcement personnel in the state of Washington. In addition, I have been a firearms instructor and for several decades have served on my county sheriff's SWAT team, where I am now point man on the entry team. Given my extensive experience dealing with violence in the workplace and at schools and colleges, I do not think professors and administrators, let alone students, should carry guns. 2

Some faculty and staff members may be capable of learning to be good shots in stressful situations, but most of them probably wouldn't practice their firearms skills enough to become confident during an actual shooting. Unless they practiced those skills constantly, there would be a high risk that when a shooting situation actually occurred, they would miss the assailant. That would leave great potential for a bullet to strike a student or another innocent bystander. Such professors and administrators could be imprisoned for manslaughter for recklessly endangering the lives of others during a crisis. 3

Although some of the legislative bills have been defeated, they may be reintroduced, or other states may introduce similar measures. Thus, colleges should at least contemplate the possibility of having armed faculty and staff members on their campuses, and ask themselves the following questions: 4

- Is our institution prepared to assume the liability that accompanies the lethal threat of carrying or using weapons? Are we financially able and willing to drastically increase our liability-insurance premium to cover all of the legal ramifications involved with allowing faculty and staff members to carry firearms?

- How much time will each faculty and staff member be given each year to spend on a firing range to practice shooting skills? Will we pay them for that time?

- Will their training include exposing them to a great amount of stress in order to simulate a real-life shooting situation, like the training that police officers go through?

- Will the firearm that each one carries be on his or her person during the day? If so, will faculty and staff members be given extensive defensive-tactics training, so that they can retain their firearm if someone tries to disarm them?

- The fact that a college allows people to have firearms could be publicized, and, under public-disclosure laws, the institution could be required to notify the general public which faculty or staff members are carrying them. Will those individuals accept the risk of being targeted by a violent student or adult who wants to neutralize the threat and possibly obtain their weapons?

- If the firearms are not carried by faculty and staff members every day, where and how will those weapons be secured, so that they do not fall into the wrong hands?

- If the firearms are locked up, how will faculty and staff members gain access to them in time to be effective if a shooting actually occurs?

- Will faculty and staff members who carry firearms be required to be in excellent physical shape, and stay that way, in case they need to fight someone for their gun?

- Will weapons-carrying faculty and staff members accept that they may be shot by law-enforcement officers who mistake them for the shooter? (All the responding officers see is a person with a gun. If you are even close to matching the suspect's description, the risk is high that they may shoot you.)

- Will faculty and staff members be prepared to kill another person, someone who may be as young as a teenager?

> "Will faculty and staff members be prepared to kill another person?"

- Will faculty and staff members be prepared for the possibility that they may miss their target (which has occurred even in police shootings) and wound or kill an innocent bystander?

- Will faculty and staff members be ready to face imprisonment for manslaughter, depending on their states' criminal statutes, if one of their bullets does, in fact, strike an innocent person?

- Even if not criminally charged, would such faculty and staff members be prepared to be the focus of a civil lawsuit, both as a professional working for the institution and as an individual, thereby exposing their personal assets?

If any of us in the law-enforcement field were asked these questions, we could answer them all with absolute confidence. We have made a commitment to train relentlessly and to die, if we have to, in order to protect others. Experienced officers have typically fired tens of thousands of rounds practicing for the time when they might need those skills to save themselves or someone else during a lethal situation. We take that commitment seriously. Before legislators and college leaders make the decision to put a gun in the hands of a professor or administrator, they should be certain they take it seriously, too.

⊖ AT ISSUE: SOURCES FOR DEVELOPING AN ETHICAL ARGUMENT

1. What is Villahermosa's thesis? Where does he state it?

2. What is Villahermosa trying to establish in paragraph 2? Do you think this paragraph is necessary?

3. In the bulleted list in paragraph 4, Villahermosa poses a series of questions. What does he want this list to accomplish? Is he successful?

4. What arguments does Villahermosa include to support his thesis? Which of these arguments do you find most convincing? Why?

5. Do you think Villahermosa is making an ethical argument here? If so, on what ethical principle does he base his argument?

6. What points does Villahermosa emphasize in his conclusion? Should he have emphasized any other points? Explain.

7. Both Villahermosa and Timothy Wheeler (p. 616) deal with the same issue—guns on campus. Which writer do you think makes the stronger case? Why?

This article is from the October 11, 2007, issue of *National Review*.

THERE'S A REASON THEY CHOOSE SCHOOLS

TIMOTHY WHEELER

Wednesday's shooting at yet another school has a better outcome than most in recent memory. No one died at Cleveland's Success Tech Academy except the perpetrator. The two students and two teachers he shot are in stable condition at Cleveland hospitals.

What is depressingly similar to the mass murders at Virginia Tech and Nickel Mines, Pennsylvania, and too many others was the killer's choice of venue—that steadfastly gun-free zone, the school campus. Although murderer Seung-Hui Cho at Virginia Tech and Asa Coon, the Cleveland shooter, were both students reported to have school-related grudges, other school killers have proved to be simply taking advantage of the lack of effective security at schools. The Bailey, Colorado, multiple rapes and murder of September 2006, the Nickel Mines massacre of October 2006, and Buford Furrow's murderous August 1999 invasion of a Los Angeles Jewish day-care center were all committed by adults. They had no connection to the schools other than being drawn to the soft target a school offers such psychopaths.

This latest shooting comes only a few weeks after the American Medical Association released a theme issue of its journal *Disaster Medicine and Public Health Preparedness*. This issue is dedicated to analyzing the April 2007 Virginia Tech shootings, in which 32 people were murdered. The authors are university officials, trauma surgeons, and legal analysts who pore over the details of the incident, looking for "warning signs" and "risk factors" for violence. They rehash all the tired rhetoric of bureaucrats and public-health wonks, including the public-health mantra of the 1990s that guns are the root cause of violence.

Sheldon Greenberg, a dean at Johns Hopkins, offers this gem: "Reinforce a 'no weapons' policy and, when violated, enforce it quickly, to include expulsion. Parents should be made aware of the policy. *Officials should dispel the politically driven notion that armed students could eliminate an active shooter*" (emphasis added). Greenberg apparently isn't aware that at the Appalachian School of Law in 2002 another homicidal Virginia student was stopped from shooting more of his classmates when another student held him at gunpoint. The Pearl High School murderer Luke Woodham was stopped cold when vice principal Joel Myrick got his Colt .45 handgun out of his truck and pointed it at the young killer.

Virginia Tech's 2005 no-guns-on-campus policy was an abject failure at deterring Cho Seung-Hui. Greenberg's audacity in ignoring the obvious is typical of arrogant school officials. What the AMA journal authors studiously avoid are on one hand the repeated failures of such feel-good steps as no-gun policies, and on the other hand the demonstrated success of armed first responders. These responders would be the students themselves, such as the trained and licensed law student, or their similarly qualified teachers.

> "Virginia Tech's . . . no-guns-on-campus policy was an abject failure."

6

In Cleveland this week and at Virginia Tech the shooters took time to walk the halls, searching out victims in several rooms, and then shooting them. Virginia Chief Medical Examiner Marcella Fierro describes the locations of the dead in Virginia Tech's Norris Hall. Dead victims were found in groups ranging from 1 to 13, scattered throughout 4 rooms and a stairwell. If any one of the victims had, like the Appalachian School of Law student, used armed force to stop Cho, lives could have been saved.

7 The people of Virginia actually had a chance to implement such a plan last year. House Bill 1572 was introduced in the legislature to extend the state's concealed-carry provisions to college campuses. But the bill died in committee, opposed by the usual naysayers, including the Virginia Association of Chiefs of Police and the university itself. Virginia Tech spokesman Larry Hincker was quoted in the *Roanoke Times* as saying, "I'm sure the university community is appreciative of the General Assembly's actions because this will help parents, students, faculty, and visitors feel safe on our campus."

8 It is encouraging that college students themselves have a much better grasp on reality than their politically correct elders. During the week of October 22–26 Students for Concealed Carry on Campus will stage a nationwide "empty holster" demonstration (peaceful, of course) in support of their cause.

9 School officials typically base violence-prevention policies on irrational fears more than real-world analysis of what works. But which is more horrible, the massacre that timid bureaucrats fear might happen when a few good guys (and gals) carry guns on campus, or the one that actually did happen despite Virginia Tech's progressive violence-prevention policy? Can there really be any more debate?

10 AMA journal editor James J. James, M.D., offers up this nostrum:

> We must meaningfully embrace all of the varied disciplines contributing to preparedness and response and be more willing to be guided and informed by the full spectrum of research methodologies, including not only the rigid application of the traditional scientific method and epidemiological and social science applications but also the incorporation of observational/empirical findings, as necessary, in the absence of more objective data.

Got that?

11 I prefer the remedy prescribed by self-defense guru Massad Ayoob. When good people find themselves in what he calls "the dark place," confronted by

the imminent terror of a gun-wielding homicidal maniac, the picture becomes clear. Policies won't help. Another federal gun law won't help. The only solution is a prepared and brave defender with the proper lifesaving tool—a gun.

⊙ AT ISSUE: SOURCES FOR DEVELOPING AN ETHICAL ARGUMENT

1. According to Wheeler, what is "depressingly similar" about the mass murders committed on campuses (para. 2)?

2. What is Wheeler's attitude toward those who said that "guns are the root cause of violence" (3)? How can you tell?

3. Why, according to Wheeler, do college administrators and bureaucrats continue to ignore the answer to the problem of violence on campus? How does he refute their objections?

4. Do you find Wheeler's argument in support of his thesis convincing? What, if anything, do you think he could have added to strengthen his argument?

5. How does Wheeler's language reveal his attitude toward his subject? (For example, consider his use of "gem" in paragraph 4 and "politically correct" in paragraph 8.) Can you give other examples of language that conveys his point of view?

6. How would you characterize Wheeler's opinion of guns? How is his opinion different from Villahermosa's (p. 613)?

7. How do you think Wheeler would respond to the ideas in "Warning Signs: How You Can Help Prevent Campus Violence" (p. 629)? Which suggestions do you think he would support? Which would he be likely to oppose? Explain.

This opinion piece was published in the *New York Times* on February 27, 2014.

WHEN MAY I SHOOT A STUDENT?

GREG HAMPIKIAN

Boise, Idaho—To the chief counsel of the Idaho State Legislature: 1

In light of the bill permitting guns on our state's college and university 2 campuses, which is likely to be approved by the state House of Representatives in the coming days, I have a matter of practical concern that I hope you can help with: When may I shoot a student?

I am a biology professor, not a lawyer, and I had never considered bring- 3 ing a gun to work until now. But since many of my students are likely to be armed, I thought it would be a good idea to even the playing field.

I have had encounters with disgruntled students over the years, some of 4 whom seemed quite upset, but I always assumed that when they reached into their backpacks they were going for a pencil. Since I carry a pen to lecture, I did not feel outgunned; and because there are no working sharpeners in the lecture hall, the most they could get off is a single point. But now that we'll all be packing heat, I would like legal instruction in the rules of classroom engagement.

At present, the harshest penalty available here at Boise State is expulsion, 5 used only for the most heinous crimes, like cheating on Scantron exams. But now that lethal force is an option, I need to know which infractions may be treated as de facto capital crimes.

I assume that if a student shoots first, I am allowed to empty my clip; but 6 given the velocity of firearms, and my aging reflexes, I'd like to be proactive. For example, if I am working out a long equation on the board and several students try to correct me using their laser sights, am I allowed to fire a warning shot?

If two armed students are arguing over who should be served next at the 7 coffee bar and I sense escalating hostility, should I aim for the legs and remind them of the campus Shared-Values Statement (which reads, in part, "Boise State strives to provide a culture of civility and success where all feel safe and free from discrimination, harassment, threats or intimidation")?

While our city police chief has expressed grave concerns about allowing 8 guns on campus, I would point out that he already has one. I'm glad that you were not intimidated by him, and did not allow him to speak at the public hearing on the bill (though I really enjoyed the 40 minutes you gave to the National Rifle Association spokesman).

Knee-jerk reactions from law enforcement officials and university presi- 9 dents are best set aside. Ignore, for example, the lame argument that some drunken frat boys will fire their weapons in violation of best practices. This view is based on stereotypical depictions of drunken frat boys, a group whose dignity no one seems willing to defend.

The problem, of course, is not that drunken frat boys will be armed; it is that they are drunken frat boys. Arming them is clearly not the issue. They would cause damage with or without guns. I would point out that urinating against a building or firing a few rounds into a sorority house are both violations of the same honor code.

> "I would point out that urinating against a building or firing a few rounds into a sorority house are both violations of the same honor code."

10

In terms of the campus murder rate—zero at present—I think that we can all agree that guns don't kill people, people with guns do. Which is why encouraging guns on campus makes so much sense. Bad guys go where there are no guns, so by adding guns to campus more bad guys will spend their year abroad in London. Britain has incredibly restrictive laws—their cops don't even have guns!—and gun deaths there are a tiny fraction of what they are in America. It's a perfect place for bad guys.   11

Some of my colleagues are concerned that you are encouraging firearms within a densely packed concentration of young people who are away from home for the first time, and are coincidentally the age associated with alcohol and drug experimentation, and the commission of felonies.   12

Once again, this reflects outdated thinking about students. My current students have grown up learning responsible weapon use through virtual training available on the Xbox and PlayStation. Far from being enamored of violence, many studies have shown, they are numb to it. These creative young minds will certainly be stimulated by access to more technology at the university, items like autoloaders, silencers, and hollow points. I am sure that it has not escaped your attention that the library would make an excellent shooting range, and the bookstore could do with fewer books and more ammo choices.   13

I want to applaud the Legislature's courage. On a final note: I hope its members will consider my amendment for bulletproof office windows and faculty body armor in Boise State blue and orange.   14

⊘ AT ISSUE: SOURCES FOR DEVELOPING AN ETHICAL ARGUMENT

1. This essay is written as a letter addressed to the chief counsel of the Idaho State legislature. What are the advantages and disadvantages of this format?

2. What is the context for Hampikian's argument? For example, what situation gave rise to the letter? What issue is Hampikian considering? How contentious is the debate concerning this issue?

3. **Satire** is the use of humor, irony, or exaggeration to ridicule a person, doctrine, or institution. In what sense is this essay satire?

4. In paragraph 10, Hampikian says, "The problem, of course, is not that drunken frat boys will be armed; it is that they are drunken frat boys." What does he mean?

5. Hampikian purposely strings together a number of fallacies in paragraph 11 to underscore the weakness of the arguments against his position. How effective is this strategy? Would a more direct approach—simply addressing opposing arguments one by one—have been more effective? Explain.

6. Hampikian concludes his essay on a humorous note. What serious point is he making? Is humor appropriate here? Why or why not?

7. How would you define Hampikian's tone? Is it humorous? Respectful? Condescending? Sarcastic? Something else? How does Hampikian's tone affect your response to his essay?

The *Washington Post* published this article on October 27, 2014.

CAN WE INVENT OUR WAY OUT OF SCHOOL VIOLENCE?

TODD C. FRANKEL

1   The idea came to her in the vulnerable early morning hours, just after the horrific shooting at Sandy Hook Elementary in Newtown, Connecticut, nearly two years ago.

2   Celisa Edwards, a teacher, was shaken. What if a gunman burst into her school in this small town outside Atlanta? She could follow lockdown procedures. Turn off the lights. Lock the door. But that didn't seem like enough to protect her seventh graders. Edwards had an idea. She hastily sketched it out and, a couple of hours later, woke up her husband. We need to make this, she told him.

3   The result was a simple metal wire with looped ends that could secure classroom doors from the inside. The Portable Affordable Lockdown System, patent pending, has been installed in one Georgia school. Edwards recently pitched it to another district.

4   Now, Edwards—whose only previous inventions involved devising lesson plans—was discussing her device with evangelical fervor during a free period late last week at Dacula Middle School. About the same time, hundreds of miles away in Maryville, Washington, a high school was going on lockdown after a student fatally shot two people and injured four others (one of whom later died). Almost immediately, the question, "What could've been done to prevent this?" was in the air.

5   "Our classrooms are not safe. There are people bent on doing wrong, doing evil," Edwards says. "And we are deterring those perpetrators."

6   A flood of school-safety inventions have hit the market in recent years, many of them created by novices stunned by what happened at Sandy Hook, where a gunman fatally shot 20 young students and six staff members in 2012. Since then, teachers and parents have come up with a range of door barricades, bulletproof backpacks, ballistic whiteboards, and online apps to monitor for homicidal plots. These products join a school security market that is expected to reach $720 million this year, according to research firm IHS. And the dozens of school shootings that have occurred since Sandy Hook only ramp up the hunt for a solution.

7   Although they could be dismissed as profiting from tragedy, inventors such as Edwards say they are motivated by fear and a sense that policymakers have failed to safeguard students and teachers.

8   Kenneth Trump, a national school safety consultant, understands the attraction of the inventions. People felt helpless after Sandy Hook, he said. And there was a major push to "do something." But the national debate over how to prevent

school shootings soon stalled out, grounded mostly by ideological divisions over gun control. And into that gaping void went these inventions, many of them focused on hardening a school's defenses. But Trump said he doubts that door locks and bulletproof materials would make a difference.

"What's really being sold here is an emotional security blanket," he said.   9

But that hasn't slowed the sales of ballistic whiteboards, made by a com- 10
pany in Pocomoke City, Maryland, that crafts anti-IED armor for the U.S. military. The small, handheld whiteboards can act as defensive shields to fend off a gunman. George Tunis, chief executive of Hardwire, said the Sandy Hook shooting convinced him that his company had a role in protecting schools.

"That's when it hit us, that these are fast events, and the armor needs to be 11
in schools," Tunis said.

Hardwire's whiteboards, which sell for $399, are in nearly 1,000 schools in 12
50 states, he said. Later this week, the Colonial School District in New Castle, Delaware, will introduce its 121 whiteboards for use in classrooms.

In Jefferson Hills, Pennsylvania, a school maintenance man invented an 13
emergency door lock after the Sandy Hook shooting. Students at Banneker High School in Washington, D.C., won a grant to develop a sleeve that jams a door's hydraulic closer. A group of teachers in Muscatine, Iowa, formed Fighting Chance Solutions to sell something similar. A company in Burlington, Vermont, released its Social Sentinel app to scour social media for signs of a school threat. And a father in Williamston, Michigan, created The Boot, a steel bar that blockades a classroom door.

Robert Couturier had been kicking around that idea a few years before 14
Sandy Hook happened. He started a company, which now has 14 full-time employees. Last week, he hired two more salesmen. He invented The Boot because he was tired of hearing about school shootings.

"I had to come up with a solution," Couturier said.   15

Since the Sandy Hook shooting, much of the discussion has been about 16
whether to arm teachers. Many states introduced bills to allow guns in schools, but only a handful enacted laws specifically allowing firearms in public schools. One of them was Georgia, which earlier this year began allowing licensed gun owners to carry weapons inside bars, nightclubs, and schools.

Trump, who has worked as a school safety consultant for three decades, 17
noted how different the response was following the 1999 Columbine High School shooting in Colorado, where 12 students and one teacher were killed. Back then, the discussion focused on training school officials to spot warning signs and offering mental health support services. But these initiatives take longer to roll out and require sustained investment, he said. The emotional intensity of the Sandy Hook shooting seemed to demand a quicker fix.

> "The emotional intensity of the Sandy Hook shooting seemed to demand a quicker fix."

"People are frustrated that there have 18
been so many steps taken and they still have this happen," Trump said.

Back at Dacula Middle School, Edwards was demonstrating her invention. 19
Her seventh graders had just filed out of the room, walking past a ball python
curled up in a glass enclosure by the door, after their discussion of the Theodore
Taylor book *The Cay*. Edwards, 48, had energetically read aloud passages.

Now, she used that same intensity to show off her device. The wire rope 20
was about two feet long and encased in plastic. Each end was looped, with a
carabiner at one end. A metal eye hook had been drilled into a concrete-block
wall, near a hand-crank pencil sharpener.

Edwards quickly hooked one end around the door handle and latched the 21
other to the eye hook. The door was secure. No one was getting in or out. The
door handle had a lock, but Edwards pointed out that administrators had keys
that a gunman could take. Her simple invention had solved that problem.

"Teachers find solutions to problems. And my passion is for classroom 22
safety," she said. "That's why I designed this."

After her demonstration, Edwards slipped the device back into a small 23
green bag and returned it to its familiar spot in her desk drawer, so she'd know
exactly where it was, if she ever needed it.

⊘ AT ISSUE: SOURCES FOR DEVELOPING AN ETHICAL ARGUMENT

1. Frankel begins and ends his essay by discussing Celisa Edwards, a teacher who invented a device to secure a classroom door. Why does he do this? What are the advantages of this strategy?

2. Although this essay does not have a stated thesis, it does make a point. On the lines below, write a one-sentence thesis statement for this essay.

   Although inventors have come up with products to stop school shootings, _____

   _____

   _____ .

3. In his essay, Frankel describes several inventions that are supposed to promote school safety. What is his opinion of these inventions? How can you tell?

4. What does Kenneth Trump mean when he says, "What's really being sold here is an emotional security blanket" (para. 9)?

5. According to Kenneth Trump, people responded differently to the Columbine High School shooting and to the shooting that took place at Sandy Hook Elementary School. Why? (Before you answer, read some background information about these shootings.)

6. In what sense, if any, could this essay be considered an argument?

This piece ran on February 18, 2015, in the *New York Times*.

A BID FOR GUNS ON CAMPUSES TO DETER RAPE

ALAN SCHWARZ

As gun rights advocates push to legalize firearms on college campuses, an 1 argument is taking shape: Arming female students will help reduce sexual assaults.

Support for so-called campus carry laws had been hard to muster despite 2 efforts by proponents to argue that armed students and faculty members could prevent mass shootings like the one at Virginia Tech in 2007. The carrying of concealed firearms on college campuses is banned in 41 states by law or by university policy. Carrying guns openly is generally not permitted.

But this year, lawmakers in 10 states who are pushing bills that would 3 permit the carrying of firearms on campus are hoping that the national spotlight on sexual assault will help them win passage of their measures.

"If you've got a person that's raped because you wouldn't let them carry a 4 firearm to defend themselves, I think you're responsible," State Representative Dennis K. Baxley of Florida said during debate in a House subcommittee last month. The bill passed.

The sponsor of a bill in Nevada, Assemblywoman Michele Fiore, said in a 5 telephone interview: "If these young, hot little girls on campus have a firearm, I wonder how many men will want to assault them. The sexual assaults that are occurring would go down once these sexual predators get a bullet in their head."

In addition to those in Florida and Nevada, bills that would allow guns on 6 campus have been introduced in Indiana, Montana, Oklahoma, South Carolina, South Dakota, Tennessee, Texas, and Wyoming.

Opponents contend that university campuses should remain havens from the gun-related risks that exist elsewhere, and that college students, with high rates of binge drinking and other recklessness, would be particularly prone to gun accidents.

7

> "Opponents contend that university campuses should remain havens."

Some experts in sexual assault said that college women were typically 8 assaulted by someone they knew, sometimes a friend, so even if they had access to their gun, they would rarely be tempted to use it.

"It reflects a misunderstanding of sexual assaults in general," said John D. 9 Foubert, an Oklahoma State University professor and national president of One in Four, which provides educational programs on sexual assault to college campuses. "If you have a rape situation, usually it starts with some sort of consensual behavior, and by the time it switches to nonconsensual, it would be nearly impossible to run for a gun. Maybe if it's someone who raped you before and is coming back, it theoretically could help them feel more secure."

Other objectors to the bills say that advocates of the campus carry laws, 10 predominantly Republicans with well-established pro-gun stances, are merely exploiting a hot-button issue.

"The gun lobby has seized on this tactic, this subject of sexual assault," 11 said Andy Pelosi, the executive director of the Campaign to Keep Guns Off Campus. "It resonates with lawmakers."

Colorado, Wisconsin, and seven other states allow people with legal carry 12 permits to take concealed firearms to campus, some with restrictions. (For example, Michigan does not allow guns in dormitories or classrooms.) Many of those states once had bans but lifted them in recent legislative cycles, suggesting some momentum for efforts in 2015.

Past debates in Colorado, Michigan, and Nevada have included testimony 13 in support of campus carry laws from Amanda Collins, who in 2007 was raped on the campus of the University of Nevada, Reno; Ms. Collins has said that had she been carrying her licensed gun, she would have averted the attack. It is unclear whether Ms. Collins will testify anywhere this year.

Some surveys have estimated that a vast majority of college presidents and 14 faculty members oppose allowing firearms on campus. Support was somewhat higher among students, but 67 percent of men and 86 percent of women still disliked the concept.

Many students who support current legislation have joined the lobbying 15 group Students for Concealed Carry. Crayle Vanest, an Indiana University senior who recently became the first woman on the group's national board, said she should be able to carry her licensed .38-caliber Bersa Thunder pistol on campus, where she said she had walked unarmed after her late-night shifts at a library food court.

"Universities are under a ton of investigation for how they handle sexual 16 assaults — that shows how safe campus maybe isn't," said Ms. Vanest, who is lobbying Indiana lawmakers. "Our female membership has increased massively. People who weren't listening before are listening now."

Some lawmakers said they expected that votes on the bills would largely be 17 along party lines. Ms. Fiore of Nevada, for example, predicted the Republican-controlled Legislature and Republican governor would enact her bill. She added that people who understood the extent of sexual assaults on college campuses, perhaps female Democrats who had been sexually assaulted themselves, "need to call their legislators and say, 'Represent us today or lose your election tomorrow.'"

A South Carolina state senator, Brad Hutto, a Democrat who will oppose 18 a campus carry bill when it is considered by the judiciary committee, said he doubted that sexual assault would swing his state's debate but, "I know that that's a card that's going to be used."

The most interesting debate could occur in Florida, where several story 19 lines intersect. Florida State University has had high-profile episodes involving sexual assault—the star football player Jameis Winston was accused of raping a fellow student in 2012 but did not face criminal charges—as well as a shooting in November in which a 31-year-old gunman opened fire at a campus library, wounding two students and an employee before being fatally shot by the police.

The university's president, John Thrasher, is a former state senator, for- 20 mer chairman of the state's Republican Party, and a vocal gun rights supporter. But he opposes guns on university grounds, in part because of a 2011 death: Ashley Cowie, a sophomore and the daughter of one of Mr. Thrasher's close friends, was shot and killed when another student, showing off his rifle in a fraternity house, did not realize the weapon was loaded.

"A college campus is not a place to be carrying guns around; our campus 21 police agree with that, and so does law enforcement," Mr. Thrasher said.

Mariana Prado, a sophomore at Stetson University in DeLand, Florida, 22 said: "I think it's a terrible idea. From what I've seen, sexual assault is often linked to situations where people are drinking, so it's not a good idea to have concealed weapons around that."

The next stop for the Florida bill will be a committee hearing in March. 23 Greg Steube, the original sponsor of the bill, said he hoped that inviting Ms. Collins, the former Nevada student who was raped in 2007, to testify would help it reach the desk of Gov. Rick Scott, a Republican, and become law.

"It's moving to hear from a young woman that had a concealed carry and 24 but for a university policy, she was raped," Mr. Steube said. "I don't know if it can get any more compelling than that."

⊘ AT ISSUE: SOURCES FOR DEVELOPING AN ETHICAL ARGUMENT

1. Schwarz begins his essay by observing that "an argument is taking shape" (para. 1). To what is he referring? Is this point self-evident, or does Schwarz need to supply proof or explanation?

2. List other points that Schwarz presents as self-evident. Next to each point, note the evidence that he could provide to support it.

3. Schwarz alludes to "opponents" (7), "some experts" (8), "other objectors" (10), and "some surveys" (14). Should he have identified the individuals to whom he refers? Why or why not?

4. In paragraph 5, Schwarz quotes Assemblywoman Michele Fiore, the sponsor of a bill to allow students to carry concealed firearms, who says, "If these young, hot little girls on campus have a firearm, I wonder how many men will want to assault them"? Do you think Fiore's statement helps or hurts her case? Explain.

5. What is Schwarz's purpose in writing this essay? To inform? To persuade? To entertain? Something else? How can you tell?

6. In his conclusion, Schwarz refers to Amanda Collins, a student who says that had she been able to carry her licensed gun on the campus of the University of Nevada, she would not have been raped. Does this conclusion support Schwarz's thesis? Why or why not? What is another concluding strategy Schwarz could have used?

This brochure is available on the website for Isothermal Community College, isothermal.edu.

WARNING SIGNS: HOW YOU CAN HELP PREVENT CAMPUS VIOLENCE

ISOTHERMAL COMMUNITY COLLEGE

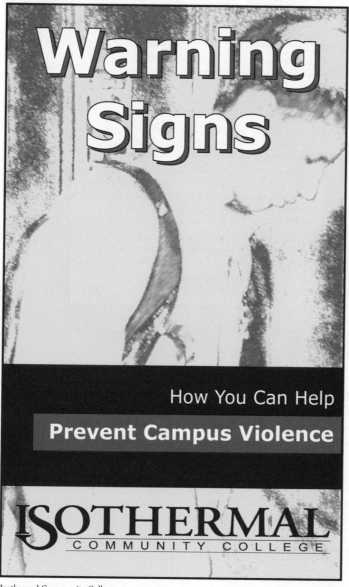

Isothermal Community College

2 ....

Things to
LOOK OUT FOR . . .

- Any direct statement about the intention to harm him/her self or other members of the community

- "Hints" that the individual intends to harm him/her self or other members of the community: For example, "I might not be around after this weekend;" "It would be a good idea for you to stay out of the cafeteria tomorrow;" "People might get hurt, if they're not careful"

- Extreme difficulty adjusting to college life; for example, the student is isolated, depressed, and/or very angry with peers

- Significant changes in behavior, appearance, habits, mood, or activities

- Statements from individuals about access to firearms and suggestions that they may be bringing them to the campus or may already have them on campus

- Behaviors that indicate that the individual is settling his/her affairs, which may include telling people goodbye, giving possessions away, and/or making statements about what they would like to have done should something happen to them

- Fascination with violence, including some types of video games and music, and/or focusing on or admiring violent "role models"

- Your own "gut feeling" that someone that you know intends to harm him/her self or others

Campus Security—289-1393. Isothermal Community College. Improve Life Through Learning. www.isothermal.edu.

At Isothermal Community College, we want all of our students, faculty, and staff to be safe and secure on campus.

In light of the tragic shootings at Virginia Tech and other recent events on college campuses and in schools around the country, it has become clear that friends, classmates, and acquaintances of troubled students may be the most likely individuals to be aware of potentially dangerous and/or self-destructive situations.

However, students often are not certain about what kinds of warning signs they should take seriously and/or whether reporting the signs to faculty or staff members is the right thing to do.

Isothermal Community College

630

. . . . 3

The tips in this brochure are aimed at helping you identify potential problems and behaviors that could lead to incidents of campus violence.

If you ever feel endangered or threatened at any time on campus, we ask that you immediately contact Isothermal security, an instructor, or an employee of the college for assistance.

Campus security can be reached at 289-1393. To contact the switchboard operator, dial **0** on any campus phone. You should also report any threatening activity to local law enforcement by dialing **911**. Don't forget to dial **9** for an outside line if using the campus phone system.

A lockdown procedure is in place for Isothermal Community College. Faculty and staff members periodically practice the procedure.

If you are informed of a lockdown situation, please cooperate with the proper authorities. Leaving the classroom or the building in such a situation may put you at greater risk.

POTENTIAL FOR VIOLENCE
Warning Signs in Others

Often people who act violently have trouble controlling their feelings. They may have been hurt by others and may think that making people fear them through violence or threats of violence will solve their problems or earn them respect. This isn't true. People who behave violently lose respect. They find themselves isolated or disliked, and they still feel angry and frustrated.

- Loss of temper on a daily basis
- Frequent physical fighting
- Significant vandalism or property damage
- Increase in use of drugs or alcohol
- Increase in risk-taking behavior
- Detailed plans to commit acts of violence
- Announcing threats or plans for hurting others
- Enjoying hurting animals
- Carrying a weapon

If you see these immediate warning signs, violence is a serious possibility:

Isothermal Community College

4 . . . .

If you notice the following signs over a period of time, the potential for violence exists:

- A history of violent or aggressive behavior
- Serious drug or alcohol use
- Gang membership or strong desire to be in a gang
- Access to or fascination with weapons, especially guns
- Threatening others regularly
- Trouble controlling feelings like anger
- Withdrawal from friends and usual activities
- Feeling rejected or alone
- Having been a victim of bullying
- Poor school performance
- History of discipline problems or frequent run-ins with authority
- Feeling constantly disrespected
- Failing to acknowledge the feelings or rights of others

Source: American Psychological Association

Isothermal Community College

⊝ AT ISSUE: SOURCES FOR DEVELOPING AN ETHICAL ARGUMENT

1. This brochure is designed to help students recognize people who have the potential to commit campus violence. What warning signs does the brochure emphasize?

2. What additional information, if any, do you think should have been included in this brochure? Why?

3. Are there any suggestions in this brochure that could possibly violate a person's right to privacy? Explain.

4. What additional steps do you think students should take to prevent campus violence?

This poster is from the UCDA Campus Violence Poster Project show at Northern Illinois University.

GONE BUT NOT FORGOTTEN

AMY DION

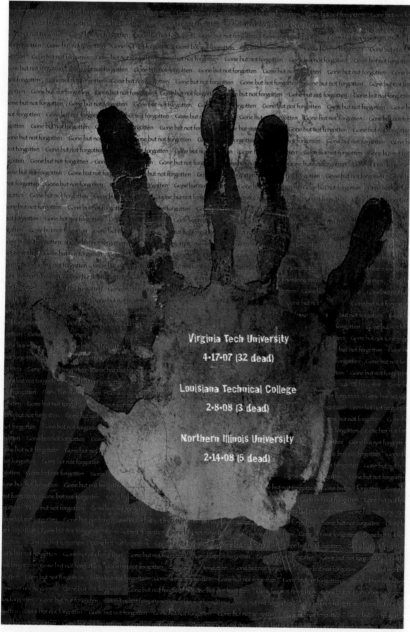

© Amy Dion, Art Director, SIU

⊙ AT ISSUE: SOURCES FOR DEVELOPING
AN ETHICAL ARGUMENT

1. This poster shows a handprint on a background that repeats the phrase "Gone but not forgotten." What ethical argument does the poster make?

2. What other images does the poster include? How do these images reinforce its message?

3. Do you think posters like this one can really help to combat campus violence? Can they serve any other purpose? Explain.

TEMPLATE FOR WRITING AN ETHICAL ARGUMENT

Write a one-paragraph ethical argument in which you answer the question, "How far should schools go to keep students safe?" Follow the template below, filling in the blanks to create your argument.

> Recently, a number of schools have experienced violence on their campuses. For example, _____. _____. Many schools have gone too far (or not far enough) in trying to prevent violence because _____
> _____
> _____
> _____. One reason _____
> _____.
> Another reason _____
> _____
> _____. Finally, _____
> _____
> _____. If schools really want to remain safe, _____
> _____
> _____
> _____.

⊙ EXERCISE 16.7

Ask your friends and your teachers whether they think any of the steps your school has taken to prevent campus violence are excessive—or whether they think these measures don't go far enough. Then, revise the paragraph you wrote in the template on the previous page so that it includes their opinions.

⊙ EXERCISE 16.8

Write an ethical argument in which you consider the topic, "How Far Should Schools Go to Keep Students Safe?" Make sure you include a clear analysis of the ethical principle that you are going to apply. (If you like, you may incorporate the material you developed in the template and in Exercise 16.7 into your essay.) Cite the readings on pages 609–634, document the sources you use, and be sure to include a works-cited page. (See Chapter 10 for information on documenting sources.)

◑ EXERCISE 16.9

Review the four pillars of argument discussed in Chapter 1. Does your essay include all four elements of an effective argument? Add anything that is missing. Then, label the key elements of your essay.

◑ WRITING ASSIGNMENTS: ETHICAL ARGUMENTS

1. Write an ethical argument in which you discuss whether hate groups have the right to distribute material on campus. Be sure to explain the ethical principle you are applying and to include several arguments in support of your position. (Don't forget to define and give examples of what you mean by *hate groups*. Remember to address arguments against your position.) You can refer to the readings on pages 165–185 to find sources to support your position.

2. Should English be made the official language of the United States? Write an ethical argument in which you take a position on this topic.

3. Many people think that celebrities have an ethical obligation to set positive examples for young people. Assume that you are a celebrity, and write an op-ed piece in which you support or challenge this idea. Be sure to identify the ethical principle on which you base your argument.

Part 5 Review: Combining Argumentative Strategies

In Chapters 12–16, you have seen how argumentative essays can use different strategies to serve particular purposes. The discussions and examples in these chapters highlighted the use of a single strategy for a given essay. However, many (if not most) argumentative essays combine several different strategies.

For example, an argument recommending that the United States implement a national sales tax could be largely a **proposal argument**, but it could present a **cause-and-effect argument** to illustrate the likely benefits of the proposal, and it could also use an **evaluation argument** to demonstrate the relative advantages of this tax as compared to other kinds of taxes.

The following two essays—"Get the Lead out of Hunting" and "Fulfill George Washington's Last Wish—a National University"—illustrate how various strategies can work together in a single argument. Note that both essays include the four pillars of argument—*thesis statement*, *evidence*, *refutation*, and *concluding statement*. (The first essay includes marginal annotations that identify the different strategies the writer uses to advance his argument.)

This opinion essay is from the December 15, 2010, *New York Times.*

GET THE LEAD OUT OF HUNTING

ANTHONY PRIETO

Cause-and-effect argument

Ethical argument

I've hunted elk, deer, and wild pigs in the American West for 25 years. Like 1
many hunters, I follow several rules: Respect other forms of life, take only
what my family can eat and the ecosystem can sustain, and leave as little
impact on the environment as possible.

That's why I hunt with copper bullets instead of lead. We've long known 2
about the collateral damage caused by lead ammunition. When bald and
golden eagles, vultures, bears, endangered California condors, and other scavengers eat the innards, called gutpiles, that hunters leave in the field after
cleaning their catch or the game that hunters wound but don't capture, they
can ingest poisonous lead fragments. Most sicken, and many die.

Cause-and-effect argument

When I began hunting, I buried the lead-laden gutpiles. It would help if 3
more hunters did this, but it's not enough. Scavengers often dig gutpiles up
anyway. And the meat that hunters take home to their families could be tainted.
I've seen X-rays of shot game showing dust-sized lead particles spread throughout the meat, far away from the bullet hole. The best solution is to stop using
lead ammunition altogether.

Proposal argument

So last summer conservationists—along with the organization I run—for- 4
mally petitioned the Environmental Protection Agency to ban lead bullets and
shot nationwide (there are limited bans for some hunting areas and game).
The E.P.A. rejected the petition, and we've since filed a lawsuit to get the
agency to address the problem.

Unfortunately, there is vocal opposition to any ammunition regulation 5
from groups like the National Rifle Association and the National Shooting
Sports Foundation, which see the campaign as an attack on hunting rights and
fear that the cost of non-lead ammunition would drive hunters away from the
sport.

But this campaign has nothing to do with revoking hunting rights; if it 6
did, I would not be involved. It's an issue of using non-toxic materials. Was
the removal of lead paint from children's toys a plot to do away with toys?
Did the switch to unleaded gas hide an ulterior motive of removing vehicles
from our roads?

Evaluation argument

And although copper bullets can be more expensive than lead ones, the 7
cost of ammunition is a small fraction of what I spend on hunting, which
includes gear, optics, food, gas, and licenses. No one will quit hunting over
spending a few more quarters per bullet. Besides, the more hunters switch
to copper, the faster prices will come down. Back in the '90s, before pre-
loaded copper cartridges could be bought over the counter, I had to hand-
load my copper bullets. But already it's easy to find them in many calibers,
including those for my Browning .270 and my Winchester .300.

The dozen friends I hunt with love shooting non-lead bullets, and it's not just because they're doing something good for the environment. The ballistics are better. I've killed more than 80 pigs and 40 deer shooting copper. These bullets travel up to 3,200 feet per second and have about a 98 percent weight retention—meaning they don't fragment as easily as lead. Copper kills cleanly. It can help keep our hunting grounds clean as well.

> "Copper kills cleanly."

8 Evaluation argument

⊙ REVIEW EXERCISE 1

1. Prieto uses various argument strategies in "Get the Lead out of Hunting," which are identified in the annotations. Why is each strategy used?

2. How does each strategy support the argument the writer makes?

3. Does one particular strategy seem to dominate the essay—that is, do you see it as largely a proposal argument, an ethical argument, or something else?

4. Where, if anywhere, could Prieto have used a definition argument? What might this strategy have added to this essay?

This article first appeared on CNN.com on March 2, 2015.

Fulfill George Washington's Last Wish—a National University

KEVIN CAREY

In 1796, in his final annual address to Congress, President George Washington   1
called for the creation of:

"... a National University; and also a Military Academy. The desirable-   2
ness of both these Institutions, has so constantly increased with every new
view I have taken of the subject, that I cannot omit the opportunity of once for
all, recalling your attention to them."

The Military Academy was soon built at West Point. But despite leaving   3
$22,222 for its establishment (a lot of money back then) in his last will and
testament, Washington's National University never came to pass.

Instead, lawmakers chose to rely on state governments and religious 4
denominations to build and finance new colleges and universities.

Today, the American higher education system is in crisis. The price of 5
college has grown astronomically, forcing students and parents to take out
loans that now exceed $1.2 trillion in outstanding debt. Many of those loans
are falling into default as graduates struggle to find work. The latest research
suggests that our vaunted universities are producing graduates who haven't
learned very much.

The time has come to revive George Washington's great idea, in 21st cen- 6
tury form. Advances in information technology that would have seemed like
pure magic in colonial times mean we can now create a 21st Century National
University that will help millions of students get a high-quality, low-cost college education—without hiring any professors, building any buildings, or
costing the taxpayers a dime.

Washington's Role

To see how, it helps to understand the three ways the federal government cur- 7
rently supports higher education.

Two of them are well known. 8
First, the Defense Department,
National Institutes of Health, and
other federal agencies spend hundreds of billions of dollars financing university-based research,
contributing to countless scientific breakthroughs and commer-

> "Second, the U.S. Department
> of Education provides $150
> billion annually in grants and
> loans to help students pay for
> college."

cial innovations. Second, the U.S. Department of Education provides $150 bil-
lion annually in grants and loans to help students pay for college.

As tuitions rise and states continue to slash funding for public universities 9
(Wisconsin Gov. Scott Walker recently proposed $300 million in new cuts),
the federal government has become the college financier of last resort.

But there is a third essential federal role in higher education that is far less 10
well known. In many ways, it's the most important of them all, and the key to
creating a 21st Century National University. In addition to funding colleges,
the federal government approves colleges.

It does this through a little-understood process called accreditation. To 11
be eligible for those billions of research and financial aid dollars, colleges
must be accredited. Technically, accreditors are nonprofit organizations run
by consortia of existing colleges. But in order to make a college eligible for
federal money, accreditors must first be approved by the federal government.
Without that approval and the money that goes along with it, both colleges
and accreditors would immediately close up shop. In other words, Uncle Sam
ultimately decides who gets to be an American college and grant college
degrees.

A University with No Buildings

So, here's the big idea: In order to build a 21st Century National University, all   12
the federal government has to do is something very simple: Approve itself.

In George Washington's days, this would have been only the first step of a   13
process subsequently involving the construction of an actual university. Doing
this today would accomplish little in solving the higher education crisis,
because physical universities cost billions of dollars to construct from scratch
and can still only enroll a handful of the many students who can't afford a
good education.

Fortunately, there's no need for new buildings—or, for that matter,   14
administrators, libraries, faculty, and all the rest. Existing colleges and universities, flush with federal dollars, have already created all the essential building
blocks for National U. Anyone with an Internet connection can log on to
Coursera, edX, saylor.org, and many other websites offering high-quality
online courses, created by many of the world's greatest universities and taught
by tenured professors, for free.

Tens of millions of students have already signed up for these courses over   15
the last four years. Yet enrollment in traditional colleges hasn't flagged, and
prices have continued to rise. The reason is clear. The free college providers
can't (or won't) give online students the one thing they need more than anything else: a college degree. Elite universities like Harvard and Stanford don't
want to dilute their exclusive brands. Nonelite universities don't want to give
away something they're currently selling for a lot of money.

That's where the federal government comes in. With some authorizing   16
language from Congress and a small, one-time start-up budget, the U.S.
Department of Education could create a nonprofit, bipartisan organization
with only two missions: approving courses and granting degrees.

Don't worry, federal bureaucrats won't be in charge of academic matters.   17
Instead, National U. would hire teams of leading scholars to evaluate and
approve courses. Some of the decisions shouldn't be difficult.

For example, this week, edX is launching a free, nine-week-long online   18
course called "Introduction to Computational Thinking and Data Science."
It will be taught by Dr. Eric Grimson, who is the chancellor of the renowned
Massachusetts Institute of Technology, and Dr. John Guttag, who leads the
MIT Computer Science and Artificial Intelligence Laboratory's Data
Driven Medical Research Group. The course materials mirror those taught
to some of the smartest students in the world on MIT's campus in
Cambridge, Massachusetts.

It seems likely that this is a good course.   19

A Degree from National U.

National U., moreover, wouldn't be limited to courses from existing colleges.   20
Any higher education provider, public or private sector, could submit a course
for approval. Those that aren't already accredited would pay a fee to cover the
cost of evaluation.

National U. would also map out which courses students need to take to   21
earn an associate or bachelor's degree. This won't be difficult, since existing
colleges have already established a standard set of requirements: a certain
number of approved lower- and upper-division courses, plus an approved
sequence in an academic major, adding up to 60 or 120 credits. Once students
complete the credits, National U. will grant them a degree.

While many of the courses will be free, students will bear small costs for   22
taking exams through secure online channels or in-person testing facilities.
(Textbooks will be free and open-source.) Students will also pay a modest fee
of a few hundred dollars for the degree itself, enough to defray the operating
costs of National U.

Lower-income students will be able to pay for those expenses using the   23
same federal grant and loan programs they currently use to pay tuition at
accredited colleges. Since National U. will likely be much cheaper, this will
actually save the taxpayers money in the long run.

If it all sounds too good to be true, keep in mind that free online courses   24
from the likes of MIT are a very recent phenomenon. Higher education policies just haven't adapted to them—yet.

The federal government's higher education approval powers are long-   25
established. Now it just needs to use them on behalf of students, instead of
traditional colleges and universities that are charging far too much. George
Washington was right all along.

⊙ REVIEW EXERCISE 2

1. What proposal argument does Carey make in this essay?

2. Label the strategies used in this essay, following the model of the
   Prieto essay on page 638.

3. Where does Carey make a cause-and-effect argument? What causes
   and effects does he identify?

4. Where does Carey make an evaluation argument? What is he evaluating? On what criteria does he base his essay?

5. Does Carey make a definition argument in this essay? Does he make
   an ethical argument? If so, where? If not, where could he add these
   strategies?

6. How does each strategy contribute to the overall effectiveness of
   Carey's argument?

Debates, Casebooks, and Classic Arguments

Are Helicopter Parents Ruining Their Children's Lives?

First used in 1969 by psychologist Haim Ginott in his book *Between Parent and Teenager,* the term *helicopter parent* refers to an overprotective parent who discourages a child's independence by taking an excessive interest in his or her life. However, the term became popular only recently, when college administrators, teachers, coaches, and others who deal with children and young adults began complaining about parental intrusion into areas that were once off-limits.

The concerns about helicopter parenting extend well beyond early childhood. Educators tell anecdotes of parents doing everything from writing their children's college admission essays to contacting professors when their children get poor grades. Students themselves report contacting their parents many times a day, relying on them financially, and seeking advice on even the smallest decisions. Even prospective employers report getting calls from nervous parents who want to make sure that their children get the job for which they are applying. One employer even tells about having an employee's parents show up at her office to see what they could do about their adult child's poor performance assessment.

In "Raising Successful Children" (p. 649), psychologist Madeline Levine argues that although parents mean well by trying to protect their children from harm and failure, "[t]he happiest, most successful children have parents who do not do for them what they are capable of doing" (p. 650). Fairly or unfairly, helicopter parenting has been blamed for ruined childhoods, lack of social connections, depression, anxiety, low self-worth, poor academic performance, and an increased tendency to engage in risky behaviors like binge drinking and shoplifting.

Helicopter parenting is not without its supporters, however. In "For Some, Helicopter Parenting Delivers Benefits" (p. 646), Don Aucoin points out that helicopter parenting is not the same as overparenting.

He claims that the current generation faces more emotional, social, sexual, and financial challenges than ever before, and that it is no wonder young adults rely more heavily on help from their parents. In other words, parents who provide this support should be praised for helping their children survive in an increasingly complicated and challenging world.

This essay first appeared on Boston.com on March 3, 2009.

FOR SOME, HELICOPTER PARENTING DELIVERS BENEFITS

DON AUCOIN

They are two words guaranteed to evoke a sneer among right-thinking people everywhere: helicopter parents. 1

According to the image cemented in the public mind, helicopter parents hover over their children (hence the name). All through high school and even after the "kids" have turned 18, 19, 20, and beyond, helicopter parents try to micromanage their lives. Eyebrow-raising stories abound of the mother who accompanies her 24-year-old son to a job fair or the father who writes a college essay for his 19-year-old daughter. 2

But wait. Beyond such undeniable excesses, a quiet reappraisal of helicopter parents is underway. Some researchers have begun to argue that late adolescence and young adulthood are such minefields today—emotional, social, sexual, logistical, psychological—that there are valid reasons for parents to remain deeply involved in their children's lives even after the kids are, technically speaking, adults. 3

Moreover, they say, with the economy in a deep swoon, helicopter parents may have a vital role to play as career counselors or even as providers of financial aid to their offspring. 4

"There is this stereotypical, oversensationalized, negative portrait, where they use 'over-parenting' and 'helicopter parenting' synonymously," says Barbara Dafoe Whitehead, a social historian and author who studies family issues. 5

"Over-parenting is not letting your kids take the consequences of their actions, swooping down to rescue them, and the result would be a spoiled brat. But helicopter parenting is entirely different, and I think it is a positive style of child-rearing." 6

Pattie Knight concurs. Even though Knight's twin daughters, Symphony and Kymberlee, are 19 and attending college, Knight remains deeply involved in their day-to-day lives. 7

[handwritten margin note: It is so hard to refuse a parent when they won't take no for an answer.]

[handwritten margin numbers: ① ②]

She goes shopping with them. She gives them advice about their relation- 8
ships. She weighs in when they are worried about an upcoming test or won-
dering which class to take. She helps decorate their dorm rooms. One night a
week, when Symphony gets off work from her part-time job, Knight drives
from her Newton home to downtown Boston, picks her up, and transports her
back to Pine Manor College.

Some of Knight's friends roll their eyes at how much she does for her 9
daughters, and she acknowledges it can be excessive at times.

For example, by her count she
and Symphony spoke on the phone
144 times in January, though she
notes her daughter did most of the
calling. "Even their boyfriends call
me, Lord have mercy," Knight says
with a laugh.

> "[B]y her count she and Symphony spoke on the phone 144 times in January."

10

But the bottom line to Knight is that her style is helping her to forge a 11
close and lasting bond with her daughters. "The thing that I like about our
relationship is that whenever they're nervous or unsure about a decision
they're about to make, that's when they need me," she says.

That reflects what Stephanie Coontz, director of research at the Council 12
on Contemporary Families, sees as an unacknowledged dividend to helicopter
parenting that is becoming more apparent: namely, the enduring friendship
often forged between the generations, in contrast to the "generation gap" of old.

"Obviously, there are horrible extremes that helicopter parents can go to, 13
where they don't allow their children to succeed or fail on their own," Coontz
says. "But in the majority of cases, this increased closeness between parents
and kids is found among healthy students, not unhealthy ones."

That was what Jillian Kinzie found—to her astonishment—when she 14
helped conduct a national survey in 2007 at 750 colleges and universities.

When Kinzie, the associate director of Indiana University's Center for 15
Postsecondary Research, first saw the results of a question about helicopter
parenting on the survey, her immediate reaction was: "This can't be right. We
have to go back and look at this again."

The survey found that college students whose parents fit the survey's defi- 16
nition of helicopter parents—they had met frequently with campus officials to
discuss issues involving their children—were more engaged in learning and
reported greater satisfaction with their colleges, even though they had slightly
lower grades than other students.

"They tended to have more interactions with the faculty, they tended to 17
be involved in active learning, collaborative learning, more often than their
peers," Kinzie says. "I have to admit I was surprised. I had the same negative
ideas about helicopter parenting. But perhaps these are students who needed a
little support to get over a hurdle, and their parents intervened, and perhaps
helped those students stay in college.

"Perhaps I'm less concerned about these helicopter parents than I used to be." 18

Still, there is far from a consensus that helicopter parenting is a plus, espe-   19
cially when it involves older children. Whitehead defines helicopter parenting
as a "high level of oversight and supervision, keeping tabs on the kids but not
interfering in every activity or decision," and she defines over-parenting as
"intrusive involvement, never allowing the kids the freedom to make a decision and live with its consequences."

Inevitably, that means the line between helicopter parenting and over-   20
parenting is a porous one, often crossed.

Susan Newman, the author of *Nobody's Baby Now: Reinventing Your*   21
Adult Relationship with Your Mother and Father, maintains that helicopter
parents "do their children an extreme disservice."

"When parents are making decisions for their children all the time and   22
protecting them, when they get out on their own they don't know a thing
about disappointment," Newman says.

"I've seen a lot of these children who are parented in the helicopter man-   23
ner who can't make a decision. They are calling home constantly: 'I don't get
along with my roommate, what should I do? My roommate ate my food, what
should I do?'"

In one case, Newman says, the college-age daughter of a helicopter parent   24
she knows called home to ask her mother whether she should have sex with a
particular young man.

Such extremes are easy to find and hard to defend. But changing eco-   25
nomic circumstances—namely, the recession—may give helicopter parenting
more legitimacy.

Financial independence will become even harder for young adults, espe-   26
cially since so many of them are leaving college burdened by tens of thousands
of dollars in debt. So they may increasingly rely on their parents for monetary
support or a temporary place to live, or both.

"Younger generations have always been poor, but rarely have they been so   27
much in debt at 21 as this generation," observes Whitehead.

Sara Christie of Swampscott does not necessarily embrace the term "heli-   28
copter parent," and says she tries to give her 16-year-old son Steve space, privacy, and room to grow.

But she makes no apologies for her close and vigilant relationship with   29
him. They are "friends" on Facebook; she still makes sure that he wears a hel-
met while bicycling and skateboarding; and if she thinks it necessary she will
text him in school to find out "what class he's in, how's it going, does he need
a ride later."

And when Steve goes to college in two years? "I want to be very involved,"   30
Christie answers, then pauses before acknowledging: "I just learned something, answering that question."

"I feel confident that I can and will be involved with my son on a daily   31
basis, even if he goes to college far away," Christie says. "That means a lot to
me."

⊖ READING ARGUMENTS

1. Where does Aucoin state his thesis? Why do you think he states it where he does?

2. In what respects is this essay a definition argument? In what respects is it an evaluation argument?

3. Aucoin cites experts—a social historian and academic researchers—to support his points. He also includes the testimony of a mother with two daughters. What are the advantages and disadvantages of each type of support? Does Aucoin provide enough evidence to support his thesis effectively? Explain.

4. What is the purpose of paragraph 19? Why is it important for the writer's argument?

5. Where does Aucoin refute arguments against his position? How effectively does he refute them?

The *New York Times* published Levine's essay in the late edition on August 5, 2012.

RAISING SUCCESSFUL CHILDREN

MADELINE LEVINE

Phrases like "tiger mom" and "helicopter parent" have made their way into 1
everyday language. But does overparenting hurt, or help?

While parents who are clearly and embarrassingly inappropriate come 2
in for ridicule, many of us find ourselves drawn to the idea that with just a
bit more parental elbow grease, we might turn out children with great talents and assured futures. Is there really anything wrong with a kind of "overparenting lite"?

Parental involvement has a long and rich history of being studied. 3
Decades of studies, many of them by Diana Baumrind, a clinical and developmental psychologist at the University of California, Berkeley, have found
that the optimal parent is one who is involved and responsive, who sets high
expectations but respects her child's autonomy. These "authoritative parents"
appear to hit the sweet spot of parental involvement and generally raise
children who do better academically, psychologically, and socially than
children whose parents are either permissive and less involved, or controlling
and more involved. Why is this particular parenting style so successful, and
what does it tell us about overparenting?

For one thing, authoritative parents actually help cultivate motivation in their children. Carol Dweck, a social and developmental psychologist at Stanford University, has done research that indicates why authoritative parents raise more motivated, and thus more successful, children.

In a typical experiment, Dr. Dweck takes young children into a room and asks them to solve a simple puzzle. Most do so with little difficulty. But then Dr. Dweck tells some, but not all, of the kids how very bright and capable they are. As it turns out, the children who are not told they're smart are more motivated to tackle increasingly difficult puzzles. They also exhibit higher levels of confidence and show greater overall progress in puzzle-solving.

This may seem counterintuitive, but praising children's talents and abilities seems to rattle their confidence. Tackling more difficult puzzles carries the risk of losing one's status as "smart" and deprives kids of the thrill of choosing to work simply for its own sake, regardless of outcomes. Dr. Dweck's work aligns nicely with that of Dr. Baumrind, who also found that reasonably supporting a child's autonomy and limiting interference results in better academic and emotional outcomes.

Their research confirms what I've seen in more than 25 years of clinical work, treating children in Marin County, an affluent suburb of San Francisco. The happiest, most successful children have parents who do not do for them what they are capable of doing, or almost capable of doing; and their parents do not do things for them that satisfy their own needs rather than the needs of the child.

The central task of growing up is to develop a sense of self that is autonomous, confident, and generally in accord with reality. If you treat your walking toddler as if she can't walk, you diminish her confidence and distort reality. Ditto nightly "reviews" of homework, repetitive phone calls to "just check if you're O.K.," and "editing" (read: writing) your child's college application essay.

Once your child is capable of doing something, congratulate yourself on a job well done and move on. Continued, unnecessary intervention makes your child feel bad about himself (if he's young) or angry at you (if he's a teenager).

> "Once your child is capable of doing something, congratulate yourself on a job well done and move on."

But isn't it a parent's job to help with those things that are just beyond your child's reach? Why is it overparenting to do for your child what he or she is almost capable of?

Think back to when your toddler learned to walk. She would take a weaving step or two, collapse, and immediately look to you for your reaction. You were in thrall to those early attempts and would do everything possible to encourage her to get up again. You certainly didn't chastise her for failing or utter dire predictions about flipping burgers for the rest of her life if she fell again. You were present, alert, and available to guide if necessary. But you didn't pick her up every time.

You knew she had to get it wrong many times before she could get it right.   12

Hanging back and allowing children to make mistakes is one of the great-   13
est challenges of parenting. It's easier when they're young—tolerating a stum-
bling toddler is far different from allowing a preteenager to meet her friends at
the mall. The potential mistakes carry greater risks, and part of being a parent
is minimizing risk for our children.

What kinds of risks should we tolerate? If there's a predator loose in the   14
neighborhood, your daughter doesn't get to go to the mall. But under normal
circumstances an 11-year-old girl is quite capable of taking care of herself for a
few hours in the company of her friends. She may forget a package, overpay
for an item, or forget that she was supposed to call home at noon. Mastery of
the world is an expanding geography for our kids, for toddlers, it's the backyard; for preteens, the neighborhood, for teens the wider world. But it is in the
small daily risks—the taller slide, the bike ride around the block, the invitation
extended to a new classmate—that growth takes place. In this gray area of just
beyond the comfortable is where resilience is born.

So if children are able to live with mistakes and even failing, why does it   15
drive us crazy? So many parents have said to me, "I can't stand to see my child
unhappy." If you can't stand to see your child unhappy, you are in the wrong
business. The small challenges that start in infancy (the first whimper that
doesn't bring you running) present the opportunity for "successful failures,"
that is, failures your child can live with and grow from. To rush in too quickly,
to shield them, to deprive them of those challenges is to deprive them of the
tools they will need to handle the inevitable, difficult, challenging, and sometimes devastating demands of life.

While doing things for your child unnecessarily or prematurely can reduce   16
motivation and increase dependency, it is the inability to maintain parental
boundaries that most damages child development. When we do things for our
children out of our own needs rather than theirs, it forces them to circumvent
the most critical task of childhood: to develop a robust sense of self.

There is an important distinction between good and bad parental involve-   17
ment. For example, a young child doesn't want to sit and do his math homework. Good parents insist on compliance, not because they need their child to
be a perfect student but because the child needs to learn the fundamentals of
math and develop a good work ethic. Compare this with the parent who
spends weeks "helping" his or her child fill out college applications with the
clear expectation that if they both work hard enough, a "gotta get into" school
is a certainty. (While most of my parent patients have graduated from college,
it is always a telltale sign of overparenting when they talk about how "we're
applying to Columbia.")

In both situations parents are using control, in the first case behavioral (sit   18
down, do your math) and in the second psychological ("we're applying"). It is
psychological control that carries with it a textbook's worth of damage to a child's
developing identity. If pushing, direction, motivation, and reward always come
from the outside, the child never has the opportunity to craft an inside. Having

tutors prep your anxious 3-year-old for a preschool interview because all your friends' children are going to this particular school or pushing your exhausted child to take one more advanced-placement course because it will ensure her spot as class valedictorian is not involved parenting but toxic overparenting aimed at meeting the parents' need for status or affirmation and not the child's needs.

So how do parents find the courage to discard the malpractice of over- 19 parenting? It's hard to swim upstream, to resist peer pressure. But we must remember that children thrive best in an environment that is reliable, available, consistent, and noninterfering.

A loving parent is warm, willing to set limits, and unwilling to breach a 20 child's psychological boundaries by invoking shame or guilt. Parents must acknowledge their own anxiety. Your job is to know your child well enough to make a good call about whether he can manage a particular situation. Will you stay up worrying? Probably, but the child's job is to grow, yours is to control your anxiety so it doesn't get in the way of his reasonable moves toward autonomy.

Parents also have to be clear about their own values. Children watch us 21 closely. If you want your children to be able to stand up for their values, you have to do the same. If you believe that a summer spent reading, taking creek walks, and playing is better than a specialized camp, then stick to your guns. Parents also have to make sure their own lives are fulfilling. There is no parent more vulnerable to the excesses of overparenting than an unhappy parent. One of the most important things we do for our children is to present them with a version of adult life that is appealing and worth striving for.

⊖ READING ARGUMENTS

1. Levine begins her essay by mentioning several terms—*tiger mom*, *helicopter parent*, and *overparenting*. Are these terms synonymous? Should Levine have defined them? Explain.

2. Find one or two **rhetorical questions** in Levine's essay. How does Levine use these questions to structure her argument?

3. Where in the essay does Levine appeal to *ethos*? Why do you think she locates the appeal where she does?

4. According to Levine, what is the "central task of growing up" (para. 8)? How does she illustrate her contention?

5. What, according to Levine, is the most effective parenting style? What effect does it have on children? What is the result of overparenting?

⊘ AT ISSUE: ARE HELICOPTER PARENTS RUINING THEIR CHILDREN'S LIVES?

1. Aucoin speaks with one parent whose son is her Facebook friend (para. 29). Levine refers to parents who make "repetitive phone calls to 'just check if you're O.K.'" (para. 8). How have new technologies—such as Facebook, Twitter, and texting—changed parent-child relationships? Do you think these changes have been positive? Harmful? Both? Neither?

2. According to Levine, researchers have found that "the optimal parent is one who is involved and responsive, who sets high expectations but respects her child's autonomy" (3). Do you think that Pattie Knight, who is mentioned in paragraph 7 of Aucoin's essay, fits this definition? Why or why not?

3. Levine writes that "it is the inability to maintain parental boundaries that most damages child development" (16). What "boundaries" do you think she is referring to? Why are they so important?

⊘ WRITING ARGUMENTS: ARE HELICOPTER PARENTING RUINING THEIR CHILDREN'S LIVES?

Both Aucoin and Levine define and evaluate different parenting styles. Using their essays as starting points, write an essay that defines the parenting style that you experienced. Address the important issues raised by Aucoin and Levine. For example, how do you define "involved and engaged parenting" on the one hand and "*over*parenting" on the other? Make sure your essay argues for or against the parenting style you discuss.

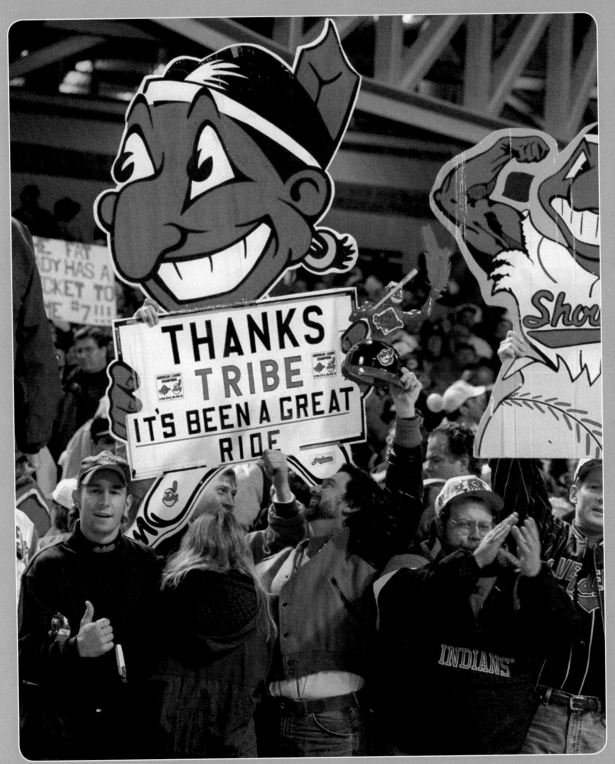

THANKS
TRIBE
IT'S BEEN A GREAT
RIDE

AP Photo/Mark Duncan

DEBATE

Should Controversial Sports Mascots Be Replaced?

The controversy over sports mascots that some consider offensive is not new. Encouraged by the civil rights era's increasing emphasis on tolerance, equality, and diversity, the National Congress of American Indians began a campaign against these stereotypes in 1968. In the late 1960s, Dartmouth College became one of the first colleges to drop its Indian mascot. The school was responding to concerns expressed by its Native American undergraduates, who found the war-paint-and-feathers imagery offensive, and also to the Dartmouth board of trustees, who considered this symbolism incompatible with the school's academic mission. Not everyone supported this action, however. For some Dartmouth faculty, undergraduates, and alumni, the school's disavowal of its Indian mascot undermined tradition and represented a drift toward hypersensitive identity politics. Since that time, many college athletic programs and sports organizations have dropped their Native American mascots. Others, however—including professional teams such as the Atlanta Braves, the Cleveland Indians, and the Washington Redskins—have not.

The broad contours of the debate have remained the same throughout the decades. For their detractors, these mascots evoke offensive, dehumanizing ethnic stereotypes and the specter of historical oppression. Viewed in this light, the Cleveland Indians' red-faced "Chief Wahoo" logo is insulting to Native Americans. In contrast, defenders of these mascots argue that they capture the collective spirit of a college community, support sports traditions, and even honor the heritage of Native Americans. They argue that, at the college and professional levels, the importance of team logos goes well beyond their value to the giant merchandising industry that has developed around them, and maintain that because these logos are central to regional sports identities, eliminating them is akin to erasing Native American heritage from the broader culture.

The two essays that follow explore the key issues of this debate. Jack Shakely acknowledges that the subject of Indian sports mascots may seem "trivial" on the surface, but he argues that these stereotypes are an assault on human dignity. For Ellie Reynolds (who, like Shakely, is Native American), the controversy surrounding the continued use of Indian mascots seems overblown, fueled by political correctness; therefore, she opposes a local bill that would change longtime sports mascots.

This essay was published in the *Los Angeles Times* on August 25, 2011.

INDIAN MASCOTS—YOU'RE OUT

JACK SHAKELY

I got my first lesson in Indians portrayed as sports team mascots in the early 1
1950s when my father took me to a Cleveland Indians–New York Yankees game. Dad gave me money to buy a baseball cap, and I was conflicted. I loved the Yankees, primarily because fellow Oklahoman Mickey Mantle had just come up and was being touted as rookie of the year. But being mixed-blood Muscogee/Creek, I felt a (misplaced) loyalty to the Indians. So I bought the Cleveland cap with the famous Chief Wahoo logo on it.

When we got back to Oklahoma, my mother took one look at the cap with 2
its leering, big-nosed, buck-toothed redskin caricature just above the brim, jerked it off my head, and threw it in the trash. She had been fighting against Indian stereotypes all her life, and I had just worn one home. I was only 10 years old, but the look of betrayal in my Creek mother's eyes is seared in my memory forever.

So maybe I shouldn't have been surprised when half a century later, a *Los* 3
Angeles Times editorial about legislators in North Dakota struggling over whether the University of North Dakota should be forced to change its team name and mascot from the Fighting Sioux provoked such a strong reaction. It was an irritant, like a long-forgotten piece of shrapnel working its way to the surface.

Most stories about sports teams and their ethnic mascots are treated like tempests in a teacup. The *Times*' editorial writer, however, while noting that the solons probably had better things to do,

> "It is a small matter, perhaps, but far from trivial." 4

understood the sensitivity and pain that can accompany such a seemingly trivial subject. It is a small matter, perhaps, but far from trivial.

Many of the fights over team names and mascots cover familiar territory. 5
Usually the team name in question has been around so long as to lose a good
bit of its meaning. The University of Illinois' Fighting Illini, for example, refers
to an Indian nation, but now that its Chief Illiniwek mascot has been aban-
doned, few people make the connection. Nor do they think twice about what
the Atlanta Braves or Edmonton Eskimos or Florida State Seminoles represent
other than sports franchises. But that doesn't necessarily make the brands
benign. And the irony that the football team in our nation's capital is called
the Redskins is not lost on a single Native American.

The controversy over changing ethnocentric mascot names is not a sim- 6
ple matter of stodgy white alums holding on to college memories. Indians, too,
are conflicted. In a 2002 study on the subject, *Sports Illustrated* reported that
84 percent of Native Americans polled had no problem with Indian team
names or mascots. Although the methods used by the magazine to reach these
figures were later criticized, that misses the point. If 16 percent of a population
finds something offensive, that should be enough to signal deep concern.
There are many things in this country that are subject to majority rule; dignity
and respect are not among them.

And it is dignity and respect we are talking about. Since the creation of 7
the National Coalition on Racism in Sports and Media in 1991, that group
of Native American organizations has been protesting negative portrayals of
Indians, hammering away at what's behind our discomfort with Indian sports
mascots. Many of these mascots—maybe most of them—act like fools or savage cutthroats.

When I went to an Atlanta Braves game in the 1970s, the Braves name 8
wasn't the biggest problem. It was that cringe-worthy Chief Noc-A-Homa
who came stomping and war-dancing his way out of a tepee in center field
every time the Braves hit a home run that got to me. He was dressed in a Plains
Indian chief's eagle bonnet and acted like a village idiot. To their credit, the
Braves retired Chief Noc-A-Homa and his girlfriend Princess Win-A-Lot in
1983, amid assertions by the Braves' home office that the protesters were over-
dramatizing the issue.

Few people complain about Florida State University calling itself the 9
Seminoles. But its war-painted and lance-threatening mascot Chief Osceola is
intended to be menacing, and that's the take-away many children will have.
Such casual stereotyping can breed callousness. In the "only good Indian" cat-
egory, in 1999 the *New York Post* entitled an editorial about the pending New
York–Cleveland baseball playoffs, "Take the Tribe and Scalp 'Em."

It isn't easy or inexpensive to remove ethnic and racial stereotypes from 10
college and professional sports. When Stanford University changed from the
Indians to the Cardinals in 1972, recriminations were bitter. Richard Lyman, a
friend of mine, was president of Stanford at the time. He said the university
lost millions of alumni dollars in the short run, but it was the right thing to do.

In 21st-century America, to name a sports team after an African American, 11
Asian, or any other ethnic group is unthinkable. So why are Native Americans

still fair game? As benign as monikers like Fighting Sioux and Redskins or mascots like Chief Osceola may seem, they should take their place with the Pekin, Ill., Chinks and the Atlanta Black Crackers in the dust bin of history. It is the right thing to do.

⊘ READING ARGUMENTS

1. How does Shakely incorporate personal narrative and anecdotal evidence into his argument? Do you find this kind of material convincing? Explain.

2. What point does Shakely make in his fourth paragraph? How is this point related to his thesis?

3. In what sense is this essay an ethical argument?

4. In paragraph 6, Shakely cites a poll that indicated that 84 percent of Native Americans "had no problem with Indian team names or mascots." How does he use this evidence to reinforce his own position? How might this evidence also support a counterargument?

5. Where does Shakely make a cause-and-effect argument?

This guest commentary ran online at DenverPost.com on March 29, 2015.

NATIVE AMERICANS HAVE BECOME A POLITICAL PAWN

ELLIE REYNOLDS

State Rep. Joe Salazar, D-Thornton, is sponsoring House Bill 1165, a mis-   1
guided effort to ban Native American mascots in Colorado's public schools. On the heels of the Washington Redskins' national controversy, Salazar's legislation would prevent public schools from using a name, mascot, or school symbol referencing Native Americans unless that school is granted a waiver from the originating tribe.

I grew up outside of the Pine Ridge reservation in South Dakota. My   2
great-grandfather, Orville Sr. "Paha Ska" Salway, was an honorary chief of the Oglala Sioux tribe. Many of the schools located on the reservations themselves have controversial school names and mascots, too. For instance, the Red Cloud Indian School mascot, the Crusader, uses the symbol of a buffalo skeleton with a Native American on a horse throwing an arrow as their mascot. This symbolizes their history.

As a member of the Oglala Sioux tribe, the suffocating political correctness policing of every aspect of our lives concerns me. In Salazar's well-intentioned attempt to prevent anyone from suffering offense, he is actually perpetuating our inability to even discuss important issues of race, power, and American history. 3

The entire purpose of a school mascot is to provide a single rallying symbol from which a community can celebrate unity. In this day of perpetual outrage, the suppression of these symbols will do little more than to further highlight the divide between Natives and everyone else. 4

In a society so consumed by political correctness, this bill could be detrimental to its stated purpose and actually prevent meaningful conversations about other cultures and races. Salazar's bill mentions nothing about Trojans, Vikings, Fighting Irish, or any other historical or ethnic group. He carves out only Native-based mascots for scrutiny and elimination. 5

Rep. Paul Lundeen, R-Monument, asked a vital question recently as the bill was being heard in the House Education committee: "What other legislation has been needed to change mascots?" 6

Salazar responded, "There wasn't any." 7

As Lundeen pointed out, throughout history mascot changes based on political correctness have been community initiatives, not legislative answers. More government is not the answer to a community concern. Not only is this not the proper role of government, this bill is a form of government coercion with a bankrupting fine. 8

> "More government is not the answer to a community concern."

Native Americans have long fought government overreach into our culture. This is yet another example of government going way too far, creating a solution in search of a problem. 9

HB 1165 demands that public schools receive special permission from the Native tribe from which their mascot or team name originated for its use. If schools with Native mascots don't comply with this new legislation, they will be fined $25,000 per month until the situation is remedied. These massive fines will ultimately be paid with taxpayer dollars. 10

The fines are so large they could quickly wipe out a high school's entire athletics budget. They are so clearly designed to be punitive in nature, many schools across the state will just change their mascots rather than risk the fine. 11

Yes, some people are offended by Native-based mascots, but it is not the government's job to prevent every person from ever feeling offended. It sends the strong message to all Coloradans that discussion, celebration of, and rallying behind a Native symbol might be so offensive to someone it requires a special carve-out. Especially to Colorado students, this message will stifle pride and unity. Salazar's legislation may, in fact, further alienate our culture from the mainstream. 12

This legislation doesn't teach Colorado's children to engage and to recognize our Native population; it teaches them to avoid offending us by avoiding the conversation at all. 13

Political correctness does not solve this, or any problem. In fact, by failing   14
to acknowledge the contributions of Native American culture to the fabric of
American culture, we create a greater problem, selectively erasing history.

Have we as a country become so haunted by political correctness and cen-   15
sorship that we have created the very barriers we say we want to overcome?
When we aren't free to communicate on issues pertaining to race, gender,
religion, or sexual orientation, we are doomed to perpetuate the stigma. We
can be mindful of how our attitudes and actions are influenced by prejudices
and how our words reinforce those prejudices and stereotypes without rules
on discourse handed down from government.

HB 1165, otherwise known as the Mascot Bill, is forceful government cen-   16
sorship, and the cost is real conversation about Native American culture. This
bill will affect Colorado public schools, our children, and our communities at
the high price tag of our freedom.

❍ READING ARGUMENTS

1. Where in her argument does Reynolds appeal to *ethos*? Do you find
   this appeal effective? Why or why not?

2. Reynolds describes Salazar's proposed legislation as "well-intentioned"
   (para. 3). Why do you think she concedes this point? Is this concession
   consistent with the overall tone of her argument? Explain.

3. How does Reynolds characterize our current social and political climate? Do you agree with her? Why or why not?

4. In what respects is this essay a cause-and-effect argument? In what
   respects is it a definition argument?

5. Reynolds writes that "it is not the government's job to prevent every
   person from ever feeling offended" (12). In the broader context of
   debates about sports mascots, is Reynolds setting up a **straw man**?
   Why or why not?

❍ AT ISSUE: SHOULD CONTROVERSIAL SPORTS MASCOTS BE REPLACED?

1. Shakely writes, "If 16 percent of a population finds something offensive, that should be enough to signal deep concern. There are many
   things in this country that are subject to majority rule; dignity and
   respect are not among them" (para. 6). How do you think Reynolds
   would respond to this claim? What is your response?

2. Reynolds makes several references to "political correctness" in her
   essay, as when she asks, "Have we as a country become so haunted

by political correctness and censorship that we have created the very barriers we say we want to overcome?" (para. 15). What does "political correctness" mean? What connotations does it have? Do you think political correctness is as big a problem as Reynolds thinks it is? Explain.

3. According to Shakely, "[C]asual stereotyping can breed callousness" (9). What do you think he means by this statement, particularly in light of his use of the adjective "casual"? Do you agree?

⊙ WRITING ARGUMENTS: SHOULD CONTROVERSIAL SPORTS MASCOTS BE REPLACED?

Write an essay that takes a position on the issue of controversial sports mascots. Should they be replaced at the professional, college, and high school levels?

The Boston Globe/Getty Images

Under What Circumstances Do Bystanders Have an Ethical Obligation to Intervene?

In 1964, twenty-eight-year-old Kitty Genovese was stabbed to death in her New York City neighborhood at 3:30 in the morning. The *New York Times* reported that thirty-eight of her neighbors heard her screams and did nothing to help, but recent research reveals that this account was overstated and that some of Genovese's neighbors actually did help—for example, one called out the window for her attacker to stop, two called the police, and another held her while she lay dying. Only two men who saw what happened failed to respond—one fled and the other was drunk. Still, the original, false story reinforced the public's fears that people could watch someone be murdered and do nothing to help. As a result, the story of Kitty Genovese entered the social consciousness, and we have been using it to ponder our ethical responsibility to help in a crisis ever since.

Some writers, such as Joe Nocera, the author of "It's Hard to Be a Hero," say that we have an unqualified obligation to help those in need. They praise individuals who respond in a crisis and condemn those who find reasons not to. Even if the Genovese case is wildly overstated, scenarios like it—with more accurately documented group apathy—occur all the time. Nocera and others examine the "bystander effect," a psychological phenomenon popularized following Genovese's murder, which suggests that the larger the number of bystanders, the less likely any one of them is to help in an emergency.

On the other side of the debate, writers like Lenore Skenazy claim that we have taken our collective social guilt about Kitty Genovese too far, and as a result, we intervene when we should simply stand by and watch. This tendency leads to concerned neighbors' calling authorities whenever they see unaccompanied children walking down the street or playing in a park, whether they are in danger or not. The cost of this overabundant concern is substantial: it is expensive for law enforcement to respond to calls, and reacting to nonexistent problems pulls police away from situations in which they might actually be needed.

As you read the two essays that follow, try to think of ways to address this debate question. For example, how does the widespread ability to take pictures and videos with smartphones affect people's inclination to step in and help? Which group of bystanders are you most likely to fall into: those who act heroically, those who do nothing or those who panic and flee?

This essay appeared in *Time* on March 13, 2014.

HOW KITTY GENOVESE DESTROYED CHILDHOOD

TIME

LENORE SKENAZY

Kitty Genovese was stabbed to death 50 years ago today. She was 28. A tragedy. 1
The press reported 38 onlookers heard her screams and decided not to intervene. That account has since come under fire, but it nonetheless created a perception of ourselves (and certainly New Yorkers) as unconscionably reluctant to get involved.

We've been making up for it ever since—and that's too bad.   2

We may once have been too slow to call the cops (though that's still dis- 3
puted), but today we are definitely too fast. Oh, I don't mean we shouldn't dial 911 if we see someone being murdered, or threatened, or hurt. Of course we should! In fact, the simple 911 number to call for emergencies was developed partly in response to the Genovese murder: Now everyone could have a quick, easy way to summon the cops anytime, anyplace. A great leap forward.

The leap sideways, or perhaps downward, came as the general public grad- 4
ually became convinced that it not only had an obligation to help anyone in danger, it had the obligation to call the cops anytime it noticed people who could be in danger, especially kids, even if they were fine and dandy at the time.

This has given rise to a near mania for calling the cops when people spot a 5
child on his or her own anywhere in public. And so we have a Connecticut mom charged with "risk of injury to a minor" and failure to appear after police said she allowed her seven- and 11-year-old children to walk to buy pizza unsupervised.

That's right. Someone noticed kids off to get pizza and alerted the cops, as if stopping a potential tragedy.   6

> "Someone noticed kids off to get pizza and alerted the cops, as if stopping a potential tragedy."

Then there's the dad who was arrested for child endangerment after a woman noticed "two children playing on the swings and slides alone without a guardian" in a suburban Pittsburgh park for two hours. (The charges were later dropped.)

And let's not forget the mom in Jonesboro, Arkansas, who made her 10-year-old son walk 4.6 miles to school after he'd been suspended from the school bus for bad behavior. A bank guard saw him walking alone—horrors!—and called the cops. The mom was arrested for child endangerment. In the end, she plead[ed] guilty and was fined $520.

None of these kids encountered any danger other than a concerned citizen with 911 on speed dial. It has become so unusual to see children outside on their own that a nervous public immediately picks up the phone at such a sight, hyperventilating about danger.

"'If in doubt, call 911 to play it safe.' That's the lesson that was taken from Kitty Genovese," says David Pimentel, a professor of law at Ohio Northern University. "But it stems from a faulty assumption, which is that there's no harm in calling." But unless the child is in true danger, "There is harm done. The harm that comes from the overreaction of everybody to this." The courts get involved, CPS gets involved. There are fines, arrests, the threat (and sometimes the reality) of jail time.

Most of the folks calling the cops—and most of the cops themselves—remember walking to school and playing outside as kids. They are convinced that times have changed and made these activities dicey, even though, nationally, the crime rate is down from what it was in the '70s, '80s, and '90s. (And that's not because we don't let kids go outside anymore. The crime rate against adults is down, too, and we don't helicopter them.)

So anyone who walked to the post office or the pizza shop as a kid was no safer than a kid today. But back then, bystanders didn't dial 911 when they saw kids on their own. They waved.

Maybe the lesson from the Kitty Genovese era should be this: Let's get more people back outside, including children. That way we can be looking out for each other, instead of freaking out.

➲ READING ARGUMENTS

1. Throughout this article, Skenazy uses the first-person plural (*we*). How does this usage affect the tone of her argument? How would her argument be different if she wrote entirely in the third-person plural (*they*)?

2. What cause-and-effect relationship does Skenazy try to establish in her three opening paragraphs? Do you find this introduction convincing?

3. Skenazy refers to a "near mania for calling the cops when people spot a child on his or her own anywhere in public" (para. 5). Does she provide enough evidence to support this assertion? Explain.

4. What specific problem does Skenazy address in this essay, and what is her suggestion for solving this problem? Would it be accurate to call this essay a proposal argument? Why or why not?

Nocera's opinion piece ran on December 7, 2012, in the *New York Times*.

IT'S HARD TO BE A HERO

JOE NOCERA

On a crisp January day in 2007, a 50-year-old construction worker named 1 Wesley Autrey became a New York hero when he rescued a man who had fallen onto the subway tracks.

A train had just left the station, so the platform was nearly empty except 2 for Autrey, his two daughters, and a young man who was having a seizure of some sort. The man fell onto the tracks, in a position, Autrey told me recently, "where he was going to lose his limbs." With another train fast approaching, Autrey instinctively jumped onto the tracks, positioned the man's body safely between the rails, and lay on top of him. Five cars passed over them before the train screeched to a halt.

What prompted me to telephone Autrey was the death on Monday of 3 Ki-Suck Han, a Queens man who was pushed onto the 49th Street subway tracks, allegedly by Naeem Davis, a drifter with whom police said he had been having an altercation. This time, there were plenty of people on the platform, most notably R. Umar Abbasi, a photographer who took some horrifying pictures as the subway train closed in on Han.

The 22 seconds or so between Han being pushed and the train reaching 4 him was about the same amount of time that Autrey had nearly six years earlier. Yet, on Monday, no one on the crowded platform made a move to help Han until it was too late. (A doctor tried to administer C.P.R., but he was already dead.)

"People were just standing in fear and shock, not really knowing what was 5 going on," one bystander told a crowd of reporters. "Some people started running out of the platform. Other people just stood there."

When one of Abbasi's gruesome photographs landed on the front page of 6 the *New York Post*, the reaction was fierce. "Someone's taking that picture," said Al Roker on NBC's *Today Show*. "Why aren't they helping this guy up?"

Abbasi defended himself in part by saying he used his flash to warn the conductor, but he was also quick to point the finger at others: "Why didn't the people who were close enough help him?" he asked. "If I had reached him in time, I would have pulled him up," he insisted. We all harbor the hope that if we found ourselves in the same position as Wesley Autrey—or Umar Abbasi— we would act with courage instead of cowardice.

Yet behavioral science suggests otherwise. The most famous case of bystanders failing to act took place in 1964, when Kitty Genovese, a young woman living in a quiet Queens neighborhood, was brutally stabbed to death. Despite her repeated screams for help, some 38 people who heard her from their apartments did nothing—not even call the police.

A. M. Rosenthal, the renowned former executive editor of the *Times*, who was then the metropolitan editor—and who had gotten the tip that led to the story—wrote a short book called *Thirty-Eight Witnesses*. In it, Rosenthal asked

> "Why didn't anyone do anything?"

the question that haunted the country in the aftermath of the murder: *Why?*

Why didn't anyone do anything?

Rosenthal could only guess at the answer because there had been no research on what is now known as "pro-social behavior." But after the story gripped the country, two young social scientists—Bibb Latané, then at Columbia University, and John Darley, who taught at New York University— conducted a series of experiments on the behavior of bystanders.

Their startling conclusion, which is now known as the bystander effect, is that the more people who witness a crime, the less likely any one of them will come to the aid of the victim. Partly this is because when people see others not doing anything, they become confused, not sure if it really is an emergency— "a collective ignorance," says Latané. Another reason, though, is something called the diffusion of responsibility. "You think to yourself, there are all these other people here. This isn't entirely my problem," says Latané.

Go back to the beginning of this column. The crucial detail in 2007, when viewed through the prism of behavioral science, is that the subway platform was nearly empty. Autrey acted heroically—even leaving his two young children unattended to do so—because there was no one else who could help. On Monday, the 49th Street subway platform was full of people, each possibly thinking that someone else was closer, someone else was stronger, someone else should be responsible for the heroic act. As a result, no one acted.

"I wouldn't do the wrong thing," one man waiting for a subway train told the *Times* on Tuesday. That's what we all want to think. It's why we are so quick to condemn those who do nothing at such moments.

But let's be honest: We don't really know how we'd act until the moment is upon us. Sadly, the science says we're more likely to do nothing than respond like Wesley Autrey.

⊙ READING ARGUMENTS

1. What prompted Nocera to write his essay? What question (or questions) did he want to answer?

2. According to Nocera, what is the "bystander effect"? What is the "diffusion of responsibility" (para. 12)?

3. What "crucial detail" (13) reveals the difference between Wesley Autrey's behavior and the behavior of those who failed to help Ki-Suck Han? How does this detail help explain Autrey's actions?

4. Nocera quotes a subway passenger who says, "I wouldn't do the wrong thing" (14). Is Nocera making an ethical argument here? If not, should he be doing so?

5. How would you describe Nocera's tone? Judgmental? Pedantic? Sarcastic? Neutral? Something else? Explain your answer.

⊙ AT ISSUE: UNDER WHAT CIRCUMSTANCES DO BYSTANDERS HAVE AN ETHICAL OBLIGATION TO INTERVENE?

1. Both Skenazy and Nocera mention the case of Kitty Genovese, but they use it to make different points. Explain how each writer interprets the story's significance and how each writer uses it to support his or her argument. Which writer uses the story more effectively? Why?

2. As Skenazy concedes, the commonly known version of the Kitty Genovese murder—in which no one helped Genovese—has "come under fire" (para. 1). According to contemporary accounts, several people did actually try to help Genovese. Does this factual discrepancy matter? Why do you think the original version of the event (regardless of its accuracy) continues to resonate?

3. Nocera writes that all of us would like to think we would act heroically to save another person in an emergency; as a result, he asserts, we are "quick to condemn those who do nothing at such moments" (para. 14). Do you agree with his conclusion? Why or why not?

⊘WRITING ARGUMENTS: UNDER WHAT CIRCUMSTANCES DO BYSTANDERS HAVE AN ETHICAL OBLIGATION TO INTERVENE?

According to Skenazy, the public has passed a turning point, becoming "convinced that it not only had an obligation to help anyone in danger" but also had "the obligation to call the cops anytime it noticed people who could be in danger" (para. 4). In contrast, Nocera suggests that powerful social forces discourage people from helping those in danger. Using these two selections as sources, write an essay offering your own view of the ethical obligations of bystanders. (You might begin by considering fundamental differences between Skenazy's and Nocera's arguments.)

20

DEBATE

DEBATE

Should Bottled Water Be Banned on College Campuses?

Three decades ago, the bottled-water industry barely existed in the United States. Although imports such as sparkling Perrier had snob appeal, most Americans saw water as a public utility that flowed from a tap. However, in response to both successful advertising and consumers' health concerns, sales of bottled water soared in the 1990s, and brands like Evian and Poland Spring emerged as fashion accessories and markers of personal taste and social status. In 2011, Americans bought 9 billion gallons of bottled water; every year, the $22 billion industry grows by over 5 percent.

This growth has its benefits. In a country that favors soft drinks and struggles with obesity, the popularity of a healthy, convenient, calorie-free alternative to sugary soda is a good thing. However, critics of bottled water have become increasingly vocal, citing the environmental effects of manufacturing and disposing of billions of plastic containers. They also point to the expense of bottled water compared to its low-cost alternative from the tap and argue that the bottled-water industry's aggressive marketing obscures the fact that tap water is generally held to higher health and safety standards than its bottled counterpart. As a result, numerous U.S. colleges, including Washington University and the University of Vermont, now ban the sale of plastic bottles of water on their campuses. Of course, the bottled-water industry has responded with its own campaign, which seeks to correct (in the words of the International Bottled Water Association) "misinformation" and the "highly emotional and incorrect" claims of critics.

The two essays in this debate have different perspectives on the question of whether or not to ban bottled water on campus. The staff of Harvard University's newspaper, the *Crimson*, urges the student body to vote "yes" on the initiative to ban bottled water, arguing that the alternatives (water fountains and refill stations) will "take less time, cost . . . less money, and help the environment." Although investigative journalist

Charles Fishman shares some of these concerns, he dismisses the idea of banning bottled water on campus, saying this idea is sillier than bottled water itself.

This article appeared in the *Harvard Crimson*, a student newspaper, on November 15, 2013.

VOTE YES ON THE BOTTLED WATER BAN

THE *CRIMSON* STAFF

It's mid-morning, and you have a few minutes between classes. You're thirsty, 1
and being health conscious, you make your way to the Science Center and purchase a bottle of water. You chug the water, throw out the bottle, and book it back to your classes. In the process, you've dropped $1.25 and used up some finite resources—not as productive as you'd hoped your morning would be.

On Nov. 18, Harvard students will vote to make their mid-morning water 2
breaks more environmentally friendly—as well as more convenient. If the Environmental Action Committee's referendum passes, the Undergraduate Council will urge administration to end the sale of single-use plastic water bottles on campus while installing water fountains and refill stations in all academic and residential buildings. We at the *Crimson* suggest that you vote for this measure.

Single-use plastic water bottles represent one of the most easily obviated 3
threats currently plaguing the environment. As the EAC notes on its homepage, the production of bottled water releases millions of tons of harmful chemicals— such as CO_2—into the environment. After the water's consumption, those very same

> "We at the *Crimson* suggest that you vote for this measure."

bottles often end up in overflowing landfills or swirling, oceanic garbage heaps. Ending the sale of bottled water on campus would constitute a step toward addressing this problem and advancing President Faust's explicitly stated goal of mitigating the University's environmental impact.

The referendum's measures would also improve students' daily lives. 4
Since the measure also calls for more water fountains placed throughout campus, students would have access to cheaper, cleaner, and more convenient water. Here in Massachusetts, we benefit from some of the strictest water supply regulations in the country, and there is no reason to avoid water fountains or tap water for fear of water quality. Bottled water is not held to the same exacting standards—it simply isn't cleaner than tap water.

Imagine a world in which you didn't have to book it to the Science Center 5 and shell out your money just to get some water. Instead, imagine quenching your thirst for free at a conveniently located water fountain, or using a refill station to fill your reusable bottle. The whole endeavor would take less time, cost you less money, and help the environment.

In her letter opposing fossil-fuel divestment, President Faust said that "we 6 need to strengthen . . . our approach to sustainable investment," and the coming referendum provides us with just that opportunity. This is a common-sense measure that will help the environment and improve our daily lives. We hope you vote "yes" on the bottled water ban, and that Harvard quickly enacts it.

spurious quote?

◉ READING ARGUMENTS

1. In paragraph 4, the writers mention the strict water supply regulations in Massachusetts. How is this point important to their argument?

2. The writers describe the bottled-water ban as a "common-sense measure" (para. 6). Is this point as self-evident as the writers seem to think it is? Explain.

3. The writers do not address arguments against their position. Would this editorial be stronger if they had summarized and refuted opposing arguments? Why or why not?

4. In what sense is this a **cause-and-effect** argument? In what respects is it a **proposal** argument?

National Geographic published this essay in its "Voices" section on February 2, 2013.

BOTTLED WATER IS SILLY—BUT SO IS BANNING IT

CHARLES FISHMAN

I remember the moment when the silliness of bottled water became vividly 1 clear to me. I was standing in the factory in San Pellegrino, Italy, at the foot of the Italian Alps, where San Pellegrino water is sealed in those shapely green bottles.

Leave aside that the glass bottles weigh more than the water they contain, 2 or the journey those bottles of water have to make, by truck and ship and truck again, to land on a grocery shelf or café table in Manhattan or St. Louis.

The bottles themselves have to be washed before being filled. And as 3
Pellegrino's wizened factory operations manager explained, they wash the bottles with . . . Pellegrino water. Before filling them with Pellegrino water.

Of course they do. 4

But then the silliness took a leap. Where, I asked, do the bubbles in 5
Pellegrino come from? The plant manager's eyes lit up. Pellegrino water
comes out of the ground uncarbonated, in fact. Pellegrino has another
spring to the south in central Italy that is naturally carbonated. The company harvests the carbon dioxide from that spring, purifies it, compresses it,
trucks it north to Pellegrino, and injects it into the water as part of the bottling process.

seriously?

No matter how far your Pellegrino water has traveled to get to you, the 6
dancing Italian bubbles that make it so delightful have traveled just a little
farther.

San Pellegrino, which is now owned by the conglomerate Nestlé, has a sto- 7
ried history—as a town, as a spring, as a water—but let's be clear: It's a product
no one needs. It's refreshing, it's appealing, but it is a pure indulgence. Whether
you live in Milan, just down the road, or Mexico City, where Pellegrino is on
the shelves at Wal-Mart. And I say that as someone whose wife and 13-year-old
son both love San Pellegrino.

In fact, unless you're struggling in the aftermath of a natural disaster, 8
unless you live in a developing world nation without safe tap water, all bottled
water really falls into that category: luxury, indulgence, convenience.

That's okay, of course, lots of things I like are indulgences: Oreos, *The* 9
Good Wife, Italian Merlot, even the ice cubes I all-but-require in the glass of
water that sits on my desk through the work day.

There is a fresh burst of controversy about bottled water on college cam- 10
puses, specifically, around whether bottled water should be sold in the dining
halls of U.S. and Canadian universities. Last week, the University of Vermont
became the latest of 15 campuses in the U.S. and Canada to ban the sale of
bottled water, according to figures from the Association for the Advancement
of Sustainability in Higher Education (AASHE).

Dozens more campuses have active campaigns to discourage bottled 11
water purchases—including giving out free reusable water bottles to students, and providing elegant, easy-to-use bottle filling stations. (Try to fill a
water bottle from a water fountain sometime—you'll be lucky to get halfway
full.)

Over the weekend, NPR's food blog had a story about college students 12
squaring off against the bottled water industry which drew more than 100
comments. Columbia University's Water Center posted an essay last week
asking, "Should Universities Ban Bottled Water?" which is getting a little
Twitter attention.

The essay doesn't answer the question, but I will: Of course bottled water 13
shouldn't be banned.

Virtually all the bans are the result of well-intentioned student activism on campus.

> "Virtually all the bans are the result of well-intentioned student activism on campus." 14

15

But I don't understand how campuses can ban sale of bottled water while continuing to sell Coke, Pepsi, Mountain Dew, Vitamin Water, and Red Bull.

What do the fired-up campus environmentalists think Coke is, anyway? 16 Regular Coke is about 95 percent water; Diet Coke is 99 percent water.

The reasoning runs something like this: Water is available on campus— 17 from taps, from spigots, from filtered water-filling stations. Students and staff don't need it delivered in plastic bottles. Coke and Red Bull aren't available the same way. (Although sodas, of course, are often delivered on tap in dining halls.)

The environmental contrail from bottled water (which I wrote about in a 18 magazine story that took me to both Fiji and Poland Spring, Maine) is astonishing. It takes a fleet equivalent to 40,000 18-wheelers just to deliver the bottled water Americans buy every week.

But how is the fleet of trucks delivering water in bottles any different than 19 the fleets delivering caramel-colored, caffeinated water in bottles? It takes 2.5 liters of water to produce every liter of Coke products.

I can understand cities banning the purchase of bottled water with 20 city funds for city offices—as San Francisco, Seattle, and New York have done. That's about both money and symbolism. Those cities run tap water systems—why would their employees need bottled water paid for by taxpayers?

I can understand vigorous on-campus awareness efforts to create a cul- 21 ture where carrying a bottle of Evian or Deer Park or SmartWater into class causes raised eyebrows. (No college student appears to be able to make it through a class these days without a drink of some kind—coffee, soda, water— as if scholarship had become seriously dehydrating. Not so long ago, students wouldn't have thought of stepping into a lecture hall with a cup of coffee or a can of soda.)

Indeed, you can start with the fact that buying water in a bottle makes 22 absolutely no economic sense. The water in a half-liter bottle typically costs 3,000 times what the same amount of water from a spigot costs. Buy a single bottle of Poland Spring for $1.29 at the college store, and you can refill the bottle every day for 8 years—college plus medical school!—before the tap water costs what the original Poland Spring cost.

exactly

The very university food service systems that proudly announce bottled 23 water bans offer products with at least as much environmental impact that also have all kinds of dietary impact. Froot Loops at breakfast? Chocolate chip cookies at dinner? Frozen yogurt on tap 16 hours a day?

Bottled water bans are not just oddly hypocritical—taking bottled water 24 out of campus vending machines while leaving soda in those machines—they seem oddly misplaced in a setting where people are supposed to be thinking for themselves.

I love seeing college students leading an imaginative revival of the drink- 25 ing fountain—and it would be great if the revival spilled beyond campuses into cities. Why do people buy bottled water? Because cities don't have public water fountains that are easy to use, clean, and safe. *we used to.*

The bottled water debate is a great way of waking people up to the big 26 water issues almost every community faces—scarcity, purity, reuse, sustainability. But the conversation has to move on from bottled water to the water supply itself.

Banning bottled water doesn't really teach anyone anything. 27

❯ READING ARGUMENTS

1. Fishman spends the first six paragraphs narrating and describing his experience visiting the San Pellegrino bottling factory. How do these paragraphs support his position on the issue? How else might he have introduced his argument?

2. In what sense is this essay a **Rogerian argument**? Identify specific elements of this argumentation strategy.

3. Fishman thinks that the logic of bottled-water-ban proponents is flawed. From Fishman's point of view, what seems illogical about their argument?

4. In paragraph 20, Fishman says that when it comes to water, there is a difference between cities and college campuses. What differences does he identify? According to Fishman, why might a bottled-water ban make sense for cities?

5. In what way is this essay an **evaluation** argument? In what way is it a **proposal** argument?

❯ AT ISSUE: SHOULD BOTTLED WATER BE BANNED ON COLLEGE CAMPUSES?

1. Both Fishman and the *Crimson* writers consider the economic and environmental issues surrounding bottled water. Does either of these readings make ethical arguments, implicitly or explicitly? Explain.

2. Fishman writes, "Bottled water bans . . . seem oddly misplaced in a setting where people are supposed to be thinking for themselves" (para. 24). What does he mean? Do you agree?

3. How do you think the editorial writers of the *Crimson* would respond to Fishman's claim that banning bottled water on campus is "silly"?

⊘WRITING ARGUMENTS: SHOULD BOTTLED WATER BE BANNED ON CAMPUSES?

Dozens of schools across America are curbing, banning, or otherwise restricting the sale and use of bottled water in plastic containers. Would you support such restrictions on your campus? Why or why not? Write an essay in which you take a stand on this issue.

Should Every American Go to College?

Since Harvard College was founded in 1636, American higher education has reflected the history of the United States—economically, socially, and culturally. In the early days of the country, a college education was a privilege for the elite few. The nineteenth century—a period of economic expansion—saw the development of the state university system, which educated many engineers, teachers, agricultural experts, and other professionals who participated in the country's industrial boom. After World War I, the City College of New York provided a free, quality college education to many working-class students, including immigrants, at a time when they were effectively barred from other colleges. However, the most significant expansion in American higher education occurred after World War II, when the GI Bill gave returning veterans money for tuition and living expenses so they could attend college. Enrollment skyrocketed, and many people credit the GI Bill for helping to create postwar prosperity and a large middle class.

In the decades since the first GI Bill was passed, the number of colleges and universities in the United States has increased steadily: as of 2012, there were over 4,700 degree-granting institutions in the United States. Nearly 40 percent of Americans now have at least a two-year college degree, and roughly two thirds of high school graduates enroll in college after graduation. Statistics show that college graduates earn an average of about $17,500 more annually than those who have only a high school diploma. This financial reality, along with the need for a highly educated and competitive workforce in an increasingly global marketplace, has led some to argue that the federal government should do more than it already does to make sure that more—and perhaps even all—Americans attend college. Such proposals raise fundamental questions about higher education. How should colleges maintain academic standards even as they admit more students? How should such institutions control costs? Is higher education a right in the same way that a high school education is? Should everyone go to college? Wouldn't high-quality vocational training make more sense for many?

The following four essays address these and other questions, exploring the importance of a college degree and suggesting new ways of viewing post-secondary education. In "College's Value Goes Deeper Than the Degree," Eric Hoover argues that a college education offers many tangible and intangible benefits. In "When a Two-Year College Degree Pays Off," Liz Weston argues that contrary to popular belief, a two-year degree is not inferior to a four-year degree and can, in many instances, lead to a high-paying career. In "What's Wrong with Vocational School?" Charles Murray argues that too many people are going to college and that some should consider vocational school as a viable alternative. Finally, in "Is College for Everyone?" Pharinet makes the point that as a society, we should accept the fact that certain people simply should not attend college.

The *Chronicle of Higher Education* published this essay on April 22, 2015.

COLLEGE'S VALUE GOES DEEPER THAN THE DEGREE

ERIC HOOVER

Scholastic skepticism is contagious. Pundits and parents alike continue to 1 second-guess the value of a college degree. After all, the recession has changed the way many Americans look at big-ticket purchases; plenty of families worry that today's expenses will not pay off tomorrow.

Not surprisingly, today's cost-conscious public views college price tags 2 with a wary eye. According to the Pew Research Center survey of the American public, only 35 percent said colleges were doing a "good" job in terms of providing value to students and parents; 42 percent said "only fair," and 15 percent said "poor."

A curious thing happened when college graduates were asked about the 3 value of their own degrees, however. In the Pew survey, 84 percent of those with degrees said college had been a good investment; only 7 percent said it had not.

Why? Perhaps it's because assessing the value of a college education is not a 4 hard-and-fast calculation. Sure, diplomas help Americans land better jobs and earn higher salaries, and one can estimate the financial return on those investments. Yet the perceived benefits of attending college go well beyond dollars.

In the Pew survey, all respondents were asked about the "main purpose" 5 of college. Forty-seven percent said "to teach knowledge and skills that can be used in the workplace," 39 percent said "to help an individual grow personally and intellectually," and 12 percent said "both equally."

These findings echo the words graduates often use to describe the benefits of their college experiences. Typically, those benefits are intangible, immeasurable, and untethered to narrow questions about what a particular degree "got" them.

Evan Bloom's diploma will tell you only so much about him. As an undergraduate at the University of California at Berkeley, Mr. Bloom considered several majors. He wanted to take hands-on courses that would require creative thinking. Finally, he settled on architecture.

After graduating, in 2007, Mr. Bloom worked in construction management for a few years, but life inside a cubicle bored him. Recently, he decided to pursue a passion for which he has no credentials: cooking.

Mr. Bloom, 25, is the co-founder of Wise Sons Jewish Delicatessen, a catering business in San Francisco. The venture, which serves the public out of rented space once a week, has yet to become a full-time, brick-and-mortar business. That's likely to change as soon as investors come aboard.

Mr. Bloom believes his out-of-classroom experiences prepared him to become a restaurateur. At Berkeley he was active in the student government, honing his networking skills. As a member of the university's Hillel chapter, he and a friend, Leo Beckerman, cooked weekly meals for groups of 250. The experience inspired them to start Wise Sons together.

More than once, Mr. Bloom has thought about the power of connections made in college. An alumnus of his fraternity helped him get an internship with the contractor for whom he later worked. And had he not met Mr. Beckerman at a bar one night years ago, he might still be doing something he enjoys less than making pastrami and rye bread.

"My classes were great, but it was really everything else I was doing that mattered the most," Mr. Bloom said. "It was tapping into this whole sphere of influences."

"Basic, Fundamental Training"

The way her life unfolded, Vanessa Mera didn't end up needing her bachelor's degrees in psychology and economics. After graduating from the University of Miami in 2001, she and her sister took over their parents' import-export-distribution business, called VZ Solutions Inc., in Miami.

Still, Ms. Mera, 31, says her time in college was crucial. As a freshman, she had expected to major in biology and go on to medical school. Over time, she realized that she didn't want to become a doctor. "In college, you come in thinking one thing about yourself," she said, "and you leave thinking in a completely different way."

Ms. Mera, who had attended a private all-girls high school, believes that interacting with people of different backgrounds helped her overcome her shyness. So, too, did the time she spent studying in Spain.

Surrounded by many high-achieving students at Miami, Ms. Mera developed a competitive streak. If you want to land a good internship, she learned, you must put yourself out there.

"I realized that just because you had good grades didn't mean you were 17
going to get anywhere," Ms. Mera said. "Without those four years, I wouldn't
be the businessperson I am today. I wouldn't have the confidence."

Jane Knecht can relate. She enrolled at the University of Virginia in the 18
late 1970s, unsure of what she wanted to study. She signed up for an introductory rhetoric course. "I didn't even know what the word meant," she said.

Soon, Ms. Knecht couldn't get enough. In a course on rhetoric and social 19
theory, she recalled, a professor gave students three unrelated pieces of writing
and told them to synthesize an argument that tied them all together. At first,
she froze up, worried that she couldn't do it. Then the writing flowed.

As Ms. Knecht practiced public speaking and wrote a mountain of papers, 20
her self-confidence soared: "It was basic, fundamental training."

Ms. Knecht graduated in 1982 with a degree in speech communications. 21
She had planned to go to law school, but instead spent seven years at home
with her two children before entering the work force. At 52, she's now director
of business development at the Water Environment Research Foundation, in
Alexandria, Virginia.

Without a bachelor's degree, Ms. Knecht figures, she wouldn't have been 22
considered for the job. Many of her colleagues have master's degrees or
Ph.D.'s. Moreover, she believes college prepared her for day-to-day challenges.

"Everything in my job is relationship-based," said Ms. Knecht, who on a 23
recent afternoon was preparing to run a conference call with business associates in Australia, followed by a board meeting. "My classes helped me recognize the importance of listening and effective negotiating, and how to go into
new situations, which I do all the time."

Billy Ray, 59, described his degree as a door that led him to prosperity. 24
His parents were poor, as were most of his childhood friends. "We were on the
bottom rung," he said. "I didn't like where I was, and I wanted to change that."

When Mr. Ray enrolled at Stephen F. Austin State University in 1970, he 25
found himself surrounded by people with fatter wallets and high aspirations.
This inspired him. "I was associating with a different level of people," he said.
He put himself through college by working for a construction company during the summers.

Mr. Ray says the contacts he made in college were just as crucial as the 26
courses he took. After graduating with a degree in business administration,
Mr. Ray went to work for the construction company as a licensed plumber.
Later, a good friend from Stephen F. Austin offered him a job selling trucks at
a dealership. "I went from making good money to really good money," he said.

Mr. Ray, who lives in Lufkin, Texas, is now a regional manager for De 27
Lage Landen, a financial-services company. He and his wife, Alys, own a
3,000-square-foot house, and they recently purchased a second home, in
Austin, where both of their sons graduated from the University of Texas.

Having written all those tuition checks, Mr. Ray understands why some 28
people question the value of college. "You're losing four years of work time
and thousands of dollars," he said. "Do you ever get it back?"

Still, Mr. Ray, the only one of three brothers to finish college, said he would have a much lower-paying job without a bachelor's degree (his current position requires one). And the

> "And the value of going to college, he believes, is only increasing." 29

value of going to college, he believes, is only increasing. "If they don't get that degree," he said, "they're going nowhere."

⊘ READING ARGUMENTS

1. In your own words, paraphrase Hoover's thesis.

2. Where does Hoover state his thesis? Why does he wait so long to do so? What information does he present before he states it? Why?

3. What is the relationship between paragraphs 6 and 7? What transition is Hoover making at this point in the essay?

4. Hoover supports his thesis with several anecdotal examples. What point do these examples make? What are the strengths and weaknesses of this kind of evidence? What other types of evidence could Hoover have included?

5. In what respects is this essay an evaluation argument?

This article first appeared on April 21, 2015, on Time.com.

WHEN A TWO-YEAR COLLEGE DEGREE PAYS OFF

LIZ WESTON

TIME

Steven Polasck of Corpus Christi, Texas, liked math and science in high 1 school. He considered attending a four-year college but ultimately decided to use his strengths to get a two-year degree in instrumentation from Texas State Technical College. He has not looked back.

"I went to work on the Monday after graduation," said Polasck, 27, who 2 monitors and fixes systems at a Valero Energy Corp refinery. "The first year I made almost $80,000."

An associate's degree has long been considered an inferior alternative to a 3 bachelor's degree. Now that more states are tracking their graduates' incomes, however, it is becoming apparent that some two-year degrees offer much higher earnings than the typical four-year degree—at a fraction of the cost.

Making more students and parents aware of these better-paying options 4 could help ease the college affordability crisis, which has so far led to more than $1 trillion in student loan debt.

The average net annual cost of a community college education—for 5 tuition, fees, room and board, minus financial aid—is just under $6,000, according to the College Board. The average undergraduate at a four-year public college pays twice that amount out of pocket, and most students attending a public school now take five or more years to complete their degrees.

The fact that people still think a bachelor's degree is always the better option 6 is probably due to popular charts that hang in many high school guidance counselor offices, said Michael Bettersworth, vice chancellor and chief policy officer for Texas State Technical College, which has nearly 30,000 enrolled students.

The "chart" is a graphic representation of earnings by educational attainment, using Bureau of Labor Statistics data showing professional degrees at the top, bachelor's degrees in the middle, and associate's degrees just above high school diplomas. 7

Median weekly earnings for those with bachelor's degrees last year 8 reached $1,101, or $57,252 a year, compared to $792, or $41,184 annually, for those with an associate's degree, according to BLS.

But the chart fails to capture the full range of salaries earned by those with 9 two-year degrees, particularly those in technical fields, Bettersworth said.

"It's far more important what you study than how much you study," he said. 10

While the average starting salary for somebody with a bachelor's degree 11 in Texas is around $40,000 per year, many technical associate's degrees offer first-year pay of more than $70,000, according to College Measures, which tracks earnings and other outcomes for higher education.

Some well-paying jobs require less than two years of study. A line worker 12 certification, a requisite for working on electrical power lines, takes about a year and brings an average starting salary of $70,000, Bettersworth said.

Texas is one of the states that has been gathering income data as a way to gauge and improve the success of its public college graduates. Other states conducting similar studies include Arkansas, Colorado, Florida, Tennessee, and Virginia. 13

> "Some well-paying jobs require less than two years of study."

The earnings advantage of some two-year degrees can persist throughout a 14 worker's lifetime. More than one in four people with associate's degrees end up making more than the average of somebody with a bachelor's degree, according to a 2011 report by Georgetown University's Center on Education and the Workplace.

Four of the 30 fastest-growing job categories according to BLS require   15
associate's degrees. The jobs include dental hygienist (median annual earnings
of $70,210), diagnostic medical sonographers ($65,860), occupational therapy
assistants ($53,240), and physical therapist assistant ($52,160).

Other jobs with strong growth and above-average pay that require two-year   16
degrees are funeral service managers ($66,720), web developers ($62,500), electrical and electronics drafters ($55,700), nuclear technicians ($69,060), radiation
therapists ($77,560), respiratory therapists ($55,870), registered nurses ($65,470),
cardiovascular technologists and technicians ($52,070), radiologic technologists
($54,620), and magnetic resonance imaging technologists ($65,360).

Polasck said it is not unusual for experienced people with his type of   17
degree to make up to $150,000 a year with "reasonable" amounts of overtime.
Job prospects are good even with declining oil prices, since refineries produce
gas and other byproducts regardless of prevailing prices.

"If I can go to this school for two years, and not be in much debt at all at   18
the end, and be making pretty good money to start, why wouldn't I do that?"
Polasck said. "It's common sense."

⊘ READING ARGUMENTS

1. How does this essay challenge widely held assumptions about
   college degrees? At what points in the essay does Weston specifically
   address these assumptions?

2. According to the Bureau of Labor Statistics, four of the fastest-
   growing job categories require associate degrees. What are these
   jobs? What do they have in common?

3. Weston quotes Michael Bettersworth, an administrator at a technical
   college that grants two-year degrees. Is he an objective source? Is he
   credible? Explain.

4. Weston includes a number of statistics to support her thesis. Where
   did she get these statistics? What are the strengths and weaknesses
   of this kind of evidence?

5. This essay begins by referring to Steven Polasck, a student who decided
   to attend a two-year school rather than a four-year school. It ends with a
   quotation from the same student. How effective is this strategy? What
   other options did Weston have for opening and closing her essay? What
   are the advantages and disadvantages of these alternatives?

The *Wall Street Journal* published this opinion piece on January 17, 2007.

WHAT'S WRONG WITH VOCATIONAL SCHOOL?

CHARLES MURRAY

The topic yesterday was education and children in the lower half of the intelligence distribution. Today I turn to the upper half, people with IQs of 100 or higher. Today's simple truth is that far too many of them are going to four-year colleges. 1

Begin with those barely into the top half, those with average intelligence. To have an IQ of 100 means that a tough high-school course pushes you about as far as your academic talents will take you. If you are average in math ability, you may struggle with algebra and probably fail a calculus course. If you are average in verbal skills, you often misinterpret complex text and make errors in logic. 2

These are not devastating shortcomings. You are smart enough to engage in any of hundreds of occupations. You can acquire more knowledge if it is presented in a format commensurate with your intellectual skills. But a genuine college education in the arts and sciences begins where your skills leave off. 3

In engineering and most of the natural sciences, the demarcation between high-school material and college-level material is brutally obvious. If you cannot handle the math, you cannot pass the courses. In the humanities and social sciences, the demarcation is fuzzier. It is possible for someone with an IQ of 100 to sit in the lectures of Economics 1, read the textbook, and write answers in an examination book. But students who cannot follow complex arguments accurately are not really learning economics. They are taking away a mishmash of half-understood information and outright misunderstandings that probably leave them under the illusion that they know something they do not. (A depressing research literature documents one's inability to recognize one's own incompetence.) Traditionally and properly understood, a four-year college education teaches advanced analytic skills and information at a level that exceeds the intellectual capacity of most people. 4

There is no magic point at which a genuine-college-level education becomes an option, but anything below an IQ of 110 is problematic. If you want to do well, you should have an IQ of 115 or higher. Put another way, it makes sense for only about 15 percent of the population, 25 percent if one stretches it, to get a college education. And yet more than 45 percent of recent high school graduates enroll in four-year colleges. Adjust that percentage to account for high-school dropouts, and more than 40 percent of all persons in their late teens are trying to go to a four-year college—enough people to absorb everyone down through an IQ of 104. 5

No data that I have been able to find tell us what proportion of those students 6
really want four years of college-level courses, but it is safe to say that few people
who are intellectually unqualified yearn for the experience, any more than someone who is athletically unqualified for a college varsity wants to have his shortcomings exposed at practice every day. They are in college to improve their chances of
making a good living. What they really need is vocational training. But nobody will
say so, because "vocational training" is second class. "College" is first class.

Large numbers of those who are intellectually qualified for college also do 7
not yearn for four years of college-level courses. They go to college because
their parents are paying for it and college is what children of their social class
are supposed to do after they finish high school. They may have the ability to
understand the material in Economics 1 but they do not want to. They, too,
need to learn to make a living—and would do better in vocational training.

Combine those who are unqualified with those who are qualified but 8
not interested, and some large proportion of students on today's college
campuses—probably a majority of them—are looking for something that the
four-year college was not designed to provide. Once there, they create a demand
for practical courses, taught at an intellectual level that can be handled by
someone with a mildly above-average IQ and/or mild motivation. The
nation's colleges try to accommodate these new demands. But most of the
practical specialties do not really require four years of training, and the best
way to teach those specialties is not through a residential institution with the
staff and infrastructure of a college. It amounts to a system that tries to turn
out televisions on an assembly line that also makes pottery. It can be done, but
it's ridiculously inefficient.

Government policy contributes to the problem by making college 9
scholarships and loans too easy to get, but its role is ancillary. The demand for
college is market-driven, because a college degree does, in fact, open up access
to jobs that are closed to people without one. The fault lies in the false premium that our culture has put on a college degree.

For a few occupations, a college
degree still certifies a qualification. For
example, employers appropriately
treat a bachelor's degree in engineering
as a requirement for hiring engineers.
But a bachelor's degree in a field such
as sociology, psychology, economics,
history, or literature certifies nothing. It
is a screening device for employers. The college you got into says a lot about
your ability, and that you stuck it out for four years says something about your
perseverance. But the degree itself does not qualify the graduate for anything.
There are better, faster, and more efficient ways for young people to acquire
credentials to provide to employers.

> "[A] bachelor's degree in a field such as sociology, psychology, economics, history, or literature certifies nothing."

10

The good news is that market-driven systems eventually adapt to reality, 11
and signs of change are visible. One glimpse of the future is offered by the

nation's two-year colleges. They are more honest than the four-year institutions about what their students want and provide courses that meet their needs more explicitly. Their time frame gives them a big advantage—two years is about right for learning many technical specialties, while four years is unnecessarily long.

Advances in technology are making the brick-and-mortar facility increasingly irrelevant. Research resources on the Internet will soon make the college library unnecessary. Lecture courses taught by first-rate professors are already available on CDs and DVDs for many subjects, and online methods to make courses interactive between professors and students are evolving. Advances in computer simulation are expanding the technical skills that can be taught without having to gather students together in a laboratory or shop. These and other developments are all still near the bottom of steep growth curves. The cost of effective training will fall for everyone who is willing to give up the trappings of a campus. As the cost of college continues to rise, the choice to give up those trappings will become easier. 12

A reality about the job market must eventually begin to affect the valuation of a college education: The spread of wealth at the top of American society has created an explosive increase in the demand for craftsmen. Finding a good lawyer or physician is easy. Finding a good carpenter, painter, electrician, plumber, glazier, mason—the list goes on and on—is difficult, and it is a seller's market. Journeymen craftsmen routinely make incomes in the top half of the income distribution while master craftsmen can make six figures. They have work even in a soft economy. Their jobs cannot be outsourced to India. And the craftsman's job provides wonderful intrinsic rewards that come from mastery of a challenging skill that produces tangible results. How many white-collar jobs provide nearly as much satisfaction? 13

Even if forgoing college becomes economically attractive, the social cachet of a college degree remains. That will erode only when large numbers of high-status, high-income people do not have a college degree and don't care. The information technology industry is in the process of creating that class, with Bill Gates and Steve Jobs as exemplars. It will expand for the most natural of reasons: A college education need be no more important for many high-tech occupations than it is for NBA basketball players or cabinetmakers. Walk into Microsoft or Google with evidence that you are a brilliant hacker, and the job interviewer is not going to fret if you lack a college transcript. The ability to present an employer with evidence that you are good at something, without benefit of a college degree, will continue to increase, and so will the number of skills to which that evidence can be attached. Every time that happens, the false premium attached to the college degree will diminish. 14

Most students find college life to be lots of fun (apart from the boring classroom stuff), and that alone will keep the four-year institution overstocked for a long time. But, rightly understood, college is appropriate for 15 a small minority of young adults—perhaps even a minority of the people who have IQs high enough that they could do college-level work if they wished. People who go to college are not better or worse people than anyone else; they are merely different in certain interests and abilities. That is the way college should be seen. There is reason to hope that eventually it will be.

➲READING ARGUMENTS

1. Construct a syllogism for the deductive argument Murray uses in his opening paragraphs. Do you find this argument persuasive? Why or why not?

2. Murray makes a distinction between engineering and the natural sciences (on the one hand) and the humanities and social sciences (on the other). What difference does he identify? Why is this difference important to his argument?

3. Murray claims that too many people are going to four-year colleges. What **cause-and-effect** arguments does he use to support this claim? How do these arguments support his position on the issue?

4. More than once in his essay, Murray notes that the "intellectually unqualified" probably do not want to attend a four-year college, and he implies that if given the chance, they would choose not to. Do you think this is true? Do you believe Murray's emphasis on personal choice strengthens his argument? Explain.

5. According to Murray, more people should go to vocational schools. What advantages does he see for those who choose careers in trades and crafts?

This essay appeared in an AssociatedContent.com blog posting dated April 25, 2007.

IS COLLEGE FOR EVERYONE?

PHARINET

"You won't get anywhere without your education." We hear this refrain from   1
the time we are in elementary school. This may be true, but is college for everyone? More and more individuals are enrolling in two- and four-year postsecondary schools, but why? Often, a desire for learning is not what

drives students to attend college. Factors that determine reasons for attending college vary from personal to professional. These factors are the key to our discussion.

There is no doubt that education is important. There is also no doubt that every person has the right to an education. However, not every person should attend college. There are too many students enrolled in school who simply don't belong there. Though drop-out rates vary, it is estimated that in the U.S., approximately 50 percent of students who begin college never graduate. There exist students who are not yet ready for the academic and financial challenges of college. There exist students who do not have the desire for college or learning. Some students may be better suited for a different type of education, if any.

> "There are too many students enrolled in school who simply don't belong there."

2

The student who is not yet ready for the academic and financial chal-   3 lenges of college is the most common. While the cost of college can be offset by grants, scholarships, and work-study programs, too many students find themselves in desperate financial situations by the end of their first semester. The cost of books can run several hundred dollars per semester. There are living expenses that students may not have planned for, including the cost of food, rent, gasoline, spending money, and supplies other than books. Students find themselves working full-time jobs while attending school full-time, and their minds, bodies, and grades end up suffering. While it may take a while longer to graduate, many students who find themselves in a position where they must work may do better to drop themselves to part-time student status, taking fewer classes. This lowers the cost of education each semester (though requires a longer-term commitment) and increases the chances of classroom success. There is more time to dedicate to course-work without overloading and overscheduling. Perhaps, certain individuals should consider a different life choice, as the long-term responsibility of repaying student loans can be overwhelming. However, the best financial planning in the world will not prepare a student for the academic challenges that await them.

Believe it or not, there are students who cannot read [but who are]   4 attending college. While this is an extreme case, it is symptomatic of the problems with the idea that "college is for everyone." If college is for everyone, why do we rely on SAT scores and high school transcripts? Why doesn't every school have an open admissions policy? Quite simply, because not everyone should attend college. If individuals are unable to read, they benefit more from a literacy program than a college course. There are also plenty of literate students who are not up for the challenge. They may have graduated from a high school that did not expect much from them, academically. They may not have the maturity necessary to dedicate themselves to the coursework. For many, this is the first time they have had personal freedom and responsibility without their parents. They aren't necessarily prepared to be "grown ups" yet. College prep courses don't often teach students about being responsible. Teaching responsibility and time and stress management may prepare some students for their college experience, but many will still fall victim to their first taste of "freedom."

"C's get degrees." One of my own students said this to me when inquiring about his progress this semester. Unfortunately, this is an all too common mentality among college students. There is no real desire for learning. Students are "going through the motions" to earn their degrees, hoping to settle into a comfortable job that will pay them well because that "C degree" hangs on their wall. Motivating students to learn is the biggest challenge most educators face. While it may be possible to ignite a spark in some, most students who don't wish to learn simply won't learn. What good is there, then, in attending college? None. What happens when this type of student enters the workforce? Do they exhibit the same lack of motivation in their careers? If so, what type of value is actually attached to that degree?

Once upon a time, college was a place you went when you wished to learn. Now, college is the place you go when you want to get a good job, or appease your parents, or because you are "finding yourself." While admissions representatives and administration share some of the blame (college is a business, after all), it is important to examine other reasons why students who don't belong in college end up there anyway. Students and parents need to examine their options. Is it really going to benefit you (or your child) to attend college? What other options exist? Is a trade school the best option? Perhaps allowing yourself to take a year or two to carefully consider who you are and what you want will save you time and money, and better prepare you should you decide to attend college. Society, too, plays a part in pushing students into college classrooms. We need to start distinguishing between the right to an education, and the benefit of an education. College does not benefit everyone. Not everyone should attend college. It is OK to say this! It is OK to believe this! You are not putting anyone down by saying these things. You may be doing them a favor by letting them know that it is OK not to attend college. Higher education is not the key to happiness and success for every person.

Many people have found happiness in careers that do not require a college education. If we continue to tell everyone to acquire a college degree, we lessen the pool of people who will do the jobs that keep our world running smoothly. There are jobs that do not require a college education. Some work can be learned on the job or from a trade school. We need fork lift drivers, factory workers, sales clerks, and cashiers. What would we do without tractor-trailer drivers, mail carriers, and construction workers? Refuse to accept the political correctness that says all of our citizens should receive a higher education. Embrace the reality that college is not for everyone.

⊘ READING ARGUMENTS

1. In her second paragraph, the writer claims that there is "no doubt that every person has the right to an education" but also asserts that "not every person should attend college." Why is this distinction important to her argument? Is it in any sense a contradiction?

2. In her conclusion, the writer advises, "Refuse to accept the political correctness that says all of our citizens should receive a higher education." Do you agree that "college for everyone" has its roots in "political correctness"?

3. According to the writer, what is the biggest challenge that educators face?

⊘ AT ISSUE: SHOULD EVERY AMERICAN GO TO COLLEGE?

1. In paragraph 5 of his essay, Hoover cites a Pew Research Survey that asked college graduates about the main purpose of college: "Forty-seven percent said 'to teach knowledge and skills that can be used in the workplace,' 39 percent said 'to help an individual grow personally and intellectually,' and 12 percent said 'both equally.'" How would you answer this question about the main purpose of college?

2. Murray bases his argument on the IQ, or "intelligence distribution" (para. 1), among the general population. What are the strengths and weaknesses of his focus on IQ?

3. Pharinet writes, "Once upon a time, college was a place you went when you wished to learn," but now people go to "get a good job," "appease" their parents, or find themselves (para. 6). Do you agree with her? If so, do you see this shift as a problem? If not, why not? Explain your reasoning.

⊘ WRITING ARGUMENTS: SHOULD EVERY AMERICAN GO TO COLLEGE?

1. After reading and thinking about the four essays in this casebook, do you think more people should be encouraged to attend college, or do you think some people should be discouraged from doing so? Do you see higher education as a "right" (and a necessity) for most, or even all citizens? Write an argumentative essay in which you answer these questions.

2. Pharinet says, "Motivating students to learn is the biggest challenge most educators face" (para. 5). Based on your own observations, what is the biggest challenge—or challenges—that most *students* face as they make their way through a postsecondary education?

CHAPTER

22

Should We Eat Meat?

As health experts increasingly worry about heart disease and obesity, this is an especially good time for Americans to evaluate the merits of meat-eating. This issue goes well beyond health and nutrition, however. According to the Vegetarian Resource Group, the over 8 million vegetarians and vegans who live in the United States become vegetarians for a variety of reasons—nutritional, ethical, environmental, and religious. In other words, their choice to forego meat is not only personal but also cultural. As Jonathan Safran Foer writes in "Let Them Eat Dog," "Food is not rational. Food is culture, habit, craving, and identity."

As shown by the increasing popularity of organic and locally grown food as well as by the popularity of books such as Jonathan Safran Foer's *Eating Animals* (2009) and documentaries such as *Food, Inc.* (2008) and *Fed Up* (2014), our culture seems obsessed with healthy eating. Of course, dietary controversies are not new—and neither is vegetarianism, which has long been associated with certain religious traditions (Jainism and various sects of Hinduism, for example). Western philosophers from Pythagoras to Jean-Jacques Rousseau and René Descartes also advocated forms of vegetarianism. In the eighteenth and nineteenth centuries, a vegetarian diet was associated with radical politics. The English Romantic poet Percy Bysshe Shelley endorsed the practice of vegetarianism—and even blamed some of the excesses of the French Revolution on meat-eating. In the United States, vegetarianism has had strong advocates dating back to the founding of our country. Presbyterian minister and dietary reformer Sylvester Graham, for example, helped found the American Vegetarian Society in 1850. He touted the benefits of a high-fiber diet of fruits and vegetables—the staple of which was the "Graham cracker," made of whole-wheat flour and bran. According to the zealous Graham, who attracted a sizable following, a meatless diet improved both health and personal morality.

Although the language and aims of vegetarians may have changed, many still see the choice to eat—or not eat—meat as a profoundly moral and ethical decision, not just a matter of personal choice. All the writers in this casebook agree that the choice to eat meat depends on a variety of social, environmental, and cultural factors. In an essay modeled on Jonathan Swift's famous satire "A Modest Proposal," Jonathan Safran Foer highlights the logical and ethical inconsistency of those who justify consuming animals such as chickens, pigs, and cows for food even though they would be horrified by killing and eating domesticated dogs and cats. Rancher Nicolette Hahn Niman addresses the connection between food production and climate change but corrects some common misperceptions about the relative environmental effects of vegetarianism and meat-eating. Daniel Payne argues that human beings are ultimately omnivores but that when making dietary choices, people must consider the realities of the way animals are raised. He argues that those who eat meat should consume only "humane" meat; in contrast, longtime vegan and activist Sunaura Taylor makes the case that the phrase *humane meat* is a contradiction in terms.

This essay is from the October 31, 2009, *Wall Street Journal*.

LET THEM EAT DOG

JONATHAN SAFRAN FOER

Despite the fact that it's perfectly legal in 44 states, eating "man's best friend"   1
is as taboo as a man eating his best friend. Even the most enthusiastic carnivores won't eat dogs. TV guy and sometimes cooker Gordon Ramsay can get pretty macho with lambs and piglets when doing publicity for something he's selling, but you'll never see a puppy peeking out of one of his pots. And though he once said he'd electrocute his children if they became vegetarian, one can't help but wonder what his response would be if they poached the family pooch.

Dogs are wonderful, and in many ways unique. But they are remarkably   2
unremarkable in their intellectual and experiential capacities. Pigs are every bit as intelligent and feeling, by any sensible definition of the words. They can't hop into the back of a Volvo, but they can fetch, run and play, be mischievous, and reciprocate affection. So why don't they get to curl up by the fire? Why can't they at least be spared being tossed on the fire? Our taboo against dog eating says something about dogs and a great deal about us.

The French, who love their dogs, sometimes eat their horses.   3

The Spanish, who love their horses, sometimes eat their cows.   4

The Indians, who love their cows, sometimes eat their dogs.   5

While written in a much different context, George Orwell's words (from   6
Animal Farm) apply here: "All animals are equal, but some animals are more equal than others."

So who's right? What might be the reasons to exclude canine from the   7
menu? The selective carnivore suggests:

Don't eat companion animals. But dogs aren't kept as companions in all 8 of the places they are eaten. And what about our petless neighbors? Would we have any right to object if they had dog for dinner?

OK, then: Don't eat animals with significant mental capacities. If by "sig- 9 nificant mental capacities" we mean what a dog has, then good for the dog. But such a definition would also include the pig, cow, and chicken. And it would exclude severely impaired humans.

> "Properly cooked, dog meat poses no greater health risks than any other meat." 10

Then: It's for good reason that the eternal taboos—don't fiddle with your crap, kiss your sister, or eat your companions—are taboo. Evolutionarily speaking, those things are bad for us. But dog eating isn't a taboo in many places, and it isn't in any way bad for us. Properly cooked, dog meat poses no greater health risks than any other meat.

Dog meat has been described as "gamey," "complex," "buttery," and "flo- 11 ral." And there is a proud pedigree of eating it. Fourth-century tombs contain depictions of dogs being slaughtered along with other food animals. It was a fundamental enough habit to have informed language itself: the Sino-Korean character for "fair and proper" (yeon) literally translates into "as cooked dog meat is delicious." Hippocrates praised dog meat as a source of strength. Dakota Indians enjoyed dog liver, and not so long ago Hawaiians ate dog brains and blood. Captain Cook ate dog. Roald Amundsen famously ate his sled dogs. (Granted, he was really hungry.) And dogs are still eaten to overcome bad luck in the Philippines; as medicine in China and Korea; to enhance libido in Nigeria; and in numerous places, on every continent, because they taste good. For centuries, the Chinese have raised special breeds of dogs, like the black-tongued chow, for chow, and many European countries still have laws on the books regarding postmortem examination of dogs intended for human consumption.

Of course, something having been done just about everywhere is no kind 12 of justification for doing it now. But unlike all farmed meat, which requires the creation and maintenance of animals, dogs are practically begging to be eaten. Three to four million dogs and cats are euthanized annually. The simple disposal of these euthanized dogs is an enormous ecological and economic problem. But eating those strays, those runaways, those not-quite-cute-enough-to-take and not-quite-well-behaved-enough-to-keep dogs would be killing a flock of birds with one stone and eating it, too.

In a sense it's what we're doing already. Rendering—the conversion of 13 animal protein unfit for human consumption into food for livestock and pets—allows processing plants to transform useless dead dogs into productive members of the food chain. In America, millions of dogs and cats euthanized in animal shelters every year become the food for our food. So let's just eliminate this inefficient and bizarre middle step.

This need not challenge our civility. We won't make them suffer any more 14 than necessary. While it's widely believed that adrenaline makes dog meat taste better—hence the traditional methods of slaughter: hanging, boiling alive, beating to death—we can all agree that if we're going to eat them, we should kill them quickly and painlessly, right? For example, the traditional Hawaiian means of holding the dog's nose shut—in order to conserve blood—must be regarded (socially if not legally) as a no-no. Perhaps we could include dogs under the Humane Methods of Slaughter Act. That doesn't say anything about how they're treated during their lives, and isn't subject to any meaningful oversight or enforcement, but surely we can rely on the industry to "self-regulate," as we do with other eaten animals.

Few people sufficiently appreciate the colossal task of feeding a world of 15 billions of omnivores who demand meat with their potatoes. The inefficient use of dogs—conveniently already in areas of high human population (take note, local-food advocates)—should make any good ecologist blush. One could argue that various "humane" groups are the worst hypocrites, spending enormous amounts of money and energy in a futile attempt to reduce the number of unwanted dogs while at the very same time propagating the irresponsible no-dog-for-dinner taboo. If we let dogs be dogs, and breed without interference, we would create a sustainable, local meat supply with low energy inputs that would put even the most efficient grass-based farming to shame. For the ecologically minded it's time to admit that dog is realistic food for realistic environmentalists.

For those already convinced, here's a classic Filipino recipe I recently 16 came across. I haven't tried it myself, but sometimes you can read a recipe and just know.

Stewed Dog, Wedding Style

First, kill a medium-sized dog, then burn off the fur over a hot fire. Carefully remove the skin while still warm and set aside for later (may be used in other recipes). Cut meat into 1" cubes. Marinate meat in mixture of vinegar, peppercorn, salt, and garlic for 2 hours. Fry meat in oil using a large wok over an open fire, then add onions and chopped pineapple and sauté until tender. Pour in tomato sauce and boiling water, add green pepper, bay leaf, and Tabasco. Cover and simmer over warm coals until meat is tender. Blend in purée of dog's liver and cook for additional 5–7 minutes.

There is an overabundance of rational reasons to say no to factory-farmed 17 meat: It is the No. 1 cause of global warming, it systematically forces tens of billions of animals to suffer in ways that would be illegal if they were dogs, it is a decisive factor in the development of swine and avian flus, and so on. And yet even most people who know these things still aren't inspired to order something else on the menu. Why?

Food is not rational. Food is culture, habit, craving, and identity. Responding 18 to factory farming calls for a capacity to care that dwells beyond information. We know what we see on undercover videos of factory farms and slaughterhouses is wrong. (There are those who will defend a system that allows for occasional animal cruelty, but no one defends the cruelty, itself.) And despite it being entirely reasonable, the case for eating dogs is likely repulsive to just about every reader of this paper. The instinct comes before our reason, and is more important.

⊘ READING ARGUMENTS

1. Evaluate Foer's title. First, look up the famous line "Let them eat cake." Who is supposed to have said this, and under what circumstances? Considering Foer's audience and the subject matter and purpose of his essay, is this an effective title? Why or why not?

2. Several times in his essay, Foer uses the term *taboo*—for example, when he refers to the "eternal taboos" in paragraph 10. What is a taboo? Why do you think Foer uses this word rather than a neutral word, such as *rule*?

3. In what respects is this essay a proposal argument? What is Foer proposing?

4. Paraphrase Foer's thesis. Where is it located?

5. What is Foer's purpose? For example, does he want to change readers' minds? Inspire them to take some kind of action? Something else?

This opinion essay is from the October 31, 2009, edition of the *New York Times*.

THE CARNIVORE'S DILEMMA

NICOLETTE HAHN NIMAN

Is eating a hamburger the global warming equivalent of driving a Hummer? 1 This week an article in the *Times* of London carried a headline that blared: "Give Up Meat to Save the Planet." Former Vice President Al Gore, who has made climate change his signature issue, has even been assailed for omnivorous eating by animal rights activists.

It's true that food production is an important contributor to climate 2 change. And the claim that meat (especially beef) is closely linked to global warming has received some credible backing, including by the United Nations and University of Chicago. Both institutions have issued reports that have been widely summarized as condemning meat-eating.

But that's an overly simplistic conclusion to draw from the research. To a rancher like me, who raises cattle, goats, and turkeys the traditional way (on grass), the studies show only that the prevailing methods of producing meat—that is, crowding animals together in factory farms, storing their waste in giant lagoons, and cutting down forests to grow crops to feed them—cause substantial greenhouse gases. It could be, in fact, that a conscientious meat eater may have a more environmentally friendly diet than your average vegetarian.

So what is the real story of meat's connection to global warming? Answering the question requires examining the individual greenhouse gases involved: carbon dioxide, methane, and nitrous oxides.

> "So what is the real story of meat's connection to global warming?"

Carbon dioxide makes up the majority of agriculture-related greenhouse emissions. In American farming, most carbon dioxide emissions come from fuel burned to operate vehicles and equipment. World agricultural carbon emissions, on the other hand, result primarily from the clearing of woods for crop growing and livestock grazing. During the 1990s, tropical deforestation in Brazil, India, Indonesia, Sudan, and other developing countries caused 15 percent to 35 percent of annual global fossil fuel emissions.

Much Brazilian deforestation is connected to soybean cultivation. As much as 70 percent of areas newly cleared for agriculture in Mato Grosso State in Brazil is being used to grow soybeans. Over half of Brazil's soy harvest is controlled by a handful of international agribusiness companies, which ship it all over the world for animal feed and food products, causing emissions in the process.

Meat and dairy eaters need not be part of this. Many smaller, traditional farms and ranches in the United States have scant connection to carbon dioxide emissions because they keep their animals outdoors on pasture and make little use of machinery.

Moreover, those farmers generally use less soy than industrial operations do, and those who do often grow their own, so there are no emissions from long-distance transport and zero chance their farms contributed to deforestation in the developing world.

In contrast to traditional farms, industrial livestock and poultry facilities keep animals in buildings with mechanized systems for feeding, lighting, sewage flushing, ventilation, heating, and cooling, all of which generate emissions. These factory farms are also soy guzzlers and acquire much of their feed overseas. You can reduce your contribution to carbon dioxide emissions by avoiding industrially produced meat and dairy products.

Unfortunately for vegetarians who rely on it for protein, avoiding soy from deforested croplands may be more difficult: as the Organic Consumers

Association notes, Brazilian soy is common (and unlabeled) in tofu and soy-milk sold in American supermarkets.

Methane is agriculture's second-largest greenhouse gas. Wetland rice 11 fields alone account for as much as 29 percent of the world's human-generated methane. In animal farming, much of the methane comes from lagoons of liquefied manure at industrial facilities, which are as nauseating as they sound.

This isn't a problem at traditional farms. "Before the 1970s, methane 12 emissions from manure were minimal because the majority of livestock farms in the U.S. were small operations where animals deposited manure in pastures and corrals," the Environmental Protection Agency says. The E.P.A. found that with the rapid rise of factory farms, liquefied manure systems became the norm and methane emissions skyrocketed. You can reduce your methane emissions by seeking out meat from animals raised outdoors on traditional farms.

Critics of meat-eating often point out that cattle are prime culprits in 13 methane production. Fortunately, the cause of these methane emissions is understood, and their production can be reduced.

Much of the problem arises when livestock eat poor-quality forages, 14 throwing their digestive systems out of balance. Livestock nutrition experts have demonstrated that by making minor improvements in animal diets (like providing nutrient-laden salt licks) they can cut enteric methane by half. Other practices, like adding certain proteins to ruminant diets, can reduce methane production per unit of milk or meat by a factor of six, according to research at Australia's University of New England. Enteric methane emissions can also be substantially reduced when cattle are regularly rotated onto fresh pastures, researchers at University of Louisiana have confirmed.

Finally, livestock farming plays a role in nitrous oxide emissions, which 15 make up around 5 percent of this country's total greenhouse gases. More than three-quarters of farming's nitrous oxide emissions result from manmade fertilizers. Thus, you can reduce nitrous oxide emissions by buying meat and dairy products from animals that were not fed fertilized crops—in other words, from animals raised on grass or raised organically.

In contrast to factory farming, well-managed, non-industrialized animal 16 farming minimizes greenhouse gases and can even benefit the environment. For example, properly timed cattle grazing can increase vegetation by as much as 45 percent, North Dakota State University researchers have found. And grazing by large herbivores (including cattle) is essential for well-functioning prairie ecosystems, research at Kansas State University has determined.

Additionally, several recent studies show that pasture and grassland areas 17 used for livestock reduce global warming by acting as carbon sinks. Converting croplands to pasture, which reduces erosion, effectively sequesters significant amounts of carbon. One analysis published in the journal *Global Change Biology* showed a 19 percent increase in soil carbon after land changed from cropland to pasture. What's more, animal grazing reduces the need for the fertilizers and fuel used by farm machinery in crop cultivation, things that aggravate climate change.

Livestock grazing has other noteworthy environmental benefits as well. 18 Compared to cropland, perennial pastures used for grazing can decrease soil erosion by 80 percent and markedly improve water quality, Minnesota's Land Stewardship Project research has found. Even the United Nations report acknowledges, "There is growing evidence that both cattle ranching and pastoralism can have positive impacts on biodiversity."

As the contrast between the environmental impact of traditional farming 19 and industrial farming shows, efforts to minimize greenhouse gases need to be much more sophisticated than just making blanket condemnations of certain foods. Farming methods vary tremendously, leading to widely variable global warming contributions for every food we eat. Recent research in Sweden shows that, depending on how and where a food is produced, its carbon dioxide emissions vary by a factor of 10.

And it should also be noted that farmers bear only a portion of the blame 20 for greenhouse gas emissions in the food system. Only about one-fifth of the food system's energy use is farm-related, according to University of Wisconsin research. And the Soil Association in Britain estimates that only half of food's total greenhouse impact has any connection to farms. The rest comes from processing, transportation, storage, retailing, and food preparation. The seemingly innocent potato chip, for instance, turns out to be a dreadfully climate-hostile food. Foods that are minimally processed, in season and locally grown, like those available at farmers' markets and backyard gardens, are generally the most climate-friendly.

Rampant waste at the processing, retail, and household stages compounds 21 the problem. About half of the food produced in the United States is thrown away, according to University of Arizona research. Thus, a consumer could measurably reduce personal global warming impact simply by more judicious grocery purchasing and use.

None of us, whether we are vegan or omnivore, can entirely avoid foods 22 that play a role in global warming. Singling out meat is misleading and unhelpful, especially since few people are likely to entirely abandon animal-based foods. Mr. Gore, for one, apparently has no intention of going vegan. The 90 percent of Americans who eat meat and dairy are likely to respond the same way.

Still, there are numerous reasonable ways to reduce our individual contri- 23 butions to climate change through our food choices. Because it takes more resources to produce meat and dairy than, say, fresh locally grown carrots, it's sensible to cut back on consumption of animal-based foods. More important, all eaters can lower their global warming contribution by following these simple rules: avoid processed foods and those from industrialized farms; reduce food waste; and buy local and in season.

⊙ READING ARGUMENTS

1. Where does Niman use an appeal to *ethos*? What role does this appeal play in her argument?

2. Where does Niman address arguments against her position? Are her refutations of these opposing arguments effective? Why or why not? How would you characterize her attitude toward those who disagree with her?

3. What kinds of specific evidence does Niman use to support her points? What other kinds of evidence could she use?

4. According to Niman, how can we "reduce our individual contributions to climate change" (para. 23)?

5. What different argumentative strategies does Niman use in this essay? For example, in what respects is this essay a cause-and-effect argument? What other strategies does she use?

Payne's essay appeared on TheFederalist.com on June 24, 2014.

WHY YOU SHOULD EAT "HUMANE" MEAT

DANIEL PAYNE

While driving around Richmond the other day, I noticed, on the back of a car, 1
a remarkably candid bumper sticker: "Humane meat is yuppie bullshit," it claimed, and advised the reader to "ask any cow" to confirm this.

Judging by the license plate above this profound eight-word manifesto, 2
the driver of the vehicle was an adherent of straight-edge veganism, a philosophy which, if you're not in the know, combines the absolute worst aspects of both Jainism and alternative music: straight-edge vegans consume no meat (indeed, no animal products at all), drink no alcohol, and obsess over a preachy sub-genre of hardcore music that, to any reasonable observer, is patently unlistenable. You will know if you ever encounter one of these mosh-happy latter-day Temperance Leaguers, if only because you will remember the fervency and the tiresome moral zeal with which they endure their uninspiring diet and their atrocious music.

But back to that erudite bumper sticker: "Humane meat is yuppie bullshit." 3
The logic being, of course, that no meat can be "humane," if only because eating meat involves killing animals, and killing animals is allegedly wrong. There are a great many interesting and compelling arguments in favor of vegetarianism, and maybe (maybe) even one or two to be made in favor of veganism;

nevertheless, there are many more arguments in favor of eating animals, and they are better than the ones the vegetarians and vegans make. Humans will probably always eat animals, and this is, in the end, as it should be.

But it remains a valid question as to *how* humans shall eat the meat they will inevitably consume, and in this regard I will disagree with the percipient slogan to be found on the vegan bumper sticker: "humane" meat is great, it is ethically logical, and it should be what you're eating if you're eating animals.   4

> "Humans will probably always eat animals, and this is, in the end, as it should be."

What Is "Humane Meat"?

First, let's define what "humane meat" really means. The definition changes a little bit depending upon the animals, but for nearly all farm livestock it will mean a life spent entirely on pasture (aside from the short trip to the slaughterhouse), with abundant room to move and engage in habits and tendencies specific to its evolutionary biology. That's a mouthful (meat always is), but it's a fairly accurate summation of what my brother and sister-in-law refer to as "happy meat."   5

One must be so specific because a fairly successful advertising campaign utilizes clever marketing language such as "all natural" and "farm fresh," utterly meaningless phrases, to trick you into thinking you're getting something you're not. Shopping for price is always wise; shopping against hucksterism should be encouraged, as well. If one is committed to eating humanely, one needs to be as judicious a customer as many companies wish you not to be.   6

What would this look like in practice? Taking as an example the lovely farm outside of Richmond from which I get most of my meat and dairy, this means beef and dairy cows on grass for their entire lives, eating from the same; laying hens and meat birds on grass as well, fed from both the pasture floor and the grain supplement they receive; and pigs both wallowing in paddocks and wandering in a nearby forest (if you've got one of the latter). These kinds of farms are invariably local, which means you'll probably find most of this kind of meat at the nearest farmer's market.   7

There are a number of truly excellent national suppliers from which you can order this type of meat in bulk, if you've no good farm nearby, but buying local from the market is easier, and more viscerally appealing: a great deal of ink has been spilled singing the praises of "getting to know your farmer," but truthfully, there really is something to be said for it. There is a reason we feel so special when we personally know the chef who's preparing our food, after all—then, too, there is a reason your mother's cooking tastes so uniquely good.   8

Isn't This Some Sort of Gimmick?

The $64,000 question, which invariably and appropriately arises, is: Why should we eat this way? It is more expensive, after all, and while there are many more farmers' markets than there used to be, they are still less conve-   9 nient than the nearby supermarket or Wal-mart, the latter two of which offer a greater abundance and variety of meats—of foods in general—than humanity has ever known. Why give up getting your meat as conveniently and as cheaply as possible?

Simply put, the convenience and price advantage afforded by industrial food does not justify the suffering to which industrial farm animals are subject. It *cannot*, unless we are prepared to invert the concepts of both suffering and justification: modern factory farms are hellhouses of animal suffering writ large. The literature with which vegetarians and vegans often make their points, while wrong in its desired outcome, is nonetheless correct about the circumstances it unveils. Pig factory farming, in particular, is a uniquely brutal form of torture to inflict upon a very intelligent type of animal, cramming pigs into slum tenement conditions, forcing pregnant sows into brutal gestation crates, and creating conditions ripe for the abuse of animals. Cows are forced into similar crowded conditions on their own factory farms and made to eat a diet of grain that makes them sick, and they must wade around in a knee-deep, toxic sea of their own waste while they're doing it. Chickens raised for meat in an industrial setting are, as usual, crowded into impossibly dense conditions, and they often suffer from skeletal problems and organ failure due to how fast they grow; their lot, however, is roses compared with laying hens, which are subject to conditions that can only be described as nightmarish. 10

And of course, the industrial farm feeds into the industrial slaughter-house, which is usually the apex of factory farm suffering. It is almost impossible to have avoided seeing at least one surreptitious PETA video of industrial abattoirs—and what one usually sees is unmitigated misery in shocking abundance. Surely many animals enter and exit the slaughterhouse with blessed unawareness; it is doubtless that many are processed with a Prussian efficiency that allows for minimal suffering. Nevertheless, the industrial system has permitted animal agony in spades, and it has shown little inclination to curb the worst of its abuses in any systematic sense. That is to say, the system itself begets the problems, and the overseers of factory farming have no desire to change the system. 11

No Need for Government Regulation

The standard response for many is to stop eating meat, or, if you're an utterly simpleminded Progressive or left-liberal, to call for more government regulation of the agriculture industry (as if it wasn't already regulated enough). There is a better solution, one that acknowledges the healthy benefits and the basic ethicality of eating meat and also recognizes the flagrant inability of the U.S. government to do anything right. Humanely raised meat does not allow for these savage abuses of morality and of nature's and God's design. Most humane farmers, after all, are, well, *humane*, and in any event there is no efficiency in abusing your animals within these types of operations: when nature is respected and good ethics are followed, you tend not to have any need or desire to be cruel to your livestock. 12

It is true that this type of eating is more expensive, and there are a number 13 of reasonable objections to a heftier price tag for any kind of food. One of the most frequent that I have heard, for instance, is that local, humanely raised meat is too expensive for poorer people to purchase, so we should not encourage it as a viable agricultural model. This is a concerning and valid complaint to the higher expense to be found in humane meat, and we should certainly be aware of the price tag that can act as a barrier for low-income people to buying any good product. Nevertheless, poor peoples' tight budgets are a strange reason to beg off doing the right thing yourself, and in any event most of the things we take for granted today, such as refrigerators and dishwashers and computers, were at first completely unaffordable for the poor.

More farmers, and hence more competition, may lower the price of such 14 food in the future; it is also worthwhile to fight against asinine government regulations that make good meats harder and more expensive to obtain for rich, middle-class, and poor people alike. In the meantime, if you can afford humane meat, you should buy it. With all due respect to low-income folks, it is fairly silly to try and align your purchasing habits with the poor in order to effect an odd display of solidarity with them. Even poor people would probably agree.

This kind of devotion to ethical treatment can be taken too far (to 15 vegetarianism or veganism, say), but it doesn't have to be. I have eaten factory-farmed meat on numerous occasions when nothing else was available. I will not go hungry or lightheaded in order to prove a point. I do try and eat as best as I can whenever I can: like Harvey Ussery, the modern guru of small-scale chicken farming, I try and eat seafood if there is no "good" meat available, usually when I'm on the road, if only because the seafood I eat is usually wild-caught and, from what I understand, much less prone to feel pain and suffering than are land animals. Nevertheless, all but a vanishing fraction of my meat and dairy products come from the type of farms I feel are best for both the animals and for the ethical justification of eating them.

There are a host of other reasons to eat like this; it supports the farm- 16 ers, for one (American industrial farming rests upon an impossibly idiotic set of economic pillars, and American industrial farmers can barely make enough money off of their product to survive); there is also abundant evidence that grass-fed beef, for one, is far healthier than its industrial cousin. That being said, the best initial reason to start eating humanely is that switching to this kind of meat will end a great deal of physical agony and psychological torment for a great number of animals. Contra the bumper sticker to which I was treated, "humane meat" is not "yuppie bullshit"; it is, rather, a wonderful recognition that the animals that provide us with healthy, life-giving food deserve not to be subject to torment and agony and immeasurable misery. Vegans and vegetarians may have a problem with dead animals, but for meat eaters, it is crucial that we consider them while they are alive.

⊘ READING ARGUMENTS

1. In paragraph 2, Payne defines "straight-edge veganism," a set of beliefs that he assigns to the driver of the car with the "Humane meat is yuppie bullshit" bumper sticker. How does he define this philosophy? Do you find his approach in this paragraph persuasive? Why or why not?

2. How would you describe Payne's style and tone in this essay? Do you find it appealing? Is it appropriate for the subject of his argument? Explain.

3. What purpose is paragraph 3 intended to serve? Do you think it achieves this purpose? Why or why not?

4. Who is the intended audience for this essay—vegetarians, meat-eaters, or both? What makes you think so?

5. Payne implies that vegetarians are committing a logical fallacy in response to the suffering in factory farms. What is this fallacy? Do you think he is right?

YES! Magazine published this essay in its Spring 2011 edition.

HUMANE MEAT? NO SUCH THING

SUNAURA TAYLOR

I recently debated Nicolette Hahn Niman at an art event in California. Niman 1
is a cattle rancher and author of *Righteous Porkchop*. I am a 28-year-old disabled artist, writer, and vegan. The event was held in a largely inaccessible building in front of an audience that had just dined on grass-fed beef—a rather ironic scenario for a wheelchair-using animal advocate like me!

[handwritten: interesting way to situate his credibility.]

My perspective as a disabled person and as a disability scholar profoundly 2
influences my views on animals. The field of disability studies raises questions that are equally valid in the animal-rights discussion. What is the best way to protect the rights of those who are not physically autonomous but are vulnerable and interdependent? How can society protect the rights of those who cannot protect their own, or those who can't understand the concept of a right?

[handwritten: so – disabled people are like animals?]

Throughout the debate I argued that limited interpretations of what is 3
natural and normal lead to the continued oppression of both disabled people and animals. Of the 50 billion animals killed every year for human use, many are literally manufactured to be disabled—bred to be "mutant" producers of meat, milk, eggs, and other products but unable to function in many ways.

Niman and her family are leading proponents for raising animals 4
humanely for slaughter. But during the debate, we agreed on something rather

surprising—a basic tenet of animal rights: Animals are sentient, thinking, feeling beings, often with complex emotions, abilities, and relationships. We agreed that livestock animals can experience deep suffering and pleasure.

Former cattlemen Howard Lyman and Harold Brown also agree that ani- 5 mals are sentient, but this realization led them to become vegan. They gave up their livelihoods and risked alienation from their communities for something greater: their consciences.

Lyman and Brown reject animal slaughter on both practical and moral 6 grounds. They point out that meat is not necessary for human health, a position endorsed by organizations from the World Health Organization to the American Dietetic Association. They cite growing evidence that animal agriculture is a major contributor to environmental problems; A 2009 report from Worldwatch Institute estimated that livestock production generates close to 51 percent of global greenhouse gases.

But Lyman and Brown go beyond the merely practical: An animal, they 7 say, is not a piece of property for human beings to use but instead an individual creature living a life that should belong to him or her alone. As Brown says on his website, "Animal rights, to me, is quite simply respecting animals as the sentient beings that they are."

But Niman—along with others who support sustainable meat—says 8 that animals' emotions are not an argument against eating meat—just an argument against cruelty. These conscientious omnivores argue that the justification for meat-eating lies elsewhere. They say we must overcome our empathy with an individual animal's will to live to grasp something greater—Nature.

Nature is one of the most common justifications for animal exploitation. 9 The arguments range from romantic declarations about the cycles of nature to nuanced discussions of sustainable farming. But the assertion that something is "natural" (or "unnatural") has long been used to rationalize terrible things.

As a disabled person I find arguments based on what's "natural" highly 10 problematic. Throughout history and all over the world, I would have, at worst, been killed at birth or, at best, culturally marginalized—and nature would have been a leading justification.

Disability is often seen as a personal tragedy that naturally leads to mar- 11 ginalization, rather than as a political and civil rights issue. Many people now reject using "nature" to justify things like sexism, white supremacy, and homophobia but still accept it as a rationale for animal exploitation and disability discrimination.

Michael Pollan, one of the pioneers of the conscientious food movement, 12 would say I am missing the point when I apply human standards to animals. Pollan argues that animal husbandry isn't oppression but rather a "mutualism or symbiosis between species"—the very reason domesticated animals exist. But our understanding of nature cannot be separated from human culture and biases, especially because we understand nature through a long and pervasive historical paradigm of human domination over animals.

The distinction that Pollan makes is especially troubling when one con- 13
siders that slavery and patriarchy were both seen as simply natural at one time.
The argument that co-evolution justifies animal exploitation is similar to an
argument that patriarchy is justified by thousands of years of history, culture,
and genetics. One cannot argue that the domesticated animal chose slaughter
any more than one could argue that women chose patriarchy.

Niman uses nature as a justification for animal slaughter in another way, 14
arguing that, since it is normal and natural for animals to eat other animals
and humans are animals, we are justified in eating meat. But violent, painful
deaths are also "normal and natural" in nature. Would Niman argue that we
have no moral obligation to kill animals humanely?

Niman and others have suggested that vegans aren't helping to change the 15
world's food production systems, whereas conscientious omnivores are. I'd
suggest it's the opposite. For a movement that supposedly advocates eating
minimal meat, the humane-meat movement sure praises and glorifies the
stuff. Trendy, socially conscious events serve sustainable animal products,
while articles praise the mouthwatering taste, showing glamorous photos of
young hipster butchers and "compassionate" farmers.

Of course all of these articles mention that we need to be eating less and 16
better meat, but one doesn't have to be an advertising expert to see that what is
being sold is "delicious" animal foods—not lentils and kale.

A 2008 Carnegie Mellon University study showed that avoiding red meat 17
and dairy one day a week achieves more greenhouse gas reductions than eating a week's worth of local food. A vegan is also able to easily buy organic and
local or, if that's not possible, to buy fair trade, which, according to the book
The Ethics of What We Eat, is arguably just as environmentally vital as buying
organic and local, if you are considering issues of global justice.

Studies show that being a vegan or a conscientious omnivore (whose ani- 18
mal products actually come from small, sustainable farms) are about equal in
environmental impact.

But I believe we must weigh environmental impact against other ethical 19
concerns, such as the treatment of animals and global access to food and
water. The more important question is which diet is more just for animals and
more realistic for a planet with nearly 7 billion people and counting? The
Worldwatch Institute calls for quick replacement of livestock products with
other protein sources. Scientists are not saying that sustainable animal farming can't be done, but many are saying that it's not a realistic solution for a
planet as hungry as ours.

Another argument is that veganism isn't realistic—that we can't grow sus- 20
tainable food without farm animals. The principal claim is that manure is necessary to maintain soil fertility. But animals do not need to be killed to poop.
In fact all of the supposedly necessary effects that domesticated animals have
on crops and soil come while the animals are alive.

Even if a practical argument in favor of eating small amounts of meat can 21 be made—whether based on soil fertility or on use of land that can't support food crops—that doesn't answer the moral argument against it.

In fact, vegan-organic farming may be a realistic option. Farmers in the 22 United Kingdom have developed a certification process for "stock-free" farming, a term that "broadly means any system of cultivation that excludes artificial chemicals, livestock manures, animal remains," and so forth. Humans have not prioritized farming methods that minimize harm to animals so we actually have no idea what is possible. That animal-free methods are not widely known says more about the belief in human domination over animals than it does about the possibility of sustainable, compassionate agriculture.

Humane meat is an oxymoron— and it seems that its advocates' consciences know it. Conscientious omnivores appear to struggle with their own empathy toward animals: From Michael Pollan overcoming his hesitance and shame in hunting a wild boar, to newspaper stories on the new meat movement where people try to overcome their uneasiness about killing animals by taking a butchering class, to the Nimans' own stories of their grief when sending their animals to slaughter. 23

> "Humane meat is an oxymoron—and it seems that its advocates' consciences know it."

Ex-cattlemen like Lyman and Brown show that empathy should be some- 24 thing that human beings have toward animals not only while they are living on our farms or after they have been killed and are on our plates being thanked or prayed over, but at that crucial moment when the decision is made to kill them for food or not.

Nicolette Hahn Niman and I agree about the horrors of factory farming. 25 We also agree on the importance of environmentally sustainable agricultural practices. But I don't agree with her that slaughtering sentient animals for food is righteous—even if it's done on a small family farm.

There are better ways to be humane. 26

⊖ READING ARGUMENTS

1. In her opening paragraph, Taylor—who uses a wheelchair—notes that her debate with Nicolette Hahn Niman (p. 699) "was held in a largely inaccessible building in front of an audience that had just dined on grass-fed beef." Why does she include these details? Do they strengthen her argument? Explain.

2. As a person with a disability, Taylor makes a strong appeal to *ethos* in this essay. Identify specific places where she does so. What does she hope to achieve with this kind of appeal? Is she successful? Explain.

3. Where does Taylor use analogy to make a point? Do you find her comparison(s) effective? Why or why not?

4. Where does Taylor introduce moral arguments against meat-eating? What are these arguments?

5. Does Taylor's essay include any elements of Rogerian argument? If so, where?

6. In paragraph 23, Taylor claims that "humane meat is an oxymoron." What is an *oxymoron*? Why is this concept important to her argument?

⊘AT ISSUE: SHOULD WE EAT MEAT?

1. In paragraph 9, Taylor writes, "Nature is one of the most common justifications for animal exploitation," and in paragraphs 12–14, she gives specific examples of this justification from humane meat advocates such as Nicolette Hahn Niman. What other examples can you identify? Do you believe that saying our behavior is natural is enough to justify our eating meat? Why or why not?

2. To a greater or lesser degree, all of the writers in this casebook use logic and evidence to make their arguments, but how effective are appeals to *logos* in the context of this topic? As Foer points out, "Food is not rational. Food is culture, habit, craving, and identity" (para. 18). How are your own eating practices—including the decision whether to eat meat—shaped by "culture, habit, craving, and identity"? Are these practices open to persuasion and argument? Explain.

⊘WRITING ARGUMENTS: SHOULD WE EAT MEAT?

All of the writers in this casebook consider the ethics of eating. Foer examines a number of implicitly moral standards that supposedly guide food choices—for instance, "Don't eat animals with significant mental capacities" (para. 9); Niman considers the environmental consequences of eating meat, with an implied ethical assumption that people should reduce their "individual contributions to climate change" (23); Taylor refers explicitly to the "moral argument" against eating meat (21); and Payne considers the "ethical justification" for eating animals (15). Write an argumentative essay in which you take a position on the issue of eating meat. Do you think it is morally and ethically acceptable? Be sure to address opposing arguments presented by the writers in this casebook.

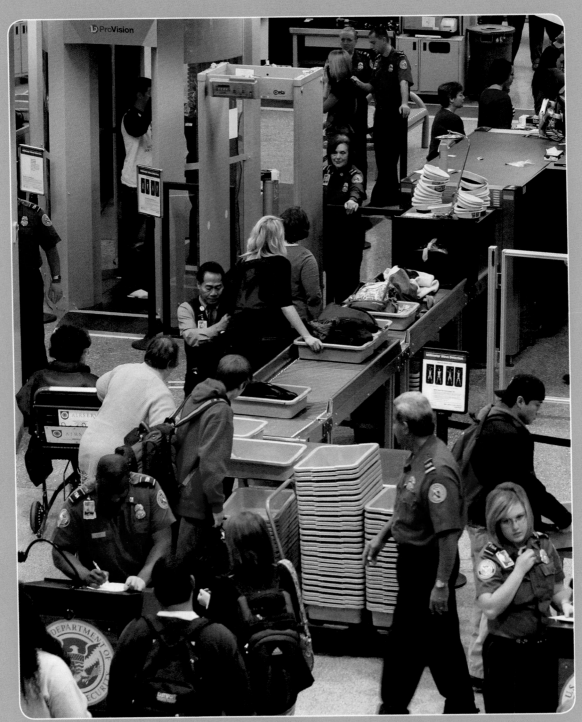

Bloomberg/Getty Images

Is America Safer Now Than Before 9/11?

In a speech on the tenth anniversary of the September 11, 2001, terrorist attacks, former New York mayor Rudolph W. Giuliani said, "As with Pearl Harbor and the John F. Kennedy assassination, these defining events have a big impact on a nation because they're not just a shared experience; they're a shared memory." There is no doubt that the attacks profoundly affected our country's policies, politics, economy, society, and even collective psychology. Moreover, in addition to sharing the immediate experience of September 11, Americans have dealt with its consequences in the years since.

In the immediate aftermath of 9/11, the United States heightened security at home while applying military force overseas. In Afghanistan, the United States toppled the ruling Taliban (a regime that provided sanctuary for al-Qaeda) and in 2003 began the politically contentious Iraq war. President George W. Bush set forth the nation's new challenges in a speech to Congress, saying, "Our war on terror begins with al-Qaeda, but it does not end there. It will not end until every terrorist group of global reach has been found, stopped, and defeated."

Most Americans have experienced the long-term effects of 9/11 through the actions of new agencies, such as the Transportation Security Administration and the Department of Homeland Security, as well as the provisions of the Patriot Act. For example, Americans have grown accustomed to removing their shoes and submitting to invasive searches at airport security checkpoints. In addition to these relatively obvious responses to the threat of terrorism, a large, complex, expensive, and largely hidden security apparatus has come into being. According to a 2010 *Washington Post* report, "Some 1,271 government organizations and 1,931 private companies work on programs related to counterterrorism, homeland security, and intelligence in about 10,000 locations across the United States." All this comes at considerable cost—over $1 trillion since the 9/11 attacks. Given that at least thirty planned terrorist attacks have been thwarted since that time, many argue that the government's actions are justified. Others worry about excessive—and possibly unconstitutional—infringements of privacy and civil liberties in the name of national security. The basic question, however, still remains: even with all these measures, are Americans really any safer now than they were before 9/11?

The four essays in this casebook evaluate the nation's long-term responses to the September 11, 2001 attacks. In "Ten Years after 9/11, We're Still in the Dark," Omar Ashmawy, a U.S. Air Force veteran, examines America's approach to interrogating and detaining suspected terrorists, claiming, "After so many years and so much sacrifice, nothing has changed" (para. 1). In "Remembering 9/11: How Safe Are We Today?" Paul Brandus lists the major terrorist attacks that have occurred since 2001 but still asserts that Americans' level of fear is not really justified. Jonathan Rauch agrees, questioning the extent of our fear and even asserting, in "Be Not Afraid," "Never have so many feared so little, so much" (para. 13). Finally, in "The TSA Has Never Kept You Safe: Here's Why," Christopher Elliott reports on a test of TSA screening that revealed its ineffectiveness but argues that the agency's purpose was never to keep the United States safe.

This essay was published in the *Washington Post* on September 9, 2010.

TEN YEARS AFTER 9/11, WE'RE STILL IN THE DARK

OMAR ASHMAWY

I joined the U.S. military after law school to help my country defend itself 1 against the threat of Islamic extremism. My final assignment in my eight years in the Air Force was as a war crimes prosecutor in Guantanamo Bay, Cuba. With access to our nation's most intimate secrets, I shuttled between Guantanamo and the Pentagon from the summer of 2007 to the winter of 2009. I learned many lessons, but on the anniversary of the Sept. 11 attacks, the most important lesson I can share is the most alarming: After so many years and so much sacrifice, nothing has changed.

Our greatest weakness remains today what it was 10 years ago, and what it 2 was eight years before that, when the World Trade Center was bombed in 1993. We don't understand Islam or Arab culture, and that ignorance prevents us from accurately predicting our relationship with Arab and Muslim countries and identifying our enemies.

From our government to the front lines, individuals are making decisions 3 based on inaccurate, biased information. The White House's August announcement on combating radical Islam acknowledged this reality. Our soldiers, agents, and analysts don't have the facts they need to make informed decisions about whom to trust, what to believe, and how to keep the threat at bay.

Whether it's the FBI recommending its agents read books by a known 4 anti-Muslim author, misplaced anxiety over "sharia law," the near absence of linguistic and cultural training in the military, or our government's collective surprise at the Arab Spring, the effect of what we don't know reverberates through U.S. policy. But the result is the same: We are caught off guard by events we should have anticipated, or, worse, we confuse our enemy's propaganda with knowledge.

> "We are caught off guard by events we should have anticipated."

As an American Muslim born and raised in New Jersey, I am frustrated 5 that America still struggles with the basics: We don't understand the difference between Islam and Islamic extremism or that Arab culture is not the same as the religion. We divide Muslims into secularists and extremists and can't tell the devout from the radical, the sympathizer from the opportunist.

Two of the most enduring examples are the military commissions and 6 Guantanamo Bay—intractable problems that will never be resolved to anyone's satisfaction. They're once and future disasters built by people who should have known better—people America trusted to know more. Both were operated and sustained by individuals so uninformed of our enemy's religion, language, and culture that they could not accurately process the information available to them. Attorneys couldn't tell good cases from bad ones, and the agents assigned to the commissions didn't know what questions to ask detainees.

I saw it firsthand. From lawyers to interrogators, the vacuum was enormous. It filled Guantanamo Bay with men who did not need to be there and 7 barred their release. It was fuel on a fire set by a legal process that initially conflated the mutually exclusive missions of intelligence-gathering and the rendering of justice. The absence of knowledge and leadership permitted the worst of what happened—reports of the abuse of prisoners, the desecration of holy books, the legal pantomimes—and continues to prevent a resolution to the human drama playing out on that island.

We cannot close Guantanamo because the trials of the detainees who 8 remain would be tainted by evidence from botched interrogations and because the men there are now radicalized—the result of decisions based in an ignorance tantamount to racism.

This ignorance is a degenerative disease that debilitates our efforts to protect our nation. It was tempting to think that with Osama bin Laden's death 9 we could end this conflict, if only we could end the wars in Iraq and Afghanistan. While those wars must be concluded, neither their end nor the death of any individual terrorist will secure us against another attack by Islamic extremists. We're not fighting a single enemy but a decentralized patchwork of groups that adhere to the same twisted, bankrupt ideology. Whether it is Jemaah Islamiah in Southeast Asia or al-Shabab in Somalia, our enemies are motivated and wait—patiently—until we forget.

As we honor the past, we must also commit to the future. This commit- 10 ment must include an expectation that all Americans responsible for protecting us possess the education and knowledge to do so and be committed to accuracy and learning. A good place to start would be language and culture training for our soldiers, and training in Islam and Arab culture and history for policy-makers. Similar education should be made available to local law enforcement and community leaders. At the height of the Cold War, we encouraged our best and brightest to study Russian language and history. Ten years after Sept. 11, this is a basic but necessary step. Ignorance is our vulnerability, and we must begin somewhere. Those individuals we remember Sunday deserve better. We all do.

◑ READING ARGUMENTS

1. In what sense is this essay an evaluation argument? In what respects is it a proposal argument? Identify the specific elements of each argumentative strategy.

2. According to Ashmawy, what is the United States' "greatest weakness" (para. 2) in dealing with the threat of terrorism?

3. Ashmawy uses first-person plural pronouns (such as *we* and *our*) in this essay, particularly in paragraphs 2–5. Why do you think he does this? Does this choice strengthen his argument? Why or why not?

4. Where in this essay does Ashmawy appeal to *ethos*? Why is his personal background important to his argument?

This article was published online at TheWeek.com on September 11, 2013.

REMEMBERING 9/11: HOW SAFE ARE WE TODAY?

PAUL BRANDUS

As we mark the 12th anniversary of the September 11, 2001, terror attacks, 1 and honor the memory of the nearly 3,000 people who died that day, I think of the debate we've had this year on our security, and just how much privacy we have given up over the years to be (or at least feel) safer.

More than a decade after the towers fell, the Pentagon burned, and a 2 Pennsylvania field was scarred, we still don't feel all that much safer. A Gallup survey taken in April said 40 percent of Americans are either "very worried" or "somewhat worried" about terrorism. Just 10 days after the 2001 attacks? 49 percent.

This makes no sense when you consider how few people have actually ₃ died on U.S. soil from terrorist attacks since September 11, 2001. First, let's define "terrorism." The federal government's National Counterterrorism Center (NCTC) calls it "premeditated, politically motivated violence, perpetrated against noncombatant targets by subnational groups or clandestine agents." Using this benchmark, I argue that the number is 35:

> Fall 2001: Five people die in a series of anthrax attacks.
>
> July 4, 2002: Two Israelis are killed at Los Angeles airport.
>
> July 28, 2006: One woman is killed in an attack on a Jewish organization in Seattle.
>
> July 27, 2008: Two people are killed in an attack on a church in Knoxville, Tennessee.
>
> May 30, 2009: Three people, all members of the same family, are killed by a militia group.
>
> May 31, 2009: An abortion doctor is gunned down in church.
>
> June 1, 2009: One soldier is killed at a recruiting center in Arkansas.
>
> June 10, 2009: One man is killed in a shooting at the National Holocaust Museum in Washington, D.C.
>
> November 5, 2009: 13 soldiers are killed during a shooting rampage at Fort Hood, Texas.
>
> February 18, 2010: One person is killed after a man flies a small plane into an IRS facility in Austin, Texas.
>
> September 23, 2011: A man is killed in his home during an attack by three members of the Aryan Brotherhood.
>
> April 15, 2013: Three people die in the Boston Marathon bombing; a fourth person—a policeman—is shot and killed three days later.

Again, in 12 years, only 35 deaths from terrorist acts. That's less than three a year.

Now, I'm not including such horrors as the 2002 sniper shootings in the ₄ Washington area (10 killed) or last December's elementary school massacre in Connecticut (27, not counting the killer). These incidents certainly terrorized their respective communities and instilled fear—but we're using the NCTC's narrower definition of "politically motivated violence" here.

Now let's add the number of Americans killed in terrorist attacks abroad. ₅ The NCTC has been collecting this data since 2005, and says between then and 2011, 158 U.S. lives were lost—with the vast majority occurring in Iraq and Afghanistan. Unless you plan on traveling to Helmand province in the near future, you probably have nothing to worry about.

Here's the bottom line: Your odds of getting killed in a terrorist attack are ₆ absurdly low: about one in 20 million. You're far more likely to meet your demise from a bee sting, gun, car accident—or from behavior that you can control: smoking, sitting on the couch stuffing your face with junk food, not exercising.

So why do tens of millions of Americans worry about terrorism? Because ₇ humans, flawed creatures that we are, don't consider probabilities with level-headed analytical reasoning. We do so with our emotions. Terrorism is meant to intimidate us, and for many, that's exactly what it does.

But there is less reason to be fearful today, in my view, because we're doing a much better job of countering the threat. Let's remember that the 19 hijackers who changed our world a dozen years ago were in many cases living right under our noses. Had we been less complacent about our security and more competent about connecting the dots, it's entirely possible, if not probable, that the attack never would have happened. As for the tradeoff we have made between civil liberty and national security ever since, I suspect that's one reason why the death toll from terrorism is so low.

> "Terrorism is meant to intimidate us, and for many, that's exactly what it does."

Since 2001, some plots—the Times Square bomber, the underwear 9 bomber, and others—came close to succeeding; others were disrupted before they became operational. In 2001, I wondered what more could we have done; now we're doing it. There are more cameras watching us in public. The government we like to bash is doing a better job of data mining, sharing information, and being more proactive about disrupting possible threats. It has made mistakes and, yes, in some cases it has gone too far and there have been abuses. We live in an imperfect world. We can do better, and I'm confident we will.

And this, in the end, is the real tradeoff: What is going too far in the name 10 of security—and what is not far enough?

⊖ READING ARGUMENTS

1. Brandus believes that Americans should not fear an imminent terrorist attack. Why then does he include a long list of attacks in his essay? Does this list strengthen or weaken his argument? Explain.

2. In what respects is this essay an evaluation argument? In what respects is it a cause-and-effect argument?

3. In assessing the number of terrorist attacks since September 11, 2001, why does Brandus exclude "horrors" such as the 2002 sniper shootings around Washington, D.C., and the 2012 school shootings in Connecticut? Do you agree with his decision?

4. In paragraph 9, Brandus discusses the U.S. government's anti-terrorism measures, such as public surveillance and data mining. What point is he making here? Explain why you agree or disagree with him.

5. Do you think the December 2015 terrorist attack in San Bernardino, California (which occurred after Brandus wrote this essay), challenges this essay's thesis? Explain your reasoning.

This essay was published in the March 2015 issue of the *Atlantic.*

BE NOT AFRAID

JONATHAN RAUCH

It often befalls presidents to be most criticized in office for what later turn out 1
to have been their particular strengths. Disparaged at the time as simplemind-
edness, timidity, and slickness, Ronald Reagan's firmness, George H. W.
Bush's caution, and Bill Clinton's adaptability look in hindsight like features,
not bugs. (Unfortunately, George W. Bush's bugs still look like bugs.) President Obama catches flak for his supposed underreaction to crises in the Middle East, Ukraine, and elsewhere. Instead of leading, the professorial president
lectures the American public not to be so darned worried. "If you watch the
nightly news, it feels like the world is falling apart," he said last August. "I
promise you things are much less dangerous now than they were 20 years ago,
25 years ago, or 30 years ago. This is not something that is comparable to the
challenges we faced during the Cold War." Blame social media, he tells us, for
shoving so much upsetting stuff in our faces.

Naturally, Obama's pontifications draw protests. "I strongly disagree with 2
the president's assertion last night that America is safer," said Senator John
McCain. "By no objective measurement is America safer." Danger abounds! In
2012, General Martin Dempsey, the chairman of the Joint Chiefs of Staff, pronounced the world "more dangerous than it has ever been." That was before the
Islamic State, or ISIS, took over swaths of Iraq. Senator Lindsey Graham has
warned that failure to defeat ISIS "will open the gates of hell to spill out on the
world." Obama appears to have his doubts: a few months after Chuck Hagel,
then the defense secretary, pronounced ISIS an "imminent" threat, not just to
the United States but "to every stabilized country on Earth," Obama sacked him.

The American people deserve to 3
hear complex, multifaceted debates
about any number of complex, multifaceted matters. This is not one of them.
Obama is simply right. The alarmists
are simply wrong. America is safer than
it has ever been and very likely safer

> "America is safer than it has ever been and very likely safer than any country has ever been."

than any country has ever been, a fact that politicians and the public are curi-
ously reluctant to believe.

Danger is a broad category. In principle, it includes everything from 4
workplace accidents and natural disasters to infectious diseases and pollution.
In pretty much all of those categories, we're doing well, although we have
much work to do. For present purposes, however, let's limit ourselves to
threats in the usual political sense: malevolent violence against Americans.
The major menaces here would be warfare, crime, and terrorism.

Historically, warfare has been the biggest violent killer of humans. 5
According to Steven Pinker, the author of *The Better Angels of Our Nature: Why Violence Has Declined*, today is probably the most peaceful time in human history. By the numbers, he writes, "the world was a *far* more dangerous place" in the 1960s, '70s, and '80s. According to the Uppsala Conflict Data Program, armed conflicts have declined by almost 40 percent since right after the end of the Cold War. "Today," write Micah Zenko and Michael A. Cohen in *Foreign Affairs*, "wars tend to be low-intensity conflicts that, on average, kill about 90 percent fewer people than did violent struggles in the 1950s." War between major nation-states has dwindled to the verge of extinction. In the context of human evolution, this is an astounding development.

Of course, the world remains turbulent, but most of today's military con- 6
flict, as in Syria right now, takes the form of civil war rather than war between nations, and implicates American interests but not American lives (unless America enters the fighting). The United States faces no plausible military invader or attacker. All we are really talking about, when we discuss threats from Iran or North Korea or ISIS, is whether our margin of safety should be very large or even larger. "No great power in world history comes close to enjoying the traditional state security that the United States does today," writes Stephanie Rugolo in *A Dangerous World? Threat Perception and U.S. National Security*, a new collection of essays from the Cato Institute.

Here at home, criminal violence is, as ever, a serious problem. But its 7
reduction over the past couple of decades is one of the great success stories of our time. The violent-crime rate (which excludes homicides) has declined by more than 70 percent since the early 1990s. The homicide rate has declined by half, and in 2011 it reached the lowest level since 1963. According to the National Crime Victimization Survey, between 1995 and 2010 the rate of rape and sexual assault fell from five per 1,000 females to two.

And how do Americans celebrate this extraordinary success? By deny- 8
ing it. Every year Gallup asks whether crime has gone up or down since the previous year. Every year, rain or shine, the public insists, usually by overwhelming margins (63 percent to 21 percent in 2014), that crime has risen. "Most Americans Unaware of Big Crime Drop Since 1990s," announced the Pew Research Center in 2013; only 10 percent of those surveyed knew that gun crimes had gone down since the 1990s. Criminologists say that many people get angry when told that crime is decreasing.

Perception is even more skewed where terrorism is concerned. "Terror- 9
ism Worries Largely Unchanged," ran another Pew headline, also in 2013. That year, 58 percent of the public was worried about another terrorist attack in the United States, a rate not all that much lower in October 2001, immediately after the 9/11 attacks, when 71 percent of the public was worried. A few months ago, perhaps influenced by ISIS's atrocities, a large plurality of respondents told NBC News/*Wall Street Journal* pollsters that the country is less safe than it was before 9/11.

Reality, once again, tells us otherwise. State-sponsored international   10
terrorism, writes the intelligence analyst Paul R. Pillar in Cato's *A Dangerous
World?*, "is today only a shadow of what it was in the 1970s and 1980s."
As for the risk posed by terrorism inside the United States, to characterize it
as trivial would be very generous. Americans are about four times as likely to
drown in their bathtub as they are to die in a terrorist attack. John Mueller of
Ohio State University and Mark G. Stewart of Australia's University of New-
castle estimate the odds of such deaths at one in 950,000 and one in 3.5 million, respectively.

Surely we can at least agree to worry about a nuclear Iran, or nuclear ter-   11
rorism, or ISIS? All are indeed worrisome, but Mueller persuasively argues
that none merits the alarm it begets. Since Nagasaki in 1945, the few countries
that have obtained nuclear weapons—including dangerous rogue states like
Mao's China, the Iran of its day—have consistently found them militarily and
diplomatically useless, except as ego boosters and perhaps as defensive weapons to forestall attack. The odds of terrorists' obtaining and deploying nuclear
weapons are much lower than most people appreciate, for a host of technical
and political reasons. ISIS, meanwhile, is an unusually vicious and destabiliz-
ing actor in a region that is full of them, but its menace has been almost
entirely local. (In this issue's cover story, Graeme Wood examines this threat,
and the appropriate response, in detail.)

Pinker, a psychologist at Harvard, mused in a recent speech about   12
Americans' odd refusal to appreciate their security. The bad news for
Obama, if Pinker is correct, is that presidential palaver will have no effect,
because people are hardwired to overreact to threats, real or perceived. In
today's world, where intricate social systems keep us safer than our forebears
could ever have imagined, overreaction is maladaptive: it is often more disruptive and damaging than whatever provoked it. In the world we evolved
for, however, humans needed to be hyperalert. Something rustling in the
bush was more likely to be a predator or an enemy than a friend with glad
tidings. Moreover, Pinker says, people are biased to overestimate the likelihood of the sorts of events that stand out in our memory, as violence and
mayhem do, and as peace and quiet do not. Add alarmism's usefulness to
politicians and pressure groups, and you have a standing order for overreaction—always, not just now.

Still, now is special. Given how safe we are, and how frightened people   13
nonetheless feel, it seems unlikely that Americans' threat perception has ever
before been quite as distorted as it is today. Never have so many feared so little, so much. In an era of overreaction, a president who lectures the public
about its insecurities, instead of pandering to its fears, necessarily seems
impolitic, out of touch, tone-deaf, pedantic, negligent, complacent—choose
your adjective. For precisely that reason, we can be grateful his instinct is to
underreact. Historians will thank him, even if we don't, for his steadfastness in
the face of unprecedented safety.

❂ READING ARGUMENTS

1. What is Rauch's position on the issue of Americans' safety? Where does he state his thesis? Is this location the best choice? Why or why not?

2. In paragraph 6, Rauch concedes, "Of course, the world remains turbulent. . . ." How does he refute this statement, which seems to challenge his position?

3. Where does Rauch use definition? Why is definition essential to his overall argument?

4. What, according to Rauch, has been the "biggest violent killer of humans" (para. 5)? How is this "violent killer" different now from what it was in the past?

5. According to Rauch, what should Americans be worried about? What should we *not* be worried about? Why?

This article was published on Fortune.com, the website for *Fortune* magazine, on June 2, 2015.

THE TSA HAS NEVER KEPT YOU SAFE: HERE'S WHY

CHRISTOPHER ELLIOTT

The Transportation Security Administration's timing couldn't have been   1
any worse. Just a few days after the busy summer travel season started—a time when inexperienced and nervous air travelers clog the nation's airports—word leaked that the TSA screeners missed 95 percent of mock explosives and banned weapons smuggled through checkpoints by screeners testing the system.

And the reaction was swift. Department of Homeland Security Secretary   2
Jeh Johnson "reassigned" the TSA administrator, Melvin Carraway, and the president nominated Coast Guard Vice Admiral Pete Neffenger to the post. Meanwhile, critics called for the agency to be reformed or disbanded, which is a familiar refrain to anyone who watches the agency assigned to protect America's transportation systems.

The larger question is: What's wrong with airport security?   3

And the surprise answer is, absolutely nothing. TSA defenders will tell   4
you that there hasn't been a single successful terrorist attack on America's air-

ports since the creation of the agency in 2001. What's more, they'd point out that the recent assessments were conducted by the TSA's "red team," which routinely conducts covert tests at domestic airports, evaluating security systems, personnel, equipment, and procedures. The point isn't to embarrass the agency, but to get a snapshot of the effectiveness of airport passenger security checkpoint screening, among other things.

Put differently, members of the red team knew where to hide the dummy 5 explosives, because they're aware of the places screeners are less likely to look for them. Terrorists aren't.

But agency critics say the lack of a new terrorist attack doesn't mean the 6 TSA is doing its job. It simply means there hasn't been another successful terrorist attack. They point out that the agency is corrupt, inefficient, and constantly in the news for violating the civil rights of passengers. Even the most level-headed and patient detractors now believe the time for reform is long past and that the agency needs to be re-imagined from the bottom up. In other words, those calls for eliminating the TSA aren't as fringe as they might have been a decade ago.

> "In a sense, the TSA was never meant to protect anyone from terrorism."

In a sense, the TSA was never meant 7 to protect anyone from terrorism. Experts know that no aviation security procedure, no matter how airtight it seems, can repel a truly determined terrorist. As Bruce Schneier, a security technologist, explained to *Vanity Fair*, "The only useful airport security measures since 9/11 were locking and reinforcing the cockpit doors, so terrorists can't break in, positive baggage matching and teaching the passengers to fight back. The rest is security theater."

All the talk about the layers of aviation security is really just that: talk. It's 8 not meant to stop terrorists from attacking a plane or airport, and they aren't even meant to make the bad guys think they can't pull off another 9/11. No, the TSA and its so-called "security circus"—which seems so much more like a carnival in the bright glare of the red team revelations—is meant to make *us* feel safer. That's the real job of the TSA. Next time you go to the airport and see the long lines and the full-body scanners, the screeners giving pregnant mothers and senior citizens "pat downs," and passengers being "swabbed" and having the samples submitted into a fancy explosive detection machine, remember that.

It's a $7 billion-a-year show put on for *you*. 9

And remember that when a terrorist finally succeeds in blowing up 10 another plane, too. There will be a similar reaction. Heads will roll at the agency. Maybe the president will ask for the Secretary of Homeland Security's resignation this time, maybe not. Critics will say, "We told you so." But in the end, we'll decide that having an incompetent TSA is better than having no TSA at all.

Wash. Rinse. Repeat. [11]

There's nothing wrong with airport security, and there's nothing wrong [12] with the TSA. It's doing exactly what we wanted it to.

⊙ READING ARGUMENTS

1. In June 2015, the Transportation Security Administration (TSA) tested its own security measures. What, specifically, did the TSA find?

2. Were you surprised by the results of this investigation? Why or why not?

3. In paragraph 3, Elliott asks, "What's wrong with airport security?" What does he conclude? Do you agree with him?

4. In paragraph 6, Elliott summarizes the views of TSA critics. Does he refute these criticisms effectively, or does he need to do more? Explain.

5. What, according to Elliott, is the real purpose of the TSA's security measures? What other purpose (or purposes) could they have?

6. Some critics of the TSA believe that the agency should be eliminated entirely. Does Elliott? What might be gained and lost if this agency were eliminated?

7. Does Elliott believe that we are safer today than we were before 9/11? Explain.

⊙ AT ISSUE: IS AMERICA SAFER NOW THAN BEFORE 9/11?

1. Ashmawy is critical of the U.S. government's approach to capturing, detaining, and interrogating suspects after 9/11: "It was fuel on a fire set by a legal process that initially conflated the mutually exclusive missions of intelligence-gathering and the rendering of justice" (para. 7). What specific distinction is Ashmawy making? Why is this distinction important to his argument? Do you agree that these two "missions" are (or should be) "mutually exclusive"? Why or why not?

2. After documenting the general decline in "malevolent violence against Americans" (para. 4), Rauch asks: "And how do Americans celebrate this extraordinary success? By denying it" (8). What factors do you think contribute to this "denial"? Do you think this denial is harmful, or might it have some benefits?

⊙ WRITING ARGUMENTS: IS AMERICA SAFER NOW THAN BEFORE 9/11?

1. Brandus writes, "As for the tradeoff we have made between civil liberty and national security . . . I suspect that's one reason why the death toll from terrorism is so low" (para. 8). Do you agree with his judgment that the tradeoff of privacy and civil liberties has been worth it because of the safety it may have brought Americans? Why or why not? Write an essay that takes a position on this question.

2. After reading these four selections, do you think America is safer now than before 9/11? Write an argumentative essay that presents your position on this issue.

SCIENCE

CAN TELL YOU HOW TO CLONE A TYRANNOSAURUS REX

HUMANITIES

CAN TELL YOU WHY THIS MIGHT BE A BAD IDEA

The University of Utah, College of Humanities

CHAPTER 24

Does It Pay to Study the Humanities?

At one time, students went to college to grow intellectually, to consider what they wanted to become, and to engage in the give-and-take of academic discourse. In the process, they could reexamine their ideas, develop new perspectives, and expand as thinkers and as human beings. Now, because students (and their parents) often have to take out loans to defray the high cost of tuition, they see a college education as an investment, not as a vehicle for intellectual growth. For this reason, they feel a great deal of pressure to ensure a return on their investment, and degrees in STEM subjects—an acronym that refers to courses in Science, Technology, Engineering, and Math—offer this return because STEM graduates earn more money than liberal arts majors. As a result, students flock to STEM majors in increasing numbers, and the humanities—art, literature, music, and history—become less and less important on college campuses. What good, students ask, is Michelangelo when it comes to developing a newer, better Web app? How can an understanding of Tolstoy contribute to building a smarter smartphone?

Even though advocates for the humanities might concede that Tolstoy cannot help us to make a smartphone smarter, they would argue that all of us could benefit from reading Tolstoy. In addition, supporters of the humanities are concerned about what would be lost if we cut down on—or even eliminate—humanities courses. Although most people would agree that something is lost when we favor career skills over the humanities, they would have a difficult time pinpointing exactly what that "something" is. It is even harder to make the case for a liberal arts education when the average cost of a four-year degree is over $40,000 at a state school and over $135,000 at a private college.

In the following chapter, you will read some essays that address the question of whether it pays to study the humanities. In "The Economic Case for Saving the Humanities," Christina H. Paxson, the president of Brown University, makes the point that society will benefit if it actively supports the humanities. In "Major Differences: Why Undergraduate Majors Matter," Anthony P.

Carnevale and Michelle Melton argue that colleges have an obligation to give students the information they need to make intelligent decisions about their majors and their lives. In "Is It Time to Kill the Liberal Arts Degree?" Kim Brooks questions whether colleges are downplaying the obstacles that liberal arts graduates face when they try to find full-time employment. Finally, in "Course Corrections," Thomas Frank contends that in order to effectively defend the humanities, academics must first address the high cost of tuition.

Paxson's essay was published on August 20, 2013, in the *New Republic*.

THE ECONOMIC CASE FOR SAVING THE HUMANITIES

CHRISTINA H. PAXSON

What can we do to make the case for the humanities? Unlike the STEM disciplines (science, technology, engineering, and mathematics), they do not—on the surface—contribute to the national defense. It is difficult to measure, precisely, their effect on the GDP, or our employment rates, or the stock market. 1

And yet, we know in our bones that secular humanism is one of the greatest sources of strength we possess as a nation, and that we must protect the humanities if we are to retain that strength in the century ahead. 2

I do not exactly hail from the center of the humanities. I'm an economist, with a specialization in health and economic development. When you ask economists to weigh in on an issue, the chances are good that we will ultimately get around to a basic question: "Is it worth it?" Support for the humanities is more than worth it. It is essential. 3

We all know that there has been a fair amount of hostility to this idea recently in Congress and in State Houses around the country. Sometimes it almost feels as if there is a National Alliance against the Humanities. There are frequent potshots by radio commentators, and calls to reduce government spending in education and scholarship in the humanities. 4

It has become fashionable to attack government for being out of touch, bloated, and elitist; and humanities funding often strikes critics as an especially muddle-headed form of government spending. For that reason, the humanities are in danger of becoming even more of a punching bag than they already are. 5

In the current economic environment, these attacks have the potential to sway people. Any expenditure has to be clearly worth it. "Performance funding" links government support to disciplines that provide high numbers of jobs. Or, as in a Florida proposal that emerged last year, a "strategic" tuition structure would essentially charge more money to students who want to study the humanities and less money for those going into the STEM disciplines. 6

As a result, there is grave cause for concern. Federal support for the humanities is
heading in the wrong direction. In fiscal year
2013, the National Endowment for the
Humanities was funded at $139 million,
down $28.5 million from FY 2010, at a time

> "Federal support
> for the humanities
> is heading in the
> wrong direction." 7

when science funding stayed mostly intact. This is part of a pattern of long-term
decline since the Reagan years.

I believe the question is fair. Are the humanities worth it? To push back against 8
the recent tide of criticism, I'd like to offer several strategies.

First, we need to argue that there are real, tangible benefits to the humanis- 9
tic disciplines—to the study of history, literature, art, theater, music, and languages. In the complex, globalized world we are moving toward, it will obviously
benefit American undergraduates to know something of other civilizations, past
and present. Any form of immersion in literary expression is helpful when we
are learning to communicate and defend our thoughts. And it should not be that
difficult to concur that a thorough and objective grounding in history is helpful
and even inspiring when applying the lessons of our past to the future.

This point came home to me when, in my previous role as Dean of 10
Princeton's Woodrow Wilson School, I went to the university archives to read
the reports and correspondence that concerned the formation of the School in
1929. The founding director of the School, DeWitt Clinton Poole, wrote that
the need was not for "young men minutely trained in specific technicalities"
but, instead, for a "broad culture that will enlarge the individual's mental scope
to world dimensions." Accordingly, the curriculum was designed to ground
students in both the social sciences and the humanities. At that time—on the
eve of the Great Depression—there was concern that such an "impractical"
education would be of little value. Indeed, one alumnus wrote that the curriculum "is not immediately useful to the boy who has to earn a living." Yet, if one
looks back over the course of the school's rich history, it is evident that many of
the men and women who were exposed to that curriculum went on to positions
of genuine leadership in the public and private sectors.

We know that one of the best aspects of the undergraduate experience is 11
the fact that it is so multifaceted. Our scientists enjoy studying alongside our
humanists and vice versa. They learn more that way, and they do better on
each side of that not-very-precise divide. When I ask any of Brown's business-
leader alumni what they valued most during their years at Brown, I am just as
likely to hear about an inspirational professor of classics or religion as a course
in economics, science, or mathematics.

Second, we need to better defend an important principle that centuries of 12
humanism have taught us—that we do not always know the future benefits of
what we study and therefore should not rush to reject some forms of research
as less deserving than others. In 1939, Abraham Flexner, the founding director
of the Institute for Advanced Studies in Princeton, wrote an essay on this topic

titled "The Usefulness of Useless Knowledge." It was published in *Harper's* in 1939, on the eve of World War II, a time when we can assume there was a high priority placed on military and scientific knowledge. In this essay, Flexner argued that most of our really significant discoveries have been made by "men and women who were driven not by the desire to be useful but merely the desire to satisfy their curiosity."

Flexner's essay underscores a very important idea—that random discov- 13 eries can be more important than the ones we think we are looking for, and that we should be wary of imposing standard criteria of costs and benefits on our scholars. Or perhaps I should put it more precisely: We should be prepared to accept that the value of certain studies may be difficult to measure and may not be clear for decades or even centuries.

After September 11, experts in Arabic and the history of Islam were sud- 14 denly in high demand—their years of research could not simply be invented overnight. Similarly, we know that regional leaders like Brazil, Indonesia, and South Africa will rise in relevance and connectivity to the United States over the next few decades, just as China and India already have. To be ready for those relationships, and to advance them, we need our humanists fully engaged.

And third, the pace of learning is moving so quickly that I would argue it is 15 all the more important that we maintain support for the humanities, precisely to make sure that we remain grounded in our core values. As many previous generations have learned, innovations in science and technology are tremendously important. But they inevitably result in unintended consequences. Some new inventions, if only available to small numbers, increase inequity or competition for scarce resources, with multiplying effects. We need humanists to help us understand and respond to the social and ethical dimensions of technological change. As more changes come, we will need humanists to help us filter them, calibrate them, and when necessary, correct them. And we need them to galvanize the changes that are yet to come. Our focus should not be only on training students about the skills needed immediately upon graduation. The value of those skills will depreciate quickly. Instead, our aim is to invest in the long-term intellectual, creative, and social capacity of human beings.

I started by saying that we should embrace the debate about the value of the 16 humanities. Let's hear the criticisms that are often leveled, and do what we can to address them. Let's make sure we give value to our students, and that we educate them for a variety of possible outcomes. Let's do more to encourage cross-pollination between the sciences and the humanities for the benefit of each. Let's educate all of our students in every discipline to use the best humanistic tools we have acquired over a millennium of university teaching—to engage in a civilized discourse about all of the great issues of our time. A grounding in the humanities will sharpen our answers to the toughest questions we are facing.

We don't want a nation of technical experts in one subject. We want a 17 scintillating civil society in which everyone can talk to everyone. That was a quality that Alexis de Tocqueville wrote of when he visited the United States at the beginning of the 1830s. Even in that era before mass communication, before the telegraph, before the Internet, we were engaged in an American conversation that stretched from one end of the country to another. In a similar manner, Martin Luther King Jr. sketched a "web of mutuality" in his "Letter from Birmingham Jail," fifty years ago this year. We want politicians who have read Shakespeare—as Lincoln did. We want bankers and lawyers who have read Homer and Dante. We want factory owners who have read Dickens.

It is really important we get this right. A mountain of empirical evidence 18 indicates a growing inequality in our society. There is no better way to check this trend than to invest in education. And there is no better way to invest in education than to invest fairly, giving attention to all disciplines and short shrift to none.

Earlier generations have weighed these questions, and answered in the 19 affirmative. An early graduate of Brown, Horace Mann, trained in the humanities, was instrumental in creating the public school system of the United States. He knew that a broad, secular education, open to all, was one of the foundations of our democracy, and that it was impossible to expect meaningful citizenship without offering people the tools to inform themselves about all of the great questions of life. Horace Mann said, "Be ashamed to die until you have won some victory for humanity." In that spirit, let's continue this conversation, eager to engage the critics in a spirited conversation whose very richness depends on the humanistic values we cherish.

And in conclusion: yes, it's worth it. 20

⊖ READING ARGUMENTS

1. Paxson begins by acknowledging the difficulty of making "the case for the humanities" (para. 1). Why? Does this opening strategy undercut her argument in any way? Explain.

2. Does Paxson make a valid point in paragraph 2, or is she **begging the question**? Explain.

3. Where in the essay does Paxson appeal to *ethos*? Is this appeal effective in the context of her argument? Why or why not?

4. Paxson writes that "the humanities are in danger of becoming even more of a punching bag than they already are" (5). What evidence does she present to support this claim? Is this sufficient?

5. Paxson offers three strategies to stem the tide of criticism against the humanities. What are they? How effective have they been in stemming the "recent tide of criticism" (8)?

6. What point does Paxson make in her conclusion? Would a different concluding strategy have been more effective? Explain.

This essay was published in the Fall 2011 issue of *Presidency*, a publication of the American Council on Education.

MAJOR DIFFERENCES: WHY UNDERGRADUATE MAJORS MATTER

ANTHONY P. CARNEVALE AND MICHELLE MELTON

In the United States today, there is no more certain investment than a college 1 education. In spite of the current gloomy economic forecast, college is still worth it. In fact, rising demand, coupled with the persistent undersupply of college-educated workers over the last 30 years, has driven up relative wages for these workers. On average, **college graduates make 84 percent more over a lifetime** than their high school–educated counterparts—up from 75 percent in 1999. While the current unemployment rate among recent college graduates is high (9 percent), it is still far lower than the average unemployment rate for recent high school graduates (35 percent). When it rains long enough and hard enough, everyone gets a little wet. Still, a college education is the best umbrella to shelter individuals from economic storms.

But that doesn't mean that all bachelor's degrees are created equal. While 2 the focus recently has been on the value of higher education in general, we have failed to connect the dots between specific college majors and specific career trajectories. College offers many non-financial benefits, but there is new evidence of the oversize influence that certain majors have in preparing students for careers. Average salaries mask very real discrepancies between the economic advantages of different undergraduate majors. While everyone who attends college can expect a significant return on their investment, different undergraduate majors lead to markedly different careers—and significantly different earnings.

Disparity in Degrees

As we found in our recent study, *What's It Worth?: The Economic Value of* 3 *College Majors*, because of the role it plays in occupational training, the choice of undergraduate major is as critical a choice as whether to get a college degree at all. In one of the most extreme examples, for instance, Counseling Psychology majors make an average of $29,000 per year, compared to $120,000 for Petroleum Engineering majors. That's a difference of 314 percent—or $4.1 million over a 45-year lifetime of work. A more typical example is the difference between two of the most popular majors, General Business and Elementary Education. A General Business major earns $60,000 annually, compared with $40,000 for an Education major. Over a lifetime, that's a difference in earnings of about $900,000.

Majors are so decisive for an individual's earnings because they are not 4 just educational categories; majors are an essential component of career training. Critics constantly disparage higher education for not being more connected with the "real world," and for failing to more tightly align higher education and curricula with labor markets. Such criticism is off the mark; since the end of the Second World War, the growth in higher education has been in programs that connect learning with careers. Very few people today actually major in Ancient Greek, and you won't see any subway advertisements promoting class offerings in Classics. Fewer than 10 percent of bachelor's degrees in the U.S. economy are in Humanities and Liberal Arts. The growth areas of higher education have been, and will continue to be, in educational programs which stress career training. The for-profit sector has recognized this fact, and has profited handsomely from it. All of higher education would benefit from making the implicit relationships between education and careers more explicit.

The point is a simple one: while it is important to discuss the benefits of col- 5
lege in general, for too long we have treated all college degrees as though they had the same economic value. We have glossed over the differences between workers with a major in Mathematics and workers with a major in Drama and Theater Arts to the detriment of students. The plain truth is that the labor market does not treat these workers the same—and students deserve to know that. A love of Shakespeare should not deter students from becoming English majors. But we believe that students

> "We have glossed over the differences between workers with a major in Mathematics and workers with a major in Drama and Theater Arts to the detriment of students."

should know how their educational choices will affect the rest of their adult lives, in terms of the careers they will have, their expected earnings, and whether they are likely to need graduate education—which they may need to take out loans to get.

We found that, for example, a Nursing major nearly always leads to a 6
career in the Health Services industry, as do many other health preparatory majors (82 percent of Nursing majors end up in Health Professional occupations, and 6 percent are in management). Likewise, well over two-thirds of Education majors—especially Special Needs Education, Elementary Education, and Educational Administration and Supervision majors—end up in the Education Services industry.

Making the Arts Pay

That these particular majors lead to specific careers may be obvious—but 7
what about Arts majors? Do most people who major in Arts actually become artists? In fact, only a quarter of Arts majors end up in Arts occupations, while about a third end up in either Office, Sales, or Education occupations. In other words, majoring in Arts only rarely leads to a career as an artist. Potential Arts majors should know this, and that they can expect median annual earnings of $44,000.

Of course, some Arts majors will end up going on to get a graduate degree 8
(in fact, less than a quarter of Arts majors, 23 percent, do get a graduate degree).
But Arts majors who get a graduate degree see a 23 percent boost in earnings.

Although it is slightly more remunerative than Arts, Humanities and Lib- 9
eral Arts majors are in the middle of the pack in terms of earnings ($47,000)
and graduate degree attainment (41 percent of Humanities and Liberal Arts
majors go to graduate school). Humanities and Liberal Arts majors that do go
on to graduate school see a 48 percent earnings boost for doing so, making
their median earnings $65,000 per year. This is a comfortable living, to be
sure, but even with a graduate degree, Humanities and Liberal Arts majors still
make significantly less than an Engineering major with a bachelor's degree.
Moreover, in terms of all graduate earnings, Humanities and Liberal Arts
majors are still in the middle of the pack. They earn more than the Arts majors
do, but significantly less than many other major groups with a graduate
degree, including Engineering, Health, Social Sciences, and Agriculture and
Natural Resources.

In short, the Humanities and Liberal Arts may have unlimited intrinsic 10
value, but in terms of their more measurable market value, these graduates
simply do not fare as well as students whose majors equip them with more
technical and scientific skills.

The point is not for students to slavishly choose the majors with the high- 11
est earnings, instead of being driven by their interests. It is to provide the
information to students so that they are not solely driven by incomplete, anecdotal, or speculative evidence about their likely success, and to balance their
interests—both economic and humanistic—in making a decision about their
working lives.

Given information, students might make different decisions. We already 12
know that such decisions are complex and based on a combination of interests, values, knowledge, skills, and abilities. If a Social Work major is motivated by the desire to interact with and help others, he or she might decide
that, compared with $39,000 in Social Work, Nursing (at $60,000) might be a
better option that would also allow him or her to pursue interacting with and
helping others. The same might be true of a Biology major ($50,000), to whom
Nursing might be an appealing alternative path. Similarly, an English major
($48,000) might decide that the small boost from majoring in Journalism
($51,000) isn't worth the switch.

We have been embarrassingly slow to provide students with information 13
that will help them make these decisions. For the most part, this is because
higher education is balancing competing—and often contradictory—missions.
Many educators are wary about subjugating higher education's traditional
role to an economic one. Some are upset about the increasingly tight ties that
bind work and education. While training foot soldiers for capitalism is not the
sole mission of our education system, the inescapable reality is that ours is a
society based on work. Those who are not equipped with the knowledge and
skills necessary to get—and keep—good jobs are denied full social inclusion

and tend to drop out of the mainstream culture, polity, and economy. In the worst cases, they can be drawn into alternative cultures, political movements, and economic activities that are a threat to mainstream American life. Therefore, if postsecondary educators cannot fulfill their economic mission to help students become successful workers and to better link postsecondary education with careers, they also will fail in their cultural and political missions to create good neighbors and good citizens.

⊘ READING ARGUMENTS

1. In paragraph 3, Carnevale and Melton say that "the choice of undergraduate major is as critical a choice as whether to get a college degree at all." What evidence do they provide to support this statement? Is this evidence convincing?

2. Carnevale and Melton write, "Critics constantly disparage higher education for not being more connected with the 'real world,' and for failing to more tightly align higher education and curricula with labor markets" (para. 4). Why do they believe that this criticism is "off the mark" (4)?

3. According to Carnevale and Melton, their purpose is to provide information about the "economic and humanistic" (11) trade-offs of different majors. Do you agree with the writers that many—or most— college students make decisions about their major based on "incomplete, anecdotal, or speculative evidence" (11)? Why or why not?

4. In what respects is this essay an evaluation argument? In what sense is it a proposal argument?

5. Where in this essay do the authors develop a **causal chain**? What point are they trying to make with this strategy? Are they successful? Explain.

This piece initially appeared in *Salon* on June 19, 2011.

IS IT TIME TO KILL THE LIBERAL ARTS DEGREE?

KIM BROOKS

Every year or two, my husband, an academic advisor at a prestigious 1 Midwestern university, gets a call from a student's parent. Mr. or Mrs. So-and-so's son is a sophomore now and still insistent on majoring in film studies, anthropology, Southeast Asian comparative literature or, god forbid . . . English. These dalliances in the humanities were fine and good when little Johnny was a freshman, but isn't it time now that he wake up and start thinking seriously about what, one or two or three years down the line, he's actually going to do?

My husband, loyal first and foremost to his students' intellectual develop-   2 ment, and also an unwavering believer in the inherent value of a liberal arts education, tells me about these conversations with an air of indignation. He wonders, "Aren't these parents aware of what they signed their kid up for when they decided to let him come get a liberal arts degree instead of going to welding school?" Also, he says, "The most aimless students are often the last ones you want to force into a career path. I do sort of hate to enable this prolonged adolescence, but I also don't want to aid and abet the miseries of years lost to a misguided professional choice."

Now, I love my husband. Lately, however, I find myself wincing when he   3 recounts these stories.

"Well," I sometimes say, "what *are* they going to do?"   4

The answer, at least according to a recent article in the *New York Times*,   5 is rather bleak. Employment rates for college graduates have declined steeply in the last two years, and perhaps even more disheartening, those who find jobs are more likely to be steaming lattes or walking dogs than doing anything even peripherally related to their college curriculum. While the scale and severity of this post-graduation letdown may be an unavoidable consequence of an awful recession, I do wonder if all those lofty institutions of higher learning, with their noble-sounding mission statements and soft-focused brochure photos of campus greens, may be glossing over the serious, at-times-crippling obstacles a B.A. holder must overcome to achieve professional and financial stability. I'm not asking if a college education has inherent value, if it makes students more thoughtful, more informed, more enlightened and critical-minded human beings. These are all interesting questions that don't pay the rent. What I'm asking is far more banal and far more pressing. What I'm asking is: Why do even the best colleges fail so often at preparing kids for the world?

When I earned my diploma from the University of Virginia in the spring   6 of 2000, it never occurred to me before my senior year to worry too seriously about my post-graduation prospects. Indeed, most of my professors, advisors, and mentors reinforced this complacency. I was smart, they told me. I'd spent four years at a rigorous institution honing my writing, research, and critical-thinking skills. I'd written an impressive senior thesis, gathered recommendations from professors, completed summer internships in various journalistic endeavors. They had no doubt at all that I would land on my feet. And I did (kind of), about a decade after graduating.

In the interim, I floundered. I worked as a restaurant hostess and tutored   7 English-as-a-second-language without a formal work visa. I mooched off friends and boyfriends and slept on couches. One dreary night in San Francisco, I went on an interview to tend bar at a strip club, but left demoralized when I realized I'd have to walk around in stilettos. I went back to school to complete the pre-medical requirements I'd shunned the first time through, then, a week into physics, I applied to nursing school, then withdrew from that program after a month when I realized nursing would be an environment where my habit of spacing out might actually kill someone. I landed a $12-an-hour job as a paralegal at an asbestos-related litigation firm. I got an MFA in fiction.

Depending on how you look at it, I either spent a long time finding 8 myself, or wasted seven years. And while all these efforts hardly add up to a tragedy (largely because I had the luxury of supportive parents willing to supplement my income for a time), I do have to admit feeling disillusioned as I moved from one gig to another, feeling as though my undergraduate education, far from preparing me for any kind of meaningful and remunerative work, had in some ways deprepared me, nurturing my natural strengths and predilections—writing, reading, analysis—and sweeping my weaknesses in organization, pragmatic problem-solving, decision-making under the proverbial rug.

Of course, there are certainly plenty of B.A. holders out there who, 9 wielding the magic combination of competency, credentials, and luck, are able to land themselves a respectable, entry-level job that requires neither name tag nor apron. But for every person I know who parlayed a degree in English or anthropology into a career-track gig, I know two others who weren't so lucky, who, in that awful, post-college year or two or three or four, unemployed and uninsured and uncommitted to any particular field, racked up credit card debt or got married to the wrong person or went to law school for no particular reason or made one of a dozen other time- and money-wasting mistakes.

And the common thread in all these stories seems to be how surprised these graduates were by their utter unemployability, a feeling of having been misled into complacency, issued reassurances about how the pedigree or prestige of the institution they'd attended would save them. This narra- 10
tive holds true whether their course of study was humanities or social sciences. My baby sitter, for example, who earned a degree in psychology from a Big Ten university, now makes $15 an hour watching my kids.

> "[T]he common thread in all these stories seems to be how surprised these graduates were by their utter unemployability."

"I was not the most serious student," she admits. "But I do wonder, why 11 was I allowed to decide on a major without ever sitting down with my advisor and talking about what I might do with that major after graduating? I mean, I had to write out a plan for how I'd fit all my required courses into my schedule, but no one seemed to care if I had a plan once I left there. I graduated not knowing how to use Excel, write out a business plan, do basic accounting. With room and board and tuition, my time there cost $120,000."

I asked Sarah Isham, the director of career services of the College of   12
Arts and Sciences at my alma mater about this discrepancy between curriculum and career planning, and she repeats the same reassurances I heard
10 years ago: "What we do is help students see how the patterns and themes
of their interests, skills, and values, might relate to particular arenas. We do
offer a few self-assessment tests, as well as many other resources to help
them do this."

When I ask how well the current services are working—that is, how many   13
recent graduates are finding jobs, real jobs that require a degree—she can only
say that, "The College of Arts and Sciences does not collect statistics on post-
graduation plans. I could not give you any idea of where these students are
going or what they are doing. Regrettably, it's not something in place at this
time."

I went on to ask her how the college's curriculum was adapting to   14
meet the demands of the recession and the realities of the job market, and
she directed me to a dean who asked not to be identified, and who
expressed, in no uncertain terms, how tired he was of articles like mine
that question the rationale, rigor, or usefulness of a liberal arts education.
He insisted that while he had no suggestions regarding how a 22-year-old
should weather a recession, the university was achieving its goal of creating citizens of the world.

When I asked him how a 22-year-old with no job, no income, no health   15
insurance, and, in some cases, six figures of college debt to pay off is supposed
to be a citizen of the world, he said he had no comment, that he was the wrong
person to talk to, and he directed me to another dean, who was also unable to
comment.

The chilliness of this response was a bit disheartening, but not terribly   16
surprising. When I was an undergrad, it seemed whenever I mentioned my
job-search anxieties, my professors and advisors would get a glassy look in
their eyes and mutter something about the career center. Their gazes would
drift toward their bookshelves or a folder of ungraded papers. And at the time,
I could hardly blame them. These were people who'd published dissertations
on Freud, written definitive volumes on Virginia Woolf. The language of real-
world career preparation was a language they simply didn't speak.

And if they did say anything at all, it was usually a reiteration of the typi-   17
cal liberal arts defense, that graduating with a humanities degree, I could do
anything: I could go on to earn a master's or a law degree or become an editor
or a teacher. I could go into journalism or nonprofit work, apply to medical
school or the foreign service. I could write books or learn to illustrate or bind
them. I could start my own business, work as a consultant, get a job editing
pamphlets for an alumni association, or raise money for public radio. The
possibilities were literally limitless. It was a like being 6 years old again and
trying to decide if I'd become an astronaut or a ballerina. The advantage to a
humanities degree, one professor insisted, was its versatility. In retrospect,
though, I wonder if perhaps this was part of the problem, as well; freedom can

promote growth, but it can also cause paralysis. Faced with limitless possibilities, a certain number of people will just stand still.

"So let me ask you something," my husband says, my wonderfully incisive 18 husband who will let me get away with only so much bitterness. "If your school had forced you to declare a career plan or take an accounting class or study Web programming instead of contemporary lit, how would you have felt about it at the time, without the benefit of hindsight?"

It's a good question, and the answer is, I probably would have transferred. 19

There were courses I took in college, courses in Renaissance literature and 20 the anthropology of social progress and international relations of the Middle East and, of course, writing, that will, in all likelihood, never earn me a steady paycheck or a 401K, but which I would not trade for anything; there were lectures on Shakespeare and Twain and Joyce that I still remember, that I've dreamt about and that define my sensibility as a writer and a reader and a human being. Even now, knowing the lost years that followed, I still wouldn't trade them in.

A new Harvard study suggests that it's not an abandonment of the 21 college curriculum that's needed, but a reenvisioning and better preparation. The study compares the U.S. system unfavorably to its European counterparts where students begin thinking about what sort of career they'll pursue and the sort of preparation they'll need for it in middle school. Could that be the answer?

At the end of my interview with Sarah Isham, she asks me if I might come 22 back to Charlottesville to participate in an alumni career panel. "We always have a lot of students interested in media and writing and the arts. It would be wonderful," she says "to have you come and talk to them." She asks me this, and I can't help but laugh.

"I don't think I'd be much of a role model," I say. "I don't have what you'd 23 call a high-powered career. I mostly do freelance work. Adjunct teaching. That sort of thing."

"Oh, that's fine," she insists. "Our students will love that. So many of them 24 are terrified of sitting in a cubicle all day."

They should be so lucky, I think. But I would never say that—not to them 25 and not to my own students. They'll have plenty of time later to find out just what a degree is and isn't good for. Right now, they're in those four extraordinary, exceptional years where ideas matter; and there's not a thing I'd do to change that.

⊙ READING ARGUMENTS

1. At two points in her essay, Brooks discusses her husband. Do you think these discussions help her advance her argument? If so, how?

2. Brooks's thesis occurs at the end of paragraph 5. Is this a logical place for it, or should it come earlier?

3. What evidence does Brooks use to support her points? Is this support convincing? What other kinds of evidence could she have used? What are the advantages and disadvantages of using such evidence?

4. What does Brooks mean when she says that the liberal arts graduates she interviewed have "a feeling of having been misled into compla-cency" (para. 10)?

5. How would you describe the tone of Brooks's essay? How does this tone affect your response to her argument?

6. What does Brooks think the purpose of college should be? Do you agree with her? Why or why not?

Harper's published this essay in its October 2013 issue.

COURSE CORRECTIONS

THOMAS FRANK

To the long list of American institutions that have withered since the dawn of the 1980s—journalism, organized labor, mainline Protestantism, small-town merchants—it may be time to add another: college-level humanities. Those ancient pillars of civilization are under assault these days, with bulldozers advancing from two different directions.

On the one hand, students are migrating away from traditional college subjects like history and philosophy. After hitting a postwar high in the mid-1960s, enrollments in the humanities dropped off sharply, and still show no signs of recovering. This is supposedly happening because recent college grads who chose to major in old-school subjects have experienced more difficulty finding jobs. Indeed, the folly of studying, say, English Lit has become some-thing of an Internet cliché—the stuff of sneering "Worst Majors" listicles that seem always to be sponsored by personal-finance websites.

On the other hand, an impressive array of public figures are eager to give the exodus from the humanities an additional push. Everyone from President Obama to Thomas Friedman knows where public support for education has to be concentrated in order to yield tangible returns both for individuals and for the nation: the STEM disciplines (science, technology, engineering, and math). *These* are the degrees American business is scream-ing for. These are the fields of study that will give us "broadly shared economic prosperity, international competitiveness, a strong national defense, a clean energy future, and longer, healthier, lives for all Americans," as a White House press release puts it.

Where does that leave the humanities, which don't contribute in any obvious way to national defense or economic prosperity? The management theorist and financier Peter Cohan, addressing unemployment among recent college grads in the pages of *Forbes*, proposes a course of straightforward erasure: "To fix this problem, the answer is simple enough: cut out the departments offering majors that make students unemployable." Certain red-state governors seem eager to take up the task. Governor Pat McCrory of North Carolina, for example, dismisses gender studies as elitist woolgathering and announces, "I'm going to adjust my education curriculum to what business and commerce needs." Governor Rick Scott of Florida declares that "we don't need a lot more anthropologists in the state," while a panel he convened in 2012 has called for tuition prices to be subsidized for those willing to acquiesce to the needs of business and study practical things. Those who want to study silly stuff like divinity or Latin will have to pay ever more to indulge in their profligate pastimes.

> "Where does that leave the humanities, which don't contribute in any obvious way to national defense or economic prosperity?"

4

And so the old battle is joined again: the liberal arts versus professional (i.e., remunerative) studies. This time around, of course, it is flavored by all the cynical stratagems of contemporary politics. Take the baseline matter of STEM workers, the ones who supposedly hold our future in their hands. According to a recent study by the Economic Policy Institute, there is actually no shortage of STEM workers in the United States—and by extension, no need for all the incentives currently on the table to push more students into those fields. Oh, the demand of the business community for an ever greater supply of STEM grads is genuine enough. But their motive is the same as it was when they lobbied for looser restrictions on STEM workers from abroad: to keep wages down. Only this time the high-handed endeavor is being presented as a favor to students, who must be rescued from a lifetime of philology-induced uselessness.

5

A similar logic explains the larger attack on the humanities. The disciplines in the crosshairs have been the right's nemeses for many years. Maybe, in the past, conservatives stumped for some idealized core curriculum or the Great Books of Western Civ—but now that the option of demolishing these disciplines is on the table, today's amped-up right rather likes the idea. After all, universities are not only dens of liberal iniquity but also major donors to the Democratic Party.[1] Chucking a few sticks of dynamite into their comfy world is a no-brainer for any politician determined to "defund the left."

6

---

[1]According to statistics compiled by Neil Gross in *Why Are Professors Liberal and Why Do Conservatives Care?*, the most left-leaning divisions of the American university are the social sciences, closely followed by the humanities.

Fans of the banality of evil might appreciate the language with which this   7
colossal act of vandalism is being urged upon us. Florida's blue-ribbon commission, for example, sets about burying the humanities with a sandstorm of
convoluted management talk:

> Four key policy questions must be addressed to accelerate Florida's pro-
> gression toward world-class recognition as a system, particularly as its
> measurement framework transitions from simply reporting to collaborat-
> ing toward clear goals. . . . Boards can advance effective cost management
> by helping to shape the conversation about aligning resources with goals
> and creating a culture of heightened sensitivity to resource management
> across the campus.

Let us assess the battle so far. In one corner, we have rhetoric like this: empty,   8
pseudoscientific jargon rubber-stamped by a Chamber of Commerce hack . . .
who was appointed by the governor of Florida . . . who was himself elected by the
Tea Party. It is not merely weak, it is preposterous; it is fatuity at a gallop.

In the other corner, we have the university-level humanities. Now, here   9
is an antagonist at the height of its vast mental powers. In polite and affluent
circles, it is respected by all. Its distinctive, plummy tone seems daily to
extend itself into more and more aspects of American life. The Opinion section of the Sunday *New York Times*, for example, is one long succession of
professorial musings. So is much of NPR's programming. Former humanities students occupy many of the seats in President Obama's Cabinet.

That the exalted men and women of higher learning might take the field   10
against opponents like the authors of the Florida report and be defeated—it's
almost impossible to believe. And yet that's precisely what is happening.

Stung by the attacks on their livelihood, the nation's leading humanists   11
have closed ranks, taken up their pencils, and tried to explain why they
exist. The result is a train wreck of desperate rationalizations, clichés, and
circular reasoning.

They insist that their work must not be judged by bogus metrics like the   12
employability of recent graduates. They scold journalists for getting the story
wrong in certain of its details. They express contempt for the dunces in state
legislatures. They tear into the elected philistines who badger them with what
the academic superstar Homi Bhabha calls a "primitive and reductive view of
what is essential."

And with touching earnestness, they argue that the humanities are   13
plenty remunerative. They tell of CEOs who demand well-rounded young
employees rather than single-minded, vocationally focused drudges. They
remind us that humanities grads get into law and medical schools, which in
turn lead (as everyone knows, right?) to the big money. Besides, they point
out, the humanist promise of explaining our mysterious country draws
foreign students—and foreign currency—to college towns across the land.
They even play the trump card of national security: wouldn't we have done

better in the global "war on terror" if we had trained more Arabic linguists prior to the start of hostilities?

Their mission, after all, is not about money: it is about molding young   14
citizens for democracy! In making this traditional argument, no one today will venture quite as far as Bruce Cole, a former chairman of the National Endowment for the Humanities, who in 2004 claimed that the humanities were "part of our homeland defense." But we're getting pretty close. Consider the report issued a few months ago by the American Academy of Arts & Sciences, which asserts that our political system itself "depends on citizens who can think critically, understand their own history, and give voice to their beliefs while respecting the views of others." As proof, the authors of the report cite Thomas Jefferson's fondness for liberal education, and then proceed to trumpet the humanities as nothing less than "the keeper of the republic"—a phrase that is doubtless meant to out-patriot the various conservatives nipping at the academy's ankles.[2]

Others want nothing to do with such hackneyed arguments. Harvard Uni-   15
versity's effort to explain the high station of the humanities, a dense and confusing text issued in June, insists that these disciplines are designed in part to "unmask the operations of power," not to buttress them. The document then disavows Harvard's *previous* justification for the humanities, which had stressed the "civic responsibilities of American citizens living in and aspiring to preserve a free democratic society." No, that was last century's model—jingoistic junk. In 2013, the humanities are all about embracing ambiguity. And about determining exactly what the humanities are about. The humanists write:

> At the same time, therefore, that we aspire to ground our sense of ourselves on some stable understanding of the aim of life (e.g., the responsible citizen in a free society), we must constantly aspire to discover anew what the best way to characterize and cultivate such an aim might be. The humanities are the site where this tension is cultivated, nurtured, and sustained.[3]

The nurturing and sustaining of tensions—that's the stuff. Of course, some tensions are more desirable than others, and for all their excitement about the unmasking of power, the Harvard humanists have little interest in

---

[2]The very same month that the Academy issued this report, its president was found not to have earned the Ph.D. ascribed to her on the organization's website.

[3]This deeply unpersuasive idea—that the humanities exist to teach us how to ponder the humanities—is so seductive to the authors that they repeat it, in slightly different form, a few pages later: "An understanding of the power of the humanistic enterprise, therefore, and an understanding of how responsibly to engage it and employ it, should be the central aims of any education in the humanities."

unmasking their own. Nor should their genuflection at the altar of ambiguity be taken as a call to knock down the disciplinary walls. No, according to Bhabha's navel-gazing appendix, even students interested in interdisciplinary studies will be D.O.A. unless they first encounter "disciplinary specificity *in its most robust expression.*" Ambiguity is a stern taskmaster, I guess.

Most touching, perhaps, is the argument advanced by Stanley Fish in a   16
2010 *New York Times* Opinionator column. After shooting down the many absurd defenses of the humanities that are floating around these days, Fish advises inhabitants of academia's more rarefied regions to forget even *trying* to explain themselves to the public. Don't ask what "French theory" does for the man in the street, Fish writes. Instead, ask whether its

> insights and style of analysis can be applied to the history of science, to the puzzles of theoretical physics, to psychology's analysis of the human subject. In short, justify yourselves to your colleagues, not to the hundreds of millions of Americans who know nothing of what you do and couldn't care less and shouldn't be expected to care.

Once, academics like Fish dreamed of bringing young people to a full understanding of their humanity, and maybe even of changing the world. Now their chant is: We're experts because other experts say we're experts. We critique because we critique because we critique—but all critique stops at the door to the faculty lounge.

One thing the humanities warriors don't talk about very much is the cost of it   17
all. In the first chapter of Martha Nussbaum's otherwise excellent *Not for Profit*, the author declares that while the question of "access" to higher ed is an important one, "it is not, however, the topic of this book."

Maybe it should have been. To discuss the many benefits of studying the   18
humanities absent the economic context in which the humanities are studied is to miss the point entirely. When Americans express doubts about whether (in the words of Obama pollster Joel Benenson) "a college education was worth it," they aren't making a judgment about the study of history or literature that needs to be refuted. They are remarking on its price.

Tellingly, not a single one of the defenses of the humanities that I   19
read claimed that such a course of study was a good deal for the money. The Harvard report, amid its comforting riffs about ambiguity, suggests that bemoaning the price is a "philistine objection" not really worth addressing. (It also dismisses questions of social class with a footnote.) The document produced by the American Academy of Arts & Sciences contains numerous action points for sympathetic legislators, but devotes just two paragraphs to the subject of student debt and tuition inflation, declaring blandly that "colleges must do their part to control costs," then suggesting that the *real* way to deal with the problem is to do a better job selling the humanities.

But ignoring basic economics doesn't make them go away. It is supposed   20
to be a disaster when right-wingers in state legislatures threaten to destroy
academic professions. However, one reason the world has so little sympathy
for those professions is that everyone knows how they themselves cranked out
Ph.D.'s for decades without considering whether there was a demand for said
Ph.D.'s, thereby transforming their own dedicated disciples into the most pite-
ous wretches on campus.

Still, the wretchedness they ought to be considering is of a different mag-   21
nitude altogether. The central economic fact of American higher ed today
is this: It costs a lot. It costs a huge amount. It costs so much, in fact—
more than $60,000 a year for tuition plus expenses at a growing number
of top private schools—that young people routinely start their postcolle-
giate lives with enormous debt loads. It's like forcing them to take out a
mortgage when they turn twenty-two, only with no white picket fence to
show for it.

This is the woolly mammoth in the room. I know the story of how it got   22
there is a complicated one. But regardless of how it happened, that staggering
price tag has changed the way we make educational decisions. Quite naturally,
parents and students alike have come to expect some kind of direct, career-
prep transaction. They're out $240,000, for Christ's sake—you can't tell them
it was all about embracing ambiguity. For that kind of investment, the gates to
a middle-class life had better swing wide!

No quantity of philistine-damning potshots or remarks from liberal-   23
minded CEOs will banish this problem. Humanists couldn't stop the
onslaught even if they went positively retro and claimed they were needed to
ponder the mind of God and save people's souls. The turn to STEM is motivated by something else, something even more desperate and more essential
than that.

What is required is not better salesmanship or reassuring platitudes. The   24
world doesn't need another self-hypnotizing report on why universities exist.
What it needs is for universities to stop ruining the lives of their students.
Don't propagandize for your institutions, professors: Change them. Grab the
levers of power and pull.

❯ READING ARGUMENTS

1. Frank observes that the debate about the value of a liberal arts education is nothing new: "And so the old battle is joined again: the liberal
   arts versus professional (that is, remunerative) studies. This time
   around, of course, it is flavored by all the cynical stratagems of contemporary politics" (para. 5). What evidence does Frank provide to
   support this statement? Does he seem to favor one political party
   over another? Explain.

2. Frank quotes specific language from both detractors of a liberal arts education (such as the Florida commission in paragraph 7) and its defenders (such as the "Harvard humanists" in paragraph 15). Why does he focus on their language? How does his analysis support his main argument?

3. Frank repeatedly uses the word *philistine*—for example, when he refers to the "elected philistines who badger" liberal arts professors (12). What is a "philistine"? Why is the word significant in the context of this debate?

4. According to Frank, what is the "central economic fact of American higher ed today" (21)?

5. In his conclusion, Frank advises universities to "grab the levers of power and pull" (24). What does he mean? What other point (or points) could he have emphasized here?

⊙ AT ISSUE: DOES IT PAY TO STUDY THE HUMANITIES?

1. Carnevale and Melton write about the difficulties colleges and universities have trying to balance conflicting missions:

   > Many educators are wary about subjugating higher education's traditional role to an economic one. Some are upset about the increasingly tight ties that bind work and education. While training foot soldiers for capitalism is not the sole mission of our education system, the inescapable reality is that ours is a society based on work (para. 13).

   Do you agree that there is a tension between these two "missions"? How should educators maintain a balance between their intellectual mission and the more practical demands of preparing graduates for work?

2. In her essay, Brooks asks, "Why do even the best colleges fail so often at preparing kids for the world?" (para. 5). How would you answer this question? When it comes to your college, do you agree or disagree with Brooks's contention?

3. According to Paxson, "We don't want a nation of technical experts in one subject. We want a scintillating civil society in which everyone can talk to everyone" (para. 17). What does she mean? For example, what is a "civil society"? How are the values conveyed by the liberal arts related to civil society and public discourse? What problems might arise from having a nation composed almost entirely of highly specialized "technical experts in one subject"?

⊘ WRITING ARGUMENTS: DOES IT PAY TO STUDY THE HUMANITIES?

1. After reading the arguments in this casebook, develop your own ideas about whether it pays to study the humanities. Then, using these essays as sources, write an essay in which you argue for your position.

2. As Frank points out, educators, policymakers, politicians, and others have been strongly encouraging young Americans to major in a STEM discipline (Science, Technology, Engineering, or Math). Are you planning on studying one of these disciplines? If not, have you felt pressure from parents, teachers, or friends to pursue science, technology, engineering, or math? Write an essay that answers these questions and takes a position on the issue.

Plato

Jonathan Swift

James Baldwin

Rachel Carson

Betty Friedan

CLASSIC ARGUMENTS

THE ALLEGORY OF THE CAVE
PLATO

Plato (428 BCE–347 BCE) was an important Greek philosopher. In The Republic, *from which "The Allegory of the Cave" is drawn, Plato examines the nature of reality, how we know what we know, and how we should act. An* **allegory** *is a dramatic representation of abstract ideas by characters and events in a story or image. "The Allegory of the Cave" is an imagined dialogue between Plato's teacher (Socrates) and brother (Glaucon).*

And now, I said, let me show in a figure how far our nature is enlightened or 1 unenlightened:—Behold! human beings living in an underground den, which has a mouth open towards the light and reaching all along the den; here they have been from their childhood, and have their legs and necks chained so that they cannot move, and can only see before them, being prevented by the chains from turning round their heads. Above and behind them a fire is blazing at a distance, and between the fire and the prisoners there is a raised way; and you will see, if you look, a low wall built along the way, like the screen which marionette players have in front of them, over which they show the puppets.

I see. 2

And do you see, I said, men passing along the wall carrying all sorts of 3 vessels, and statues and figures of animals made of wood and stone and various materials, which appear over the wall? Some of them are talking, others silent.

You have shown me a strange image, and they are strange prisoners. 4

Like ourselves, I replied; and they see only their own shadows, or the 5 shadows of one another, which the fire throws on the opposite wall of the cave?

True, he said; how could they see anything but the shadows if they were 6 never allowed to move their heads?

And of the objects which are being carried in like manner they would 7 only see the shadows?

Yes, he said. 8

And if they were able to converse with one another, would they not sup- 9 pose that they were naming what was actually before them?

Very true. 10

And suppose further that the prison had an echo which came from the 11
other side, would they not be sure to fancy when one of the passers-by spoke
that the voice which they heard came from the passing shadow?

No question, he replied. 12

To them, I said, the truth would be literally nothing but the shadows of 13
the images.

That is certain. 14

And now look again, and see what will naturally follow if the prisoners are 15
released and disabused of their error. At first, when any of them is liberated
and compelled suddenly to stand up and turn his neck round and walk and
look towards the light, he will suffer sharp pains; the glare will distress him,
and he will be unable to see the realities of which in his former state he had
seen the shadows; and then conceive someone saying to him, that what he saw
before was an illusion, but that now, when he is approaching nearer to being
and his eye is turned towards more real existence, he has a clearer vision—
what will be his reply? And you may further imagine that his instructor is
pointing to the objects as they pass and requiring him to name them,—will he
not be perplexed? Will he not fancy that the shadows which he formerly saw
are truer than the objects which are now shown to him?

Far truer. 16

And if he is compelled to look straight at the light, will he not have a pain 17
in his eyes which will make him turn away to take refuge in the objects of
vision which he can see, and which he will conceive to be in reality clearer
than the things which are now being shown to him?

True, he said. 18

And suppose once more, that he is reluctantly dragged up a steep and 19
rugged ascent, and held fast until he is forced into the presence of the sun himself, is he not likely to be pained and irritated? When he approaches the light
his eyes will be dazzled, and he will not be able to see anything at all of what
are now called realities.

Not all in a moment, he said. 20

He will require to grow accustomed to the sight of the upper world. And 21
first he will see the shadows best, next the reflections of men and other objects
in the water, and then the objects themselves; then he will gaze upon the light
of the moon and the stars and the spangled heaven; and he will see the sky and
the stars by night better than the sun or the light of the sun by day?

Certainly. 22

*Earth's star, often associated
in Plato's work with reason,
absolute good, intellectual
illumination, and God*

Last of all he will be able to see the sun,° and not mere reflections of him 23
in the water, but he will see him in his own proper place, and not in another;
and he will contemplate him as he is.

Certainly. 24

He will then proceed to argue that this is he who gives the season and the 25
years, and is the guardian of all that is in the visible world, and in a certain way
the cause of all things which he and his fellows have been accustomed to behold?

Clearly, he said, he would first see the sun and then reason about him. 26

And when he remembered his old habitation, and the wisdom of the den 27 and his fellow prisoners, do you not suppose that he would felicitate himself on the change, and pity them?

Certainly, he would. 28

And if they were in the habit of conferring honors among themselves on 29 those who were quickest to observe the passing shadows and to remark which of them went before, and which followed after, and which were together; and who were therefore best able to draw conclusions as to the future, do you think that he would care for such honors and glories, or envy the possessors of them? Would he not say with Homer,°

Better to be the poor servant of a poor master,

and to endure anything, rather than think as they do and live after their manner?

Yes, he said, I think that he would rather suffer anything than entertain 30 these false notions and live in this miserable manner.

Imagine once more, I said, such a one coming suddenly out of the sun to 31 be replaced in his old situation; would he not be certain to have his eyes full of darkness?

To be sure, he said. 32

And if there were a contest, and he had to compete in measuring the 33 shadows with the prisoners who had never moved out of the den, while his sight was still weak, and before his eyes had become steady (and the time which would be needed to acquire this new habit of sight might be very considerable), would he not be ridiculous? Men would say of him that up he went and down he came without his eyes; and that it was better not even to think of ascending; and if any one tried to loose another and lead him up to the light, let them only catch the offender, and they would put him to death.

No question, he said. 34

This entire allegory, I said, you may now append, dear Glaucon,° to the 35 previous argument; the prison house is the world of sight, the light of the fire is the sun, and you will not misapprehend me if you interpret the journey upwards to be the ascent of the soul into the intellectual world according to my poor belief, which, at your desire, I have expressed—whether rightly or wrongly God knows. But, whether true or false, my opinion is that in the world of knowledge the idea of good appears last of all, and is seen only with an effort; and, when seen, is also inferred to be the universal author of all things beautiful and right, parent of light and of the lord of light in this visible world, and the immediate source of reason and truth in the intellectual; and that this is the power upon which he who would act rationally either in public or private life must have his eye fixed.

I agree, he said, as far as I am able to understand you. 36

Moreover, I said, you must not wonder that those who attain to this 37 beatific vision are unwilling to descend to human affairs; for their souls are ever hastening into the upper world where they desire to dwell; which desire of theirs is very natural, if our allegory may be trusted.

A blind Greek poet from the eighth century BCE, author of the epics The Iliad *and* The Odyssey

Plato's brother, who responds to the questions, ideas, and arguments Socrates poses in The Republic

Yes, very natural. 38

And is there anything surprising in one who passes from divine contem- 39
plations to the evil state of man, misbehaving himself in a ridiculous manner;
if, while his eyes are blinking and before he has become accustomed to the surrounding darkness, he is compelled to fight in courts of law, or in other places,
about the images or the shadows of images of justice, and is endeavoring to
meet the conceptions of those who have never yet seen absolute justice?

Anything but surprising, he replied. 40

Anyone who has common sense will remember that the bewilderments of 41
the eyes are of two kinds, and arise from two causes, either from coming out of
the light or from going into the light, which is true of the mind's eye, quite as
much as of the bodily eye; and he who remembers this when he sees anyone
whose vision is perplexed and weak, will not be too ready to laugh; he will first
ask whether that soul of man has come out of the brighter life, and is unable to
see because unaccustomed to the dark, or having turned from darkness to the day
is dazzled by excess of light. And he will count the one happy in his condition and
state of being, and he will pity the other; or, if he have a mind to laugh at the soul
which comes from below into the light, there will be more reason in this than in
the laugh which greets him who returns from above out of the light into the den.

That, he said, is a very just distinction. 42

But then, if I am right, certain professors of education must be wrong 43
when they say that they can put a knowledge into the soul which was not there
before, like sight into blind eyes.

They undoubtedly say this, he replied. 44

Whereas, our argument shows that the power and capacity of learning 45
exists in the soul already; and that just as the eye was unable to turn from
darkness to light without the whole body, so too the instrument of knowledge
can only by the movement of the whole soul be turned from the world of
becoming into that of being, and learn by degrees to endure the sight of being,
and of the brightest and best of being, or in other words, of the good.

Very true. 46

And must there not be some art which will effect conversion in the easiest 47
and quickest manner; not implanting the faculty of sight, for that exists already,
but has been turned in the wrong direction, and is looking away from the truth?

Yes, he said, such an art may be presumed. 48

And whereas the other so-called virtues of the soul seem to be akin to 49
bodily qualities, for even when they are not originally innate they can be
implanted later by habit and exercise, the virtue of wisdom more than anything
else contains a divine element which always remains, and by this conversion is
rendered useful and profitable; or, on the other hand, hurtful and useless. Did
you never observe the narrow intelligence flashing from the keen eye of a
clever rogue—how eager he is, how clearly his paltry soul sees the way to his
end; he is the reverse of blind, but his keen eyesight is forced into the service of
evil, and he is mischievous in proportion to his cleverness?

Very true, he said. 50

But what if there had been a circumcision of such natures in the days of 51
their youth; and they had been severed from those sensual pleasures, such as eating and drinking, which, like leaden weights, were attached to them at their
birth, and which drag them down and turn the vision of their souls upon the
things that are below—if, I say, they had been released from these impediments
and turned in the opposite direction, the very same faculty in them would have
seen the truth as keenly as they see what their eyes are turned to now.

Very likely. 52

Yes, I said; and there is another thing which is likely, or rather a necessary 53
inference from what has preceded, that neither the uneducated and uninformed of the truth, nor yet those who never make an end of their education, will be able ministers of State; not the former, because they have no single
aim of duty which is the rule of all their actions, private as well as public; nor
the latter, because they will not act at all except upon compulsion, fancying
that they are already dwelling apart in the islands of the blessed.

Very true, he replied. 54

Then, I said, the business of us who are the founders of the State will be to 55
compel the best minds to attain that knowledge which we have already shown
to be the greatest of all—they must continue to ascend until they arrive at the
good; but when they have ascended and seen enough we must not allow them
to do as they do now.

What do you mean? 56

I mean that they remain in the upper world: but this must not be allowed; 57
they must be made to descend again among the prisoners in the den, and partake of their labors and honors, whether they are worth having or not.

But is not this unjust? he said; ought we to give them a worse life, when 58
they might have a better?

You have again forgotten, my friend, I said, the intention of the legislator, 59
who did not aim at making any one class in the State happy above the rest; the
happiness was to be in the whole State, and he held the citizens together by
persuasion and necessity, making them benefactors of the State, and therefore
benefactors of one another; to this end he created them, not to please themselves, but to be his instruments in binding up the State.

True, he said, I had forgotten. 60

Observe, Glaucon, that there will be no injustice in compelling our philos- 61
ophers to have a care and providence of others; we shall explain to them that in
other States, men of their class are not obliged to share in the toils of politics:
and this is reasonable, for they grow up at their own sweet will, and the government would rather not have them. Being self-taught, they cannot be expected
to show any gratitude for a culture which they have never received. But we have
brought you into the world to be rulers of the hive, kings of yourselves and of
the other citizens, and have educated you far better and more perfectly than
they have been educated, and you are better able to share in the double duty.
Wherefore each of you, when his turn comes, must go down to the general
underground abode, and get the habit of seeing in the dark. When you have

acquired the habit, you will see ten thousand times better than the inhabitants of the den, and you will know what the several images are, and what they represent, because you have seen the beautiful and just and good in their truth. And thus our State, which is also yours, will be a reality, and not a dream only, and will be administered in a spirit unlike that of other States, in which men fight with one another about shadows only and are distracted in the struggle for power, which in their eyes is a great good. Whereas the truth is that the State in which the rulers are most reluctant to govern is always the best and most quietly governed, and the State in which they are most eager, the worst.

Quite true, he replied. 62

And will our pupils, when they hear this, refuse to take their turn at the 63 toils of State, when they are allowed to spend the greater part of their time with one another in the heavenly light?

Impossible, he answered; for they are just men, and the commands which we 64 impose upon them are just; there can be no doubt that every one of them will take office as a stern necessity, and not after the fashion of our present rulers of State.

Yes, my friend, I said; and there lies the point. You must contrive for your 65 future rulers another and a better life than that of a ruler, and then you may have a well-ordered State; for only in the State which offers this, will they rule who are truly rich, not in silver and gold, but in virtue and wisdom, which are the true blessings of life. Whereas if they go to the administration of public affairs, poor and hungering after their own private advantage, thinking that hence they are to snatch the chief good, order there can never be; for they will be fighting about office, and the civil and domestic broils which thus arise will be the ruin of the rulers themselves and of the whole State.

Most true, he replied. 66

And the only life which looks down upon the life of political ambition is 67 that of true philosophy. Do you know of any other?

Indeed, I do not, he said. 68

❍ READING ARGUMENTS

1. Do you find Plato's allegory persuasive? What are its strengths and weaknesses?

2. According to Plato, what are the benefits of becoming educated about the true nature of reality? What are the drawbacks and costs of this process?

3. "The Allegory of the Cave" contains elements of a proposal argument. What does Plato propose? In what sense, if any, does his proposal apply to contemporary politics?

4. This argument is presented in the form of a dialogue, in which Glaucon responds to Socrates. How do Glaucon's responses move Plato's argument along?

⊙ WRITING ARGUMENTS

Both Plato and Thomas Jefferson (p. 764) discuss political leadership. How are their views similar? Where do their beliefs about the proper conduct and nature of political leaders differ? Which writer's argument seems more persuasive, and why? Develop your ideas in an argumentative essay.

TO HIS COY MISTRESS

ANDREW MARVELL

Andrew Marvell (1621–1678) was a member of the English Parliament for twenty years, starting in 1658. His poetry, which he wrote for his own enjoyment, was not published until after his death. "To His Coy Mistress" is his best-known poem.

Had we but world enough, and time,   1
This coyness, lady, were no crime.
We would sit down, and think which way
To walk, and pass our long love's day.
Thou by the Indian Ganges° side   5 *A river in India*
Should'st rubies find: I by the tide   *A river in England that flows*
Of Humber° would complain.° I would   *past the city of Hull*
Love you ten years before the Flood,   *To write poems or songs of*
And you should, if you please, refuse   *unrequited love*
Till the conversion of the Jews.°   10 *The belief that Jews would*
My vegetable love° should grow   *be converted to Christianity*
Vaster than empires, and more slow.   *during the Last Judgment;*
An hundred years should go to praise   *the end of time*
Thine eyes, and on thy forehead gaze: *A slow-growing love*
Two hundred to adore each breast: 15
But thirty thousand to the rest.
An age at least to every part,
And the last age should show your heart.
For, lady, you deserve this state,
Nor would I love at lower rate.   20
    But at my back I always hear
Time's winged chariot hurrying near;
And yonder all before us lie
Deserts of vast eternity.

Thy beauty shall no more be found,
Nor in thy marble vault shall sound   25
My echoing song; then worms shall try
That long preserved virginity,
And your quaint honor turn to dust,
And into ashes all my lust.   30
The grave's a fine and private place,
But none, I think, do there embrace.
        Now therefore, while the youthful hue
Sits on thy skin like morning dew,
And while thy willing soul transpires   35
At every pore with instant fires,
Now let us sport us while we may;
and now, like am'rous birds of prey,
Rather at once our time devour,

Slowly chewing jaws Than languish in his slow-chapt° power,   40
Let us roll all our strength, and all
Our sweetness, up into one ball;
And tear our pleasures with rough strife

Through Thorough° the iron gates of life.
Thus, though we cannot make our sun   45
Stand still, yet we will make him run.

⟳ READING ARGUMENTS

1. "To His Coy Mistress" is divided into three sections. Paraphrase each section's main idea in a single sentence.

2. What does the phrase "coy mistress" suggest about the occasion and audience for the poem? How do you think the "coy mistress" would respond to the speaker's arguments?

3. How does the speaker's attitude toward time—and toward his relationship with the lady he addresses—change in line 21? How does this shift support his argument? What does he say will happen to the lady if she is not persuaded by his poem?

4. The concluding stanza of the poem begins with the phrase, "Now therefore." How does the speaker develop a deductive argument in the lines that follow?

⟳ WRITING ARGUMENTS

1. Write a letter from the "coy mistress" to the poem's speaker refuting his arguments.

2. "To His Coy Mistress" is generally considered to be a poem on the theme of *carpe diem,* which means "seize the day." The full quotation comes from the Roman poet Horace: "Seize the day, and place no trust in tomorrow." Does this seem like a good philosophy of life? Write an argumentative essay that develops your position on this issue.

A MODEST PROPOSAL

JONATHAN SWIFT

Jonathan Swift (1667–1745) was a Protestant clergyman (dean of St. Patrick's Cathedral in Dublin) and a member of the Irish ruling class. His other works include A Tale of a Tub *(1704) and* Gulliver's Travels *(1726). "A Modest Proposal," written in 1729, addresses the wretched condition of the Irish people under English rule: drought had caused crop failures in Ireland, and English landowners ignored the widespread famine while thousands died of starvation.*

It is a melancholy object to those who walk through this great town or travel in the country, when they see the streets, the roads, and cabin doors, crowded with beggars of the female sex, followed by three, four, or six children, all in rags and importuning every passenger for an alms. These mothers instead of being able to work for their honest livelihood, are forced to employ all their time in strolling to beg sustenance for their helpless infants: who as they grow up either turn thieves for want of work, or leave their dear native country to fight for the pretender in Spain,° or sell themselves to the Barbadoes.°

I think it is agreed by all parties that this prodigious number of children in the arms, or on the backs, or at the heels of their mothers, and frequently of their fathers, is in the present deplorable state of the kingdom a very great additional grievance; and, therefore, whoever could find out a fair, cheap, and easy method of making these children sound, useful members of the commonwealth, would deserve so well of the public as to have his statue set up for a preserver of the nation.

But my intention is very far from being confined to provide only for the children of professed beggars; it is of a much greater extent, and shall take in the whole number of infants at a certain age who are born of parents in effect as little able to support them as those who demand our charity in the streets.

As to my own part, having turned my thoughts for many years upon this important subject, and maturely weighed the several schemes of our projectors, I have always found them grossly mistaken in their computation. It is true, a

1

2

3

4

James Francis Edward Stuart (1688–1766), descendant of the Stuart royal line. After the Stuarts were expelled from Protestant England in 1689, they took refuge in Catholic countries.

A New World colony in the Caribbean. The poor sometimes emigrated from Ireland to Barbados to find work.

Just born

child just dropped from its dam° may be supported by her milk for a solar year, with little other nourishment; at most not above the value of 2s., which the mother may certainly get, or the value in scraps, by her lawful occupation of begging; and it is exactly at one year old that I propose to provide for them in such a manner as instead of being a charge upon their parents or the parish, or wanting food and raiment for the rest of their lives, they shall on the contrary contribute to the feeding, and partly to the clothing, of many thousands.

There is likewise another great advantage in my scheme, that it will pre- 5 vent those voluntary abortions, and that horrid practice of women murdering their bastard children, alas! too frequent among us! sacrificing the poor inno- cent babes I doubt more to avoid the expense than the shame, which would move tears and pity in the most savage and inhuman breast.

The number of souls in this kingdom being usually reckoned one million 6 and a half, of these I calculate there may be about 200,000 couple whose wives are breeders; from which number I subtract 30,000 couple who are able to maintain their own children (although I apprehend there cannot be so many, under the present distress of the kingdom); but this being granted, there will remain 170,000 breeders. I again subtract 50,000 for those women who mis- carry, or whose children die by accident or disease within the year. There only remain 120,000 children of poor parents annually born. The question there- fore is, how this number shall be reared and provided for? which, as I have already said, under the present situation of affairs, is utterly impossible by all the methods hitherto proposed. For we can neither employ them in handicraft nor agriculture; we neither build houses (I mean in the country) nor cultivate land; they can very seldom pick up a livelihood by stealing, till they arrive at six years old, except where they are of towardly parts, although I confess they learn the rudiments much earlier, during which time they can, however, be properly looked upon only as probationers; as I have been informed by a prin- cipal gentleman in the county of Cavan, who protested to me that he never knew above one or two instances under the age of six, even in a part of the kingdom so renowned for the quickest proficiency in that art.

I am assured by our merchants, that a boy or a girl before twelve years old 7 is no salable commodity; and even when they come to this age they will not yield above 3£. or 3£. 2s. 6d. at most on the exchange; which cannot turn to account either to the parents or kingdom, the charge of nutriment and rags having been at least four times that value.

I shall now therefore humbly propose my own thoughts, which I hope 8 will not be liable to the least objection.

I have been assured by a very knowing American of my acquaintance in 9 London, that a young healthy child well nursed is at a year old a most deli- cious, nourishing, and wholesome food, whether stewed, roasted, baked, or broiled; and I make no doubt that it will equally serve in a fricassee or a ragout.

I do therefore humbly offer it to public consideration that of the 120,000 10 children already computed, 20,000 may be reserved for breed, whereof only one-fourth part to be males; which is more than we allow to sheep, black cattle, or swine; and my reason is, that these children are seldom the fruits of marriage, a circumstance not much regarded by our savages; therefore one male will be sufficient to serve four females. That the remaining 100,000 may, at a year old, be offered in sale to the persons of quality and fortune through the kingdom; always advising the mother to let them suck plentifully in the last month, so as to render them plump and fat for a good table. A child will make two dishes at an entertainment for friends; and when the family dines alone, the fore and hind quarter will make a reasonable dish, and seasoned with a little pepper or salt will be very good boiled on the fourth day, especially in winter.

I have reckoned upon a medium that a child just born will weigh 11 12 pounds, and in a solar year, if tolerably nursed, will increase to 28 pounds.

I grant this food will be somewhat dear, and therefore very proper for 12 landlords, who, as they have already devoured most of the parents, seem to have the best title to the children.

Infants' flesh will be in season throughout the year, but more plentiful in 13 March, and a little before and after: for we are told by a grave author, an eminent French physician, that fish being a prolific diet, there are more children born in Roman Catholic countries about nine months after Lent than at any other season; therefore, reckoning a year after Lent, the markets will be more glutted than usual, because the number of popish infants is at least three to one in this kingdom: and therefore it will have one other collateral advantage, by lessening the number of papists° among us.

Catholics. The term papists suggests their allegiance to the Pope rather than to the Church of England.

I have already computed the charge of nursing a beggar's child (in which 14 list I reckon all cottagers, laborers, and four-fifths of the farmers) to be about 2s. per annum, rags included; and I believe no gentleman would repine to give 10s. for the carcass of a good fat child, which, as I have said, will make four dishes of excellent nutritive meat, when he has only some particular friend or his own family to dine with him. Thus the squire will learn to be a good landlord, and grow popular among the tenants; the mother will have 8s. net profit, and be fit for work till she produces another child.

Those who are more thrifty (as I must confess the times require) may flay 15 the carcass; the skin of which artificially dressed will make admirable gloves for ladies, and summer boots for fine gentlemen.

As to our city of Dublin, shambles° may be appointed for this purpose in 16 *Butcher shops* the most convenient parts of it, and butchers we may be assured will not be wanting: although I rather recommend buying the children alive, and dressing them hot from the knife as we do roasting pigs.

A very worthy person, a true lover of his country, and whose virtues I 17 highly esteem, was lately pleased in discoursing on this matter to offer a refinement upon my scheme. He said that many gentlemen of this kingdom, having of late destroyed their deer, he conceived that the want of venison might be well supplied by the bodies of young lads and maidens, not exceeding fourteen years of age nor under twelve; so great a number of both sexes in every country being now ready to starve for want of work and service; and these to be disposed of by their parents, if alive, or otherwise by their nearest relations.

But with due deference to so excellent a friend and so deserving a patriot, I cannot be altogether in his sentiments; for as to the males, my American acquaintance assured me from frequent experience that their flesh was generally tough and lean, like that of our schoolboys by continual exercise, and their taste disagreeable; and to fatten them would not answer the charge. Then as to the females, it would, I think, with humble submission be a loss to the public, because they soon would become breeders themselves: and besides, it is not improbable that some scrupulous people might be apt to censure such a practice (although indeed very unjustly), as a little bordering upon cruelty; which, I confess, has always been with me the strongest objection against any project, how well soever intended.

George Psalmanazar (1679?–1763), who falsely claimed to be the first person from Formosa (modern-day Taiwan) to visit Europe. He described Formosan native customs that included cannibalism.

Chinese nobles, court officials, or magistrates

A post for hanging; a gallows

A small coin

But in order to justify my friend, he confessed that this expedient was put 18 into his head by the famous Psalmanazar,° a native of the island Formosa, who came from thence to London about twenty years ago: and in conversation told my friend, that in his country when any young person happened to be put to death, the executioner sold the carcass to persons of quality as a prime dainty; and that in his time the body of a plump girl of fifteen, who was crucified for an attempt to poison the emperor, was sold to his imperial majesty's prime minister of state, and other great mandarins° of the court, in joints from the gibbet,° at 400 crowns. Neither indeed can I deny, that if the same use were made of several plump young girls in this town, who without one single groat° to their fortunes cannot stir abroad without a chair, and appear at the playhouse and assemblies in foreign fineries which they never will pay for, the kingdom would not be the worse.

Some persons of a desponding spirit are in great concern about the vast 19 number of poor people, who are aged, diseased, or maimed, and I have been desired to employ my thoughts what course may be taken to ease the nation of so grievous an encumbrance. But I am not in the least pain upon that matter, because it is very well known that they are every day dying and rotting by cold and famine, and filth and vermin, as fast as can be reasonably expected. And as to the young laborers, they are now in as hopeful condition: They cannot get work, and consequently pine away for want of nourishment, to a degree that if at any time they are accidentally hired to common labor, they have not strength to perform it; and thus the country and themselves are happily delivered from the evils to come.

I have too long digressed, and therefore shall return to my subject. I think 20 the advantages by the proposal which I have made are obvious and many, as well as of the highest importance.

For first, as I have already observed, it would greatly lessen the number of 21 papists, with whom we are yearly overrun, being the principal breeders of the nation as well as our most dangerous enemies; and who stay at home on purpose to deliver the kingdom to the Pretender, hoping to take their advantage by the absence of so many good Protestants, who have chosen rather to leave their country than stay at home and pay tithes against their conscience to an Episcopal curate.

Secondly, The poor tenants will have something valuable of their own, 22 which by law may be made liable to distress° and help to pay their landlord's rent, their corn and cattle being already seized, and money a thing unknown.

Able to be seized to pay a debt

Thirdly, Whereas the maintenance of 100,000 children from two years 23 old and upward, cannot be computed at less that 10s. a-piece per annum, the nation's stock will be thereby increased £50,000 per annum, beside the profit of a new dish introduced to the tables of all gentlemen of fortune in the kingdom who have any refinement in taste. And the money will circulate among ourselves, the goods being entirely of our own growth and manufacture.

Fourthly, The constant breeders beside the gain of 8s. sterling per annum 24 by the sale of their children, will be rid of the charge of maintaining them after the first year.

Fifthly, This food would likewise bring great custom to taverns, where the 25 vintners will certainly be so prudent as to procure the best receipts for dressing it to perfection, and consequently have their houses frequented by all the fine gentlemen, who justly value themselves upon their knowledge in good eating; and a skillful cook who understands how to oblige his guests, will contrive to make it as expensive as they please.

Sixthly, This would be a great inducement to marriage, which all wise 26 nations have either encouraged by rewards or enforced by laws and penalties. It would increase the care and tenderness of mothers toward their children, when they were sure of a settlement for life to the poor babes, provided in some sort by the public, to their annual profit instead of expense. We should see an honest emulation among the married women, which of them would bring the fattest child to the market. Men would become as fond of their wives during the time of their pregnancy as they are now of their mares in foal, their cows in calf, their sows when they are ready to farrow; nor offer to beat or kick them (as is too frequent a practice) for fear of a miscarriage.

Many other advantages might be enumerated. For instance, the addition 27 of some thousand carcasses in our exportation of barreled beef, the propagation of swine's flesh, and improvement in the art of making good bacon, so much wanted among us by the great destruction of pigs, too frequent at our table; which are no way comparable in taste or magnificence to a well-grown, fat, yearling child, which roasted whole will make a considerable figure at a lord mayor's feast or any other public entertainment. But this and many others I omit, being studious of brevity.

Supposing that 1,000 families in this city would be constant customers for 28 infants' flesh, besides others who might have it at merry-meetings, particularly at weddings and christenings, I compute that Dublin would take off annually about 20,000 carcasses; and the rest of the kingdom (where probably they will be sold somewhat cheaper) the remaining 80,000.

I can think of no one objection that will possibly be raised against this 29 proposal unless it should be urged that the number of people will be thereby much lessened in the kingdom. This I freely own, and it was indeed one principal design in offering it to the world. I desire the reader will observe, that I calculate my remedy for this one individual kingdom of Ireland and for no other that ever was, is, or I think ever can be upon earth. Therefore let no man talk to me of other expedients: of taxing our absentees at 5s. a pound: of using neither clothes nor household furniture except what is of our own growth and manufacture: of utterly rejecting the materials and instruments that promote foreign luxury: of curing the expensiveness of pride, vanity, idleness, and gaming in our women: of introducing a vein of parsimony, prudence, and temperance: of learning to love our country, in the want of which we differ even from Laplanders,° and the inhabitants of Topinamboo:° of quitting our animosities and factions, nor acting any longer like the Jews, who were murdering one another at the very moment their city° was taken: of being a little cautious not to sell our country and conscience for nothing: of teaching landlords to have at least one degree of mercy toward their tenants: lastly, of putting a spirit of honesty, industry, and skill into our shopkeepers; who, if a resolution could now be taken to buy only our native goods, would immediately unite to cheat and exact upon us in the price, the measure, and the goodness, nor could ever yet be brought to make one fair proposal of just dealing, though often and earnestly invited to it.

Therefore I repeat, let no man talk to me of these and the like expedients,   30
till he has at least some glimpse of hope that there will be ever some hearty and sincere attempt to put them in practice.

But as to myself, having been wearied out for many years with offering   31
vain, idle, visionary thoughts, and at length utterly despairing of success, I fortunately fell upon this proposal; which, as it is wholly new, so it has something solid and real, of no expense and little trouble, full in our own power, and whereby we can incur no danger in disobliging England. For this kind of commodity will not bear exportation, the flesh being of too tender a consistence to admit a long continuance in salt, although perhaps I could name a country° which would be glad to eat up our whole nation without it.

After all, I am not so violently bent upon my own opinion as to reject any   32
offer proposed by wise men, which shall be found equally innocent, cheap, easy, and effectual. But before something of that kind shall be advanced in contradiction to my scheme, and offering a better, I desire the author or authors will be pleased maturely to consider two points. First, as things now stand, how they will be able to find food and raiment for 100,000 useless mouths and backs. And secondly, there being a round million of creatures in human figure throughout this kingdom, whose subsistence put into a common stock would leave them in debt 2,000,000£. sterling, adding those who are beggars by profession to the bulk of farmers, cottagers, and laborers, with the wives and children who are beggars in effect; I desire those politicians who dislike my overture, and may perhaps be so bold as to attempt an answer, that they will first ask the parents of these mortals, whether they would not at this day think it a great happiness to have been sold for food at a year old in the

The indigenous Sami people of northern European countries, including Sweden, Norway, and Finland. The term is now considered pejorative.

Brazil

Jerusalem, which was conquered by the Roman commander Titus in 70 CE

England

manner I prescribe, and thereby have avoided such a perpetual scene of misfortunes as they have since gone through by the oppression of landlords, the impossibility of paying rent without money or trade, the want of common sustenance, with neither house nor clothes to cover them from the inclemencies of the weather, and the most inevitable prospect of entailing the like or greater miseries upon their breed for ever.

I profess, in the sincerity of my heart, that I have not the least personal 33 interest in endeavoring to promote this necessary work, having no other motive than the public good of my country, by advancing our trade, providing for infants, relieving the poor, and giving some pleasure to the rich. I have no children by which I can propose to get a single penny; the youngest being nine years old, and my wife past childbearing.

⊖READING ARGUMENTS

1. Swift's "A Modest Proposal" is **satire**: it takes a position that is so extreme that readers must necessarily disagree with it. By taking such a position, Swift ridicules the English political system that he considers corrupt and insensitive and implies another, more reasonable argument that the reader must infer. What is the real argument that Swift is making in "A Modest Proposal"? What social reforms does he propose?

2. Where does "A Modest Proposal" use inductive reasoning?

3. In what sense is "A Modest Proposal" an ethical argument?

4. Swift's use of **irony**—saying one thing but meaning another—is a useful technique for making an argument, yet it also has limitations. What are some of these limitations?

5. What elements of a proposal argument appear in this essay? Which elements, if any, are missing?

⊖WRITING ARGUMENTS

1. Write your own "modest proposal." Choose a contemporary issue or controversy (political, cultural, or social). Then, write an argumentative essay that uses **irony**, **satire**, and **hyperbole** (intentional exaggeration) to make your point.

2. "A Modest Proposal" includes population data, economic projections, and other kinds of support. What point do you think Swift is making about actual proposals to solve social or political problems? Do you think his point is relevant today? Why or why not?

THE DECLARATION OF INDEPENDENCE

THOMAS JEFFERSON

Thomas Jefferson, born in 1743, was one of the founding fathers of the United States. He served in the Virginia House of Burgesses and the Continental Congress, as governor of Virginia, minister to France, secretary of state in President George Washington's cabinet, vice president, and president of the United States for two terms. He also founded the University of Virginia. In 1776, he was chosen to draft the Declaration of Independence, the founding document of American liberties. Jefferson died on July 4, 1826.

In Congress, July 4, 1776
The Unanimous Declaration of the
Thirteen United States of America

When in the Course of human events it becomes necessary for one people to   1
dissolve the political bands which have connected them with another, and to
assume among the powers of the earth, the separate and equal station to which
the Laws of Nature and of Nature's God entitle them, a decent respect to the
opinions of mankind requires that they should declare the causes which impel
them to the separation.

We hold these truths to be self-evident, that all men are created equal,   2
that they are endowed by their Creator with certain unalienable Rights, that
among these are Life, Liberty, and the pursuit of Happiness. That to secure
these rights, Governments are instituted among Men, deriving their just
powers from the consent of the governed. That whenever any Form of Government becomes destructive of these ends, it is the Right of the People to
alter or to abolish it, and to institute new Government, laying its foundation
on such principles and organizing its powers in such form, as to them shall
seem most likely to effect their Safety and Happiness. Prudence, indeed, will
dictate that Governments long established should not be changed for light
and transient causes; and accordingly all experience hath shewn that mankind are more disposed to suffer, while evils are sufferable, than right themselves by abolishing the forms to which they are accustomed. But when a
long train of abuses and usurpations, pursuing invariably the same Object
evinces a design to reduce them under absolute Despotism, it is their right, it
is their duty, to throw off such Government, and to provide new Guards for
their future security. Such has been the patient sufferance of these Colonies;
and such is now the necessity which constrains them to alter their former
Systems of Government. The history of the present King of Great Britain is a

history of repeated injuries and usurpations, all having in direct object the establishment of an absolute Tyranny over these States. To prove this, let Facts be submitted to a candid° world.

Impartial, without prejudice

He has refused his Assent to Laws, the most wholesome and necessary for the public good. 3

He has forbidden his Government to pass laws of immediate and pressing importance, unless suspended in their operation till his Assent should be obtained; and when so suspended, he has utterly neglected to attend to them. 4

He has refused to pass other Laws for the accommodation of large districts of people, unless those people would relinquish the right of Representation in the Legislature, a right inestimable to them and formidable to tyrants only. 5

He has called together legislative bodies at places unusual, uncomfortable, and distant from the depository of their Public Records, for the sole purpose of fatiguing them into compliance with his measures. 6

He has dissolved Representative Houses repeatedly, for opposing with manly firmness his invasions on the rights of the people. 7

He has refused for a long time, after such dissolutions, to cause others to be elected; whereby the Legislative Powers, incapable of Annihilation, have returned to the People at large for their exercise; the State remaining in the mean time exposed to all the dangers of invasion from without, and convulsions within. 8

He has endeavored to prevent the population of these States; for that purpose obstructing the Laws for Naturalization of Foreigners; refusing to pass others to encourage their migration hither, and raising the conditions of new Appropriations of Lands. 9

He has obstructed the Administration of Justice, by refusing his Assent to Laws for establishing Judiciary Powers. 10

He has made Judges dependent on his Will alone, for the tenure of their offices, and the amount and payment of their salaries. 11

He has erected a multitude of New Offices, and sent hither swarms of Officers to harass our people, and eat out their substance. 12

He has kept among us, in times of peace, Standing Armies without the Consent of our legislatures. 13

He has affected to render the Military independent of and superior to the Civil Power. 14

He has combined with others to subject us to a jurisdiction foreign to our constitution, and unacknowledged by our laws; giving his Assent to their Acts of pretended Legislation: For quartering large bodies of armed troops among us: For protecting them, by a mock Trial, from punishment for any Murders which they should commit on the Inhabitants of these States: For cutting off our Trade with all parts of the world: For imposing Taxes on us without our Consent: For depriving us in many cases, of the benefits of Trial by Jury: For transporting us beyond Seas to be tried for 15

Quebec, whose residents were deprived of political representation by the British government in 1774

pretended offenses: For abolishing the free System of English Laws in a neighboring Province,° establishing therein an Arbitrary government, and enlarging its Boundaries so as to render it at once an example and fit instrument for introducing the same absolute rule into these Colonies: For taking away our Charters, abolishing our most valuable Laws and altering fundamentally the Forms of our Governments: For suspending our own Legislatures, and declaring themselves invested with power to legislate for us in all cases whatsoever.

He has abdicated Government here, by declaring us out of his Protection 16 and waging War against us.

He has plundered our seas, ravaged our Coasts, burnt our towns, and 17 destroyed the lives of our people.

He is at this time transporting large Armies of foreign Mercenaries to 18 complete the works of death, desolation and tyranny, already begun with circumstances of Cruelty & Perfidy scarcely paralleled in the most barbarous ages, and totally unworthy the Head of a civilized nation.

He has constrained our fellow Citizens taken Captive on the high Seas to 19 bear Arms against their Country, to become the executioners of their friends and Brethren, or to fall themselves by their Hands.

He has excited domestic insurrections amongst us, and has endeavored to 20 bring on the inhabitants of our frontiers, the merciless Indian Savages, whose known rule of warfare, is an undistinguished destruction of all ages, sexes, and conditions.

In every stage of these Oppressions We have Petitioned for Redress in 21 the most humble terms: Our repeated Petitions have been answered only by repeated injury. A Prince, whose character is thus marked by every act which may define a Tyrant, is unfit to be the ruler of a free people.

Nor have We been wanting in attention to our British brethren. We have 22 warned them from time to time of attempts by their legislature to extend an unwarrantable jurisdiction over us. We have reminded them of the circumstances of our emigration and settlement here. We have appealed to their native justice and magnanimity, and we have conjured them by the ties of our common kindred to disavow these usurpations, which would inevitably interrupt our connections and correspondence. They too have been deaf to the voice of justice and of consanguinity. We must, therefore, acquiesce in the necessity, which denounces our Separation, and hold them, as we hold the rest of mankind, Enemies in War, in Peace Friends.

We, THEREFORE the Representatives of the UNITED STATES OF 23 AMERICA, in General Congress, Assembled, appealing to the Supreme Judge of the world for the rectitude of our intentions, do, in the Name, and by Authority of the good People of these Colonies, solemnly publish and declare, That these United Colonies are, and of Right ought to be FREE AND INDEPENDENT STATES; that they are Absolved from all Allegiance to the British Crown, and that all political connection between them and the State of Great Britain, is and ought to be totally dissolved; and that as Free and Independent States, they have full Power to levy War, conclude Peace, contract Alliances, establish Commerce, and to do all other Acts and Things which Independent States may of right do. And for the support of this Declaration, with a firm reliance on the protection of Divine Providence, we mutually pledge to each other our Lives, our Fortunes, and our sacred Honor.

⊘ READING ARGUMENTS

1. What are the purposes of the first and second paragraphs of the Declaration of Independence? Do these opening paragraphs present information deductively or inductively?

2. In paragraph 2, Jefferson writes, "Governments long established should not be changed for light and transient causes." Why is this qualification important to his argument? What objections does it anticipate?

3. According to the Declaration, what is the purpose of government? What makes a government legitimate?

4. In what sense is the Declaration of Independence a cause-and-effect argument?

5. What specific evidence does Jefferson supply to support his case? How effective is this evidence? What do you consider his most convincing piece of evidence?

⊘ WRITING ARGUMENTS

1. Write a one-page rhetorical analysis of the Declaration of Independence in terms of the Toulmin model. Begin by identifying the claim, the grounds, and the warrant. (See Chapter 6 for more on Toulmin argument; see Chapter 4 for information on writing a rhetorical analysis.)

2. Jefferson writes that revolutionary action should not be taken for "light and transient causes" (para. 2). After an armed uprising several years before the American Revolution, he also said, "God forbid we be 20 years without such a rebellion. . . . The tree of liberty must be refreshed from time to time with the blood of patriots and tyrants." In your view, what conditions or actions on the part of an established government justify its overthrow? Explain your answer in an argumentative essay.

THE GETTYSBURG ADDRESS
ABRAHAM LINCOLN

Abraham Lincoln (1809–1865) was the sixteenth president of the United States. Raised in frontier Kentucky and Indiana, he rose from rural poverty to become a lawyer, an Illinois state legislator, and a member of the U.S. House of Representatives. He also became one of America's mythic figures. Elected to the White House in 1861 and again in 1864, Lincoln led the United States through the cataclysm of the Civil War and was assassinated in 1865. His 1863 Gettysburg Address, delivered at the dedication of the Soldier's National Cemetery in Gettysburg, Pennsylvania, is arguably the most famous speech in American history.

Four score and seven years ago our fathers brought forth on this continent, a 1
new nation, conceived in Liberty, and dedicated to the proposition that all men are created equal.

Now we are engaged in a great civil war, testing whether that nation, or 2
any nation so conceived and so dedicated, can long endure. We are met on a great battle-field of that war. We have come to dedicate a portion of that field, as a final resting place for those who here gave their lives that that nation might live. It is altogether fitting and proper that we should do this.

But, in a larger sense, we can not dedicate—we can not consecrate—we 3
can not hallow—this ground. The brave men, living and dead, who struggled here, have consecrated it, far above our poor power to add or detract. The world will little note, nor long remember what we say here, but it can never forget what they did here. It is for us the living, rather, to be dedicated here to the unfinished work which they who fought here have thus far so nobly advanced. It is rather for us to be here dedicated to the great task remaining before us—that from these honored dead we take increased devotion to that cause for which they gave the last full measure of devotion—that we here highly resolve that these dead shall not have died in vain—that this nation, under God, shall have a new birth of freedom—and that government of the people, by the people, for the people, shall not perish from the earth.

⊃ READING ARGUMENTS

1. According to Lincoln, what is the obligation of "the living" (para. 3)? Explain this obligation in your own words.

2. Does the Gettysburg Address make an argument? If so, is it a deductive argument or an inductive argument? Explain.

3. Lincoln gave this speech at the dedication of a cemetery, yet he concedes that "in a larger sense, we can not dedicate—we can not consecrate—we can not hallow—this ground" (3). Is he undercutting his own implicit purpose here? How does this concession support his larger point?

4. What strategies does Lincoln use to support his position? Does he make an ethical argument? A cause-and-effect argument? Is this speech in any sense a proposal argument?

⊙ WRITING ARGUMENTS

1. Consider Lincoln's prose style—in particular, its rhythm and word choice. For example, is "Four score and seven years ago" (para. 1) the clearest, simplest phrasing he could have chosen? Rewrite this sentence—or any other sentence—in your own words. How does your version compare to Lincoln's? What do you learn about Lincoln's language—and his argument—when you try to paraphrase his speech?

2. In a well-known 1920 essay, the American critic H. L. Mencken lauded the Gettysburg Address as "eloquence brought to a pellucid and almost gem-like perfection—the highest emotion reduced to a few poetical phrases." However, Mencken qualified his praise of Lincoln's speech by saying, "But let us not forget that it is poetry, not logic; beauty, not sense." He said of Lincoln's main point: "It is difficult to imagine anything more untrue." How do you respond to Mencken's assessment? Do you find Lincoln's argument "true" or "untrue"? Do you think the speech's "eloquence," "poetry," and "beauty" undercut its "logic," "sense," and "truth"? Why or why not?

DECLARATION OF SENTIMENTS AND RESOLUTIONS

ELIZABETH CADY STANTON

Elizabeth Cady Stanton (1815–1902) was a prominent leader in the struggle for the rights of women, advocating for the right of women to vote, divorce, and be equal to men under law. In 1848, when Stanton's "Declaration of Sentiments and Resolutions" was written for a women's rights convention in Seneca Falls, New York, married women were not allowed to own property. Stanton's declaration is modeled on Thomas Jefferson's Declaration of Independence.

When, in the course of human events, it becomes necessary for one portion of   1
the family of man to assume among the people of the earth a position different
from that which they have hitherto occupied, but one to which the laws of
nature and of nature's God entitle them, a decent respect to the opinions of
mankind requires that they should declare the causes that impel them to such
a course.

We hold these truths to be self-evident: that all men and women are cre-   2
ated equal; that they are endowed by their Creator with certain inalienable
rights; that among these are life, liberty, and the pursuit of happiness; that to
secure these rights governments are instituted, deriving their just powers from
the consent of the governed. Whenever any form of government becomes
destructive of these ends, it is the right of those who suffer from it to refuse
allegiance to it, and to insist upon the institution of a new government, laying
its foundation on such principles, and organizing its powers in such form, as
to them shall seem most likely to effect their safety and happiness. Prudence
indeed, will dictate that governments long established should not be changed
for light and transient causes; and accordingly all experience hath shown that
mankind are more disposed to suffer, while evils are sufferable, than to right
themselves by abolishing the forms to which they were accustomed. But when
a long train of abuses and usurpations, pursuing invariably the same object
evinces a design to reduce them under absolute despotism, it is their duty to
throw off such government, and to provide new guards for their future security. Such has been the patient sufferance of the women under this government, and such is now the necessity which constrains them to demand the
equal station to which they are entitled.

The history of mankind is a history of repeated injuries and usurpations   3
on the part of man toward woman, having in direct object the establishment
of an absolute tyranny over her. To prove this, let facts be submitted to a candid world.

He has never permitted her to exercise her inalienable right to the elective   4
franchise.

He has compelled her to submit to laws, in the formation of which she   5
had no voice.

He has withheld from her rights which are given to the most ignorant and   6
degraded men—both natives and foreigners.

Having deprived her of this first right of a citizen, the elective franchise,   7
thereby leaving her without representation in the halls of legislation, he has
oppressed her on all sides.

He has made her, if married, in the eye of the law, civilly dead.   8

He has taken from her all right in property, even to the wages she earns.   9

He has made her, morally, an irresponsible being, as she can commit many   10
crimes with impunity, provided they be done in the presence of her husband.
In the covenant of marriage, she is compelled to promise obedience to her husband, he becoming, to all intents and purposes, her master—the law giving him
power to deprive her of her liberty, and to administer chastisement.

He has so framed the laws of divorce, as to what shall be the proper causes, 11
and in case of separation, to whom the guardianship of the children shall be
given, as to be wholly regardless of the happiness of women—the law, in all
cases, going upon a false supposition of the supremacy of man, and giving all
power into his hands.

After depriving her of all rights as a married woman, if single, and the 12
owner of property, he has taxed her to support a government which recognizes her only when her property can be made profitable to it.

He has monopolized nearly all the profitable employments, and from 13
those she is permitted to follow, she receives but a scanty remuneration. He
closes against her all the avenues to wealth and distinction which he considers
most honorable to himself. As a teacher of theology, medicine, or law, she is
not known.

He has denied her the facilities for obtaining a thorough education, all 14
colleges being closed against her.

He allows her in Church, as well as State, but a subordinate position, 15
claiming Apostolic authority for her exclusion from the ministry, and, with
some exceptions, from any public participation in the affairs of the Church.

He has created a false public sentiment by giving to the world a different 16
code of morals for men and women, by which moral delinquencies which
exclude women from society, are not only tolerated, but deemed of little
account in man.

He has usurped the prerogative of Jehovah himself, claiming it as his right 17
to assign for her a sphere of action, when that belongs to her conscience and to
her God.

He has endeavored, in every way that he could, to destroy her confidence 18
in her own powers, to lessen her self-respect, and to make her willing to lead a
dependent and abject life.

Now, in view of this entire disfranchisement of one-half the people of this 19
country, their social and religious degradation—in view of the unjust laws above
mentioned, and because women do feel themselves aggrieved, oppressed, and
fraudulently deprived of their most sacred rights, we insist that they have immediate admission to all the rights and privileges which belong to them as citizens
of the United States.

In entering upon the great work before us, we anticipate no small amount 20
of misconception, misrepresentation, and ridicule; but we shall use every
instrumentality within our power to effect our object. We shall employ agents,
circulate tracts, petition the State and National legislatures, and endeavor to
enlist the pulpit and the press in our behalf. We hope this Convention will be
followed by a series of Conventions embracing every part of the country.

⟐READING ARGUMENTS

1. Why do you think Stanton chose to echo the style and structure of the
   Declaration of Independence? What point was she trying to make?

2. How do Stanton's general political aims contrast with Jefferson's goals in the Declaration of Independence (p. 764)?

3. According to Stanton, "The history of mankind is a history of repeated injuries and usurpations on the part of man toward woman, having in direct object the establishment of an absolute tyranny over her" (para. 3). How does she support this generalization? Do you find her evidence convincing? Why or why not?

4. Stanton writes that man has "usurped the prerogative of Jehovah himself, claiming it as his right to assign for [women] a sphere of action" (17). What do you think she means? Do you think her point is valid today?

5. In her conclusion, Stanton summarizes how women will fulfill the goals of her declaration. What specific steps does she expect women to take?

⊖ WRITING ARGUMENTS

1. Stanton accuses male-dominated society not only of "monopoliz[ing] nearly all the profitable employments" (para. 13) but also of "giving to the world a different code of morals for men and women" (16). Do you think these gender restrictions and double standards still exist today? Write an argumentative essay that takes a stand on this issue.

2. In paragraph 2, Stanton quotes Thomas Jefferson's claim that "all experience hath shown that mankind are more disposed to suffer, while evils are sufferable, than to right themselves by abolishing the forms to which they were accustomed." What view of human nature is implied here? Do you agree with this view? Do you think it is still held by people today? Explain your views in an argumentative essay.

POLITICS AND THE ENGLISH LANGUAGE
GEORGE ORWELL

George Orwell was the pen name of journalist, critic, and novelist Eric Blair (1903–1950), best known for his allegorical satire Animal Farm *(1945) and his dystopian novel* 1984 *(1949). Orwell also wrote nonfiction about many different subjects, from his experiences in the Spanish Civil War to his affection for English cooking. He was especially preoccupied with language and political writing—for example, the ways in which political orthodoxy leads to a "lifeless, imitative style." Orwell himself rejected orthodoxy: he was a democratic socialist who criticized socialism, a lover of England who attacked British colonialism, and a literary highbrow who enjoyed popular culture. Although it was written in 1946, "Politics and the English Language" remains an excellent guide for avoiding the bad writing habits of "political conformity."*

Most people who bother with the matter at all would admit that the English language is in a bad way, but it is generally assumed that we cannot by conscious action do anything about it. Our civilization is decadent and our language—so the argument runs—must inevitably share in the general collapse. It follows that any struggle against the abuse of language is a sentimental archaism, like preferring candles to electric light or hansom cabs to aeroplanes. Underneath this lies the half-conscious belief that language is a natural growth and not an instrument which we shape for our own purposes. 1

Now, it is clear that the decline of a language must ultimately have political and economic causes: it is not due simply to the bad influence of this or that individual writer. But an effect can become a cause, reinforcing the original cause and producing the same effect in an intensified form, and so on indefinitely. A man may take to drink because he feels himself to be a failure, and then fail all the more completely because he drinks. It is rather the same thing that is happening to the English language. It becomes ugly and inaccurate because our thoughts are foolish, but the slovenliness of our language makes it easier for us to have foolish thoughts. The point is that the process is reversible. Modern English, especially written English, is full of bad habits which spread by imitation and which can be avoided if one is willing to take the necessary trouble. If one gets rid of these habits one can think more clearly, and to think clearly is a necessary first step towards political regeneration: so that the fight against bad English is not frivolous and is not the exclusive concern of professional writers. I will come back to this presently, and I hope that by that time the meaning of what I have said here will have become clearer. Meanwhile, here are five specimens of the English language as it is now habitually written. 2

These five passages have not been picked out because they are especially bad—I could have quoted far worse if I had chosen—but because they illustrate various of the mental vices from which we now suffer. They are a little below the average, but are fairly representative samples. I number them so that I can refer back to them when necessary: 3

> (1) I am not, indeed, sure whether it is not true to say that the Milton who once seemed not unlike a seventeenth-century Shelley had not become, out of an experience ever more bitter in each year, more alien [*sic*] to the founder of that Jesuit sect which nothing could induce him to tolerate.
> Professor Harold Laski (Essay in *Freedom of Expression*)

(2) Above all, we cannot play ducks and drakes with a native battery of idioms which prescribes such egregious collocations of vocables as the basic *put up with* for *tolerate* or *put at a loss* for *bewilder*.

Professor Lancelot Hogben (*Interglossa*)

(3) On the one side we have the free personality: by definition it is not neurotic, for it has neither conflict nor dream. Its desires, such as they are, are transparent, for they are just what institutional approval keeps in the forefront of consciousness; another institutional pattern would alter their number and intensity; there is little in them that is natural, irreducible, or culturally dangerous. But *on the other* side, the social bond itself is nothing but the mutual reflection of these self-secure integrities. Recall the definition of love. Is not this the very picture of a small academic? Where is there a place in this hall of mirrors for either personality or fraternity?

Essay on psychology in *Politics* (New York)

(4) All the "best people" from the gentlemen's clubs, and all the frantic fascist captains, united in common hatred of Socialism and bestial horror of the rising tide of the mass revolutionary movement, have turned to acts of provocation, to foul incendiarism, to medieval legends of poisoned wells, to legalize their own destruction of proletarian organizations, and rouse the agitated petty-bourgeoisie to chauvinistic fervour on behalf of the fight against the revolutionary way out of the crisis.

Communist pamphlet

(5) If a new spirit *is* to be infused into this old country, there is one thorny and contentious reform which must be tackled, and that is the humanization and galvanization of the B.B.C. Timidity here will bespeak cancer and atrophy of the soul. The heart of Britain may be sound and of strong beat, for instance, but the British lion's roar at present is like that of Bottom in Shakespeare's *Midsummer Night's Dream*—as gentle as any sucking dove. A virile new Britain cannot continue indefinitely to be traduced in the eyes or rather ears, of the world by the effete languors of Langham Place, brazenly masquerading as "standard English." When the Voice of Britain is heard at nine o'clock, better far and infinitely less ludicrous to hear aitches honestly dropped than the present priggish, inflated, inhibited, school-ma'amish arch braying of blameless bashful mewing maidens!

Letter in *Tribune*

Each of these passages has faults of its own, but, quite apart from avoid-   4
able ugliness, two qualities are common to all of them. The first is staleness of imagery: the other is lack of precision. The writer either has a meaning and cannot express it, or he inadvertently says something else, or he is almost indifferent as to whether his words mean anything or not. This mixture of vagueness and sheer incompetence is the most marked characteristic of modern English prose, and especially of any kind of political writing. As soon as certain topics are raised, the concrete melts into the abstract and no one seems

able to think of turns of speech that are not hackneyed: prose consists less and less of *words* chosen for the sake of their meaning, and more and more of *phrases* tacked together like the sections of a prefabricated hen-house. I list below, with notes and examples, various of the tricks by means of which the work of prose-construction is habitually dodged:

Dying Metaphors

A newly invented metaphor assists thought by evoking a visual image, while 5 on the other hand a metaphor which is technically "dead" (e.g., *iron resolution*) has in effect reverted to being an ordinary word and can generally be used without loss of vividness. But in between these two classes there is a huge dump of worn-out metaphors which have lost all evocative power and are merely used because they save people the trouble of inventing phrases for themselves. Examples are: *Ring the changes on, take up the cudgels for, toe the line, ride roughshod over, stand shoulder to shoulder with, play into the hands of, no axe to grind, grist to the mill, fishing in troubled waters, on the order of the day, Achilles' heel, swan song, hotbed.* Many of these are used without knowledge of their meaning (what is a "rift," for instance?), and incompatible metaphors are frequently mixed, a sure sign that the writer is not interested in what he is saying. Some metaphors now current have been twisted out of their original meaning without those who use them even being aware of the fact. For example, *toe the line* is sometimes written *tow the line.* Another example is *the hammer and the anvil,* now always used with the implication that the anvil gets the worst of it. In real life it is always the anvil that breaks the hammer, never the other way about: a writer who stopped to think what he was saying would be aware of this, and would avoid perverting the original phrase.

Operators or Verbal False Limbs

These save the trouble of picking out appropriate verbs and nouns, and at the 6 same time pad each sentence with extra syllables which give it an appearance of symmetry. Characteristic phrases are: *render inoperative, militate against, make contact with, be subjected to, give rise to, give grounds for, have the effect of, play a leading part (role) in, make itself felt, take effect, exhibit a tendency to, serve the purpose of,* etc., etc. The keynote is the elimination of simple verbs. Instead of being a single word, such as *break, stop, spoil, mend, kill,* a verb becomes a *phrase,* made up of a noun or adjective tacked on to some general-purposes verb such as *prove, serve, form, play, render.* In addition, the passive voice is wherever possible used in preference to the active, and noun constructions are used instead of gerunds (*by examination of* instead of *by examining*). The range of verbs is further cut down by means of the *-ize* and *de-* formation, and the banal statements are given an appearance of profundity by means of the *not un-* formation. Simple conjunctions and prepositions are replaced by such phrases as *with respect to, having regard to, the fact that, by dint of, in view of, in the interests of, on the hypothesis that;* and the ends of sentences are saved from anticlimax by such resounding commonplaces as *greatly to be desired, cannot be left out of account, a development to be expected in the near* *future, deserving of serious consideration, brought to a satisfactory conclusion,* and so on and so forth.

Pretentious Diction

Words like *phenomenon, element, individual (as noun), objective, categorical,*   7
effective, virtual, basic, primary, promote, constitute, exhibit, exploit, utilize, eliminate, liquidate, are used to dress up simple statements and give an air of scientific impartiality to biased judgments. Adjectives like *epoch-making, epic, historic, unforgettable, triumphant, age-old, inevitable, inexorable, veritable,* are used to dignify the sordid processes of international politics, while writing that aims at glorifying war usually takes on an archaic color, its characteristic words being: *realm, throne, chariot, mailed fist, trident, sword, shield, buckler, banner, jackboot, clarion.* Foreign words and expressions such as *cul de sac, ancien régime, deus ex machina, mutatis mutandis, status quo, gleichschaltung, weltanschauung,* are used to give an air of culture and elegance. Except for the useful abbreviations *i.e., e.g.,* and *etc.,* there is no real need for any of the hundreds of foreign phrases now current in English. Bad writers, and especially scientific, political, and sociological writers, are nearly always haunted by the notion that Latin or Greek words are grander than Saxon ones, and unnecessary words like *expedite, ameliorate, predict, extraneous, deracinated, clandestine, subaqueous,* and hundreds of others constantly gain ground from their Anglo-Saxon opposite numbers.[1] The jargon peculiar to Marxist writing (*hyena, hangman, cannibal, petty bourgeois, these gentry, lackey, flunky, mad dog, White Guard,* etc.) consists largely of words and phrases translated from Russian, German, or French; but the normal way of coining a new word is to use a Latin or Greek root with the appropriate affix and, where necessary, the *-ize* formation. It is often easier to make up words of this kind (*deregionalize, impermissible, extramarital, nonfragmentatory,* and so forth) than to think up the English words that will cover one's meaning. The result, in general, is an increase in slovenliness and vagueness.

Meaningless Words

In certain kinds of writing, particularly in art criticism and literary criticism, it is   8
normal to come across long passages which are almost completely lacking in meaning.[2] Words like *romantic, plastic, values, human, dead, sentimental, natural,*

---

[1] An interesting illustration of this is the way in which the English flower names which were in use till very recently are being ousted by Greek ones, *snapdragon* becoming *antirrhinum, forget-me-not* becoming *myosotis,* etc. It is hard to see any practical reason for this change of fashion: it is probably due to an instinctive turning-away from the more homely word and a vague feeling that the Greek word is scientific.

[2] Example: "Comfort's catholicity of perception and image, strangely Whitmanesque in range, almost the exact opposite in aesthetic compulsion, continues to evoke that trembling atmospheric accumulative hinting at a cruel, an inexorably serene timelessness . . . Wrey Gardiner scores by aiming at simple bull's-eyes with precision. Only they are not so simple, and through this contented sadness runs more than the surface bittersweet of resignation" (*Poetry Quarterly*).

vitality, as used in art criticism, are strictly meaningless in the sense that they not only do not point to any discoverable object, but are hardly ever expected to do so by the reader. When one critic writes, "The outstanding feature of Mr. X's work is its living quality," while another writes, "The immediately striking thing about Mr. X's work is its peculiar deadness," the reader accepts this as a simple difference of opinion. If words like *black* and *white* were involved, instead of the jargon words *dead* and *living*, he would see at once that language was being used in an improper way. Many political words are similarly abused. The word *Fascism* has now no meaning except in so far as it signifies "something not desirable." The words *democracy, socialism, freedom, patriotic, realistic, justice*, have each of them several different meanings which cannot be reconciled with one another. In the case of a word like *democracy*, not only is there no agreed definition, but the attempt to make one is resisted from all sides. It is almost universally felt that when we call a country democratic we are praising it: consequently the defenders of every kind of régime claim that it is a democracy, and fear that they might have to stop using the word if it were tied down to any one meaning. Words of this kind are often used in a consciously dishonest way. That is, the person who uses them has his own private definition, but allows his hearer to think he means something quite different. Statements like *Marshal Pétain was a true patriot, The Soviet Press is the freest in the world, The Catholic Church is opposed to persecution*, are almost always made with intent to deceive. Other words used in variable meanings, in most cases more or less dishonestly, are: *class, totalitarian, science, progressive, reactionary, bourgeois, equality*.

Now that I have made this catalog of swindles and perversions, let me give 9
another example of the kind of writing that they lead to. This time it must of its nature be an imaginary one. I am going to translate a passage of good English into modern English of the worst sort. Here is a well-known verse from *Ecclesiastes*:

> I returned and saw under the sun, that the race is not to the swift, nor the battle to the strong, neither yet bread to the wise, nor yet riches to men of understanding, nor yet favor to men of skill; but time and chance happeneth to them all.

Here it is in modern English:

> Objective consideration of contemporary phenomena compels the conclusion that success or failure in competitive activities exhibits no tendency to be commensurate with innate capacity, but that a considerable element of the unpredictable must invariably be taken into account.

This is a parody, but not a very gross one. Exhibit (3), above, for instance, 10
contains several patches of the same kind of English. It will be seen that I have not made a full translation. The beginning and ending of the sentence follow the original meaning fairly closely, but in the middle the concrete illustrations—race, battle, bread—dissolve into the vague phrase "success or failure in competitive

activities." This had to be so, because no modern writer of the kind I am discussing—no one capable of using phrases like "objective consideration of contemporary phenomena"—would ever tabulate his thoughts in that precise and detailed way. The whole tendency of modern prose is away from concreteness. Now analyze these two sentences a little more closely. The first contains forty-nine words but only sixty syllables, and all its words are those of everyday life. The second contains thirty-eight words of ninety syllables: eighteen of its words are from Latin roots, and one from Greek. The first sentence contains six vivid images, and only one phrase ("time and chance") that could be called vague. The second contains not a single fresh, arresting phrase, and in spite of its ninety syllables it gives only a shortened version of the meaning contained in the first. Yet without a doubt it is the second kind of sentence that is gaining ground in modern English. I do not want to exaggerate. This kind of writing is not yet universal, and outcrops of simplicity will occur here and there in the worst-written page. Still, if you or I were told to write a few lines on the uncertainty of human fortunes, we should probably come much nearer to my imaginary sentence than to the one from *Ecclesiastes*.

As I have tried to show, modern writing at its worst does not consist in 11 picking out words for the sake of their meaning and inventing images in order to make the meaning clearer. It consists in gumming together long strips of words which have already been set in order by someone else, and making the results presentable by sheer humbug. The attraction of this way of writing is that it is easy. It is easier—even quicker, once you have the habit—to say *In my opinion it is a not unjustifiable assumption that* than to say *I think*. If you use ready-made phrases, you not only don't have to hunt about for words; you also don't have to bother with the rhythms of your sentences, since these phrases are generally so arranged as to be more or less euphonious. When you are composing in a hurry—when you are dictating to a stenographer, for instance, or making a public speech—it is natural to fall into a pretentious, Latinized style. Tags like a *consideration which we should do well to bear in mind* or a *conclusion to which all of us would readily assent* will save many a sentence from coming down with a bump. By using stale metaphors, similes, and idioms, you save much mental effort, at the cost of leaving your meaning vague, not only for your reader but for yourself. This is the significance of mixed metaphors. The sole aim of a metaphor is to call up a visual image. When these images clash—as in *The Fascist octopus has sung its swan song, the jackboot is thrown into the melting pot*—it can be taken as certain that the writer is not seeing a mental image of the objects he is naming; in other words he is not really thinking. Look again at the examples I gave at the beginning of this essay. Professor Laski (1) uses five negatives in fifty-three words. One of these is superfluous, making nonsense of the whole passage, and in addition there is the slip *alien* for akin, making further nonsense, and several avoidable pieces of clumsiness which increase the general vagueness. Professor Hogben (2) plays ducks and drakes with a battery which is able to write prescriptions, and, while disapproving of the everyday phrase *put up with*, is unwilling to look *egregious* up in the dictionary and see what it means. (3), if one takes an uncharitable attitude towards it, is simply meaningless: probably one could work out its intended meaning by reading the whole of the article in which it occurs. In (4), the writer knows more or less what he wants to say, but an accumulation of stale phrases chokes him like tea leaves blocking a sink. In (5), words and meaning have almost parted company. People who write in this manner usually have a general emotional meaning—they dislike one thing and want to express solidarity with another—but they are not interested in the detail of what they are saying. A scrupulous writer, in every sentence that he writes, will ask himself at least four questions, thus: What am I trying to say? What words will express it? What image or idiom will make it clearer? Is this image fresh enough to have an effect? And he will probably ask himself two more: Could I put it more shortly? Have I said anything that is avoidably ugly? But you are not obliged to go to all this trouble. You can shirk it by simply throwing your mind open and letting the ready-made phrases come crowding in. They will construct your sentences for you—even think your thoughts for you, to a certain extent—and at need they will perform the important service of partially concealing your meaning even from yourself. It is at this point that the special connection between politics and the debasement of language becomes clear.

In our time it is broadly true that political writing is bad writing. Where it   12
is not true, it will generally be found that the writer is some kind of rebel, expressing his private opinions and not a "party line." Orthodoxy, of whatever color, seems to demand a lifeless, imitative style. The political dialects to be found in pamphlets, leading articles, manifestos, White Papers, and the speeches of under-secretaries do, of course, vary from party to party, but they are all alike in that one almost never finds in them a fresh, vivid, home-made turn of speech. When one watches some tired hack on the platform mechanically repeating the familiar phrases—*bestial atrocities, iron heel, bloodstained tyranny, free peoples of the world, stand shoulder to shoulder*—one often has a curious feeling that one is not watching a live human being but some kind of dummy: a feeling which suddenly becomes stronger at moments when the light catches the speaker's spectacles and turns them into blank discs which seem to have no eyes behind them. And this is not altogether fanciful. A speaker who uses that kind of phraseology has gone some distance towards turning himself into a machine. The appropriate noises are coming out of his larynx, but his brain is not involved as it would be if he were choosing his words for himself. If the speech he is making is one that he is accustomed to make over and over again, he may be almost unconscious of what he is saying, as one is when one utters the responses in church. And this reduced state of consciousness, if not indispensable, is at any rate favorable to political conformity.

In our time, political speech and writing are largely the defense of the in-   13
defensible. Things like the continuance of British rule in India, the Russian purges and deportations, the dropping of the atom bombs on Japan, can indeed be defended, but only by arguments which are too brutal for most people to face, and which do not square with the professed aims of political parties.

Thus political language has to consist largely of euphemism, question-begging, and sheer cloudy vagueness. Defenseless villages are bombarded from the air, the inhabitants driven out into the countryside, the cattle machine-gunned, the huts set on fire with incendiary bullets: this is called *pacification*. Millions of peasants are robbed of their farms and sent trudging along the roads with no more than they can carry: this is called transfer of *population* or *rectification of frontiers*. People are imprisoned for years without trial, or shot in the back of the neck, or sent to die of scurvy in Arctic lumber camps: this is called *elimination of unreliable elements*. Such phraseology is needed if one wants to name things without calling up mental pictures of them. Consider for instance some comfortable English professor defending Russian totalitarianism. He cannot say outright, "I believe in killing off your opponents when you can get good results by doing so." Probably, therefore, he will say something like this:

"While freely conceding that the Soviet régime exhibits certain features 14 which the humanitarian may be inclined to deplore, we must, I think, agree that a certain curtailment of the right to political opposition is an unavoidable concomitant of transitional periods, and that the rigors which the Russian people have been called upon to undergo have been amply justified in the sphere of concrete achievement."

The inflated style is itself a kind of euphemism. A mass of Latin words falls 15 upon the facts like soft snow, blurring the outlines and covering up all the details. The great enemy of clear language is insincerity. When there is a gap between one's real and one's declared aims, one turns as it were instinctively to long words and exhausted idioms, like a cuttlefish squirting out ink. In our age there is no such thing as "keeping out of politics." All issues are political issues, and politics itself is a mass of lies, evasions, folly, hatred, and schizophrenia. When the general atmosphere is bad, language must suffer. I should expect to find—this is a guess which I have not sufficient knowledge to verify—that the German, Russian, and Italian languages have all deteriorated in the last ten or fifteen years, as a result of dictatorship.

But if thought corrupts language, language can also corrupt thought. A 16 bad usage can spread by tradition and imitation, even among people who should and do know better. The debased language that I have been discussing is in some ways very convenient. Phrases like a *not unjustifiable assumption, leaves much to be desired, would serve no good purpose, a consideration which we should do well to bear in mind*, are a continuous temptation, a packet of aspirins always at one's elbow. Look back through this essay, and for certain you will find that I have again and again committed the very faults I am protesting against. By this morning's post I have received a pamphlet dealing with conditions in Germany. The author tells me that he "felt impelled" to write it. I open it at random, and here is almost the first sentence that I see: "(The Allies) have an opportunity not only of achieving a radical transformation of Germany's social and political structure in such a way as to avoid a nationalistic reaction in Germany itself, but at the same time of laying the foundations of a cooperative and unified Europe." You see, he "feels impelled" to write—feels, presumably, that he has something new to say—and yet his words, like cavalry horses answering the bugle, group themselves automatically into the familiar dreary pattern. This invasion of one's mind by ready-made phrases (*lay the foundations, achieve a radical transformation*) can only be prevented if one is constantly on guard against them, and every such phrase anaesthetizes a portion of one's brain.

I said earlier that the decadence of our language is probably curable. 17 Those who deny this would argue, if they produced an argument at all, that language merely reflects existing social conditions, and that we cannot influence its development by any direct tinkering with words and constructions. So far as the general tone or spirit of a language goes, this may be true, but it is not true in detail. Silly words and expressions have often disappeared, not through any evolutionary process but owing to the conscious action of a minority. Two recent examples were *explore every avenue* and *leave no stone unturned*, which were killed by the jeers of a few journalists. There is a long list of flyblown metaphors which could similarly be got rid of if enough people would interest themselves in the job; and it should also be possible to laugh the *not un-* formation out of existence,[3] to reduce the amount of Latin and Greek in the average sentence, to drive out foreign phrases and strayed scientific words, and, in general, to make pretentiousness unfashionable. But all these are minor points. The defense of the English language implies more than this, and perhaps it is best to start by saying what it does not imply.

To begin with it has nothing to do with archaism, with the salvaging 18 of obsolete words and turns of speech, or with the setting up of a "standard English" which must never be departed from. On the contrary, it is especially concerned with the scrapping of every word or idiom which has outworn its usefulness. It has nothing to do with correct grammar and syntax, which are of no importance so long as one makes one's meaning clear, or with the avoidance of Americanisms, or with having what is called a "good prose style." On the other hand it is not concerned with fake simplicity and the attempt to make written English colloquial. Nor does it even imply in every case preferring the Saxon word to the Latin one, though it does imply using the fewest and shortest words that will cover one's meaning. What is above all needed is to let the meaning choose the word, and not the other way about. In prose, the worst thing one can do with words is to surrender to them. When you think of a concrete object, you think wordlessly, and then, if you want to describe the thing you have been visualizing you probably hunt about till you find the exact words that seem to fit. When you think of something abstract you are more inclined to use words from the start, and unless you make a conscious effort to prevent it, the existing dialect will come rushing in and do

---

[3]One can cure oneself of the *not un-* formation by memorizing this sentence: *A not unblack dog was chasing a not unsmall rabbit across a not ungreen field.*

the job for you, at the expense of blurring or even changing your meaning. Probably it is better to put off using words as long as possible and get one's meaning as clear as one can through pictures or sensations. Afterwards one can choose—not simply *accept*—the phrases that will best cover the meaning, and then switch round and decide what impression one's words are likely to make on another person. This last effort of the mind cuts out all stale or mixed images, all prefabricated phrases, needless repetitions, and humbug and vagueness generally. But one can often be in doubt about the effect of a word or a phrase, and one needs rules that one can rely on when instinct fails. I think the following rules will cover most cases:

1. Never use a metaphor, simile, or other figure of speech which you are used to seeing in print.

2. Never use a long word where a short one will do.

3. If it is possible to cut a word out, always cut it out.

4. Never use the passive where you can use the active.

5. Never use a foreign phrase, a scientific word, or a jargon word if you can think of an everyday English equivalent.

6. Break any of these rules sooner than say anything outright barbarous.

These rules sound elementary, and so they are, but they demand a deep 19 change of attitude in anyone who has grown used to writing in the style now fashionable. One could keep all of them and still write bad English, but one could not write the kind of stuff that I quoted in those five specimens at the beginning of this article.

I have not here been considering the literary use of language, but merely 20 language as an instrument for expressing and not for concealing or preventing thought. Stuart Chase and others have come near to claiming that all abstract words are meaningless, and have used this as a pretext for advocating a kind of political quietism. Since you don't know what Fascism is, how can you struggle against Fascism? One need not swallow such absurdities as this, but one ought to recognize that the present political chaos is connected with the decay of language, and that one can probably bring about some improvement by starting at the verbal end. If you simplify your English, you are freed from the worst follies of orthodoxy. You cannot speak any of the necessary dialects, and when you make a stupid remark its stupidity will be obvious, even to yourself. Political language—and with variations this is true of all political parties, from Conservatives to Anarchists—is designed to make lies sound truthful and murder respectable, and to give an appearance of solidity to pure wind. One cannot change this all in a moment, but one can at least change one's own habits, and from time to time one can even, if one jeers loudly enough, send some worn-out and useless phrase—some *jackboot, Achilles' heel, hotbed, melting pot, acid test, veritable inferno,* or other lump of verbal refuse—into the dustbin where it belongs.

⊘READING ARGUMENTS

1. What two qualities do Orwell's "five specimens" (para. 2) share? According to Orwell, what is the "most marked characteristic of modern English prose, and especially of any kind of political writing" (4)?

2. Where in this essay does Orwell use deductive reasoning?

3. How does Orwell use cause-and-effect argument in his essay? For instance, how does he use it to explain why political speech and writing are bad? What other examples of cause-and-effect argument can you identify?

4. Orwell argues that "political language" consists "largely of euphemism, question-begging, and sheer cloudy vagueness" (13). What is a euphemism? What does "question-begging" mean?

5. Where does Orwell make a proposal argument? What does he propose?

⊘WRITING ARGUMENTS

1. In paragraph 16, Orwell concedes, "Look back through this essay, and for certain you will find that I have again and again committed the very faults I am protesting against." Find three examples of these "faults" in Orwell's prose. Then, write a paragraph for each "fault," explaining why it meets his standard for "bad" writing.

2. Surveying the state of the English language in 1946, Orwell asserts that "it is broadly true that political writing is bad writing" (12). Is this still "broadly true"? Reread paragraphs 12–15 of Orwell's essay. Then, develop your own argument about the language of contemporary politics, updating Orwell's examples with contemporary examples.

THE OBLIGATION TO ENDURE

RACHEL CARSON

Rachel Carson (1907–1964) received a master's degree in zoology and worked as editor-in-chief of publications for the U.S. Bureau of Fisheries. Her books include Under the Sea-Wind *(1941);* The Sea around Us *(1951), a bestseller and winner of the National Book Award;* The Edge of the Sea *(1955); and* The Sense of Wonder *(published in 1965 after her death). Her most famous work is*

Silent Spring (1962), from which "The Obligation to Endure" is drawn. In this book, Carson argues that agricultural pesticides are destructive to wildlife and to the environment, an idea that predates the modern environmental movement and to this day remains controversial. Silent Spring, *an extremely influential work, led to bans of DDT as well as other chemicals.*

The history of life on earth has been a history of interaction between liv- 1
ing things and their surroundings. To a large extent, the physical form and the habits of the earth's vegetation and its animal life have been molded by the environment. Considering the whole span of earthly time, the opposite effect, in which life actually modifies its surroundings, has been relatively slight. Only within the moment of time represented by the present century has one species—man—acquired significant power to alter the nature of his world.

During the past quarter century this power has not only increased to 2
one of disturbing magnitude but it has changed in character. The most alarming of all man's assaults upon the environment is the contamination of air, earth, rivers, and sea with dangerous and even lethal materials. This pollution is for the most part irrecoverable; the chain of evil it initiates not only in the world that must support life but in living tissues is for the most part irreversible. In this now universal contamination of the environment, chemicals are the sinister and little-recognized partners of radiation in changing the very nature of the world—the very nature of its life. Strontium 90, released through nuclear explosions into the air, comes to earth in rain or drifts down as fallout, lodges in soil, enters into the grass or corn or wheat grown there, and in time takes up its abode in the bones of a human being, there to remain until his death. Similarly, chemicals sprayed on croplands or forests or gardens lie long in soil, entering into living organisms, passing from one to another in a chain of poisoning and death. Or they pass mysteriously by underground streams until they emerge and, through the alchemy of air and sunlight, combine into new forms that kill vegetation, sicken cattle, and work unknown harm on those who drink from once pure wells. As Albert Schweitzer has said, "Man can hardly even recognize the devils of his own creation."

It took hundreds of millions of years to produce the life that now inhabits 3
the earth—eons of time in which that developing and evolving and diversifying life reached a state of adjustment and balance with its surroundings. The environment, rigorously shaping and directing the life it supported, contained elements that were hostile as well as supporting. Certain rocks gave out dangerous radiation; even within the light of the sun, from which all life draws its energy, there were short-wave radiations with power to injure. Given time—time not in years but in millennia—life adjusts, and a balance has been reached. For time is the essential ingredient; but in the modern world there is no time.

The rapidity of change and the speed with which new situations are cre- 4
ated follow the impetuous and heedless pace of man rather than the deliberate
pace of nature. Radiation is no longer merely the background radiation of
rocks, the bombardment of cosmic rays, the ultraviolet of the sun that have
existed before there was any life on earth; radiation is now the unnatural creation of man's tampering with the atom. The chemicals to which life is asked
to make its adjustment are no longer merely the calcium and silica and copper
and all the rest of the minerals washed out of the rocks and carried in rivers to
the sea; they are the synthetic creations of man's inventive mind, brewed in his
laboratories, and having no counterparts in nature.

To adjust to these chemicals would require time on the scale that is 5
nature's; it would require not merely the years of a man's life but the life of
generations. And even this, were it by some miracle possible, would be futile,
for the new chemicals come from our laboratories in an endless stream;
almost five hundred annually find their way into actual use in the United
States alone. The figure is staggering and its implications are not easily
grasped—500 new chemicals to which the bodies of men and animals are
required somehow to adapt each year, chemicals totally outside the limits of
biologic experience.

Among them are many that are used in man's war against nature. Since 6
the mid-1940's over 200 basic chemicals have been created for use in killing
insects, weeds, rodents, and other organisms described in the modern vernacular as "pests"; and they are sold under several thousand different brand
names.

These sprays, dusts, and aerosols are now applied almost universally to 7
farms, gardens, forests, and homes—nonselective chemicals that have the
power to kill every insect, the "good" and the "bad," to still the song of birds
and the leaping of fish in the streams, to coat the leaves with a deadly film, and
to linger on in soil—all this though the intended target may be only a few
weeds or insects. Can anyone believe it is possible to lay down such a barrage
of poisons on the surface of the earth without making it unfit for all life? They
should not be called "insecticides," but "biocides."

The whole process of spraying seems caught up in an endless spiral. Since 8
DDT° was released for civilian use, a process of escalation has been going on
in which ever more toxic materials must be found. This has happened because
insects, in a triumphant vindication of Darwin's principle of the survival of the
fittest, have evolved super races immune to the particular insecticide used,
hence a deadlier one has always to be developed—and then a deadlier one
than that. It has happened also because, for reasons to be described later,
destructive insects often undergo a "flareback," or resurgence, after spraying,
in numbers greater than before. Thus the chemical war is never won, and all
life is caught in its violent crossfire.

Along with the possibility of the extinction of mankind by nuclear war, 9
the central problem of our age has therefore become the contamination of
man's total environment with such substances of incredible potential for

*Dichlorodiphenyltrichloroeth-
ane, a synthetic pesticide that
was widely used to control
disease-spreading insect
populations*

harm—substances that accumulate in the tissues of plants and animals and even penetrate the germ cells to shatter or alter the very material of heredity upon which the shape of the future depends.

Some would-be architects of our future look toward a time when it will be possible to alter the human germ plasm by design. But we may easily be doing so now by inadvertence, for many chemicals, like radiation, bring about gene mutations. It is ironic to think that man might determine his own future by something so seemingly trivial as the choice of an insect spray. 10

All this has been risked—for what? Future historians may well be amazed by our distorted sense of proportion. How could intelligent beings seek to control a few unwanted species by a method that contaminated the entire environment and brought the threat of disease and death even to their own kind? Yet this is precisely what we have done. We have done it, moreover, for reasons that collapse the moment we examine them. We are told that the enormous and expanding use of pesticides is necessary to maintain farm production. Yet is our real problem not one of *overproduction*? Our farms, despite measures to remove acreages from production and to pay farmers *not* to produce, have yielded such a staggering excess of crops that the American taxpayer in 1962 is paying out more than one billion dollars a year as the total carrying cost of the surplus-food storage program. And is the situation helped when one branch of the Agriculture Department tries to reduce production while another states, as it did in 1958, "It is believed generally that reduction of crop acreages under provisions of the Soil Bank will stimulate interest in use of chemicals to obtain maximum production on the land retained in crops." 11

All this is not to say there is no insect problem and no need of control. I am saying, rather, that control must be geared to realities, not to mythical situations, and that the methods employed must be such that they do not destroy us along with the insects. 12

The problem whose attempted solution has brought such a train of disaster in its wake is an accompaniment of our modern way of life. Long before the age of man, insects inhabited the earth—a group of extraordinarily varied and adaptable beings. Over the course of time since man's advent, a small percentage of the more than half a million species of insects have come into conflict with human welfare in two principal ways: as competitors for the food supply and as carriers of human disease. 13

Disease-carrying insects become important where human beings are crowded together, especially under conditions where sanitation is poor, as in time of natural disaster or war or in situations of extreme poverty and deprivation. Then control of some sort becomes necessary. It is a sobering fact, however, as we shall presently see, that the method of massive chemical control has had only limited success, and also threatens to worsen the very conditions it is intended to curb. 14

Under primitive agricultural conditions the farmer had few insect problems. These arose with the intensification of agriculture—the devotion of immense acreages to a single crop. Such a system set the stage for explosive 15 increases in specific insect populations. Single-crop farming does not take advantage of the principles by which nature works; it is agriculture as an engineer might conceive it to be. Nature has introduced great variety into the landscape, but man has displayed a passion for simplifying it. Thus he undoes the built-in checks and balances by which nature holds the species within bounds. One important natural check is a limit on the amount of suitable habitat for each species. Obviously then, an insect that lives on wheat can build up its population to much higher levels on a farm devoted to wheat than on one in which wheat is intermingled with other crops to which the insect is not adapted.

16   The same thing happens in other situations. A generation or more ago, the towns of large areas of the United States lined their streets with the noble elm tree. Now the beauty they hopefully created is threatened with complete destruction as disease sweeps through the elms, carried by a beetle that would have only limited chance to build up large populations and to spread from tree to tree if the elms were only occasional trees in a richly diversified planting.

17   Another factor in the modern insect problem is one that must be viewed against a background of geologic and human history: the spreading of thousands of different kinds of organisms from their native homes to invade new territories. This worldwide migration has been studied and graphically described by the British ecologist Charles Elton in his recent book *The Ecology of Invasions.* During the Cretaceous Period, some hundred million years ago, flooding seas cut many land bridges between continents and living things found themselves confined in what Elton calls "colossal separate nature reserves." There, isolated from others of their kind, they developed many new species. When some of the land masses were joined again, about 15 million years ago, these species began to move out into new territories—a movement that is not only still in progress but is now receiving considerable assistance from man.

18   The importation of plants is the primary agent in the modern spread of species, for animals have almost invariably gone along with the plants, quarantine being a comparatively recent and not completely effective innovation. The United States Office of Plant Introduction alone has introduced almost 200,000 species and varieties of plants from all over the world. Nearly half of the 180 or so major insect enemies of plants in the United States are accidental imports from abroad, and most of them have come as hitchhikers on plants.

19   In new territory, out of reach of the restraining hand of the natural enemies that kept down its numbers in its native land, an invading plant or animal is able to become enormously abundant. Thus it is no accident that our most troublesome insects are introduced species.

20   These invasions, both the naturally occurring and those dependent on human assistance, are likely to continue indefinitely. Quarantine and massive chemical campaigns are only extremely expensive ways of buying time. We are faced, according to Dr. Elton, "with a life-and-death need not just to find new technological means of suppressing this plant or that animal";

instead we need the basic knowledge of animal populations and their relations to their surroundings that will "promote an even balance and damp down the explosive power of outbreaks and new invasions."

Much of the necessary knowledge is now available but we do not use it. We 21 train ecologists in our universities and even employ them in our governmental agencies but we seldom take their advice. We allow the chemical death rain to fall as though there were no alternative, whereas in fact there are many, and our ingenuity could soon discover many more if given opportunity.

Have we fallen into a mesmerized state that makes us accept as inevitable 22 that which is inferior or detrimental, as though having lost the will or the vision to demand that which is good? Such thinking, in the words of the ecologist Paul Shepard, "idealizes life with only its head out of water, inches above the limits of toleration of the corruption of its own environment. . . . Why should we tolerate a diet of weak poisons, a home in insipid surroundings, a circle of acquaintances who are not quite our enemies, the noise of motors with just enough relief to prevent insanity? Who would want to live in a world which is just not quite fatal?"

Yet such a world is pressed upon us. The crusade to create a chemically 23 sterile, insect-free world seems to have engendered a fanatic zeal on the part of many specialists and most of the so-called control agencies. On every hand there is evidence that those engaged in spraying operations exercise a ruthless power. "The regulatory entomologists . . . function as prosecutor, judge and jury, tax assessor and collector and sheriff to enforce their own orders," said Connecticut entomologist Neely Turner. The most flagrant abuses go unchecked in both state and federal agencies.

It is not my contention that chemical insecticides must never be used. I do 24 contend that we have put poisonous and biologically potent chemicals indiscriminately into the hands of persons largely or wholly ignorant of their potentials for harm. We have subjected enormous numbers of people to contact with these poisons, without their consent and often without their knowledge. If the Bill of Rights contains no guarantee that a citizen shall be secure against lethal poisons distributed either by private individuals or by public officials, it is surely only because our forefathers, despite their considerable wisdom and foresight, could conceive of no such problem.

I contend, furthermore, that we have allowed these chemicals to be used 25 with little or no advance investigation of their effect on soil, water, wildlife, and man himself. Future generations are unlikely to condone our lack of prudent concern for the integrity of the natural world that supports all life.

There is still very limited awareness of the nature of the threat. This is an 26 era of specialists, each of whom sees his own problem and is unaware of or intolerant of the larger frame into which it fits. It is also an era dominated by industry, in which the right to make a dollar at whatever cost is seldom challenged. When the public protests, confronted with some obvious evidence of damaging results of pesticide applications, it is fed little tranquilizing pills of half truth. We urgently need an end to these false assurances, to the sugar coating of unpalatable facts. It is the public that is being asked to assume the risks that the insect controllers calculate. The public must decide whether it wishes to continue on the present road, and it can do so only when in full possession of the facts. In the words of Jean Rostand, "The obligation to endure gives us the right to know."

⊘ READING ARGUMENTS

1. In her opening paragraphs, Carson makes broad and provocative claims about human beings and their place in the natural world. What evidence does she use to support these assertions? Do you find this evidence convincing?

2. According to Carson, what problem (in addition to the threat of nuclear war) was the greatest threat to human beings in the middle of the twentieth century?

3. In what sense is "The Obligation to Endure" an evaluation argument?

4. In paragraph 2, Carson refers to "man's assaults upon the environment." How does she characterize human beings throughout her essay? For example, how does she describe their interaction with the environment? How does her characterization of human beings support her essay's main point?

5. Where in her essay does Carson address opposing arguments? Do you think she refutes them effectively? Why or why not?

⊘ WRITING ARGUMENTS

1. Carson contrasts the "heedless pace of man" with the "deliberate pace of nature" (para. 4). Is this distinction valid? Do you think her view of people and their relationship with the environment is accurate? For example, do you think human beings are engaged in a "war against nature" (6)? Do you generally share Carson's view of scientific progress and industrial society? Write an argumentative essay that takes a stand for or against her views.

2. As a result of Carson's book, DDT was banned worldwide. Since then, the World Health Organization has called for its limited use indoors in African countries to combat malaria, but it remains banned in the United States. Given the dramatic rise of insect-borne diseases (such as the West Nile virus, the Zika virus, Lyme disease, and Chagas disease), do you think the United States should reconsider its response to Carson's book and permit the use of DDT in some situations? Write an essay explaining your position.

THE IMPORTANCE OF WORK

BETTY FRIEDAN

An activist, an author, and the first president of the National Organization for Women, Betty Friedan (1921–2006) sparked the second wave of American feminism with her manifesto The Feminine Mystique. *This 1963 book examined the "problem that has no name"—the deep dissatisfaction of American women, who were trapped by domestic roles and feminine ideals that limited their individuality, freedom, and growth. In the following excerpt from this book, Friedan argues that women need "to break out of their comfortable concentration camps"—a metaphor that, like the book, remains shocking and controversial more than fifty years later.*

The question of how a person can most fully realize his own capacities and 1
thus achieve identity has become an important concern of the philosophers and the social and psychological thinkers of our time—and for good reason. Thinkers of other times put forth the idea that people were, to a great extent, defined by the work they did. The work that a man had to do to eat, to stay alive, to meet the physical necessities of his environment, dictated his identity. And in this sense, when work was seen merely as a means of survival, human identity was dictated by biology.

But today the problem of human identity has changed. For the work that 2
defined man's place in society and his sense of himself has also changed man's world. Work, and the advance of knowledge, has lessened man's dependence on his environment; his biology and the work he must do for biological survival are no longer sufficient to define his identity. This can be most clearly seen in our own abundant society; men no longer need to work all day to eat. They have an unprecedented freedom to choose the kind of work they will do; they also have an unprecedented amount of time apart from the hours and days that must actually be spent in making a living. And suddenly one realizes the significance of today's identity crisis—for women, and increasingly, for men. One sees the human significance of work—not merely as the means of biological survival, but as the giver of self and the transcender of self, as the creator of human identity and human evolution.

For "self-realization" or "self-fulfillment" or "identity" does not come 3
from looking into a mirror in rapt contemplation of one's own image. Those who have most fully realized themselves, in a sense that can be recognized by the human mind even though it cannot be clearly defined, have done so in the service of a human purpose larger than themselves. Men from varying disciplines have used different words for this mysterious

process from which comes the sense of self. The religious mystics, the philosophers, Marx, Freud—all had different names for it: man finds himself by losing himself; man is defined by his relation to the means of production; the ego, the self, grows through understanding and mastering reality—through work and love.

The identity crisis, which has been noted by Erik Erikson° and others in recent years in the American man, seems to occur for lack of, and be cured by finding, the work, or cause, or purpose that evokes his own creativity. Some never find it, for it does not come from busy-work or punching a time clock. It does not come from just making a living, working by formula, finding a secure spot as an organization man. The very argument, by Riesman and others, that man no longer finds identity in the work defined as a paycheck job, assumes that identity for man comes through creative work of his own that contributes to the human community: the core of the self becomes aware, becomes real, and grows through work that carries forward human society.

4 Erik Erikson (1902–1994): A German-born American psychologist who coined the phrase "identity crisis"

Work, the shopworn staple of the economists, has become the new frontier of psychology. Psychiatrists have long used "occupational therapy" with patients in mental hospitals; they have recently discovered that to be of real psychological value, it must be not just "therapy," but real work, serving a real purpose in the community. And work can now be seen as the key to the problem that has no name. The identity crisis of American women began a century ago, as more and more of the work important to the world, more and more of the work that used their human abilities and through which they were able to find self-realization, was taken from them.

Until, and even into, the last century, strong, capable women were needed to pioneer our new land; with their husbands, they ran the farms and plantations and Western homesteads. These women were respected and self-respecting members of a society whose pioneering purpose centered in the home. Strength and independence, responsibility and self-confidence, self-discipline and courage, freedom and equality were part of the American character for both men and women, in all the first generations. The women who came by steerage from Ireland, Italy, Russia, and Poland worked beside their husbands in the sweatshops and the laundries, learned the new language, and saved to send their sons and daughters to college. Women were never quite as "feminine," or held in as much contempt, in America as they were in Europe. American women seemed to European travelers, long before our time, less passive, childlike, and feminine than their own wives in France or Germany or England. By an accident of history, American women shared in the work of society longer, and grew with the men. Grade- and high-school education for boys and girls alike was almost always the rule; and in the West, where women shared the pioneering work the longest, even the universities were coeducational from the beginning.

The identity crisis for women did not begin in America until the fire and strength and ability of the pioneer women were no longer needed, no longer used, in the middle-class homes of the Eastern and Midwestern cities, when the pioneering was done and men began to build the new society in industries and professions outside the home. But the daughters of the pioneer women had grown too used to freedom and work to be content with leisure and passive femininity.

It was not an American, but a South African woman, Mrs. Olive 8 Schreiner, who warned at the turn of the century that the quality and quantity of women's functions in the social universe was decreasing as fast as civilization was advancing; that if women did not win back their right to a full share of honored and useful work, woman's mind and muscle would weaken in a parasitic state; her offspring, male and female, would weaken progressively, and civilization itself would deteriorate.

The feminists saw clearly that education and the right to participate in 9 the more advanced work of society were women's greatest needs. They fought for and won the rights to new, fully human identity for women. But how very few of their daughters and granddaughters have chosen to use their education and their abilities for any large creative purpose, for responsible work in society? How many of them have been deceived, or have deceived themselves, into clinging to the outgrown, childlike femininity of "Occupation: housewife"?

It was not a minor matter, their mistaken choice. We now know that the 10 same range of potential ability exists for women as for men. Women, as well as men, can only find their identity in work that uses their full capacities. A woman cannot find her identity through others—her husband, her children. She cannot find it in the dull routine of housework. As thinkers of every age have said, it is only when a human being faces squarely the fact that he can forfeit his own life, that he becomes truly aware of himself, and begins to take his existence seriously. Sometimes this awareness comes only at the moment of death. Sometimes it comes from a more subtle facing of death: the death of self in passive conformity, in meaningless work. The feminine mystique prescribes just such a living death for women. Faced with the slow death of self, the American woman must begin to take her life seriously.

"We measure ourselves by many standards," said the great American psy- 11 chologist William James, nearly a century ago. "Our strength and our intelligence, our wealth and even our good luck, are things which warm our heart and make us feel ourselves a match for life. But deeper than all such things, and able to suffice unto itself without them, is the sense of the amount of effort which we can put forth."

If women do not put forth, finally, that effort to become all that they have 12 it in them to become, they will forfeit their own humanity. A woman today who has no goal, no purpose, no ambition patterning her days into the future, making her stretch and grow beyond that small score of years in which her body can fill its biological function, is committing a kind of suicide. For that future half a century after the child-bearing years are over is a fact that an American woman cannot deny. Nor can she deny that as a housewife, the world is indeed rushing past her door while she just sits and watches. The terror she feels is real, if she has no place in that world.

The feminine mystique has succeeded in burying millions of American 13
women alive. There is no way for these women to break out of their comfortable concentration camps except by finally putting forth an effort—that human effort which reaches beyond biology, beyond the narrow walls of home, to help shape the future. Only by such a personal commitment to the future can American women break out of the housewife trap and truly find fulfillment as wives and mothers—by fulfilling their own unique possibilities as separate human beings.

⊙ READING ARGUMENTS

1. In what respects is this essay a definition argument? What key term is being defined? Why is the meaning of this term essential to Friedan's argument?

2. According to Friedan, how do modern people establish their identities? What gives these identities meaning?

3. In paragraph 6, Friedan writes about eighteenth- and nineteenth-century women who helped "to pioneer" the United States. How does she characterize these women? Why is their history important to her overall point?

4. In her next-to-last paragraph, Friedan refers to "a kind of suicide." What does she mean?

⊙ WRITING ARGUMENTS

1. According to Friedan, men and women need work that satisfies their creativity and contributes to human society. Do you agree with her implication that doing paid work is the only way to create a meaningful life? Is it possible to find fulfillment by focusing on domestic tasks such as child-rearing? How do you view such questions in the context of your own life and career ambitions? Write an essay that responds to Friedan's argument about the importance of work—that is, of meaningful paid employment.

2. This essay is from Friedan's 1963 book *The Feminine Mystique*. Does the "identity crisis" that Friedan describes still exist? Many aspects of society have changed over the last five decades. Do her arguments seem relevant to men and women today? Why or why not? Write an essay that presents your point of view.

IF BLACK ENGLISH ISN'T A LANGUAGE, THEN TELL ME, WHAT IS?

JAMES BALDWIN

Although the Harlem-born novelist, playwright, poet, and critic James Baldwin spent much of his life abroad, he remained an American writer. That is evident in well-known works like Go Tell It on the Mountain *(1953),* Notes of a Native Son *(1955), and* The Fire Next Time *(1963), which explore the problem of race in the United States. He also wrote powerfully about class, culture, and sexual identity in both his fiction and his essays. Baldwin was especially perceptive about the complex relationship between "self" and "society," as is clear in the following essay. For Baldwin, language "reveals the private identity, and connects one with, or divorces one from, the larger, public, or communal identity."*

The argument concerning the use, or the status, or the reality, of black English 1 is rooted in American history and has absolutely nothing to do with the question the argument supposes itself to be posing. The argument has nothing to do with language itself but with the role of language. Language, incontestably, reveals the speaker. Language, also, far more dubiously, is meant to define the other—and, in this case, the other is refusing to be defined by a language that has never been able to recognize him.

People evolve a language in order to describe and thus control their cir- 2 cumstances or in order not to be submerged by a situation that they cannot articulate. (And if they cannot articulate it, they are submerged.) A Frenchman living in Paris speaks a subtly and crucially different language from that of the man living in Marseilles; neither sounds very much like a man living in Quebec; and they would all have great difficulty in apprehending what the man from Guadeloupe, or Martinique, is saying, to say nothing of the man from Senegal—although the "common" language of all these areas is French. But each has paid, and is paying, a different price for this "common" language, in which, as it turns out, they are not saying, and cannot be saying, the same things: They each have very different realities to articulate, or control.

What joins all languages, and all men, is the necessity to confront life, in 3 order, not inconceivably, to outwit death: The price for this is the acceptance, and achievement, of one's temporal identity. So that, for example, though it is not taught in the schools (and this has the potential of becoming a political issue) the south of France still clings to its ancient and musical Provençal, which resists being described as a "dialect." And much of the tension in the Basque countries, and in Wales, is due to the Basque and Welsh determination not to allow their languages to be destroyed. This determination also feeds the flames in Ireland for among the many indignities the Irish have been forced to undergo at English hands is the English contempt for their language.

It goes without saying, then, that language is also a political instrument, means, and proof of power. It is the most vivid and crucial key to identity: It reveals the private identity, and connects one with, or divorces one from, the larger, public, or communal identity. There have been, and are, times and places, when to speak a certain language could be dangerous, even fatal. Or, one may speak the same language, but in such a way that one's antecedents are revealed, or (one hopes) hidden. This is true in France, and is absolutely true in England: The range (and reign) of accents on that damp little island make England coherent for the English and totally incomprehensible for everyone else. To open your mouth in England is (if I may use black English) to "put your business in the street." You have confessed your parents, your youth, your school, your salary, your self-esteem, and, alas, your future.

Now, I do not know what white Americans would sound like if there had never been any black people in the United States, but they would not sound the way they sound. *Jazz*, for example, is a very specific sexual term, as in *jazz me, baby*, but white people purified it into the Jazz Age. *Sock it to me*, which means, roughly, the same thing, has been adopted by Nathaniel Hawthorne's° descendants with no qualms or hesitations at all, along with *let it all hang out* and *right on! Beat to his socks*, which was once the black's most total and despairing image of poverty, was transformed into a thing called the Beat Generation,° which phenomenon was, largely, composed of *uptight*, middle-class white people, imitating poverty, trying to *get down*, to *get with it*, doing their *thing*, doing their despairing best to be *funky*, which we, the blacks, never dreamed of doing—we were funky, baby, like *funk* was going out of style.

Now, no one can eat his cake, and have it, too, and it is late in the day to attempt to penalize black people for having created a language that permits the nation its only glimpse of reality, a language without which the nation would be even more *whipped* than it is.

I say that the present skirmish is rooted in American history, and it is. Black English is the creation of the black diaspora. Blacks came to the United States chained to each other, but from different tribes. Neither could speak the other's language. If two black people, at that bitter hour of the world's history, had been able to speak to each other, the institution of chattel slavery could never have lasted as long as it did. Subsequently, the slave was given, under the eye, and the gun, of his master, Congo Square, and the Bible—or, in other words, and under those conditions, the slave began the formation of the black church, and it is within this unprecedented tabernacle that black English began to be formed. This was not, merely, as in the European example, the adoption of a foreign tongue, but an alchemy that transformed ancient elements into a new language: *A language comes into existence by means of brutal necessity, and the rules of the language are dictated by what the language must convey.*

Nathaniel Hawthorne (1804–1864), an American novelist and short story writer whose work often focused on Puritan New England

A group of post–World War II American writers that valued freedom, authenticity, spontaneous expression, antimaterialism, and nonconformity

There was a moment, in time, and in this place, when my brother, or my   8
mother, or my father, or my sister, had to convey to me, for example, the danger in which I was standing from the white man standing just behind me, and
to convey this with a speed and in a language, that the white man could not
possibly understand, and that, indeed, he cannot understand, until today. He
cannot afford to understand it. This understanding would reveal to him too
much about himself and smash that mirror before which he has been frozen
for so long.

*Toni Morrison (1931–) an
African-American writer
who won the 1993 Nobel
Prize in Literature*

Now, if this passion, this skill, this (to quote Toni Morrison)° "sheer intel-   9
ligence," this incredible music, the mighty achievement of having brought a
people utterly unknown to, or despised by "history"—to have brought this
people to their present, troubled, troubling, and unassailable and unanswer-
able place—if this absolutely unprecedented journey does not indicate that
black English is a language, I am curious to know what definition of languages
is to be trusted.

A people at the center of the western world, and in the midst of so hostile   10
a population, has not endured and transcended by means of what is patroniz-
ingly called a "dialect." We, the blacks, are in trouble, certainly, but we are not
inarticulate because we are not compelled to defend a morality that we know
to be a lie.

The brutal truth is that the bulk of the white people in America never had   11
any interest in educating black people, except as this could serve white purposes. It is not the black child's language that is despised. It is his experience.
A child cannot be taught by anyone who despises him, and a child cannot
afford to be fooled. A child cannot be taught by anyone whose demand, essentially, is that the child repudiate his experience, and all that gives him sustenance, and enter a limbo in which he will no longer be black, and in which he
knows that he can never become white. Black people have lost too many black
children that way.

And, after all, finally, in a country with standards so untrustworthy, a   12
country that makes heroes of so many criminal mediocrities, a country unable
to face why so many of the nonwhite are in prison, or on the needle, or standing, futureless, in the streets—it may very well be that both the child, and his
elder, have concluded that they have nothing whatever to learn from the people of a country that has managed to learn so little.

⊖ READING ARGUMENTS

1. How does Baldwin use deductive reasoning in the first three paragraphs of this essay? Construct a syllogism for this argument. Do you
   find the syllogism's conclusion persuasive? Why or why not?

2. Baldwin writes, "It goes without saying, then, that language is also a
   political instrument, means, and proof of power" (para. 4). What does he

mean? Does this really "go without saying"? In other words, is this point self-evident? How does he support his claim?

3. According to Baldwin, black people "created a language that permits the nation its only glimpse of reality" (6). What does he mean? Do you agree? Why or why not?

◎ WRITING ARGUMENTS

1. For Baldwin, language is the "most vivid and crucial key to identity" (para. 4). He points out that when you speak, you reveal "your parents, your youth, your school, your salary, your self-esteem, and, alas, your future" (4). In your experience, have you found this to be true? Are these aspects of your life evident in the sounds of your own speech? Write an essay that presents your point of view on these questions.

2. Baldwin discusses black contributions to American English. He also points out how white Americans "purified" (5) certain black terms from jazz culture and transformed black poverty into the "Beat Generation." Why would people imitate the language of poverty? Is this process still at work today? If so, where do you see it? Address these questions in an argumentative essay, using examples to support your points.

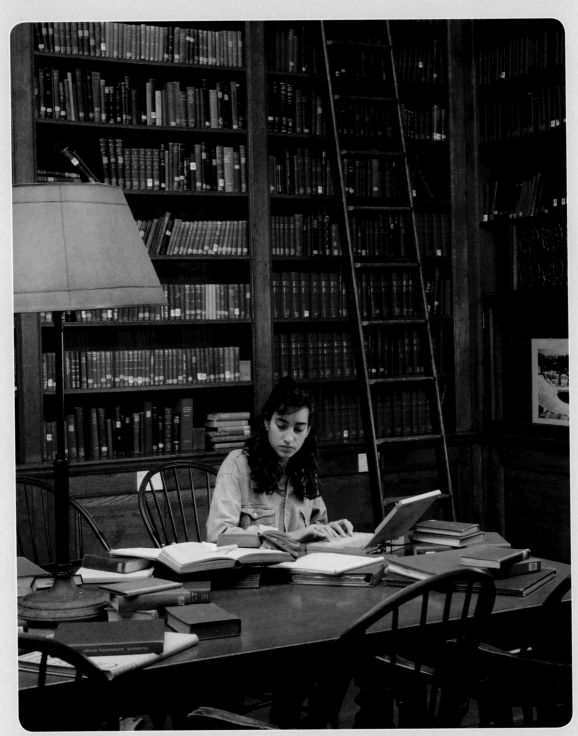

APPENDIX

A

Writing Literary Arguments

When you write an essay about literature, you have a number of options. For example, you can write a **response** (expressing your reactions to a poem, play, or story), or you can write an **explication** (focusing on a work's individual elements, such as a poem's imagery, meter, figurative language, and diction). You can also write an **analysis** of a work's theme, a character in a play or a story, or a work's historical or cultural context. Another option, which is discussed in the pages that follow, is to write a literary argument.

What Is a Literary Argument?

When you write a literary argument, you do more than just respond to, explicate, or analyze a work of literature. When you develop a **literary argument**, you take a position about a literary work (or works), support that position with evidence, and refute possible opposing arguments. You might, for example, take the position that a familiar interpretation of a well-known work is limited in some way, that a work's impact today is different from its impact when it was written, or that two apparently very different works have some significant similarities.

It is important to understand that not every essay about literature is a literary argument. For example, you might use a discussion of Tillie Olsen's short story "I Stand Here Ironing," with its sympathetic portrait of a young mother during the Great Depression, to support an argument in favor of President Franklin D. Roosevelt's expansion of social welfare programs. Alternatively, you might use Martín Espada's poem "Why I Went to College" to support your own decision to continue your education. However, writing a literary argument involves much more than discussing a literary work in order to support a particular position or referring to a character to shed light on your own intellectual development or to explain a choice you made. A literary argument *takes a stand* about a work (or works) of literature.

Stating an Argumentative Thesis

When you develop an argumentative thesis about literature, your goal is to state a thesis that has an edge—one that takes a stand on your topic. Like any effective thesis, the thesis of a literary argument should be clearly worded and specific; it should also be more than a statement of fact.

INEFFECTIVE THESIS (TOO GENERAL)	In "A&P," Sammy faces a difficult decision.
EFFECTIVE THESIS (MORE SPECIFIC)	Sammy's decision to quit his job reveals more about the conformist society in which "A&P" is set than about Sammy himself.
INEFFECTIVE THESIS (STATES A FACT)	The theme of *Hamlet* is often seen as an Oedipal conflict.
EFFECTIVE THESIS (TAKES A STAND)	Although many critics have identified an Oedipal conflict in *Hamlet*, Shakespeare's play is also a story of a young man who is struggling with familiar problems—love, family, and his future.

Here are three possible thesis statements that you could support in a literary argument:

- Charlotte Perkins Gilman's short story "The Yellow Wallpaper," usually seen as a feminist story, is actually a ghost story.

- The two characters in August Strindberg's play *The Stronger* seem to be rivals for the affection of a man, but they are really engaged in a professional rivalry to see who gives the better performance.

- Although many readers might see Wilfred Owen's "Dulce et Decorum Est" as the more powerful poem because of its graphic imagery of war, Carl Sandburg's understated "Grass" is likely to have a greater impact on modern readers, who have been overexposed to violent images.

(For more on developing a thesis statement, see Chapter 7.)

Choosing Evidence

Like any argument, a literary argument relies on evidence. Some of this evidence can be found in the literary work itself. For example, to make a point about a character's antisocial behavior, you would cite specific examples of such behavior from the work. To make a point about a poet's use of biblical allusions, you would present examples of such allusions from the poem.

> **NOTE**
>
> Be careful not to substitute plot summary for evidence. For example, summarizing everything that happens to a character will not convince your readers that the character is motivated by envy. Choose only *relevant* examples—in this case, specific instances of a character's jealous behavior, including relevant quotations from the literary work.

Evidence can also come from **literary criticism**—scholarly articles by experts in the field that analyze and evaluate works of literature. For example, to argue that a particular critical theory is inaccurate, outdated, or oversimplified, you would quote critics who support that theory before you explain why you disagree with their interpretation. (For more on evaluating potential sources for your essay, see Chapter 8.)

Writing a Literary Argument

The structure of a literary argument is similar to the structure of any other argument: it includes a **thesis statement** in the introduction, supporting **evidence**, **refutation** of opposing arguments, and a strong **concluding statement**. However, unlike other arguments, literary arguments follow specific conventions for writing about literature:

- In your essay's first paragraph, include the author's full name and the title of each work you are discussing.

- Use present tense when discussing events in works of literature. For example, if you are discussing "I Stand Here Ironing," you would say, "The mother *worries* [not *worried*] about her ability to provide for her child." There are two exceptions to this rule. Use past tense when referring to historical events: "The Great Depression *made* things difficult for mothers like the narrator." Also use past tense to refer to events that came before the action described in the work: "The mother is particularly vulnerable because her husband *left* her alone to support her children."

- Italicize titles of plays and novels. Put titles of poems and short stories in quotation marks.

- If you quote more than four lines of prose (or more than three lines of poetry), indent the entire quotation one inch from the left-hand margin. Do not include quotation marks, and add the parenthetical documentation after the end punctuation. Introduce the quotation with a colon, and do not add extra line spaces above or below it.

- When mentioning writers and literary critics in the body of your essay, use their full names ("Emily Dickinson") the first time you mention them and their last names only ("Dickinson," not "Miss Dickinson" or "Emily") after that.

- Use **MLA documentation style** in your paper, and include a works-cited list. (See Chapter 10 for information on MLA documentation.)

- In your in-text citations (set in parentheses), cite page numbers for stories, act and scene numbers for plays, and line numbers for poems. Use the word *line* or *lines* for the first in-text citation of lines from each poem. After the first citation, you may omit the word *line* or *lines*.

🔽 The following literary argument, "Confessions of a Misunderstood Poem: An Analysis of 'The Road Not Taken,'" takes a stand in favor of a particular way of interpreting poetry.

CONFESSIONS OF A MISUNDERSTOOD POEM: AN ANALYSIS OF "THE ROAD NOT TAKEN"

MEGAN MCGOVERN

Introduction (identifies titles and authors of works to be discussed)

In his poem "Introduction to Poetry," Billy Collins suggests that   1 rather than dissecting a poem to find its meaning, students should use their imaginations to experience poetry. According to Collins, they should "drop a mouse into a poem / and watch him probe his way out" (lines 5–6). However, Collins overstates his case when he implies that analyzing a poem to find out what it might mean is a brutal or deadly process, comparable to tying the poem to a chair and "beating it with a hose" (15). Rather than killing a poem's spirit, a careful and methodical dissection can often help the reader better appreciate its subtler meanings. In fact, with patient coaxing, a poem often has much to "confess." One such poem is Robert Frost's familiar but frequently misunderstood "The Road Not Taken." An examination of Frost's "The Road Not Taken" reveals a complex and somewhat troubling message about the arbitrariness of our life choices and our need to idealize those choices.

On the surface, Frost's poem seems to have a fairly simple meaning. The poem's speaker talks about coming to a fork in the road and choosing the "less-traveled" path. Most readers see the fork in the road as a metaphor: the road represents life, and the fork represents an individual's choices in life. By following the less-traveled road, the speaker is choosing the less conventional—and supposedly more emotionally rewarding—route. At the end of the poem, the speaker indicates his satisfaction when he says his choice "made all the difference" (line 20). However, Frost himself, referring to "The Road Not Taken," advised readers "'to be careful of that one; it's a tricky poem—very tricky,'" encouraging readers not to accept the most appealing or obvious interpretation (qtd. in Savoie 7–8). Literary critic Bojana Vujin urges readers to look for "poetic booby traps such as irony or deceit" in this poem and to enjoy the pleasures and rewards of discovering instances of "deliberate deceit on the poet's part" (195). In fact, after the speaker's tone and word choice are carefully examined, the poem's message seems darker and more complicated than it did initially.

The speaker's tone in the first three stanzas suggests indecision, regret, and, ultimately, lack of power. Rather than bravely facing the choice between one common path and one uncommon path, the speaker spends most of the poem considering two seemingly equal roads, "sorry" not to be able to "travel both" (2). Even after choosing "the other" road in line 6, the speaker continues for two more stanzas to weigh his options. The problem is that the two roads are, in fact, indistinguishable. As several critics have observed, "the difference between the two roads, at least when

The word *lines* is omitted from the in-text citation after the first reference to lines of a poem.

Thesis statement

2 Refutation of opposing argument

3 Evidence: Analysis and explication of Frost poem

it comes to the amount of treading they have been exposed to, is but an illusion: "'they both that morning equally lay' and neither is particularly travelled by" (Vujin 197). The roads are worn "really about the same" (10). If there is virtually no difference between the two, then why does Frost draw our attention to this fork in the road—this seemingly critical moment of choice? If Frost had wanted to dramatize a meaningful decision, the roads would be different in some significant way.

One critic, Frank Lentricchia, argues that Frost is demonstrating   4 "'that our life-shaping choices are irrational, that we are fundamentally out of control'" (qtd. in Savoie 13). Similarly, another critic contends that Frost wants his readers "to feel his characters' inner conflicts and to feel as conflicted as his characters, who are all too often lost in themselves" (Plunkett). These two critical views help to explain the speaker's indecision in the first three stanzas. The speaker impulsively chooses "the other" road but cannot accept the arbitrariness of his choice; therefore, he cannot stop considering the first road. He exclaims in the third stanza, "Oh, I kept the first for another day!" (13). In the next two lines, when he finally gives up the possibility of following that first road, he predicts, "Yet knowing how way leads on to way, / I doubted if I should ever come back" (14–15). Here, the speaker further demonstrates a lack of control over his own decisions. He describes a future guided not by his own active, meaningful choices but rather by some arbitrary force. In a world where "way leads on to way," he is a passive traveler, not a decisive individualist.

Given the indecision that characterizes the previous stanzas, the   5 poem's last two lines are surprisingly decisive: "I took the one less traveled by / And that has made all the difference" (19–20). Is the speaker contradicting himself? How has he suddenly become clear about the rightness of his decision? In fact, the last stanza does not make sense unless the reader perceives the irony in the speaker's tone. The speaker is imagining himself in the future, "ages and ages hence," telling the story of his moment at the crossroads (17). He imagines how he will, in hindsight, give his choice meaning and clarity that it did not have at the time. As Vujin argues, the poem's speaker is

Evidence: Literary criticism

Evidence: Literary criticism

Evidence: Analysis and explication of Frost poem

Evidence: Analysis and explication of Frost poem

already "mythologizing his self and his life" (198). The narrator, rather than anticipating the satisfaction that will come from having made the right and braver choice, is anticipating rewriting his own life story to make sense of an ultimately arbitrary chain of events. Vujin explains, "This is not a poem about individuality; this is a poem about self-deceit and the rewriting of one's own history" (198). Reading the last stanza ironically allows readers to make sense of the poem as a whole.

Evidence: Literary criticism

There are many possible interpretations of "The Road Not Taken," most of which can be supported with evidence from the poem itself. However, to understand these interpretations, readers need to take the poem apart, look at how its parts fit together, and reach a thoughtful and logical conclusion. To do so, readers must go against some of Billy Collins's well-meaning advice and be willing to tie the poem—and themselves—to a chair: to read it carefully, ask questions, and stay with it until it confesses.

6 Conclusion

Works Cited

Collins, Billy. "Introduction to Poetry." *Sailing Alone around the Room.* Random House, 1998, p. 16.

Frost, Robert. "The Road Not Taken." *Mountain Interval.* Henry Holt, 1920, *Bartleby.com*, www.bartleby.com/119/1.html.

Plunkett, Adam. "Robert Frost Was Neither Light Nor Dark." *New Republic*, 13 Jun. 2014, newrepublic.com/article/118046/art-robert-frost -tim-kendall-reviewed-adam-plunkett.

Savoie, John. "A Poet's Quarrel: Jamesian Pragmatism and Frost's 'The Road Not Taken.'" *New England Quarterly*, vol. 77, no. 1, 2004, pp. 5–24. *Academic Search Premier*, www.ebscohost.com/academic /academic-search-premier.

Vujin, Bojana. "'I Took the Road Less Traveled By': Self-Deception in Frost's and Eliot's Early Poetry." *Annual Review of the Faculty of Philosophy*, vol. 36, no. 1, 2011, pp. 195–203.

⊘ The following literary argument, "Not Just a 'Girl,'" argues against the commonly held position that a key character in the 1925 Ernest Hemingway short story "Hills Like White Elephants" is a stereotype.

NOT JUST A "GIRL"

LOREN MARTINEZ

Introduction

In Ernest Hemingway's famous story "Hills Like White Elephants," a couple, "the American and the girl with him," talk and drink while waiting for a train to Madrid (Hemingway 69). Most readers agree that the subject of their discussion is whether "the girl," called Jig, should have an abortion. Most of the story is told through dialogue, and although the word *abortion* is never mentioned, most readers agree that the pregnancy is the source of the tension between them. However, there are other aspects of the story about which readers do not agree. For example, some critics believe that Hemingway's portrayal of "the girl" is unfair or sexist. More specifically, some see in her the qualities of "the typically submissive Hemingway woman" (Nolan 19). How-

Thesis statement

ever, a close reading of the story reveals the opposite to be true: "the girl" is not a one-dimensional stereotype but a complex, sympathetically drawn character.

Refutation of opposing arguments

Most critics who see Hemingway's portrayal of Jig as sexist base their interpretation on Hemingway's reputation and not on the story itself. For example, feminist critic Katherine M. Rogers points out that because Hemingway himself "openly expressed fear of and hostility to women" (263), it "seems fair" to see his male characters "as representative of Hemingway himself" (248). However, although "the American" in this story may see Jig as just "a pleasant pastime," it would be an oversimplification to confuse the character's opinion of her with the writer's as Rogers would encourage us to do (251). For example, one could argue (as many critics have done) that because the name "Jig" has sexual connotations, it reveals the author's sexism (Renner 38). However, as critic Howard Hannum points out, she is referred to by this name only twice in the story, both times by the male character himself, not by the narrator (qtd. in Renner 38). Critic Stanley Renner agrees with Hannum, rejecting the idea that Hemingway's choice to refer to the character as "the girl" is equally "belittling" (38).

1

2

Renner argues that this use of the word *girl* is necessary to show how the character changes and matures in this story. In fact, he sees "her achievement of mature self-knowledge and assertion [as] the main line of development in the story" (39). All in all, the evidence suggests that "the girl," not "the American," is actually the story's protagonist. Given this central focus on "the girl" and the complexity of her character, the accusations that Hemingway's sexism has led him to create a stereotype do not seem justified.

When students who are not familiar with Hemingway's reputation as a misogynist read "Hills Like White Elephants," they tend to sympathize more often with "the girl" than with "the American" (Bauer 126) and to see the female character's thoughtfulness and depth. Although "the American" refers to the abortion as "'really an awfully simple operation'" (Hemingway 72), downplaying its seriousness, "the girl" has a "more mature understanding" of what her decision might mean (Bauer 130). She recognizes that it is not so "simple," and she is not naive enough to think that having the baby will save the relationship. In fact, she responds to his own naive comments with sarcasm. He claims that they will be "'all right and happy'" if she goes through with the operation; he says he's "'known lots of people who have done it.' 'So have I,' said the girl. 'And afterward they were all so happy'" (Hemingway 73). Despite her sarcasm and her resistance to his suggestions, the man continues to insist that this problem will be easy to fix. Finally, the girl becomes irritated with him and, as readers can see by the dashes that end his lines midsentence, cuts him off, finishing his lines for him as he tries to tell her again how "perfectly simple" the operation is (Hemingway 76). Readers understand her pain and frustration when she finally says, "'Would you please please please please please please please stop talking?'" (Hemingway 76).

The argument that "the girl" is a flat, stereotypical character portrayed in sexist terms is hard to support. In fact, a stronger argument could be made that it is the man, "the American," who is the stereotype. As critic Charles J. Nolan Jr. points out, "Hemingway highlights Jig's maturity and superiority as he excoriates the selfishness and insensitivity of her companion" (19). Moreover, "the girl" is certainly the central character in this story—the one in conflict, the one who must

3 Evidence: First point in support of thesis

4 Evidence: Second point in support of thesis

make the final decision, and the one who grows over the course of the story. At times, she seems willing to listen to the man, even going so far as to say, "'Then I'll do it. Because I don't care about me'" (Hemingway 74). However, soon after, she responds defiantly to his comment, "'You mustn't feel that way'" with "'I don't feel any way'" (Hemingway 75). Thus, as Renner notes, Hemingway's dialogue reveals "the self-centered motives of his male character" while at the same time dramatizing the female character's complex inner struggle (38). By the end of the story, the shallow "American" still expects things to be all right between them. But when the man asks, "'Do you feel better?'" Hemingway shows the girl's quiet power—and her transformation—by giving her the final understated words of the story: "'I feel fine. . . . There's nothing wrong with me. I feel fine'" (Hemingway 77). Although we do not learn what her decision is, we can see that she is now in control: she has decided to shut down the conversation, and what the man has to say no longer matters.

Conclusion

In "Hills Like White Elephants," "the girl" proves herself to be neither "'weak *in* character'" nor "'weak *as* character'" as some have described Hemingway's female characters (Bauer 126). Far from being weak *in* character, she constantly questions and pushes against the male character's suggestions. And far from being weak *as* a character, she acts as the protagonist in this story, winning the reader's sympathies. A stereotypically drawn female character would not be able to

Concluding statement

carry off either of these feats. Although Hemingway may demonstrate sexism in his other stories—and demonstrate it in his own life—readers who evaluate *this* story will discover a complex, conflicted, sympathetic female character.

5

Works Cited

Bauer, Margaret D. "Forget the Legend and Read the Work: Teaching Two Stories by Ernest Hemingway." *College Literature*, vol. 30, no. 3, 2003, pp. 124–37. *Academic Search Premier*, www.ebscohost.com/academic/academic-search-premier.

Hemingway, Ernest. "Hills Like White Elephants." *Men without Women*. Charles Scribner's, 1927, pp. 69–77.

Nolan, Charles J., Jr. "Hemingway's Women's Movement." *Hemingway Review*, vol. 4, no. 1, 1984, pp. 14–22. *Academic Search Premier*, www.ebscohost.com/academic/academic-search-premier.

Renner, Stanley. "Moving to the Girl's Side of 'Hills Like White Elephants.'" *Hemingway Review*, vol. 15, no. 1, 1995, pp. 27–41. *Academic Search Premier*, www.ebscohost.com/academic/academic-search-premier.

Rogers, Katherine M. *The Troublesome Helpmate: A History of Misogyny in Literature*. U of Washington P, 1996.

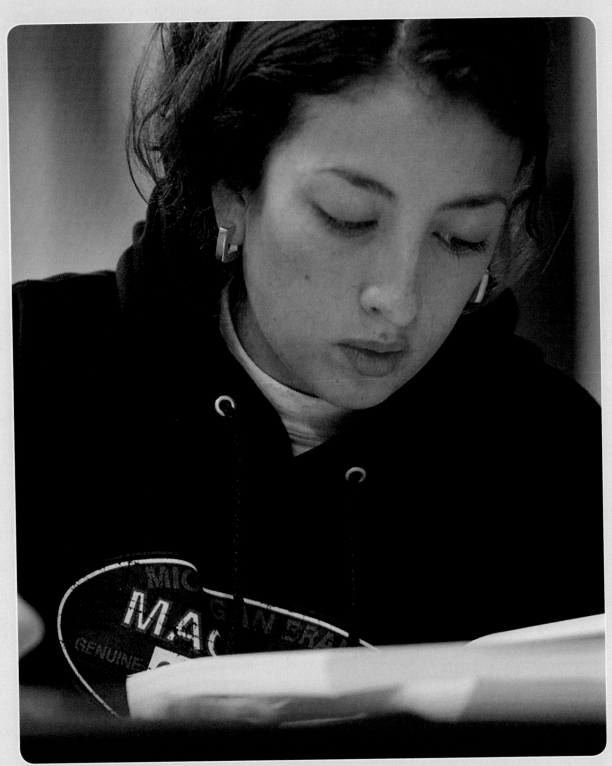

AP Photo/The Journal and Courier, Tom Leniniger

B

Documenting Sources: APA

American Psychological Association (APA) documentation style is commonly used in the social sciences. In APA style, parenthetical references refer readers to sources in the list of references at the end of the paper.* Parenthetical citations must be provided for all sources that are not common knowledge, whether you are summarizing, paraphrasing, or quoting.

Using Parenthetical References

In APA style, parenthetical references refer readers to sources in the list of references at the end of the paper. A typical parenthetical reference includes the author's last name (followed by a comma) and the year of publication: (Vang, 2015). Here are some guidelines for specific situations.

- If the author's last name appears in the text, follow it with the year of publication, in parentheses: According to Vang (2015), recent studies suggest . . .

- When quoting from a source, include a page number, if available: (Vang, 2015, p. 33). Once you have cited a source, you can refer to the author a second time without the publication date so long as it is clear you are referring to the same source: Vang also found . . .

- If no author is identified, use a shortened version of the title: ("Mind," 2015).

- If you are citing multiple works by the same author or authors published in the same year, include a lowercase letter with the year: (Peters, 2014a), (Peters, 2014b), and so on.

---

*American Psychological Association, *Publication Manual of the American Psychological Association*, Sixth Edition (2010).

- When a work has two authors, cite both names, separated by an ampersand, and the year: (Tabor & Garza, 2006). For three to five authors, in the first reference, cite all authors, along with the year; for subsequent references, cite just the first author, followed by et al. When a work has six or more authors, cite just the first author, followed by et al. and the year: (McCarthy et al., 2010).

- Omit page numbers or dates if the source does not include them. (Try to find a .pdf version of an online source; it will usually include page numbers.)

- If you quote a source found in another source, cite the original author and the source in which you found it: Psychologist Gary Wells asserted . . . (as cited in Doyle, 2005, p. 122).

- Include in-text references to personal communications and interviews by providing the person's name, the phrase "personal communication," and the date: (J. Smith, personal communication, February 12, 2015). Do not include these sources in your reference list.

If a direct quotation is forty words or less, include it within quotation marks without separating it from the rest of the text. When quoting a passage of more than forty words, indent the entire block of quoted text one-half inch from the left margin, and do not enclose it in quotation marks. It should be double-spaced, like the rest of the paper. Place parenthetical documentation one space after the final punctuation.

Preparing a Reference List

Start your list of references on a separate page at the end of your paper. Center the title References at the top of the page, and follow these guidelines:

- Begin each reference flush with the left margin, and indent subsequent lines one-half inch. Double-space the reference list within and between entries.

- List your references alphabetically by the author's last name (or by the first major word of the title if no author is identified).

- If the list includes references for two sources by the same author, alphabetize them by title.

- Italicize titles of books and periodicals. Do not italicize article titles or enclose them in quotation marks.

- For titles of books and articles, capitalize the first word of the title and subtitle as well as any proper nouns. Capitalize words in a periodical title as they appear in the original.

When you have completed your reference list, go through your paper and make sure that every reference cited is included in the list in the correct order.

Examples of APA Citations

The following are examples of APA citations.

Periodicals

Article in a journal paginated by volume

Shah, N. A. (2006). Women's human rights in the Koran: An interpretive approach. *Human Rights Quarterly, 28*, 868–902.

Article in a journal paginated by issue

Lamb, B., & Keller, H. (2007). Understanding cultural models of parenting: The role of intracultural variation and response style. *Journal of Cross-Cultural Psychology, 38*(1), 50–57.

Magazine article

Von Drehle, D. (2015, April 20). Line of fire. *Time, 185*(14), 24–28.

Newspaper article

DeParle, J. (2009, April 19). Struggling to rise in suburbs where failing means fitting in. *The New York Times,* pp. A1, A20–A21.

Books

Books by one author

Jordan, Jennifer A. (2015). *Edible memory: The lure of heirloom tomatoes and other forgotten foods.* Chicago, IL: University of Chicago Press.

Books by two to seven authors

McFadden, J., & Al-Khalili, J. (2014). *Life on the edge: The coming of age of quantum biology.* New York, NY: Crown.

Books by eight or more authors

Barrett, J. M., Smith, V., Wilson, R. T., Haley, V. A., Clarke, P., Palmer, N. B., . . . Fraser, D. (2012). *How to cite references in APA style.* New York: Cambridge University Press.

Edited book

Brummett, B. (Ed.). (2008). *Uncovering hidden rhetorics: Social issues in disguise.* Los Angeles, CA: Sage.

Essay in an edited book

Alberts, H. C. (2006). The multiple transformations of Miami. In H. Smith & O. J. Furuseth (Eds.), *Latinos in the new south: Transformations of place* (pp. 135–151). Burlington, VT: Ashgate.

Translation

Piketty, T. (2015). *The Economics of inequality* (A. Goldhammer, Trans.). Cambridge, MA: Harvard University Press.

Revised edition

Johnson, B., & Christensen, L. B. (2008). *Educational research: Quantitative, qualitative, and mixed approaches* (3rd ed.). Los Angeles, CA: Sage.

Internet Sources

Entire website

Secretariat of the Convention on Biological Diversity. (2015). *Convention on biological diversity.* Retrieved from https://www.cbd.int/

Web page within a website

The great divide: How Westerners and Muslims view each other. (2006, July 6). In *Pew global attitudes project.* Retrieved from http://pewglobal.org/reports/display.php?ReportID=253

University program website

National security archive. (2009). Retrieved from George Washington University website: http://www.gwu.edu/~nsarchiv/

Journal article found on the Web with a DOI

Because websites change and disappear without warning, many publishers have started adding a **Digital Object Identifier (DOI)** to their articles. A DOI is a unique number that can be retrieved no matter where the article ends up on the Web.

To locate an article with a known DOI, go to the DOI system website at http://dx.doi.org/ and type in the DOI number. When citing an article that has a DOI (usually found on the first page of the article), you do not need to include a URL in your reference or the name of the database in which you may have found the article.

> Geers, A. L., Wellman, J. A., & Lassiter, G. D. (2009). Dispositional optimism and engagement: The moderating influence of goal prioritization. *Journal of Personality and Social Psychology, 94,* 913–932. doi:10.1037/a0014746

Journal article found on the Web without a DOI

> Bendetto, M. M. (2008). Crisis on the immigration bench: An ethical perspective. *Brooklyn Law Review, 73,* 467–523. Retrieved from http://brooklaw.edu/students/journals/blr.php/

Journal article from an electronic database

The name and URL of the database are not required for citations if a DOI is available. If no DOI is available, provide the home page URL of the journal or of the book or report publisher.

> Staub, E., & Pearlman, L. A. (2009). Reducing intergroup prejudice and conflict: A commentary. *Journal of Personality and Social Psychology, 11,* 3–23. Retrieved from http://www.apa.org/journals /psp/

Electronic book

> Katz, R. N. (Ed.). (2008). *The tower and the cloud: Higher education in an era of cloud computing.* Retrieved from http://net .educause.edu/ir/library/pdf/PUB7202.pdf

Video blog post

> Green, J. (2015, July 7). Understanding the financial crisis in Greece [Video file]. Retrieved from https://www.youtube.com /watch?v=tigaryz-1y4

Presentation slides

> Hall, M. E. (2009) *Who moved my job!? A psychology of job-loss "trauma"* [Presentation slides]. Retrieved from http://www.cew .wisc.edu/docs/WMMJ%20PwrPt-Summry2.ppt

Student Essay

The following research paper, "The High Cost of Cheap Counterfeit Goods,"
follows APA format as outlined in the preceding pages.

APA PAPER GUIDELINES

- An APA paper should have a one-inch margin all around and be
  double-spaced throughout.

- The first line of every paragraph should be indented, and all
  pages of the paper, including the first, should be numbered
  consecutively.

- Every page should have a page header (an abbreviated title in all
  upper-case letters) typed one-half inch from the top of the page.

- An APA paper has four sections: the *title page*, the *abstract*, the *body
  of the paper*, and the *reference list*:

  1. The **title page** (page 1) should include a running head (in all
     upper-case letters) at the top:

     Running Head: COUNTERFEIT GOODS

  2. The title page should also include the title of the paper (upper-
     and lower-case letters), your name (first name, middle initial, last
     name), and your school.

  3. The **abstract** (page 2) should be a 150- to 250-word summary of
     the paper. Type the word **Abstract** (centered); skip one line; and
     do not indent. After the abstract, skip one line and type *Keywords*
     (italicized and indented), followed by keywords that will help
     researchers find your essay in a database.

  4. The **body of the paper** should begin on page 3. After the title
     page, each page of the paper should include the running head (in
     all upper-case letters), typed flush left, one-half inch from the top
     of the page:

     COUNTERFEIT GOODS

  5. The **reference list** should begin on a new page, after the body of
     the paper. (See pages A-14–A-15 for a discussion of how to for-
     mat the reference list.)

- Citations should follow APA documentation style.

The High Cost of Cheap Counterfeit Goods

Deniz A. Bilgutay

Humanities 101, Section 1

Professor Fitzgerald

March 4, 2015

COUNTERFEIT GOODS 2

Abstract

The global trade in counterfeit products costs manufacturers of luxury goods millions of dollars each year. Although this illegal trade threatens the free market, employs underage labor, and may even fund terrorism, many people consider it a victimless crime. Studies show that some consumers even take pride in buying knock-off products. But a closer look at this illicit trade in counterfeit goods shows that consumers in the United States—and around the world—do not understand the ethical implications of the choices they make. Consumers should stop supporting this illegal business, and law enforcement officials should prosecute it more vigorously than they currently do. In the final analysis, this illegal practice hurts legitimate businesses and in some cases endangers the health and safety of consumers.

Keywords: counterfeiting, terrorism, ethics, crime

COUNTERFEIT GOODS   3

The High Cost of Cheap Counterfeit Goods

For those who do not want to pay for genuine designer products, a fake Louis Vuitton bag or knock-off Rolex watch might seem too good to pass up. Such purchases may even be a source of pride. According to one study, two-thirds of British consumers said they would be "proud to tell family and friends" that they bought inexpensive knock-offs (Thomas, 2007). The trade in counterfeit goods, however, is a crime—and not a victimless crime. A growing body of evidence suggests that the makers and distributers of counterfeit goods have ties to child labor, organized crime, and even terrorism. In addition, the global economic cost of counterfeiting is esti-mated at $600 billion a year, according to recent data from the International Chamber of Commerce (Melik, 2011). For these reasons, consumers should stop buying these products and funding the illegal activities that this activity supports.

Much of the responsibility for the trade in counterfeit goods can be placed on the manufacturers and the countries that permit the production and export of such goods. For exam-ple, China, which dominates the world counterfeit trade, is doing very little to stop this activity. According to a recent arti-cle in *USA Today* by Calum MacLeod (2011), "a major obstacle is China's *shanzhai* culture, whereby some Chinese delight in making cheap imitations, sometimes in parody, of expensive, famous brands." Chinese counterfeiters have gone so far as to create entire fake stores: fake Starbucks stores, fake Abercrom-bie & Fitch stores, and even fake Apple stores. Although some of these copycats have been prosecuted, there is a high level of tolerance, even admiration, for counterfeiting in China. This attitude towards *shanzhai* is reflected in the country's lax intellectual property protection laws. As one Chinese intellectual property lawyer observed, "The penalties don't

Introduction

Thesis
statement

outweigh the benefits" (as cited in MacLeod, 2011). Given this situation, the production of counterfeit goods in China is not likely to slow down any time soon.

Despite such cultural justifications for counterfeiting, there is still an ethical problem associated with the purchase of knock-offs. As Dana Thomas (2007) has written in *The New York Times*, many of these counterfeit products are made by children who are "sold or sent off by their families to work in clandestine factories." To American consumers, the problem of children laboring in Chinese factories may be remote, but it is serious. If it is reasonable to place blame for this flourishing market on the countries that allow it, it is also reasonable to blame the people who buy most of the counterfeit goods—namely, consumers in the United States and Europe. According to a report by U.S. Customs and Border Patrol, 62% of fake goods seized in the United States in 2011 were produced in China (as cited in Coleman, 2012). In Europe, the numbers are even higher. According to *The Wall Street Journal*, 85% of goods seized in the European Union come from China (Nairn, 2011). Conse-quently, the simple act of buying a counterfeit Coach handbag implicates the consumer in the practice of forced child labor.

Immoral labor practices are not the only reason why the counterfeit market needs to be stopped. Organized crime is behind much of the counterfeit trade, so "every dollar spent on a knockoff Gap polo shirt or a fake Kate Spade handbag may be supporting drug trafficking, . . . and worse" ("Editorial: The True Cost," 2007). Consumer dollars may also be supporting narcotics, weapons, and child prostitution (Thomas, 2007).

This illicit international system also helps to finance groups even more sinister than crime syndicates. American consumers of counterfeit goods should understand that profits from

Evidence: Point 1

Evidence: Point 2

COUNTERFEIT GOODS   5

counterfeit goods support terrorist and extremist groups, including Hezbollah, paramilitary organizations in Northern Ireland, and
FARC, a revolutionary armed faction in Colombia (Thomas, 2007).
According to the International Anti-Counterfeiting Coalition, the
sale of knock-off T-shirts may even have funded the 1993 attack
on the World Trade Center. Some observers speculate that terrorists annually receive about 2% of the roughly $500 billion trade in
counterfeit goods ("Editorial: The True Cost," 2007). According to
Ronald K. Noble, secretary-general of the international law
enforcement agency Interpol, crime involving counterfeit merchandise "is becoming the preferred method of funding for a
number of terrorist groups" (as cited in Langan, 2003).

Evidence:
Point 3

    Beyond the moral and ethical implications of its links to
child labor, crime, and terrorism, counterfeit merchandise also
undermines the mainstay of Western business—respect for intellectual property. In the context of a vast international market of
counterfeit luxury goods, the issue of intellectual property can
seem insignificant. But the creation of new products requires
time, energy, and money, and "unrestrained copying robs creators of the means to profit from their works" (Sprigman, 2006).
Copyright law exists to make sure that inventors and producers
will be motivated to create original work and be fairly compensated for it. This principle applies to the designers of luxury
goods and fashion items as well. Christopher Sprigman (2006)
disagrees, however, noting that although intellectual property
law does little to protect fashion designs, this is as it should be.
"Trend-driven consumption," says Sprigman, is good for the
fashion industry because the industry's ability to create trends
"is based on designers' relative freedom to copy." But even
this argument—which addresses the influences of legitimate
fashion designers and manufacturers—cannot be used to
justify allowing counterfeiters to copy Prada handbags or Hugo

Evidence:
Point 4

Opposing
argument

Refutation

COUNTERFEIT GOODS   6

Boss suits and pass them off as genuine branded articles. Such illicit activity creates no trends—other than perhaps increasing the market for counterfeit products, which siphons off more profits from original designers.

Evidence: Point 5

    The knock-off market is not limited to fashion and luxury goods. For example, fake products such as shoddy brake pads have directly injured many consumers. In addition, each year millions of people in the United States and abroad buy counterfeit drugs that do not work and in many cases are dangerous. Some sources estimate that the majority of drugs used to treat life-threatening diseases in Africa are counterfeit. Not coincidentally, many of the same people who are making and distributing counterfeit luxury goods are also manufacturing these drugs ("Editorial: The True Cost," 2007).

Conclusion

    It is time for people to realize the harm that is done by counterfeit merchandise and stop buying it. One way to combat this problem is to educate consumers about the effects of their purchases. As James Melik (2011) of the BBC explains, "People try to save money without realising that the purchase of counterfeit goods can actually harm themselves, the economy and ultimately, their own pockets." Melik urges consumers to "think twice" before buying "products which promote and fund crime." Another way to confront the problem is for law enforcement to address this issue aggressively. Not only should local authorities do more to stop this illegal trade, but national governments should also impose sanctions on countries that refuse to honor international treaties concerning intellectual property. Only by taking this issue seriously can we ensure that this "victimless" crime does not continue to spread and claim more victims.

COUNTERFEIT GOODS   7

References

Coleman, S. (2012, January 20). China still accounts for majority of US counterfeit goods. *Canadian Manufacturers and Exporters*. Retrieved from http://www.cme-mec.ca/?lid =JCKNC-E742G-1W6JA&comaction=show&cid=DVU6K -CVBRZ-C6TZQ

Editorial: The true cost: Illegal knockoffs of name-brand products do widespread harm [Editorial]. (2007, December 2). *The Columbus* [OH] *Dispatch*, p. 4G.

Langan, M. (2003, July 24). Counterfeit goods make real terrorism. *Pittsburgh Post-Gazette*, p. A17.

MacLeod, C. (2011, August 2). China takes knock-offs to a new level, copying entire stores. *USA Today*. Retrieved from http://www.usatoday.com/money/industries /technology/2011-07-31-China-counterfeiting-fake-Western -goods-stores_n.htm

Melik, J. (2011, December 18). Fake goods save money but at what cost? *BBC News*. Retrieved from http://www.bbc .co.uk/news/business-16087793

Nairn, G. (2011, October 18). Countering the counterfeiters. *The Wall Street Journal*. Retrieved from http://online.wsj.com /article/SB10001424052970204226204576600462442044764 .html

Sprigman, C. (2006, August 22). The fashion industry's piracy paradox [Online forum comment]. Retrieved from http:// www.publicknowledge.org/node/597

Thomas, D. (2007, August 30). Terror's purse strings. *The New York Times*, p. A23.

Accurate evidence: Evidence from reliable sources that is quoted carefully and in context.

Ad hominem fallacy: The logical fallacy of undermining an argument by attacking the person who is making the argument instead of addressing the argument itself.

Allusion: A reference within a work to a person, literary or biblical text, or historical event. This shorthand device reminds the reader of something that enlarges the context of the situation being written about.

Analogy: An extended comparison that explains an unfamiliar item, concept, or situation by comparing it to a more familiar one.

Annotating: Making notes of your questions, reactions, and ideas on the document itself.

Antithesis: An opposing statement that tests whether an argumentative **thesis** is debatable.

Appeal to doubtful authority: The use of nonexperts to support an argument.

Applied ethics: The field of philosophy that applies **ethical principles** to real-life issues (such as abortion, the death penalty, animal rights, or doctor-assisted suicide).

Argument: A logical and persuasive presentation of **evidence** that attempts to convince people to accept (or at least to consider) the writer's position.

Argument by analogy: An argument that claims that its position is valid because it is similar in some ways to a position on another issue that readers are likely to accept.

Backing: In a **Toulmin argument**, the evidence that supports the warrant.

Bandwagon appeal: An attempt to convince people that something is true because it is widely held to be true.

Begging-the-question fallacy: An illogical assumption that a statement is self-evident (or true) when it actually requires proof.

Bias: Preconceived ideas or prejudices, which are often used in an argument instead of factual **evidence**.

Brainstorming: Making quick notes on a topic to generate ideas.

Causal chain: A sequence of events in which one event causes the next, which in turn causes the next, and so on.

Cause-and-effect argument: An argument that explains an event or a situation by considering its likely causes or outcomes.

Circular reasoning: An attempt to support a statement by simply repeating the statement in different terms.

Claim: In a **Toulmin argument**, the main point, usually stated as a **thesis**.

Clustering: Creating a diagram to map out your thoughts.

Common ground: Points of agreement that are shared by those on opposing sides of an argument.

Common knowledge: Factual information (such as a writer's date of birth, a scientific fact, or the location of a famous battle) that can be found in several credible sources. Common knowledge does not require documentation.

Conclusion: The last part of a **syllogism**.

Confirmation bias: The tendency that people have to accept information that supports their own beliefs and to ignore information that does not.

Confrontational argument: A kind of argument that is characterized by conflict and opposition.

Contributory causes: The less important causes in a **causal argument**.

Credibility: Trustworthiness. A credible source is believable.

Criteria for evaluation: Standards by which a subject (or source) is evaluated.

Critical response: A passage in which a writer examines the ideas that are presented in an argument and evaluates them.

Current source: A source containing up-to-date information. Current sources are especially important in discussions of scientific subjects and may be less important in other subjects.

Debatable thesis: A thesis statement that presents a position with which people might disagree.

Deductive reasoning: A form of reasoning that moves from general statements (or **premises**) to specific conclusions. See **inductive reasoning**.

Definition argument: An argument that is based on the idea that something fits or does not fit a particular definition of a key term.

Dictionary definition: A structure for definition that consists of the term to be defined, the general class to which the term belongs, and the qualities that differentiate the term from other items in the same class.

Dilemma: A choice between two or more unfavorable alternatives.

Distortion: An unfair tactic of argument in which the writer misrepresents evidence—for example, by presenting an opponent's view inaccurately or by exaggerating his or her position.

Documentation: Information that identifies the sources used in an argument.

Editing and proofreading: The final steps in the writing process, which check that an essay is well organized, convincing, and clearly written and has no distracting grammatical, spelling, and mechanical errors.

Either/or fallacy: Faulty reasoning that presents only two choices when there are actually three or more choices.

Enthymeme: A **syllogism** with one or two parts of its argument (usually the major premise) missing.

Equivocation: The use of two different meanings for the same key term in an argument.

Ethical argument: An argument that focuses on whether something should be done because it is good or right.

Ethical dilemma: A conflict between two or more possible actions, each of which will potentially have negative outcomes.

Ethical principles: A set of ideas or standards that guides someone to an ethically correct conclusion.

Ethics: The field of philosophy that studies the standards by which an act can be judged right or wrong or good or bad.

Ethos: An appeal to the trustworthiness or credibility of a speaker or writer.

Evaluate: To express an opinion about the quality of something.

Evaluation argument: An argument that presents a positive or negative judgment, asserts that someone else's positive or negative judgment is not accurate or justified, or demonstrates that one thing is or is not superior to another.

Evidence: The facts, observations, expert opinion, examples, and statistics that support a thesis statement. In a **Toulmin argument**, the evidence is called the **grounds**.

Fact: A statement that can be verified (proven to be true).

Fallacy: An error in reasoning that undermines the logic of an argument.

False dilemma: See **either/or fallacy**.

Formal argument: An argument developed according to set rhetorical principles in academic discussion and writing. See **informal argument**.

Formal outline: A presentation of an essay's main and subordinate points that uses a number/letter system to designate the order in which the points will be discussed.

Freewriting: Writing continuously for a set time to generate ideas without worrying about spelling or grammar.

Grounds: In a **Toulmin argument**, the evidence that is used to support the claim.

Hasty generalization: An error in reasoning that occurs when a conclusion is based on too little evidence or when the gap between the evidence and conclusion is too wide.

Highlighting: Using underlining and symbols to identify an essay's most important points.

Identifying tag: A phrase that identifies the source of a **quotation**, **paraphrase**, or **summary**.

Immediate cause: In a **causal argument**, the cause that occurs right before an event.

Inductive leap: In **inductive reasoning**, a stretch of the imagination that enables a writer to draw a reasonable conclusion from the existing information.

Inductive reasoning: A form of reasoning that begins with specific observations (or evidence) and moves to a general conclusion. See **deductive reasoning**.

Inference: A statement that uses what is known to draw a conclusion about what is unknown.

Informal argument: An **argument** that occurs in daily life about politics, sports, social issues, and personal relationships. See **formal argument**.

Informal outline: A list of the ideas that will be discussed in an essay. See **formal outline**.

Jumping to a conclusion: See **hasty generalization**.

Logic: The principles of correct reasoning that enable someone to tell whether a conclusion correctly follows from a set of statements or assumptions.

Logical fallacy: A flawed argument.

Logos: An appeal to logic.

Main cause: In a **causal argument**, the most important cause.

Major premise: See **syllogism**.

Means of persuasion: The appeals—*logos*, *pathos*, and *ethos*—that writers use to persuade their audience.

Metaphor: A comparison in which two dissimilar things are compared without the word *like* or *as*.

Middle term: The term in a **syllogism** that appears in both the major and minor premises but not in the conclusion.

Minor premise: See **syllogism**.

Misuse of statistics fallacy: When data are misrepresented.

Non sequitur fallacy: Illogical reasoning that occurs when a conclusion does not follow from the premises or is supported by weak or irrelevant evidence or by no evidence at all.

Objective source: A source that is not unduly influenced by personal opinions or feelings.

Operational definition: A definition of how something acts or works that transforms an abstract concept into something concrete, observable, and possibly measurable.

Opinion: A personal judgment; therefore, an idea that is open to debate.

Parallelism: The use of the same or a similar structure in the repetition of words, phrases, or clauses.

Paraphrase: A passage that presents a source's ideas in detail, including its main idea and key supporting points and perhaps key examples.

Parenthetical references: In MLA and APA **documentation**, citations that identify the source of a paraphrase, quotation, or summary.

Pathos: An appeal to the emotions.

Peer review: The process of having colleagues examine and critique written work. Informally, school work is read by friends or classmates; formally, scholarly work is read by experts in the field to confirm its accuracy.

Persuasion: The act of influencing an audience to adopt a particular belief or to follow a specific course of action.

Plagiarism: The use of the words or ideas of another person without attributing them to their rightful author.

Popular magazine: A periodical that is aimed at general readers. It generally is not an acceptable source for research.

Post hoc fallacy: Faulty reasoning that asserts that because two events occur closely in time, one event must have caused the other.

Premises: Statements or assumptions on which an **argument** is based or from which a conclusion is drawn.

Previewing: During active reading, forming a general impression of a writer's position on an issue, the argument's key supporting points, and the context for the writer's remarks.

Propaganda: Biased or misleading information that is spread about a particular viewpoint, person, or cause.

Proposal argument: An argument that attempts to convince people that a problem exists and that a particular solution is both practical and desirable.

Qualifiers: In a **Toulmin argument**, statements that limit the **claim**.

Quotation: Words or sentences taken directly from a source.

Quoting out of context: Removing a quotation from its original setting for the purpose of distorting its meaning.

Reading critically: Questioning or challenging material instead of simply accepting it as true. This often involves assessing the accuracy of facts in sources and considering the evidence that supports them.

Reason: In a **Toulmin argument**, a statement that supports the **claim**.

Rebuttals: In a **Toulmin argument**, refutations of opposing arguments.

Red herring fallacy: An irrelevant side issue that diverts attention from the real issue.

Refutation: The section of an argumentative essay that identifies opposing arguments and presents arguments against them.

Refute: To disprove or call into question.

Relevant evidence: **Evidence** that applies specifically (not just tangentially) to the topic under discussion.

Remote causes: In a **causal argument**, incidents that occurred in the past but may have had a greater impact than more recent events.

Representative evidence: **Evidence** that is drawn from a fair range of sources, not just from sources that support a particular position.

Revision: The careful and critical review of a draft.

Rhetoric: The effect of various elements working together to form a convincing and persuasive **argument**.

Rhetorical analysis: A systematic examination of the strategies that a writer employs to achieve his or her purpose.

Rhetorical question: A question that encourages readers to reflect on an issue but does not call for a reply.

Rhetorical situation: The combination of the writer, the writer's purpose, the writer's audience, the topic, and the context.

Rhetorical strategies: The ways in which argument writers present ideas and opinions, including but not limited to thesis, organization, evidence, and stylistic techniques (**simile**, **metaphor**, **allusion**, **parallelism**, repetition, and **rhetorical questions**).

Rhetorical triangle: A graphic representation of the three kinds of appeals in an argument—*logos* (reason), *ethos* (credibility), and *pathos* (values and beliefs).

Rogerian argument: A model of argument that assumes that people of good will can avoid conflict by identifying **common ground** and points of agreement. It is based on the work of Carl Rogers, a twentieth-century psychologist who felt that traditional confrontational arguments could be counterproductive.

Scholarly journal: A periodical that is usually written by experts, documented, and peer reviewed.

Scientific method: A way of using induction to find answers to questions. It involves proposing a hypothesis, making a series of observations to test the hypothesis, and arriving at a conclusion that confirms, modifies, or disproves the hypothesis.

Self-evident: A proposition that requires no proof or explanation.

Simile: A figure of speech that compares two unlike things by using *like* or *as*.

Skeptical: Having an open mind but still needing to be convinced.

Slanting: An unfair tactic that makes an argument appear stronger by presenting only evidence that supports a particular position and ignoring evidence that challenges it.

Slippery-slope fallacy: An illogical argument that holds that one thing will cause a series of events that ends in an inevitable, unpleasant conclusion, usually with no evidence that such a sequence will actually occur.

Straw man fallacy: An intentional oversimplification of an opposing argument to make it easier to refute.

Sufficient evidence: Evidence that includes enough facts, statistics, and expert opinion to support the essay's thesis.

Summary: A concise restatement of the main idea of a passage (or article or book) without the examples, explanations, and stylistic devices of the source.

Sweeping generalization: See **hasty generalization**.

Syllogism: A model for **deductive reasoning** that includes a **major premise**, a **minor premise**, and a **conclusion**. Some types of syllogisms are:

Sound syllogism: A syllogism that is both true and valid.

True syllogism: A syllogism in which the **premises** are consistent with the **facts**.

Valid syllogism: A system in which a conclusion follows logically from its premises.

Synthesis: A combination of **summary**, **paraphrase**, **quotation**, and a writer's own ideas that supports an original conclusion.

Taking a stand: Expressing a position in the form of a **thesis statement**.

Thesis: The position that an argument supports.

Thesis statement: A single sentence in an argumentative essay that states a position on an issue.

Thinking critically: Questioning rather than accepting ideas at face value.

Toulmin argument: An argument that includes the **claim** (the main point), the grounds (the **evidence** a writer uses to support the claim), and the **warrant** (the inference—either stated or implied—that connects the claims to their grounds).

Unfair appeal: An appeal to an audience's fears or prejudices.

Visual: An image—such as a chart, graph, table, photo, drawing, or diagram.

Visual argument: An advertisement, chart, graph, table, diagram, Web page, photograph, painting, or other representation that communicates a position through images.

Warrant: In a **Toulmin argument**, the inference or assumption, either stated or implied, that connects a claim to its grounds.

Works-cited list: An alphabetical list of sources that appears at the end of an essay that follows MLA style.

Writing process: The process of planning, drafting, revising, and editing an argument.

You-also fallacy (*tu quoque*): An illogical assertion that a statement is false because the speaker has said or done the opposite. It attacks a person for doing the thing that he or she is arguing against.

ACKNOWLEDGMENTS

Text Credits

Sam Adolphsen. "Student Loan Debt: It's Not the Government's Fault." From *The Maine Wire*, May 1, 2012. © 2012 Maine Heritage Policy Center. Reproduced with the permission.

American Psychological Association. "Violence in Mass Media." Copyright © 2016 by the American Psychological Association. From the *Council Policy Manual*. Reproduced with permission. The official citation that should be used in referencing this material is http://www.apa.org/about/policy/media.aspx. No further reproduction or distribution is permitted without written permission from the American Psychological Association.

Dan Ariely. "Essay Mills: A Coarse Lesson in Cheating." From *Los Angeles Times*, June 17, 2012. Reproduced with the permission of the author.

Omar Ashmawy. "Ten Years After 9/11, We're Still In The Dark." From *The Washington Post*, September 9, 2010. Copyright © 2010 Omar Ashmawy. Reproduced with permission of the author. All rights reserved.

Don Aucoin. "For Some, Helicopter Parenting Delivers Benefits." From *The Boston Globe*, March 3, 2009. © 2009 Boston Globe Media Partners. All rights reserved. Used by permission and protected by the Copyright Laws of the United States. The printing, copying, redistribution, or retransmission of this Content without express written permission is prohibited.

Austin American-Statesman. "Cheaters Never Win." From *The Austin American-Statesman*, August 11, 2006. Copyright © 2006 Austin American-Statesman. Reproduced with permission. All rights reserved.

James Baldwin. "If Black English Isn't A Language, Then Tell Me, What Is?" From *The New York Times*, July 29, 1979. Collected in *James Baldwin: Essays*, published by Library of America. Copyright © 1979 James Baldwin. Reproduced by arrangement with the James Baldwin Estate.

K. Balibalos and J. Gopalakrishnan. "'Okay or Not?' A New Poll Series about Plagiarism." From *WriteCheck*, July 24, 2013. Copyright © 2013 Turnitin, LLC. Reproduced with permission.

Paul Brandus. "Remembering 9/11: How safe are we today?" From *The Week*, September 11, 2013. © 2013 The Week. Reproduced with permission.

Kim Brooks. "Is it time to kill the liberal arts degree?" From *Salon*, June 19, 2011. © 2011 Salon Media Group, Inc. This article first appeared in Salon.com, at http://www.Salon.com. An online version remains in the Salon archives. Reprinted with permission.

Tony Brummel. "Practical Experience Trumps Fancy Degrees." From *Bloomberg Business Week*, March 2011. Reproduced with permission of Bloomberg L.P. Copyright © 2015. All rights reserved.

Patrick Buchanan. "Immigration Time-Out." From http://buchanan.org/blog/immigration-time-out-163, October 31, 1994. Copyright © 1994 Patrick Buchanan. Reproduced with permission of Friedman, Inc. All rights reserved.

Chris Bustamante. "The Risks And Rewards Of Online Learning." From *The Community College Times*, November 16, 2011. Copyright © 2011 American Association of Community and Junior Colleges. Reproduced with permission. All rights reserved.

Dylan Byers. "Plagiarism and BuzzFeed's Achilles' Heel." From Politico, July 25, 2014. Copyright © 2014 Politico. Reproduced with permission of Politico via Copyright Clearance Center.

Kevin Carey. "Fulfill George Washington's Last Wish—A National University." From CNN.com, March 2, 2015. Copyright © 2015 Turner Broadcast Systems, Inc. All rights reserved. Used by permission and protected by the Copyright Laws of the United States. The printing, copying, redistribution, or retransmission of this content without express written permission is prohibited.

Kevin Carey. "The U.S. Should Adopt Income-Based Loans Now." From *The Chronicle of Higher Education*, October 23, 2011. Copyright © 2011 Kevin Carey. Reproduced with permission of the author. All rights reserved.

Anthony P. Carnevale and Michelle Melton. "Major Differences: Why Undergraduate Majors Matter." From *The Presidency*, Fall 2011. © 2011 American Council on Education. Republished with permission. Permission conveyed through Copyright Clearance Center, Inc.

Ben Carson. "Vaccinations Are for the Good of the Nation." From *National Review*, February 11, 2015. © 2015 National Review. Reproduced with permission.

Rachel Carson. "The Obligation to Endure." From *Silent Spring*. Copyright © 1962 Rachel L. Carson, renewed 1990 by Roger Christie. Reprinted by permission of Houghton Mifflin Harcourt Publishing Company. All rights reserved. Electronic rights by permission of Frances Collin, Trustee. All copying, including electronic, or re-distribution of this text, is expressly forbidden.

Adam Cohen. "Should Self-Driving Cars Be Legal?" From *Time*, January 14, 2015. © 2015 Time Inc. All rights reserved. Reprinted from TIME and published with permission of Time Inc. Reproduction in any manner in any language in whole or in part without written permission is prohibited.

John Crisp. "Short Distance Learning." From *The Metro West Daily News*, December 14, 2011. Copyright © 2011 John Crisp. Reproduced with permission of the author. All rights reserved.

Mary C. Daly and Leila Bengali. "Is It Still Worth Going to College?" From *FRBSF Economic Letter*, May 5, 2014. © 2014 Federal Reserve Bank of San Francisco. Reproduced with permission.

Craig Desson. "My Creepy Instagram map knows where I live." From *The Toronto Star*, February 27, 2015. © 2015 Copyright Toronto Star Newspapers Ltd. Reproduced with permission.

Christopher Elliot. "The TSA has never kept you safe: here's why." From *Fortune*, June 2, 2015. © 2015 Time Inc. All rights reserved. Reprinted from FORTUNE and published with permission of Time Inc. Reproduction in any manner in any language in whole or in part without written permission is prohibited.

Susan Engel. "Teach Your Teachers Well." From *The New York Times*, November 2, 2009. Copyright © 2009 The New York Times. All rights reserved. Used by permission and protected by the Copyright Laws of the United States. The printing, copying, redistribution, or retransmission of this Content without express written permission is prohibited.

Nora Ephron. "The Chicken Soup Chronicles." From *The New York Times*, January 13, 2008. Copyright © 2008 The New York Times. All rights reserved. Used by permission and protected by the Copyright Laws of the United States. The printing, copying, redistribution, or retransmission of this Content without express written permission is prohibited.

Charles Fishman. "Bottled Water Is Silly, But So Is Banning It." From *National Geographic*, February 13, 2012. Reproduced with permission of the author.

Shelley Fralic. "Fralic: Don't fall for the myths about online privacy." From *Calgary Herald*, October 17, 2015. © 2015 Postmedia Network Inc. Material republished with the express permission of Calgary Herald, a division of Postmedia Network Inc.

Thomas Frank. "Course Corrections." From *Harper's Magazine*, October 2013. Copyright © 2013 Harper's Magazine. All rights reserved. Reproduced from the October issue by special permission.

Todd C. Frankel. "Can a Wave of New Inventions Stop School Shootings?" From *The Washington Post*, October 27, 2014. Copyright © 2014 Washington Post Company. All rights reserved. Used by permission and protected by the Copyright Laws of the United States. The printing, copying, redistribution, or retransmission of this Content without express written permission is prohibited.

Betty Friedan. "The Importance of Work." From *The Feminine Mystique*. Copyright © 1983, 1974, 1973, 1963 Betty Friedan. Reproduced with permission of W. W. Norton & Company, Inc.

Thomas L. Friedman. "Get It Right on Gas." From *The New York Times*, August 4, 2012 © 2012. The New York Times. All rights reserved. Used by permission and protected by the Copyright Laws of the United States. The printing, copying, redistribution, or retransmission of this Content without express written permission is prohibited.

Trip Gabriel. "Plagiarism Lines Blur For Students In Digital Age." From *The New York Times*, August 1, 2010. Copyright © 2010 The New York Times. All rights reserved. Used by permission and protected by the Copyright Laws of the United States. The printing, copying, redistribution, or retransmission of this Content without express written permission is prohibited.

Ej Garr. "Athlete Vs. Role Model." From *The Rainmaker*, September 1, 2014. Reproduced with permission of the author.

Jennifer Golbeck. "All Eyes on You." From *Psychology Today*, September/October 2014. Reproduced with permission of the author.

Clyde Haberman. "A Discredited Vaccine Study's Continuing Impact on Public Health." From *The New York Times*, February 1, 2015. Reproduced with permission of the author.

Greg Hampikian. "When May I Shoot a Student?" From *The New York Times*, February 27, 2014. Copyright © 2014 The New York Times. All rights reserved. Used by permission and protected by the Copyright Laws of the United States. The printing, copying, redistribution, or retransmission of this Content without express written permission is prohibited.

The Harvard Crimson. "Vote Yes on the Bottled Water Ban." From *The Harvard Crimson*, November 15, 2013. Copyright © 2013 The Harvard Crimson, Inc. Reproduced with permission.

Andrew Herman. "Raise The Drinking Age to 25." From *The BG News*, August 22, 2007. Copyright © 2007 BG News. Reproduced with permission. All rights reserved.

Lawrence M. Hinman. "How To Fight College Cheating." From *The Washington Post*, September 3, 2004. Copyright © 2004 Lawrence Hinman. Reproduced with permission of the author. All rights reserved.

Eric Hoover. "College's Value Goes Deeper than the Degree." From *The Chronicle of Higher Education*, May 15, 2011. Used with permission of The Chronicle of Higher Education Copyright © 2016. All rights reserved.

Alison Hudson. "Stop *Wikipedia* Shaming." From *Skeptiod*, December 1, 2014. © 2014 Skeptoid.com. Reproduced with permission.

Internet Encyclopedia of Philosophy. "Statement of Purpose." From http://www.iep.utm.edu/home/about/. Reproduced with permission of The Internet Encyclopedia of Philosophy.

Isothermal Community College. "Warning Signs: How You Can Help Prevent Campus Violence." From http://www.isothermal.edu/publications/Warning%20Signs.pdf. Copyright © Isothermal Community College, Spindale, NC. Reproduced with permission. All rights reserved.

Sharon Jayson. "Online and Mobile Dating Face Privacy, Safety Concerns." From *USA Today*, March 27, 2014. Copyright © 2014 Gannett. All rights reserved. Used by permission and protected by the Copyright Laws of the United States. The printing, copying, redistribution, or retransmission of this Content without express written permission is prohibited.

Gerard Jones. "Violent Media Is Good For Kids." From *Mother Jones*, June 28, 2000. Copyright © 2000 The Foundation for National Progress. Reproduced with permission of The Foundation for National Progress. All rights reserved.

INDEX OF TITLES AND AUTHORS